*physiological
psychology*

physiological psychology

THOMAS S. BROWN
DePaul University

PATRICIA M. WALLACE
Clarion State College

ACADEMIC PRESS
New York
San Francisco
London
A Subsidiary of
Harcourt Brace Jovanovich,
Publishers

Cover illustration on photograph by D. L. Cramer

ACADEMIC PRESS, INC.
111 Fifth Avenue, New York, New York 10003

United Kingdom Edition published by
ACADEMIC PRESS, INC. (LONDON) LTD.
24/28 Oval Road, London NW1 7DX

ISBN: 0-12-136660-X
Library of Congress Catalog Card Number: 79-52344

PRINTED IN THE UNITED STATES OF AMERICA

contents

There is an air of enthusiasm in a field like physiological psychology that is very typical of young sciences. The excitement even infects the general public as more and more TV specials and magazine articles appear which deal with topics in this field. We hope we will convey some of this enthusiasm to the students who read this book, some of whom will continue with their training and go on to explore the fascinating relationship between physiology and behavior.

Our aim in writing this book was to present an introduction to a field that is rapidly growing and changing. This area of study combines the talents of psychologists, biologists, chemists, physicists, engineers, nutritionists, and many others interested in the relationship between biology and behavior. Though a young field, it is accumulating significant information very rapidly, partly because of the development of new techniques and new approaches, and partly because of the growing awareness that we cannot understand human behavior without "looking inside" the body. This book is intended for an undergraduate course usually called physiological psychology, but which may also go under such names as biological psychology, psychobiology, brain and behavior, or physiology and behavior.

The book's organization reflects the most recent trends in the field of physiological psychology. We begin with basic information about the nervous system and the neuron, and then discuss the topics about which physiological psychologists know the most: the sensory systems. The next section examines the physiological bases of some of the more "primitive" behaviors, such as hunger and thirst, reproduction, sleep, and emotion. The last section explores the topics of development, and of learning and memory, from the standpoint of plasticity in the nervous system. This approach acknowledges a major change in the way scientists are viewing the nervous system. An approach that we believe will lead to a better understanding of the way the nervous system is able to change in response to internal and external events. The final chapter deals with the higher processes such as thinking, decision making, attention, and language; it describes ground-breaking studies that are actually exploring the physiological bases of human consciousness.

In a field as interdisciplinary as this, there will be many students who do not have extensive backgrounds in psychology, biology, or the other sciences that have contributed to knowledge in the area. We have written the book with this in mind. And no strong science prerequisites are necessary in order to understand the material. Even so, we recognize that physiological psychology is not an easy subject, and we have given much thought and effort to designing a book that will provide students with as much help as possible.

One simple technique we use is tightly organized chapters. Every chapter is preceded by an outline, and within the chapter are running summaries that review each major section. This technique will not only improve the student's understanding of the material, it will allow instructors to assign parts of chapters without causing confusion. Key terms are typed in bold face, and are listed at the end of each chapter, along with a list of suggested readings. All key terms are defined in an extensive glossary at the end of the book.

Another technique we employ to help the student is the use of many human experiments and applications. The effects of drugs on feeding behavior in a rat are certainly fascinating to physiological psychologists, but students usually want to know how these findings might apply to humans.

Within each chapter we emphasize the logical progression of experiments which lead to specific conclusions in every subject area, and we spend extra time examining the methods used to arrive at conclusions. It is particularly important for students to understand "how you get there from here," and to be able to evaluate the methods scientists use to test hypotheses. No method, whether it is a lesion, a pharmacological manipulation, an electrical recording, or any other, is free from complications in interpretation. Yet valid conclusions can be drawn based on the weight of the evidence from several kinds of studies. When a question is attacked from several angles, the experimental results often begin to fit a pattern, and the pieces of the puzzle gradually fall into place. The knowledge base of physiological psychology has benefited from this multifaceted approach, and we emphasize it throughout the book, explaining the advantages and limitations of each technique. There is no separate chapter on techniques—this material is interwoven into each of the subject areas. We have found that students are far more likely to appreciate methodological issues when they can see how they affect the interpretations of specific experimental results.

It may be acceptable to understate the significance and relevance of experimental findings among colleagues, but students appreciate an explanation of why a specific experiment was performed, and how the results fit into and support (or refute) a general hypothetical framework. In each chapter, we emphasize the relevance of experimental results and try to show why each set of experiments answers some questions and raises still more. We also frequently point out the relevance of findings in one chapter to issues presented in another. The division of a book into chapters might lead a student to believe that there are discrete subsystems of behavior, each of which has its own set of physiological underpinnings. We tried to counteract this by cross-referencing between chapters, without sacrificing the independence of each chapter.

A unique feature of this book is the inclusion of a brief atlas of the human brain. Our students have frequently been exasperated by the numerous anatomical terms, and it seemed quite logical to provide them with a detailed map to help them find their way in this novel terrain.

A comprehensive study guide accompanies and parallels the book, which contains more features to help the student. The guide recapitulates the important points in each chapter, and includes multiple choice, essay, and matching questions for self-examination. There are anatomical diagrams to provide practice in identifying and labeling those structures mentioned in the text. The study guide also contains useful projects which can be conducted by the student, or by the instructor as class demonstrations. Another feature of the study guide is the section on "Ideas for Research Topics," with suggested sources. It has been our experience that students often have difficulty finding a topic for a research paper, and this section was included to help alleviate that problem.

No book is the work of its authors alone, and this one is no exception. Our reviewers, some of whom stayed with us through the writing of the entire manuscript, provided valuable advice, criticism, and suggestions. We would like to thank Paul D. Coleman, University of Rochester Medical Center; Michael Gabriel, University of Texas at Austin; William T. Greenough, University of Illinois at Urbana-Champaign; John E. Kelsey, Indiana University; Richard A. King, University of North Carolina at Chapel Hill; Dale W. McAdam, University of Rochester; and Margaret White, California State University at Fullerton. Our editors, and the people at Academic Press, deserve special thanks. Those on the publishing end of a book rarely receive enough credit, yet their ideas, suggestions, and long, hard hours of work are an important component of the book's quality. We would like to thank Raelene Seelbach and Melissa Preston for assistance with the seemingly endless details of writing, typing, filing, and obtaining copyright permissions. For moral support, we thank Julian Jones and the sorely missed and lovingly remembered Poukah.

Last, but far from least, we gratefully acknowledge the contributions of our students, for their suggestions and advice, their challenging questions, and their sometimes astonishing insights. Some of their suggestions are worth quoting:

"More graphics, not necessarily pictures, but graphs and diagrams."

"Less jargon . . . please."

"Write for us, not for other professors who already know it."

"Why don't you write a book on human sexuality?"

"How could anyone know enough to write an entire textbook?"

"Give it some humanity . . . I'm not just a black box filled with nuts and bolts."

We took most of these suggestions to heart, and especially tried to "give it some humanity." We hope we have succeeded.

Thomas S. Brown
Patricia Wallace

*physiological
psychology*

1

introduction

introduction In recent years, news stories have carried titles such as "Emotional Stress and Sudden Death" (Engel, 1977), "Mind Controllers: CIA Testing" (Getlein, 1977), "Biorhythms: A Key to Your Ups and Downs (Bolch, 1977), and "Pain Control with Hypnosis" (Holden, 1977). Reading through these, one feels a combination of emotions, sometimes outrage and indignity, sometimes fear, and sometimes a nervous optimism about what scientists can accomplish. It is one thing to learn that our moods and actions are related to environmental events. But it is quite another to learn that these same moods and actions may be related to the action of certain chemicals in specific parts of the brain. Can our very thoughts, our most private emotions, be studied by a detached scientist and reduced to the mere action of a few chemicals in the brain? Worse, can they be controlled by simply changing brain chemistry or neural activity? The glimmerings of a major assault on the very nature of human beings are on the horizon.

This book is about physiological psychology—the physiological bases of behavior. In many ways, the fears and hopes that people are developing about this field are a credit to its enormous growth and success in learning about the brain. In this book, we will discuss what is known about how physiological events relate to behavior, and often how behavior can be changed, even controlled, by modifying the physiological events. But the experiments and findings we are about to explain will have a large impact on the way that human beings perceive themselves, and their relationship to the world. So before we begin, we will examine some of these philosophical issues.

the mind—body problem Historically, philosophers have hypothesized that the mind and the body are two different elements. Even though the brain is highly complex, and certainly has a lot to do with our behavior, it is still part of the body, and thus merely matter. The "mind," the "consciousness," the "I" that thinks, decides, feels, and understands is something nonphysical—or a different element. Descartes (1596–1650) was one of the foremost proponents of this **dualistic position.**

While physiologically oriented psychologists were studying simple behaviors like reflexes, this issue remained in the background. Even later, with the advent of behaviorism in the beginning of this century, scientists limited themselves to the study of overt behavior, and the issue still did not present too much of a problem. "Mind" and "consciousness" were not studied by scientists because they are not overt behaviors. They are hidden, subjective experiences. During the behavioristic era, they were considered not suitable for scientific inquiry.

But in recent years, there has been an incredible burgeoning of knowledge about how the brain works, and how its workings are related to our behavior. And very recently, scientists have dared to enter the previously forbidden terrain of the study of "consciousness." As we learn more about the brain, we find that physiological events are related to emotions like anger, fear, love, and even to decision making, perception, and intellect. Right now, the knowledge that we have about the physiological correlates of the hidden thoughts and feelings of a human being are very rudimentary. But we have enough so that people are beginning to wonder whether "mind" is indeed something separate. Is it possible that the workings of the brain can account for the subjective experience of "mind?" Can physical events account for "me?"

Scientists are very often conservative people, and do not like to take a stand without data to back them up. There are not yet any data available to settle this issue, and some would say that there never will be. Many scientists prefer to think of the **mind–body problem** as a philosophical issue that does not concern scientists. But others have entered the debate.

Wilder Penfield (1975), for example, has performed hundreds of neurosurgical operations on epileptic patients, some of which included electrical stimulation of brain tissue. His observations have led him to the belief that mind and brain are intimately related, but that the workings of the brain cannot, by themselves, explain the mind:

When I have caused a conscious patient to move his hand by applying an electrode to the motor cortex of one hemisphere, I have often asked him about it. Invariably his response was, "I didn't do that. You did!" When I caused him to vocalize, he said, "I didn't make that sound. You pulled it out of . me." . . . For my own part, after years of striving to explain the mind on the basis of brain action alone, I have come to the conclusion that it is simpler (and far easier to be logical) if one adopts the hypothesis that our being does consist of two fundamental elements. (Penfield, 1975)

Other scientists argue that the mind is not a separate element, that the mind can be explained by the workings of the brain. Sagan (1977) states this position quite forcefully:

My fundamental premise about the brain is that its workings—what we sometimes call "mind"—are a consequence of its anatomy and physiology, and nothing more. "Mind" may be a consequence of the action of the components of the brain severally or collectively. Some processes may be a function of the brain as a whole. A few students of the subject seem to have concluded that, because they have been unable to isolate and localize all higher brain functions, no future generation of neuroanatomists will be able to achieve this objective. But absence of evidence is not evidence of absence. (Sagan, 1977)

Steven Rose (1973) also takes this position:

In particular, consciousness and mind are seen . . . as being an inevitable consequence of the evolution of particular brain structures which developed in a series of evolutionary changes in the pathway of man's own emergence. The hypothesis is advanced that consciousness is a consequence of the evolution of

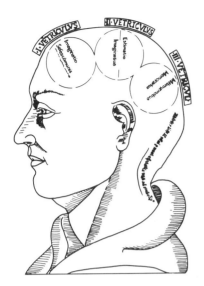

Figure 1.1
An anatomical drawing by Albertus Magnus (1206–1280). [From Clarke and Dewhurst (1972).]

a particular level of complexity and degree of interaction among the nerve cells (neurons) of the cerebral cortex, while the form it takes is profoundly modified for each individual brain by its development in relationship with the environment. (Rose, 1973)

Rose suggests that the mind–body problem may be one caused by semantic difficulties. The study of mind on a mentalistic level (which might on the surface make it seem as though there are two fundamental elements underlying mind and brain) is really simply a different hierarchical analysis of the correlates of human behavior. Neurobiology understands human behavior on one level, and psychology and sociology understand it on quite another.

The implications of the proposition that mind and brain are one and the same are profound. If it is true, and it becomes widely accepted, human beings will have to change the way that they view themselves. Perhaps even our own values have physiological roots. Wilson (1978) argues this point in his book *On Human Nature*:

Innate censors and motivators exist in the brain that deeply and unconsciously affect our ethical premises: from these roots, morality evolved as instinct. If that perception is correct, science may soon be in a position to investigate the very origin and meaning of human values, from which all ethical pronouncements and much of political practice flow. . . .
Because the guides of human nature must be examined with a complicated arrangement of mirrors, they are a deceptive subject, always the philosopher's deadfall. The only way forward is to study human nature as part of the natural sciences, in an attempt to integrate the natural sciences with the social sciences and humanities. I can conceive of no ideological or formalistic shortcut. Neurobiology cannot be learned at the feet of a guru. . . . (Wilson, 1978)

To many people, these are frightening, even revolutionary ideas. They attack the very core of human philosophy and come into conflict with ideas about religion, free will, and the concept of the human soul. As more and more is learned about the workings of the brain, the question of who and what we are will loom larger. A major rethinking may be needed.

localization of function Another issue which has been disputed throughout the centuries, and which reflects in some ways the mind–body problem, is the issue of **localization of function.** Two opposing viewpoints hold that (1) consciousness and other functions of human beings cannot be localized within particular areas of the brain, and (2) different areas within the brain handle different kinds of behaviors.

The concept of localization of function is a very old one, and even during the Middle Ages, people believed that different areas of the brain served different functions. During this time, they concentrated on the ventricles of the brain, which circulate cerebrospinal fluid. Figure 1.1 shows an anatomical drawing from the thirteenth century. The three circles represent the ventricles of the brain, each of which is devoted to a particular kind of behavior. The first cell contained the "sensus communis" (common sense), and "imaginativa" (imagination); the second cell contained more "imaginativa" and also "aestimativa" (judgment); the last cell contained "memorativa" (memory) and "membro motiva" (control of motion). It is interesting that the medieval scientists did not consider brain tissue important enough to even be included in the anatomical diagrams.

In the seventeenth and eighteenth centuries, interest in the convolutions of the cortex evolved, and eventually culminated in the extreme viewpoint of the **phrenologists.** They believed that the brain was a repository of the mind, and that specific mental and moral faculties were located in specific places along its surface. Examination of bumps on the cranium would reveal deficits and strengths in the personality. At its most extreme, some phrenologists were identifying over 100 separate "traits," each with its own area on the cranium and face (see Figure 1.2). Some of these traits were preposterously precise. For example, 149 was "Republicanism," 148 (right next to 149) was "Faithful Love," and 149A was "Responsibility." The labels seem to demonstrate more about the political biases of the labeler than about brain function.

Modern brain scientists tend to regard phrenology as comical in the extreme but with enough grain of truth to have stimulated interest in the specific functions of structures within the brain. Clearly, certain areas of the brain are more involved than others in specific functions, as we shall see in this book. But the areas within the brain are connected by pathways and fiber systems. Modern theories about brain function emphasize the importance of pathways and integrations between various brain areas in the control of behavior. Nevertheless, this issue has not yet been completely resolved, especially for some of the higher brain functions such as memory.

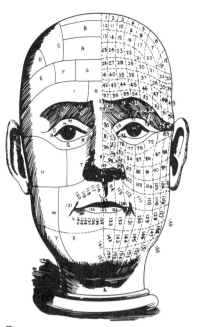

Figure 1.2
A phrenological diagram. [From Clarke and Dewhurst (1972).]

A third issue with which physiological psychologists have had to grapple involves the controversy about **nature versus nurture.** On one extreme is the viewpoint that the human being is basically a product of heredity. On the other is the viewpoint that humans are a product of their environment. If one adheres to the first viewpoint, then statements like "He is basically dumb," or "She is innately aggressive," are possible. The implication is that human beings have genes which make them behave in certain ways regardless of environmental events. If one adheres to the second viewpoint, then it is a logical

nature versus nurture

proposition that all human beings start out with identical equipment. What makes them behave differently is the fact that they have developed in different environments.

Questions like "Are we innately aggressive?" or "Are women biologically more emotional than men?" carry with them the implication that there are certain prescriptions for change. If the nature argument is correct, then we need to change the genes (or their by-products) in order to change behavior. If the nurture argument is correct, then we need to change the environment in order to see a change in the way that humans behave.

In recent years, it has become very clear that opposing viewpoints about the importance of nature and nurture in human behavior are extremely simplistic. Human beings cannot exist without both their genes and their environment. The two interact in complex ways throughout development. Waddington (1957) proposed a rather elegant analogy to describe the interaction between genes and environment during development. Development of a trait, whether it is eye color, body build, intelligence, or emotionality, is like a ball rolling down the slopes of a hill. Each trait, or ball, glides down its own part of the hill, and its course is affected by many ridges and valleys on the hill's landscape. For some traits, those ridges and valleys form a deep channel, so that the ball's course is fairly rigidly predetermined. Thus one can predict with a fair degree of accuracy where the ball will land at the bottom. For the other traits, the channels are not so deep, and they widen considerably as the ball rolls down the hill. For these traits, it is not so easy to predict where the ball will land, but it is still more likely to land in some places than in others.

The task is not to determine whether genes or environment are at the root of our individual differences. It is to discover how "wide the channels" are for various traits. This is a very complex problem, and it is likely that some unknown environments might widen the channels even further. As it stands now, for example, the "channels" are not as wide as we might like for the ball which represents the development of intelligence (as measured by IQ tests). Perhaps some environments (which we don't yet know about) might be able to provide children with the chance to develop their abilities further than they are now. The study of gene—environment interactions is still in its infancy. But people tend to react to comments about genetic predispositions to develop certain traits (like schizophrenia) with emotions like defiance or resignation. It is frightening to find that one's genes, over which one has no control, might be pushing our behavior in directions that we would not choose.

the organization Before we begin to talk about behavior, we will discuss the neuron
of this book and the nervous system. Chapters 2 and 3 introduce the details about the building block of the nervous system—the neuron. First we de-

scribe how information gets from one end to the other (Chapter 2), and then we explain how neurons communicate with each other (Chapter 3). In Chapter 4, we present a brief overview of the nervous system, so that you will have a road map of the structures and pathways which will be discussed in the remainder of the book.

In Chapters 5 through 8, we discuss the sensory systems: vision, audition, the chemical senses (olfaction and taste), and the somatosensory and vestibular systems. An understanding of how an organism gets information about the environment is critical to understanding how that information might affect behavior. We do not see all there is to see, and we even receive distorted messages about physical reality during the process of sensing our world. We begin with the senses because physiological psychologists have studied them for so long, and because we know a great deal about how they work. The chapters on the senses are followed by a discussion of the motor systems (Chapter 9), a topic which is intimately related to sensation. Even the brain areas which are involved with sensation and with movement are very close to one another, and they interact very intimately.

The next sections of the book (Chapters 10 through 13) deal with emotion and motivation, subjects closer to the heart of human beings, and closer to the profound issues which we discussed in the beginning of this chapter. First we discuss the physiological correlates of emotions, and we will find that emotions can indeed be related to specific kinds of brain activity. In some cases, they can even be controlled by appropriate physiological means. Drugs called "uppers" and "downers," and electrical stimulation of certain brain regions, can have quite an impact on our emotions. In Chapters 11, 12, and 13 we discuss motivation for food and water, sex, and sleep. Each of these are very important for our very survival, and we will see that the phylogenetically older parts of the brain play major roles.

In the last three chapters we will take up the topics which bear directly on the philosophical issues which we discussed. First, we will examine the kinds of plasticity which our nervous systems are capable of, first through development, and second as it relates to learning and memory. The final chapter deals with higher processes, such as thinking, deciding, and reasoning, and also considers language. Although studies which try to find out if there are neural correlates of consciousness are still only scratching the surface, they make us aware that we have come a long way since the days when people believed that the "mind" was in the heart. They also make us aware that physiological psychology is a very powerful discipline—an awakening giant that has the power to change the way that humans view themselves as profoundly as Copernicus did when he described the movement of the planets around the sun, or as Darwin did when he formulated the principles of evolution.

KEY
TERMS
dualistic position
mind—body problem
localization of function
phrenology
nature versus nurture

SUGGESTED
READINGS
Clarke, E., and Dewhurst, K. (1972). *An Illustrated History of Brain Function.* University of California Press, Berkeley. (A fascinating collection of anatomical drawings from antiquity through modern times which shows how ideas about mind and brain have changed.)

Penfield, W. (1975). *The Mystery of the Mind.* Princeton University Press, Princeton, New Jersey. (The famous neurosurgeon describes his research, and his philosophical conclusions about the relationship between mind and brain.)

Rose, S. (1973). *The Conscious Brain.* Alfred A. Knopf, New York. (A survey of the brain and its evolution which presents the author's views about how consciousness emerged during the course of evolution.)

Sagan, C. (1977). *The Dragons of Eden: Speculations on the Evolution of Human Intelligence.* Ballantine, New York. (The famous astronomer presents his views on the mind—body controversy, and how human intelligence has evolved.)

2

*the neuron:
axonal
conduction*

introduction Of all the different kinds of cells in our body, the most important for our behavior are the neurons. An example of a neuron, showing its major parts, is shown in Figure 2.1. These are the building blocks of the nervous system; they form a vast and complex network of cells whose main function is to process information. Everything we do, think, feel, remember, depends upon the activity of these tiny specialized cells, so it is very important to understand their advantages and limitations. Their value lies in the fact that they can code information, integrate the information, and then pass it on to other parts of the nervous system. Before we plunge into the neuron's structure, we will discuss what we mean by **information,** and what we mean by **processing.**

the information In everyday conversation the term information usually means something more complex than the way that we use it in physiological psychology. It may mean the evening news, or it may mean the concepts that you pick up from a textbook. But in the study of the nervous system, the term information simply means message; and the message may seem extremely simple. For example, the lighting level in the room qualifies as information. The message that your brain sends to the muscles in your legs to walk is a kind of information. The temperature that you feel when you put your hand on a hot plate is also information.

Since neurons don't use the English language, they must use another kind of language to code and process information. The information contained in the phrase "the plate is getting hotter" can be coded in many different ways. Figure 2.2 shows some of the ways that are possible. One kind of code (Figure 2.2a) might involve the release of more and more chemical as the temperature of the hot plate went up.

Figure 2.1
A neuron.

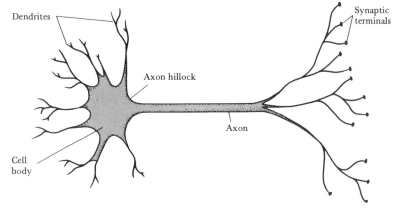

Dendrites

Synaptic terminals

Axon hillock

Axon

Cell body

Another kind, which looks a little like Morse code, might involve a change in the rate of identical units such as "dots" across time (Figure 2.2b). When the plate is cool, the "dots" on a telegraph key come very slowly; as the plate heats up they come faster and faster. A computer might use a similar kind of code in which each component can be in only one of two states (yes or no).

In this chapter, and in the next one, we will see that the neuron uses two methods to code information. One method is a **digital code,** similar to the one in Figure 2.2b. When a neuron is moving information from one end to the other, it uses a digital code in which each "dot" is identical in size. The information is carried in the rate and pattern of "dots." (We will explain what the "dots" are in this chapter.) But when a neuron is communicating with another neuron, it uses an **analog code,** much like the one in Figure 2.2a. The same information which was coded in a digital fashion is converted to an amount rather than a rate. For example, if the neuron was producing a very fast rate of "dots," then it would release a very large amount of chemical which would then affect the next neuron. In this analog code, it is the amount of chemical released at any given moment that carries the information.

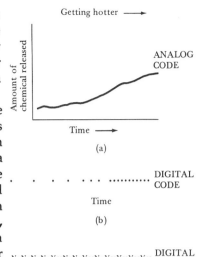

Figure 2.2
Different ways to code the same information.

Each neuron is involved in three different kinds of information processing: (1) moving the information from one end to the other, or **axonal conduction;** (2) transmitting the information to the next neuron, or **synaptic transmission;** and (3) **integration** of information. Figure 2.3 shows a schematic network of neurons that we will use to provide an overview of these three kinds of information processing. Neurons only move information in one direction, so in this figure the information is moving from left to right.

For this example, let us suppose that the information to be moved is a shock to the first neuron at point *A*. From the animal's point of view,

the processing

Figure 2.3
Schematic neural network showing three types of information processing: (1) axonal conduction, (2) synaptic transmission, and (3) integration.

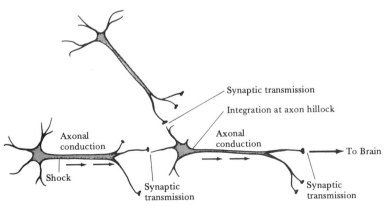

this could be a dangerous situation involving pain and perhaps some response, such as escape. So it is important to move the information quickly to the brain.

axonal conduction. The first thing that must happen to get the information on its way is axonal conduction. The axon uses a digital code, one which involves "dots" called **action potentials.** If it is a very strong shock, the axon might fire off a very rapid volley of action potentials. Action potentials are due to the movement of charged particles across the axon's membrane, and thus basically involve an electrical process. Once the action potential reaches the end of the neuron, the information must be carried to the next neuron.

synaptic transmission. When an action potential reaches the end of the axon, a small amount of chemical, called **neurotransmitter** is released. Thus the digital code is converted to an analog code. The chemical diffuses across the tiny space between the axon ending and the next neuron, and affects the membrane of the next neuron. This chemical process is called synaptic transmission.

integration. The third kind of information processing is a type of decision making, called integration, which occurs at the first segment of the neuron's axon (**axon hillock**). The changes in the neuron's membrane which are produced by the effects of the neurotransmitter spread to the axon hillock. If the changes are large enough, and of the right kind, the axon hillock will fire off its own action potential. The integration comes in because this neuron is receiving input from a

Figure 2.4
Some different types of neurons: (a) pyramidal, (b) bipolar, (c) unipolar.

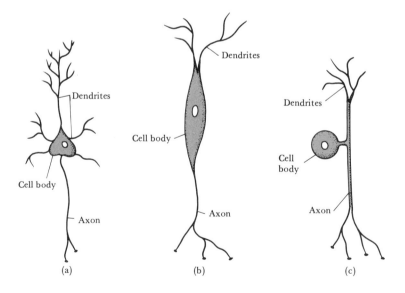

great many other sources, not just from the neuron that received the shock. The input from the shocked neuron must be integrated with the input from the other sources before the axon hillock makes its decision about whether to pass on the information about the shock.

In this chapter, and in the next one, we will examine these three basic information processing functions in more detail. First, we will look more closely at the structure of the neuron, and then discuss how the axon conducts information from one end to the other using a digital code. Secondly, we will see how the axon hillock integrates the information that is coming in from many sources, and makes its decision about firing off its own action potentials. In the next chapter, we will explore the process of synaptic transmission. Since this is basically a chemical process, while the other two are more electrical in nature, it will be discussed in a separate chapter. It will involve us in a discussion of drugs and behavior, because many drugs act by affecting the process of synaptic transmission.

In some ways, the neuron is very much like the other cells in the body. It has a nucleus which contains DNA, a cell membrane, and cytoplasm. It also contains various organelles such as mitochondria, the source of energy for the cell. It has to synthesize proteins, take up nutrients, and dispose of waste products, just like other cells. But in order to perform its special information processing functions it has several features which are not present in the other cells of the body.

Figure 2.4 shows some neurons which are present in the nervous system. Each neuron has **dendrites,** a **cell body** or **soma,** an **axon,** and **synaptic terminals** at the ends of the axon branches. Figure 2.5 shows a "typical neuron" with more detail. We will refer to this schematic drawing as we examine each of the neuron's parts.

the structure of the neuron

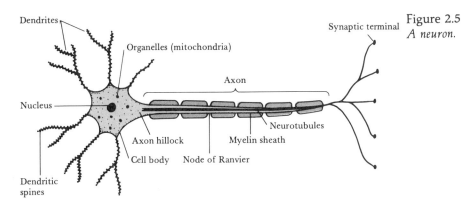

Figure 2.5
A neuron.

the dendrites The dendrites are a special adaptation of the neuron that receives input. Messages are received at the dendrites and passed along to the cell body. Because a single neuron can receive messages from hundreds of other cells, the dendrites of a single neuron can be quite complicated. They often arrange themselves into **dendritic trees** with first, second, and third-order branches. Figure 2.6 shows a cell from the brain with an enormous amount of branching. In some of these cells, the dendritic trees are so large that some scientists have estimated that the ratio of dendritic surface to cell body surface might be as high as 15 to 1.

Much of the increased surface area on the dendrites is due to the presence of **dendritic spines,** or tiny knoblike branches. These spines are places where axon endings from other cells communicate with the neuron through synaptic transmission.

The amount of branching, and also the number of spines on the dendrites is turning out to be very important because it is related to some interesting environmental events. In Chapter 14, we shall see how an animal which is reared in an enriched environment develops more complicated dendritic trees compared to one which is reared in a less-than-stimulating standard lab cage. If more dendritic branching is present, the animal presumably has the capability to make more connections between neurons. The ability to make more connections would lead to more advanced information processing and perhaps more flexibility in the animal's behavior.

the cell body Also called the soma, the cell body is the part of the neuron that contains the nucleus and most of the organelles that maintain the life of the cell. A particular type of neuron is often given a name which reflects the shape or location of the cell body. For example, **pyramidal neurons** (shown in Figure 2.4) have a cell body shaped like a pyramid.

the axon Another major specialized structure of the neuron is the axon, the long extension protruding from the cell body. It is the output end of the cell; every neuron has only one, although the axon itself can have considerable branching at its end. The portion of the axon that emerges from the cell body is called the axon hillock, and this part is very important in the integration process.

Surrounding some axons, although absent at the axon hillock, is a fatty sheath called **myelin.** The myelin sheath insulates the neuron from the surrounding tissue. Along the length of the sheath there are gaps, called **nodes of Ranvier,** where the membrane of the axon is exposed to extracellular fluid. As we shall see later in this chapter, myelination of neurons is important not only because of its insulating properties, but also because it permits neural messages to travel much faster down the length of the axon. Various neurological diseases are characterized by the degeneration of the myelin sheath, such as multiple sclerosis.

The ends of the axon, called **synaptic terminals,** are slightly swollen and contain **synaptic vesicles.** These are small enclosed bodies that hold the chemicals which will be used to communicate with the next neuron. Most axons terminate near the dendrites or the cell body of the next neuron, and make their connections with those parts of the cell, but as we shall see in the next chapter, an axon might also terminate near the axon of another cell. They can also terminate near endocrine organs, or near blood capillaries where they release the chemicals from the vesicles into the bloodstream, thereby affecting very remote target organs.

The **cell membrane** of the neuron is particularly important because it *the cell membrane* functions in the conduction of the neural message along the axon, and also in the reception of the message by the dendrites. Its principle chemicals are proteins and **phospholipids** (a kind of fat). The phospholipids form a layer when they are in contact with water, with the **hydrophilic** (water-seeking) phosphate head in the water, and the **hydrophobic** (water-repelling) fatty acid tail outside; this is very similar to the way a layer of fat will float on top of a pan of water. When there are two surfaces of water, however, as there are inside and outside the neuron, *two* layers of phospholipids are formed. The fatty acid tails are on the inside of the "bilayer sandwich," and the phosphate heads are on the outside, in contact with the two surfaces of water.

The status of the membrane proteins is less clear. Modern theories of the cell membrane suggest that the proteins are inserted inside the two layers of phospholipid, and may float on it, or even pass right through it.

The important function of the membrane is to act as a "molecular sieve" by which the molecules entering and leaving the cell can be controlled. The semipermeable membrane has pores that permit the movement of some substances, but limit others. The membrane is more permeable to lipid-soluble molecules than to water-soluble ones; and small molecules tend to penetrate faster than large ones. Very large molecules may not be able to penetrate the membrane at all. Furthermore, the permeability of the neuron's membrane varies a good deal, depending upon whether the neuron is resting, receiving a message from another cell, or passing along an action potential. We will learn more about the critical role of the cell membrane in information processing in this chapter and the next one.

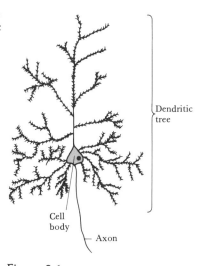

Dendritic tree

Cell body

Axon

Figure 2.6
A neuron with a very extensive dendritic tree.

The main components of the neuron are (1) the *dendrites*, (2) the *cell body* or *soma*, (3) the *axon*, and (4) the *cell membrane*. The dendrites receive input from other cells, and often are dotted with *dendritic spines*. Dendrites often have complicated branching patterns, thus making it possible for a neuron to receive input from many other neurons. The cell body contains the nucleus, and is the place where most of the organelles are located which maintain the life of the cell.

The axon is the output end of the cell, and is a long extension protruding from the cell body. Many axons are surrounded by a *myelin sheath* that serves to insulate it from the extracellular fluid. Gaps along the sheath are called *nodes of Ranvier*. The axon ends in *synaptic terminals*, which contain *synaptic vesicles*. The vesicles contain the neurotransmitter, which carries information from the end of one neuron to the beginning of the next. Substances which are produced in the cell body can be transported down the axon via the *neurotubules*, using *axoplasmic transport*.

Surrounding the entire neuron is a cell membrane, composed of proteins and phospholipids. The permeability of the membrane is capable of changing; this feature plays a critical role in the process of axonal conduction.

axonal conduction

In this section we will see how the properties of the axon's membrane make it ideally suited for transmitting messages down its length. Axonal conduction is basically an electrical process, and involves the movement of charged ions across the cell's membrane. But before we

Figure 2.7
Forces which tend to move ions across a semipermeable membrane.

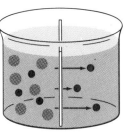
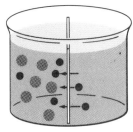
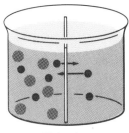

Na$^+$

Cl$^-$

Chloride ions move down their osmotic gradient

Chloride ions move down their electrostatic gradient

An equilibrium between osmotic and electrostatic forces is established. Left side has net positive charge

can discuss how messages are transmitted we will explain the state of the axon when it is not conducting any messages—when it is in its resting state.

forces which act to move ions

In order to understand the kinds of forces which act to move ions, imagine a glass of water that is divided in half by a semipermeable piece of cloth, as shown in Figure 2.7. The pores in the piece of cloth are easily large enough to allow the passage of water molecules, so the water molecules distribute themselves equally on both sides of the membrane.

Now suppose we drop a teaspoonful of salt into one side of the glass. The first thing that would happen is the dissociation of the two ions, sodium (Na^+) and chloride (Cl^-). In solution, many compounds break into their ionic components, each with its own charge.

The next thing that would happen is that the sodium and chloride ions would disperse evenly throughout the water. But in this example, the piece of cloth has pores which are large enough to allow the passage of the small chloride ions, but too small to allow the larger sodium ions to pass through. This means that the chloride ions can disperse throughout the glass, but the sodium ions must remain on the left side. Across a semipermeable membrane, ions tend to move from regions of higher concentrations to regions of lower concentrations, at least as far as they are able to; this force is called *osmosis*. Some of the chloride ions would move to the region of lower concentration on the right, down their **osmotic gradient.** The sodium ions would also move down their osmotic gradient if they were able to.

Osmosis is not the only force that moves ions around. The other important force for our purposes is the **electrostatic gradient.** Like charges repel one another, and unlike charges tend to attract. In the glass of salty water, the force of osmosis is tending to move some of the chloride ions over to the right. But the electrostatic force is tending to push them back to the left, since they are repelled by one another and attracted to the positively charged sodium ions.

Because of these two opposing forces, the chloride ions are in a state of flux. They establish a standoff between moving down their osmotic gradient and moving down their electrostatic gradient. The ultimate result is a state of equilibrium in which the two forces are balanced—a kind of compromise between the effects of the osmotic gradient and the electrostatic gradient. As long as the two forces remain balanced, the concentration of chloride ions on each side remains stable, even though individual chloride ions may be moving back and forth.

the membrane potential

Whenever there is a semipermeable membrane that limits the flow of some ions but not others, there is likely to be a difference in the number of positive ions on either side. In our glass of water, for example, the equilibrium that developed resulted in more positive ions on the left. The left side wound up with a net positive charge. The difference in charge between one side of a membrane and the other is called the **membrane potential.** Its size depends on a number of things, including the concentration of ions on each side, the temperature of the solution, and the permeability characteristics of the membrane. It is possible to measure the size of the membrane potential using a voltmeter. With one electrode placed into the solution on one side of the membrane, and the other placed on the other side, the voltmeter will tell you what the voltage difference is across the membrane. The membrane potential across the axon's membrane is not very large, but it plays a critically important role in axonal conduction.

the resting potential Because the cell membrane of the axon is semipermeable, we can expect that it permits the flow of some molecules more easily than others. Thus we can also expect that the distribution of ions across the membrane will not be equal. Table 2.1 shows the concentration of the four most important ions which are present in the cytoplasm of the axon (the **axoplasm**) and in the fluid surrounding the axon.

When the axon is at rest, its membrane is impermeable to the large negatively charged protein molecules, called **anions,** and practically impermeable to the sodium ions. The anions remain inside the axon and most of the sodium ions remain outside. However, the membrane is fairly permeable to the other two ions, chloride and potassium (K^+). These two distribute themselves on either side of the membrane and reach an equilibrium which balances the forces of the osmotic and electrostatic gradients. The concentrations listed in Table 2.1 for potassium and chloride are the result of this equilibrium.

Table 2.1
The concentration of the four important ions inside and outside the axon (expressed in millimoles/liter)

Ion	Concentration inside the axon	Concentration outside the axon
Sodium (Na^+)	50	460
Potassium (K^+)	400	10
Chloride (Cl^-)	40	560
Anions (A^-)	345	0

Just as in our glass of water, the presence of a semipermeable membrane results not only in the unequal distribution of the ions, but also in a membrane potential. If we measured the voltage difference between the inside and the outside of the axon, we would find that the inside was slightly more negative than the outside. Our voltmeter would record a difference of about −70 millivolts (mV), which is about one-fifteenth the difference between the positive and negative poles of a flashlight battery. This membrane potential which exists while the axon is at rest is called the **resting potential.** As long as the membrane is not disturbed, and no one artificially tries to change the concentration of ions in the solutions, we will continue to record a resting potential of about −70 mV, as shown in Figure 2.8.

Thus when the axon is at rest, there is a membrane potential across the membrane of −70 mV. But the axon's function is to conduct information from one end to the other. As we mentioned in the beginning of this chapter, the axon uses a digital code, and produces "dots" like a telegraph key, at varying rates. In the next section we will see

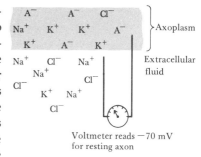

Voltmeter reads −70 mV
for resting axon

Figure 2.8
The axon at rest has a membrane potential of −70 mV. The inside of the axon is slightly more negative relative to the outside.

Figure 2.9
Hyperpolarizations and depolarizations at the axon hillock.

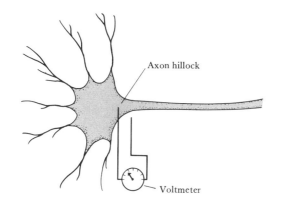

Axon hillock

Voltmeter

Membrane potential

+50

0

−50
−70

Depolarization

Hyperpolorization

Time

how a sudden change in the voltage difference across the membrane constitutes a single "dot," called an action potential.

the action potential *the threshold of the axon.* If we were to place the electrodes of our voltmeter at the axon hillock, as in Figure 2.9, we would find that the resting potential was not as stable as it was further down the axon. Messages, in the form of fluctuations in the membrane potential are coming into the axon hillock all the time. (We will explain the origin of these messages later.) Sometimes the membrane potential increases, and the inside of the axon becomes even more negative relative to the outside. These increases in membrane potential are called **hyperpolarizations.** The membrane potential might increase to −80 mV or −85 mV. Other times, the membrane potential might decrease to −65 mV or −60 mV, and the inside of the axon becomes less negative relative to the outside. These decreases in the membrane potential are called **depolarizations.** (Actually they should be called "hypopolarizations," since "depolarization" means the absence of any membrane potential. But since nearly everyone uses the term "depolarization," we will too.)

Again, recording at the axon hillock, we might notice a rather large depolarization followed by an event which would make us think that the voltmeter had broken down. The membrane potential would suddenly decrease all the way to zero and then go positive, to as high as +50 mV. Just as suddenly, it would drop back down to zero and then increase to a negative value again, as shown in Figure 2.10. This sudden change in the membrane potential is called the **action potential,**

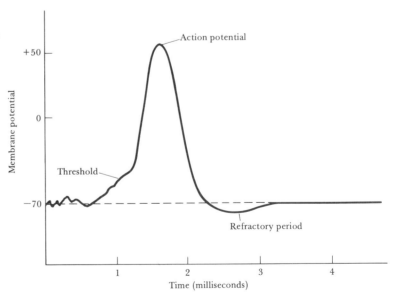

Figure 2.10
The action potential.

and it constitutes the "dot." The large depolarization which occurred just before the action potential reached the axon's **threshold.** When a depolarization at the axon hillock is large enough to reach the axon's threshold (around -55 mV), the axon will fire off an action potential down its length, an event that is also called a "spike."

ionic movements during an action potential. When a depolarization reaches the axon's threshold at the hillock, the characteristics of the axon's membrane at this spot suddenly change. As if a door was thrown open, the membrane's permeability to sodium suddenly becomes very high. Sodium ions rush into the axon, down their osmotic and electrostatic gradients. This influx of positively charged sodium ions is what caused our voltmeter to jump. The inside of the axon gains positive charges, and the inside becomes more positive relative to the outside.

At the peak of the action potential the permeability of the membrane changes. It becomes relatively impermeable to sodium again, and even more permeable to potassium ions than it normally is. Since the inside of the cell is now positive, the forces which were acting on the potassium ions have changed. The positive interior of the axon now pushes the positively charged potassium ions out, down their electrostatic gradient. These ions are also moving down their own osmotic gradient since the concentration of potassium is much lower outside the cell. The movement of the potassium ions out of the cell is what caused the membrane potential to go back to a negative level.

refractory period. In fact, the movement of the potassium ions out of the cell produces a brief **refractory period,** in which the membrane potential goes to around -75 mV. Only gradually does the membrane potential return to its resting level of -70 mV.

When the axon hillock has just fired off an action potential, and that area of the membrane is in the refractory period, it is much less likely that another action potential can be triggered. This is because any depolarizations which reached the axon hillock would not only have to reach threshold, but they would have to overcome the hyperpolarization which is associated with the refractory period. Thus the duration of the action potential itself, combined with the duration of the refractory period sets a limit on the rate at which an axon can transmit action potentials. The duration of the action potential is less than one-thousandth of a second, and the refractory period may last a few milliseconds. So an axon can transmit well over 100 action potentials per second. The telegraph key analogy thus falls apart—no one could press the key that fast.

the sodium–potassium pump. The sudden influx of sodium ions, followed by the efflux of potassium ions, would suggest that the axon would eventually lose all of its potassium and fill up with sodium. Actually, the amount of sodium that is gained with each action potential is very small. In the area of axoplasm right next to the membrane, however, it is enough to change the membrane potential to +50 mV. But after many action potentials, the gain of sodium and the loss of potassium would eventually make the osmotic gradients, down which the ions must flow during an action potential, much less steep. To prevent this, the axon has a **sodium–potassium pump**—a metabolic mechanism which carries the sodium ions back outside and carries the potassium ions back inside the cell. Since the pump has to move these ions against their osmotic gradients it must use energy. In fact some scientists have proposed that the sodium–potassium pump uses 40% of the neuron's energy.

One hypothesis to account for the movement of potassium and sodium ions against their osmotic gradients involves a carrier molecule that would move through the membrane. On its way out, it would carry sodium, and on its way back in, it would pick up potassium. The unknown carrier molecule might have varying affinities for sodium and potassium depending on the different ionic concentrations inside and outside the cell.

conducting the action potential down the axon

the all-or-none principle of axonal conduction. If we were recording the membrane potential at some distance from the axon hillock, we would not see the small hyperpolarizations and depolarizations that we saw at the hillock. These small changes in the membrane potential decay long before they reach the end of the axon. But we would see the action potentials. A depolarization large enough to reach threshold at the hillock triggers an action potential. An action potential is such a large depolarization that it immediately reaches the threshold of the part of the axon which is right next to it, and sets off an action potential there. The wave moves right down the axon. This means that an axon either transmits an action potential down its length, or it does not. This feature of axonal conduction is called the **all-or-none principle** of axonal conduction. The size of the action potential remains the same along the entire length of the axon. The fluctuations which appear at the hillock never reach the other end; only the action potentials arrive.

saltatory conduction in myelinated axons. Most axons in the vertebrates are surrounded by myelin, and the membrane is only exposed to the extracellular fluid at the nodes of Ranvier. This means that an action potential can only occur at the nodes, not in the myelinated segments. An action potential which is triggered at the unmyelinated axon hillock will move down the axon, diminishing in size and decaying, just as though it were a very large depolarization. But because an action potential is such a large depolarization it is easily still large enough to trigger another action potential at the first node of Ranvier. This new action potential travels to the next node, and it is still large enough when it gets there to reach the threshold and trigger yet another action potential. At each node, the action potential is amplified back to its original size, so it reaches the axon endings with the same strength. This kind of "skipping" that occurs in myelinated axons is called **saltatory conduction.**

The advantage to saltatory conduction may not be immediately obvious, but it is quite an important advantage. In unmyelinated axons, the speed with which an axon can move an action potential down its length is fairly slow. The movement of ions in every segment of the membrane takes some time. But in myelinated axons, the action potential can skip from node to node. Ionic movements only have to occur in a few places along the axon, rather than over the entire membrane. To give you an idea how fast these myelinated axons can transmit information, some mammalian axons can move an action potential as fast as 224 miles per hour.

Another advantage to myelination is the conservation of energy which is required by the sodium—potassium pump. Since sodium is gained and potassium is lost only at the nodes of Ranvier, the pump does not have to work so hard to maintain the ionic concentrations inside the axoplasm.

The process by which information is moved from one end of the axon to the other is basically electrical and involves the movement of ions across the membrane. At rest, the concentration of ions inside the axon is slightly different from the concentration outside because the axon's membrane is semipermeable. *Osmotic* and *electrostatic* forces balance one another so that at rest, the four important ions (sodium, potassium, chloride, and anions) are unequally distributed inside and outside the cell. There is much more sodium (Na^+) outside, for example, and the outside has a net positive charge. The difference between the charge inside and outside the axon at rest is called the *resting potential,* and is about -70 mV.

At the axon hillock, messages are coming in from all over the cell body and dendrites in the form of *hyperpolarizations* and *depolarizations.* During a hyperpolarization the membrane potential might increase to -75 mV, and during a depolarization it might decrease to -65 mV. If one of these depolarizations is large enough to reach the axon's *threshold,* the axon hillock will fire off an *action potential.* The axon's membrane at this spot becomes very permeable to sodium and these ions rush into the axon down their osmotic and electrostatic gradients. The inside of the axon, having gained positive ions, becomes more positive; during the action potential the difference in voltage between the inside and the outside changes to about $+50$ mV.

summary
Axonal Conduction

At the peak of the action potential, the membrane closes its doors to sodium, and becomes even more permeable to potassium. Potassium ions leak out of the axon down their osmotic and electrostatic gradients. This brings the membrane potential back down to a negative value, and even overshoots the resting potential of −70 mV. During this *refractory period*, it is more difficult to trigger another action potential.

In unmyelinated axons, the action potential moves like a wave down the axon. The action potential on one segment of the axon is a very large depolarization which easily reaches the threshold of the next spot. Thus the axon will either fire or not fire off an action potential. The small hyperpolarizations and depolarizations which occur at the axon hillock, and which do not trigger an action potential, decay long before they travel very far down the axon. This is called the *all-or-none principle* of axonal conduction.

In myelinated axons, the all-or-none principle still applies, but action potentials are only triggered at the nodes of Ranvier. Between the nodes they decay slightly, but are still large enough to trigger another action potential at the next node.

The gain in sodium and the loss of potassium during action potentials might eventually change the concentrations of ions inside and outside the axon. But a metabolic pump, which uses energy, carries the sodium outside and the potassium back in to prevent this from happening. This metabolic machinery is called the *sodium–potassium pump.*

---

integration at the axon hillock

Another kind of information processing which the neuron must conduct is integration. The axon hillock is integrating all the messages which are coming into it, and making a decision about whether to fire off an action potential based on the integration process. Messages, in the form of hyperpolarizations and depolarizations, are arriving from all over the dendrites and the cell body. (In the next chapter we will see where these messages come from, but for the moment it is enough to know that they are produced by the effect of neurotransmitter from other neurons.) The axon hillock uses the processes of **spatial summation** and **temporal summation** to perform the integration.

spatial summation

Figure 2.11 shows a neuron that is receiving two inputs, from two different places on the dendrites. One place is receiving a hyperpolarization message and transmitting it to the axon hillock; the other place is receiving a depolarization message and is also sending it to the axon hillock. Both of these messages begin to decay as they spread toward the axon hillock, since the cell body's membrane cannot produce action potentials. But they are still fairly large by the time they reach the hillock.

They arrive at the axon hillock at exactly the same moment in time. At the hillock, the integration process takes place. The two messages

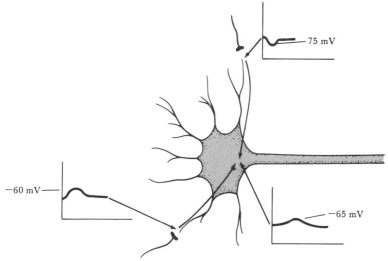

Figure 2.11
Spatial summation of two inputs (one depolarization and one hyperpolarization) at the axon hillock.

are algebraicly added together, and the result is a small depolarization which changes the resting potential from -70 mV to about -68 mV. This kind of integration is called spatial summation. Spatial summation also means that two depolarizing inputs, each of which is too small to trigger an action potential at the hillock, can sum together to reach threshold.

Normally, since many neurons are providing input to the neuron which is doing the integrating, the axon hillock is spatially summating quite a number of inputs. Whenever the spatial summation of all the inputs which reach the axon hillock at the same time produces a depolarization which reaches the axon's threshold, the axon hillock will fire off an action potential.

Integration of inputs at the axon hillock involves the summation of messages across time, as well as space. A small depolarization arriving at the hillock lasts for a millisecond or more, so another one coming right after it can be added to the first. This phenomenon is shown in Figure 2.12.

temporal summation

By the same token, a suprathreshold depolarization that would normally trigger an action potential can be inhibited if a hyperpolarization arrives just before it. The axon hillock is summing its inputs, both in time and in space, and then deciding whether to trigger an action potential. The decision-making process is entirely based on whether the summed integration reaches the axon's threshold of excitation.

The effect of this integration process is that a chain of neurons does not act like a row of dominoes. Just because one neuron in the chain fires off an action potential, and thus sends a message to the next neu-

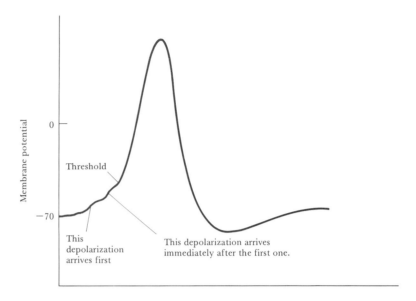

Figure 2.12
Temporal summation of two small but successive depolarizations which together reach the threshold at the axon hillock.

In the figure: Membrane potential (vertical axis), 0, Threshold, −70, This depolarization arrives first, This depolarization arrives immediately after the first one.

ron, does not mean that the next neuron will fire. The second neuron's behavior depends upon *all* of its inputs.

summary

Integration at the Axon Hillock

Inputs in the form of hyperpolarizations and depolarizations are coming into the axon hillock from all over the dendrites and cell body. The hillock uses the processes of *spatial* and *temporal summation* to integrate all of these messages. Spatial summation means that two inputs which arrive at the same time, and which are coming from two different places on the cell body or dendrites, will be algebraicly summated. A hyperpolarization might cancel out the effects of a depolarization, and no action potential will be triggered. Two small depolarizations might sum together to trigger an action potential.

Inputs are also temporally summated because a depolarization or a hyperpolarization last for a millisecond or more. An input which follows one of these events will be added to it. For example, a small depolarization which is followed by another small one might reach the axon's threshold and the axon will fire off an action potential. Normally, a single neuron receives input from perhaps hundreds of other neurons, so the integration process might involve the summation of hundreds of different inputs.

In this chapter we discussed how the neuron performs two of its information processing functions: axonal conduction and integration. In the next chapter we will see how it performs the third kind of information processing: synaptic transmission.

KEY
TERMS

information processing
digital code
analog code
axonal conduction
synaptic transmission
integration
action potential
neurotransmitter
axon hillock
dendrites
cell body
soma
axon
synaptic terminals
dendritic trees
dendritic spines
pyramidal neurons
myelin
nodes of Ranvier
synaptic vesicles

cell membrane
phospholipids
hydrophilic
hydrophobic
neurotubules
axoplasmic transport
osmotic gradient
electrostatic gradient
membrane potential
axoplasm
resting potential
threshold of the axon
hyperpolarizations
depolarizations
refractory period
sodium–potassium pump
all-or-none principle
saltatory conduction
spatial summation
temporal summation

SUGGESTED
READINGS

Eccles, J. C. (1973). *The Understanding of the Brain*. McGraw-Hill, New York.
Katz, B. (1966). *Nerve, Muscle and Synapse*. McGraw-Hill, New York.
(Both of these books provide more detail about the process of axonal conduction.)
Keynes, R. D. (1971). The nerve impulse and the squid. In *Physiological Psychology* (R. F. Thompson, ed.), pp. 128–135. W. H. Freeman and Company, San Francisco. (This edited book contains many readings from *Scientific American*. This one by Keynes details some of the experiments on the squid's giant axon.)

3

the neuron: synaptic transmission

introduction In this chapter we will see how neurons communicate with one another at the site of their connection, called the synapse. The neurons used a digital code to carry information down the length of their axon. But to pass information to the next neuron they use an analog code—one which is chemical in nature, rather than electrical. When an action potential reaches the synaptic terminals, a small amount of chemical called neurotransmitter is released. This chemical diffuses across the small gap between the synaptic terminal and the membrane of the next cell. When the chemical reaches the next cell, it produces a change in the membrane which results in a small hyperpolarization or depolarization. These spread to the axon hillock where they are integrated with messages coming into the neuron from other places on the dendrites and cell body.

The study of synaptic transmission has been one of the most fascinating stories in physiological psychology. At first, people thought that the end of one neuron and the beginning of the next actually touched each other, and the message was carried electrically throughout the nervous system. (Some neurons actually do touch each other, but these **gap junctions** are less well understood, and are also less usual in vertebrates.) When anatomists observed that neurons did not touch and that there was a small space between them, people suspected that the action potential might be carried across the space like a spark. But eventually it became clear that the synapse uses a completely different coding process for passing along information—one that involves the release of one of several different neurotransmitters.

In this chapter we will first discuss the structure of the synapse. Then we will explore the process of synaptic transmission which involves three basic steps: (1) release of neurotransmitter, (2) the effect of the neurotransmitter on the next cell, and (3) inactivation of the

Figure 3.1
The synapse.

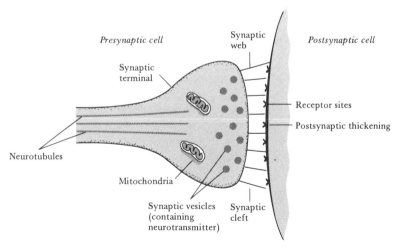

Presynaptic cell

Synaptic web

Postsynaptic cell

Synaptic terminal

Receptor sites

Postsynaptic thickening

Neurotubules

Mitochondria

Synaptic vesicles (containing neurotransmitter)

Synaptic cleft

neurotransmitter. The next section of this chapter examines some of the alternative ways that neurons can communicate with one another. Last, we will look at some of the neurotransmitters, particularly those which appear again and again throughout this book.

The synapse, shown in Figure 3.1, is composed of three basic parts: (1) the axon endings, or **synaptic terminals** of the **presynaptic cell** (the neuron sending the message), (2) the space between the neurons, also called the **synaptic cleft,** and (3) the portion of the **postsynaptic cell** which is across from the terminal and which receives the message by means of the **postsynaptic membrane.**

the structure of the synapse

As the axon reaches its destination, it shows a great deal of branching. At the end of each branch is a small swelling called the synaptic terminal. This is the structure that contains the chemical released in response to the neuron's action potentials. The terminal contains a large number of **synaptic vesicles,** which are the storehouses for the neurotransmitter substance. In addition to the vesicles, the terminal also contains mitochondria (to provide energy) and neurotubules (used in axoplasmic transport).

the synaptic terminals

The gap between the pre- and postsynaptic cell can range from 120 to 200 angstrom units (one angstrom unit, abbreviated Å, is 10^{-8} cm), and so does not present a tremendous distance which must be crossed by the neurotransmitter molecules. In some synapses, particularly those which are prevalent in the invertebrates, very small gaps have been seen. These connection points are the gap junctions that we mentioned earlier. It is likely that information is passed across these junctions in an electrical way, rather than in the chemical process that is used in most vertebrate synapses.

the synaptic cleft

Recently anatomists have observed that the synaptic cleft is not just filled with extracellular fluid. It also contains a **synaptic web** which appears to bind the presynaptic membrane to the postsynaptic membrane. The web is a system of filaments but its function in synaptic transmission is not known.

The membrane that is directly opposite from the synaptic terminal is called the postsynaptic membrane, and it often appears to be slightly thickened compared to places which are not functioning in synaptic transmission. The postsynaptic membrane also contains **receptor sites** which receive the molecules of transmitter substance.

the postsynaptic membrane

Usually, the information from the presynaptic cell is passed, via a synapse, to places on the dendrites of the postsynaptic cell. This is why we referred to the dendrites as the input end of the cell in Chapter 2. This kind of synaptic contact is called **axo–dentritic,** because it involves the axon endings of one cell, and the dendrites of the next. But axons also terminate in places other than the dendrites of the next cell. Terminations on the cell body, for example, are called **axo–somatic contacts.** Some axon endings even terminate on the axon of another cell in **axo–axonic contacts.** Another kind of contact, called **dendro–dendritic,** does not even involve the axon or its terminals. As its name implies, it involves the dendrites of two neurons.

The postsynaptic cell need not even be another neuron. Later in the book we will see that axons terminate on muscle cells, producing a synapse called a **neuromuscular junction.** They can also terminate on blood vessels, intestines, endocrine glands, or they even might release the contents of their vesicles directly into the bloodstream. The nervous system is anything but a closed system, and neurons are capable of controlling the activity of many body functions.

---

summary
The Structure of the Synapse

The synapse, which is the connection point between two neurons, has three basic parts: (1) the axon endings or *synaptic terminals* of the *presynaptic cell,* (2) the space between the neurons, or *synaptic cleft,* and (3) the portion of the *postsynaptic cell* which receives the message.

The synaptic terminals are swollen knobs that contain *synaptic vesicles.* Stored inside the vesicles is the neurotransmitter substance which is released into the synaptic cleft when an action potential courses down the axon. The postsynaptic membrane is often thickened, and it contains receptor sites that receive the molecules of neurotransmitter substance. Synapses can occur between the axon endings of one cell and the dendrites of another (*axo–dendritic*), or between the axon endings and the cell body of another cell (*axo–somatic*), or even between two axons (*axo–axonic*) or two dendrites (*dendro–dendritic*). Axons can also terminate on muscle cells (*neuromuscular junction*), near blood vessels, or on body organs.

---

synaptic transmission　In this section we will discuss the process of synaptic transmission as it occurs in axo–dendritic and axo–somatic contacts. These appear throughout the nervous system and are very basic to the understanding of physiological psychology. Axo–axonic and dendro–dendritic contacts will be discussed later in this section because the details of transmission at these synapses are slightly different.

Synaptic transmission involves three basic events: (1) the release of the neurotransmitter substance, (2) the **postsynaptic potentials,** which are produced by the effects of the neurotransmitter on the postsynaptic membrane, and (3) the inactivation of the neurotransmitter.

When the depolarizing action potential courses down the axon and then through all of its branches, it eventually results in the rapid depolarization of the membrane of the synaptic terminals. As a result of this depolarization one or more of the vesicles releases its contents into the synaptic cleft. The amount of neurotransmitter depends on the rapid change in membrane potential from its resting level (-70 mV) to its level at the peak of an action potential ($+50$ mV). Normally, since all action potentials are the same size, the amount of neurotransmitter released with each spike is the same. (We shall see later that axo–axonic contacts can vary the amount of transmitter released, however.)

release of neurotransmitter

Figure 3.2 shows the process, called **exocytosis,** by which the synaptic vesicles fuse with the presynaptic membrane and spill their contents into the synaptic cleft. The vesicle migrates to the membrane of the synaptic terminal and fuses with it. The combined membrane then ruptures, and the neurotransmitter contained within the vesicle spills into the cleft. Eventually the vesicle's membrane is recycled and used again.

Once the molecules of neurotransmitter have been spilled into the cleft, they diffuse across the gap and affect the postsynaptic membrane. When they get there, they attach very briefly to the receptor sites on the postsynaptic membrane. The permeability of the membrane is slightly altered when the neurotransmitter attaches, and the concentration of ions inside and outside the membrane changes.

postsynaptic potentials

If we were to record from the postsynaptic cell immediately after neurotransmitter had been released, we would see one of two events: a graded depolarization, as shown in Figure 3.3, or a graded hyperpolarization. These are called postsynaptic potentials or PSPs for short. A PSP which happens to be a depolarization is called an **excitatory postsynaptic potential (EPSP)** because this kind of event will tend to increase the probability that an action potential will be triggered at the axon hillock. A PSP which happens to be a hyperpolarization is called an **inhibitory postsynaptic potential (IPSP)** because it will tend to inhibit the triggering of an action potential when it reaches the axon hillock.

Whether the release of neurotransmitter results in an EPSP or an IPSP in the postsynaptic cell depends upon two things. First, it depends upon what kind of neurotransmitter substance is used by the presynaptic cell. We shall see later in the chapter that a few neurotransmitters seem to always produce either an EPSP or an IPSP in every synapse in which they are used. But some neurotransmitters can produce EPSPs or IPSPs at different synapses. This is because of the nature of the receptor site. A neurotransmitter that combines with one

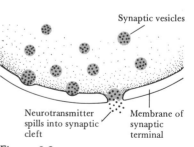

Figure 3.2
The process of exocytosis.

Synaptic vesicles

Neurotransmitter spills into synaptic cleft

Membrane of synaptic terminal

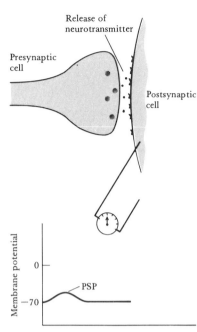

Figure 3.3
A graded excitatory (depolarizing) postsynaptic potential recorded immediately after the presynaptic cell released neurotransmitter.

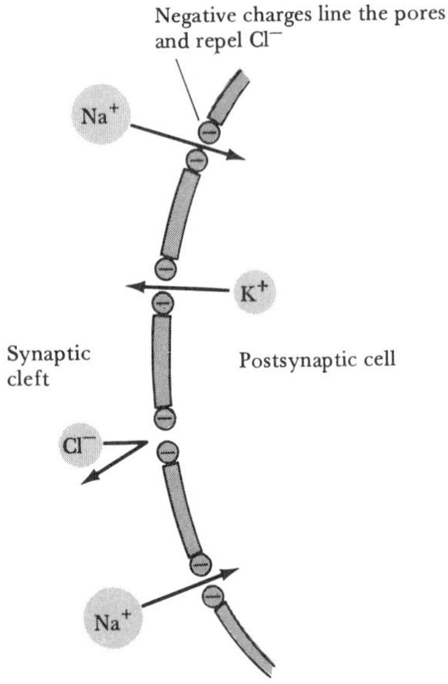

Figure 3.4
Ionic movements during an EPSP.

kind of receptor site might result in an EPSP; but if it attaches to another kind of receptor site at a different synapse, the same neurotransmitter might produce an IPSP.

These PSPs are not like action potentials—there is no sudden change in the potential of the membrane. They are graded changes which will quickly spread to the axon hillock and be integrated with the rest of the input that the neuron is receiving. It is important to remember the distinction between these graded potentials and the kind of all-or-none spikes which develop in the axon. However a graded EPSP might *lead* to the triggering of an action potential, *if* it is large enough to reach threshold, and *if* there are very few IPSPs arriving at the axon hillock about the same time which might cancel it out.

The exact nature of the receptor sites and the effects of the neurotransmitter substance on them is not yet clear. Perhaps the receptor sites act like little doors over the pores in the membrane which control the flow of ions; the neurotransmitter molecules might be able to open some of the doors. We can speculate on the changes that must occur in the membrane since we know that they are producing depolarizations and hyperpolarizations. These must involve the movement of ions across the membrane.

ionic movements during an EPSP. When a neurotransmitter produces an EPSP in the postsynaptic cell, the concentration of positive ions inside the cell increases. Eccles (1965) proposed that the EPSP is due mostly to the influx of sodium ions. When the neurotransmitter combines with the receptor sites, the pores in the membrane open slightly wider and admit some sodium ions into the cell. This would make the inside slightly more positive, and would explain the depolarization which occurs during an EPSP. One problem with this hypothesis is that any pore large enough to admit sodium would also be large enough to allow potassium and chloride ions to pass through. Eccles has proposed that some potassium does leak out of the cell during an EPSP. If it did not, the EPSP would be even larger. But the negatively charged chloride ions, which would tend to move into the cell along with the sodium ions down their osmotic gradient, are prevented from passing through because the pores are lined with negative charges, as shown in Figure 3.4. The negative charge would repel the negatively charged chloride ions, but would attract the positively charged sodium and potassium ions.

ionic movements during an IPSP. When a neurotransmitter produces an IPSP, then the inside of the cell becomes even more negative relative to the outside than it normally is. This phenomenon is probably due to the opening of pores large enough to allow the passage of potassium and chloride ions, but too small to allow sodium to pass through. The events shown in Figure 3.5 demonstrate how these ions would move about. When the neurotransmitter combined with the receptor sites, small pores would allow K⁺ to leak out down its osmotic gradient. Some chloride would also leak out because it would be traveling down its electrostatic gradient. But the net loss of potassium would lead to a hyperpolarization.

The EPSPs and IPSPs which occur in the postsynaptic cell when neurotransmitter is released by the presynaptic cell spread across the cell body's membrane and arrive very quickly at the axon hillock. There they are integrated and the axon hillock will fire off an action potential if the integration results in a net depolarization which reaches the axon's threshold. A single neuron may be receiving input in the form of IPSPs and EPSPs from many synapses which are spread over the dendrites and cell body. All of them are integrated using the processes of spatial and temporal summation, which we discussed in the last chapter.

Once the neurotransmitter is released by the synaptic terminal, it is very important that it only have a very brief effect on the postsynaptic membrane. The molecules of neurotransmitter should not remain permanently attached to the receptor sites because this would make it impossible for the postsynaptic membrane to receive new messages. Synapses have two mechanisms to make sure that the neurotransmitter's effect on the postsynaptic membrane is very brief: **inactivation by enzymes** and **re-uptake.**

inactivation of the neurotransmitter

inactivation by enzymes. One mechanism for terminating the effect of the neurotransmitter involves enzymes. These enzymes are located on the postsynaptic membrane so that as soon as the neurotransmitter arrives, it is broken down by an enzyme. Then the broken pieces of the neurotransmitter molecules are no longer capable of interacting with the receptor sites. One example of an inactivating enzyme is **acetylcholinesterase** (called AChE for short), which inactivates the neurotransmitter **acetylcholine** (ACh). Later in this chapter we will discuss the synthesis and breakdown of several of the neurotransmitters; you will notice that enzymes always end in − ase, which makes them easy to spot.

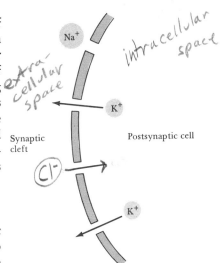

Figure 3.5
Ionic movements during an IPSP.

re-uptake. Instead of being inactivated by enzymes on the postsynaptic membrane, some neurotransmitters are taken back up directly into the synaptic terminal. As soon as the neurotransmitter is released, the synaptic terminal takes the chemical back up so that it only has a brief time in which to affect the postsynaptic membrane. Synapses which use the neurotransmitter **norepinephrine,** for example, use this re-uptake mechanism to terminate the effects of the neurotransmitter on the next cell.

alternative kinds of communication between neurons The process of synaptic transmission which we have been discussing applies mainly to axo—dendritic and axo—somatic contacts. But there are other kinds of synapses in which transmission is slightly different. The events of synaptic transmission at the neuromuscular junction, for example, are similar; but since the postsynaptic cell is a muscle cell, rather than another neuron, the events in the muscle cell are different. We will discuss these events later in the book (Chapter 9), when we deal with the control of movement. The events at axo—axonic and dendro—dendritic contacts are also slightly different, and we will discuss them here.

axo—axonic contacts. Figure 3.6 diagrams a synapse in which the axon ending of one cell terminates on the axon of another cell, very near one of its synaptic terminals. Suppose some excitatory neurotransmitter is released into the synaptic cleft because there was an action potential in the presynaptic cell. This would cause a depolarization in the membrane of the postsynaptic cell. This depolarization would not be integrated at the axon hillock, but it can have interesting effects on the postsynaptic cell nonetheless. If a spike is coursing down the axon, and it arrives at this point when the postsynaptic membrane is depolarized, then the postsynaptic cell will continue to carry the spike. But since the axon's membrane at this point was already slightly depolarized, then the difference between its potential just before and just after the spike arrived will be smaller than if the depolarization had not been there.

As we mentioned earlier, the amount of neurotransmitter which is released by the postsynaptic cell is dependent upon the rapid and very large change in membrane potential which accompanies a spike. The depolarization just before the synaptic terminal, which appeared because of the release of excitatory neurotransmitter by the presynaptic cell, diminished both the amount and the quickness of the change in membrane potential. Instead of a rapid change from the resting level of -70 mV to the peak of the action potential ($+50$ mV), the membrane near the synaptic terminal only changed from its depolarized level (e.g., -60 mV) to $+50$ mV. This may seem like only a minor difference, but it has quite an impact on the amount of neurotransmitter which is subsequently released by the postsynaptic cell. The synaptic terminal of the postsynaptic cell might now only release half as much neurotransmitter as it would have if it had not been inhibited by this axo—axonic contact. This phenomenon is called **presynaptic inhibition,** because it tends to inhibit the amount of neurotransmitter

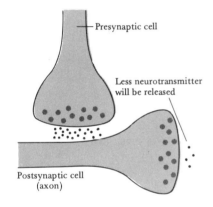

Presynaptic cell

Less neurotransmitter will be released

Postsynaptic cell (axon)

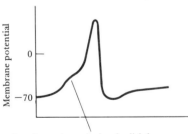

Membrane potential

0

−70

Axon's membrane is already slightly depolarized by excitatory neurotransmitter before spike arrives

Figure 3.6
Presynaptic inhibition at an axo—axonic contact.

which is released in response to an action potential in the postsynaptic cell's terminal.

Presynaptic inhibition differs from postsynaptic inhibition in that the former occurs because of the result of excitatory neurotransmitter affecting the cell just before its synaptic terminal. The latter results from the effects of inhibitory neurotransmitter affecting the dendrites or cell body. Presynaptic inhibition is a much more powerful way to inhibit the activity of a cell, because the message is not integrated at the axon hillock. It directly affects the amount of transmitter released by the synaptic terminal. This kind of synaptic contact is rather widespread, at least in the networks of neurons which carry sensory information to the brain.

An axo–axonic contact might also involve **presynaptic facilitation.** In this case, the presynaptic cell might be releasing inhibitory neurotransmitter. This would cause a hyperpolarization on the postsynaptic cell's axon, and the rate and amount of change during the spike would be larger than usual. Thus slightly more neurotransmitter would be released by the postsynaptic cell's terminal than normal.

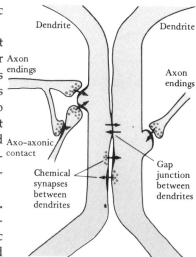

Figure 3.7
Various kinds of communication between neurons, especially dendrodendritic contacts. [Modified from Schmitt et al. (1976), Fig. 1. Copyright 1976 by the American Association for the Advancement of Science.]

dendro–dendritic contacts. Recently neuroscientists have come to the conclusion that the kinds of communication which occur between neurons is much more complex than we had previously thought (Schmitt *et al.,* 1976). Not only are neurons able to pass information along by means of their axon endings, but they are able to pass information by means of their dendrites, without ever having to go through the process of axonal conduction. Anatomists have observed that the dendrites of some neurons come into very close contact in some places, and they hypothesize that these contacts may represent actual synapses or gap junctions. Figure 3.7 shows a schematic diagram of how complex the interactions between neurons may be. The dendrites in this diagram are acting as both postsynaptic cells (as they would in the regular kinds of synapses) but also as presynaptic cells (as they would in these dendro–dendritic contacts).

These contacts between dendrites would provide a means for neurons to pass along information in "local circuits." The information, in the form of graded hyperpolarizations and depolarizations, could be moved directly from the dendrite of one cell to the dendrite of the next, without ever having to go through the axon. At the moment, not very much is known about how these contacts work, but it is clear that they exist. In fact, some cells in the eye and in the nose have no axons at all, so they must be using a form of communication which does not involve axonal conduction. We are only in the third chapter and already it has become a cliché to say that the more we learn about the brain, the more complicated it appears.

summary
Synaptic Transmission

The process of synaptic transmission at axo–dendritic and axo–somatic contacts involves three basic steps: (1) the release of the neurotransmitter by the synaptic terminal, (2) the *postsynaptic potentials,* which are produced in the postsynaptic cell, and (3) the inactivation of the neurotransmitter.

When a spike courses down the axon, the membrane of the synaptic terminal is rapidly depolarized. This causes one or more of the synaptic vesicles to move to the presynaptic membrane, fuse with it, and spill its contents into the synaptic cleft, in a process called *exocytosis.* The neurotransmitter diffuses across the cleft, locks onto receptor sites in the postsynaptic membrane, and produces a *postsynaptic potential* (PSP). The PSP might be an excitatory one which is a graded depolarization *(EPSP),* or it might be an inhibitory one which is a graded hyperpolarization *(IPSP).* Whether a neurotransmitter produces an EPSP or an IPSP depends partly on the nature of the transmitter substance, and partly on the nature of the receptor sites. During an EPSP, sodium ions leak into the postsynaptic cell and some potassium ions leak out. During an IPSP, potassium ions leak out along with some chloride ions. The neurotransmitter substance can be inactivated in one of two ways: (1) *inactivation by enzymes* that are located on the postsynaptic membrane, or (2) *re-uptake* by the presynaptic cell.

At axo–axonic and dendro–dendritic contacts, the process of transmission is slightly different. When one axon terminates near the synaptic terminal of another axon (axon–axonic contact), the release of excitatory neurotransmitter into the synaptic cleft results in *presynaptic inhibition.* The amount of transmitter subsequently released by the postsynaptic cell's terminal is reduced. The release of an inhibitory transmitter at this kind of contact would result in *presynaptic facilitation.* In dendro–dendritic contacts, axonal conduction is not involved at all. Graded hyperpolarizations or depolarizations are passed directly from the dendrite of one cell to the dendrite of another, completely bypassing the process of axonal conduction.

the neurotransmitters

To be identified as a neurotransmitter, a chemical should meet a number of criteria. One set of criteria (McLennon, 1970) includes the following: (1) the chemical should be found within the presynaptic neuron (this seems rather obvious but it is more difficult to demon- strate than you might imagine); (2) the presynaptic neuron should possess the enzymes necessary to synthesize the chemical; (3) en- zymes which inactivate the chemical should be present at the synapse; (4) application of the chemical to the postsynaptic membrane should mimic the effects of the normal neurotransmitter; and (5) during nor- mal stimulation, the chemical should be present in the extracellular fluid.

These criteria have been very challenging for any chemical to meet. But neuroscientists generally agree that several chemicals act as neurotransmitters in the nervous system, and hypothesize that some more will eventually be found. The chemicals which are thought to be neurotransmitters include *acetylcholine* (ACh), *norepinephrine* (NE), *dopamine, serotonin, epinephrine, gamma-aminobutyric acid* (GABA), and a few others. In this section we will discuss those neurotransmitters that are most involved in behavior (at least as far as we know), and which will crop up again and again throughout this book. First, we will discuss the synthesis and breakdown of the neurotransmitter, and second, we will discuss some of the drugs which are used to affect synaptic transmission at synapses which use the neurotransmitter. These drugs sometimes have complicated chemical names, but they are important because they often have quite profound effects on behavior.

Drugs can affect synaptic transmission in many different ways. For example, they might inhibit the synthesis of the neurotransmitter so that the synaptic terminal does not have enough of it to release; the synapse would then become less efficient. Or they might interfere with the inactivation of the neurotransmitter so that there is too much of it in the synapse; the synapse would then become overactive. Or a drug might have a structure which is so similar to the neurotransmitter's structure that it can mimic its actions on the postsynaptic membrane. When the drug is capable of locking onto the receptor sites, but not capable of producing a PSP, the drug is called a **false transmitter.** Drugs have become a very powerful tool in the arsenal of the physiological psychologist because they can tell us a great deal about how a network of neurons which uses a particular neurotransmitter might be involved in a particular behavior.

A synapse which uses the neurotransmitter **acetylcholine (ACh)** is called a **cholinergic synapse.** ACh is the neurotransmitter which is used by the neurons which terminate on muscle cells at the neuromuscular junction. As we shall see in Chapter 9, the release of ACh at these synapses results in a kind of EPSP in the muscle cell, so here it is an excitatory neurotransmitter. ACh is also present in other areas of the peripheral nervous system, and is thought to be used as a neurotransmitter in the brain as well. It may not act like an excitatory neurotransmitter all the time, however.

acetylcholine (ACh)

synthesis and breakdown ACh is synthesized by the following reaction:

$$\text{acetyl CoA + choline} \xrightarrow{\text{choline acetylase}} \text{ACh + CoA}$$

Coenzyme A (CoA) is a substance which takes part in many reactions in the body. In order to make ACh, enzyme coenzyme A and its attached acetate ion are broken apart and the acetate is combined with **choline**. This reaction is accomplished by the catalytic enzyme **choline acetylase**. One of the **cholinesterase** enzymes, such as

acetylcholinesterase, then breaks down ACh in the following reaction:

$$ACh + H_2O \xrightarrow[\text{cholinesterase}]{} choline + acetate$$

Some of the choline is then taken back up and reused to make new molecules of ACh. Figure 3.8 shows a cholinergic synapse and also shows some of the chemical reactions that take place.

drugs that affect cholinergic synapses. Quite a variety of drugs can affect cholinergic synapses by interfering with the neurotransmitter's synthesis, inactivation, or blocking its action on the receptor sites. **Physostigmine,** for example, inhibits acetylcholinesterase. This has the net effect of allowing ACh to accumulate in the synapse, thereby increasing the size of the PSPs in the next neuron. It causes violent muscular contractions. In the form of the Calabar bean from which it is derived, it was once used as a test of guilt or innocence in some tribes of West Africa. The suspect was asked to swallow the poison; if he was confident of his innocence, he would do this quickly and then vomit up the poison. If he were guilty, he would hesitate and die. A different form of physostigmine has a more useful purpose. It has been used in the treatment of **myasthenia gravis,** a debilitating disease which produces extremely weak muscles, presumably because the individual does not have enough acetylcholine at the neuromuscular junctions.

ACh is known to have two different kinds of receptor sites, called **muscarinic** and **nicotinic receptors.** These receptors appear in differ-

Figure 3.8
A cholinergic synapse and its various chemical reactions.

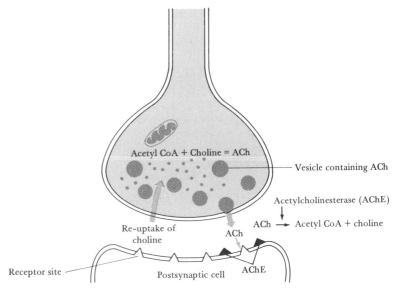

ent places in the nervous system; for example, the neuromuscular junction has nicotinic receptors, while other parts of the nervous system have the muscarinic variety. These receptors were named because of the drugs which are known to stimulate them, **muscarine** and **nicotine.** Muscarine can be extracted from one of the poison mushrooms, and it has a direct excitatory effect on the postsynaptic membranes at the ACh synapses which have muscarinic receptors. The symptoms of mushroom poisoning include profound sweating, increased salivation, pupillary constriction, and slowing of heart rate.

Another interesting drug that interferes with muscarinic receptors is **atropine.** This drug, derived from *Atropa belladonna* or deadly nightshade, causes the reverse effects of muscarine. It acts like a false transmitter by blocking the receptors but not stimulating them, like muscarine does. *Atropa belladonna* was used as a poison by medieval evildoers, and also by Roman and Egyptian women who applied small amounts of the substance to their eyelids. This made their pupils dilate and appear more beautiful, at least according to them. In fact, the word "belladonna" means beautiful woman.

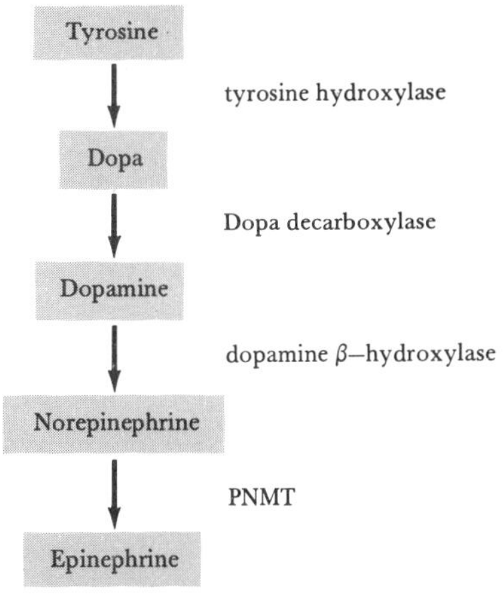

Figure 3.9
Biosynthesis of the catecholamines.

Norepinephrine (also called **noradrenaline**) is one of a group of related chemicals that fall under the term **catecholamine.** The other two transmitters that also fall under this heading are dopamine and **epinephrine** (also called **adrenaline**). Synapses that use NE are called **noradrenergic synapses.**

norepinephrine (NE)

This neurotransmitter is found in various areas of the brain and also in neurons that terminate on some organs of the body. As we shall see in later chapters, NE and the networks of neurons that use it in the brain are very much involved in mood and motivation.

synthesis and breakdown. Figure 3.9 diagrams the synthesis of NE (and also of epinephrine and dopamine). The synapses which use NE inactivate the transmitter mainly by the re-uptake mechanism. But two enzymes are present that also are involved. One is **catechol-O-methyltransferase (COMT)** which appears to act near the postsynaptic membrane. The other is **monoamine oxidase (MAO)** which is present in the presynaptic cell. This enzyme does not inactivate NE in the synaptic cleft, because it is not there. Instead it may regulate the amount of NE which is synthesized in the presynaptic terminal. MAO is also present in the presynaptic terminals which use the other catecholamines. Figure 3.10 shows a schematic diagram of a noradrenergic synapse.

drugs that affect noradrenergic synapses. The pathways in the brain that use NE have been strongly implicated in mood and in motivation.

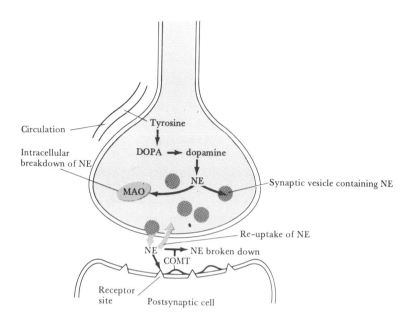

Figure 3.10
A noradrenergic synapse.

Thus many of the drugs that interfere with these synapses have effects on mood or motivation.

Reserpine, for example, prevents the storage of NE in synaptic vesicles, so the NE can be inactivated by intracellular enzymes (MAO). Reserpine is used to treat high blood pressure, and is also known to cause some depression. Various drugs which potentiate the action of NE at its synapses have the effect of elevating mood. **Amphetamine, for example, is believed to block the NE re-uptake mechanism and also raises mood. Tricyclic antidepressant** drugs which are used clinically to treat depression also block the re-uptake mechanism.

A variety of drugs can interfere with the synthesis of NE, but because the biosynthetic pathway also involves the other two catecholamines, these drugs affect activity at these other synapses as well. **Alpha-methyl-para-tyrosine (AMPT)** for example, inhibits the enzyme **tyrosine hydroxylase.** Thus this drug lowers the levels of NE and the other catecholamines in the brain.

dopamine The catecholamine **dopamine** is also found in the brain. In Chapter 9 we will see that some of the networks of neurons that use this neurotransmitter are very much involved in the control of movement. It has also been implicated as one of the neurotransmitters that is involved in schizophrenia, as we shall see in Chapter 10. Synapses that use dopamine are called **dopaminergic synapses.**

drugs that affect dopaminergic synapses. The drugs that affect the synthesis of NE also affect the synthesis of dopamine, since they are in the same biosynthetic pathway. But some drugs appear to affect dopaminergic synapses selectively. **Benzotropine,** for example, selectively inhibits the re-uptake of dopamine by the synaptic terminals. This drug increases the amount of dopamine in the synapse and thus potentiates its effects on the postsynaptic membrane. Patients with **Parkinson's disease,** which is characterized by tremors and other disorders of movement, have been treated with this drug successfully. This has led to the hypothesis that Parkinson's disease is partly due to the presence of inefficient dopaminergic synapses.

Drugs such as **haloperidol** are able to block dopamine receptor sites. This drug is commonly used in the treatment of schizophrenia, and this is the reason that many scientists believe that dopamine is involved in schizophrenia. Not surprisingly the antischizophrenic drugs also produce disorders of movement, since dopaminergic synapses are affected.

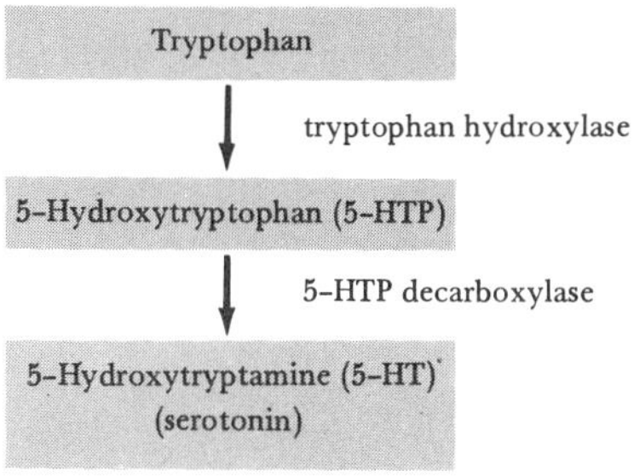

Figure 3.11
Biosynthesis of serotonin.

Serotonin is a neurotransmitter that occurs primarily in the lower parts of the brain. It is particularly involved in the sleeping and waking cycle, as we shall see in Chapter 13. Synapses that use serotonin are called **serotonergic synapses.**

serotonin

synthesis. Figure 3.11 shows the pathway by which serotonin is synthesized in brain tissue. Re-uptake appears to be the main mechanism by which serotonergic synapses inactivate the neurotransmitter.

drugs that affect serotonergic synapses. One drug that appears to interfere with these synapses is LSD, but the precise way in which it does this is not yet known. Cells which use serotonin show decreased electrical activity and also decreased amounts of serotonin when LSD is administered. But this might be due to several kinds of effects. For example, LSD might be blocking the receptor sites, or it might be directly inhibiting the serotonin containing cells in some way. At the moment, the best that can be said is that LSD appears to interfere with these synapses, but how it interferes, and how its interference might relate to the hallucinogenic effects of the drug, are not yet known.

Various other substances are believed to be neurotransmitters. For example, **GABA** appears in abundance in the brain, and many scientists hypothesize that it acts as an inhibitory transmitter substance. **Glutamic acid** also is found in the brain and is probably an excitatory transmitter. Several other chemicals are suspect, and as we learn more about the biochemistry of the nervous system, more neurotransmitters will probably be positively identified.

other neurotransmitters

summary
The Neurotransmitters

In this section we discussed those neurotransmitters that appear to be most involved in behavior, although many chemicals are believed to act as neurotransmitters and still others are probably yet to be identified.

Acetylcholine is the neurotransmitter that is used at the neuromuscular junction and other places in the nervous system. It is synthesized from *acetyl CoA* and *choline,* and inactivated by the enzyme *acetylcholinesterase* (AChE). Some of the choline is taken back up to be reused. Drugs that affect ACh include *physostigmine,* which inhibits AChE; *muscarine* and *nicotine,* which interact with each of acetylcholine's two receptor sites (called *muscarinic* and *nicotinic receptors);* and *atropine,* which acts as a false transmitter at muscarinic receptors.

Norepinephrine (NE) is one of the *catecholamines,* a group that also includes the neurotransmitters *epinephrine* and *dopamine.* It is mainly inactivated by the re-uptake mechanism, but two enzymes *(COMT* and *MAO)* also are able to break it down. Synapses that use NE are called *noradrenergic;* drugs that affect these synapses include *AMPT,* which blocks one of the enzymes used in NE's synthesis, *reserpine,* which prevents the storage of catecholamines in the synaptic vesicles, and *amphetamine,* which is believed to block the re-uptake mechanism. These drugs also affect mood, and noradrenergic synapses have been implicated in its control.

Synapses which use dopamine are called dopaminergic. Drugs which affect these synapses include *benzotropine,* which inhibits the re-uptake mechanism, and *haloperidol,* which blocks dopamine receptor sites. Most drugs which block dopamine receptor sites also have clinical uses in the treatment of schizophrenia, thus implicating this neurotransmitter in mental disorders.

Serotonin is a transmitter that has been implicated in the sleeping—waking cycle, among other behavioral systems. The hallucinogen LSD is believed to act at serotonergic synapses, but its precise mode of action is not yet known.

In the next chapter we will provide an overview of the anatomy of the nervous system. Part of Chapter 4 will deal with chemical maps that show the distribution of some of the neurotransmitters in the brain.

KEY TERMS

gap junctions
synaptic terminals
presynaptic cell
synaptic cleft
postsynaptic cell
postsynaptic membrane
synaptic vesicles
synaptic web
receptor sites
axo—dendritic contacts
axo—somatic contacts
axo—axonic contacts
dendro—dendritic contacts
neuromuscular junction
postsynaptic potential
exocytosis
excitatory postsynaptic potential
   (EPSP)
inhibitory postsynaptic potential
   (IPSP)
inactivation by enzymes
re-uptake
presynaptic inhibition
presynaptic facilitation
false transmitter
acetylcholine (ACh)
cholinergic synapse
Coenzyme A
choline
choline acetylase
cholinesterase
acetylcholinesterase
physostigmine
myasthenia gravis
muscarinic receptors
nicotinic receptors

muscarine
nicotine
atropine
Atropa belladonna
norepinephrine
noradrenaline
catecholamine
epinephrine
adrenaline
noradrenergic synapses
catechol-O-methyltransferase
 (COMT)
monoamine oxidase (MAO)
reserpine

amphetamine
tricyclic antidepressants
tyrosine hydroxylase
alpha-methyl-para-tyrosine (AMPT)
dopamine
dopaminergic synapses
benzotropine
Parkinson's disease
haloperidol
serotonin
serotonergic synapses
GABA
glutamic acid

Barchas, J. D., Berger, P. A., Ciaranello, R. D., and Elliott, G. R., eds. (1977). *Psychopharmacology: From Theory to Practice.* Oxford University Press, London and New York. (This collection contains some very readable articles on the relationship between drugs and behavior, particularly in the clinical setting.)

Cooper, J. R., Bloom, F. E., and Roth, R. H. (1974). *The Biochemical Basis of Neuropharmacology.* Oxford University Press, London and New York.

Dunn, A. J., and Bondy, S. C. (1974). *Functional Chemistry of the Brain.* SP Books, Flushing, New York. Distributed by Halstead Press, Division of John Wiley and Sons.

(The above two books provide more detail about the neurochemistry of the brain.)

Eccles, J. C. (1971). The synapse. In *Physiological Psychology* (R. F. Thompson, ed.), pp. 136–146. W. H. Freeman and Co., San Francisco. (A very easy to understand *Scientific American* article.)

Schmitt, F. O., Dev, P. and Smith, B. H. (1976). Electrotonic processing of information by brain cells. *Science* **193**, 114–120. (A description of some of the alternative kinds of communication between neurons, particularly dendro–dendritic contacts.)

SUGGESTED
READINGS

4

*overview
of the
nervous
system*

Neuroanatomy! The very word strikes terror into the hearts of most students, fearful of having to memorize long lists of strange Latin names. But we can't proceed very far into the brain without learning some of its parts. We can't begin to find out what this physical basis of mind is and how its function relates to our behavior without a road map of some kind. In this chapter we will provide a simplified road map of the nervous system (although even a simple one is rather complicated—the human nervous system is the most complicated piece of machinery on Earth). As we go through each of the behavioral systems in later chapters we will add more detail.

The anatomical study of the nervous system began with a sharp knife and the naked eye, and has progressed to the point where it is possible to see incredibly fine details of synapses and neuron structure. Early anatomists often gave parts of the nervous system a name based on the structure's appearance. Functional names might have simplified the task of studying physiological psychology, but early anatomists did not know what the functions of these structures might be. To complicate things still further, different anatomists called the same structure by different names, and sometimes both names survived.

Thankfully, anatomists have agreed upon a number of different terms and conventions which are helpful in providing an orientation for places in the nervous system. So before we go any further we will discuss these terms.

anatomical terms *directional terms.* Figure 4.1 shows a rat with some of the directional terms which are used in anatomy. The front end of the rat is the **anterior** end and the tail end is the **posterior** end. Anatomists also use the terms **rostral** for anterior and **caudal** for posterior. The back of the animal (which is actually the top) is the **dorsal** direction, and the stomach side is the **ventral** direction. Structures which are located more toward the middle of the animal are called **medial,** and those which are more toward the outside are called **lateral.** For example, the part of the rat's eye which is closer to the midline of the rat would be the medial part, and the part which is furthest from the midline would be the lateral part.

Figure 4.2 shows the directional terms which are used for the human being. We are not quite like rats and other four-legged animals because (among other reasons) our heads are attached at an angle to the rest of our bodies. But for anatomical purposes, the terms are used as though this angle did not exist and humans were actually walking around on all fours. This is why the figure shows an absurd diagram of a human in the crawling position to illustrate the compari-

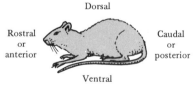

Figure 4.1
Anatomical terms indicating direction.

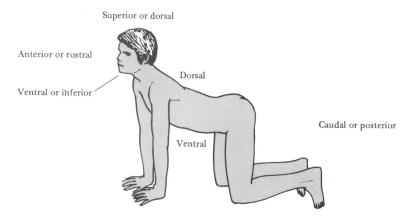

Superior or dorsal

Anterior or rostral

Dorsal

Ventral or inferior

Caudal or posterior

Ventral

Figure 4.2
Anatomical terms indicating direction for the human being.

son. For humans, dorsal refers to the direction toward the top of the head (when talking about brain structures), but to a direction toward the back (when talking about body parts). For brain structures, the term **superior** is also used to describe the dorsal direction. The term ventral refers to lower brain structures (when talking about the brain), but for the body it refers to parts which are closer to the stomach side. The term **inferior** is used synonymously with ventral when anatomists are talking about brain structures.

planes of dissection. In order to study the nervous system, it is necessary to cut it open; there are many ways to do this since it is a three-dimensional object. Figure 4.3 shows the planes of dissection which are most common. The **horizontal plane** sections the brain into an upper and lower part, the **coronal plane** sections it into a front and back part, and the **sagittal plane** divides it into right and left parts. A **midsagittal** cut would divide the brain right down the midline into its left and right halves.

terms for pathways. Terms which are used by anatomists to talk about pathways include **afferent,** which refers to pathways moving information toward the brain, and **efferent,** which refers to pathways sending information from the brain to more peripheral areas. The afferent sensory pathways, for example, bring information from the sense organs to the brain. The terms **ascending** and **descending** refer to pathways which are either moving information toward higher (more rostral), or lower (more caudal) locations in the nervous system.

Another set of terms which describes connections between structures emphasizes the interrelationships between the right and left sides of the body. **Ipsilateral** pathways refer to ones which connect structures which are on the same side of the body, and **contralateral**

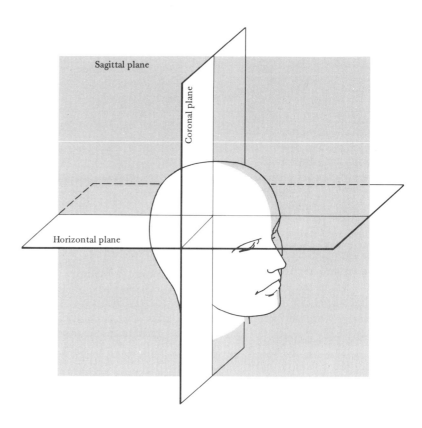

Figure 4.3
Planes of dissection.

connections refer to ones which start on one side and end on the other. Pathways are often given names which identify their point of origin and their destination. For example, the *spino-thalamic tract* would begin in the spinal cord and terminate in the thalamus.

We can now begin our road map of the nervous system. The nervous system can be divided into two major parts: the **central nervous system,** which includes the brain and spinal cord, and the **peripheral nervous system.** First we will discuss some general features of the brain, and then we will examine its anatomical subdivisions and chemical pathways. Next we will take a look at the spinal cord, and finally we will examine the components of the peripheral nervous system.

general features of the brain If you put your hands on your head, the first thing that you will feel is your hair and scalp. Under that you can feel the bones of your skull. The brain is encased in a very tough covering of bone which provides protection. Underneath the bone is another tough covering of connective tissue called the **meninges,** a term which is derived from the Greek word for "membrane." Under the meninges is the neural tissue, which for the living person, is the consistency of raw egg. In this section we will first look into the cells which make up the brain, and then examine the brain's blood supply and fluid cavities.

For our purposes, the most important components of the brain are the neurons and the **glial cells.**

cells in the brain

neurons. In Chapters 2 and 3 we discussed the structures of these important cells, and also how they moved information from one end to the other by means of axonal conduction and how they communicated with one another. In the nervous system, **gray matter** is mostly made up of cell bodies and short axoned neurons, while **white matter** is mostly made up of myelinated axons. In the brain the gray matter is mainly toward the outside, and the white matter is inside. The spinal cord, however, has its white matter on the periphery.

glial cells. The term "glia" means glue, and in many respects the glial cells act like glue. There are about 12 billion neurons in the brain, but scientists hypothesize that glial cells outnumber neurons by 10 to 1. They surround and support the neurons, and act as a buffer between the neurons and the rest of the body. At first scientists believed that the sole purpose of the glial cells was simply to serve as a matrix which supported the neurons; but now it seems clear that they serve other functions as well.

Some glial cells, called **astrocytes,** surround the blood capillaries

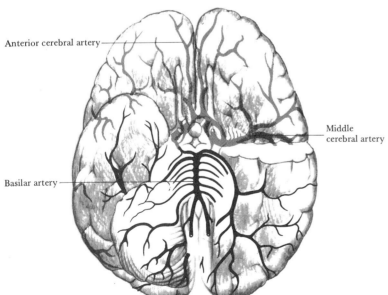

Anterior cerebral artery

Middle cerebral artery

Basilar artery

Figure 4.4
Major arterial supply to the brain.
[From Noback and Demarest (1972).]

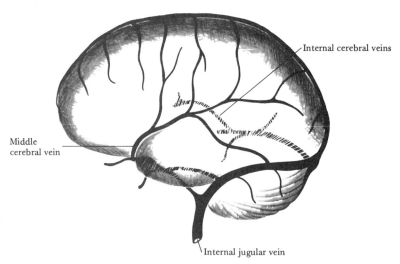

Internal cerebral veins

Middle
cerebral vein

Internal jugular vein

Figure 4.5
*Major vessels of venous drainage
of the brain. [From Noback and
Demarest (1972).]*

and thus control the materials which are transported back and forth
between the neurons and the blood. These astrocytes, along with the
tissue that makes up the blood vessels, form a **blood–brain barrier**
which protects the neurons from substances which have access to the
rest of the body. Another kind of glial cell, the **oligodendroglia,**
serves as the myelin sheath for neurons.

blood supply of the brain The brain gets about one-fifth of the blood pumped by the heart because it needs a great deal of oxygen and nourishment. But even
though the brain gets so much of the total amount of blood, the supply
is just barely enough. Consciousness is lost if the blood supply is cut
off for just a few seconds; longer periods without blood will result in
brain damage or death. But the other tissues of the body can survive
much longer periods of glucose deprivation or lack of oxygen.

Figure 4.4 shows the main arterial supply of blood to the brain, and
Figure 4.5 shows the venous drainage. The brain uses about the same
amount of blood regardless of its activity. A person may be sleeping,
running, thinking, or just sitting, but the brain still requires about the
same amount of blood.

cerebrospinal fluid Brain tissue is well protected from the outside environment by the
and the brain's ventricles skull and meninges. But it is also protected from damage by the **cerebrospinal fluid** (CSF). This fluid, produced by the meninges, consists
of water, protein, gases in solution, glucose, and various ions. The
brain floats in CSF so that rapid jerks and movements do not cause the
brain to jolt against the skull. Also, the brain has cavities, called **ven-**

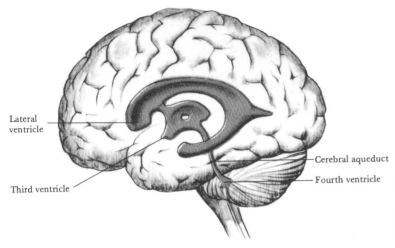

Lateral
ventricle

Third ventricle

Cerebral aqueduct

Fourth ventricle

Figure 4.6
Lateral view of the ventricles of the brain. [From Noback and Demarest (1972).]

tricles, which contain CSF. The ventricles, shown in Figure 4.6, provide additional shock absorption.

The biggest cavity is the **lateral ventricle,** and the two smaller ones are the **third** and **fourth ventricles.** These ventricles merge into the **central canal** of the spinal cord. These cavities are all interconnected, so that the bath of CSF is continuous.

In order to take certain kinds of X rays, it is necessary to remove the CSF from the brain. When this is done the person suffers from intense headaches until the meninges can produce new CSF. These headaches are due to the fact that the person's brain has no shock absorber.

---

summary
General Features of the Brain

The brain is protected by the hair, scalp, bones of the skull, and a covering of connective tissue called the *meninges.* The major cells in the brain are the neurons and the *glial cells,* which provide a matrix of support, control the flow of nutrients by means of the *blood–brain barrier,* and form myelin for axons. The brain receives about one-fifth of the total amount of blood through an extensive network of arteries. The *ventricles* of the brain contain *cerebrospinal fluid,* which acts as a kind of shock absorber.

---

subdivisions
of the brain

In this section we will discuss the five major subdivisions of the brain: the *telencephalon, diencephalon, mesencephalon, metencephalon,* and *myelencephalon.* Table 4.1 presents these 5 subdivisions, and also shows some of the alternate terms which are used to describe particular areas. The terms **forebrain, midbrain,** and **hindbrain** are very commonly used. The forebrain includes the telencephalon and diencephalon, the midbrain is the mesencephalon, and the hindbrain is the metencephalon and myelencephalon.

Table 4.1
Anatomical subdivisions of the central nervous system

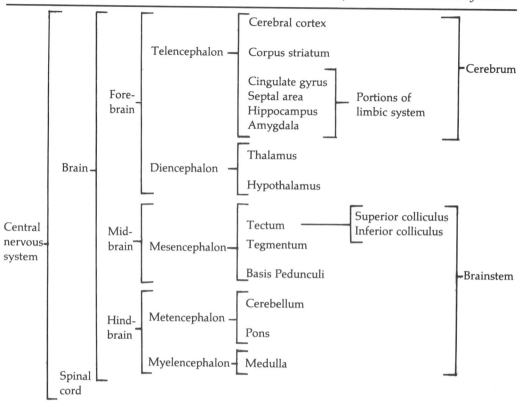

telencephalon The **telencephalon** literally means "end-brain." It includes the *cerebral cortex, corpus striatum,* and parts of the *limbic system.* Several fiber bundles, called **commissures,** connect the right and left sides of the brain at the level of the telencephalon. The largest of these is called the **corpus callosum** (shown in Figure 4.11).

cerebral cortex. The term "cortex" comes from the Latin word for "bark," and the cerebral cortex is literally the bark of the brain. The total surface area of the cortex is on the order of 20 square feet; but since the surface has many grooves, a great deal more tissue can be squeezed into the skull. These grooves are called **sulci** (from the Latin word for "plow"; singular: *sulcus)* when they are small, and **fissures** when they are large. The area between adjacent sulci or fissures is called a **gyrus** (plural: *gyri).* Figure 4.7 shows a lateral view of the brain which identifies the major fissures, sulci, and gyri. Approximately two-thirds of the cortex is buried in the depths of the sulci and fissures.

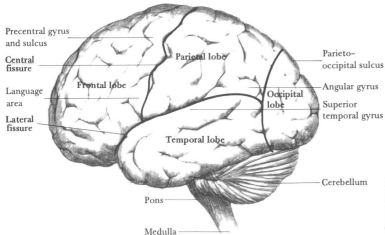

Precentral gyrus
and sulcus

**Central
fissure**

Language
area

Lateral
fissure

Parietal lobe

Frontal lobe

Occipital
lobe

Temporal lobe

Pons

Medulla

Parieto-
occipital sulcus

Angular gyrus

Superior
temporal gyrus

Cerebellum

Figure 4.7
*Side view of the human brain.
[From Noback and Demarest
(1972).]*

From the exterior surface of the cortex to the inside, the tissue appears layered or laminated, because some layers contain mostly cell bodies, and others contain mostly axons or dendrites. Scientists usually distinguish six layers of cortex, whose names are somewhat descriptive of their appearance. Figure 4.8 shows these six layers. The **molecular layer** (1) contains mostly fibers oriented in a horizontal direction, and the **external granular layer** (2) contains mostly small pyramidal cells. Layer 3, called the **medium pyramidal layer**, contains larger pyramidal cells. The **internal granular layer** (4) is a mixture of small pyramidal cells and **granule cells,** which have short branching axons and dendrites with many branches. Layer 5, the **large pyramidal layer,** contains (not surprisingly) large pyramidal cells. And layer 6, the **spindle cell layer,** contains tiny cells with horizontal dendrites and axons.

The major divisions of the cortex are called **lobes,** and include the **frontal lobe,** the **parietal lobe,** the **temporal lobe,** and the **occipital lobe.** All tissue that is anterior to the **central fissure,** and dorsal to the **lateral fissure** is called the frontal lobe. All tissue ventral to the lateral fissure is called the temporal lobe. The less obvious **parieto-occipital sulcus** is the dividing line between the parietal and occipital lobes. All of these areas can be seen in Figure 4.7.

Part of the cerebral cortex is devoted to the processing of sensory information and to the control of motor acitivity. These areas are the shaded ones in Figure 4.9. For example, the small area in the occipital lobe processes visual information. The areas surrounding the central fissure are involved with movement and with the skin senses. And the tiny area in the temporal lobe receives auditory information.

Much has been learned about these areas of the cortex by electrical stimulation studies. During neurosurgery, a patient is usually given a local anesthetic on the scalp, but remains awake during the operation.

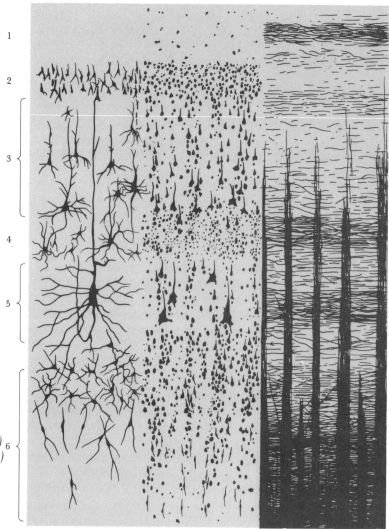

Figure 4.8
The cellular layers of the cortex: (1) molecular, (2) external granular, (3) medium pyramidal, (4) internal granular, (5) large pyramidal, and (6) spindle cell. [From Ranson and Clark (1959).]

The surgeon then can electrically stimulate different areas and watch what the patient does, or listen to what he says. For example, during stimulation of the auditory area of the temporal lobe the patient might report hearing a buzz or humm. Generally, the effects of the stimulation are felt in the ear opposite to the side of the electrical stimulation. Stimulation of the motor areas of the cortex might produce an involuntary movement in one of the limbs. We will discuss these areas of cortex in more detail when we examine each of the sensory systems and the brain areas which are involved in movement.

The white areas in Figure 4.9 represent **association cortex.** These areas do not specifically process sensory information, nor do they appear to be directly related to the control of motor activity. But as we shall see in later chapters (especially Chapter 16), these areas play very important roles in various kinds of higher processes, such as memory, decision making, thinking, and integration of sensory information. For example, when the association area of the temporal lobe is stimulated, the patient often makes some comment which appears to relate to auditory memory. In one case described by Penfield (1958), who has been a pioneer in this field, the patient said, "Yes sir, I think I heard a mother calling her little boy somewhere. . . . It seemed to happen long ago. . . . It was somebody in the neighborhood where I live." Another patient stimulated in this area said, "Yes. I heard voices down along the river somewhere, a man's voice and a woman's voice calling." This patient also noted that she seemed to see the river, and it had been one she visited as a child. Thus the association area of the temporal lobe appears not to be strictly limited to auditory memories.

As we shall see in later chapters, the association areas are involved in many diverse functions, although in many cases these functions are not entirely clear. Part of the temporal lobe on the left side of the brain (at least for most people) is devoted to language functions. And the association areas in the frontal lobes (which are huge as you can see in Figure 4.9) are very important in some kinds of memory, particularly memory for spatial tasks. These association areas are of particular interest to physiological psychologists because they are one of the features which makes the human brain so different from other animals. Figure 4.9 also shows a comparison of the size of the association areas in various animals. As you can see, even the closely related monkey cannot compare to humans in the amount of association cortex.

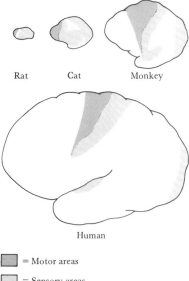

Rat   Cat   Monkey

Human

■ = Motor areas
▨ = Sensory areas
□ = Association areas

Figure 4.9
The cortex of four different species. [From Thompson (1967). Copyright © 1967 by Richard F. Thompson. Reprinted by permission of Harper & Row, Publishers, Inc.]

corpus striatum. This collection of structures includes the **caudate nucleus,** the **globus pallidus,** and the **putamen,** all of which can be seen in the coronal plane of Figure 4.10. The term **basal ganglia** is loosely used as a synonym for the corpus striatum, but the term may include other structures as well. The structures in the corpus striatum lie below the cortex of the frontal lobe, although part of the caudate nucleus extends beneath the temporal lobe.

The corpus striatum has numerous connections to other parts of the brain. For example, these structures receive and send fibers to the cortex, especially the frontal lobes. They also send fibers to lower parts of the brain, particularly the thalamus (in the diencephalon). In addition, there are numerous connections between the structures of the corpus striatum.

Because of the widespread connections of the corpus striatum, the functional importance of these structures is undoubtedly varied. But they clearly appear to be involved in movement, as we shall see in Chapter 9. For example, high-frequency stimulation of the caudate

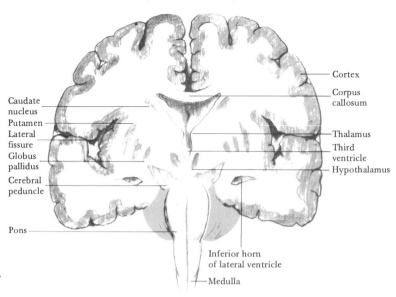

produces movements of the contralateral parts of the body (Foreman and Ward, 1957).

limbic system. The limbic system gets its name from the Latin word meaning "border." It is a collective name for a group of structures which spans both the telencephalon and the diencephalon. It forms a border or ring around the thalamus, and includes the **cingulate gyrus, the septal area,** the **hippocampus,** and the **amygdala** in the telencephalon, and the **anterior** part of the **thalamus** and the **mammillary bodies** in the diencephalon. Figure 4.11 shows these structures in a close-up sagittal view, as well as some of the connections between them.

These structures are involved in a wide variety of behaviors. For example, there is a great deal of evidence from lesion and electrical stimulation studies to indicate that the limbic system has an important role in emotional behavior. Removal of both temporal lobes, the amygdala, and large portions of the hippocampus results in some striking behavioral changes in monkeys, Animals with lesions like these show an almost complete lack of emotional expression. This syndrome, called the **Kluver–Bucy syndrome,** shows other symptoms as well. For example, the monkeys do not flee from objects like snakes and sometimes will even pick up a snake and examine it. Surgical removal of the septal area results in a pronounced increase in aggressive behavior, a phenomenon called **septal rage.** Stimulation of the amygdala in humans sometimes results in rage and aggressive assault. In Chapter 10 we will examine the role of the limbic system in

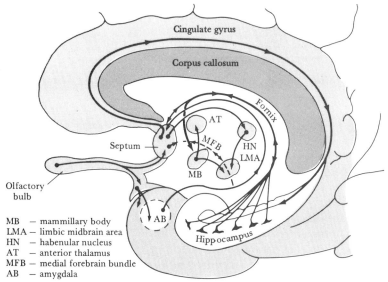

MB — mammillary body
LMA — limbic midbrain area
HN — habenular nucleus
AT — anterior thalamus
MFB — medial forebrain bundle
AB — amygdala

Figure 4.11
The limbic system and some of its connections. [From Gardner (1975).]

emotional behavior more closely. And in Chapter 15 we will see that the hippocampus plays a fascinating role in memory.

The diencephalon is the posterior portion f the forebrain, and its major structures are the *thalamus* and the *hypothalamus.* These two structures are both shown in Figure 4.10.

diencephalon

thalamus. The thalamus, a portion of which belongs to the limbic system, is the largest component of the diencephalon. It is composed of many masses or clusters of cell bodies called **nuclei.** The overall shape of this structure is much like two footballs, one in each hemisphere. One function of the thalamus is to act as a kind of "staging area" where information from the sensory receptors is received and integrated before it is relayed on to the cerebral cortex. The afferent sensory pathways which lead to the cortex, with the exception of the one coming from the nose, synapse in specific nuclei in the thalamus.

The most common way to classify the thalamic nuclei is based on their function. For example, **relay nuclei** are those whose afferent fibers come ultimately from the sensory receptors. The **lateral geniculate bodies,** which receive input from the eyes, are examples of the relay nuclei. **Association nuclei** are those which receive fibers from and project fibers to association cortex. **Nonspecific nuclei** are called nonspecific because they have widespread connections with many areas of the brain and their functions are obscure. Stimulation of these nonspecific nuclei sometimes produces widespread changes in the electrical activity of the cortex, but stimulation of the relay or association nuclei produces more localized effects, restricted to certain cortical areas. The nonspecific nuclei appear to be important in the regulation of the electrical activity of the whole cortex, and thus may play some role in sleep and wakefulness.

hypothalamus. Despite its small size, the hypothalamus plays a major role in some of our most interesting behaviors. It is located beneath the thalamus, beside the third ventricle. It contains numerous nuclei, and has two important fiber bundles running through it (the **fornix** and the **medial forebrain bundle).** Several chapters in this book will deal with this structure in more detail because it has quite a range of functions. In the midsagittal view of the brain shown in Figure 4.12, you can see that the hypothalamus lies right above the pituitary gland. These two structures communicate by both neural and endocrine means, and their communication provides a means whereby the brain and the endocrine organs of the body can interact.

The hypothalamus also receives fibers from and sends fibers to many parts of the brain, and is clearly involved in behaviors such as sex, agression, temperature control, and food and water intake. Although its range of functions is large, it seems to be most involved in those behaviors which have to do with the survival of the species, rather than any higher intellectual functions.

mesencephalon This area is a short segment between the hindbrain and the diencephalon. It has three principle components: the *tectum,* the *tegmentum,* and the *basis pedunculi.* These parts are much easier to see if we turn the brain over and look at it from underneath. Figure 4.13 shows this

Figure 4.12
Midsagittal view of the human brain. [From Houston et al. (1979).]

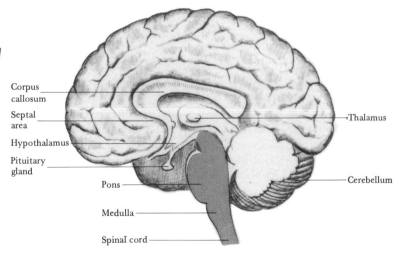

Corpus callosum
Septal area
Hypothalamus
Pituitary gland
Thalamus
Cerebellum
Pons
Medulla
Spinal cord

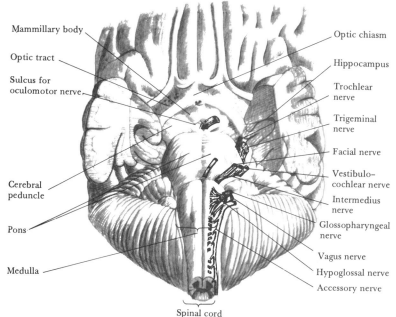

Mammillary body

Optic tract

Sulcus for
oculomotor nerve

Cerebral
peduncle

Pons

Medulla

Spinal cord

Optic chiasm

Hippocampus

Trochlear
nerve

Trigeminal
nerve

Facial nerve

Vestibulo-
cochlear nerve

Intermedius
nerve

Glossopharyngeal
nerve

Vagus nerve

Hypoglossal nerve

Accessory nerve

Figure 4.13
*View of the brain from underneath.
[From Sobotta and Figge (1974).]*

view, and Figure 4.14 shows a section through the midbrain, from the same viewpoint. Figure 4.15 shows the brainstem seen from the left.

tectum. The tectum contains four clusters of cells, two of which form the **superior colliculi,** and two the **inferior colliculi** (seen in Figure 4.15). The superior colliculi are important in the coordination of eye movement, as we shall see in Chapter 5. The inferior colliculi are important in the coordination of movement with sounds that the person hears (Chapter 6). Both colliculi play a role in a reflex system which results in the orientation of the head and eyes to sources of visual and auditory stimuli.

tegmentum. This structure lies between the tectum and the **substantia nigra,** and contains numerous ascending and descending fiber tracts. Some of its nuclei are also involved with eye movements. Another, the **red nucleus** (shown in Figure 4.14) is related to gross movements of the body. Electrical stimulation of this structure results in strange circling motions in animals; lesions result in disturbances in gait and increased muscle tone.

basis pedunculi. This group of structures is in the ventral part of the mesencephalon. It includes the **cerebral peduncles** and a cluster of pigmented neurons known as the **substantia nigra.** These structures also appear to play a role in movement. The peduncles contain fiber

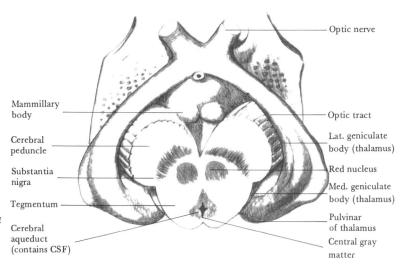

Figure 4.14
Section through the midbrain, view from behind. Compare with Figure 4.13. [From Sobotta and Figge (1974), p. 29.]

Labels on figure:
Optic nerve
Mammillary body
Optic tract
Cerebral peduncle
Lat. geniculate body (thalamus)
Substantia nigra
Red nucleus
Med. geniculate body (thalamus)
Tegmentum
Pulvinar of thalamus
Cerebral aqueduct (contains CSF)
Central gray matter

bundles which connect the motor cortex to the spinal cord; damage in the substantia nigra has been implicated in Parkinson's disease.

metencephalon The two major portions of the metencephalon are the **cerebellum** and the **pons,** both of which are easy to see in Figure 4.7 and 4.12.

cerebellum. The cerebellum, or "little brain," is involved with movement and balance. Damage to one of its lobes results in a disturbance of gait and posture in which the person tends to fall backward. Not surprisingly, birds have an enormous cerebellum, which is very useful in maintaining balance during flight. Information from many of the sensory systems, as well as information from the motor systems of the brain, comes into the cerebellum and is modulated so that the output of motor activity is smoother and more coordinated.

pons. This large rounded structure contains many nuclei, called the **pontine nuclei.** Between these clusters are fiber bundles which carry information between the cortex and the spinal cord. The pons also contains portions of the reticular formation, and some of the cranial nerves, which we shall discuss later.

myelencephalon The **myelencephalon** is the **medulla** (Figure 4.12) and is actually a continuation of the spinal cord. It contains all of the ascending and descending fiber tracts connecting the brain and spinal cord. Some of the cranial nerves, which transmit information from various parts of the body to and from the brain, enter and leave the brain at the medulla. The medulla also contains nuclei which are concerned with the control of respiration, heart action, and digestive activity.

reticular formation. This area occupies the central core of the brainstem and midbrain, and extends from the lower border of the medulla to the upper parts of the midbrain. It thus spans several of the subdivisions (the myelencephalon, mesencephalon, and metencephalon), and some scientists even include parts of the diencephalon in the reticular formation. We mention it under the myelencephalon because this is where it begins.

The **reticular formation** derives its name from the apparent random and chaotic criss-crossing of nerve fibers and location of cell bodies which make it look like a net. Indeed, the word "reticulum" means "net." The ascending fibers of the reticular formation project to the thalamus, cortex, and other areas of the brain. Some of these ascending fibers play critical roles in sleeping and waking, and are thus part of the **reticular activating system.** For example, electrical stimulation of some of these fibers awakens a sleeping animal, and lesions may

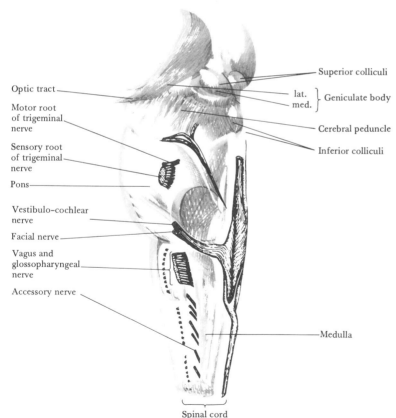

Optic tract

Motor root of trigeminal nerve

Sensory root of trigeminal nerve

Pons

Vestibulo-cochlear nerve

Facial nerve

Vagus and glossopharyngeal nerve

Accessory nerve

Superior colliculi

lat.
med. } Geniculate body

Cerebral peduncle

Inferior colliculi

Medulla

Spinal cord

Figure 4.15
Brainstem seen from left and somewhat dorsal. [From Sobotta and Figge (1974), p. 29, Figure 34.]

result in a state of coma. We will discuss this fascinating part of the brain in more detail in Chapter 13.

chemical pathways in the brain The anatomical divisions of the brain which we just discussed are very important in organizing our thoughts about the nervous system and also very important in identifying different places in the brain. But the anatomical subdivisions were in general identified long before anyone knew very much about the functions of those subdivisions. Now it is becoming clear that pathways in the brain are much more important as functional systems than are the anatomical subdivisions. These pathways are sometimes identified anatomically. For example, the limbic system, which spans two of the anatomical subdivisions, constitutes a set of interconnecting pathways which is very important functionally. But scientists are more and more interested in the chemical pathways of the brain, that is, those pathways of neurons which use the same neurotransmitter substance. These chemical pathways appear to be more important than anatomical subdivisions when we are talking about functional systems which relate to behavior.

A number of methods are available for identifying these chemical pathways. One of the most useful is the technique of **histochemical fluorescence.** This technique takes advantage of the fact that certain stains produce fluorescence in neurons which contain the catecholamines, and recent modifications even permit the researcher to determine which of the catecholamines is present. Presumably, if the neuron contains one of the catecholamines, then it uses the substance as its neurotransmitter. In this section we will briefly look at the chemical "maps" which have been drawn for some of the transmitters.

norepinephrine. Figure 4.16 shows the norepinephrine pathways in the rat brain. A number of small clusters of cell bodies (A1 through A7)

Figure 4.16
Distribution of neurons which contain norepinephrine in rat brain. [From Livett (1973), modified from Ungerstedt (1971).]

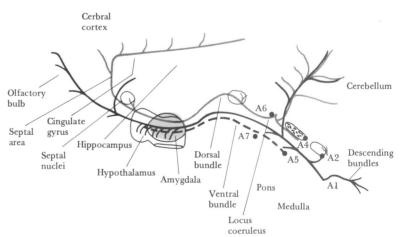

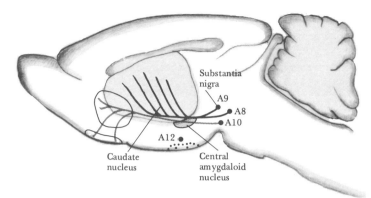

Figure 4.17
Distribution of neurons which contain dopamine in rat brain. [From Livett (1973), modified from Ungerstedt (1971). Obtained from Handbook of Psychobiology.]

are found in the brainstem. Notice that the pathways begin to divide in the midbrain to form a **dorsal bundle** and a **ventral bundle.** In later chapters we will see that these two bundles may subserve different functions. The cell clusters have ascending fibers which innervate the cerebellum, hypothalamus, cortex, and other brain areas. Norepinephrine pathways have been implicated in the control of mood, the response to environmental stress, eating behavior, and in other behavioral systems.

dopamine. The dopamine pathways (shown in Figure 4.17) are much less diffuse than the norepinephrine pathways. The cell clusters which contain dopamine are more rostral than the ones containing norepinephrine, and many of them are in or near the substantia nigra. Axons from the bundles proceed rostrally to such structures as the corpus striatum and the amygdala. Patients suffering from Parkinson's disease show a loss of dopamine from the pathway leading from the substantia nigra to the corpus striatum, suggesting that this pathway is intimately involved in motor control. However, motor activity may not be the only behavior influenced by the dopamine pathways. As we shall see in later chapters, some of the dopamine pathways have also been implicated in schizophrenia.

serotonin. The cell groups which contain serotonin lie mainly in the **raphe nucleus** of the brainstem. Their projections ascend through the tegmentum and terminate in the hypothalamus, amygdala, and other brain structures. Some descending fibers diffusely project to the reticular formation in the pons. In Chapter 13 we shall see that serotonin containing cells have been implicated in the control of sleeping and waking.

acetylcholine. Although the anatomical distribution of fibers containing acetylcholine has not yet been mapped, it has been possible to stain brain tissue for the presence of acetylcholinesterase, the enzyme which breaks down acetylcholine. This map is only reliable insofar as the presence of the enzyme indicates the presence of neurons which use acetylcholine as their neurotransmitter.

There are two main pathways. The **dorsal tegmental pathway** starts in the reticular formation and projects to the midbrain tectum, the thalamus, and other structures. The **ventral tegmental pathway** arises from the ventral tegmentum in the midbrain and projects to the basal forebrain areas as well as to all parts of the cerebral cortex.

summary
Subdivisions of the Brain

The brain is anatomically divided into five sections: the *telencephalon, diencephalon, mesencephalon, metencephalon,* and *myelencephalon.* The telencephalon is the largest subdivision, because it contains the cerebral cortex. This area is very large in humans and is involved in the processing of sensory and motor activity as well as the higher processes. From the outer surface to the inside of the cortex, the neural tissue appears laminated; scientists have named six layers based on the appearance of the cells and cell processes within each layer. The telencephalon also includes the *corpus striatum (caudate nucleus, globus pallidus,* and *putamen)* which is involved in movement, and parts of the *limbic system (cingulate gyrus, septal area, hippocampus, amygdala)* which is involved in emotion and other behavioral systems. The limbic system also includes the *anterior thalamus* and *mammillary bodies* in the diencephalon.

The major structures of the diencephalon are the *thalamus* and *hypothalamus.* The thalamus contains many nuclei, some of which serve as relay stations for sensory information on its way to the cortex.

The hypothalamus is involved with behaviors which are critical for the survival of the species, such as sex, eating and drinking, aggression, and temperature control.

The mesencephalon has three principle components: the *tectum,* which is important in a reflex system which orients the head toward sights and sounds, the *tegmentum,* and the *basis pedunculi,* both involved in movement. The metencephalon contains the *cerebellum,* which is involved in movement and balance, and the *pons.* Finally, the myelencephalon or *medulla* is a continuation of the spinal cord and contains fibers which connect the brain to the spinal cord. The *reticular formation,* which is important in sleeping and waking, begins in the medulla and extends to the upper border of the metencephalon.

Chemical pathways in the brain appear to be more important as functional systems than anatomical subdivisions. These chemical maps show which neuronal networks use the same neurotransmitter, and maps have been developed for norepinephrine, dopamine, serotonin, and acetylcholine.

the spinal cord Also part of the central nervous system, the spinal cord is the long neural tube found in the core of the vertebral column. Like the brain, it has white matter (mainly myelinated axons) and gray matter (mainly cell bodies). But in the cord, the gray matter is on the inside and the white matter is on the outside. Figure 4.18 diagrams a cross section of the spinal cord, showing the **dorsal horns** and **ventral horns.**

dorsal and ventral horns The centrally located gray area of the cord can be divided into dorsal and ventral horns. The dorsal horn is the sensory part of the gray in that afferent fibers enter the cord (through the **dorsal roots**) and termi-

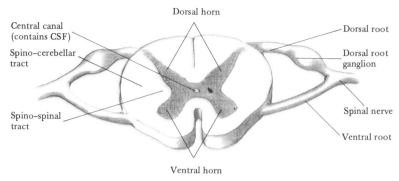

Central canal (contains CSF)
Spino-cerebellar tract
Spino-spinal tract
Dorsal horn
Dorsal root
Dorsal root ganglion
Spinal nerve
Ventral root
Ventral horn

Figure 4.18
Cross section of the spinal cord.

nate there. The ventral horn is the motor part of the cord. The nerve pathways to the muscles leave the cord by way of the ventral horn and go through the **ventral root.** Destruction of these motor neurons, which can happen during an attack of polio, results in paralysis. But diseases which affect the dorsal horn cells produce sensory deficits. For example, degeneration of some of these dorsal horn cells due to syphilis results in abnormalities of gait which are easily recognizable. These patients watch their feet while walking and slap them sharply on the ground with a shuffling gait. The people are receiving no information from their legs concerning the position of their feet, so they must rely on visual and auditory cues to determine where their feet are.

The white area of the cord contains numerous fiber tracts. The ones that extend the furthest are on the periphery, and the shorter ones are toward the middle. For example, the *spino—cerebellar tract* shown in Figure 4.18 extends all the way from the cord to the cerebellum. But the *spino—spinal tract,* in a more medial position, contains fibers which connect parts of the spinal cord to one another.

white matter in the cord

The gray matter of the cord is on the inside and consists of *dorsal* and *ventral horns.* Afferent sensory fibers come into the cord in the dorsal horns, and efferent motor fibers leave from the ventral horns. The surrounding white matter of the cord contains fiber tracts. The most peripheral travel the longest distances, while those in more medial positions travel the shortest distances.

summary
The Spinal Cord

All of the nerves which lie outside the brain and spinal cord are part of the peripheral nervous system. In this section we will discuss the *somatic nerves,* the *autonomic nerves,* and the *cranial nerves.*

the peripheral nervous system

The spinal cord is segmented in that it contains 31 pairs of spinal nerves. As these leave the cord, the sensory and motor sections coming from the dorsal and ventral roots combine into a mixed spinal

somatic nerves

nerve, as shown in Figure 4.18. The fibers in each of these mixed nerves thus contain both afferent (sensory) and efferent (motor) fibers. When the afferent and efferent fibers reach their destination in the periphery, they split up again. The region of the body which sends information to one dorsal root is called a **dermatome,** although there is considerable overlap of dermatomes. For example, the receptors in a single skin region may send messages to the brain via several dorsal roots. The efferent motor nerves innervate the skeletal musculature, and provide the means whereby the central nervous system can control muscular contractions.

The cell bodies of all the outgoing motor nerves of the ventral root are located in the inside gray matter of the cord. But the cell bodies of the dorsal root sensory fibers are located in the **dorsal root ganglia,** shown in Figure 4.18.

autonomic nerves Some of the motor neurons which leave the central nervous system through spinal nerves (and also through cranial nerves) are not destined to innervate the skeletal musculature. Instead they terminate in the smooth muscle of the heart, stomach, liver, sweat glands of the skin, adrenal glands, salivary glands, and other internal organs. These nerves form a separate section of the peripheral nervous system called the **autonomic nervous system.** It has two subdivisions: the **sympathetic division** and the **parasympathetic division.** Both of these are diagrammed in Figure 4.19.

sympathetic division. Fibers in the sympathetic division have their cell bodies in the gray matter of the cord, and leave the cord with the other motor fibers through the ventral roots and mixed nerves. But then they leave the mixed nerves and enter one of the **sympathetic ganglia,** which form a chain of ganglia running along the outside of the spinal cord. At the ganglia, these autonomic motor neurons synapse with postganglionic fibers, and then head toward their destination to innervate one of the glands or organs. Activation of the sympathetic division of the autonomic nervous system results in increased heart rate, contraction of some arteries, increased sweat gland activity, dilation of the pupils, and other effects related to the preparation of the body for an emergency.

parasympathetic division. The parasympathetic nerves, which innervate and influence the activity of many of the same body organs, emerge from the central nervous system either from the cranial nerves or from the caudal end of the spinal cord. Instead of synapsing right outside the cord these fibers travel to ganglia located near the organs which they innervate, and synapse with their postganglionic fibers there. Activation of the parasympathetic nerves results in effects which are

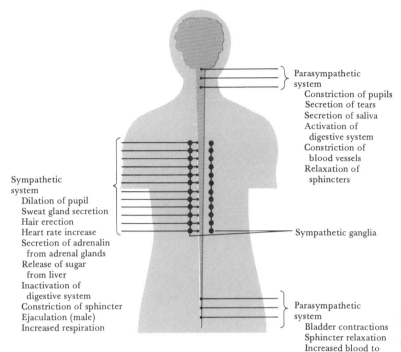

Parasympathetic
system
  Constriction of pupils
  Secretion of tears
  Secretion of saliva
  Activation of
    digestive system
  Constriction of
    blood vessels
  Relaxation of
    sphincters

Sympathetic
system
  Dilation of pupil
  Sweat gland secretion
  Hair erection
  Heart rate increase
  Secretion of adrenalin
    from adrenal glands
  Release of sugar
    from liver
  Inactivation of
    digestive system
  Constriction of sphincter
  Ejaculation (male)
  Increased respiration

Sympathetic ganglia

Parasympathetic
system
  Bladder contractions
  Sphincter relaxation
  Increased blood to
    genitals

Figure 4.19

The sympathetic and parasympathetic divisions of the autonomic nervous system. [From Houston et al. (1979).]

often opposite to those seen in sympathetic activation. For example, heart rate slows, pupils constrict, and sweat gland activity slows down.

The activation of the sympathetic nervous system prepares the organism for the "flight–fight–fright" response, behaviors which might be needed during stress. Some of these changes in physiology have been used to detect stress in the human being. The "lie detector" test, for example, actually measures sympathetic activation rather than lying, since it records blood pressure and galvanic skin response. Presumably, when a person is lying they will show some physiological signs of stress which are reflected in the activity of the sympathetic nervous system. By contrast, the activation of the parasympathetic system is related to relaxation. But parts of both systems may be active at one time, depending upon what the organism is doing. We will learn more about these two systems in Chapter 10, when we discuss emotional behavior.

The **cranial nerves** can be seen in Figure 4.13. Notice that they enter and leave the brain at irregular intervals along the brainstem. Some of the cranial nerves contain only afferent sensory fibers, others contain only motor fibers leading to musculature in the head, and still others contain both sensory and motor fibers. Table 4.2 lists the 12 cranial nerves, their functional importance, and the place where they enter or leave the brain.

cranial nerves

Table 4.2
The cranial nerves

Number	Name	Functional Importance	Origin and/or endpoint
1	Olfactory	Sensory nerve for smell	Telencephalon
2	Optic	Sensory nerve for vision	Diencephalon
3	Oculomotor	Motor nerve for eye movement	Mesencephalon
4	Trochlear	Motor nerve for eye movement	Mesencephalon
5	Trigeminal	Sensory nerve for tongue and face	Metencephalon and
		Motor nerve for chewing	Myelencephalon
6	Abducens	Motor nerve for eye movement	Myelencephalon
7	Facial	Sensory nerve for taste	Myelencephalon
		Motor nerve for salivation, and facial muscles	
8	Auditory	Sensory nerve for audition and equilibrium	Myelencephalon
9	Glossopharyngeal	Sensory nerve for taste	Myelencephalon
		Motor nerve for pharynx	
10	Vagus	Sensory nerve for taste	Myelencephalon
		Motor nerve for abdominal viscera	
11	Accessory	Motor nerve for pharynx and larynx	Myelencephalon
12	Hypoglossal	Motor nerve for tongue	Myelencephalon

summary
The Peripheral Nervous System

The main components of the peripheral nervous system are the *somatic nerves,* the *autonomic nerves,* and the *cranial nerves.* The peripheral nervous system includes all nerves which lie outside the brain and spinal cord.

The somatic nerves enter or leave the spinal cord through either the *dorsal* or *ventral roots.* Sensory and motor fibers then come together again to form a mixed nerve. The skin area which sends input to a single dorsal root is called a *dermatome.* The motor fibers which leave the cord through the ventral roots innervate the musculature of the body.

The autonomic nerves are motor neurons which leave the central nervous system through the spinal or cranial nerves and innervate various bodily organs and glands. The *sympathetic division* serves to activate the body for an emergency; for example, some motor neurons produce an increase in heart rate while others produce a slowing of stomach contractions. The *parasympathetic division* innervates many of the same organs and glands, but often produces the opposite effects, such as the slowing of heart rate.

The 12 cranial nerves leave the brain at irregular intervals along the brainstem. They carry sensory information from, and motor information to, various parts of the head and neck.

In this chapter we have provided a brief road map of the nervous system which will be useful in finding your way in the rest of the book. As you read along, you can also check the anatomical maps in the Appendix to locate particular structures. Now we are ready to begin exploring this marvelous piece of machinery, and how its function relates to our behavior.

anatomical terms
anterior, posterior
rostral, caudal
dorsal, ventral
medial, lateral
superior, inferior
horizontal plane
coronal plane
sagittal plane
afferent, efferent
ascending, descending
ipsilateral, contralateral
central nervous system (CNS)
peripheral nervous system
meninges
glial cells
gray matter
white matter
astrocytes
blood–brain barrier
oligodendroglia
cerebrospinal fluid (CSF)
ventricles (lateral, third, fourth)
central canal
forebrain
midbrain
hindbrain
telencephalon
commissures
corpus callosum
cerebral cortex
sulci, fissures, gyri
lobes (frontal, parietal, temporal,
  occipital)
central fissure
lateral fissure
parieto-occipital sulcus
corpus striatum
caudate nucleus
globus pallidus
putamen
basal ganglia
limbic system
cingulate gyrus
septal area
hippocampus

amygdala
anterior thalamus
mammillary bodies
Kluver–Bucy Syndrome
septal rage
diencephalon
thalamus
lateral geniculate bodies
association nuclei
nonspecific nuclei
hypothalamus
fornix
medial forebrain bundle
mesencephalon
tectum
superior colliculi
inferior colliculi
tegmentum
basis pedunculi
cerebral peduncles
substantia nigra
metencephalon
cerebellum
pons
myelencephalon
medulla
reticular formation
reticular activating system
histochemical fluorescence
dorsal bundle
ventral bundle
dorsal tegmental pathway
ventral tegmental pathway
dorsal horns
ventral horns
dorsal roots
ventral roots
somatic nerves
dermatome
dorsal root ganglia
autonomic nervous system
sympathetic division
parasympathetic division
sympathetic ganglia
cranial nerves

Gardner, E. (1975). *Fundamentals of Neurology: A Psychophysiological Approach*, 6th
  ed. Saunders, Philadelphia. (This book is much less difficult to understand
  than its title would suggest.)
Noback, C. R., and Demarest, R. J. (1972). *The Nervous System: Introduction and
  Review*. McGraw-Hill, New York. (A small book with marvelous drawings,
  some of which were used in this chapter.) SUGGESTED
READINGS

5

*introduction
to
the
senses
and
vision*

introduction All around us are sights we can't see, sounds we can't hear, odors we can't smell. Without special equipment, we are only able to detect those parts of our environment to which our sense organs are sensitive. But while our sense organs cannot tell us everything about what is going on in the environment, we are by no means as limited as some animals. We may only be able to imagine the vivid color the bee sees when it lands on a flower striped with ultraviolet. But we are capable of seeing many more colors than the dog. We may not be able to see as well as a cat on a dark night. But we are certainly more versatile than the sparrow, which is so dependent upon light that it will starve to death if there is none, even if it is sitting on a pile of food. Finally, we may not be able to smell marijuana through a suitcase in the customs office. But our world of odors is much more varied than the moth, whose sense of smell is limited to only a few substances.

The sensory systems are the means by which all animals receive information about their environment. Understanding what information they receive (or don't receive) and how they receive it, is critical to understanding and predicting their behavior. We began this book with discussions about the neuron and the nervous system. That information provided you with an understanding of the tools humans and animals possess—tools which enable them to interact with their environment and to coordinate their various bodily parts during that interaction. But now we are ready to see how the nervous system underlies specific behaviors, and the remainder of this book will be devoted to different types of behavior.

We begin with the sensory systems for two reasons. First, all of the other behavioral systems such as sex, learning, and eating, require interaction with the environment. It is through the sensory systems that we make this interaction. A moth cannot mate unless it can find a female, and it does this through the sense of smell. A hunting cat does not eat unless it can find and catch food, and it does this through a combination of practically all the senses. And learning in the human being is partly based upon an association between two or more environmental events which impinge upon the sensory systems in some predictable fashion. Thus an understanding of how we receive and code information, and what types of information we don't receive, is important in understanding the rest of our behavior.

The second reason we begin with the sensory systems is that this is the kind of behavior about which physiological psychology knows the most. Science usually progresses from the simpler questions to the more complex, and although questions about how the sensory systems send information to the brain are far from simple, they are nevertheless not as complex as questions about some of the other behavioral systems. Compared to the question "Why do we like sex?" the question "How do we see?" is much closer to a complete answer.

In this chapter we begin with a general discussion of the sensory systems, and the questions that are asked about each of them. First we can ask what kinds of sense organs we have, and what properties of the environment each one is most sensitive to. Second, we would like to know how the sense organ transforms the environmental energy into a neural message. This process, called **transduction**, is critical because our brains can only interpret potentials and spiking of axons, not sound, light, smells, or tastes. Third, we can ask what path the information in the form of neural energy takes in getting to the brain, which is the same as asking what the sensory afferent pathway is. Each sensory system follows its own path, but along the way the pathways cross and interact so that we are able to receive a more integrated picture of environmental events. The fourth question asks how the information is coded by the nervous system. This topic will receive a great deal of attention in this chapter, and in Chapters 6, 7, and 8, because the nature of the coding process is essentially what determines what information about the environment our brains actually receive.

The last question asks what happens to the information after it reaches the final level of the afferent sensory pathway. The answer to this question is very important because it is what determines how we respond to any stimulus, but it is only recently that the technology of physiological psychology has been advanced enough for scientists to attack this question. We still know very little about this important step, but the few glimpses we have suggest that the nervous system is still as marvelous and as full of surprises as it seemed to the first human beings who asked questions about it.

introduction to the senses

the five (or perhaps eight or ten) basic senses

Most people believe that there are five basic senses: seeing, hearing, touching, tasting, and smelling. But this simple category system has not proven adequate for explaining all that we know about what an individual is able to sense in the external world. The senses of seeing and hearing are easily placed into two separate categories. But the other three senses pose problems. For example, the sense of touch, which we shall discuss in Chapter 8, may need to be divided into several different senses, each of which transmits information about a different kind of stimulus, such as temperature change, pain, and pressure. The chemical senses, taste and smell, also pose problems because the information we receive from the nose and the tongue overlap a good deal. Our perception of the "taste" of an apple or onion is partly dependent upon odors. If you held your nose, you would have difficulty telling the difference between an apple and an onion placed on your tongue.

To complicate the picture still further, there is another sensory system that cannot be grouped into any of those "basic" five senses. The **vestibular system**, whose sense organ is located deep inside the ear, provides us with information about the orientation and movement of the head, and thus is very useful in the maintenance of balance. This sensory system will be discussed as part of the chapter on the somatosenses (Chapter 8), which will also discuss the sense (or senses) of touch.

Regardless of the exact number of sensory systems, the one main function they all have in common is to transmit information about events in the environment to the brain. In order to do this, they must first change some of the physical energy in the environment into neural energy, using the process of transduction.

transduction of physical energy

The sense organs of humans cannot transduce everything in the environment into neural energy, but they can transduce the shorter light waves, some air pressure changes (hearing), temperature and pressure changes on the skin, and some heavier molecules passing by the nose and tongue.

the adequate stimulus. The transduction process, diagrammed in Figure 5.1, begins with the physical energy striking a receptor cell of the sense organ, the part of the organ which is specialized to make the transformation. Receptor cells do not respond to all kinds of physical energy with equal vigor, however. The ones in the eye, for example,

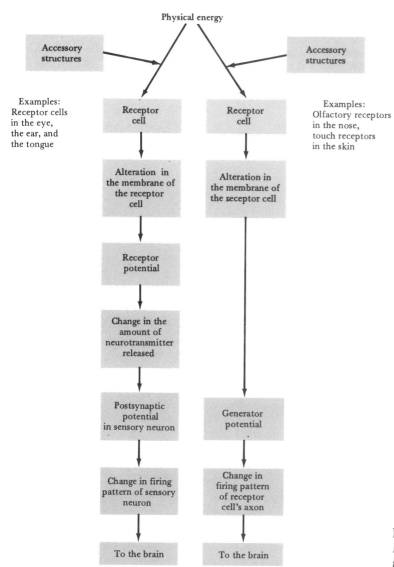

Figure 5.1
Diagram of the transduction process in two types of receptor cells.

are specialized to respond to certain light waves. They will respond weakly to some other kinds of physical energy, such as pressure, but their threshold of response is much higher. Light waves are called the **adequate stimulus** for the receptors in the eye, and each of the sense organs has its own adequate stimulus to which its threshold of response is the lowest.

receptor and generator potentials. When an adequate stimulus strikes the input end of the receptor, the cell responds by showing a change in potential—not a spike, just a slower change away from the resting potential of the cell, similar to those recorded from the postsynaptic cell after neurotransmitter has been released from the presynaptic cell. This graded change in potential is called a **receptor potential** in some receptors, such as the ones in the eye, but it is called a **generator potential** in receptors such as the ones in the nose. The difference between the two is that the receptor potential does not lead to any spiking in the same cell because this kind of receptor cell does not do any spiking—it has no axon. The receptor potential can of course eventually result in a change in the spiking activity of the **sensory neuron** on which it synapses, presumably because the change in potential results in the release of neurotransmitter into the synaptic space between the receptor potential and the sensory neuron. Receptor cells which produce generator potentials have their own axon, and the generator potential can produce a change in spiking activity in the axon part of the receptor cell.

The manner in which the physical energy is able to produce these potential changes in the receptor cells is not very clear in most of the sensory systems. The transduction process about which the most is known is in the photoreceptors of the eye. All transduction processes, however, probably involve some molecular change in the receptor cell —one which results in the movement of ions across the receptor cell's membrane. It is, after all, the movement of ions which is the underlying feature of potential changes, as we saw in Chapters 2 and 3.

accessory structures. The sense organ is composed of the receptor cell, which performs the transduction process, the sensory neuron (unless the receptor cell has its own axon), and also often has a set of **accessory structures** which modify the nature of the physical energy before it reaches the receptor cell. For example, light waves are focused by the lens and cornea of the eye, both of which are examples of accessory structures. And air pressure changes are considerably amplified before they ever reach the receptor cells of the inner ear, again by a variety of accessory structures.

Once the physical energy has been modified by the accessory structures, transduced into a graded potential by the receptor cell, and the sensory neuron (or the axon of the receptor cell) has changed its spiking activity, the information is on its way to the brain.

the afferent sensory pathway The afferent sensory pathways are the series of neurons and the synapses between them which lead from the receptor cells to the brain. Each sensory system has its own pathways, although the pathways from different sensory systems often cross and interact. For example, each sensory system (except olfaction) has one afferent pathway which reaches the cortex by passing through the thalamus—the structure which acts like a relay station. Also, some reflex pathways from two or more sensory systems interact in lower parts of the brainstem. For example, we mentioned in the last chapter that the tectum was a point of interaction between reflex pathways for the eyes and ears which served to orient the head toward sights and sounds in the environment.

convergence. A common characteristic of all sensory pathways is that there are many fewer fibers leading away from the receptor cells than there are receptor cells. This feature, called **convergence**, means that the information that the brain ultimately receives is a summary of what actually was transduced by the receptors, and some details are inevitably lost. In the eye, for example, there may be more than 100 receptors converging onto a single sensory neuron, and this is only in the first part of the afferent sensory pathway.

magnification. Some information may be lost, but some kinds of information may undergo **magnification**. Thus in the cortex there may be a disproportionate representation. In the visual cortex, for example, there is a magnified representation of information from the center of the visual field. There are many more cells devoted to central vision than to peripheral vision. Typically, the kind of information that is magnified is the kind that is most important to the animal. For example, there is magnification of information from the fingertips of primates, from the whiskers of a mouse, and from the snout of a pig.

lateral interaction. Another common feature of the afferent sensory pathways is called **lateral interaction**. This means that the activity of one receptor cell and its connections have an effect on the activity in the connnections of nearby receptor cells, regardless of whether any physical energy is hitting those nearby receptors. This effect shows up all along the afferent pathway. For example, if a tiny beam of light is shined onto a single receptor in the eye, the sensory neurons of the nearby receptor cells change their firing activity too, usually in the direction opposite from the stimulated receptor's sensory neuron. This property of the afferent sensory pathway for vision produces an interesting optical illusion, as we shall see later in this chapter.

the coding process

All of the sensory systems carry the responsibility of changing information about the environment into neural energy, and they do this by changing that information into a neural **code**. In this section we will discuss what properties of the physical energy might be coded, and in the next section we will consider the various "candidate" codes which might be used to code these properties.

The physical energy which impinges on any sense organ can vary in a number of ways, each of which may be important to the organism. First, the energy can vary in *intensity*. For example, a light can be bright or dim, or a sound can be loud or soft, or anything in between. Second, the physical energy can vary in *space*. Spatial characteristics of the environment are critically important in the senses of seeing, hearing, and touching. The remarkable ability of primates to see such finely detailed patterns in their visual world is chiefly due to the ability of their sensory system to code spatial patterns. The fact that you can read this textbook print attests to your own remarkable pattern vision.

A third characteristic of the physical environment which may be important is *time*. The matter of when a particular stimulus strikes a particular receptor may be very important to an animal, and this applies to lengthy amounts of time, as well as very short temporal intervals. We shall see in Chapter 13 (Rhythmic Behavior) that some animals are able to code time intervals as long as a day. Very short time intervals may combine with variations in the spatial characteristics of the stimulus to provide information about rapidly moving objects.

The fourth characteristic of the physical energy which should be coded is *stimulus quality*. Is the stimulus light or change in air pressure? And on a more refined level, is the stimulus blue, purple, or lime green? In the chemical senses, as we shall see in Chapter 7, the quality of the stimulus is very slippery. An odor might be described as musky, fruity, or any number of adjectives, and a taste might be salty, sweet, bitter, sour, or some combination. Stimulus quality in the sense of touch is equally problematical, particularly because it is not certain whether we have just one sense of touch with coding of different stimulus qualities, or many skin senses, each of which handles a separate stimulus quality.

the candidate codes Table 5.1 lists on the left the characteristics of the stimulus that might be coded, and on the right, lists the kinds of codes that might be used. It is important to remember that the candidate codes can only incorporate activities of which a neuron or receptor cell is capable. As we discussed in Chapter 2, a single neuron can only spike or not spike at any given point in time. During a longer time interval, however, the neuron might speed up or slow down its firing rate, change the interval between spikes, or fire in some kind of pattern. A receptor cell can only produce two kinds of receptor or generator potentials: depolarization or hyperpolarization. But the size of those graded potentials can vary, and so can the rate at which the potential rises or falls.

Since there are many neurons and receptor cells in each sensory system, a spatial code is also a candidate. Which unit, or which combination of units are active may represent some characteristic of the stimulus. The number of units which are responding, regardless of where they are, is also a candidate.

Any of these candidates might be used to code any of the stimulus

Table 5.1
Stimulus characteristics and their coding

Characteristics of the stimulus that might be coded	"Candidate" codes	
	In the receptor cell	*In the neurons of the afferent pathway*

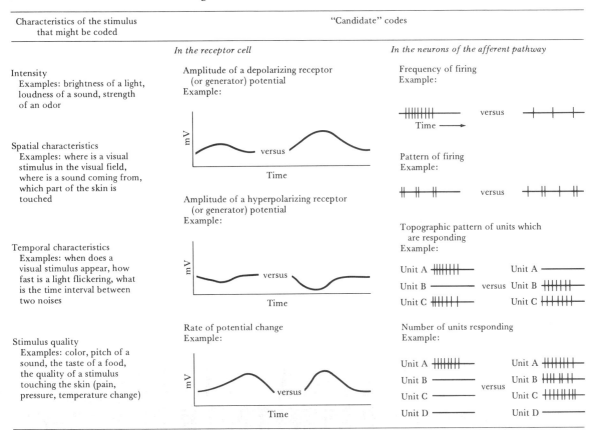

characteristics mentioned in the previous section, and in Table 5.1. For example, stimulus intensity might be coded by an increase in firing rate, or it might be coded by the number of units which are activated, or perhaps both at once. Furthermore, there is no reason to suppose that the kind of code which is used to represent some characteristic of the stimulus is the same at every level of the afferent pathway. A spatial code may be translated into a rate code, and back again. Even though any code may be used, you will no doubt notice a heavy reliance on spike frequency, partly because the technology we now have available is very good at detecting changes in spike frequency, rather than spike patterns or interspike intervals.

compression. Despite the variety of candidates which may be used to code various features of the stimulus, a number of generalizations are possible. For example, an increase in stimulus intensity is often coded

generalizations about the coding process

introduction to t

by a change in firing rate, or by the activation of more neurons. The coding of intensity also is often characterized by **compression**. For example, if one sound is twice as loud as another, a responding neuron might fire faster, but not twice as fast. This is another example of how information is lost on its way to the brain.

topographic organization. A spatial code is often used to code spatial characteristics of the stimulus, and is particularly useful because of the general **topographic organization** of the neurons which lead from most of the sense organs. For example, fibers which lead from the finger tip remain close to fibers which lead from the palm of the hand all the way to the cortex, but remain more distant from the fibers leading from the kneecap.

receptive fields. The term **receptive field** refers to the area in space within which a stimulus can produce a response of some kind in a particular neuron along the sensory pathway, as shown in Figure 5.2. For example, the receptive field of a neuron in the visual system refers to that area of the visual field within which a visual stimulus can produce a response in the neuron. In the skin senses, the receptive field of a neuron in the afferent pathway refers to an area of skin. In the auditory pathway, the term can refer to where the sound is coming from in space, or it might refer to the range of frequencies of sound which can produce a response in a particular neuron. Neurons can have receptive fields larger than the area covered by their own receptor cells, partly because of the principle of lateral interaction, discussed earlier in this chapter. The receptive field concept has proven particularly valuable in the study of vision, and as we shall see, a neuron may respond quite differently depending upon where the light strikes the receptive field.

coding of stimulus quality. Generalizations about the coding of stimulus quality are difficult to make because each sensory system handles the problem differently. It was first believed that a special kind of spatial code was used to code stimulus quality. The doctrine of **specific nerve energies** proposed that the brain was able to tell the difference between two stimulus qualities, salt and sugar, for example, by virtue of the fact that different receptors, and therefore different pathways, were activated. This theory has certainly turned out to be correct on the gross level since fibers arising from the different sense organs tend to give rise to sensations associated with that sense organ. For example, the stimulation of fibers from the receptor cells of the eye always produces some kind of visual sensation, no matter what kind of energy stimuluates these fibers. (Try pressing on your eyeball.)

But the specific nerve energy doctrine has turned out to be inadequate in explaining stimulus quality variations *within* a particular sensory system. There are no "salty" receptors which respond exclusively

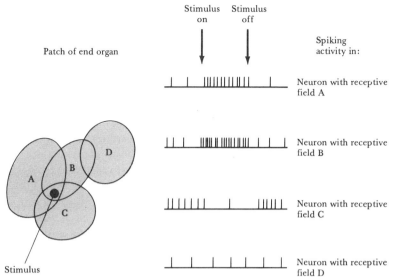

Patch of end organ

Stimulus on   Stimulus off

Spiking activity in:

Neuron with receptive field A

Neuron with receptive field B

Neuron with receptive field C

Neuron with receptive field D

Stimulus

Figure 5.2
When a stimulus appears where the dot is on this patch of end organ, it produces a change in firing in neurons A, B, and C. This stimulus is in the receptive fields of A, B, and C, but not D.

to salty tasting substances, and there are no "orange" receptors that exclusively respond to that color and no others. It is often the case that a sensory neuron will respond best to one particular sensory quality, but it will also usually respond in some way to other stimulus qualities as well.

feature detection. A recent term which was coined to explain some of the coding of many different characteristics of the stimulus in the visual system is **feature detection**. Some neurons not only require the stimulus to be in a certain area in the visual field before they will show their best response, they also show much more vigorous responses if the stimulus has some other specific characteristic as well. For example, one neuron might respond best to a vertical line, while another might respond best to a line moving in a particular direction. Thus a particular neuron may use a single code, such as a change in firing rate to code both spatial and temporal characteristics of the stimulus, and perhaps quality and intensity too. The brain apparently has not seen our neatly arranged Table 5.1 and insists on disorderly overlap. Cortical cells are particularly guilty of this kind of overlap coding.

At many levels of the afferent sensory pathway, information is not only coded and moved up toward the higher levels, but some information is moved down again, so that it might have an effect on the coding of subsequent sensory messages. A flash of light, for example, produces contraction of the pupils—an event which will affect how the receptor cells respond to whatever visual stimulus comes next. This

efferent pathways

introduction to the senses **83**

process is produced by just these kinds of efferent pathways. In Chapter 8, we shall discuss some exciting new findings on how the brain may be able to control the afferent flow of information about pain. And efferent pathways must be involved in the "cocktail party" effect. At a cocktail party, people are able to filter out a lot of conversational babble and attend to what one interesting person is saying at the other end of the room. This phenomenon must involve some control of sensory input somewhere beyond the transduction stage. The ways in which higher levels of the nervous system are able to influence the responses of neurons lower in the sensory pathways are still largely unknown. But it is becoming clear that the brain is not simply the passive recipient of incoming sensory information.

future goals One of the goals of the study of the sensory systems is to provide fuller answers to some of the questions we have just posed. This kind of work will eventually lead to an explanation of how the levels of the sensory afferent pathway transduce, then code the characteristics of the physical energy in the environment. We will then understand how variations in the physical environment are translated into neurophysiological events.

The coding processes in the cortex may be the final step in the neurophysiological coding process, but the question might be asked, "What happens then?" Ultimately we would like to relate variations in the physical environment not only to variations in neurophysiological events, but also to *behavior*. We would like to know how the final representation of a stimulus is perceived by the brain, not simply what is sensed, because it is the perception of the stimulus that is more intimately related to behavior.

The term "perception" is very difficult to define. Very often our perception of a stimulus can be explained quite well in terms of the neurophysiological events which scientists have been able to measure, and so we might say that sometimes perception is the same as sensation. Some optical illusions, for example, can be explained fairly well by referring to the lateral interaction which occurs in the visual pathway.

But other perceptions, which we measure by observing the individual's behavior or simply listening to the person's verbal description of a physical stimulus, are not so readily explainable. For example, a full explanation of the coding process will probably never be able to completely explain why a person can recognize a familiar word faster than an unfamiliar word of the same length. Lawyers have known for years that two eyewitnesses of an event will often report having seen two completely different things. The physical stimuli which were impinging on the two eyewitnesses were very similar, and the coding processes which were used to move the information to the brains of the two individuals were also probably similar. Why then do they so often report the event so differently?

Presumably, the perception of a stimulus is a conglomeration of the code which represents it in the cortex, and neural events in the brain which relate to memory, emotions, physical state, motivations, and other factors about which we know very little. During the coding process itself, much information about the stimulus is lost or modified because of convergence, and some characteristics of the stimulus may be magnified. The effects of the other factors, such as memory or emotion, may move the perception of the stimulus even further from the "true" version. As we said in the beginning of this chapter, we don't see all there is to see; to that we might add, what we do see (or perceive) may not be quite right.

Even though we don't understand the neurophysiological routes between sensation and perception, we must be confident that they are there. The cortex does not contain a little person who "decodes" the information and then sends it on to other brain areas. In the discussions of the sensory systems to follow, we will try to draw links between the physical stimulus, the neurophysiological events, and behavior. Sometimes those links are somewhat hypothetical; even when a person talks about what they have just seen or heard, the information which was coded by the sensory areas of the cortex must somehow reach the pathways in the brain which subserve language. The possiblity of a "slip 'twixt the cup and the lip" is always there. Nevertheless, very often our behavior can be predicted with remarkable accuracy by an understanding of the neurophysiological events which occur in response to changes in the environment.

---

summary
Introduction to the Senses

The basic function of the sensory systems is to provide the individual with information about events in the external world. This section discussed the questions which are asked about the sensory systems in order to learn how the systems perform this function.

(1) What kinds of sensory systems do we have? Although many people believe that there are five basic senses: seeing, hearing, touching, tasting, and smelling, the nervous system is arranged in such a way that there are probably more than just five. For example, the *vestibular sense*, located in the ear, provides information about the movement and orientation of the head, and the sense of touch is probably made up of several separate senses, each with its own route to the brain.

(2) How does the sense organ translate physical energy into neural energy? This process is called *transduction*, and is the means by which some of the physical energy in the environment can be translated into potentials and spiking of axons in the nervous system. Since each sense organ is dealing with a different form of physical energy, the details of the transduction process differ in each of the sensory systems.

(3) What path does the information follow en route to the brain? Some

sensory afferent pathways lead from the sense organ, through the thalamus (except for those leading from the nose), and from there go on to the cortex. Other pathways may be involved in reflexes, and may cross and interact in lower brain areas. On its way to the brain, some information is lost, through the process of *convergence*, but some may be *magnified*, particularly the information which is most important to the animal's life style. Information from each receptor cell is modified by the activity in neighboring receptor cells because of *lateral interaction* between the fibers of the afferent sensory pathways.

(4) How is the information coded by the nervous system? The nervous system might code several features about the physical energy, including: stimulus *intensity, spatial* and *temporal* characteristics of the stimulus, and stimulus *quality*. The candidate codes include the amplitude of receptor potentials, change in firing rate in axons, spatial pattern of firing, change in spike intervals, number of units activated, and others. (See Table 5.1.) For example, the intensity of a light may be coded by the firing rate of a neuron in the afferent sensory pathway, but this code may change at different levels of the pathway. The nervous system often uses a spatial code to represent spatial characteristics of the stimulus, particularly because of the *topographic organization* of fibers which

lead from the sense organs; however, there are exceptions to this rule.

Two terms which are important to remember which relate to the coding properties of the nervous system are *receptive field* and *feature detection*. The receptive field of a neuron refers to the patch of end organ within which a stimulus can produce a response of some kind in that neuron. Feature detection refers to the complex coding properties of visual cortical cells in particular, which often will respond best to a stimulus when it possesses a number of characteristics, such as movement in a particular direction and a particular orientation in the field.

(5) What are the efferent pathways leading from the brain? Information not only travels up the afferent pathway but some is returned to lower levels of the pathway and thus may have an effect on the coding of subsequent sensory messages. For example, efferent pathways from the brain control the muscles which result in dilation and contraction of pupils. Furthermore, the sensory information which is coded in the sensory cortex must be passed to other areas of the brain in order to affect the behavior of the individual. Little is known about these pathways, but it is these pathways that will help to explain the translation of a sensation to a perception, which is capable of affecting our behavior.

vision Of all the senses that human beings have, the one that they rely on the most is vision. Even the U.S. Government recognizes the importance of vision—it gives an extra tax exemption to blind people. But even those with the "eyes of an eagle" are limited in what they can see— limited by the special adaptations of their visual system. The primate eye can provide very detailed information about form and pattern, movement, depth, and color. But compared to many mammals, it is rather limited in providing information about the visual world when the lights are low.

In the remainder of this chapter we will first examine the visual stimulus—what properties it possesses which might be coded by the visual system. Then we will discuss the structure of the eye, particularly emphasizing the structure of the **retina**—the layer of receptor cells and their immediate connections. From there we will examine the visual pathways which move information from the retina to the brain. The next section will deal with the process of transduction in the receptor cells, and the following sections will examine how the visual pathway codes information about the visual environment. Finally, we will consider what pathways the visual information takes in leaving the brain.

Light energy is thought to be a form of electromagnetic radiation, which is a composite of particles which have wavelike properties. If this definition is confusing, it is because light is not a substance which can be easily understood—even by physicists. For the purposes of understanding the rest of this chapter, the properties of light which are of interest are **wavelength** and **intensity**.

All kinds of light energy move at the same speed, 186,000 miles per second (about 300,000 km/sec), and their movement is in a wavelike fashion. Figure 5.3 shows a wave, and also shows what is meant by wavelength. The distance from the top of one peak to the top of the next is the wavelength. Light energy can be of any wavelength, but the human eye can only detect a very small portion of the entire spectrum of wavelengths. This small portion is called the **visible spectrum**, and ranges from 380 to 760 *nanometers*, a unit of measurement which represents one-billionth of a meter.

The colors that we can see are a function of the wavelength of light; the relationship is shown in Figure 5.4. Some animals have eyes which are specialized so that they can see wavelengths which are outside of our visible spectrum. For example, the bee can detect light which has a shorter wavelength than we are able to see—we call the "color" **ultraviolet**, even though we have never seen it with the naked eye because

the visual stimulus—light

Figure 5.3
Diagram showing a theoretical light wave. The distance between points A and B represents the wavelength.

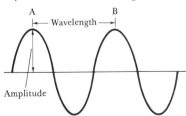

Figure 5.4
The visible spectrum.

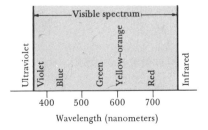

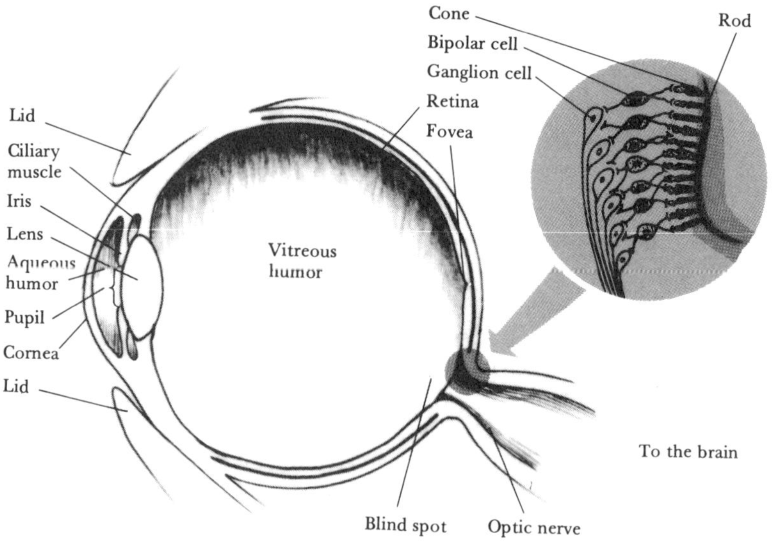
Cone
Rod
Bipolar cell
Ganglion cell
Retina
Fovea
Lid
Ciliary muscle
Iris
Lens
Aqueous humor
Pupil
Cornea
Lid
Vitreous humor
To the brain
Blind spot
Optic nerve

Figure 5.5
Cross section of the eye, and a magnified section of the retina. [From Houston et al. *(1979).]*

its wavelength is just shorter than what we see as purple. Some snakes can detect wavelengths just longer than what we see as red—we call this "color" **infrared**. Many mammals can see all the wavelengths we can, but they do not see them as different colors—their coding system does not code wavelength of light.

The intensity of light reflects how much energy is in the light waves. It can be measured in *watts*, such as in a 60-watt light bulb, or in *lumens*, which takes into account the fact that the human eye is most sensitive to light energy in the middle of the visible spectrum (around 550 nanometers). Light from a 50-watt yellowish-green bulb would appear much brighter to us than from a 50-watt red bulb, and so would be considered more intense as measured by lumens. To a large extent, the visual abilities that any animal has depend on the kind of eye it has, and human beings have one of the best in the animal kingdom—or at least one of the most versatile.

structure of the eye

The eye, situated in the bony orbit of the skull, is the sense organ for vision. Like any sense organ, it consists of receptor cells and their connections and accessory structures, shown in Figure 5.5. These accessory structures are particularly elaborate in the eye, and are designed for protection and to provide the receptor cells with the best image possible. The **cornea**, for example, is the transparent protective covering over the outside of the front of the eyeball. It accomplishes the major focusing of light onto the retina, the layer at the back of the eyeball which contains the receptor cells and their connections. The **lens** can change its thickness because the muscles to which it is attached receive neural messages from the brain. The change in thickness provides a means whereby light waves can be finely focused onto the surface of the retina. When an individual focuses on a distant object, the lens becomes flat and thin, but when the object is nearby, the muscles produce a thickening of the lens, in a process called **accommodation**.

The **iris** is an accessory structure which regulates the amount of light which is allowed to enter the eye, and which also gives the eye its color. The iris can open wide around the **pupil** to let in a great deal of light, or it can contract, much like the f-stop of a camera, to limit the amount of light. Although the pupil appears to be dark, this is only because there is no source of light inside the eyeball. If you shine a light directly on the pupil you can see the pink tissue of the retina, through the transparent liquid **vitreous humor**. The old instant cameras used to do just this when they used a flash attachment right next to the lens, and the people in the photograph looked like they had red eyes. The problem was easily solved by adding an extension so that the flash was further away from the lens. The flash still lights up part of the pink retina, but not the same part that is being photographed.

The business section of the eye, however, is not the accessory structures, but the receptor cells in the retina. These are the photosensitive cells that change light energy into a neural message to be passed along to the brain.

structure of the retina

The retina, diagrammed in Figure 5.6, is composed of the receptor cells and a number of other cells to which the receptor cells are connected. Notice in the diagram that the receptor cells are in the back of the retina, and light must pass through these other cells before it reaches them. Luckily these other cells are transparent.

rods and cones. There are two types of receptor cells in the retina of the human eye: the **rods**, which function quite well in very low light conditions but which transmit pattern information poorly, and the **cones**, which need more light but which can process finely detailed pattern and color information. The two types are not randomly distributed over the retina. The rods are mostly found on the periphery, while the cones are found in high concentrations in the center or **fovea**. The two types of receptor cells have different patterns of connection to the other cells in the retina—cells which eventually lead to the afferent sensory pathway. It is partly because the two types of receptors have different patterns of connections that they are able to perform separate functions.

neural connections for rods and cones. Both the rods and the cones are connected to **bipolar cells**, shown in Figure 5.6. The visual informa-

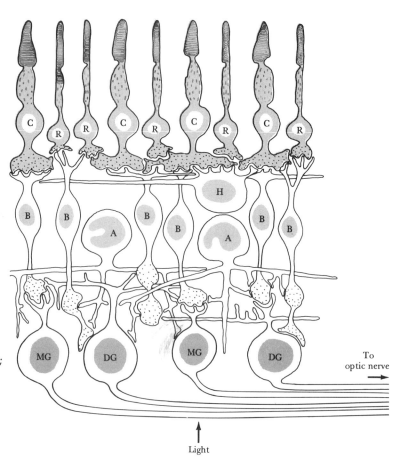

Figure 5.6
Schematic diagram of the principle elements of the primate retina: R, rod; C, cone; B, bipolar cell; A, amacrine cell; H, horizontal cell; MG, midget ganglion cell; DG, diffuse ganglion cell. [From Dowling and Boycott (1966), with slight revision by Professor Boycott.]

To optic nerve

Light

tion is then passed from the bipolar cells to the **ganglion cells**, the axons of which form a fiber bundle called the **optic nerve** which leaves the retina on its way to the higher levels of the pathway.

The difference between the connections for the rods and cones, however, rests with the number of photoreceptor cells which synapse onto the bipolar and ganglion cells. A single **diffuse ganglion cell** receives input from as many as hundreds of rods, while a **midget ganglion cell** serving the cones might only receive input from a few receptors. This means that finely detailed pattern information about the visual environment will be preserved quite well by the midget ganglion cells, but not very well by the diffuse ganglion cells. A single diffuse ganglion cell can only transmit a summary of what is going on in the hundreds of rods from which it is receiving input. Because the cones are so highly concentrated in the fovea, it is at the fovea that human beings have their best pattern vision, or visual acuity.

The rods are more sensitive to low levels of light however, partly because of the way in which they are connected in the retina. A ganglion cell connected mainly to rods may change its firing rate if light is striking any of its rods, which may be distributed over a wide area, but the ganglion cell connected to a few cones must have light striking one of those few before it will respond.

The rods and cones of the retina communicate not only with the higher visual centers of the brain by means of their own bipolar and ganglion cells, but with the ganglion cells of other photoreceptors. The **horizontal** and **amacrine cells**, shown in Figure 5.6, form a maze of neurons linking the photoreceptors, bipolars, and ganglion cells to one another. A single ganglion cell does not simply respond in an automaton-like fashion to the input of its photoreceptors—the rods and cones linked to other ganglion cells can modulate its activity through the horizontal and amacrine cells. This feature of the retina has certainly made the study of vision more complicated, but it provides marvelous versatility in visual coding, and plays an important role in lateral interaction and in the receptive field properties of the ganglion cells.

the afferent visual pathway

The optic nerve leaves the retina from a point slightly closer to your nose than the fovea (nasal side of the eye). Since there are no receptors there, each eye has a "blind spot." The optic nerve from each eye proceeds along the floor of the skull to a point immediately in front of the pituitary stalk. Here the two nerves meet, forming the **optic chiasm**. Figure 5.7 shows the pathway of these fibers, and also shows that the fibers which came from the nasal halves of the two eyes cross at the optic chiasm, while the fibers from the outside halves do not cross. Because of this partial crossing, fibers which have arisen in the right half of each retina, and which are carrying information from the left half of the visual field, travel to the right side of the brain; fibers from the left halves of each retina wind up in the left hemisphere, carrying information about the right half of the visual field.

The axons of the ganglion cells travel through the optic chiasm, proceed along the optic tract, and terminate in a part of the thalamus called the **lateral geniculate nucleus (LGN)**. The LGN consists of six layers of cells. Fibers arising from the fovea tend to terminate in the middle of this nucleus, regardless of which eye they came from. Fibers arising from the eye on the same side of the brain (ipsilateral eye) terminate in layers 2, 3, and 5, while contralateral fibers (from the eye on the other side) terminate in layers 1, 4, and 6. The neurons of the various layers of the LGN send their axons to the **striate cortex** in the occipital lobe. This area is also called Brodmann's area 17, after a famous anatomist who applied a numbering system to various parts of the brain. From there, the information is passed onto the **prestriate cortex** (Brodmann's areas 18 and 19), right next to the striate cortex. The prestriate cortex is responsible for more processing of visual in

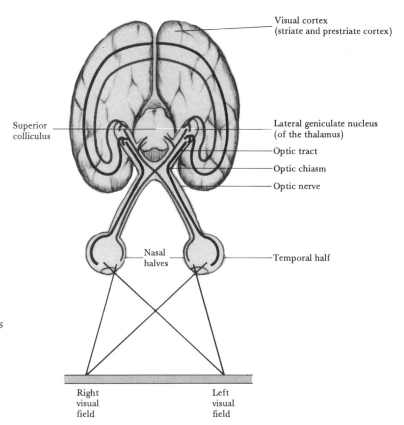

Visual cortex
(striate and prestriate cortex)

Superior
colliculus

Lateral geniculate nucleus
(of the thalamus)

Optic tract

Optic chiasm

Optic nerve

Nasal
halves

Temporal half

Right
visual
field

Left
visual
field

Figure 5.7
The afferent visual pathway. Fibers carrying information from the left part of the visual field in the two eyes travel to the left hemisphere, while fibers from the right halves of the retinas proceed to the right hemisphere. Fibers from the nasal halves of both retinas cross at the optic chiasm.

formation. The visual information also appears to reach the lower part of the temporal lobe (**inferotemporal cortex**) for some very high level processing, as we shall discuss later in this chapter and in Chapter 16 on higher processes.

There are also other pathways by which visual information can leave the ganglion cells and enter the brain. For example, some of the fibers in the optic tract send collaterals to the reticular formation, and this pathway may serve as a simple gross activator of the entire cortex, since the reticular formation is so intimately involved in sleeping and waking. Another pathway is a system of collaterals which lead from the optic tract to the superior colliculus. The responses of cells in this structure suggest that the pathway is involved in gross spatial localization and eye movement, rather than fine form perception.

topographic organization. It is possible to make a few generalizations about the afferent pathway for vision. First, the cells follow a rather regular topographic organization at every level of the pathway. The terminations of the fibers in the LGN was an example of this orderly arrangement, and we shall see later in this chapter how the cortex follows another kind of topographic arrangement—one which arranges things according to what eye the messages are coming from, rather than what part of the visual field. Topographic organization is a common characteristic of the pathways for most of the senses, as we discussed earlier in this chapter.

magnification. A second generalization has to do with magnification. The density of receptor cells is highest in the fovea, as is the density of ganglion cells. This is one kind of magnification that is already present in the retina. But the cortex may magnify foveal vision even more. Myerson and his colleagues (1977) calculated the approximate proportion of visual cells in the cortex of the owl monkey that are devoted to the processing of foveal vision, and found that this proportion far exceeded the proportion of ganglion cells in the retina that were receiving input from receptors on the fovea. It is not known whether this kind of ultramagnification is going on in human beings because of the technical problems involved. It is relatively easy to estimate cell counts in both the retina and the striate cortex of the owl monkey, but the task is enormous in the human being.

redundancy. A third generalization involves redundancy. The fibers from the LGN project to several places in the cortex, so that in the right hemisphere there are several different representations of information from the entire left visual field. In the left hemisphere, there are several different representations of the right half of the visual field. It is possible that the different representations may serve different functions with respect to the way visual information is able to influence the rest of our behavior. Redundancy is also a common characteristic of the nervous system in general.

The eye is the sense organ which changes some of the light energy in the environment (the shorter wavelengths) into neural energy. It is composed of a variety of accessory structures, such as the *cornea*, the *lens*, the *iris*, and the *retina*, or layer of receptor cells at the back of the eyeball. The accessory structures act to protect the retina, and to sharpen the image of light waves reaching the retina, while the receptor cells act to transduce the light energy into neural energy.

The *rods* and the *cones* are two types of receptor cells in the retina. The rods, which undergo a great deal of convergence before they pass their messages to the brain, are very sensitive to low light levels, but provide poor pattern vision and no color vision. The cones, which undergo much less convergence, provide good pattern and color vision. Both the rods and cones are connected to the *bipolar cells*, which are then connected to the *ganglion cells*, all of which are in the retina. The axons of the ganglion cells leave the retina by way of the *optic nerve*, on their way to the brain. Also within the retina are a maze of interconnections which include the *amacrine* and the *horizontal* cells.

The afferent pathway for vision travels from the optic nerve to the

summary
Structure of the Eye and Afferent Visual Pathway

optic chiasm, where some of the fibers cross to the other side of the brain. From the chiasm, the fibers travel to the *lateral geniculate nucleus* and then to the visual cortex. Some fibers in the pathway also travel to the superior colliculus, a structure which may mediate eye movement, to the reticular formation of the brainstem, which acts as a gross activator of behavior, and to other brain structures as well.

transduction in the photoreceptors

The function of all the structures and pathways described so far is to first transduce light energy into neural energy, and second to code the message so that the brain receives the important features and initiates some response. The transduction process in the photoreceptors is fairly well understood, and begins with the chemicals in the rods and cones.

photoreceptors and photopigment

Figure 5.8 shows a typical photoreceptor in vertebrates. The top part of the receptor, or **outer segment**, contains a substance called **photopigment** which is responsive to light. The story of how this substance reacts to light was largely worked out by George Wald and his colleagues (Wald, 1968), and it begins with the molecular structure.

The photopigment molecule, when it is in the dark, contains two parts: **retinal** and **opsin**. The retinal part of the molecule is basically unstable, because when it is exposed to light it changes from the **11-cis** form, to the **all-trans** form of retinal. This change results in a bending

Figure 5.8
Schematic drawing of a photoreceptor.

Figure 5.9
The typical dark adaptation curve. The first part of the curve represents the rapidly adapting, but less sensitive cones, while the second part represents the activity of the more slowly adapting, but very sensitive rods.

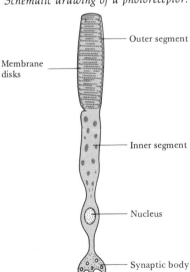

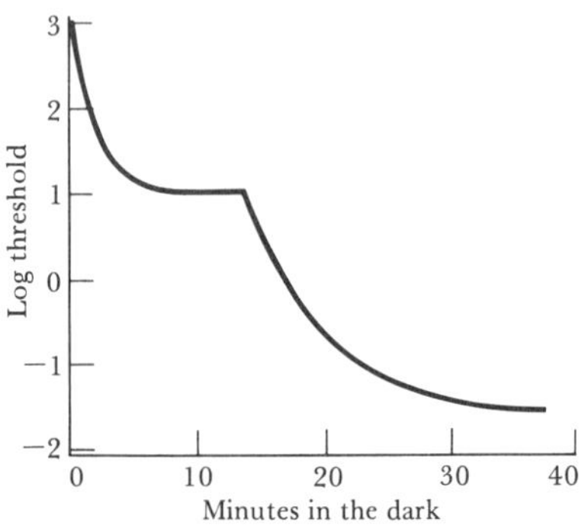

Outer segment

Membrane disks

Inner segment

Nucleus

Synaptic body

of the retinal part of the molecule, and also causes the entire retinal—opsin combination to break apart. When the opsin part of the molecule has broken off, it too changes shape, and it is this change which probably causes the membrane of the receptor cell to alter the rate at which charged ions are moving back and forth across it. This movement of ions is recorded as the receptor potential of the cell.

In vertebrates, there are four kinds of photopigments, but only one kind appears in each receptor cell. **Rhodopsin** is the type which is contained in all the rods, and the cones contain one of three different kinds, all of which are called **iodopsins**. In all the photopigments, the retinal part of the molecule is the same—it bends when it is struck by light, and breaks apart from the opsin part. But the four kinds of photopigments contain different opsins, one for the rods, and three for the cones. Each of the three photopigments in the cones is most sensitive to a different wavelength of light. This point will be very important when we discuss how the receptor cells code color.

rhodopsin and iodopsin

The recovery of the photopigment molecule, after it has broken, takes time, but eventually the all-trans retinal will change back into 11-cis retinal and recombine with the opsin part. The implications of this recovery are easily noted when you walk into a dark room from the daylight outside. At first it is very difficult to see anything, but gradually your eyes "get used to" the dark, and the room seems to get brighter. This process, called **dark adaptation**, is graphed in Figure 5.9. In the dark room, your threshold for a dim light stimulus is at first very high, meaning that the light must be fairly bright for you to see it. But after a period of about 30 minutes, the photopigments in the receptor cells recover, and your threshold is much lower, in fact sometimes more than 10,000 times lower.

dark adaptation

The typical dark adaptation curve normally shows two segments: a short, rapidly adapting segment which occurs first, and then a longer, but more slowly adapting segment which ultimately allows the eyes to reach their lowest threshold. This two segment curve is attributable to the two kinds of photoreceptors in the eye. The first part of the curve represents the dark adaptation of the cones. They adapt to the dark faster, but they never reach the low threshold of which the rods are capable. The second part of the curve represents the slower recovery of the rods. People who are completely colorblind since they have no functional cones—only rods—show only this part of the curve during dark adaptation. Although it is usually assumed that the dark adaptation curve can be explained by referring to how fast the rhodopsin and iodopsins recover, there may also be some kind of neural adaptation going on. Perhaps the bipolar cells of the retina respond to less stimulation from the receptor cells than they normally would require. Nevertheless, the process of dark adaptation is a good example of a behavior which can be explained fairly well in terms of known neurophysiological events, or in this case, biochemical events.

receptor potential In the dark, the receptor cells are depolarized and they appear to release a continuous flow of neurotransmitter. But this **dark current** is interrupted when light energy strikes the receptors. The broken-off opsin molecule produces a change in the membrane of the receptor, so that it increases its resistance to sodium and becomes hyperpolarized. Then the flow of transmitter from the receptor is slowed down or stopped. This may seem strange, but it is important to remember that a hyperpolarization and a cessation of neurotransmitter release is just as good a candidate code as a depolarization and an increase in transmitter release. The change in the amount of neurotransmitter released at the other end of the receptor cell begins the next step in the chain of coding events. In the next sections we will discuss how the visual system codes intensity, pattern and movement, depth, and finally, color.

---

summary
Transduction in the Photoreceptors

The transduction of light energy takes place in the rods and cones. The *outer segment* of these cells contains *photopigment* molecules, each of which has two parts: *retinal* and *opsin*. When light strikes the receptor cell, the retinal part changes shape by bending, and breaks off from the opsin part. The opsin part then changes its own shape, and probably produces a disturbance in the receptor cell's membrane which results in a change in the rate of ion flow across the membrane. This membrane disturbance is recorded as the receptor potential, and in vertebrates, the receptor potential in response to light is normally a hyperpolarization.

The photopigment in the rods is called *rhodopsin*, while the three different kinds of pigments in the cones are called *iodopsins*. The retinal portion of the pigment molecules is the same for all pigments, but the opsins differ.

The photopigment molecules recover quickly after they have broken apart, but the recovery process is faster in the cones. Although the process is slower for rods, the sensitivity to light which is ultimately reached by the rods is much higher. This phenomenon results in the typical two-part *dark adaptation curve*.

---

coding of intensity As good as our eyes are at coding pattern, movement, color, and depth, they are not very good at accurately coding absolute levels of intensity. The dark adaptation curve shown in the previous section demonstrates that our thresholds for light stimuli vary enormously depending on how long we've been in the dark. Apparently, absolute intensity of light is not all that important as far as the nervous system is concerned, although in the retina at least the photoreceptors respond differently depending upon the intensity of the stimulus.

Tomita and his colleagues (1967) were able to record receptor potentials from the retina of the carp, an animal which has fairly large receptor cells. They found that in the dark, the animal's cell had a resting potential of about 10–30 mV, but when they shined a light on the carp's eye, the photoreceptor showed a sustained, graded hyperpolarizing potential. This hyperpolarization, as we mentioned, is typical of receptor potentials in vertebrate eyes. But the amplitude of the potential was closely related to the intensity of the light, suggesting that the receptor potential amplitude may be serving as a code for stimulus intensity. Throughout the visual pathway, many cells respond differently to different intensities of light by changing firing rate, for example. But the coding of intensity clearly is not their only function. Other properties of the stimulus, such as quality or pattern, are much more potent in producing a change in firing rate.

Since the human being has two kinds of photoreceptors, one of which is more sensitive to low levels of illumination, our nervous system probably also uses a gross spatial code to represent intensity. For example, if the cones are not being stimulated because the light level is too low, only the neurons connected to the rods would be responding.

coding of pattern and movement

The coding of pattern and movement represents examples of how the visual system codes spatial and temporal characteristics of the stimulus. Depth vision, which is another example of the coding of spatial information, will be considered in a separate section. The visual system has evolved codes for pattern and movement which overlap to a considerable extent (anticipating Einstein's space–time continuum by millions of years). The coding of movement and pattern becomes progressively more complex and more interrelated as the messages travel along the afferent pathway, but coding in the retina is far from simple.

coding in the retina

While there are approximately 131 million photoreceptors in the human retina, there are only about 1 million ganglion cells. The information from the receptors, particularly the rods, thus has to undergo a great deal of convergence. The ganglion cells only pass along a summary of what is happening at the level of the receptors. Werblin and Dowling (1969) were able to study this summarizing process by recording from each of the various cell types in the mud puppy. Figure 5.10 shows what electrical changes occur in each cell types when the receptor on the left is stimulated by a tiny beam of light for a short period of time, and the one on the right remains in the dark. Notice

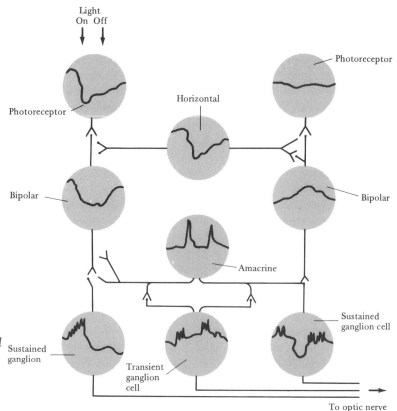

Light
On Off

Photoreceptor

Photoreceptor

Horizontal

Bipolar

Bipolar

Amacrine

Sustained
ganglion cell

Sustained
ganglion

Transient
ganglion
cell

To optic nerve

Figure 5.10
Electrical responses of the various cell types in the retina of the mud puppy when the photoreceptor on the left is stimulated by light. [Modified from Werblin and Dowling (1969).]

that it is the *third* cell in the visual pathway, the ganglion cell, that changes the amplitude code into a spike code. Both the photoreceptors and the bipolars use only graded potential changes.

The cell which is struck by light hyperpolarizes as we might expect. The receptor in the dark remains depolarized. The electrical activity in the stimulated receptor produces more hyperpolarization in both the bipolar and horizontal cells to which it is directly connected, and also results in a burst of spikes in the **sustained ganglion cell** in the lower left-hand corner, for as long as the light remains on. But notice that the cells which are connected to the unstimulated receptor are also affected. The bipolar cell on the right shows a depolarization while the ganglion cell in the lower right-hand corner shows a slowdown of firing when the light is on, then a burst of firing when the light is turned off. The **transient ganglion cell** in the center is also affected—it shows a short burst of firing when the light goes on and again when the light goes off.

The fact that hyperpolarizations of the bipolar cells are causing an increase in firing rate of the ganglion cell may be confusing because hyperpolarizations usually slow down the firing rate of the cell. But this hyperpolarization affects only neurotransmitter release, and the transmitter might be the inhibitory type, rather than the excitatory type. If, when light strikes, *less* inhibitory transmitter is released, this might result in *faster* firing in the next cell—the ganglion cell, for instance. By the same token, it should not be surprising that the depolarization in the bipolar cell on the right results in a cessation of firing in the sustained ganglion cell to which it is directly connected.

Because of this maze of interconnections, the ganglion cells can code at least two types of messages. They can of course code where the light is hitting the retina, by means of the sustained output of the ganglion cell directly in line with the photoreceptor receiving the light. But they can also code temporal information about the light, because the transient cells nearby change their firing rates when the light is turned on and off. Also, because of the interconnections between the retinal cells, every ganglion cell is capable of passing along information from a fairly large number of receptor cells, all of which contribute to the receptive field properties of the cell.

receptive fields of ganglion cells. The receptive field of a ganglion cell is usually shaped like a circle or oval, perhaps 1–2 mm across, with a *center* region and a *surround* region. Some ganglion cells, called **on-center**, respond more vigorously when a light is shined in the center of the field, but less vigorously than their spontaneous rate when the light is shined in the surround. Other cells, called **off-center**, respond in the reverse way—more vigorously to light in their surround, and less so to light in the center. The on-center ganglion cells presumably code a light spot on a dark background, while the off-center cells code a dark spot on a light background.

The two types of cells respond differently to light in their receptive fields because of the way they are connected in the retina. Recently, because of advances in dyes and in electron microscopy, it has been possible to look more closely at the kinds of connections the two types of cells make. For example, Famiglietti and his colleagues (1977) removed the carp's retina and then recorded from some of its cells while they presented dots of light. By injecting a dye into the cell after they had recorded from it, they were able to find the cell later with the microscope and plot its connections. The off-center cells connected in a different layer of the retina, compared to the on-center cells. Using a similar technique, Stell and his colleagues (1977), studying the gold-fish retina, found that off-center retinal cells made a different kind of synaptic junction with the photoreceptors, compared to the kind made by on-center retinal cells. Perhaps one kind of junction is inhibitory and the other excitatory. These kinds of studies are important because they emphasize that the coding properties of cells higher in the afferent pathway must be due to the way they make connections to cells lower in the pathway. They are not due to some intrinsic difference

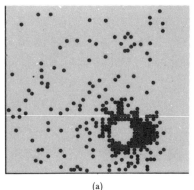

(a)

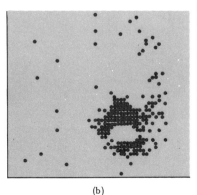

(b)

Figure 5.11

Two plots of the receptive field of a single ganglion cell in the cat's retina. In (a), the computer scanned horizontally, and a dot appears on the graph each time the cell's firing rate exceeded the criterion. In (b), the computer scanned vertically. [From Spinelli (1967).]

between the ganglion cells themselves. We shall see this kind of explanation emerge again when we examine how pattern and movement is coded in the cortex.

Spinelli (1967) was able to make a rather neat demonstration of the receptive field properties of some of the ganglion cells in the cat's eye. He placed a tiny microelectrode into a single optic nerve fiber and then began presenting dots in the visual field of the cat. His method of presenting dots, however, was via a computer which regularly moved the dot along 50 horizontal lines in a single direction. The computer also recorded the number of spikes from the optic nerve after each dot. Whenever the number of spikes exceeded some criterion, Spinelli plotted that point on a graph; an example of the responses of a ganglion cell are shown in Figure 5.11a. Notice that the cell responds above criterion very frequently in a surround region, but virtually never responds above the criterion in the center, indicating that this cell is an off-center.

Figure 5.11b shows how the same cell responded when the computer moved the dots vertically instead of horizontally. The two graphs in Figure 5.11 are not quite the same, suggesting that the receptive field of at least some cells is not simply determined by where the dot is hitting the field, but also by what direction the dot is moving. The intensity of the dots of light also has an effect on the receptive field characteristics of a single ganglion cell.

transient ganglion cells. Thus, at the level of the retina, some of the ganglion cells, called *transient*, are already combining the code for space (i.e., location on the retina) and time (i.e., movement). These transient cells are particularly responsive to movement within their receptive field if it is sudden, and they differ from the other ganglion cells in a number of ways. For example, they have larger receptive fields, in general, and these cells also have faster conduction velocities. They are also more abundant in the periphery of the retina. Some of the axons from the transient cells go directly to the superior colliculus, a structure which we mentioned earlier as part of an alternate afferent pathway by which visual information reaches the brain, and which may be involved in eye movement. Ikeda and Wright (1972) hypothesize that the transient cell-superior colliculus connection provides a means whereby a moving stimulus can elicit an orienting response from an animal. When the animal's transient cells are stimulated by sudden movement, the message quickly results in eye movement which brings the stimulus in front of the fovea, so the animal can see it more clearly. These transient cells would obviously be advantageous to a predatory animal hunting for food, or to humans as they drive cars and respond quickly to the sudden movement of a child in their peripheral vision.

The maze of interconnections which occurs in the retina, and the emergence of a receptive field coding system in the ganglion cells, certainly indicate that a great deal of lateral interaction is going on. Receptive fields of ganglion cells overlap considerably so one might imagine that if a single spot of light is striking the on-center of one ganglion cell, it might be striking the on-surround of another. The situation in the vertebrate retina is so complex that it will be much easier if we describe some classic studies on lateral interaction in the horseshoe crab visual system, studied by Hartline and his associates (Hartline *et al.*, 1956; Hartline and Ratliff, 1957, 1958; Ratliff and Hartline, 1959).

The horseshoe crab's visual system begins with separate photoreceptors, called **ommatidia** (singular: ommatidium), each of which sends its own message to the brain. Each ommatidium is also connected to those alongside it, as shown in the schematic diagram in Figure 5.12, so lateral interactions between the ommatidia are much more limited in scope compared to the maze of interconnections in the vertebrate retina. By recording from the nerve fiber beyond the place where it interacts with its neighbors, these scientists found that light shined anywhere nearby an ommatidium reduced that receptor's response to a light shined directly onto it. This also means that if light is striking one ommatidium, then all of its neighbors will produce less vigorous responses if light is then shined on them. The amount of inhibition that an ommatidium whose neighbor is being stimulated suffers depends on the intensity of the stimulus, and how far away that neighbor is.

Presumably this arrangement acts to enhance contrast. The brain of the crab gets more vigorous messages from the receptor that is being stimulated, but also gets a reduction in activity from the nearby receptors.

Mach bands and lateral interaction. An interesting visual illusion, which is probably due to a similar though much more complex type of lateral interaction in the human retina is the **Mach band**. In a dark room, if you hold a flashlight over an envelope, which is a few inches above a white sheet of paper, you will see the shadow of the envelope. The edge of the shadow presents a gradient of dark to light, and it is at this gradient that the Mach bands appear. Just as the shadow begins to change from dark to light you will see a very much darker "band," and just as the shadow is changing to completely light, you will see another "band," but this time the band appears much brighter than the nearby light areas. This phenomenon is shown in Figure 5.13a, and a graph which shows the comparison of the actual intensity of light along the gradient, compared to the perceptual experience, is shown in Fig. 5.13b. This is a good example of how our sensory systems do not always give us an accurate picture of what is out there, and it is also a fairly good example of a perceptual phenomenon that can be explained in terms of known (or at least hypothesized) neurophysiological events.

coding of pattern and movement in the LGN The cells in the LGN respond to light on the retina in much the same way as the ganglion cell. They have slightly smaller receptive fields, however, and show a sharper distinction between light in the center and light in the surround of the field. This means that the LGN probably is less responsive to diffuse light, but can sharpen the resolution of the patterns of light striking the retina.

Another change which occurs in the LGN is the reorganization of information from both eyes. Information from receptors in both the left and right eye, which receive light from the same part of the visual field, send axons to the same place in the LGN. There is some controversy over whether there are very many LGN cells which have receptive fields which include light coming from *both* eyes, so it is not clear yet how much of a role the LGN actually plays in the processing of binocular vision. But at least the axons from the two eyes, which are coding information from the same place in the visual field, are arriving in the same place in the LGN. The place where these axons group is arranged in a column, which crosses through various layers in the LGN. The receptive fields of the LGN also demonstrate some color-coding properties, which we shall discuss in a later section.

coding of pattern and movement in the cortex The study of how the cortical cells code pattern and movement information introduces the concept of feature detection in the visual system. But this concept was originated by Lettvin and his colleagues (1959, 1961) in connection with their studies on coding in the ganglion cells of the frog's retina.

feature detection in the frog's visual system. These scientists recorded from single ganglion cells, while they presented a visual stimulus in the frog's field of vision. The found a number of different types of cells, different because of the kind of stimulus which could produce a response. For example, one type responded when there was a contrast between light and dark in its receptive field, and another responded only when there was a small dark spot of light moving in its receptive field. They suggested that each of the types that they found corresponded to one of several types by virtue of a characteristic way in which it was connected to the other cells in the retina. Again this emphasizes the point that the response characteristics of any particular cell are determined by the input it receives. This moving dark spot looked suspiciously like a bug. Since the frog feeds on bugs it seems reasonable to assume that these cells alert the frog to the presence of food. The existence of these "bug detectors" initiated the concept of feature detection—a concept which suggests that the coding in the nervous system may emphasize not just any properties of the visual system, but those which are important to the animal.

feature detection in the cat's cortical cells. There is no complex feature detection of this kind in the retina of the mammal, but there may be in the cortex. Hubel and Wiesel (1959, 1962, 1965) pioneered the studies of the responses of single cortical cells in the cat and found that there were several different types of cells, each of which responded best to a different kind of stimulus in their receptive field. These studies are not simple to do since they require the animal to be immobilized, and it is only possible to record from a single cell for a short period of time, if you are going to try to record from as many cells as possible. Thus it is difficult to present all possible types of visual stimulation to a single cell since the dimensions might include shape, distance, color, movement, etc. Nevertheless, Hubel and Wiesel were able to classify the cells they found into three different types: simple, complex, and hypercomplex.

(1) **Simple cells**. These cells responded most vigorously to a straight line or bar held in front of the animal's eye at a particular angle. If the orientation of the bar is turned, the cell's response becomes less vigorous. The receptive fields of these cells still had on–off regions, like those of the LGN and ganglion cells, but the field seemed to be larger and elongated, rather than circular. Hubel and Wiesel speculate that this kind of receptive field may arise from connections with a series of LGN cells whose fields overlap one another.

(2) **Complex cells**. These cells have larger receptive fields, and the stimulus to which they responded most vigorously was a line, in a specific orientation, and moving. Also, these cells are not so fussy about where the line actually appears in the visual field, compared to the simple cells.

(3) **Hypercomplex cells**. The best response from these cells came from a bar-shaped stimulus, which was not only in a particular orientation and moving, but was of a specified length. Some of these cells were even more particular about their preferred stimulus. For example, a group of "higher order hypercomplex cells" responded best to two bars set at 90°, and thus may represent feature detectors for corners. Hypercomplex cells are most concentrated in area 19 (prestriate cortex) and possibly receive their input from the simple and complex cells in areas 17 and 18.

The cortical cells that have a similar orientation preference were arranged in columns, so that when the electrode was moved down into the brain, perpendicular to the surface of the cortex, the cells tended to

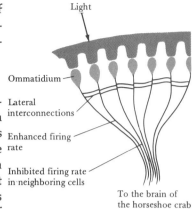

Figure 5.12
Schematic diagram of the effects of lateral interaction between the ommatidia of the horseshoe crab.

Light
Ommatidium
Lateral interconnections
Enhanced firing rate
Inhibited firing rate in neighboring cells
To the brain of the horseshoe crab

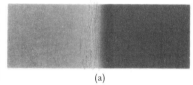

(a)

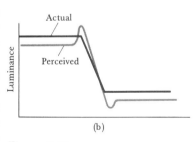

Actual
Perceived
Luminance
(b)

Figure 5.13
(a) Mach bands. (b) Graph which compares the actual luminance across the gradient to the perceptual experience of brightness across the gradient. Solid line represents actual luminance, dashed line represents perceptual experience.

coding of pattern and movement **103**

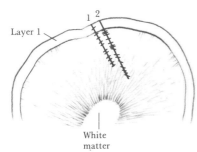

Layer 1

White
matter

Figure 5.14
Two parallel pathways of microelectrodes into the cat's visual cortex. Track 1 has apparently slid down a column, in which all of the cells have specific sensitivities in the same direction. Track 2 crosses from column to column hitting many cells with different directional sensitivities. [From Hubel and Wiesel (1963).]

show a preference for bars in the same orientation, as shown in Figure 5.14.

processing in the temporal lobe. The temporal lobe, although an area not generally included in the afferent pathway for vision, nevertheless receives many nerve fibers from areas 18 and 19. Some of these cells respond to visual stimulation, and Gross *et al.* (1972) found cells that were sensitive to movement, contrast, orientation, and so forth. But they also found cells which were extremely particular about what they would respond most vigorously to. Figure 5.15 shows the visual stimuli which were presented to a cell in the temporal lobe of the monkey. This neuron responded most vigorously to a picture of the monkey's hand. This is indeed very complex feature detection.

The concept of feature detection for visual stimuli in the cortex is controversial, because not all scientists have found that cells are so preferential in their responses. Also, it is difficult to present all the possible kinds of shapes and movements to a single cell. While Lettvin and his colleagues used stimuli that were relevant to the frog's way of life, Hubel and Wiesel presented a very restricted set of stimuli to the cat. The natural importance of these lines and bars to the cat might be questioned. Nevertheless, the concept of feature detection has changed the way that we think about visual coding, and has initiated a whole train of questions—particularly about the origin of feature detectors.

the origin of feature detectors If there really are feature detectors for certain shapes and sizes (and even distance, as we shall see in the next section), where did they come from? Was the animal born with cortical cells with such specific preferences, or do the cells become this way after experience with the environment? Or is the process some combination of the two? This question is essentially asking about the plasticity of the nervous system during development, and about how much the environment can shape the properties of the developing brain. We shall discuss this question in Chapter 14, but for the moment we will simply say that the visual environment in which an organism develops is capable of having an impact on how the cortical cells develop their coding properties. It appears that the responses of cortical cells of the newborn

Figure 5.15
Examples of shapes used to stimulate a group TE unit apparently having very complex trigger features. The stimuli are arranged from left to right in order of increasing ability to drive the neuron from none (1) or little (2 and 3) to maximum (6). [From Gross et al. (1972).]

1   1   1   2   3   3   4   4   5   6

animal are quite similar to those of the adult animal, although they may not be as sharply preferential. There are cells which respond best to vertical lines as well as horizontal lines, for example. But if the visual environment in which the animal develops is abnormal in some way, such as containing nothing but vertical lines, then the coding properties of the cortical cells can be modified.

---

summary
Coding of Intensity, Pattern, and Movement

The main features of the visual environment which must be coded include intensity, pattern and movement, depth, and color. The human visual system does not code absolute light intensity very well, particularly because our sensitivity to light varies depending upon how long we've been in the dark. However, it codes the other features of the visual environment extremely well.

The coding of pattern begins in the retina. Each ganglion cell responds when a light stimulus is in its receptive field, an area 1–2 mm across. This field is usually oval or circular, and has a *center–surround* organization. For example, the cell might fire faster if the light is in the center, but slower if the light is in its surround (on-center cell). Off-center cells respond in the opposite manner. This receptive field organization is produced by the maze of interconnections in the retina. Each ganglion cell receives input not only from its own set of photoreceptors, but also from other receptors by means of the interconnecting horizontal and amacrine cells. The lateral interaction between ganglion cells probably acts to enhance contrast and results in some interesting optical illusions. Some ganglion cells, called transient cells, are also very sensitive to sudden movement in the visual field, and these cells send some of their information to the superior colliculus—a structure which may be involved in the control of eye movement.

In the cortex, many cells code both spatial and temporal characteristics of the stimulus. For example, a single cortical neuron might only respond by an increase in firing rate if the stimulus is a line in a particular orientation that is moving in a particular direction. Cortical cells with such distinct preferences are called feature detectors. Cells with similar orientation preferences are arranged in columns in the cortex, so that an electrode moved directly into the brain, perpendicular to the surface, might encounter many cells with a preference for a line in the same orientation.

Another spatial characteristic of the visual environment which is especially important to primates, aside from pattern, is depth. Just using one eye, we can tell how far away an object is by a variety of cues. For example, we can use aerial haze, which means that the further objects are fuzzier than the closer ones, or interposition, meaning that objects which overlap objects in the visual field must be closer. The most im-

coding depth

portant cue we use to determine distance, however, is based on the fact that we have two eyes with overlapping fields of vision, and is called **retinal disparity**.

When you look at an object, the two eyes, because they are about 6 cm apart, see slightly different views of the object. The closer the object, the more disparate are the two images striking the retina. The brain fuses the two overlapping images into one, and interprets the amount of disparity as some measure of depth. The televiewer many children use to see three-dimensional pictures of Cinderella's castle uses the same principle. The camera takes two pictures of the castle, from two slightly different angles, and the televiewer projects each picture onto one of your eyes. The brain fuses the two images, using a process called **stereopsis**, and perceives the resulting image as three dimensional.

anatomical substrate for binocular vision When fibers carrying visual information leave the LGN, they are still essentially grouped according to where the information came from in the visual field. But when they reach the cortex, the arrangement changes. Rakic (1976) used the technique of **autoradiography** to follow the fiber pathways leading from each eye in the developing monkey. In this technique, a radioactively labeled protein is injected into one eye, and the protein is transported through the neurons leading from that eye, and also across the synapses which those neurons make. When the brain of the monkey is sectioned later, it is possible to make photographs of each section, which highlight the radioactive grains, and thus show where the fibers which lead from one eye go.

Using this technique he was able to confirm previous electrophysiological evidence which suggested that the cortex was arranged in columns which overlap the orientation columns mentioned earlier. These columns are called **ocular dominance columns** because they alternate between fiber terminations which are bringing information from the left eye, with those coming from the right eye. This kind of columnar arrangement, in which information from each eye is grouped together, provides the basis for binocular vision. In order to determine distance, it is necessary that the brain receive input from each eye separately, and the existence of the ocular dominance columns suggests that the brain is indeed separating the information anatomically in the cortex. But although the columns in the cortex separate the information, they also provide a means to integrate the information through the neuronal connections between columns.

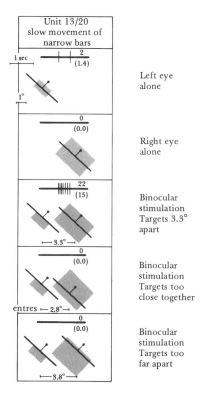

Figure 5.16
The responses of a "disparity detector" in the cat's visual cortex. This cell responded weakly when only one eye was stimulated by a slowly moving narrow bar in the visual field. But it responded vigorously when both eyes were stimulated—provided the two stimuli were 3.3° apart in the visual field. The cell did not respond if the targets were too far apart to too close together. [From Barlow et al. (1967).]

Although the ganglion cells, and most of the LGN cells, only respond to light striking the eye to which they are connected, many cortical cells receive input from both eyes, and therefore can be stimulated from either eye as long as the image is coming from the proper place in the visual field. Barlow *et al.* (1967) found what appeared to be feature detectors for depth in the cortex. They inserted microelectrodes into the visual cortex of the immobilized cat and recorded the re-

retinal disparity detectors

sponses of single cells to bar-shaped, moving stimuli which were being presented to one eye alone, or both eyes simultaneously. Figure 5.16 shows some of their results for a single cell.

When one eye was stimulated by itself, the firing rate was very slow, but when both eyes were stimulated, the cell responded vigorously. Furthermore, the places on the two retinas which were stimulated turned out to be very important. If the two stimulating lights were too far apart, or too close together, the cell would slow down its firing rate considerably. This finding is very important because it suggests that this particular cell responds best when there is a stimulus in the visual environment which is a certain distance away and therefore stimulating just the right spots on each of the retinas. They also found other cells which would respond best to a different distance between the two stimulating lights, suggesting that there may be many **disparity detectors**, each of which responds best to a visual stimulus that is a certain distance away.

---

summary
Coding Depth

The visual system of human beings is excellent for coding depth because it has two eyes with overlapping fields of vision. The image of an object on one eye is slightly different from the image of the object reaching the other eye. The amount of this *retinal disparity* is the best clue to the distance of the object. The brain fuses the two images in a process called *stereopsis*, and uses the amount of retinal disparity as an estimate of depth. In the cortex, the LGN fibers bringing information from the left eye are separate from those related to the right eye. These left eye and right eye terminations are arranged in alternating columns, called *ocular dominance columns*. In the cortex, there are also some cells, called *disparity detectors*, which preferentially respond to a stimulus when it is a certain distance away from the person, and thus is striking two specific points on the retina. There are presumably many disparity detectors, each with a preference for an object at a different distance.

---

color coding

The coding of stimulus quality in the sense of vision refers to the coding of color. The determination of stimulus quality is very simple, because different qualities lie along a continuum of wavelengths within the visible spectrum. But hypotheses about how the brain codes color information have differed substantially. One major theory, proposed by Young in 1801, and modified by Helmholtz, is called the **trichromatic theory**. It stated that color vision is mediated by three separate types of receptors, all of which are types of cones, and each of which is most responsive to a particular range of wavelengths.

The second major theory, called the **opponent process theory**, proposed by Hering in 1878, suggested that there were cells which changed their firing rates in response to different wavelengths in an opponent manner. For example, red might produce an increase in firing, but green would produce a decrease in the same cell. This theory postulated the existence of three types of cells: red–green, blue–yellow, and black–white. As we shall see, both theories turned out to be basically correct, but at different levels of the afferent pathway, reiterating the basic premise that the coding of any feature of the environment can change from one level to the next.

When we discussed the three different photopigments in the cones of *color coding in the retina* the retina, we mentioned that each one was more sensitive to a particular band of wavelengths. Marks *et al.* (1964) were able to determine what wavelengths each kind of cone absorbed by using a technique called **microspectrophotometry**. This technique, which is not quite as complicated as its name, involves shining a tiny beam of light on a single photoreceptor and also on an area of the retina containing no photoreceptors. They then measured the wavelengths of the light which was reflected back from both places, and those wavelengths that were not reflected back were absorbed. Any difference in the amount of light absorbed by the two places on the retina would then indicate the amount of light absorbed by the photoreceptor. By systematically varying the wavelength of the beams of light, they were able to obtain an entire absorption curve for each photoreceptor that they investigated.

Figure 5.17 shows that there are three types of cones: one which absorbs the most light at around 445 nanometers (nm) (blue-sensitive), another which absorbs the most at 535 (green-sensitive), and a third, which absorbs the most at 570. The third type is called red-sensitive, even though 570 is yellow, because this type shows more absorption of the red wavelengths than either the blue or the green sensitive cells. Notice in the graph that there is a considerable amount of overlap in the wavelengths to which each kind of cone is sensitive. For example, at 535 nm both the blue and the green sensitive cones will absorb some light, suggesting that our brain will have some reliable information about the color bluish-green.

These findings have clearly set to rest the controversy about how the photoreceptors code color. Young's trichromatic theory was essentially correct: there are three types of cones, each of which is broadly tuned to respond to a range of wavelengths, but also show peak sensitivities to blue, green, and red. But once the information is

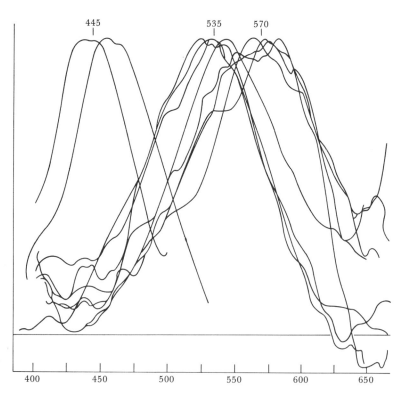

Figure 5.17
Absorption difference spectra for 10 cones, in the human and primate retina. Each curve represents the absorption of various wavelengths of light by a single cone. [From Marks et al. (1964). Copyright 1964 by the American Association for the Advancement of Science.]

moved to the ganglion cells and the LGN, the opponent process theory describes the coding situation better.

coding of color in the LGN DeValois and his colleagues (DeValois *et al.*, 1966) performed a series of studies which brought to light (no pun intended) the way in which color information is coded by the LGN. They recorded from single cells in the monkey, which has excellent color vision, while they presented 12 different flashes of light in sequence, each of which was a different wavelength. Many of the cells which they tested showed no differential response to the different colors, but many of them, the **spectral opponent cells**, did. They found four different types of these spectral opponent cells: one which inhibited its firing rate to green, but increased to red ($+R-G$); a second which inhibited to red, but increased to green ($+G-R$); a third which inhibited to yellow but increased to blue ($+B-Y$); and a fourth that inhibited to blue, but increased to yellow ($+Y-B$). Examples of the responses of two of these types, one a $+R-G$ and another a $+Y-B$, are shown in Figure 5.18. Thus the opponent process system of color coding seems to be correct by the time the information reaches the level of the LGN.

receptive fields of color. Wiesel and Hubel (1966), whom you may remember from the discussion of cortical cell receptive fields, also stud-

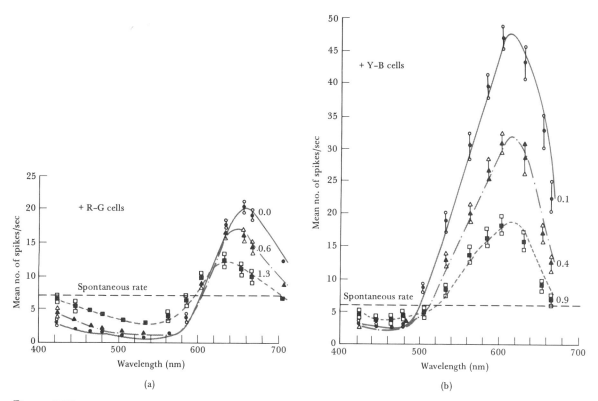

Figure 5.18
(a) The responses of a cell in the lateral geniculate body which was excited by red and inhibited by green. (b) The responses of a cell which was excited by yellow but inhibited by blue. [From DeValois et al. (1966).]

ied the receptive field properties of LGN cells to determine if there were any overlap between the coding of spatial information and the coding of stimulus quality. They presented lights of different colors in different places in the receptive field of some LGN neurons of the monkey, and found that some cells showed a characteristic center —surround organization. But this time, the cell was not simply re- sponding to the presence of light in a particular place in the field—it was also responding to its color. One type of cell that showed this property, for example, responded most vigorously when red was presented in its center, *or* when green was presented in its surround.

In the cortex, very little information is available about how color is *color coding in the cortex* coded because so few of the cells tested with colored lights showed any different responses so far. A few simple cortical cells have exhib- ited their usual bar-shaped receptive fields in which there was an exci- tatory center for red, bordered by an inhibitory region sensitive to green; so it is possible that some of the cortical cells also use an opponent process.

But some of them may be switching back to a trichromatic method of coding color. Motokawa *et al.* (1962) found a few cells which could be grouped into three categories: one with a peak response at 460 nm, another with a peak at 530 nm, and a third group which peaked at 620 nm. It is not yet clear whether most cortical cells are making this switch back to a trichromatic method of coding, because the response properties of a cortical cell are so incredibly complex. It is very difficult to find the "best" stimuli for any cortical cell, because there are so many ways to vary the stimulus.

---

summary
Color Coding

The visual pathway uses two methods to code stimulus quality or color. The first, called the *trichromatic method*, is used by the photoreceptors, and is based on the fact that there are three types of cones, each of which is maximally sensitive to a particular band of wavelengths. The three types of cones, blue-sensitive, green-sensitive, and red-sensitive, pass their information onto the ganglion cells, and then the LGN, where the second method of color coding comes into play, called the *opponent process*. Cells in this structure respond vigorously to one color, but are inhibited by another color. The four types of cells are $+R-G$, $+G-R$, $+B-Y$, and $+Y-B$. Thus far, very little information is available about color coding in the cortex, but it appears that some of the cells may be using the opponent process, and others may switch back to the trichromatic method.

---

efferent output of visual information

Efferent controls from the brain are able to modify the responses of cells lower in the pathway. For example, the muscles surrounding the eye, which result in eye movement, are innervated by axons which come from the brain. Although this efferent control system is not well understood, it is clear that messages from the visual pathway must be sent back down to the eye so that appropriate eye movements can be made. The pathway leading to the superior colliculus from the transient ganglion cells in the retina may be an example of just such a connection.

The muscles controlling the iris must also receive efferent input, since they are able to change the size of the pupil in response to the amount of light coming into the retina. There may even be efferent input directly into the retina, since among the amacrine cells, there are axon endings whose axons originated somewhere in the vicinity of the optic nerve. Thus the brain is certainly sending some of its visual information back down to lower levels of the pathway.

From the visual cortex, however, it is likely that visual information is passed to many areas of the brain, where it can be useful in affecting other behavioral systems. The study of these connections is not easy, but these are the ones that may provide some of the missing links between the coding processes in the afferent pathway and the actual perception of the stimulus.

One example of these connections which was studied by Glickstein and Gibson (1976), involves the route between the visual cortex and the cerebellum, a structure intimately involved in balance and movement. First, these scientists investigated the pathway itself in the cat, by means of a degeneration technique. They made lesions in various areas in the visual cortex, and after 10 days, removed the brains of the cats. The axons of the destroyed cell bodies degenerated, and one of the pathways of degeneration led from area 18 of the visual cortex to the pons—the structure in the midbrain which is a source of fiber input to the cerebellum. This suggested that the pons receives input from the visual cortex.

The next experiment they performed asked the question: What kind of information is the pons receiving from the visual cortical cells? To answer this question, they presented various types of visual stimuli to the cat and recorded from single cells in the pons. These cells had preferred stimuli, just as the cells in the cortex had. Nearly all of them preferred a target that was moving in a particular direction, although the speed of movement was not so critical as it is for some cells in the cortex. The precise shape of the targets was not very important, and many different shapes were capable of eliciting a vigorous response from the pontine cells—a feature which is unlike most cortical cells. Some pontine cells responded best to a moving configuration of dots, while others responded best to a single moving dot. The responses of one pontine cell are shown in Figure 5.19.

By using an interesting technique called **antidromic invasion**, they were next able to identify some of the cells in the cortex which send their information to the pons. The technique is somewhat complicated, but it involves sending a spike backward up the axon which led from the cortex to the pons, and then determining whether the cortical cell received the backward "antidromic" spike. Using this technique, they were able to identify cortico–pontine cells and then to determine their coding properties. They found that only a small subset of cortical cells send input to the pons, and their coding properties were more like the pontine cells than they were like other cortical cells. For example, they preferred moving targets, although they showed a sharper preference for line orientation than any of the cells in the pons had shown.

Glickstein and Gibson suggest that the input the pons receives about the visual field corresponds to a few naturally occurring stimuli, such as movement of a prey animal of the cat, in the case of those pontine cells that respond to single moving spots. The moving ground

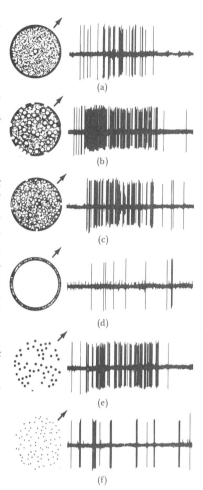

visual cortex—pons connection

Figure 5.19
The responses of a single pontine cell to various visual stimuli, moving in the same direction. All six targets evoked a response in this cell, but the most effective stimulus was a pattern of white dots on a black background that was moving in a specific direction (b). [From Glickstein and Gibson (1976).]

texture as the animal walks or runs might correspond to the natural stimuli for the cells that responded to a moving array of dots.

It is possible that these pontine cells, in sending their information to the cerebellum, contribute to the control of eye and body movement, and coordinate that control with what the animal sees. The story of where the information which the visual cortex receives goes is only beginning, but this retina–visual cortex–pons–cerebellum connection is a good example of how the story might begin. We may find that visual information from the cortex eventually gets to every part of the brain. But if the connection between the visual cortex and the pons can be used as a model for the distribution of visual information, then it may be that the different areas of the brain, for example, those involved in emotion, memory, sex behavior, or sleep, do not receive *all* the visual information, only a part of it. And the part that they receive, or at least preferentially receive, may be the part that is most important for that particular behavior. This is a tantalizing thought—one that reiterates and expands the discussion at the beginning of this chapter. We may not be able to sense everything, but we have a nervous system that senses what is important—and then may distribute the information to where it is needed.

---

summary
Efferent Output of Visual Information

Information from the higher levels of the visual pathway is returned to lower levels in order to control eye movements, pupil dilation and contraction, and probably other dynamics in the accessory structures of the eye. This efferent output from the brain will have an effect on the coding of subsequent sensory messages.

In addition to efferent messages back to the eye, information from the visual cortex probably reaches many areas of the brain. Very little is known about the pathways that it takes, but it is known that there are visual cells sending axons to the pons. This structure provides fiber input to the cerebellum, the part of the brain involved in balance and movement. The pontine cells receiving visual input are primarily sensitive to movement in the visual field, and the shape of the stimulus is less important. This suggests that the pons is receiving, and passing to the cerebellum, only a small subset of the information which the visual cortex is coding, perhaps only the information which it needs in order to control balance and movement while walking or stalking prey. Determining where the information is sent, once it is coded by the cortex, may help us to understand how we perceive what we see, and how visual information can affect our behavior.

KEY TERMS

transduction
vestibular system
adequate stimulus
receptor potential
generator potential
sensory neuron
accessory structures

convergence
magnification
lateral interaction
code
compression
topographic organization
receptive field

specific nerve energies
feature detection
retina
wavelength
intensity
visible spectrum
ultraviolet
infrared
cornea
lens
accommodation
iris
pupil
vitreous humor
rods
cones
fovea
bipolar cells
ganglion cells
optic nerve
diffuse ganglion cell
midget ganglion cell
horizontal cells
amacrine cells
optic chiasm
lateral geniculate nucleus (LGN)
striate cortex
prestriate cortex

inferotemporal cortex
outer segment
photopigment
retinal
opsin
rhodopsin
iodopsins
dark adaptation
dark current
sustained ganglion cell
transient ganglion cell
on-center
off-center
ommatidia
Mach band
simple cells
complex cells
hypercomplex cells
retinal disparity
stereopsis
autoradiography
ocular dominance columns
disparity detectors
trichromatic theory
opponent process theory
microspectrophotometry
spectral opponent cells
antidromic invasion

SUGGESTED READINGS

Glickstein, M., and Gibson, A. R. (1976). Visual cells in the pons of the brain. *Scientific American* **235**, 90–98.

Gregory, R. L. (1978). *Eye and Brain: The Psychology of Seeing.* McGraw-Hill, New York.

(These two references provide easy reading about the visual system. Gregory's book contains interesting chapters about visual illusions.)

Uttal, W. R. (1973). *The Psychobiology of Sensory Coding.* Harper and Row, New York. (An advanced level book that contains excellent information about coding in all the sensory systems.)

6

audition

introduction It is easy to imagine how difficult life would be if we could not see. We need merely to close our eyes and try to walk down the street. But since we cannot close off our sense of hearing so easily we are not able to appreciate what our lives would be like if we could not hear. Not only would we miss the pleasant sounds of the proverbial bubbling brook and whistling wind, but we would be severely impaired in communication because it would be so difficult to learn to speak and understand language. Deafness in the infant is devastating to normal development because the child is cut off from language. The ability to communicate abstract ideas verbally is the unique property of human beings—indeed, the property which makes them so different from the rest of the animal world.

But the ability to hear is certainly not unique to human beings, and Masterson (1974) notes that no species of vertebrate animal is deaf. Though some animals may exist without vision and be none the worse off since in their environments there is little or no light, none apparently can survive very long without hearing. There is no environment on earth without sound, and the ability to detect it, to analyze it, and to react to it is part of the reason the vertebrates have done so well during the course of evolution.

In this chapter we will examine the sense of hearing. First we will discuss sound—the auditory stimulus, and then we will look at the ear —the sense organ that modifies, amplifies, and finally transduces sound energy into neural energy. Next we will explore the afferent pathway for hearing—a pathway which is complicated and much less clear than the one leading from the eyes. Finally we will take up the problem of coding—from the transduction of sound energy in the receptors to the responses of cells in the auditory cortex.

sound: the auditory stimulus While the eyes transduce light energy into a neural message, the ears do the same for sound energy in the environment. The energy for the sound stimulus originates from things that move or vibrate in a medium such as air or water. The medium must have some degree of elasticity to allow for the successive changes in pressure that is sound. Also, the medium must contain particles since sound does not travel in a vacuum.

The simple sound produced by a tuning fork can illustrate the nature of the sound stimulus. When the tuning fork is struck, the prongs are set into vibratory motion, illustrated in Figure 6.1. The motion of the prongs is arbitrarily given displacement values of -1 through $+1$ in (a), and at the center point the prongs are in the zero position. Diagram (b) shows the continuously changing positions of the fork through time. The four patterns illustrate the patterns of **condensations** and **rarefactions** which occur in the air adjacent to the tuning

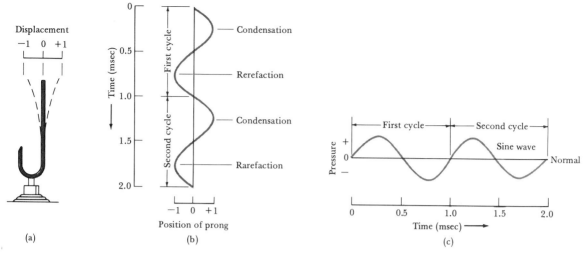

Displacement
−1 0 +1

(a)

Time (msec)
First cycle — Second cycle

Condensation
Rerefaction
Condensation
Rarefaction

−1 0 +1
Position of prong
(b)

Pressure
+
0
−

First cycle — Second cycle
Sine wave
Normal

0   0.5   1.0   1.5   2.0
Time (msec) —→
(c)

Figure 6.1
Schematic illustration of the properties of a sound wave. [*From
Hearing*: Physiology and Psychophysics, *by Lawrence Gulick.
Copyright* © *1971 by Oxford University Press, Inc. Reprinted by
permission.*]

fork. Condensation is an increase in density of the molecules, so that
the pressure of that area increases above the normal atmospheric
pressure, while rarefaction is the opposite—a decrease in the density
of the particles which results in a decrease in the air pressure below
the normal value. A condensation produces a rarefaction next to it,
and a rarefaction results in a condensation in the area adjacent. It is in
this way that a sound wave travels, and although the process might
seem clumsy, sound can actually move at a speed of 1100 ft/sec at sea
level. The sine wave pictured in Figure 6.1c represents the alternating
condensations and rarefactions as they pass through a given point
over a 2-msec time span. At time zero the air pressure at the point is
normal, but after 0.25 msec (1/1000 sec), the pressure has increased.
When 0.75 msec has passed, the pressure is reduced below its normal
value, and after 1 msec the pressure is returned to normal.

This sine wave can be used to illustrate some of the basic terms
related to sound wave motion. The **cycle** of the wave, shown in Figure
6.1, refers to the displacement of the sound source or vibrating body
from its stationary position to the maximum movement, first in one
direction and then in the other. Each cycle includes one condensation
and one rarefaction. The time required for one cycle to occur is the
period of the wave. The **wavelength** is the distance traveled by the
leading edge or wavefront in one period, and the **frequency** of a sine
wave is the number of cycles which pass a given point per unit of time.
The sine wave in Figure 6.1 is a 1000 cycles per second (cps) tone

because its period is 1 msec. Usually the number of cycles which pass a point over a 1-second period is used as a reference point in comparing sound waves. This measure of frequency is called **hertz** (Hz), named in honor of the German scientist Heinrich Hertz. The frequency of a sound wave corresponds to our perception of pitch; for example, a tuning fork which vibrates at 1024 cps or Hz is the musical pitch "C." Although tuning forks can produce near pure tones, most sounds that we hear consist of combinations of many different frequencies. If the frequency of a sound wave is repetitive, and does not vary from moment to moment, it sounds like a musical tone. The reasons why a person's speaking voice does not sound like music is because of the change in the variety of frequencies which are being produced over time.

sound intensity The amount of the displacement of the vibratory body which corresponds to the amount of pressure change from the normal to the maximum during a condensation is the **amplitude** of the wave. In Figure 6.1c, the amplitude of the wave refers to its height. The intensity of a sound wave is equal to its amplitude, and intensity corresponds roughly to our perception of loudness. All other things being equal, the greater the amplitude of the sound wave, the louder it sounds.

Although as sound travels, the form of the wave remains the same,

Table 6.1
Sound level chart[a]

Decibel	Bel	Type of Sound	Times as Loud as 0 dB
0	0	The least sound heard by a normal human ear	—
10	1	The rustle of leaves in a light breeze	10
20	2	An average whisper 4 feet away from hearer	100
30	3	Broadcasting studio when no program is in progress	1,000
40	4	Night noises in a city	10,000
50	5	Average residence	100,000
60	6	Normal conversation at 3 feet	1,000,000
70	7	An accounting office	10,000,000
80	8	A noisy city street	100,000,000
90	9	A moderate discotheque	1,000,000,000
100	10	A food blender	10,000,000,000
110	11	A pneumatic drill	100,000,000,000
120	12	A jet engine	1,000,000,000,000

[a]From Tannenbaum, B., and Stillman, M. (1973) *Understanding Sound*, p. 31. McGraw-Hill, New York. Copyright © 1973 by Beulah Tannenbaum and Myra Stillman.

the amplitude or intensity of the wave gets smaller. This principle of wave action is easily understood if you consider how a microphone works. The sound of your voice would lose much of its amplitude over a long distance, but the microphone picks up the pressure changes and the amplifier increases the amplitude without changing the form of the waves.

To measure the intensity of a wave it is customary to measure the amount of pressure exerted by the vibratory air particles upon a surface. Pressure is measured in terms of force per unit area, and the unit of measure is the **dyne** per square centimeter. Normal atmospheric pressure is about 1 million dynes per square centimeter, but the sensitivity of human hearing is such that for some frequencies we can hear pressures as small as 0.0002 dynes/cm². Furthermore the human ear is sensitive to an enormous range of intensities, and the logarithmic **decibel scale** (dB) was constructed in order to compress this range into more manageable proportions. Thus, because human beings can hear so many widely different intensities, we use decibels, which is a comparison between the sound intensity in question and the widely used standard physical pressure of 0.0002 dyne/cm², to measure the intensity of a sound. Table 6.1 shows the decibel levels of various sounds with which we are familiar.

The least intense sound that a human being can hear varies with the individual, and also depends upon the frequency of the sound. On the average, human beings can hear a 1000-Hz tone when the intensity is only 0.0002 dyne/cm². Figure 6.2 shows the thresholds or **minimum audible pressures (MAP)** over frequencies which range from 10 to 10,000 Hz. Notice that for lower frequencies, our hearing thresholds are higher, so that the sound needs to be more intense (higher decibels) in order for us to hear it. This is one reason why we usually like to turn up the volume of the base on the stereo; we do not hear the lower sound frequencies as well as the treble. Figure 6.2 also shows the decibel levels at various frequencies which produce the sensations of tickle and discomfort, rather than the sensation of hearing.

Human hearing thresholds are measured by means of **audiometry,** and the record of an individual's hearing level for certain tones is called an **audiogram.** Figure 6.3 shows an audiogram for a person with impaired hearing. The hearing for sounds conducted by the bones of the middle ear (which we will discuss later), rather than by the air medium is within the normal range except for the very high 4000-Hz tones. But enormous intensities are required for sounds transmitted through the air before the subject reports hearing the tones. For example, the subject can only hear a 1000-Hz tone at intensities of at least 40 dB. The normal individual can hear these tones at almost 0 dB. This

hearing thresholds

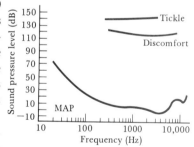

Figure 6.2
Human hearing thresholds as a function of sound frequency. Bottom curve represents the minimum audible pressure that young adults with normal hearing can hear in an earphone. Thresholds for discomfort and tickle sensations are also shown. [From Scharf (1975).]

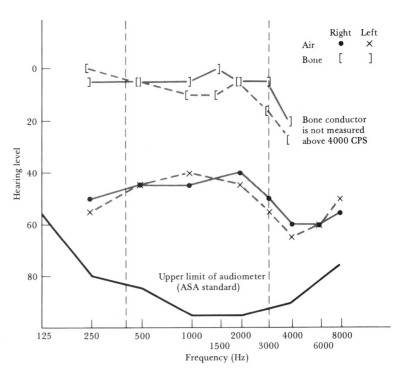

Figure 6.3
Audiogram showing the hearing levels in a hypothetical case of conductive hearing loss, with a slight additional sensory-neural loss at 4000 Hz. The vertical dashed lines indicate the band of frequencies most important for understanding speech. [From Hearing and Deafness, rev. ed., edited by Hallowell Davis and S. Richard Silverman. Copyright 1947, © 1960 by Holt, Rinehart and Winston, Inc. Reprinted by permission of Holt, Rinehart and Winston.]

pattern indicates that there is very little wrong with the person's auditory neurons and the way that the sounds are analyzed by the brain, but there is something very definitely wrong with the structures of the ear which conduct the airborne sound waves to the nerves which transduce the sound into a neural message. There are many things which can go wrong with the ear's structure which might produce the **conductive** type of **hearing loss** which this patient has, rather than a **sensory-neural hearing loss** which results from damage to the nervous system.

summary
The Auditory Stimulus

Sound is actually tiny air pressure changes consisting of alternating condensations and rarefactions in a medium such as air, which move in a wavelike fashion. One condensation and one rarefaction are contained in one *cycle* and the number of cycles which pass a point per unit time is the wave's *frequency*. The amount of pressure change above normal atmospheric pressure is the wave's *amplitude* or *intensity*, and as the wave travels it loses intensity while retaining its form. Human ears are sensitive to extremely low sound intensities, and these intensities are measured in *decibels* (dB). An *audiogram* is a graph which depicts an individual's hearing thresholds in decibels for each ear for tones of different frequencies. With this graph it is possible to determine whether a person has any hearing loss, and if so, what type it might be.

122 *physiological psychology*

Just as the sense of vision requires a number of accessory structures to modify the light energy before it is transduced to a neural message, the ear has a number of structures which modify and amplify the sound energy. The ear is divided into three parts: the *outer, middle,* and *inner* ears, each of which has its own function. The outer ear "collects" the sound, the middle ear "transmits" the sound, and the inner ear contains the sensory receptor cells which transduce the sound from mechanical to neural energy. The ear does not simply bring the sound waves passing through the air to the sensory cells; it also amplifies the waves to make the receptor cells more efficient at detecting tiny pressure changes. Figure 6.4 shows the gross structure of the ear.

The main parts of the **outer ear** include the **pinna** and the **auditory** *outer ear* **canal.** The pinna is the fleshy structure on each side of the head which is commonly called the ear, and it aids in the collection of sound pressure waves. In human beings the pinna is not quite as useful as it is in animals like the dog which can orient their pinnae toward the source of a sound, although it does help somewhat since people who have lost or damaged their pinnae have difficulty distinguishing noises originating in front from those in the back of the head.

The auditory canal is the tube through which the sound waves travel, and if it is blocked hearing will be impaired. We frequently block it deliberately with our fingers, but it can also be blocked by wax which is secreted into the canal by the epithelium lining. The wax serves two functions: it discourages entry of insects and it prevents the cells of the canal from drying out.

In humans, the auditory canal is about 2.5 to 3 cm long, with a di-

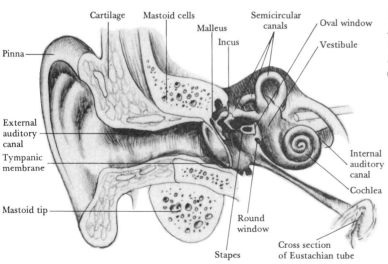

Figure 6.4
A semidiagrammatic drawing of the ear. [From Davis and Silverman (1960), in Thurlow (1971).]

ameter of about 7 mm. Stretched across the inner end of the canal is the rather taut **tympanic membrane** or ear drum. The membrane is shaped like a cone with its apex toward the inside as shown in Figure 6.4. Sound waves passing down the canal strike against the tympanic membrane and set it into vibration. Because the membrane is suspended between two bodies of air at equal pressure, it can vibrate rather freely and its vibration pattern faithfully reproduces the pattern of the sound waves. If this membrane is damaged as a result of scar tissue from the healing of a puncture or tear, small hearing losses will result. The tympanic membrane is the boundary that divides the outer and middle ear.

middle ear The small air-filled cavity behind the tympanic membrane is the **middle ear,** and its total volume varies from 2 to 8.55 cm³. Air enters the cavity from the mouth via the **Eustachian tube,** and the entrance of this air from the mouth allows the air pressure on both sides of the tympanic membrane to be equalized. This is important because any difference in air pressure across the membrane hampers the vibratory motion of the membrane, thereby lessening the efficiency of the sense of hearing. When air pressure outside the body changes, as it does during the take-off of an airplane, or during scuba diving, the air from the Eustachian tube must also change its pressure to compensate. This takes a little time, and this is why it is often difficult to hear in an airplane.

The major parts of the middle ear are the three small **bony ossicles:** the **malleus,** the **incus,** and the **stapes,** shown in Figure 6.5. The ossicles are set into vibratory motion by the movements of the tympanic membrane, to which the incus is attached, and the stapes transmits this motion to another membrane called the **oval window,** which is an opening in the bony external wall of the inner ear.

The importance of the vibrating ossicles lies in the fact that the inner ear is filled with fluid, rather than air, and fluid is much more difficult to set into motion than air. If the sound waves were to strike the oval window directly from the air, 99.9% of the energy would be reflected back. The ossicles, since they are made of bone, provide a mechanical advantage to overcome the resistance difference between the air and the inner ear fluids. They act as a series of levers to amplify the vibrations.

Damage to the ossicles results in severe hearing losses. For example, patients with **otosclerosis** have a bony growth around the stapes which restricts its movement and fixes it firmly against the oval window. Sound waves cannot reach the inner ear nearly as well because they do not have the help of the ossicles to set the fluid in motion. The surgical technique which has been used to treat this disease involves **fenestration** in which a new window to the inner ear is created, completely bypassing the useless ossicles and oval window (Walsh, 1960). Normal hearing cannot be restored, however, because the sound pressure waves from the air must now strike the new window directly, without the benefit of the mechanical advantage provided by the vibrating bony ossicles. Sometimes, it is possible to remove the growth, thereby allowing the stapes to move freely again. This procedure, called **stapes mobilization,** often results in full recovery from the hearing loss. Another technique involves the complete removal of the encrusted stapes, and the insertion of a plastic one, which is fitted against the oval window and attached to the incus. As long as there is no sensory neural damage, the patient should have good recovery, although the operation is far from simple because the stapes is about the size of a pin head.

A transient form of middle ear dysfunction is **otitis media,** which is an inflammation of the middle ear tissue which occurs during a cold in the head. Nasal secretions flow backward and infect the Eustachian tube, which then closes up and prevents the passage of air during swallowing. The imbalance of air pressure across the tympanic membrane eventually restricts the membrane's movement, causing a hearing loss. Years ago, before the introduction of penicillin, otitis media sometimes resulted in permanent hearing damage.

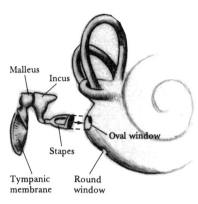

Figure 6.5
Schematic diagram of the bones of the middle ear.

On the other side of the oval window lies the bony labyrinth of the *inner ear* **inner ear.** It is made up of three cavities, two of which are filled with a fluid called **perilymph.** This fluid is similar in composition to the cerebrospinal fluid discussed in Chapter 4. The first cavity is directly behind the oval window and is called the **vestibule.** The second cavity, above and behind the vestibule, is the three **semicircular canals** which contain the sensory cells for the vestibular sensory system. (We will discuss this system in Chapter 8.) The sensory cells for hearing are located in the third cavity, the **cochlea,** shown in Figure 6.6.

The cochlea is a spiral structure similar to a snail shell, which has about two and one-half turns. In cross section, the tubelike structure can be seen to consist of three distinct tubes or canals, shown in Figure 6.6b. The **scala vestibuli** begins at the vestibule opposite the oval window. The **scala tympani** is the largest of the tubes, and at its beginning is a membrane called the **round window** which lies just below the oval window. These two canals share their fluid in common, by means of a small opening at the apex of the cochlea. But the third tube, the **scala media,** is entirely sealed off from the other two canals by means of continuous membranes, one of which is called the **basilar membrane.** This structure extends the length of the cochlea and separates the scala tympani from the scala media. The fluid inside the scala media is different from the perilymph—it contains more potassium ions, and is called the **endolymph.** The fluids of the cochlea are virtually

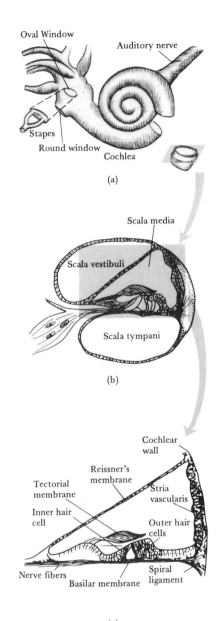

(a)

(b)

(c)

Figure 6.6
Structural and anatomical features of the cochlea. (a) The cochlea in relation to the middle ear. (b) Cross section of the cochlea. (c) The structures within the scala media. [From Green (1976).]

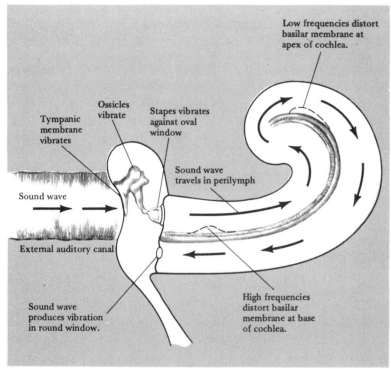

Figure 6.7
The transmission of vibrations from tympanic membrane through the cochlea.

incompressible and are encased in bone. The only pressure relief point is at the round window. When the stapes is pushed in against the oval window, energy is delivered to the fluid of the inner ear. This energy creates a pressure wave in the fluid that flows up the vestibular canal. The wave can flow because of the relief point provided by the round window, so that when the stapes and oval window are pushed in, the round window is pushed out and vice versa.

Resting on top and along the length of the basilar membrane, and shown in Figure 6.6c, is a highly complex structure called the **organ of**

Corti, which contains the sensory receptor cells for hearing. The structure contains parts which are rigid and simply serve to hold it together, but it also contains the **hair cells** and the associated **tectorial membrane** which comprise the transducing part of the organ of Corti. At the base of the hair cells are dendrites of the auditory neurons, which are part of the afferent sensory pathway for hearing. There are also axon endings from efferent fibers, which we will discuss later. Figure 6.7 diagrams the transmission of sound waves from the tympanic membrane through the cochlea.

summary
Structure of the Ear

The ear has three parts: the *outer ear,* which collects the sound and is made up of the *pinna* or fleshy exterior, and the *auditory canal;* the *middle ear,* which transmits the sound; and the *inner ear,* which contains the receptor cells that transduce the sound. As sound waves travel down the auditory canal, they set into motion the *tympanic membrane,* which divides the outer and middle ear. The movement of this membrane sets off vibrations in the three *bony ossicles* of the middle ear, which then start the vibrations of the *oval window.* This vibration starts the sound wave through the fluids of the *cochlea* in the inner ear. The cochlea is a long, tube-shaped structure wound into a snail shape. The tube is divided into three cavities all of which continue through its entire length. One of the membranes which separates two of the cavities is the basilar membrane, and this membrane vibrates when the fluids of the cochlea are carrying sound waves. On top of the basilar membrane is the *organ of Corti,* which contains the receptor cells for hearing—the *inner* and *outer hair cells.*

transduction in the ear   The transduction process in the inner ear is one of the thorniest problems in the study of audition. There is general agreement that the hair cells in the organ of Corti are the receptor cells which must accomplish the transduction process, but just how they might do this is still a question for lively scientific debate.

motion in the basilar membrane   When a sound wave travels down the fluid of the cochlea, it sets the basilar membrane in motion, actually in a wavelike motion which reproduces the form of the sound wave. (The whole basilar membrane does not vibrate at the same amplitude; however, the place which vibrates the most depends on the frequency of the sound. This property of the basilar membrane plays an important role in the coding of quality in the auditory system, and we will discuss it further in the next section.) In Figure 6.8 which is a close-up of the organ of Corti, you will notice that the inner and outer hair cells lie between the vibrating basilar membrane and the **tectorial membrane.** When the basilar membrane vibrates it produces a **shearing force** on the **cilia** of the hair cells. Somehow, this shearing force is thought to produce a recep-

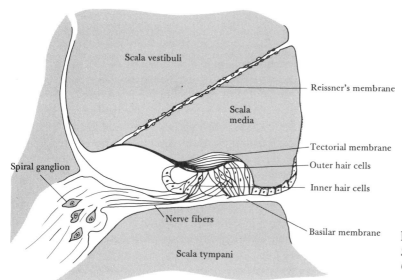

Figure 6.8
Schematic diagram of the organ of Corti.

tor potential in the hair cells which eventually results in transmitter release at the hair cells basal end.

The way in which the receptor potential is produced in the hair cell is not well understood, but speculations abound. Davis (1965), for example, has proposed that the hair cell acts like a "variable resistor" in that changes in its membrane resistance result from the shearing forces. These changes in membrane resistance would eventually result in the release of neurotransmitter from the hair cell to excite the spiral ganglion dendrite. The fluid inside the hair cell is −60 mV relative to the extracellular fluid, but the potential of the endolymph inside the cochlear canal is +80 mV relative to the perilymph of the tympanic canal (Tasaki *et al.*, 1954). Assuming that the endolymph forms the fluid chamber around the cilia of the hair cells, then the potential across the cilia membrane is on the order of 140 mV. This is quite a large electrical gradient, and any change in the properties of the hair cell membrane would result in the movement of many ions, and it is the movement of ions which constitutes a neural message and which can set off the spiking of neurons. Although which ions are moving, and how they could result in spiking is not yet clear for the auditory system, the fact that hair cells are more sensitive when potassium is added to the endolymph suggests that the ionic characteristics of this fluid play an important role in auditory transduction (Hashimoto and Katsuki, 1972).

Masterson (1974) has proposed a method by which the shearing of the hair cells might result in changes in membrane resistance. When

hypotheses about the receptor potential

the hair cells are upright, and standing close together, their membrane resistance would be high and few ions would permeate because membrane resistance is inversely related to the total surface area exposed to the extracellular fluid. But when a pressure wave sets off the shearing action, then the hair cells are moved apart, increasing the total surface area exposed, and thus decreasing the resistance of the membrane to current flow. When the pressure wave moved the shearing action in the other direction, the hair cells are even closer together, creating a hyperpolarization and even less current flow than normal. Other explanations have also been advanced to account for auditory transduction, but none of them has been universally accepted.

cochlear microphonic. One reason why the transduction process is still such an enigma is that the receptor potential has not even been unequivocally identified, although there are certainly a number of potentials which have been recorded in the cochlea, and which follow the stimulus input. Wever and Bray (1930), for example, were recording from the cat's cochlea and found that when they talked into the cat's ear, their voices could be heard over the amplifying equipment. This potential, called the **cochlear microphonic** (CM), faithfully follows the sound stimulus, and has been suggested to be the summated receptor potential from the hair cells.

Not all scientists agree that the cochlear microphonic is the receptor potential, however. It simply may be a correlated phenomenon. First of all, the CM probably is produced almost entirely by the outer hair cells, but it is the inner hair cells that are probably most important in producing activity in the afferent auditory fibers (Fex, 1974). Ninety-five percent of all auditory nerve fibers innervate only inner hair cells (Spoendlin, 1974). Furthermore, the outer hair cells can be completely destroyed without any remarkable loss of hearing abilities. For example, cats treated with **kanamycin,** a drug that preferentially destroys outer hair cells, showed very little loss in their ability to discriminate different frequencies (Nienhuys and Clark, 1978). It was only when some of the inner hair cells were destroyed—in parts of the basilar membrane associated with higher frequencies—that the cats had trouble hearing.

The role of the outer hair cells may be to modulate the activity of the afferent fibers leading from the inner hair cells. Lynn and Sayers (1970) suggest that fibers leading from the outer hair cells synapse onto the afferent fibers leading from the inner hair cells. These dendrodendritic contacts may act to "boost" the activity in the dendrite serving the inner hair cells. If these contacts do exist, they are not the only modulations of activity in the auditory nerve. Efferent fibers also synapse in the area near the base of the hair cells, but we will discuss these inputs in the last section of this chapter.

It is probably clear at this point that much needs to be learned about the cochlea before a clear picture of the transduction process can emerge. But scientists generally agree about the outline of this picture. A traveling sound wave in the fluid of the cochlea sets the basilar membrane into vibratory motion. This vibration produces a shearing force on the receptors, called *hair cells*, lying between the basilar membrane and the *tectorial membrane*. The shearing force, in some way, results in the release of neurotransmitter—an event which sets off spiking activity in the fibers of the auditory nerve.

summary
Transduction in the Auditory System

the afferent auditory pathway

The neural pathway from the organ of Corti in the cochlea to the auditory cortex is more complex than in other systems, at least in terms of the number of synapses which occur along its course. The cell bodies of the sensory afferent neurons lie in the **spiral ganglion,** shown in Figure 6.8. The axons of these neurons form the auditory component of the VIII cranial nerve, which enters the cranial cavity through an opening in the bone.

Once inside the brain, the fibers terminate in the brainstem in the **dorsal and ventral cochlear nuclei,** as indicated in Figure 6.9. Some

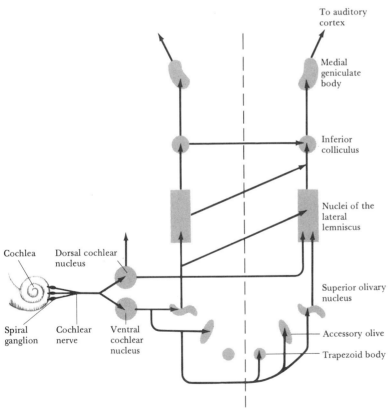

Figure 6.9
The afferent sensory pathway for audition.

fibers that leave the dorsal nucleus cross the midline of the brainstem and ascend in a nerve tract known as the **lateral leminscus.** Fibers leaving the ventral cochlear nucleus terminate in the **olivary complexes,** on both sides of the brain stem, between the pons and medulla. One of the nuclei of this complex, called the **accessory olive,** receives inputs from both ears, and it is the first place along the afferent pathway that binaural interaction can occur.

All ascending fibers synapse in the nucleus of the lateral lemniscus on either side of the brain before reaching the **inferior colliculus** at the midbrain level. From the inferior colliculus the pathway proceeds to the **medial geniculate body** of the thalamus, where interactions between all the sensory pathways occur (with the exception of olfactory pathways). From the medial geniculate, auditory fibers proceed to the auditory cortex, located in the superior part of the temporal lobes.

In the next section, we take up the problem of sound coding. The three properties of sound which need to be coded, and which we will discuss, include sound intensity, the frequency of the sound, and the location of a sound source. In addition we will examine some studies which explore how the brain codes complex sound stimuli.

the coding of sound

In this section we will discuss how the ear codes intensity, frequency, and localization in space. We will also discuss some interesting studies which deal with the coding of some very complex sounds.

coding of intensity

The range of intensities that the human ear can hear is staggering. We can detect movement of the basilar membrane which is many times smaller than the diameter of a hydrogen atom—and we can detect movement that is much larger (perhaps a trillion times larger). This enormous range of sensitivities means that intensity information must be compressed.

coding of intensity in the receptor and auditory nerve. The compression should start at the level of the receptor, but the size of the cochlear microphonic potential shows a linear relationship to sound pressure (Wever *et al.,* 1959). This is another argument against the hypothesis that the CM is the elusive receptor potential.

But even in the auditory nerve, the expected compression is not obvious. Single cell recordings of these fibers reveal that each cell behaves very idiosyncratically. Figure 6.10 shows the responses of several fibers in the auditory nerve. A single fiber shows much faster spiking as the intensity of the stimulus is increased within a particular range, but outside of this range the cell does not increase its firing, and may even show a decrease (Kiang, 1965).

To complicate the picture still further, the frequency and intensity

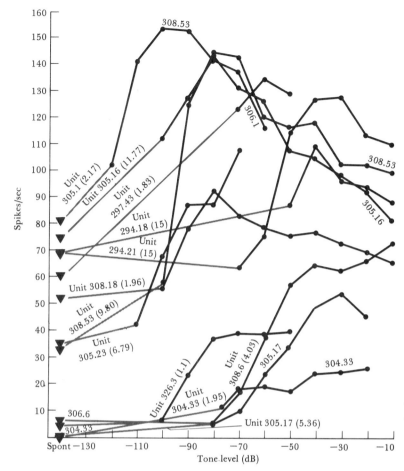

Figure 6.10
Responses of single units in the auditory nerve to sounds of varying intensities. Numbers in parentheses are the best frequencies of each neuron (in kilohertz). [From Kiang (1965) by permission of the MIT Press, Cambridge, Massachusetts.]

of the stimulus interact in the coding process. Figure 6.11 shows the responses of a single cochlear nerve fiber in the cat to a variety of tones having different frequencies and different intensities (Evans, 1975). The best frequency for this fiber, that is the one which produces the most vigorous response, is 2.2 kHz, and the neuron's range of intensities for this frequency begins at around 20 dB. At different frequencies, the cell requires a higher intensity before it will respond, but its firing rate continues to increase at higher intensities. We will see this interaction between the coding of frequency and intensity again when we discuss frequency coding.

It is clear that no single fiber in the auditory nerve could possibly code the enormous range of intensities that we are able to detect. But the pattern of firing in many cells could code this information.

coding of intensity in the auditory pathway. At higher levels of the auditory pathway, many cells show an increase and then a decrease in

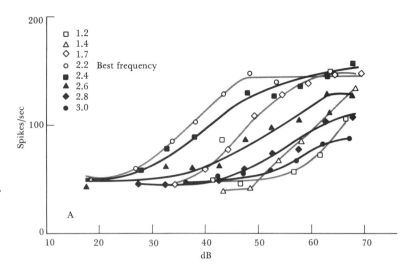

Figure 6.11
Spiking rate of a single cochlear fiber, with a best frequency of 2.2 kHz, to tones of varying frequencies and intensities. [*From Evans (1975).*]

firing in response to a sound of increasing intensities. For example, about half of the cells in the inferior colliculus respond to increasing intensities. Single cells increase their firing rate, others decrease, and still others increase and then decrease as the intensity gets higher (Goldstein *et al.*, 1968). Gross recordings from the auditory cortex, however, using larger electrodes, suggest that the general pattern is for more neural activity as the intensity of a stimulus increases (Saunders, 1970).

The auditory system is somewhat peculiar in the way that it codes intensity. The other sensory systems generally employ an increase in firing rates, with compression of information, but this code is not readily apparent in the auditory pathway. Perhaps this is partly because intensity information is often coded simultaneously with frequency information, as we shall see in the next section.

coding of frequency Quality coding in the auditory system amounts to frequency coding and the frequency of a sound wave corresponds fairly closely with the sensation of pitch. The higher musical notes have higher frequencies while the bass notes have low frequencies. The range of frequencies that human beings can hear varies from about 20 to over 20,000 Hz, but some mammals like the bat can hear much higher frequencies. Humans are very good at detecting very slight differences in frequency. Differences in frequency are translated into a spatial code on the basilar membrane. We can tell what frequency a sound is partially by where it produces the most displacement along this membrane.

Von Békésy (1960) has shown that the amplitude of a pressure wave traveling through the inner ear's fluid from the oval window to the apex of the cochlea will reach a point of maximum height and then taper off. The position along the basilar membrane where the maxi-

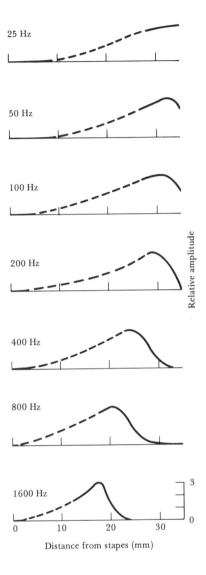

25 Hz

50 Hz

100 Hz

Relative amplitude

200 Hz

400 Hz

800 Hz

1600 Hz

3

0

0   10   20   30

Distance from stapes (mm)

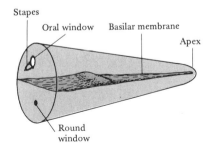

Stapes

Oral window   Basilar membrane

Apex

Round
window

Figure 6.12
*Maximum displacement of the
basilar membrane for a variety of
frequencies. Bottom diagram shows
the "unrolled" cochlea schematically.*

mum amplitude of the wave occurs depends on the frequency of the stimulus. Figure 6.12 shows the distance from the stapes at which the maximum displacement of the basilar membrane occurs, for a variety of frequencies. For example, a sound with a frequency of 25 Hz will have its maximum amplitude all the way at the apex end of the cochlea, and thus the basilar membrane will be displaced the most at that point. The higher frequencies reach their highest amplitudes very close to the stapes. The brain can tell the difference between sounds of different frequencies because different hair cells along the basilar membrane are stimulated.

tuning curves. Along the auditory pathway, the responses of single cells to frequency depends upon the intensity of the sound. To show these relationships it is possible to draw **tuning curves** for the cells as shown in Figure 6.13. To obtain a tuning curve for a cell, it is necessary to first place the microelectrode near enough to the cell so that its spikes can be recorded. Then a series of sounds of different intensities and frequencies are presented. A point is plotted on the graph for the lowest intensity at each frequency which was capable of eliciting a response from the cell. Notice in the figure that each cell can be said to have a **best frequency**—one to which it will respond at the lowest sound intensity. But all the cells will respond to other frequencies when the intensity is higher. Tuning curves are characteristically V-shaped at most levels of the auditory pathway although in the cortex the tuning curves of single cells may be U-shaped and may even have more than one best frequency (Abeles and Goldstein, 1972).

The fact that cells along the auditory pathway are fairly "broadly tuned," that is, they respond to a range of frequencies, is puzzling. Broad tuning, rather than the narrow tuning predicted by the specific nerve energy doctrine, is certainly typical of quality coding in many sensory systems. In vision, for example, we saw that even a green-sensitive photoreceptor still responds to a rather broad range of wavelengths, and we will see broadly tuned taste fibers in Chapter 7. But this does not help explain how we can detect such minor differences in frequency, usually differences of only 1 to 4 Hz when the stimuli are between 50 and 3000 Hz. This remarkable ability remains a mystery.

phase locking. Another mystery involves how we can code the low pitches. The tuning curves of Figure 6.13 do not show any fibers that have best frequencies in the low pitch range. But we can easily tell the difference between a frequency of 30 and one of 32 or 33 Hz. One phenomenon which may help to bridge the gap between our incredible hearing abilities and the events recorded in the auditory pathway is **phase locking.** Some fibers fire preferentially during a certain portion of the cycle of a sound wave—particularly when the frequency is

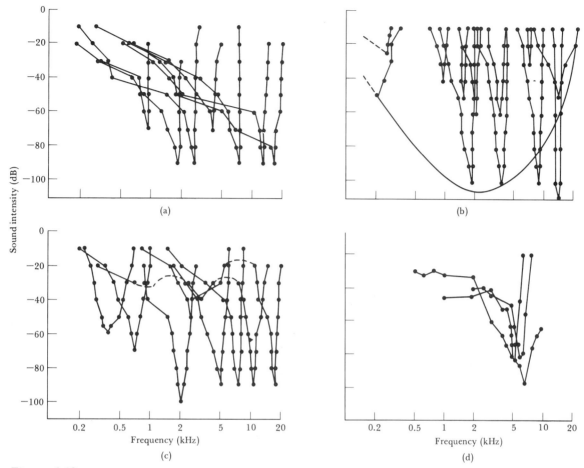

Sound intensity (dB)

Frequency (kHz)

(a)   (b)   (c)   (d)

Figure 6.13
Tuning curves for auditory neurons at different levels of the afferent pathway: (a) at the level of the cochlear nerve, (b) at the level of the inferior colliculus, (c) at the level of the trapezoid body, and (d) at the level of the thalamus. [From Katsuki (1961), in Uttal (1973) by permission of The MIT Press, Cambridge, Massachusetts.]

low (Rose *et al.*, 1967). This phenomenon is demonstrated in Figure 6.14. Some neurons might fire during the same part of every stimulus wave, and others might only fire every tenth stimulus wave—again, during the same portion of the wave. Still others might fire always during the same portion of the cycle, but with a variable number of cycles between each spike. Rose and his colleagues (1967) reported that some fibers in the auditory nerve of the squirrel monkey phase locked for frequencies up to 5000 Hz. This frequency is well beyond the rate at which any neuron can fire (around 1000 spikes/sec). But most fibers that did phase-lock did so for the lower frequencies.

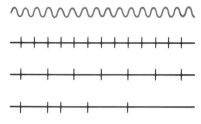

Figure 6.14
Phase-locked firing. All units fire during the lowest part of the sound wave's cycle, although not necessarily for every cycle.

If phase locking is important for quality coding of the lower pitches, it means that the auditory system not only uses a spatial code, but a temporal code for quality coding. At the lower frequencies, it may be *interspike intervals* which are important, rather than the *place* on the basilar membrane which is displaced the most. If the interspike interval is exactly 1 msec (1/1000 sec), or some multiple of 1 msec, perhaps 2, 3, or 4, msec, it would signal that the fiber is phase-locked onto a specific portion of a sound wave which has a frequency of 1000 Hz. Phase locking has also been implicated in the coding of localization in space, which we will discuss later.

topographic organization. Where the visual system is topographically organized according to space in the retina, the auditory system's topographic organization is arranged according to frequency, which is actually the space on the basilar membrane. For example, the fibers in the cochlear nerve are arranged in an orderly way so that cells with similar best frequencies are close to one another and further away from cells with very different best frequencies. This spatial code makes sense in that the fibers originated at the hair cells of the basilar membrane and the basilar membrane encodes frequency in an orderly spatial arrangement. Topographic organization is called **tonotopic organization** in the auditory system.

Higher structures in the auditory pathway also exhibit this tonotopic arrangement, so that if an electrode is pushed deeper into the structure, the best frequencies of the cells encountered change gradually. In the primary auditory cortex of the cat, cells with high best frequencies are found in the anterior region, while those with low best frequencies are usually found in the posterior (Goldstein *et al.*, 1968).

The visual cortex is functionally arranged in columns (orientation columns and ocular dominance columns) but there is no convincing evidence that the auditory cortex has any corresponding "frequency" columns. Abeles and Goldstein (1972) point out that neurons with similar best frequencies might be loosely arranged in very small columns, but that the "hard-walled" columns typical of the visual cortex do not appear to be present.

locating sounds in space Human beings are very good at coding properties of the spatial environment. In the visual system we saw that a spatial code was the primary method by which visual patterns are coded. But in the auditory system space is coded by time. Since we have two ears, one on either side of the head, a sound wave from a click originating on the left side of the head reaches the left ear first. The auditory system, however, uses two separate methods to determine which ear is receiving the wave first: *phase differences* and *intensity differences*.

For lower frequency sounds, the auditory system detects the difference in the portions of the cyclic wave which reach each ear. As a wave moves through space the wave front will be in a different portion of its cycle with every passing moment, and since the two ears are separated, the portion of the wave which strikes the tympanic membranes will be different—unless the sound source is directly in front of or behind the person. The phase-locked fibers from each ear may be very important in sound localization of the low frequencies. A low frequency sound to the left may set off a phase-locked fiber a fraction of a second sooner in the left ear compared to its counterpart in the right ear.

For the higher frequency sounds, a difference in intensity between the two ears is important for sound localization. Because the head is a much denser medium compared to air, the high frequency sounds lose much of their intensity as the waves move through the head, if the sound source is toward the side. Thus high frequency sound waves originating to your left are much less intense by the time they reach your right ear. Intensity differences are not very useful for the low frequency sounds because they lose very little intensity as they pass through the dense medium of your head. (No offense intended.)

The visual system has no binocular interaction until at least the level of the thalamus, but binaural interaction occurs much earlier. Since timing differences are so crucial for sound localization, the interaction must occur earlier, or else the interference of time delays from synapses might blur the time difference information.

Cells in the olivary nuclei respond to input from both ears (Goldberg and Brown, 1969). Typically those cells with best frequencies in the low range are most sensitive to phase differences between the sound waves arriving at each ear, and those with best frequencies in the high range are most sensitive to intensity differences. This makes good sense in light of the behavioral data.

phase difference detectors. In the inferior colliculus, there are some cells that are not only sensitive to phase differences, but to *particular* phase differences. Rose *et al.* (1966) presented stimuli of the same intensity to the two ears of a cat, but they varied the time delay between the two stimuli. The responses of one cell are shown in Figure 6.15. This particular cell was sensitive not to just any phase difference; it varied its firing rate depending upon the amount of phase difference (which is a function of time delay between stimulus presentations). Other cells showed similar patterns but different characteristic time delays.

These cells might be called feature detectors for phase differences between the two ears. Their behavior must depend upon the kind of connections they make with cells lower in the auditory pathway, and Licklider (1959) proposed a model many years ago to account for these kinds of connections, diagrammed in Figure 6.16. A **phase difference detector** must receive input from left and right ears and for it

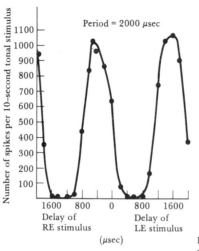

Period = 2000 μsec

Figure 6.15
Responses of a cell in the inferior colliculus of a cat as a function of the amount of time delay between the stimulus in the right ear and the one in the left. [From Rose et al. (1966).]

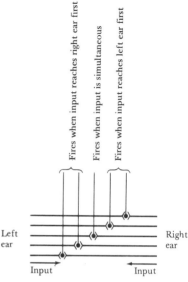

Figure 6.16
Hypothetical connections to explain the behavior of cells which localize sound in space.

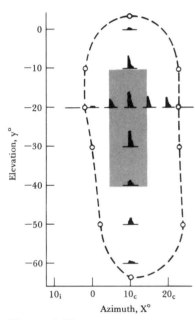

Figure 6.17
The receptive field of an auditory neuron in the owl's brain. This neuron responded best when the sound stimulus was coming from a particular location in space. Each of the small histograms represents the cell's response during a 200-msec presentation of the sound stimulus. [From Knudsen and Konishi (1978). Copyright 1978 by the American Association for the Advancement of Science.]

to fire maximally, the detector must receive the input simultaneously. The detector in the middle, for example, would only fire if the two ears were receiving the sound wave in exactly the same portion of its phase, because the input from both ears travels the same distance to get to the middle. The detector on the left would only fire if the sound wave hit the right ear first, because that information would take longer to reach the detector. This model is attractively simple, but it is not known whether these connections actually exist. What is clear, however, is that information about location in space is first changed into a temporal code—by time differences between the two ears—but then is apparently changed back into a place code. Different cells in the inferior colliculus respond to characteristic time delays between the two ears.

receptive fields for auditory space. More recently, cells with receptive fields in auditory space have been found in a brain structure of the owl which is homologous to the inferior colliculus (Knudsen and Konishi, 1978). A cell would respond maximally only when the speaker was in a particular area in space relative to the owl's head. They found that the receptive fields of several cells overlapped one another, and were shaped like vertically oriented ellipsoids. When the speaker was moved up and down, the cell continued to respond, but when it was moved horizontally, the cell quickly ceased responding. The receptive field of one cell is shown in Fig. 6.17. This study on the owl shows clearly how spatial coding is being used in the brain to code auditory space, because each cell had its own receptive field in space.

Some cells in the auditory cortex may be preferentially sensitive to complex characteristics of the sound stimulus. We noted such complex coding properties of visual cortical cells, and it is certainly not unreasonable to suppose that there are cells in the auditory cortex that are doing some very sophisticated coding.

Some cells in the cat, for example, do not have a best frequency, and indeed do not respond at all to steady tones. Instead, they respond to frequency-modulated tones, ones which change frequency from moment to moment (Whitfield and Evans, 1965). Some of these cells only responded to the rising portion of the FM tone, while others responded only during the falling portion.

coding biologically relevant sounds. Some cells have been found which respond to even more complex sounds. The squirrel monkey has a complex signaling system which includes some 25 to 30 separate calls (Winter *et al.*, 1966), and neurons in the auditory cortex of this animal responded to many of these calls (Newman and Wollberg, 1973). Although the cells fired vigorously to many of the calls, they also discriminated between one or more pairs of acoustically similar calls. Furthermore, the responses of different cells to the same call often showed considerable variation. Figure 6.18 shows the firing patterns of two cells in the auditory cortex in response to the "err-chuck" call. The first cell did not respond at all to the "err" part of the call, but increased after the "chuck." The second responded only to the "err" component.

Some interesting studies on the bat have reinforced the hypothesis that an animal's sensory systems are adapted to code biologically relevant information. The bat uses *echolocation* for moving around, a system in which the animal emits complex noises and then listens for the echoes to find out where the obstacles and the food (insects) are. Some cells in the cortex of the bat are exquisitely sensitive to the kinds of sounds the bat makes. For example, one sound made by the mustache bat consists of about 30 msec of a constant 60,000-Hz tone followed by a few milliseconds of a downward sweeping FM sound. In the cortex, there are cells that respond quite selectively to this particular combination of sounds (Suga *et al.*, 1978).

The problems involved in uncovering complex coders like the ones in the cat and the bat are very difficult because auditory stimuli, like visual stimuli, can vary along a number of different dimensions. The emphasis upon a search for cells which code biologically relevant stimuli is in part an attempt to narrow down the range of stimuli which might elicit preferential responding from cortical neurons—and

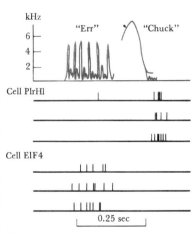

Figure 6.18
Responses of two cells in the auditory cortex of the squirrel monkey to the "err–chuck" call. The top part of the diagram shows the frequencies of sound present in each part of the call. The first cell responded only to the "chuck" part of the call, while the second cell responded only to the "err" part. [From Winter and Funkenstein (1973).]

this strategy has been rewarded by the findings in the bat. But the bat is a somewhat esoteric animal in that certain very important complex sounds must be coded or else it will go bump in the night. We can only speculate whether we, as humans, have any sounds that are any more biologically relevant than others, and for which we have complex coders in our cortex.

---

summary
The Coding of Sound

In this section we examined the characteristics of the sound stimulus that are coded by the auditory system, and what codes are used for each one. The three characteristics of sound which were discussed include (1) sound intensity, (2) frequency, and (3) location in space.

As a first approximation, most neurons in the afferent pathway lower than the cortex increase their firing rate as a sound becomes more intense. But they only increase within a particular range of intensities, and that range depends on the frequency of the sound. The range of intensities that we can detect is enormous, and thus we would expect to see a great deal of compression of information—but that compression is not obvious in the way that single units respond. It is likely that intensity information of a single sound is not coded by single neurons, but rather in the pattern of firing in many neurons.

The frequency of a sound represents its quality, and it corresponds closely to our sensation of pitch. The basilar membrane vibrates at the same frequency as the sound wave, but the place along this membrane which is deformed the most by the traveling wave depends upon the frequency of the sound. High-frequency sounds produce the most displacement close to the stapes, while low sounds produce the most toward the apex of the cochlea. Thus stimulus quality is translated into a place code at the basilar membrane. This place code is maintained by the *tonotopic* organization of neurons throughout the auditory pathway. Cells responding to a particular frequency are found nearby cells which respond to sounds of similar frequencies. Thus where the visual system codes spatial characteristics of the stimulus with its topographic organization, the auditory system codes stimulus quality this way.

Auditory neurons receiving input from the hair cells in the cochlea each have a *best frequency*, which corresponds to the location of the hair cells on the basilar membrane, but each neuron is fairly broadly tuned in that it will respond to other frequencies as well, provided the tones are louder. Recordings from single auditory neurons typically yield a V-shaped *tuning curve* which demonstrates the relationship between the responses of the fiber and the frequency and intensity of the sound stimulus. For low frequencies, auditory neurons are sometimes *phase-locked* to the sound wave; the neuron fires only during a specific portion of the wave's cycle.

Spatial characteristics of the stimulus are coded by means of temporal differences between the two ears. A click coming from the left would produce effects in the left ear slightly before the right ear. The auditory system uses phase differences between the wave reaching the two ears for low-frequency sounds; for high-frequency sounds, intensity differences are used. Binaural interaction occurs very early in the auditory pathway. Cells in the olivary nuclei, for example, can be stimulated by input from both ears, and some cells are most sensitive to phase differences, some are most sensitive to intensity differences, and others are sensitive to both. Higher in the afferent pathway of some animals are some cells which have receptive fields that correspond to sounds coming from a particular area in space. Thus the temporal code may be changed back into a place code with the introduction of these feature detectors.

There may also be more complex coders in the auditory cortex. Some cortical cells in the cat respond best to frequency modulated tones rather than constant frequency tones, some in the monkey respond best to particular parts of one of the monkey's vocalizations, and some in the bat fire preferentially to specific orientation sounds used by the bat in echolocation.

---

olivo—cochlear bundle. Fibers from the higher levels of the auditory pathway are able to affect the activity of neurons lower in the pathway and thus alter the way that subsequent sounds are coded. One example of these efferent effects is the **olivo—cochlear bundle** (OCB)—a fiber system that runs from the olivary complex to the base of the hair cells in the organ of Corti. Some of the fibers from each olivary nucleus go directly to the ear on the same side of the brain, but most of them cross to the other side going to the opposite ear, and it is this crossed bundle that we know the most about.

The axon terminals from these fibers end very close to the hair cells, as shown in Figure 6.19. They probably terminate directly onto the base of outer hair cells, but for the inner hair cells, they look as if they synapse onto the dendrites of the auditory neurons.

When these fibers are stimulated electrically, the activity of the auditory neurons, and of other fibers in the afferent pathway, is inhibited, so the main function of this efferent system is an inhibitory one. Those synapses at the base of the hair cells must contain an inhibitory transmitter substance, and evidence is accumulating that the best candidate is acetylcholine (Fex, 1974). For example, acetylcholinesterase, one of the enzymes which is needed to break down acetylcholine, is present in those axon terminals (Churchill and Schuknecht, 1959). Also, some drugs which block ACh activity also block the inhibitory effects of

efferent effects in the auditory system

efferent effects on the ear

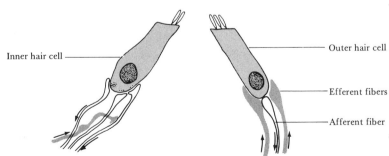

Inner hair cell

Outer hair cell

Efferent fibers

Afferent fiber

Figure 6.19
Schematic sketch showing the pattern of synaptic termination of efferent olivo—cochlear fibers (in black) onto either the auditory dendrite of the inner hair cells, or the base of the outer hair cells. [From Desmedt (1975).]

stimulating the crossed olivo—cochlear bundle. As we mentioned in Chapter 3, however, it is very difficult to nail down precisely what transmitter is being used at a synapse, so other candidates, particularly glycine, still remain in the running. Although some of the details of the way this system works are becoming clear, its function is still in doubt. Perhaps this system of efferent control is involved in the "cocktail party" effect. There is no doubt that we are able to filter out certain sounds and attend to others, depending upon what they mean to us.

middle ear reflex. Another efferent system, whose pathway goes from the auditory neurons to the brain stem and then to motor neurons which control muscles in the ear, involves the **middle ear reflex.** When a very loud sound is presented, two muscles in the middle ear contract and this results in a reduction in the amount of sound transmitted to the cochlea. The contraction of the muscles moves the ossicles, changing the mechanical advantage provided by the ossicular chain. Across most frequencies, the reflex is elicited when the sound is about 80 dB above the normal threshold, and the function of this system is probably to extend the dynamic range of intensities to which the ear is sensitive and to protect the inner ear from damage from loud noises. Unfortunately this reflex cannot even begin to close off the ear completely to sound pressure, as the eyelid does for the eye, but it is able to reduce the sound transmission by about 0.6 or 0.7 dB for every decibel increase in sound intensity (Møller, 1973).

where does auditory information go? The question of where auditory information goes after it has been coded by the cortex will no doubt take a long time and much more research to answer. Very likely the information, or parts of it, reaches many areas of the brain just as does most sensory input. Some of it probably goes back to the ear by way of efferent fibers to the olivary nuclei, some of it probably goes to motor areas, and some probably goes to other processing areas in the cortex.

One such cortico—cortical projection may involve the **insular—temporal cortex,** which is just beneath the primary auditory cortex, shown in Figure 6.20. This area has long been considered an auditory area, because the neurons there become active when sounds are presented. But Colavita (1977) has recently proposed that this area has some more complicated functions. He suggests that this part of the cortex receives projections from many sensory areas, and is involved in temporal pattern discrimination. For example, in order for a cat to discriminate the sequence A—B—A from B—A—B, when A and B are sounds of different intensities, or lights of different brightnesses, or even two separate tactile stimuli, the animal must have an intact insular—temporal cortex. Perhaps this part of the cortex is receiving projections from many sensory areas in the cortex, and/or subcortex, and it functions in detecting patterns. It might be called a polysensory association area. Certainly more research is needed to determine what kinds of input this part of the cortex receives, and how these cells code that input, but it is clear that organisms are able to perform these pattern discriminations so some neural activity somewhere must be involved. Even though ideas such as this one are somewhat speculative, they represent important leaps in the study of the brain. We are approaching the state in physiological psychology where we have learned a great deal about how simple sensory stimuli are coded by the brain. This research has been slow, but very rewarding, partly because it has provided a basis for moving to the study of more complicated information processing. It is true that how you code a "click" may not seem terribly important to finding out how you think; but it is, and how you can tell the difference between "click–beep–click" and "beep–click–beep" is getting even closer to the neurological underpinnings of complex thought.

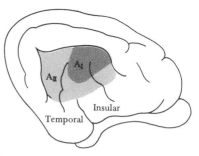

Figure 6.20
The insular–temporal region of the cat's cortex, in relation to the auditory cortex. [From Colavita (1977).]

---

summary
Efferent Effects in the Auditory System

Two examples of how higher levels of the auditory pathway can influence lower levels were given. One efferent system involves the *olivo–cochlear bundle* which produces inhibition in lower level auditory neurons. The terminals from this fiber system synapse near the base of the hair cells and they probably use acetylcholine as their inhibitory transmitter. The second efferent system is the *middle ear reflex*. When a loud noise is present, two muscles in the middle ear contract and reduce the ability of the tympanic membrane to transmit sound.

The paths of efferent output from the auditory cortex are largely unknown. However, there may be output which projects to the *insular–temporal* cortex, a structure which may receive input from several sensory modalities and which may be involved in temporal pattern discriminations.

KEY TERMS

condensations
rarefactions
cycle
period
wavelength
frequency
hertz
amplitude
dyne
decibel scale
minimum audible pressure
audiometry
audiogram
conductive hearing loss
sensory-neural hearing loss
outer ear
pinna

auditory canal
tympanic membrane
middle ear
Eustachian tube
bony ossicles
malleus
incus
stapes
oval window
otosclerosis
fenestration
stapes mobilization
otitis media
inner ear
perilymph
vestibule
semicircular canals

cochlea
scala vestibuli
scala tympani
round window
scala media
basilar membrane
endolymph
organ of Corti
hair cells
tectorial membrane
cochlear microphonic
kanamycin
spiral ganglion
dorsal and ventral cochlear nuclei

lateral lemniscus
olivary complex
accessory olive
inferior colliculus
medial geniculate body
tuning curves
best frequency
phase locking
tonotopic organization
phase difference detector
olivo–cochlear bundle
middle ear reflex
insular–temporal cortex

SUGGESTED READINGS

Green, D. M. (1976). *An Introduction to Hearing.* Lawrence Erlbaum Assoc., Hillsdale, New Jersey. (A lower level book on hearing.)

Katz, J. (1978). *Handbook of Clinical Audiology,* 2nd ed. Williams & Wilkins Co., Baltimore. (Contains a wealth of information about hearing disorders.)

Møller, A. R., ed. (1973). *Basic Mechanisms in Hearing.* Academic Press, New York. (A collection of advanced level articles on the neurophysiology of hearing.)

7

the
chemical
senses

introduction   A male silk moth has just emerged from its cocoon and rests quietly on a twig. He will live for only a short time and will certainly not waste any energy on eating or drinking. The only thing which will occupy his short life is the search for a mate. But to find a female, the moth must be stimulated by her and she may be hundreds of yards away. The sensory signal that our male moth will use is an odor released by the sex glands of the female, which is received by the olfactory receptors on the male's antennae. His olfactory receptors are not confused by other odors, since the vast majority of these receptors are only responsive to the female's sex attractant. He only needs a single molecule of this important substance for him to begin his search. Following the trail toward higher concentrations of the odor, he may, if he is lucky, come upon a receptive female moth who will find him attractive enough to mate with him. Then he will die.

You may think of your chemical senses as nice to have and occasionally useful—especially during a French food repast when the tastes and aromas of the crepes suzettes create an extraordinary experience. But to our hapless moth, an acute sense of smell is the only thing between dying childless and leaving his genes to populate the world in the next generation. And insects are not the only creatures which rely heavily on their chemical senses—the mammals, and the rodents in particular, use these senses to find food and avoid poisons, to elude predators, to mate, to fight, and generally to survive.

Human beings may not get any tax breaks if they lose their sense of smell or taste, and these losses may not be so devastating as the loss of sight or hearing. But the chemical senses are extremely important to the lower animals, and some scientists hypothesize that they may be more important to humans than most of us realize. The industries which concentrate on perfumes, deodorants, and food flavorings are certainly not going broke.

In this chapter we will first discuss the stimulus for the chemical senses, then we will go on to consider the sense of taste, and finally the olfactory system.

the chemical stimulus   The study of the chemical senses has lagged behind the study of vision and audition, partly because taste and olfaction are considered less important to human beings. The chemical senses have also been much more difficult to study because it is very difficult to identify the stimulus.

identifying the stimulus   In the chemical senses, the intensity of the stimulus represents the concentration of molecules which are presented to the receptor cells in the nose or on the tongue. The experimenter can specify the number of molecules that may be present in a stimulus puff of air or a drop of taste solution but, at the same time, be unable to determine the number of molecules that actually reach the receptor cells. For example, it has been estimated that only two percent of the molecules which enter the nose come into contact with the olfactory receptor cells.

In the chemical senses, spatial characteristics of the stimulus are not coded like those of vision. This is as it should be. Odorous molecules, obeying the gas laws, would diffuse away from a source equally in all directions unless there are air currents. In natural settings, however, there are air currents and thus intensity gradients. Many animals use the intensity gradient to find where the strongest concentration of the odor is, and then move in that direction. The moth, for example, can find his mate that way. Predators, if they are to be successful, must remain downwind as they stalk their prey.

coding the chemical stimulus

The concept of stimulus quality in the chemical senses is much more perplexing. In vision, stimulus quality is color—or wavelength, and in hearing, it is frequency of sound. Thus in those two senses, stimulus quality variations represent variations along only one dimension. But although we are able to detect a huge variety of stimulus qualities of odors and tastes, no one is quite certain what properties of the molecules are important. Molecules can differ from one another in quite a number of ways; for example, their molecular weight, their shape, composition, electrical charges, or pH. Whereas we can simply measure the wavelength of light to determine its quality, we can not simply measure a substance's pH to find out its odorous or taste quality.

primary qualities. Most scientists have at least tacitly assumed that there are taste and odor **primary qualities,** which form the basis for chemical quality sensation. In taste, for example, there are the four primaries of salty, sweet, bitter and sour; in odor, different scientists have proposed different primaries, but they usually include such qualities as musky, fruity, or flowery. Not all scientists agree that primaries actually exist, however (Erickson and Schiffman, 1975). It may be that both of the sensory systems determine quality by relying on continuous properties of molecules, particularly molecular weight and pH. Thus there would not be discrete categories of quality, like salty or sweet, but rather continuous gradations between all of the possible qualities.

If there were receptor cells on the tongue which were specifically responsive to salty or sweet tastes, then this would settle the issue and we would know that there are indeed primaries. But unfortunately, as we shall see in the section on coding, this is not the case. At the moment, the coding of sensory quality in the chemical senses is still very confusing, but there is little doubt that the quality of a taste or an odor cannot be coded by a single fiber.

summary
The Chemical Stimulus

The chemical senses are peculiar for a number of reasons. First, they are much more difficult to study compared to audition or vision because identifying the stimulus is a problem. Although one can specify the concentration of an odorant or taste stimulus, no one can tell how much of the stimulus actually reaches the receptor cells. The coding of chemical stimuli is also slightly different. For example, many animals learn something about the spatial characteristics of an odor by following an odor gradient, and thus using intensity cues. Stimulus quality in the chemical senses is a particularly troublesome issue. Most scientists assume that there are *primary qualities* (such as salty and sweet, or fruity and musky) in both gustation and olfaction. But the evidence for these primary qualities is not terribly convincing.

gustation   The sense of taste, also called gustation, provides both a savory sensation for beneficial foods as well as a warning signal for potentially harmful ones. The sense of taste has saved many an animal from eating poisonous foods.

It is the opinion of most researchers that the sense of taste consists of four basic qualities—sweet, sour, salty and bitter. Though there is some disagreement on this point, as noted in the previous section, several lines of evidence do support the notion of the four basic or primary qualities. For example, whenever two or more taste stimuli are mixed no new qualities appear. The component qualities of the mixture can still be identified. Naturalistic observations tend to link the different qualities to different biological survival functions. Salt is needed for maintaining optimal body fluid balance. Sweet taste tends to signal calories. Bitter tasting substances tend to be poisonous. The sour taste signals an acidic or low pH substance and may therefore be a warning stimulus, because of the corrosive properties of acids.

The phenomenon of **cross-adaptation** provides a separate and much stronger line of evidence in support of the basic qualities. Cross-adaptation can be easily demonstrated. It occurs whenever prolonged stimulation with a given taste quality, e.g., sodium chloride to elicit the salty taste, results in a reduced response not only to sodium chloride but also to all other taste stimuli which elicit the salty taste. The reduced responsiveness occurs both at the level of afferent nerve activity and also at that level of perceived intensity. Another important point of cross-adaptation is that prolonged stimulation within one quality does not affect the responsiveness of the taste system to stimuli of any other quality. The interested reader should consult McBurney (1974) for a more complete discussion of the question of primary qualities. This chapter accepts the position that the sense of taste does consist of the four basic qualities. The sensory cells for taste are found primarily on the tongue, and to some extent in the pharynx and larynx.

The tongue is a striated muscle, consisting of bundles which are oriented in all three planes, and which cross one another at right angles. This makes it possible to move the tongue in many different directions, a feature which undoubtedly contributes to its usefulness in the formation of speech sounds. It is about 3 inches in length with its anterior end free, and its posterior end attached to the floor of the mouth.

the taste buds. The anterior end of the tongue is covered with many tiny projections called **papillae,** some of which are surrounded by circular trenches. Most of the receptor organs, or **taste buds,** are found lining the walls of the trenches, and the **taste pore,** or opening in the taste bud, opens up into the trench. A typical taste bud is shown in Figure 7.1

The taste bud is a cluster which may contain anywhere from 15 to 60 elongated cells, depending upon both the type of papilla and the animal species. There has been much disagreement over the types of cells which are present in the taste bud. Some scientists maintain that there are four or five different types, each with its own function, while others hypothesize that the different appearances of the cells merely represent different stages of development, rather than different cell types. It is not clear at the moment which of the cells in the bud is the receptor cell for taste, but it is clear that the cells which act as receptors must have **microvilli,** fine finger-like projections which extend into the taste pore opening. The molecules which stimulate the taste receptors probably drop into the taste pore and interact with the microvilli of the receptor cells.

At the bottom of the cells in the taste bud is a membrane called the **basement membrane.** The intactness of the taste bud depends upon its innervation by nerve fibers which enter the bud through its basement membrane. If these nerves are cut, the cells degenerate and the taste bud disappears. Taste buds, however, will often regenerate when the nerve fibers regenerate, a characteristic that makes them different from the receptor cells for vision or audition (Guth, 1958).

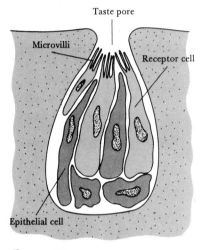

Figure 7.1
Schematic drawing of the taste bud.

The cells within the taste bud synapse on the dendrites of three separate cranial nerves: the facial (VII), the glossopharyngeal (IX), and the vagus (X). The buds in the front of the tongue are serviced by a branch of the facial nerve (VII), called the **chorda tympani.** The chorda tympani passes near the tympanic membrane in the middle ear, hence its

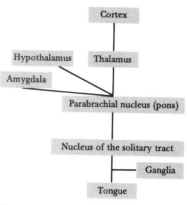

Figure 7.2
The afferent pathway for gustation.

name. The posterior third of the tongue is innervated by the glosso-pharyngeal (IX) nerve, and the vagus nerve (X) innervates the taste buds of the pharynx and larynx. This arrangement means that the chorda tympani carries taste information from the anterior two-thirds of the tongue, while the glossopharyngeal carries information from the posterior one-third.

After these nerve fibers enter the brain, their axons terminate in the brainstem in an area called the **nucleus of the solitary tract.** The three taste nerves terminate in this tube-shaped nucleus in an orderly spatial arrangement with the chorda tympani fibers in the dorsal tip, the glossopharyngeal fibers in the middle, and the vagal fibers in the ventral half. The cell bodies of these neurons are in separate ganglia just outside the brainstem.

Neurons leaving the nucleus of the solitary tract proceed rostrally to a small area of the pons, the **parabrachial nucleus** (Norgren and Leonard, 1973). From this pontine taste area, some neurons proceed to the thalamic taste nucleus. The projection from each pontine area is bilateral to the thalamic taste relay nucleus. In addition, there are fibers from the pontine taste area to the hypothalamus and amygdala (Norgren, 1976). This latter projection is probably involved in the pleasant–unpleasant aspects of taste sensations, that is, the acceptance or rejection of certain stimuli.

From the thalamus, axons project to the cortex, particularly the somatosensory cortex which subserve the face region. The afferent pathway is diagrammed in Figure 7.2.

transduction in the taste buds Although there is a great deal of information about how each level of the brain codes visual information, the same cannot be said for the chemical senses. The taste pathway has received less attention, and the responses of the neurons along it have often been mystifying. Even the first step in the coding of the stimulus, that of transduction in the taste bud, is still a matter of controversy.

Before information about the taste stimulus can be transmitted to the brain, it must be transduced to a receptor potential which can alter the firing rates of the neurons along the sensory pathway. Most researchers agree that the taste stimulus molecule must attach itself to the membrane of the taste receptor cell, presumably in the region of the cell's microvilli, but how that is accomplished, and how it results in a receptor potential which can communicate information about stimulus quality and strength, are unknown.

coding of stimulus strength—adsorption. To account for the transduction of information about stimulus strength, Beidler (1954) proposed that there are a finite number of sites on a receptor cell membrane where molecules can be attached or adsorbed. **Adsorption** is a reversible process, so that as some molecules are being adsorbed, others are being desorbed until an equilibrium is attained. Figure 7.3 shows the relationship between the number of molecules being adsorbed and the concentration of the molecule in the liquid on the tongue. Using a summated or integrated measure of the response of the chorda tympani nerve bundle, Beidler (1953) was able to determine the amount of response of nerve fibers in relation to the concentration of a salt solution, shown in Figure 7.3b. The curves in (a) and (b) are very similar, suggesting that the amount of adsorption onto the membrane is reflected by a correlated amount of activity in the taste pathway.

This proposal only partially accounts for the ability of the transduction process to tell the brain something about the concentration of the stimulus. When taste molecules strike the tongue, there is an initial burst of firing in the chorda tympani, followed by a sustained but reduced rate of activity throughout the period of stimulation. Beidler's (1954) theory only accounts for the sustained firing, not the initial burst. But there is reason to believe that the inital burst is very important in guiding the behavior of an animal. Halpern and Tapper (1971), for example, found that rats can encode quality information about a stimulus within 400–500 msec, a time duration which falls within the initial burst of activity. Rats might even be able to recognize a particular taste within a period of 84 msec (Halpern and Marowitz, 1973). But the equilibrium state of adsorption onto the receptor cell membrane occurs long after 84 msec.

coding of stimulus strength—rate of adsorption. Another hypothesis has been proposed which attempts to account for the rat's rapid recognition of taste stimuli, which suggests that the neural response is proportional to the *rate* of adsorption, rather than the amount (Heck and Erickson, 1973). The rate of adsorption would be greatest when the molecules fall onto a membrane devoid of other taste stimuli, but would decline rapidly as the membrane receptor sites filled up. Figure 7.4a plots the relationship between the rate of adsorption and the time after the molecules strike a surface, while Figure 7.4b shows the relationship between the number of impulses per second and the time after the taste stimulus is presented. The two curves are very similar, suggesting that the rate of adsorption may be more important in determining the firing rates of neurons along the taste pathway, and thus passing along information about stimulus concentration. Bealer (1978) has shown that the early transient portion of the chorda tympani response is both necessary and sufficient for behavioral intensity discriminations by the rat. This result along with the data of Halpern and his colleagues provides strong evidence for the importance of the early transients in the afferent nerve. This suggests that the rate of adsorption is more important for behavior than the final steady state condition.

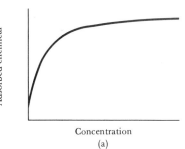

Concentration

(a)

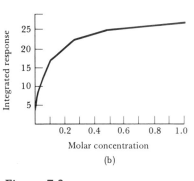

(b)

Figure 7.3
(a) The relationship between the amount of chemical adsorbed to a solid surface at equilibrium and the concentration of the chemical. (b) The relationship between response in the chorda tympani nerve of rats, and the concentration of the taste stimulus (sodium chloride). [From Heck and Erickson (1973).]

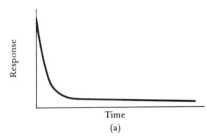

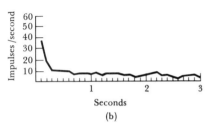

Figure 7.4
(a) The hypothetical relationship between the rate of adsorption (right ordinate), the time since stimulus presentation, and neural responses. (b) Observed relationship between neural response in the chorda tympani and the time since the presentation of a taste stimulus. [From Heck and Ericson (1973).]

coding of stimulus quality—receptor sites? The way in which the taste receptors transduce information about taste quality is also open to speculation. The process of transduction is probably quite similar for both taste and olfactory receptor cells. Both are chemical senses. That means that the transduction process begins whenever a stimulus molecule adsorbs onto the receptor cell membrane.

For this reason, transduction in the chemical senses may be similar to the previously discussed processes which occur when a molecule acts on the membrane of a cell. Two such occasions are during synaptic transmission and the action of a hormone on the membrane of its target cell. Physiologists speak of receptor sites which both the hormone and the transmitter molecule occupy, and thereby, initiate the events of neurotransmission and hormone action.

It seems probable, therefore, that stimulus molecules for taste (and olfaction) may also occupy receptor sites, and thereby trigger the transducer functions of the receptor cell. This notion received experimental support when a "sweet receptor protein" was isolated from the tongue epithelium of the cow (Dastoli and Price, 1966). The protein binds or forms complexes with sweet-tasting substances (Prince, 1972). For example, this protein molecule forms complexes with the sweet tasting D-amino acids, but not with the L-amino acids, which do not taste sweet.

The molecular structure of the sweet sensitive protein remains to be identified. The speculation is that this protein is part of the receptor cell membrane, and it undergoes a change in its structural arrangement whenever it forms a complex with a sweet tasting substance. This change, in turn, alters the permeability of the membrane that leads to a depolarization of the receptor cell. It is not known, however, what events follow the change in membrane permeability (Price and Desimone, 1977).

It remains to be determined whether there are separate receptor molecules for each of the four basic taste qualities. One line of evidence suggests that there may be different transducer mechanisms. For example, sweet, sour, and salty stimuli induce receptor cell depolarization with a decrease in membrane resistance which is the usual case. Bitter-tasting stimuli, on the other hand, depolarize the receptor cell but with an *increase* in membrane resistance rather than a decrease (Akaike and Sato, 1976). The difference in action of bitter substances compared to the other qualities does not argue against the notion of a bitter-sensitive receptor molecule. It merely suggests that this molecule, if there is one, alters membrane permeability in a different way than the other stimuli.

receptor potentials Although it is not clear how molecules can affect the receptor cells, it is clear that a receptor potential is generated in these cells whenever a stimulus is passed over the tongue. Taste bud cells in the papillae of the rat show a resting potential ranging from 20–80 mV (Ozeki and Sato, 1972). Some of the cells showed depolarization when taste stimuli were presented, but others did not, suggesting that some of the cells in the taste bud are not receptors.

Each receptor cell in the rat responds to more than two of the four taste qualities: salty, sour, bitter, and sweet. But the magnitude of the response usually differs. For example, the receptor potential measured in one cell was 22 mV for salt, 2 mV for sucrose, and 16 mV for quinine, a very bitter substance (Kimura and Beidler, 1961). The amplitude of the receptor potential increased with increasing stimulus concentrations, regardless of the quality of the stimulus.

receptor cell response profiles. Each receptor cell exhibits a unique response profile, and even cells in the same taste bud possess different profiles (Ozeki and Sato, 1972). Furthermore, there is no correlation between the nature of the profiles and the location of the receptor cell on the rat's tongue. This is surprising because the back of the tongue is usually more sensitive to bitter tastes, while the front is more sensitive to sweet substances. There are no "salty receptors" or "sweet receptors" but there are cells which respond maximally to these qualities and minimally to other qualities. This suggests that coding at the level of the receptor does not divide the stimuli into four basic categories, but rather arranges them along one or more continua.

Although taste information is relayed to the brain by means of three *coding in the cranial nerves* different cranial nerves, most investigators have concentrated on the chorda tympani. This branch of the facial nerve is a favorite of experimenters because it carries only taste information, while the others also carry tactile messages. (The chorda tympani is also much easier to reach.)

receptive field organization. Each chorda tympani fiber which leaves the tongue is receiving information from as many as seven to eight different papillae (Beidler, 1969), and these papillae constitute the receptive field of that fiber. These show characteristics very similar to the center–surround receptive field organization in the visual system. Using a technique in which papillae can be stimulated individually, Miller (1971) found that of the various papillae contributing to the excitability of a single fiber, the most sensitive papilla provided over one-half of the fiber's response output. The fiber's response was enhanced if both this sensitive papilla and the others were stimulated by the same substance, but the fiber's response was depressed if the sensitive papilla or center was stimulated by one substance, and others which might be called the surround were stimulated by a different

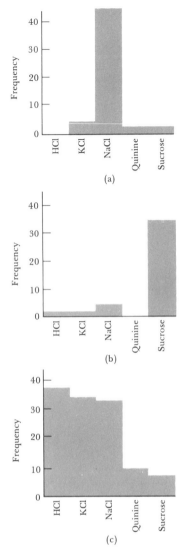

Figure 7.5

Response profiles from three different neurons in the rat's taste pathway. Each neuron was stimulated by five different taste stimuli, and each responded to at least two of those stimuli, but with different rates of response. [From Pfaffman (1955).]

taste stimulus. It is not known how these interactions, especially the depression, occur.

response profiles of papillae leading to a single fiber. The individual papillae which are providing input to a single fiber have about the same response profile (Oakley, 1975). For example, if one papilla in a fiber's receptive field is most responsive to salty tastes, chances are that the other papillae also are. This suggests that the papillae to which a given fiber is connected are not determined at random, even though they may be millimeters apart.

across-neuron response patterns. The responses from individual neurons in the chorda tympani also show different profiles as shown in Figure 7.5. Each neuron alters its firing rate to many different stimuli, but is usually maximally sensitive to one. Pfaffmann (1955) proposed that the afferent information for taste quality is not to be found in mutually exclusive subsets of fibers, but rather in the relative amounts of nerve activity produced in many different fibers. This suggestion has been developed into a model of the **across-neuron response pattern** (Erickson *et al.*, 1965), in which each taste stimulus will activate a large number of nerve fibers, each to a different degree. Thus a pattern of nerve activity across many separate neurons would result from a particular taste stimulus, and this pattern would be different for each stimulus.

This model may prove useful in predicting how any particular substance will taste. If the across-neuron response pattern is similar for two substances, then their tastes should be similar. For example, Figure 7.6 shows the responses of 13 different neurons, labeled *A* through *M*, to three "salt" tastes: ammonium chloride, potassium chloride, and sodium chloride. The response pattern to the potassium and ammonium salts was quite similar, suggesting that the rat should perceive their tastes to be similar. But the response to the sodium salt was very different, so that its taste should be different (Erickson, 1963). In behavioral tests using rats which had been trained to avoid drinking ammonium chloride, because they had been made sick after tasting the substance, the rats also tended to avoid potassium chloride. Their aversion response presumably generalized to a similar tasting substance. But they did not avoid sodium chloride to as great an extent, suggesting that this substance tastes different.

Erickson and his co-workers (1965) have prepared a table of correlations between different substances which reflect the degree of similarity between the across-neuron response pattern in the chorda tympani. If the correlation is high between two compounds then behavioral testing should reveal that they taste similar, and several studies are bearing out the utility of this model. For example, Nachman (1963) induced an aversion to lithium chloride in rats, and then tested

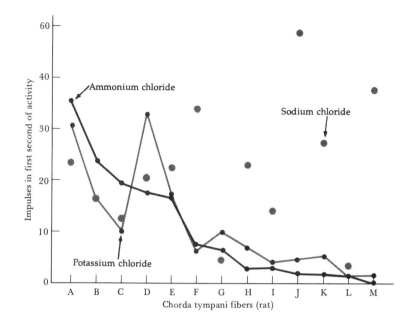

Figure 7.6
Responses of 13 chorda tympani fibers to 3 taste stimuli. The 13 fibers are arranged along the baseline in order of decreasing responsiveness to ammonium chloride. [From Erickson (1963).]

them to see if their aversion would generalize to other chloride salts. They avoided sodium chloride more than chloride salts of potassium and ammonia. Erickson's table of correlations predicts this result because the correlation between the neuron response patterns of lithium and sodium chloride is 0.91. The correlations between lithium chloride and potassium chloride is only 0.03, and that between lithium and ammonium chloride is 0.11.

The response of individual fibers in the glossopharyngeal nerve have received much less attention, but they probably also respond to many different taste stimuli, but with different rates of firing. These fibers show a greater responsiveness to bitter substances than those of the chorda tympani (Pfaffman *et al.*, 1967), which agrees well with the fact that the glossopharyngeal innervates the back of the tongue, where our threshold for bitter is lowest. Thus the increased sensitivity for bitterness in the back may be the result of differences in cranial nerve response, rather than differences in the receptor potentials generated in the taste buds.

The neurons in this nucleus maintain the across-neuron response pattern to various taste stimuli, wherein each neuron fires with its own individual profile to many different tastes. The pattern of response across neurons to sodium chloride and lithium chloride is very similar and different from the patterns for ammonium or potassium chloride, just as they are in the chorda tympani (Doetsch and Erickson, 1970). It would be possible to predict the similarity of taste substances on the

coding in the nucleus of the solitary tract

basis of neuronal firing patterns in this nucleus, just as it has been done using the patterns in the chorda tympani.

An interesting feature of the neurons in this nucleus is that their firing rates are much higher than those in the cranial nerves, sometimes as much as 4.6 times higher (Ganchrow and Erickson, 1970). The pattern is maintained for different taste substances, although sometimes a neuron does not increase its firing rate for increases in concentration of the same stimulus. The reason for this higher firing rate is unknown.

convergence of odor and taste information. Another very interesting feature of the nucleus of the solitary tract is that there appears to be some convergence here between taste and odor information (Van Buskirk and Erickson, 1977). These scientists found that single units in this nucleus in the rat responded not only to taste stimuli, but to odors as well. They suggest that this nucleus is involved not just with taste, but with the array of stimuli that an animal needs to process when it is sniffing and tasting food. This kind of neural convergence may be one reason why the taste of food is so dependent upon its odor.

coding in the thalamus Neurons from the nucleus of the solitary tract proceed rostrally to the pontine taste area, but since this area was only recently demonstrated to be involved with taste, it has not yet received much attention. From the pons, the neurons go to both sides of the brain to the medial tip of the ventromedial nucleus in the thalamus. Thalamic neurons respond differently from those mentioned so far in a number of ways, however. For example, sodium chloride and hydrochloric acid (a sour-tasting substance) evoke greater responses in the earlier parts of the pathway than either sucrose or quinine hydrochloride. At the thalamus, the response rate is approximately the same for all four stimuli, suggesting that this area is more attuned to complex substances, perhaps those which may have more biological relevance, like sucrose. Thalamic neurons also lack the initial burst of firing when the stimulus is first applied, perhaps because many of the neurons in this area *decrease* their firing rate in response to a stimulus (Scott and Erickson, 1971). The thalamus performs more complicated integrative functions than the lower structures in most of the sensory systems, and these differences in the response patterns of the neurons may reflect finer tuning of the coded information for taste.

coding in the cortex Cells which respond to taste stimuli can be found in the somatosensory cortex (Cohen *et al.,* 1957; Landgren, 1957), but many of these often responded to tactile stimulation as well, suggesting òral—tactile convergence. The rat probably does most of the coding for taste before the information ever reaches the cortex since cortical lesions do not result in very devastating effects on the sense of taste. The results of lesions along the taste pathway are shown in Figure 7.7. The normal rat can detect a quinine hydrochloride solution when the concentration is only 15 parts per million, and with a cortical lesion in the taste area the rat's threshold is raised to 80 parts per million. Lesions in the thalamus or in the solitary nucleus are much more devastating to the rat's ability to detect the substance, however, and there is much less recovery after a few weeks. Whether or not human beings depend on lower structures more than their cortex for taste coding is unknown.

summary
Gustation

The receptors for the sense of taste are in the *taste buds,* most of which are located in trenchlike *papillae* on the tongue. Some of the cells within the bud have *microvilli* which project out into the *taste pore,* or opening of the taste bud. Molecules on the tongue apparently stimulate the taste receptors via the microvilli.

The receptor cells within the taste buds synapse onto the dendrites of cranial nerves. After entering the brain, fibers from the taste receptor cells project to the nucleus of the solitary tract, the pontine taste area, the thalamus, and finally part of the somatosensory cortex which subserves the mouth and tongue area.

Transduction by the taste receptors is largely unknown, but presumably involves the adsorption of molecules onto the membrane of the receptor. Neural response to a taste stimulus is generally proportional to the rate of adsorption, which would correspond roughly to stimulus intensity. The quality of a taste substance might be differentially transduced by different receptor sites. When a stimulus is passed over the tongue, the taste receptors produce a receptor potential, which increases in size with increases in the concentration of the stimulus. Most receptors respond to more than one kind of stimulus, such as salty, sweet, bitter, or sour, although they generally respond maximally to only one kind.

Afferent fibers which synapse onto the receptors might service seven or eight different papillae, an area which constitutes the fiber's receptive field. Responses from these fibers are much like those in the receptor cells, in that firing rate increases for increasing stimulus concentrations, and each fiber usually responds to more than one of the four primary tastes. Because of this, taste quality is probably coded by means of an *across-neuron response pattern,* in which the individual can tell what the taste is by virtue of the activity in many neurons, rather than in just one. Coding in the nucleus of the solitary tract is similar to that in the cranial nerves, except that the firing rate is much higher, and there is convergence between odor and taste stimuli. Many neurons in this nucleus also respond to odors.

The thalamus and cortical areas for taste probably do even more integrating of taste information. For example, cells in the cortex also respond to tactile stimulation of the tongue. Since an animal can perform taste discriminations very well, even though some of the higher afferent areas have been lesioned, most taste coding is probably accomplished fairly completely by the lower levels of the pathway.

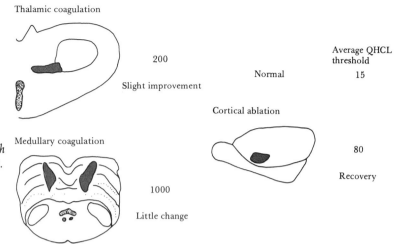

Thalamic coagulation

200

Slight improvement

Medullary coagulation

1000

Little change

Normal

Cortical ablation

80

Recovery

Average QHCL
threshold

15

Figure 7.7
*Comparison of average quinine
hydrochloride thresholds for rats with
lesions in different areas of the brain.
Comments below threshold values
indicate amount of improvement in
taste thresholds 12–15 weeks after
the operation. [From Burton and
Benjamin (1971).]*

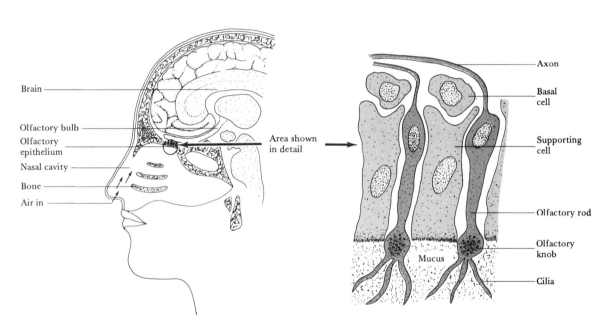

Brain

Olfactory bulb

Olfactory
epithelium

Nasal cavity

Bone

Air in

Area shown
in detail

Axon

Basal
cell

Supporting
cell

Olfactory rod

Olfactory
knob

Cilia

Mucus

Figure 7.8
*Anatomy of the olfactory system and a detail of the structure of the olfactory
epithelium. [From Coren et al. (1979).]*

The sense of smell in human beings is extremely good. In fact, your nose is more sensitive than the finest instruments when it comes to detecting small amounts of odorous molecules in the air. And the sense of olfaction is not just extremely sensitive to low intensities, it is also capable of discriminating slight differences between odorants.

In this section, we will discuss the sense organ for olfaction, the afferent sensory pathway, and transduction in the olfactory receptors. Finally, we will consider the coding of olfactory information at various levels of the afferent pathway.

olfaction

The nose serves as both the sense organ for smell and the structure through which air is warmed and filtered before it reaches the lungs. It contains several passages, but the area that is used for olfaction is a lining in the back of the nasal cavity called the **olfactory epithelium.** The area of sensory epithelial tissue varies from species to species, and can be taken as a gross index of olfactory sensitivity. For example, human beings have about 2 to 4 cm² of olfactory epithelial tissue (Graziadei, 1971), but the German shepherd has about 150 cm² (Dröscher, 1969).

olfactory structures

The olfactory epithelium has three different types of cells: the receptors, the **support cells,** and the **basal cells,** as shown in Figure 7.8.

The receptor cell is a bipolar neuron which has a small, generally oval shaped cell body, and two fine extensions: one oriented toward the brain, which is the axon of the cell, and the other oriented toward the nasal surface of the epithelium. This latter extension is called the **olfactory rod,** and at its tip are a number of even finer extensions called the **olfactory cilia.** It is on the cilia where odorous molecules probably interact with the receptor cell and where transduction begins.

The name of the support cells suggests that they support something, but they may be more intimately involved in olfaction than was previously thought. They are elongated cells which surround the receptors, and they contain an unusually large concentration of organelles, particularly endoplasmic reticulum. They also release tiny granules when a strong odor reaches the epithelium, but whether they actually play a role in olfaction is unknown (Graziadei, 1971).

The basal cells form a single row along the basement membrane of the epithelium. The basal cells have two important functions in olfaction. The first is that they provide the sheath system for the receptor cell axons leaving the epithelium. The basal cells also provide a source for new olfactory receptors. The olfactory receptor cells, like those in taste, are continually renewed. The source of the new receptors is the basal cells (Harding *et al.,* 1977). The olfactory receptors, however, have their own axons. This formation of new neurons from undifferentiated cells in *adult* animals is perhaps unique.

the afferent olfactory pathway The receptor cell for olfaction is different from those in the ear or eye because it does not simply transduce information; it also spikes and forms the first stage in the afferent olfactory pathway. The very slim axons from each receptor emerge from the basement membrane and group together in bundles, sheathed by the basal cells. Groups of these bundles are then sheathed in Schwann cells, and this **olfactory nerve** proceeds to the **olfactory bulbs.**

In vertebrates the olfactory bulbs, which lie before the main forebrain mass, are rather complicated structures. The axons enter the bulb and make their first synapse in the **glomeruli,** spherical masses of axon terminals from the receptor cells and the dendritic branches of the **mitral cells** and **tufted cells,** whose cell bodies lie deeper in the bulb. The axons of the mitral and tufted cells proceed out of the bulb via the **lateral olfactory tract.** Within the bulb is another class of cells called the **granule cells,** which make intrabulb connections between the various cell types. They are analagous to the amacrine cells in the retina.

The lateral olfactory tract is the pathway from the olfactory bulb to other areas of the brain. It has an orderly topographical organization, as seen in all sensory pathways. Fibers originating from the mitral and tufted cells in the dorsal, lateral, and ventral areas of the bulb are found in the dorsal, middle, and ventral parts of the tract, respectively (Shepherd and Haberly, 1970). The structures in which the axons of the tract terminate include the **anterior olfactory nucleus,** the **olfactory tubercle, prepyriform cortex,** and parts of the amygdala, all of which are below the level of the cortex.

The thalamus and the hypothalamus receive secondary projections from the bulb. For example, fibers from the olfactory tubercle extend into the hypothalamus. Fibers from various parts of the brain also send efferent pathways back down to the olfactory bulb, creating a feedback loop wherein the bulb and the other parts of the brain can mutually affect each other's activity. The afferent pathway is shown in Figure 7.9.

olfactory transduction Very little is known about how the olfactory receptor cell transduces information about odorous molecules into a neural message. Amoore (1952) proposed a stereochemical theory of olfaction which postulated that the odor of a compound is correlated with the physical fit of its molecules into certain "sites" on the membrane surface of the cell. Molecules of the same shape fit into the same receptor sites and evoke identical, or highly similar odor sensations. An underlying notion here is that the occupation of the receptor site by the odorous molecule would alter the cell's membrane permeability and thereby give rise to an action potential. Amoore postulated that there were seven primary odor qualities. Five of them (ethereal, camphoraceous, musky, floral, and minty) were determined by the shape of the molecule, and two (pungent and putrid), by the electrical charge on the molecule.

specific anosmias. Over the years Amoore and his colleagues did show correlation between molecular shape and perceived similarity of odor that ranged from 0.51 to 0.66 for the seven primary qualities. But in 1965 he began to revise his procedures for determining primary qualities and thereby extend his theory. Amoore began the study of **specific anosmia.** This is the condition in which a person of otherwise normal olfactory acuity cannot perceive a particular compound at a concentration such that its odor is obvious to most other people. Specific anosmia, therefore, may be considered analogous to color blindness.

The hypothesis is that each type of specific anosmia results from a specific defect in the olfactory receptor cells. For example, the cells may lack or have a reduced number of membrane-bound receptor molecules that would bind with the stimulus molecule. Each occurrence of specific anosmia, therefore, should reveal one of the fundamental odors. An accurate determination of the actual primary qualities should result from the determination of the occurrences of specific anosmias.

In a recent review, which the interested reader should read, Amoore (1977) summarized his efforts for the delineation of the primary olfactory qualities. He has identified six primary odors thus far. The odors, as well as the odorant which yields the largest anosmic deficit, are listed in Table 7.1.

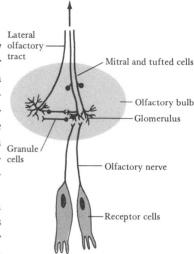

Figure 7.9
Schematic diagram of the afferent pathway for olfaction.

Table 7.1
The olfactory primaries as determined from investigations of specific anosmia[a]

Odor Quality	Odorant	Percent Frequency of Occurrence of Anosmia
Sweaty	Isovaleric acid	3
Spermous	1-Pyrroline	16
Fishy	Triethylamine	6
Malty	Isobutyraldehyde	36
Urinous	5α-Androst-16-en-3-one	47
Musky	ω-Pentadecalactone	12

[a]Modified from Amoore (1977).

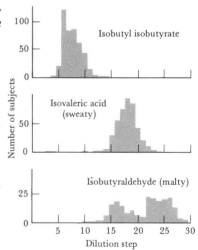

Figure 7.10
Olfactory threshold distributions in the population for three different odorants. [From Amoore (1977).]

One should remember that specific anosmia is an elevation of the detection threshold for a particular odorous stimulus. It is not an absolute loss of olfactory sensitivity. A brief description of the way in which Amoore measures the anosmia demonstrates the relative nature of the deficit. The subject has to identify which two of five flasks contain 20 ml of an odorous solution. The other three contain 20 ml of pure water. If the subject is correct, he or she is then tested with a stimulus concentration one-half that of the preceding trial. If the subject is wrong, the stimulus concentration is raised. The threshold is determined by the lowest consecutive concentration step that is correctly identified. Figure 7.10 shows the distribution of thresholds for three odorants, two of which are the odorants for the qualities of sweaty and malty.

The top histogram of Figure 7.10 shows a relatively normal distribution of scores for the odorant isobutyl isobutyrate. The distribution for isovaleric acid also shows a relatively normal distribution, but there are eight subjects that have relatively high thresholds. These subjects are considered as anosmic for isovaleric acid. Their thresholds range from 5 to 15 dilution steps from the mean of the other subjects. The distribution for isobutyraldehyde, the malty primary, is bimodal. Amoore (1977) divided the subjects at dilution step 20. Those subjects to the right (more than 20) were considered to have normal thresholds for the odorant while those to the left (less than 20) were considered to be anosmic for isobutyraldehyde.

Amoore's primary odorants. The structural formulas of the six primary odorants are shown in Figure 7.11. The molecules belong to common chemical groups, and there is nothing unusual in their structure. Perhaps the most important feature of the primary odorants is that they

Figure 7.11
Structural formulas of the six primary odorants. [From Amoore (1977).]

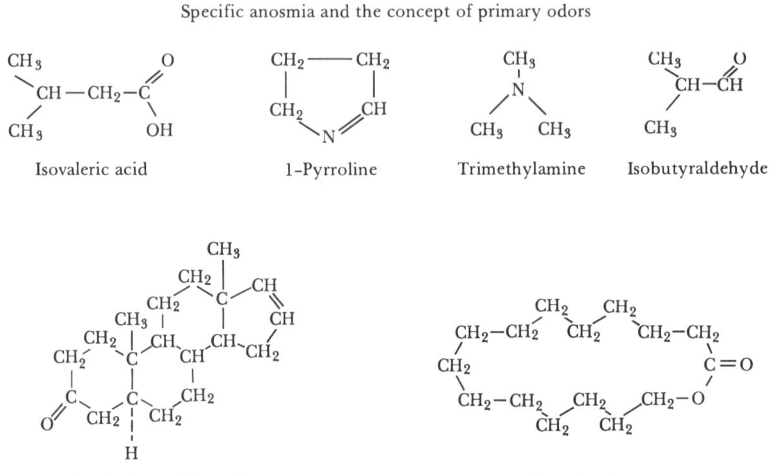

Specific anosmia and the concept of primary odors

Isovaleric acid   1-Pyrroline   Trimethylamine   Isobutyraldehyde

5α–Androst–16–en–3–one

ω–Pentadecalactone

occur in nature. They may be the biological signals that are important for survival both of the species and the organism. This topic of chemical signals, pheromones, is discussed later in the chapter.

It seems probable that the primary odorants bind with receptor proteins that are embedded in the membranes of the olfactory sensory cells. Amoore (1977) hypothesized that specific anosmia could result from the genetic defect in the synthesis of the receptor protein. In fact, such evidence does exist for the primary odorant ω-pentadecalactone.

responses of receptor cells to odorants. Regardless of how the receptor cell transduces the information, it is clear that when odorous molecules strike the epithelium, the cell responds by firing. Figure 7.12 shows the response of a single receptor cell to four different odors: musk xylene, nitrobenzene, benzonitrite, and pyridine. The cell responds to the first three compounds, albeit at different magnitudes, and does not respond at all to the pyridine (Gesteland *et al.*, 1963). The olfactory receptors were similar to the fibers along the taste pathway in that individual receptors show their own profile of response and usually respond to many different odor qualities. There may be a number of different receptor sites distributed over the surface of the olfactory cilia, and the responsiveness of a cell would reflect the variation of the receptor sites.

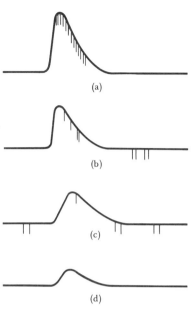

Figure 7.12
Responses of a single unit to four different odors: (a) musk xylene, (b) nitrobenzene, (c) benzonitrite, and (d) pyridine. [From Gesteland et al. *(1963).]*

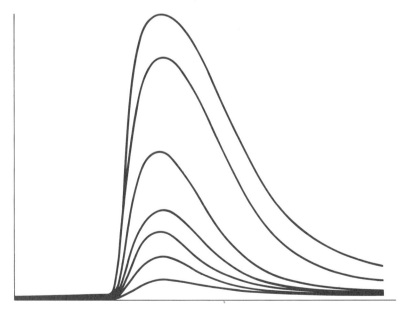

Figure 7.13
The electro-olfactograms of the frog's olfactory mucosa in response to brief stimulations of a single odor in varying strengths. [From Ottoson (1956).]

coding in the olfactory pathway The study of the coding processes in the olfactory system has been especially difficult partly because the relevant stimulus parameters are still unknown. The task of recording from single cells is also difficult, particularly in the olfactory receptors, because the axons are very slim and close together, and often unsheathed. Nevertheless, the picture which is emerging is one of a coding process similar to the one in the taste system. Neurons at every step of the pathway respond to a wide variety of stimuli, although each unit may respond maximally to a particular odor. Most units increase their firing rates with increases in stimulus strength.

coding of stimulus strength. The receptor cells of the olfactory epithelium constitute the first step in the olfactory pathway, and it is possible to record from both large populations of receptor cells, as well as single units. The **electro-olfactogram** is a measure of the electrical activity of a large population of olfactory cells, and its general waveform reflects the intensity of the stimulus. Figure 7.13 shows the electro-olfactograms of the frog's olfactory mucosa in response to brief stimulations of a single odor in varying strengths. Ottoson (1956) proposed that this change in voltage represents the generator potential in the olfactory system. The latency of the potential varies from 200–400 msec, and rises to a peak, the size of which depends upon the concentration of the odor.

Electro-olfactograms and recordings from single units have recently been taken from young rats (Gesteland and Sigwart, 1977). The electro-olfactograms look much like those taken from the olfactory receptors of frogs. They increase in amplitude with increases in the stimulus intensity.

Gesteland and Sigwart (1977) found that different odors might excite a single unit in the young rat's olfactory apparatus, suppress spontaneous activity, or have no effect on the cell. But if an odor did produce excitation in a single unit, then the concentration of the odor was related to the amount of excitation. Figure 7.14 shows the re-

Figure 7.14

Responses of a single receptor cell to various concentrations of ethyl butyrate. The horizontal bar at the top indicates the stimulus duration. [From Gesteland and Sigwart (1977).]

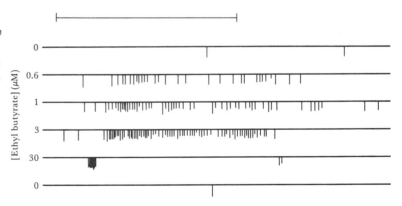

sponses of a single unit during stimulation by increasing concentrations of ethyl butyrate. At low intensities, the firing rate increased right after the onset of the stimulus, and continued for the duration of the odor presentation. At higher intensities, the firing rate was higher, and the higher rate was still maintained during the entire stimulus presentation. But at very high intensities, the cell showed a rapid burst of firing followed by a sustained suppression of spike activity.

coding in the olfactory bulb and cortex. In the olfactory bulb, single units increase their firing rate to increases in stimulus intensity also. These units also show a broad tuning, in that they will generally respond to several different odors, by excitation and by inhibition (Doving, 1964).

Although some units in the prepyriform cortex show changes in firing rate when odors are presented (Haberly, 1969), lesions in this area do not affect the animal's ability to make olfactory discriminations. Indeed, lesions in any area of the brain, except the olfactory bulb or lateral olfactory tract, have little effect on the sense of smell, suggesting that the bulb can do most of the processing of odors by itself, without the need for higher brain structures. The sense of smell is a very primitive function which evolved long ago, and it is reasonable to conclude that it does not require the remarkable abilities of the cortex, which are absent in many animals which have an excellent sense of smell.

Presumably, any information that is coded by the olfactory system *coding of biologically* should be biologically relevant to the animal—otherwise, it wouldn't *relevant information* code it. But some scientists have used odor stimuli which are clearly very relevant, such as the odor of females or of food.

Rats, for example, can tell whether or not a female is in estrous by the urine's odor. Pfaff and Gregory (1971) used urine from estrous and ovariectomized females as an odor stimulant, while recording from single units in various brain areas. Units in the olfactory bulb responded to both odors very similarly, suggesting that the rat's behavioral preference for sniffing the estrous female's urine was not due to coding by the olfactory bulbs. But single units in the preoptic area near the hypothalamus, which receives secondary projections from the olfactory pathway, were also tested. Many of these units responded differentially to the two urine odors. The olfactory bulb units were more likely to respond differentially to the nonurine odors, however, suggesting that the bulb certainly is capable of coding.

The coding of some biologically relevant information may in part depend upon efferent influences from other areas of the brain. For example, it is possible that a female rat may code the odor of a male differently depending upon whether she is in estrous. The coding of food odors may also be different, depending upon whether the animal is hungry. For example, the odor of steak smells wonderful to a person who is very hungry, but rather unexciting when the same person is satiated.

Pager (1978) found that the activity of the mitral cells in the olfactory bulb in response to food odors is quite different, depending upon whether the animal is hungry or satiated. One important difference had to do with the rate of habituation. Using a multiunit recording, she found that the integrated activity of the mitral cells was first very high in response to any odor, regardless of whether the animal was hungry or satiated. Figure 7.15 shows that when the odor is not food, habituation occurs very rapidly. The multiunit activity of the mitral cells drops down to about 20% of its maximum response after the same odor has been presented several times. Even when the odor is food, but the animal is satiated, the multiunit activity also habituates very rapidly. But if the animal is hungry, and the odor presented over and over is food, then habituation to the repeated presentations is much slower.

Pager (1978) also found that lesioning some of the efferent fibers, which lead back to the olfactory bulb and the mitral cells, had a significant effect on mitral cell activity in hungry and satiated rats. This would suggest that this kind of modulation on coding in the olfactory bulb is in fact due to input to the olfactory bulbs coming from other brain areas.

---

summary
Olfaction

The receptor cells for olfaction are located in the *olfactory epithelium.* They are bipolar neurons with two fine extensions. The extension which is oriented toward the brain is the axon of the cell. The extension which is oriented toward the nasal surface is called the *olfactory rod,* and it contains tiny *olfactory cilia.* It is the surface of these cilia which interact with odorous molecules and begin the process of transduction.

Since the receptor cell has its own axon, it not only transduces olfactory information, it spikes. Olfactory information proceeds from the receptor cells along the *olfactory nerve* to the *olfactory bulbs,* where interactions between cells are common. From the bulb, the information travels via the *lateral olfactory tract* to various areas of the brain, including the *anterior olfactory nucleus,* the *olfactory tubercle,* and the

prepyriform cortex. The thalamus and the hypothalamus receive secondary projections from the olfactory bulb.

One hypothesis to account for the transduction of olfactory information suggests that the cilia contain several different kinds of receptor sites with which odorous molecules can interact. Each kind of receptor site would transduce information about one of the primary qualities of odors. By studying people with *specific anosmias* (people who are deficient in the ability to smell a particular substance, but not others) Amoore has been able to identify six primary odorants. Their specific anosmia may be due to a genetic defect which results in the absence of one of the receptor proteins.

Although it is not yet clear exactly how the receptor cells transduce the olfactory information, it is clear that

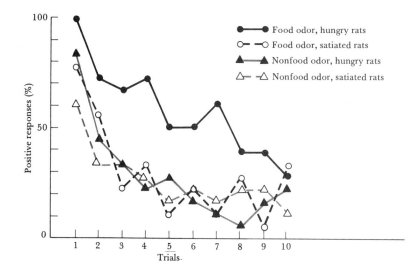

Figure 7.15
Habitation of positive multiunit
mitral cell responses during a
stimulation series.

the receptor cells fire when odorous molecules strike the epithelium. Each receptor usually responds to many different olfactory qualities, but maximally to one, much like the receptor cells for taste. This suggests that the across-neuron response pattern is used to code for stimulus quality in the olfactory system as well as the sense of taste.

Most neurons respond with faster firing rates to increases in stimulus intensity. The *electro-olfactogram,* which measures electrical activity of a large population of olfactory cells, also shows an increase with increases in stimulus strength. Cells in the olfactory bulb show a similar pattern for the coding of stimulus intensity. Most olfactory processing is probably done in the olfactory bulb (at least in the rat), since lesions in any area of the brain except the olfactory bulb or lateral olfactory tract have little effect on the sense of smell.

The coding of odors may in part depend upon the biological significance of the odor to the animal. For example, single units in the preoptic area of the male rat (an area which is involved in sexual behavior) respond differently to the odor of female rat urine depending upon whether the female rat is in estrous. Also, the responses of cells in the olfactory bulb to food odors vary depending upon whether the rat is hungry or not.

In the last two chapters, we have seen a trend toward using stimuli which might be biologically more relevant when studying sensory coding processes. In vision, for example, we discussed the "bug detectors" in the frog. And in audition, we mentioned some work on the bat's echolocation signals.

Earlier in this chapter, we explored some studies using sexually significant odors, as well as odors and tastes that were related to food. But we feel that the topic of biological relevance in the chemical senses deserves a little more attention, because its importance may not be

biological relevance of the chemical senses

quite as obvious. The sense of taste, for example, has come under scrutiny not only because it provides information about the taste of foods, but because it aids in the selection of nutritious foods and avoidance of the poisonous ones. The sense of smell has received attention because odors may do more than simply inform us of fire and of rotting food. They may serve as a primitive communication system —informing the attentive as to the sex, reproductive state, and identity of another animal.

special taste abilities Just as our sense of vision has evolved in conjunction with our lifestyles as daytime primates, so have our chemical senses. Our ability to taste a wide variety of substances, salty, sweet, bitter, and sour, is probably due to our reliance on a wide variety of foods during our evolution. Not all animals are as omnivorous as human beings, however. For example, cats are indifferent to sweet substances (Kare and Ficken, 1963) undoubtedly because sweet foods, like ripe fruits, are not part of their daily fare.

Sociobiologists suggest that our preferences for certain tastes, particularly sweet tastes, have evolved to ensure that we eat ripe fruits. These foods provided good nutrition to the primates which ate them, so that the animals which preferred this taste left more offspring. There was no selection pressure on cats to develop a preference for sweet foods, since the cat's survival depended on a preference for raw meat. The general dislike for bitter tasting substances probably evolved in conjunction with poisonous plants. The question "Why is sugar sweet?" is not answered by something in the intrinsic properties of sugar. Sugar is sweet because during our evolutionary history, foods with sugar in them were nutritious (Barash, 1977).

Unfortunately, the same cannot be said for foods with sugar in them today. Yet most of us like candy bars, not because they are good for us, but because our biological evolution has not been able to catch up with the ingenuity of the food industry. We can take some small comfort in the fact that we are not the only omnivores which can be so easily fooled. The rat also much prefers sweetened water, and drinks huge quantities of it (Valenstein *et al.*, 1967).

Whether or not taste preferences are as adaptive as they once were, the fact remains that they exist. They usually differ between species, and they also change over time in the same individual. Some of the species differences in taste preference can be readily explained by differences in life-styles, but others are not so easy to explain. For example, humans generally like the two sweetening agents, saccharin and dulcin. But rats prefer only the saccharin and monkeys only like dulcin (Fisher *et al.*, 1965).

specific hungers. Within an individual, taste preferences can change for a number of reasons, but particularly because of a physiological deficit. If an animal is deprived of sodium, perhaps because of an adrenalectomy (which would interfere with the ability to conserve sodium), it develops a **specific hunger** for the substance. For example, Epstein and Stellar (1955) deprived adrenalectomized rats of sodium for the first 10 postoperative days. Prior to the operation these animals drank virtually none of a 3% sodium chloride solution, but as soon as they had access to it, they dramatically increased their intake. This sudden change in the rat's taste preferences is very unusual because the rat does not need to have any experience with sodium loss, or the taste of sodium, in order to prefer it during the physiological deficit. The increased sodium intake is probably not the result of any change in sensitivity to the substance because neural thresholds and firing rates have not changed (Pfaffmann and Bare, 1950; Nachman and Pfaffman, 1963). The change in taste preference is not at the level of the tongue, but is presumably in some higher part of the central nervous system.

learned specific hungers and flavor aversions. Except for a change in preference for sodium, most changes are due to learning. For example, rats that are fed a diet which is deficient in Vitamin B learn to prefer a diet which has the nutrient, whereas nondeficient rats show no preference (Harris *et al.*, 1933). More recent studies have revealed that rats will prefer any novel diet over one which is deficient in some needed substance (Rodgers and Rozin, 1966). This phenomenon, called a **learned specific hunger,** is closely related to the phenomenon of **flavor aversion,** in which an organism will learn to avoid a taste which resulted in sickness. For example, if an animal is fed a novel food, and several hours later it becomes ill, it will usually not eat the food again. This amazing feat has not only saved many a rat from going back to a poisonous food for seconds, but it has also created many problems for traditional learning theory which insists that an effective punishment should follow the response immediately, not come hours later. Furthermore, the animal can often learn to avoid the novel food after tasting it only once. Strangely, the animal does not avoid other stimuli associated with the illness, such as the food cup, or any auditory stimulation—it only avoids the taste of the food.

The special abilities which are present in the sense of taste of rats, and perhaps of human beings, include (1) inherent taste sensitivities and preferences, which may or may not be as valuable as they once were, and (2) the ability to change taste preferences in response to physiological and environmental needs. This latter ability is particularly remarkable in that it occurs very rapidly in spite of the less than optimal conditions for learning.

The neural bases for these abilities are completely unknown at the present. But with the trend toward the study of biologically relevant stimuli, it is likely that answers will be forthcoming. For example, Pager and Royet (1976) found that when a rat is trained to avoid a food because of a food aversion, the odor of the food no longer can produce the unusually large activity in the olfactory bulb typical of those produced by a food odor in the hungry rat. Admittedly, this finding was in the olfactory system, not the gustatory system, but similar kinds of modulation of coding processes after a flavor aversion experience are likely to appear in the afferent pathway for taste also.

special olfactory abilities   Human beings have an extremely good sense of smell—perhaps not as sensitive as the dog's, but nevertheless sensitive to a very wide array of compounds. One of the characteristic features of odors is that they are usually associated with some kind of emotion. Perhaps because the olfactory afferent pathway includes subcortical structures which are involved with emotional behaviors such as sex and aggression, odors are often used to communicate information which are relevant to these behaviors. These "communication odors" are called **pheromones.**

pheromones.   Pheromones are very common among insects, and the sex attractant of the female moth, which had such a potent effect on the male at the beginning of this chapter, is one example. This kind of pheromone is called a **releaser,** because it elicits a specific behavioral response, in this case attraction to the female. The isolation and synthesis of these compounds has generated much interest because of their potential value in the environmental control of insect populations.

The sense of smell also plays an important role in the communication of mammals, and the pheromones of mice have received the most attention so far (Whitten and Bronson, 1970). When female mice are housed together, away from males, their estrous cycles become very erratic (Lee and Boot, 1955). But if the odor from male urine is blown into the cage, their estrous cycles synchronize and they become behaviorally receptive to the male within a couple of days (Whitten *et al.,* 1968). The male's urine also has an effect on a recently inseminated female. If she becomes pregnant by one male, and a strange male's odor is then introduced into the cage, she will often abort the pregnancy and come into estrous again (Bruce, 1959, 1960). Whether these effects are mediated by one or more pheromones is unknown, and to date it has been impossible to isolate any chemical from the urine which can be identified as the pheromone. Table 7.2 lists the odors which have physiological and behavioral significance for the mouse.

Rhesus monkeys may also use pheromones in communicating messages about sexual state. Michael and Keverne (1968) reported that male monkeys perform a bar pressing task in order to have access

Table 7.2
Odors of physiological and behavioral significance for the mouse

Odor	Source	Effect	Reference
1. Female odor	Not known, maybe urine	Mutual distrubance of estrous cycles when females are housed together	Lee and Boot (1955)
2. Familiar male	Urine	Increased synchrony in mating when odor is placed with group of females	Whitten (1956)
3. Alien male	Urine	Blocks pregnancy of recently mated females	Bruce (1959)
4. Individual odor	?		Bowers and Alexander (1967)
5. Individual odor	Sweat glands of pads	—	Ropartz (1966)
6. Group odor	Coagulating glands of male genital tract	—	Ropartz (1966,1968)
7. Alarm odor	?		Muller-Vetten (1966)
8. Female odor	Probably urine	Indicated estrous status to mates	—

to a receptive female, but not a nonreceptive one. The cue that they were using to make the distinction must have been an olfactory one, since they did not perform the response if their nasal passages were blocked. Attempts to isolate the vaginal compound responsible for the male monkey's attraction have pointed to a short-chained aliphatic acid (Michael *et al.*, 1971). Although these studies are controversial (Goldfoot *et al.*, 1978), they do suggest the possibility that monkeys may communicate with pheromones, even though they may not rely on this form of communication very much.

Whether human beings use odors for communication has been the subject of much speculation (Comfort, 1971; Schneider, 1971), although little hard evidence is available to support the hypothesis. The substances which may act as pheromones in monkeys are also present in human females, and their concentrations fluctuate across the menstrual cycle (Michael *et al.*, 1974). This finding suggests that the female's odors may vary across the menstrual cycle, which might provide an olfactory cue which could be used to determine what phase of the cycle she is in. But there is no evidence which suggests that human beings actually use that olfactory cue.

Wallace (1977) found that humans can discriminate the odors from two different individuals, and that women in particular were quite efficient at the task. Subjects were less able to discriminate between a pair of identical twins, particularly if they were on the same diet, indicating that both diet and genetics contribute to an individual's unique odor. These findings suggest that there is an olfactory cue available which might be useful in recognizing individuals, and which is certainly used by tracking dogs. But again, there is no evidence which suggests that people actually use the cue, except perhaps when they have lost their sight. Nevertheless, much olfactory processing goes on below the level of the cortex, and human beings may be using some of these cues without actually realizing it. The amount of money which is spent every year on perfumes and deodorants certainly suggests that human beings are concerned about their odors, and this area of research will no doubt continue to receive attention.

summary
Biological Relevance of the Chemical Senses

As we saw in the chapters on vision and audition, the sensory systems for any particular animal cannot code all kinds of environmental information. The same is true for the chemical senses. Much of the information which they have evolved to code has some particular biological relevance.

In the sense of taste, for example, it is likely that human beings evolved the four basic primary qualities in conjunction with their diet. Sweet foods (like ripe fruits) were generally nutritious, and we have evolved a preference for them (as well as a good ability to code sweet taste information). Cats, which did not rely on fruits, have not evolved an acute sense of taste for "sweet" information. Thus the sense of taste varies between species, depending upon evolutionary factors. It is interesting to speculate how bamboo shoots taste to the panda bear, a species which relies on that food substance.

The sense of taste can also vary across time within the same individual, depending upon experience and physiological need. For example, a rat which requires more sodium (because of an adrenalectomy) develops a *specific hunger* for salt and consumes much more of it than usual. Changes in the sense of taste can also be produced by a flavor aversion. If an animal eats a novel food and becomes sick hours later, the animal will avoid that taste in the future. This ability is peculiar (but very adaptive) because although it looks like a typical learning experience, it violates some of the traditional principles of learning. The neural substrate for specific hungers and flavor aversions are not known yet.

The sense of smell has some special abilities as well. Many animals, insects and mammals in particular, use biological odors in their communication systems. These odors are called *pheromones*. In moths, for example, the odor of the female is what attracts the male.

The pheromonal communication system of the mouse has received a great deal of attention. In particular, the odor of the male's urine can have an impact on the female's behavior and physiology. For example, male urine odor can bring noncycling females into estrous.

The status of pheromonal communication in primates and human beings is less clear. It appears that rhesus monkeys use female odors to determine estrous, although they can use other cues as well. Whether or not human beings use some kind of pheromonal communication is not yet known. Although the human olfactory system is sensitive enough to detect biological odors easily, and they are able to tell the difference between two individuals by odor, it is not yet clear whether they actually use the odor cues as a primitive form of communication. Nevertheless, this is an exciting area for research, and much speculation exists. Since much olfactory information is processed subcortically, it is possible that we might use olfactory information (and perhaps pheromones) subconsciously.

KEY TERMS

primary qualities
cross-adaptation
papillae
taste buds
taste pore
basement membrane
chorda tympani
nucleus of the solitary tract
parabrachial nucleus
adsorption
across-neuron response pattern
olfactory epithelium
support cells
basal cells
olfactory rod
olfactory cilia
olfactory nerve
olfactory bulbs
glomeruli
mitral cells
tufted cells
lateral olfactory tract
granule cells
anterior olfactory nucleus
olfactory tubercle
prepyriform cortex
specific anosmia
electro-olfactogram
specific hunger
learned specific hunger
flavor aversion
pheromones
releaser

SUGGESTED READINGS

Amoore, J. E. (1977). Specific anosmia and the concept of primary odors. *Chemical Senses and Flavor,* **2,** 267–281.

McBurney, D. H. (1974). Are there primary tastes for man? *Chemical Senses and Flavor,* **1,** 17–28.

McBurney, D. H., and Gent, J. F. (1979). On the nature of taste qualities. *Psychological Bull.* **86,** 151–167.

(The above three articles review the literature on the question of whether there are primary qualities in the chemical senses.)

Uttal, W. R. (1973). *The Psychobiology of Sensory Coding.* Harper and Row, New York. (This book presents an excellent review of the chemical senses, as well as the other sensory systems.)

8

*the somato-
sensory and
vestibular
systems*

introduction In this chapter we will discuss the somatosensory system and the vestibular system. The somatosenses include the **skin senses** (touch, temperature change, and pain) and the **kinesthetic sense,** which provides information about the position of the body. The **vestibular system** processes information about movement and position of the head, information which we need for balance and posture.

the skin senses When you sit on a tack a lot of information reaches your brain. You can tell where the tack is, whether it is very hot or very cold, how much pressure, and how fast the tack penetrated, and needless to say you can also feel the pain—first a sharp pain, then a dull ache. In this section we will explore how all of this is possible. First we will look at the kinds of stimuli in the environment which your skin can sense, and what properties of the stimuli might be coded by the nervous system. Second, we will examine the skin's structure, and then the structure of the receptors and possible transduction mechanisms. The routes the information takes to the brain will be covered in the section on the afferent sensory pathway. Finally we will look at how pressure or touch, temperature change, and pain are coded by the nervous sys-

tem. The section on pain is particularly important because it emphasizes the role of efferent effects from the brain and how we might be
able to control pain.

We can feel a great variety of sensations from our skin, and we describe them with a host of adjectives such as painful, cold, smooth,
sharp, greasy, rough, itchy, and so forth. It might seem reasonable to
label these sensory qualities, but they do not vary along only one dimension, as the sensory qualities do in vision or hearing. Sensory
quality in vision represents color, but color is a function of wavelength
and thus stimulus quality depends on variations along only one dimension. The same is true for stimulus quality (or frequency) in hearing. We saw a similar problem with stimulus quality when we
discussed the chemical senses.

are there several skin senses? Rather than considering the skin senses to
be one sensory system which codes many different stimulus qualities,
many scientists hypothesize that there are really several skin senses.
This system is probably made up of a grab bag of senses, each with its
own coding properties (Uttal, 1973). This hypothesis does solve some
problems, but it also raises more questions. How many different skin
senses are there? Some would say that there are three: one for pain,
one for touch, and a third for temperature. But others might list
"tickle" as a fourth, or perhaps insist on separating pain into "sharp
pain" and "ache." It might seem a simple matter to record from single
fibers leading away from the skin, and find out which kind of stimulus
produces a response from that fiber. If there are fibers which respond
only to pressure, and nothing else, then we would know that pressure
is one of the skin senses. And if there are fibers that respond only to
temperature change, or only to painful stimuli, then these would also
be separate skin senses. However, as we shall see in later sections,
many fibers respond to two or more of these different stimuli, so we
are pushed back to square one. It would appear that the skin senses
are not one unitary system, but neither are they completely separate.

In later sections we will consider the coding of touch, pain, and temperature, even though it is not yet clear whether these are separate
senses, or simply different stimulus qualities, or something in between (which is often the case). Also in the sections on coding, we will
examine how the skin senses handle intensity differences between
stimuli, and how they handle the spatial characteristics of a stimulus.
But before we take up the coding problems, we must look at the sense
organ. The skin has an area of about two square meters, and represents about 16% of the total body weight. Since it serves protective
functions as well as sensory ones, it is very complicated.

the structure of skin The skin's two major layers are the **epidermis** and the **dermis,** shown in Figure 8.1. The epidermis is the outer layer of cells that forms the protective sheathing for the organism, cells which are continuously sloughed off. New cells divide in lower layers of the epidermis and migrate to the surface to replace those which are lost. The thickness of the epidermis varies across the body surface, but is very thick on the **glabrous skin** (smooth, hairless) of the palms and soles of the feet. The epidermis of the hairy skin is much thinner, and is usually only between 0.07 and 0.12 mm thick. Underneath the epidermis is the dermis, which varies in thickness between 1 and 2 mm and contains glands, blood vessels, hair follicles, free nerve endings, and nerve endings with a variety of encapsulations.

the receptors Hidden among this array of various structures is a network of fibers, both myelinated and unmyelinated, which are the receptor cells. Many of the fibers branch out into layers of the skin without any encapsulations, and these are called **free nerve endings.** But others have their ends surrounded by a bewildering variety of encapsulations. The receptor cells with encapsulations have been given names such as **Pacinian corpuscle, Krause end-bulb, Merkel cell,** and **Ruffini ending.** With improvements in anatomical techniques, even more varieties are being described. It would make a very tightly knit story if each of the different types of encapsulations were responsible for the transmission of a different kind of sensation. But this does not seem to be the case. Figure 8.1 shows what some of the end organs look like,

Figure 8.1
A piece of hairy skin in cross section. [Based upon Woolard, Weddell, and Harpman (1940); from Coren et al. (1979).]

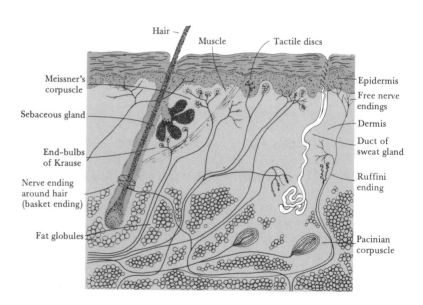

but the structures vary a good deal over time and in different individuals.

One type of encapsulation which shows some specificity for the kind of stimulation to which it will respond, however, is the Pacinian corpuscle. Its structure is not complicated, and is simply the input end of a receptor cell surrounded by layers of connective tissue. Most of the receptor cells in the skin are like the olfactory receptor cells, in that they not only transduce energy into a graded generator potential, they also spike—thus forming the first step in the afferent pathway to the brain.

The Pacinian corpuscle is a receptor for touch that has been studied in detail. When something presses on the outer layer of the corpuscle, the pressure is transmitted toward the inside until it reaches the receptor ending. The pressure produces, in some as yet unknown way, a generator potential in the cell which travels to the first node of Ranvier. If this generator potential is large enough, it will generate a spike in the neuron at the node, which will course throughout the cell and carry its information to the spinal cord and beyond. Table 8.1 summarizes the process. *transduction in the Pacinian corpuscle*

The two processes of transduction and spike production are different, and although they are occurring in the same cell, they are spatially separate. The first occurs in the nerve ending surrounded by the layers

Table 8.1
Transduction in the Pacinian corpuscle

External stimulus

↓

Membrane strain

↓

Transducer Process

↓

Generator Potential

↓

Impulse Process

of connective tissue, and the second occurs at the first node of Ranvier, located just within the corpuscle (Loewenstein and Mendelson, 1965).

adaptation. The Pacinian corpuscle is said to be a **rapidly adapting mechanoreceptor** because it transmits a generator potential at the on-set of a touch stimulus but does not maintain the potential if the pressure continues. Loewenstein and Skalak (1966) proposed that the pressure on all the layers of the corpuscle is uniform when the touch is first presented, but then the layers tend to conform to the pressure. As they do, the pressure on the outer layer increases, and that on the inner layer—next to the nerve—decreases. Even if the touch is constant for a long time, no pressure will reach the nerve cell because it is all absorbed by the outer layers of the corpuscle. But as soon as the touch stimulus is removed, the pressure change is again transmitted to the inner layers, and another generator potential is produced. The Pacinian corpuscle's structure provides a means whereby the touch receptor is sensitive to *changes* in the environment, rather than static conditions, and this property is very common in sensory receptors. Many cells within the visual system, for example, are also responsive only to changes in the visual field, rather than constant conditions. Not only are environmental changes more important to an organism, but it would certainly be inconvenient if our brains were constantly receiving information about the static pressure of our clothing.

Although the Pacinian corpuscle's layers certainly contribute to the rapid adaptation of the generator potential after the onset of a touch stimulus, they do not seem to play any role in the transduction process. If the corpuscle is stripped away, the nerve cell can still produce a potential at the onset and offset of the stimulus, but the potentials do not decay so rapidly (Loewenstein and Rathkamp, 1958). Figure 8.2 shows the characteristics of the generator potential when a touch stimulus is presented. In Figure 8.2, the nerve fiber with the Pacinian corpuscle stripped away still shows the potential, but it does not decay so fast, and therefore would presumably continue to result in spikes to the spinal cord for some time after the stimulus is first applied.

the afferent sensory pathway The axons leaving the receptor cells in the skin all over the body (ex-cept for the head) enter the various segments of the spinal cord through the large dorsal root ganglia. There are 31 pairs of dorsal root ganglia, and the part of the body which is subserved by the fibers entering one of the ganglia is called its **dermatome.** Once the fibers have entered the cord, they proceed to the brain by either the **lemnis-cal pathway,** or one of the more diffuse **extralemniscal pathways.** The lemniscal pathway primarily carries information about touch, particularly its precise localization. The other pathways carry mostly pain and temperature information. The lemniscal pathway has relatively

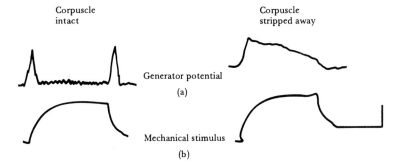

Corpuscle intact

Corpuscle stripped away

Generator potential
(a)

Mechanical stimulus
(b)

Figure 8.2
(a) Generator potentials from the nerve ending within a Pacinian corpuscle when the corpuscle is intact and when it is stripped away. (b) Represents the amplitude of the mechanical stimulus. [From Loewenstein and Rathkamp (1958).]

few synapses so the information using this route gets to the brain quickly and directly. The more diffuse extralemniscal pathways have many synapses so the movement of information takes longer.

the lemniscal pathway. The receptor cells which follow this route (shown in Figure 8.3) begin in the skin. Their cell bodies are just outside the spinal cord and their axons do not terminate until they

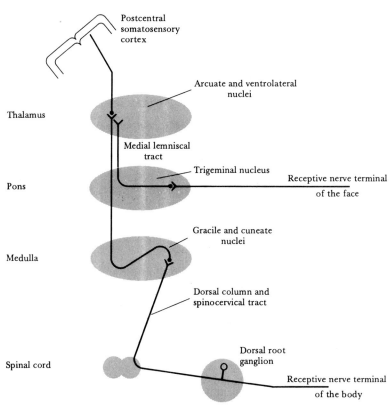

Postcentral somatosensory cortex

Arcuate and ventrolateral nuclei

Thalamus

Medial lemniscal tract

Trigeminal nucleus

Receptive nerve terminal of the face

Pons

Gracile and cuneate nuclei

Medulla

Dorsal column and spinocervical tract

Dorsal root ganglion

Spinal cord

Receptive nerve terminal of the body

Figure 8.3
A schematic drawing of the lemniscal pathway. [From Uttal (1973).]

have reached the brainstem. You can imagine that some of them are very long, particularly those coming from the toe. These axons course along the spinal cord in the **dorsal columns,** on each side of the cord, and the columns get thicker higher up on the cord because more and more axons are added from the higher body regions. The dorsal column maintains a topographic organization, because the axons which are added higher up on the body are added to the column in more and more lateral positions.

The axons of the neurons in the dorsal columns finally terminate in the **dorsal column nucleus** in the medulla, and synapse on second-order neurons which cross over to the opposite side of the brain. These crossing over neurons form the **medial lemniscus** and their axons project to the ventrobasal complex of the thalamus. Because all of the axons cross at the medial lemniscus, information from the right half of the body reaches the left side of the brain, and vice versa. From the thalamus, axons project to the **somatosensory cortex,** located just behind the central fissure in the parietal lobe.

extralemniscal system. One of the pathways followed by some receptors is called the **spinothalamic tract.** These axons terminate in the **dorsal horn** of the spinal cord, synapse onto other neurons which cross to the opposite side of the cord, and begin ascending in a nerve bundle called the spinothalamic tract—hence, its name. These axons terminate in the thalamus, and from there project to a variety of brain areas such as the cerebellum, reticular formation of the brainstem, and perhaps to other parts of the thalamus. Eventually some of the axons reach the somatosensory cortex, but the route is rather indirect. The extralemniscal pathways are also completely crossed, except that the crossing is done in the spinal cord as soon as the fibers enter, rather than in the medial lemniscus in the brainstem. Those cells in the dorsal horn of the spinal cord which form a part of this afferent pathway will be discussed again in conjunction with the coding of pain.

information from the head and face. Receptor cells in the head and face do not pass their information to the brain by means of the spinal cord, but enter via one of the three cranial nerves: the **trigeminal nerve,** the **facial nerve,** and the **vagus nerve.** Their axons synapse in the medulla, and the second-order neurons proceed to the thalamus and project to the somatosensory cortex.

---

summary
Structure of Skin and the Afferent Sensory Pathway

The stimuli which are changed into neural energy by the skin senses include touch, temperature, pain, and perhaps others. It is likely that the nervous system codes these different sensations in a complicated and interacting way, so that the skin senses cannot be called three separate senses, nor can they be called a single unitary sense. The receptors which perform the transduction process are in the skin, and the skin has two layers: the *epidermis,* or outer layer, and the lower bottom layer called the *dermis.*

The skin contains free nerve endings and a variety of encapsulated end organs such as the *Pacinian corpuscle.* These receptors are not specifically related to particular sensations, except for the Pacinian corpuscle, which is a mechanoreceptor. Most of these receptor cells not only produce a generator potential in response to some kind of stimulation, they also spike.

The transduction process in most of the receptor cells is not understood. In the Pacinian corpuscle, mechanical energy is transmitted via the surrounding layers of connective tissue to the nerve ending inside. A generator potential is only produced during changes of pressure on the outer layers of the corpuscle, but not during static pressure. Even without the layers, the receptor ending can still produce a potential in response to touch. So the major role of the corpuscle is not to aid in the transduction process, since the nerve ending can do that, but rather to provide rapid adaptation to pressure changes.

The fibers leading from the skin enter the cord through the dorsal root ganglia, and travel up either the *lemniscal pathway* or the *extralemniscal pathway.* The lemniscal pathway carries information about precisely localized stimulation, and first-order afferents following this route do not synapse until they reach the brainstem. The *spinothalamic tract* which is an extralemniscal pathway, carries information mainly about pain and temperature, and its route has more synapses and is less direct. Information from the skin receptors ultimately reaches the *somatosensory cortex.*

As we mentioned earlier, it is not clear whether certain receptor types are associated with particular sensations, except for the mechanoreceptive Pacinian corpuscle. It is even possible that the various receptor endings of a single afferent fiber might be different. Because of this situation, much of the information on coding is from fibers whose receptor endings are unknown. Recordings are made from a single fiber or a group of fibers while a stimulus, such as pressure or a cooling probe, is applied to the skin.

Three types of information which must be coded by the skin senses include the spatial characteristics of the stimulus, its intensity, and whether the stimulus is painful, mechanical, or a change in temperature. Spatial characteristics are partly coded by the familiar topographic organization of the nervous system.

general features of coding in the skin senses

the lemniscal pathway and thalamus. As the fibers from the skin enter the cord, and proceed up the lemniscal pathway, they are organized so that fibers from the bottom part of the body are in the medial portion of the cord, and those from the top are added laterally. This means that cells which transmit information from a particular area of the body are grouped together. This topographic organization is maintained at every level of the nervous system. For example, in the ventrobasal complex of the thalamus, neurons which receive information

topographic organization

from the toe are grouped together, and those which receive information from the ankle are nearby. Each neuron in the thalamus has a receptive field on the skin, and stimulation in that field produces a response in the thalamic neuron. Neurons which are receiving information from the very sensitive body parts, such as the hands or face, have very small receptive fields, while those receiving information from less sensitive areas have larger receptive fields. The receptive fields of the thalamic neurons have inhibitory and excitatory regions, much like the ones in the visual pathway. Stimulation in the "off" region produces inhibition in the corresponding neuron in the thalamus, while stimulation in the "on" region of the skin results in excitation. In skin areas where the receptive fields are small, it is very easy to tell precisely where a touch stimulus strikes, because the touch will be striking the excitatory areas of some receptive fields and the inhibitory areas of others.

somatosensory cortex. The somatosensory cortex also maintains a topographic organization, with neurons receiving information from specific body parts grouped together. Figure 8.4 shows this part of the brain, and shows the way the area is mapped. There is an enormous

Figure 8.4
(a) Location of the somatosensory cortex in the human brain. [From Schwartz (1973).] (b) Topographical organization of the somatosensory cortex. [From Penfield and Rasmussen (1950), in Schwartz (1973).]

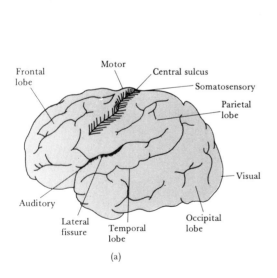

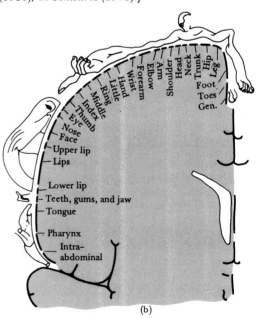

magnification of information about the hands and face; less cortical space is devoted to the less sensitive body parts.

extralemniscal pathway. The neurons which follow the extralemniscal pathways do not show such a neat topographic organization anywhere along the path. For example, neurons in the **posterior nuclear group** of the thalamus, which receives extralemniscal projections, have extremely large receptive fields. Some even respond to a touch anywhere on the body. In the part of the somatosensory cortex that receives extralemniscal projections the mapping is also somewhat haphazard. The neurons which follow this path probably do not provide very much information about the location of a stimulus, but since they primarily carry information about pain and temperature, they may perform other important functions.

stimulus intensity

In olfaction, a stronger stimulus is one with a higher concentration of odorous molecules, and in audition, a more intense stimulus is one whose sound waves have a greater amplitude. But in the skin senses, "strong" can mean a lot of different things. For example, it might mean that a mechanical stimulus exerts more pressure, or that it causes more pain. Or if the stimulus is a cooled probe, then the probe is downright freezing rather than just cool. For these reasons, it is somewhat more difficult to determine how the nervous system codes the strength of a stimulus which strikes the skin.

One way in which this information is transmitted is simply by the involvement of more receptor cells, and hence more nerve fibers. Another way is the faster firing rates of the cells which have been stimulated. But there may also be special kinds of fibers which transmit specific information about certain types of stimulus intensity. For example, there are some fibers which transmit information about the velocity with which a single hair is moved. The faster the velocity of the displacement, the faster the fiber will spike.

It is not at all clear how the fibers which respond to temperature changes code the stimulus strength. For example, fibers which respond to cold continue firing at a constant rate to a very wide range of temperatures, but more will be said about this later, particularly about how the pattern of firing may be a candidate code. The fact that the skin senses consist of at least three different but overlapping and interacting types of sensation means that the coding of even stimulus intensity is likely to be very intricate and varied codes are likely to be used.

One of the most frustrating problems in sensory coding is how we can tell what kind of stimulus is touching the skin. The answer clearly

what is the stimulus?

does not lie in the nature of the encapsulations in the dermis, except for the Pacinian corpuscle, as we have mentioned.

Nevertheless, the "labeled line" theory whereby different stimulus qualities are mediated by different receptors and afferent fibers, is difficult to discard. For the skin senses, the theory was originally proposed by Von Frey, who suspected that the different types of encapsulations of the receptor cells meant that each type would be stimulated by a particular type of stimulus quality. This was found to be incorrect, and many neurons respond with changes in firing rates to two or more different kinds of stimulation. The "labeled line" theory is thus inadequate to explain how the nervous system codes stimulus quality in the skin senses.

Some scientists proposed that the receptor cells had absolutely no specificity and that a person could tell whether a stimulus was touch, temperature change, an itch, pain, or something else by the pattern of firing in the neurons which were stimulated (Nafe, 1929). This theory assumed that several neurons must be activated before the person could recognize the quality of the stimulus.

The fibers which lead from the skin tend to be neither completely specific in their responses to different types of stimulation, nor completely nonspecific, so that the answer to the problem of sensory coding of stimulus quality probably lies somewhere between these two extreme theories. A few fibers are quite specific, and will only respond when, for example, a thermal stimulus is present; but most of them respond to at least two types of stimulation, but with different patterns of firing.

summary
General Features of Coding in the Skin Senses

Spatial characteristics of the stimulus are coded mainly by the topographic organization of the afferent pathways. Fibers from specific skin areas are grouped together as they proceed up the spinal cord. Thalamic neurons sensitive to stimulation on the skin sometimes have receptive fields with "on" and "off" regions—stimulation in the on region produces increased firing in the thalamic neuron and stimulation in the off region of the skin produces decreased firing. The somatosensory cortex maintains the topographic organization, but there is magnification of the information coming from the skin on the hands and face. Fibers which use the extralemniscal routes do not maintain such a neat topographical organization.

The coding of stimulus intensity may be partly accomplished by the involvement of more receptor cells, or by the increased firing rates of cells in the afferent pathway.

How the skin senses are able to code the type of stimulus (thermal, mechanical, painful) is still somewhat of a mystery. The "labeled line" theory proposed that each of the different receptors was responsible for coding a single type of sensation. But this theory is not correct, since some receptors are responsive to several kinds of stimulation. It appears that the fibers leading from the skin are neither completely specific in the kind of stimulation to which they will respond nor are they completely nonspecific.

When mechanical pressure is applied to the skin, an individual can tell a great deal about that stimulus. The fibers that are responsive to touch, even though they may respond weakly to other kinds of stimulation, are called mechanoreceptors. To illustrate some of the properties of the mechanoreceptor's response to touch, we will discuss two topics: **adaptation** and **flutter-vibration.**

adaptation

When we discussed transduction in the Pacinian corpuscle, we pointed out that the biggest generator potential occurs during any change in pressure, rather than during static pressure. This general principle is also true of many of the fibers that transmit mechanical information. These fibers are called *rapidly adapting* and show a burst of firing when the stimulus is applied and another when it is removed.

These rapidly adapting mechanical receptors are extraordinarily sensitive. Studies on the human hand reveal that a stimulus just strong enough to elicit one or two action potentials from the fiber is enough for the person to report that a sensation was present (Knibestöl and Vallbo, 1970).

Aside from the rapidly adapting mechanoreceptive fibers, there are also slowly adapting mechanoreceptors. These units are much less numerous, at least in human glabrous skin, and are also not quite as sensitive. With both rapidly adapting and slowly adapting units serving the same area of skin, it is easy to see how we can be aware of static pressure and also be alerted when there is any change.

flutter-vibration

A series of experiments which illustrates how mechanoreceptors code a temporal property of touch involves the application of a sinusoidal stimulus to an area of skin (Talbot *et al.*, 1968). The stimulus is a mechanical vibrator that can be adjusted to different frequencies. When the vibrator is set on low frequencies, between 5 and 40 Hz, the human being reports that the sensation feels like a "flutter" or an oscillation. But at higher frequencies above 60 to 80 Hz the sensation changes to a vibration or a hum. Because there are two different kinds of sensation there may be two different coders working here.

Assuming that the monkey would also feel the two sensations of flutter and vibration even though it could not report it, Talbot and colleagues (1968) recorded from single units in the afferent pathway in response to the sinusoidal stimulus. These scientists made recordings from slowly and rapidly adapting fibers, and also afferents from the Pacinian corpuscles. They found that the behavior of the rapidly adapting receptors corresponded very well with the human being's verbal description of flutter at low frequencies, and the behavior of the Pacinian afferents corresponded well to the vibration sensation. They thus concluded that the slowly adapting fibers played little or no role in the sensations of flutter and vibration. Studies like this one, in which electrophysiological records are taken from the monkey and combined with psychophysical data from humans, can be very valuable.

Some of the fibers that responded to the vibrating stimulus showed time-locking, or firing at the same frequency as the stimulus. This time-locking appears in the somatosensory cortex also, although it is not quite as clear and sharp as it is in the peripheral fibers which lead away from the hand (Mountcastle et al., 1969). The importance of this time-locking is not understood, but this kind of phenomenon appears often in the nervous system. For example, some auditory neurons lock onto the frequency of a sound, and some neurons which respond to knee bending, a kinesthetic stimulation, lock onto the frequency of repetitive, back-and-forth knee bends.

---

summary
The Coding of Touch

The location of a touch stimulation is coded by means of the topographic organization of the nervous system. In the somatosensory cortex there is magnification of the most sensitive body parts, particularly the hands and face.

One of the properties which characterizes the response of many mechanoreceptive fibers is rapid adaptation. When a touch stimulation is applied to a fiber's receptive field on the skin, the fiber responds with a burst of firing, but then its firing rate rapidly drops to spontaneous levels. There are also less numerous slowly adapting fibers, which are able to code static pressure.

Stimulus intensity is probably coded by faster firing rates, or the involvement of more neurons. Some temporal aspects of the stimulus are coded by a kind of spatial code. When the skin is stimulated by a vibrating stimulus, two sensations are produced. Low frequency vibration is described as flutter, while high-frequency stimulation is labeled vibration. Two different sets of fibers apparently mediate these two different sensations. Some fibers time-lock onto the vibrating stimulus, and fire each time the sinusoidal stimulus goes through a cycle.

---

the coding of temperature

For a nerve fiber to be classified as a thermoreceptor, it must exhibit the following features: (1) a static discharge at a constant temperature, (2) a dynamic response to temperature changes, and (3) no response to mechanical stimuli which are within reasonable limits of intensity. Some fibers have met all these criteria (e.g., Hensel and Boman, 1960).

cold and warm fibers

Thermoreceptors can be classified as either **cold fibers** or **warm fibers** depending on the stimuli which cause firing pattern changes. The cold fibers have a static response which falls off as the temperature goes above about 43°C and which cease firing as temperatures fall below

5°C (Hensel and Kenshalo, 1969). The warm fibers are much more specific in their preferred temperatures. They show a maximal response around 45–47°C, and their firing rates rapidly fall off when the temperature goes above or below that range. These responses are shown in Figure 8.5.

These patterns of firing suggest that if an individual relies entirely on spike frequency in warm fibers, they won't know what the temperature is, because warm fibers fire at about the same rate for many pairs of temperatures. However, if one is using relative activity in both warm and cold fibers, then there would be less ambiguity.

Another factor that might shed light on the ambiguous temperature information that seems to be coming from the thermoreceptors is interspike intervals. Figure 8.6 shows the responses of a cold receptor in the hair skin of the monkey (Iggo and Iggo, 1971). The temperature of the skin was lowered from 40° to 15°C at a rate of 0.27°/sec., and the tracings show the responses of the fiber at various intervals during the cooling process. Notice that when the fiber is cooled to 31°C, the impulses appear in a continuous stream with regular interspike intervals. But with further cooling, the spikes begin to appear in groups. Thus at different temperatures this cold unit may respond with the same rate of firing, but with a different kind of grouping of spikes, that is a different interspike interval (Iggo and Young, 1975).

This study emphasizes the fact that a change in spike frequency is not the only way that a fiber can code aspects of the stimulus, as we discussed in Chapter 5. Even though spike frequency is the same, it does not necessarily mean that the information being transmitted is

temperature and firing patterns

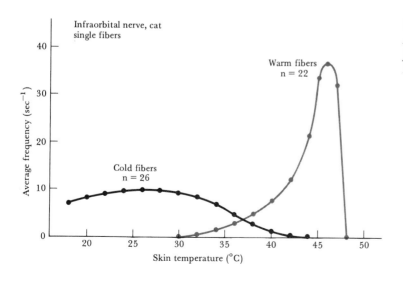

Figure 8.5
Average frequency of thermoreceptors for various temperatures. [From Hensel and Kenshalo (1969).]

ambiguous. Another study which emphasizes this point deals with the apparently ambiguous information transmitted by the fibers that respond to several kinds of stimulation, not just temperature change. For example, Hensel and Boman (1960) studied responses in the fibers of the human forearm and found that many responded to both cooling and touch. But the pattern of firing was different. Touch elicited an initial burst of firing, which rapidly died down, while cooling elicited a slower change which was maintained for a longer period of time. The different patterns of response to different types of stimulation may explain how a single fiber can code for separate stimulus qualities.

Other studies have shown that pattern differences may be important in fibers that respond to even more than two kinds of stimulation. Wall and Cronly-Dillon (1960) studied cells in the spinal cord of the cat, and found that in a single cell, the response varied widely depending on the type of stimulus applied. To a touch stimulus in the receptive field of the single unit, there would be a sharp burst of firing that died down before the touch was removed, a phenomenon very typical

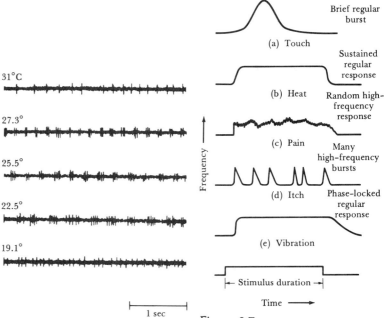

Figure 8.6
Records from a monkey cold receptor during the change in skin temperature from 40° to 15°C. The temperatures at the start of each trace are indicated at the left-hand side. [From Iggo and Iggo (1971).]

Figure 8.7
Drawings of the spike action potential frequency pattern in spinal neurons of the cat as a function of the quality of the stimulus. [From Wall and Cronly-Dillon (1960), adapted by Uttal (1973). Copyright 1960, American Medical Association.]

of cells responsive to touch. But the cell would respond with a sustained but regular discharge when the skin was warmed. And if the stimulus was painful, the cell responded with a high-frequency, but random discharge of spikes. These responses are shown in Figure 8.7. It would appear that there are specific neurons which provide information about temperature changes, but many of them can pass along messages about other characteristics of the stimulus as well, via the pattern of firing.

The kind of end organ which transmits temperature information is not known, and it is possible that more than one type of end organ and even free nerve endings are involved. Even when a "cold" or "warm" fiber has been identified, it is very difficult to determine what receptor structures are connected to it, and it is of course possible that the fiber receives information from many different kinds of receptor structures. Hensel (1973), however, was able to identify the terminals that converged upon a cold fiber in the cat's nose. The fiber was a thin myelinated axon which branched into a number of fine unmyelinated terminal endings. The endings appeared to enter the cells of the epidermal layer.

The nature of the transduction process for temperature changes is even more obscure. Somehow, a change in temperature in the skin must be transmitted to the receptor cell, which then must move ions across the membrane to produce a generator potential. But how this happens is unknown. Certainly temperature affects reaction rates and molecular movement in all cells, so that it is not difficult to imagine that many and perhaps most receptors might be able to transmit some information about temperature changes, although this may or may not be their primary function.

---

summary
The Coding of Temperature

Temperature coding is accomplished by two sets of fibers: one set of warm fibers and another set of cold fibers. Warm fibers respond maximally to temperature changes in the range of 45°–47°C, while the cold fibers respond to changes in a much broader, but cooler range of temperatures. The coding of absolute temperature may be rather ambiguous because a single cold fiber, for example, fibers at the same rate at vastly different temperatures. However, the fiber may employ different firing patterns for the different temperatures, even though the rate is about the same. Pattern differences in firing may also be important when a fiber responds to two or more different kinds of stimulation, such as cooling and touch.

---

the coding of pain

The method the brain uses to code painful stimulation is undoubtedly very complex and probably different from the coding of touch or temperature. Pain not only involves some localized sensation, but an emotional component as well, so many brain areas and pathways are likely to be involved. In this section we will begin with a discussion of the **nociceptors,** the receptors and fibers in the skin which transmit painful information to the spinal cord. Then we will consider hypotheses about how pain is coded in the spinal cord and the brain. Finally, we will look at some very exciting studies which point to the importance of descending fibers from the brain in the transmission and sensation of pain, and how the activation of these fibers may be related to the pain relief afforded by the opiates.

nociceptors Most researchers agree that the receptors in the skin which are primarily sensitive to noxious stimulation are the free nerve endings, although other receptors may transduce painful stimulation as well. Unfortunately very little is known about how the transduction process occurs, although many hypothesize that it has something to do with the release of chemicals during tissue damage. However, much more is known about the responses of fibers to painful stimulation. Some of these fibers, particularly the thinly myelinated **A-delta** and unmyelinated **C fibers,** are even uniquely responsive to pain. The activation of thinly myelinated fibers is correlated with the feeling of sharp pain, while the activation of the unmyelinated ones is correlated with the sensation of ache.

Figure 8.8 shows the responses of one of these nociceptors (Perl, 1968). The spike discharges illustrate the neuron's responses to a mechanical probe placed on the skin. The neuron shows no response to this, as shown in Fig. 8.8, even when the weight of the probe reaches 100. The tracing in (B) illustrates the cell's response when a needle tip is placed on the skin, again with an increase in pressure up to 100. When the needle first hits the skin, with very minor pressure, the neuron shows a burst of firing but by the time the pressure reaches 100, the response has virtually adapted out. The third tracing shows the cell's response to a pinch with forceps. The cell shows a rapid adaptation to this painful stimulation on the skin also. The quick adaptation of this cell to noxious stimulation may seem surprising, but the initial response is probably all the brain requires for the organism to localize the pain and to begin some appropriate defensive reaction. Furthermore, just because this particular cell has ceased sending messages does not mean that the sensation of pain has stopped. Pain is very much a central nervous system phenomenon also, as we shall see in later sections. But before we consider central mechanisms of pain, let us examine what happens to the painful messages when they reach the spinal cord.

pain and the spinal cord As pain messages reach the cord, the axons carrying them make synapses with a variety of interneurons within the dorsal horn. Two classes of interneurons within this structure are now known to play some role in the transmission of pain, but that role is not completely understood.

The **class 1 cells** are similar to the nociceptors in that some of them at least respond specifically to painful stimulation. But the **class 2 cells** must also be important, even though they are not so specific, because it appears that activation of these cells may be a sufficient condition for the experience of pain (Mayer *et al.*, 1975). In one study, these scientists (and surgeons) were performing an operation to remove part of the spinal cord in a patient, for the purpose of relieving pain, and during the operation, they electrically stimulated parts of the cord. They recorded the current thresholds and also the current frequencies which elicited pain in the patient and then compared them with the thresholds and frequencies which were optimal for eliciting activity from the two classes of dorsal horn cells in the monkey. Their conclusion was that the kind of stimulation of the cord which elicited pain from humans was the same kind of stimulation that was best for eliciting activity from the class 2 dorsal horn cells in the monkey, rather than the class 1 cells.

A very important theory which was proposed some years ago to account for the transmission of pain through the spinal cord emphasized pain responsive cells in the dorsal horn; it is called the **gate control theory** of pain (Melzack and Wall, 1965). These scientists proposed that there is a neural "gate" in the spinal cord that compares the relative amount of activity in the large and small afferent fibers which carry information about pain. The gate is opened when the small fibers are very active relative to the larger ones, but it closes when the reverse is true. The main parts of the theory are diagrammed in Figure 8.9. When the gate is open, the **transmission cells** in the cord are active, and this is when painful messages are sent to the brain. Furthermore, the activity of the transmission cells is affected not only by the relative activity of the small and large afferent fibers, but also by the activity of descending fibers which reach the transmission cells.

There is clinical evidence which supports the part of this theory which emphasizes the relative activity in small and large fibers. For example, studies in which chronic pain is reduced when the large fibers are stimulated support the gate control theory (Wall and Sweet, 1967), and the theory makes some intuitive sense. For example, if your knee hurts, it often helps to rub it, thereby stimulating the large afferent fibers. Perhaps this is the reason why the rubbing is effective. More support for the theory comes from patients with a disease which preferentially destroys large-diameter fibers. The chronic pain of these patients can be treated with electrical stimulation, again increasing the activity of the large fibers which are left (Nathan and Wall, 1974).

the gate control theory of pain

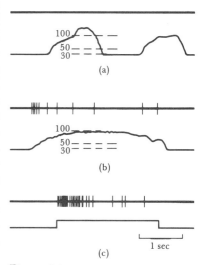

(a)

(b)

(c)

1 sec

Figure 8.8
Responses of a nociceptor. Upper traces in (a), (b), and (c) represent firing of fiber. Lower traces in (a) and (b) show weight of mechanical probe and needle tip, respectively. In (c), the receptive field of the neuron was pinched with forceps. [From Perl (1968), in Burgess and Perl (1973).]

Figure 8.9
Schematic diagram of the gate control theory of pain mechanism. L, large diameter fibers; S, small diameter fibers. The fibers project to the substantia gelatinosa (SG) and first central transmission (T) cells in the spinal cord. The inhibitory effect exerted by SG on the afferent fiber terminals is increased by activity in L fibers and decreased by activity in S fibers. The central control trigger is represented by a line running from the large fiber system to the central control mechanisms; those mechanisms in turn, project back to the gate control system. The T cells project to the entry cells of the action system: +, excitation; −, inhibition. [From Melzack and Wall (1965), in Melzack (1973). Copyright 1965 by the American Association for the Advancement of Science.]

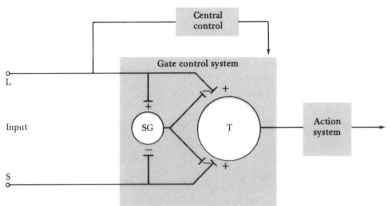

The phenomenon of acupuncture has had a stormy history in this country, but some researchers believe that part of its effectiveness may lie in the stimulation of large diameter fibers. Tiny needles are inserted into nerve fibers at specified locations on the body, and this procedure often results in analgesia. Thus far, many researchers hypothesize that stimulation by acupuncture does not cause any more relief from pain than does stimulation of the nerve fibers by electricity. Nevertheless acupuncture is sometimes used as the only form of analgesia for surgery patients in China, so for some patients it must be quite effective. In China, the procedure involves a great deal more than simply sticking pins into the patient. It is performed in a milieu of proper explanation, rapport between the physician and patient, and a whole culture which believes in its utility. This milieu may significantly contribute to the effectiveness of the analgesia produced by acupuncture, perhaps by involving higher brain mechanisms in the control of pain, mechanisms which may also be involved when any placebo treatment is able to relieve pain. It is important to remember that the effectiveness of a placebo treatment does not mean that the pain never existed, or that the person for whom the "sugar pills" worked is a hypochondriac. It probably means that the higher centers in the brain are capable of controlling the transmission of painful messages from the spinal cord.

evidence against the gate control theory. In spite of the clinical observations which attest to the importance of the relative activity in large and small fibers, the gate control hypothesis must not be completely correct because several studies have failed to support it. In a direct test of the hypothesis, Nathan and Rudge (1974) induced large fiber activity in the upper arm of normal people by electrical stimulation and then administered different kinds of pain, such as radiant heat, a pin prick, and pressure. According to the theory, the people should have reported less pain from these stimuli, but they did not. The theory has undergone many modifications as more and more has been learned about the spinal cord, but this theory has contributed a great deal to pain research. First it has emphasized the importance of patterns of neural response in different fibers, and second, it has directed attention to the descending fibers from the brain.

Many areas of the brain receive input from the spinal columns which transmit pain messages, and one of them, the **nucleus gigantocellularis** (NGC) in the reticular formation, has received a lot of attention. Many cells in this region respond maximally to activation of the sparsely myelinated A-delta fibers, as well as the unmyelinated C fibers in the periphery, although they respond to other types of peripheral stimulation as well (Casey, 1971). When the cells in this area of the brain are stimulated, it must produce some aversive experience for an animal, because it will learn to perform a task in order to escape the stimulation.

brain areas responsive to pain

In many ways, these cells in the NGC are much like the class 2 cells in the dorsal horn. For example, they respond maximally, but not only, to noxious stimulation. They also tend to have very large receptive fields, and can be activated by painful stimulation coming from a large area on the skin, again like the Class 2 dorsal horn cells. This would suggest that the activation of these cells is related to the emotional component of a painful stimulus, rather than the simple sensory stimulation that precisely localizes the stimulus. Liebeskind and Paul (1977) suggest that this area of the brain, and others in which units have been found which respond best to painful stimulation, are activated by neurons arriving via the extralemniscal routes mentioned earlier. The role of this pathway, which includes cells in the NGC, may be to produce an emotional response so that the organism can effectively prepare for some emergency. Precise information about the spatial and temporal characteristics of the painful stimulus is probably mediated by neurons traveling along the lemniscal pathway, which also carries information about touch, and which ultimately reaches the somatosensory cortex.

As information about pain moves from a remote body area to the brain, it must be diffusely spread around, because lesions in various areas have not been very effective in reducing pain. This certainly makes sense if we consider that pain really has two components—the one serving the sensory-discriminative aspects, and the other, much more diffuse component, which subserves the emotional aspects. There is no "pain center" which can be conveniently removed to alleviate chronic and debilitating pain. However, there may be other ways

efferent effects on the transmission of pain

to alleviate pain—ones which rely on the fact that areas of the brain send efferent messages back down to the spinal cord. These efferent messages can have a very powerful influence on the individual's experience of pain.

analgesia produced by electrical stimulation of the brain. When particular areas of the brainstem, such as the **central gray** and the **nucleus raphe magnus**, are stimulated electrically, the organism feels much less pain from a noxious stimulus (e.g., Mayer and Liebeskind, 1974). For example, if one applies radiant heat to a rat's tail, the rat will ordinarily perform a tail-flick. But if the rat has received brain stimulation in one of these areas, then it will take several seconds and more heat before the rat will do any flicking. After only a few seconds of brain stimulation, the analgesic effect may last for several hours or more, and the effect is as strong as a large dose of morphine. There is much evidence to suggest that the reason this stimulation can produce analgesia is because it is activating a descending fiber system, one which inhibits the transmission of painful messages from the spinal cord.

One piece of evidence that has led to this hypothesis is that this kind of brain stimulation in the cat can lead to the total inhibition of activity in the class 2 dorsal horn cells in response to painful stimulation (Oliveras *et al.*, 1974). But even though the cat's dorsal horn cells are not responding to painful stimulation, which they ordinarily would do, they *are* responding to other kinds of stimulation which are not painful. Also, when the descending fibers of the nucleus raphe magnus are destroyed by lesion in the spinal cord, the analgesic effect of brain stimulation in that nucleus does not appear (Basbaum *et al.*, 1976). Thus the analgesic effects of brain stimulation, in that area at least, are dependent upon the presence of intact descending fibers. Liebeskind and Paul (1977) suggest that compared to the kind of analgesia which is available through peripheral mechanisms, such as stimulation of large fibers, the analgesic effects of descending controls may be much more powerful.

brain stimulation and the opiates There are a number of remarkable parallels between the way in which brain stimulation produces analgesia and the way in which the opiates, such as morphine, produce it. For example, **naloxone,** a drug which blocks the analgesic effects of morphine, also partially blocks the analgesic effects of brain stimulation (Akil *et al.*, 1976). Also, analgesia from morphine and from brain stimulation can both be blocked by PCPA, a drug which depletes serotonin (Akil and Mayer, 1972). Those descending fibers from the nucleus raphe magnus, which when cut, also block analgesia from brain stimulation, are known to contain the neurotransmitter serotonin.

There are other pieces of the puzzle which also suggest that morphine and brain stimulation are producing analgesia in similar ways. An individual quickly becomes tolerant to morphine, so that the more the person takes, the more they need to relieve the same amount of pain. The same is true of brain stimulation. There is also cross-tolerance between the two analgesics, so that if an organism takes morphine, it will become tolerant to brain stimulation, and vice versa (Mayer and Hayes, 1975). Another very unfortunate similarity between the two is that they both produce physical dependence (Wei, cited in Liebeskind and Paul, 1977).

the enkephalins. The similarity between the two analgesics is intriguing. And it appears that it may be more than just a coincidence, because in a recent series of rather startling developments, it has been learned that the brain produces its own morphine-like compounds (Hughes *et al.*, 1975). The first of these to be discovered were two short-chained peptides called **enkephalins,** but many more have since been isolated. The enkephalins act very much like morphine, except that they are more potent. Their analgesic effect can be reversed by the drug naloxone, and they occupy the same receptor sites in the brain as do the opiates. These receptor sites are located along the same brain pathways that pain messages are known to travel. The connection between brain stimulation analgesia and morphine analgesia may be that when the brain is electrically stimulated, it results in the release of these enkephalins from certain areas; then the enkephalins go on to produce morphine-like analgesia. Stimulation of the central gray area produces the release of these chemicals (Stein, cited in Liebeskind and Paul, 1977), or ones very similar, and this may be the route that stimulation analgesia generally takes.

how do the enkephalins produce analgesia?

The next question to be asked is how the enkephalins, or opiates for that matter, produce analgesia. The answer to this question is not completely understood, but we do have some leads. For example, we mentioned earlier that brain stimulation was not effective in producing analgesia unless the serotonin-containing descending fibers from the brain were intact. The same is true of morphine. This suggests that morphine, and possibly enkephalins, act by stimulating descending brainstem mechanisms, which then transmit their information to the cord—messages which shut down the transmission of painful messages back to the brain. The descending fiber influence, suggested by the gate control theory, may actually have the potency to close the gate completely, regardless of how much pain is being transmitted to the cord.

the effects of enkephalins on nerve cells. On a cellular level, both the opiates and the enkephalins, when applied to neurons generally have an in-

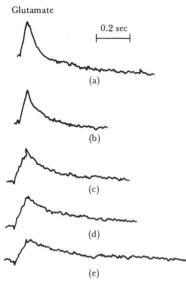

Glutamate

0.2 sec

(a)

(b)

(c)

(d)

(e)

Figure 8.10
*The depolarization produced by
the application of glutamate to a
spinal cord neuron (a). The
depression of the glutamate
depolarization when enkephalin
is added (b)–(e). [From Barker
et al. (1978). Copyright 1978 by
the American Association for the
Advancement of Science.]*

hibiting effect on firing rates. Some have suggested that the enkephalins are actually another neurotransmitter (Snyder, 1977). In the brain they are found in nerve terminals, rather than cell bodies or axons, and their distribution closely parallels the distribution of the opiate receptors throughout the brain. Recently Barker *et al.* (1978) have proposed another role for these fascinating substances. They recorded from spinal cord neurons which had been grown *in vitro* from mouse embryo tissue while they applied various substances to the neurons. When they applied glutamate, which is a putative neurotransmitter, they noted a large depolarization of the membrane of the neuron. But when they applied both glutamate and one of the enkephalins to the neuron, the size of the depolarization was depressed. These responses are shown in Figure 8.10. The depression was not large, but with increasing amounts of enkephalins, the depolarization only reached about 50% of its size when only glutamate was applied. They also found that naloxone, the opiate antagonist, partially reversed the depressing effects of the enkephalin, so that the depolarization by glutamate came nearly to the normal level.

the enkephalins as neuromodulators. These scientists believe that the enkephalin is not acting like a neurotransmitter in their experiments, but rather like a **neuromodulator.** They make a very interesting analogy to explain this new type of communication between neurons. They suggest that the neurohormones, like some of those from the pituitary, communicate with the nervous system like a radio broadcast. The message is sent out all over, but only those with antennae tuned to the correct wavelengths receive the message. The neurohormone would be the message, while the cells with the antennae would be those with receptor sites for that neurohormone. Chemical transmission at a synapse is likened to a telephone conversation; it is both very private between two neurons, and it requires hard wiring. Neuromodulation would be a form of gain control imposed on the private conversation between two neurons—it would affect the "volume" of the conversation.

*what activates the
enkephalin analgesia?* However the electrical stimulation of efferent pathways or the release of enkephalins produce analgesia, we would like to know how these mechanisms are activated in the first place. Under what conditions are these antinociceptive devices brought into play so that the individual will be relieved from the pain?

   Although it may be hard to believe, pain is really a very desirable sensation. It gives us a warning that something is wrong so that we can take some action. Even a dog does not need to be told to keep its weight off a cut paw, so the cut stays cleaner and heals faster. A person who does not feel any pain, and there are some, is not lucky and often dies young because they don't get these warnings.

analgesia under stress. There are times when the sensation of pain would be detrimental even though an injury is present—and these times may be the ones when the efferent antinociceptive mechanisms are activated. Suppose you are attacked by a dog; the dog bites you on the leg and is about to bite you again unless you start running. Pain sensations from your injured leg would only make you limp and run slower, so you would be better off if you could inhibit the pain sensations for awhile.

The analgesia experienced in situations like this have been documented time and time again. Soldiers wounded in battle report feeling no pain, at least until they are out of danger, and people injured in car wrecks often are able to perform amazing feats of strength to save someone else.

This antinociception under stress has been found in laboratory animals also; and there is reason to believe that the efferent mechanisms we have been discussing, particularly the release of enkephalin, is involved. Chance and his colleagues (1978) conditioned a group of rats to be afraid of a cage which had an electrical grid. The rats were placed onto the grid and shocked for 15 seconds every day for 8 days. A control group of rats were also placed on the grid, but they were not shocked, so their conditioned fear of the procedure was considerably less. At the end of the 8 days, they placed each rat on the grid again, and measured the rat's response to a tail-flick test, described earlier. The rats which were afraid—those that had been shocked—were much slower to flick their tails, indicating that they were less sensitive to the painful radiant heat being directed on their tails. Thus they had activated some antinociceptive mechanism.

To find out *what* mechanism, they took the brains of all the rats, right after the tail-flick test, homogenized them and added radioactively labeled enkephalin. The reason for this procedure was to find out whether the opiate receptors, which bind enkephalin, were already occupied in the rat's brain. If they were occupied, presumably by enkephalin released by the rat's own brain, then there would be very few sites left for the labeled enkephalin to occupy. If the rat's brain had not released its own enkephalin, then they would find a great deal of labeled enkephalin bound to the receptor sites.

Figure 8.11 shows what they found. The rats with conditioned fear (dark circles) had the longest tail-flick latencies, as we mentioned. They also had less labeled enkephalin in their brains, suggesting that the opiate receptors were already occupied by naturally released enkephalin. This study suggests that a scared rat releases enkephalins, thereby producing analgesia.

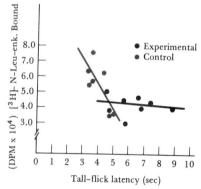

Figure 8.11
The relationship between tail-flick latency and amount of bound, labeled enkephalin, in the brains of fear-conditioned rats (dark circles) and control rats (light circles). See text for explanation. [From Chance et al. (1978).]

conclusions There has been a considerable increase in the attention devoted to the efferent brain mechanisms which can affect the transmission of painful messages. The findings have given rise to very tantalizing hypotheses to explain why an individual is often able to control pain, during stress or fear. There may even be other ways to activate these pain control mechanisms. Pain relief during hypnosis, by placebo, or by the milieu surrounding the use of acupuncture in China, may also be partly mediated by these descending controls.

Some people may be able to activate these analgesic devices voluntarily, simply by concentrating. Certain individuals can walk over hot coals, or stick needles in their arms or neck and consistently report feeling no pain. If parts of the brainstem have such a powerful influence over the transmission of pain messages from the spinal cord, then it is possible that some individuals have developed a neural path of access to these "pain inhibition" areas—probably a path which begins in the higher brain areas, but which results in the release of the individual's personal supply of potent analgesic. Whether this is indeed what they are doing, and whether the rest of us can take advantage of our own pain inhibition mechanisms, are questions to be answered by future research.

---

summary
The Coding of Pain

Pain is different from touch or temperature change, because it not only involves a localized sensation and sensory discriminative aspect, but also an emotional component. The peripheral fibers which transmit painful information from the skin are called *nociceptors,* and many of them terminate in free nerve endings in the skin. The sparsely myelinated *A-delta* fibers, and the unmyelinated *C fibers* are the ones which carry painful sensations to the spinal cord.

In the dorsal horn of the spinal cord, there are two classes of cells which respond to painful stimulation. *Class 1* cells respond only to noxious stimulation, while the *class 2* cells can be stimulated by other kinds of stimulation as well. A theory which was proposed to explain the transmission of painful messages through the cord is called the *gate control theory,* and it suggests that pain is only transmitted when there is more activity in the small peripheral fibers, relative to the large ones, via a gating mechanism in the cord. Support for this theory comes from the finding that there are cells in the dorsal horn which respond to painful stimulation, and also from studies in which stimulation of large fibers has resulted in the relief from pain in people with certain diseases. But there is more to transmission of pain through the cord than the simple gating mechanism, because stimulation of large fibers does not produce analgesia in normal subjects.

Neurons in the brain which are responsive to pain are found in several places, including the *nucleus gigantocellularis* in the reticular formation. But since these brain cells are not generally exclusively responsive to painful stimulation, they are probably part of pathways that contribute to the emotional component of pain. The localization of pain is probably mediated by the lemniscal pathway, which can accurately pinpoint the location of touch sensations, while the extralemniscal routes, by which neurons in the nucleus gigantocellularis are probably activated, may produce the emotional response to painful stimulation.

The gate control theory suggested that the cells which transmit pain in the cord are also affected by descending fibers. These fibers are particularly important in the sensation of pain. When certain areas of the brainstem are electrically stimulated, such as the *central gray* or *nucleus raphe magnus,* analgesia results. This analgesia may be mediated by the activation of descending serotonin-containing fibers from the nucleus raphe magnus. The fibers, when activated, inhibit the cells in the dorsal horn—the ones which carry the painful messages.

Pain is also inhibited by the opiates, such as morphine, and brain stimulation and the opiates act in similar ways. The brain produces its own morphine-like factors, called *enkephalins,* which occupy opiate receptor sites, and which also produce analgesia. Brain stimulation probably results in the release of enkephalins from the brain, which then occupy the opiate receptor sites, and activate the descending pain inhibiting mechanism.

Natural events which produce analgesia include stress and conditioned fear. These events also seem to result in the release of enkephalins from the brain, so that they may also be able to activate the pain inhibiting mechanism.

---

kinesthesia

The somatosensory system not only includes the sensations arising from the skin, but also those arising from the muscles, tendons, and joints—sensations which provide information about the position and movement of the body. The system which provides these sensations is the *kinesthetic system.* Although we are not generally aware of these sensations, they are very important in maintaining balance and posture, and also in providing feedback during movement. Even with your eyes closed, you know what position your arms or legs are in because the sensory receptors of the kinesthetic system are sending this information to the brain. This kind of information is called **proprioceptive,** meaning that the messages are about things happening in the internal rather than the external environment.

In each joint of your body are sensory receptors called **joint receptors,** and these are the main avenues for kinesthetic sensations. There are also receptors placed onto the muscle tissue and the tendons, but the involvement of muscle receptors is a subject of controversy. Since the muscle receptors will be discussed in Chapter 9 on the control of movement, and since their role in kinesthesia is not certain, we will not discuss them in this section. Instead we will concentrate on the joint receptors, particularly the ones in the cat's knee joint. You may have noticed that the cat is a favored animal in sensory research, and even the cat's knees have not escaped scrutiny.

In this section we will begin with the receptors and the afferent sensory pathway. Then we will discuss the coding of proprioceptive information by the neurons in the pathway leading from the joint receptors.

joint receptors The kinds of receptor endings found in joints are very similar to those found in the skin. In the cat's knee joint capsule, for example, there are free nerve endings, and encapsulated end organs that look very much like the Pacinian corpuscles discussed earlier. There is also a spray type that looks like another receptor located in the skin called the Ruffini ending.

The way that these endings transduce the mechanical energy of movement of the limbs into neural energy is not clear. Since the three types of endings are so much like those in the skin, they presumably transduce energy in a similar way.

afferent sensory pathway
for the joint receptors The receptors in the joint are also similar to many receptors in the skin because the receptor cell not only transduces, it also spikes. It thus forms the first neuron in the afferent pathway. These fibers travel to the spinal cord, synapse, and then travel up the lemniscal pathway in the cord—the same one used by cutaneous fibers. Kinesthetic information projects to the thalamus, and also the somatosensory cortex, just like cutaneous information. There are also projections of these fibers to the cerebellum, which makes sense considering that this structure is so intimately related to balance and movement.

sensory coding of
kinesthetic information When the cat's knee is bent back and forth, the afferent fibers respond by increasing their firing rates. But the fibers can provide much more information than simply that the knee was bent. They also code how fast the bending occurs and what angle the knee joint is in.

rapidly and slowly adapting fibers. There are two types of fibers—those which rapidly adapt to any movement of the joint and those which slowly adapt. When the joint is bent, the rapidly adapting fibers increase their firing frequency, but then quickly drop back to spontaneous firing levels. The much more numerous slowly adapting fibers do not drop back to spontaneous levels so quickly. Instead, they decrease to a new level of firing depending upon what angle the knee joint ends up in. Thus the rapidly adapting fibers can code simple movement, and probably how fast that movement occurred, but the slowly adapting fibers can provide information about the precise angle of the joint.

Most of the slowly adapting fibers respond best when the joint is either fully extended or fully bent, but there are also fibers which respond best at intermediate angles. Figure 8.12 shows the responses of some of these intermediate neurons. For example, one neuron had its

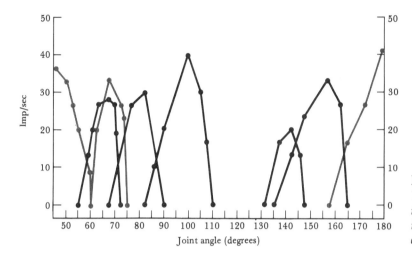

Figure 8.12
The responses of eight single units innervating slowly adapting receptors in the capsule of the knee joint of the cat. [From Skoglund (1956).]

highest adapted firing level when the angle of the knee joint was about 65°, while another showed the best response to an angle of about 95° (Skoglund, 1956). Thus precise information is provided about the exact angle of the knee joint by the fact that different neurons respond best to different angles. The angles of the knee joint which can activate the neuron represent a kind of receptive field for kinesthetic fibers.

coding of movement. At higher levels of the afferent pathway, the coding of kinesthetic information seems to emphasize movement rather than static angular position of the knee. For example, Yin and Williams (1976) recorded from cells in the ventral posterolateral nucleus of the thalamus and found cells which were specifically responsive to movements of the cat's knee joint. Most of the cells were rapidly adapting, rather than slowly adapting, and did not respond best to particular angles of the joint, like the first-order afferent fibers did. Instead they responded to movement, particularly when it was a specific speed of movement.

phase-locking. These scientists noticed that some of the cells exhibited **phase-locking.** For example, when the joint was bent quickly back and forth through an angle of only about 5° at a frequency of three times per second, one cell responded at three times per second. The cell was phase-locked in the sense that it tended to fire during the same portion of each cycle of movement. Since this cell did not respond best to any static position of the knee angle, but rather to movements, and since it phase-locked to different frequencies of movements, it would appear that the thalamic cells are very good at detecting velocity of movement. The faster the movement back and forth, the faster would be the firing of the phase-locked thalamic neurons.

Information from the joint receptors sometimes converges with information from other sensory systems, so that some cells respond to stimulation from more than one sensory modality. We will see examples of this kind of convergence between kinesthetic and vestibular information in the next section.

summary
Kinesthesia

Sensory receptors in the muscles, tendons, and joints all provide proprioceptive information about what is going on in the internal environment. The receptors in the joints, however, probably provide the most important information about the position and movement of the limbs. These *joint receptors* are of three types, and look very much like those located in the skin. They include free nerve endings, spray type endings, and modified Pacinian corpuscles. The afferent pathway for the joint receptors follows the same route as that for the skin senses, through the lemniscal pathway. The kinesthetic information also projects to the cerebellum.

Sensory coding in the first-order afferent neurons emphasizes the static angle of the joint. The slowly adapting fibers respond best when the joint is in or near a particular angle, that is in its receptive field, but the less numerous rapidly adapting fibers respond to any movement of the joint. Neurons in the higher parts of the afferent pathway, particularly the thalamus, emphasize the coding of movement velocity. Some cells in the thalamus are phase-locked to the movements of the joint and fire at the same rate as repetitive back-and-forth movements of the joint.

the vestibular system

The last sensory system which we examine is the vestibular system—the one that provides information about rotation, inclination, and acceleration of the head. Like the information provided by the kinesthetic system, it is not the kind we are generally aware of, unless we are falling through space or spinning wildly around. But the information is very important for maintaining balance.

In this section we will consider the properties of the vestibular system in the same order that we have for all the other sensory systems. First we will discuss the sense organ and the receptors, then the afferent pathway, and finally coding.

the vestibular organ

Situated right next to the cochlea of the inner ear is the vestibular organ, shown in Figure 8.13. It is made up of five fluid-filled cavities: two oval bulbs called the **saccule** and **utricule** and three **semicircular canals.** The semicircular canals are arranged in space so that each one generally corresponds to one of the three planes of the head. One canal is roughly sagittal in orientation, another is horizontal, and the third is roughly coronal. Each one detects the acceleration of movement of the head best when the direction of movement is in the canal's plane.

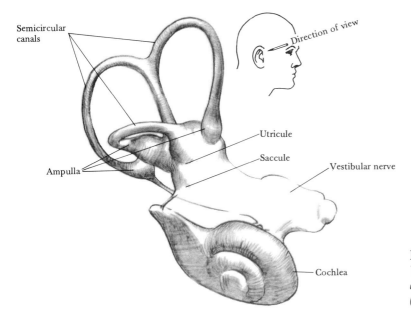

Figure 8.13
The main features of the vestibular organ. [Modified from Hardy (1934).]

The ends of each canal terminate on the surface of the utricule, in bulblike regions called **ampullae.** It is the inner surface of these ampullae and the inner surface of the saccule and utricule that contain the **hair cells**—the receptors for the vestibular system.

stimulation of the vestibular system. The stimuli that activate the hair cells in the ampullae and those in the saccule and utricule are different, because the accessory structures surrounding the receptor cells are different. The receptors in the ampullae at the end of the semicircular canals are covered by a gelatinous mass called the **cupula.** When the fluid in the canals moves, it produces movement in the cupula, and hence there is a shearing force on the hair cells in the ampullae. The only time the fluid in the canals moves and produces this effect is when the head is changing velocity, but not when it is moving at a constant rate. If you imagine what happens when you lift a cup of coffee, you'll see how this happens. The only time the coffee itself moves relative to the cup is when there is a change in velocity, such as when you first start lifting it, or when you stop. The stimulus that is the adequate one for the receptors in the ampullae is thus acceleration or deceleration—not steady movement.

The receptors in the saccule and utricule, however, are designed for detecting steady movement. The cilia of these hair cells are embedded in a fine layer of calcium salts, called **otoconia.** When the head is moved at a steady rate, the weight of the otoconia shift and produce a shearing force on the hair cells.

the receptors The hair cells of the vestibular system are very much like those found in the cochlea. There are two types, shown in Figure 8.14. As you can see in the diagram, they have cilia, which are embedded in either the cupula or the otoconia. The cilia are attached to the **cuticular plate,** which overlies the rest of the hair cell. The afferent connections to one type of hair cell surround the whole distal end, but in the other type, the synapse simply connects to a small portion of the receptor cell. Both types of hair cells also have efferent connections, although their function is unknown.

The transduction process in the hair cells is probably similar to the one in the cochlea. When the cupula or the otoconia shift, it produces a shearing force on the hair cells, which is probably transmitted in some way through the cuticular plate to the rest of the hair cell. This shearing force in some way causes a movement of ions so that a receptor potential is produced—one which ultimately results in the release of transmitter in the synapse to the afferent sensory neuron. Although this is the most likely explanation for the transduction process, it is just as speculative as it was in the discussion on audition.

the afferent sensory pathway The pathway that vestibular information travels is shown in Figure 8.15. The cell bodies of the first-order sensory neurons, which synapsed with the hair cells, are located in the **vestibular ganglion** in the medulla. From there, some fibers go to the cerebellum, but most

Figure 8.14
The hair cells of the vestibular system. [Modified from Uttal (1973).]

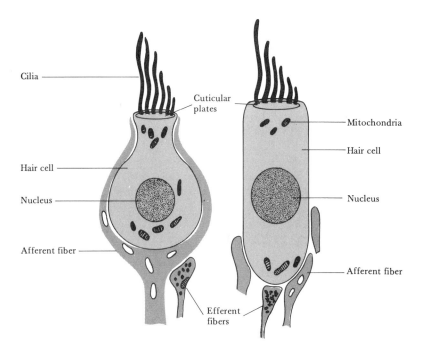

Cilia

Cuticular plates

Mitochondria

Hair cell

Hair cell

Nucleus

Nucleus

Afferent fiber

Afferent fiber

Efferent fibers

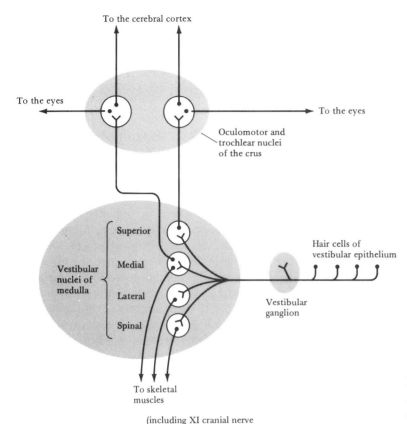

To the cerebral cortex

To the eyes

To the eyes

Oculomotor and
trochlear nuclei
of the crus

Superior

Medial

Vestibular
nuclei of
medulla

Lateral

Spinal

Hair cells of
vestibular epithelium

Vestibular
ganglion

To skeletal
muscles

(including XI cranial nerve
which supplies neck muscles)

Figure 8.15
*Schematic drawing of part of the
ascending vestibular pathway.
[Modified from Uttal (1973).]*

branch off into four separate **vestibular nuclei** and terminate there.
From the vestibular nuclei are projections to motor nuclei which control eye movement. Other fibers from the vestibular nuclei go directly
to the ventral roots in the spinal cord. This connection is a direct link
to motor neurons which control the skeletal muscles.

Although some third-order neurons reach the cerebral cortex, it
would appear that much vestibular information does not actually
reach the higher levels of the nervous system. At least it does not go
there very directly, and this may be one reason why we are not generally aware of vestibular sensations.

Even though you may not usually be aware of vestibular sensations,
your nervous system nonetheless codes the information. But studies
on how single afferent fibers react to vestibular stimulation are very
difficult to do because rotation of the head is likely to jar the electrode,
particularly if it is fast. In spite of this problem progress has been
made.

*sensory coding in the
vestibular system*

In the squirrel monkey, for example, first-order afferent fibers respond to angular acceleration (Goldberg and Fernandez, 1971). When the monkey's head was rotated, so that the cupula in the horizontal canal was deflected toward the utricule, the fibers increased their firing rate. When the head was rotated in the opposite direction, the fibers decreased their firing rate.

polysensory stimulation of vestibular fibers. One of the most interesting properties of vestibular neurons is that many of them, if not most of them, are responsive to other forms of sensory stimulation as well. For example, in the thalamus of the squirrel monkey there are neurons which respond by increasing their firing rate when electrical pulses are applied to the vestibular nerve. Many of the thalamic vestibular neurons are also sensitive to somatosensory stimulation (Liedgren *et al.*, 1976). When these vestibular cells were tested to see if they would respond to touch on the skin, pressure, or movement of joints, many of them often did indeed respond. In fact, these scientists found very few cells that only responded to vestibular stimulation. And even those few might have responded to some other kind of stimulation that was not presented in the experiment.

This kind of convergence was particularly noticeable between vestibular stimulation and joint movement. This suggests that these thalamic cells are acting like a kind of integrator for vestibular and somatosensory (especially proprioceptive) information. It is probably this integration of information that is passed along to the cortex for further analysis—and this may be another reason why one is generally unaware of vestibular information. Integration between vestibular and proprioceptive information is very convenient since they are both involved in balance and movement.

integration in the vestibular nuclei. Another place at which some integration occurs is the vestibular nuclei—right near the beginning of the afferent sensory pathway. In the cat many of the cells in these nuclei respond to somatosensory stimulation as well as vestibular stimulation, just like those in the thalamus (Fredrickson *et al.*, 1966). But virtually all of them which were tested by Waespe and Henn (1977) also responded to movement in the visual field. These scientists recorded from single units in the vestibular nuclei of awake rhesus monkeys while they performed some interesting manipulations. One of these was rotation of the monkey in the dark, and this constituted pure vestibular stimulation. Another was rotation of the monkey in the light, and this counted as both visual and vestibular stimulation. And the third involved keeping the monkey still, but rotating a cylinder painted with black-and-white stripes around the monkey's head—this was pure visual stimulation.

Figure 8.16 shows the average responses of six neurons during the

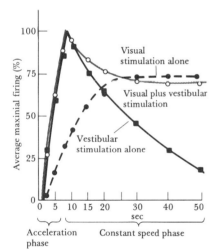

Figure 8.16
Average frequency responses from six neurons during chair rotation in the dark (dark line), chair rotation in the light (light line), and cylinder rotation around the stationary animal (broken line). [Adapted from: Waespe and Henn (1977).]

rotations. During the first 7.5 sec shown on the horizontal axis the monkey or the cylinder was accelerating, but during the rest of the time the monkey or the cylinder maintained a constant speed of rotation. The vertical axis represents average percent of maximal firing for the six neurons.

During and immediately following the acceleration, the neurons responded the same regardless of whether they were receiving vestibular stimulation alone or visual and vestibular stimulation combined. But these same neurons fired much more slowly during this acceleration phase when the monkey's head was not moving but the cylinder was. This means that the firing patterns in these neurons easily code the difference between rotation of the monkey and rotation of the visual field. But during the constant speed phase, rotation of the monkey in the light and the rotation of the cylinder by itself produced the same firing frequency in these six neurons. These neurons could code rotation in the dark, of course, because their firing rate drops off considerably during this manipulation. But the monkey may have some difficulty telling the difference between its own rotation and rotation of the visual field, when the rotation speed is held constant.

The monkey's nervous system may have other ways of reducing this ambiguity of course. Also, it's difficult to imagine that this situation would pose any problems for an animal because constant speed would not be maintained for very long. Nevertheless, one of your authors is reminded of a pleasant experience during childhood which might represent an illusion produced by this kind of ambiguity. If you lie down on one of those small playground merry-go-rounds while it is rotating, with your head in the middle, you will at first be fully aware that the contraption is rotating. But sometimes, if you watch the sky, the sensation will completely change. It seems just as if the sky were rotating, rather than you and the merry-go-round.

This concludes our discussion of the vestibular system, and indeed of all the sensory systems. The last few paragraphs are particularly good to end with because they provide a glimpse of how the brain is integrating the bombardment of sensory information which is always present. Right now you may be looking at this book, drinking a Coke, listening to the radio, and even activating your vestibular system (by leaning on your elbow and suddenly falling as you nod off) all at the same time. We may not know too much about how this integrating is done at the moment, but by analyzing each sensation separately, seeing what each one can do, and what it cannot do, we are slowly putting the pieces together.

---

summary
The Vestibular System

This system provides information about rotation of the head, and its sense organ is located in the inner ear. It is made up of five cavities: the *utricule* and *saccule* and the three *semicircular canals*. The hair cell receptors in the utricule and saccule detect constant speed movements of the head. The hair cells in the *ampullae* of the semicircular canals are stimulated when there is a change in velocity during head movements.

Fibers which synapse onto the hair cells proceed to the vestibular nuclei in the medulla or to the cerebellum. At the vestibular nuclei, they synapse and second-order afferents go to the spinal cord and to motor nuclei which control eye movements. Projections also go to the thalamus and to the cortex.

Usually first-order afferent fibers increase their firing rate to rotations in one direction and decrease it to rotations in the other direction. But vestibular neurons throughout the pathway often respond to stimulation in other sensory modalities as well. For example, vestibular thalamic neurons respond to somatosensory stimulation, and even neurons in the vestibular nuclei are not specifically sensitive to head rotation. They also respond to gross movement in the visual field. The information coded by vestibular neurons is usually converged with information from other sensory pathways.

KEY TERMS

skin senses
kinesthetic system
vestibular system
epidermis
dermis
glabrous skin
free nerve endings
Pacinian corpuscle
Krause end-bulb
Merkel cell
Ruffini ending
rapidly adapting mechanoreceptor
dermatome
lemniscal pathway
extra lemniscal pathways
dorsal columns
dorsal column nucleus
medial lemniscus
somatosensory cortex
spinothalamic tract
dorsal horn
trigeminal nerve
facial nerve
vagus nerve
posterior nuclear group
adaptation

flutter-vibration
cold fibers
warm fibers
nociceptors
A-delta fibers
C fibers
Class 1 cells
Class 2 cells
gate control theory
nucleus gigantocellularis
central gray
nucleus raphe magnus
naloxone
enkephalins
neuromodulator
proprioceptive
joint receptors
phase-locking
saccule
utricule
semicircular canals
ampullae
hair cells
otoconia
vestibular ganglion
vestibular nuclei

SUGGESTED READINGS

Messing, R. B., and Lytle, L. D. (1977). Serotonin-containing neurons: their possible role in pain and analgesia. *Pain 4*, 1–21.

Snyder, S. H. (1977). Opiate receptors and internal opiates. *Scientific American* **236**, 44–56.

Wall, P. D. (1975). The somatosensory system. In: *Handbook of Psychobiology* (Gazzaniga, M. S., and Blakemore, C., eds.), Academic Press, New York, pp. 373–393.

Uttal, W. R. (1973). *The Psychobiology of Sensory Coding.* Harper and Row, New York.

(The first two articles provide more information about pain and analgesia, while the last two references provide detail about the somatosensory system.)

9

*the
motor
system
of
the
brain*

introduction Professor Alf Brodal, an internationally known neuroanatomist, suffered a cerebral stroke in 1972. Shortly after awaking one morning, he experienced an unusual dizziness, double vision, and a marked **paresis,** or weakness, of the left arm and leg. Because of his vast knowledge of the nervous system, Professor Brodal realized that his own personal observations concerning his stroke and recovery would be of importance in aiding neuroscientists to understand further the workings of the brain. He recorded these observations (Brodal, 1973) and what follows is a short excerpt from that article:

It was a striking and repeatedly made observation that the force needed to make a severely paretic muscle contract is considerable. . . . Subjectively this is experienced as a kind of mental force, a power of will. In the case of a muscle just capable of being actively moved the mental effort needed was very great. Subjectively it felt as if the muscle was unwilling to contract, and as if there was a resistance which could be overcome by very strong voluntary innervation. The greater the degree of paresis of such a muscle, the greater was the mental effort needed to make it contract and to oppose voluntarily even a very weak counter-force. . . .

This force of innervation is obviously some kind of mental energy *which cannot be quantified or defined more closely, but the result of which is seen as a contraction of the muscle(s) in question. The expenditure of this mental energy is very exhausting, a fact of some importance in physiotherapeutic treatment. . . .*

For some forty years the patient has used a bow tie almost daily and has tied it every morning. When he had to do this for the first time again after the stroke (some two months later) it was, as expected, very difficult and he had to make seven to ten attempts before he finally succeeded. The appropriate finger movements were difficult to perform with sufficient strength, speed and coordination, but it was quite obvious to the patient that the main reason for the failure was something else.

Under normal conditions the necessary numerous small delicate movements had followed each other in the proper sequence almost automatically, and the act of tying when first started had proceeded without much conscious attention. Subjectively the patient felt as if he had to stop because "his fingers did not know the next move. . . ." It was felt as if the delay in the succession of movements (due to paresis and spasticity) interrupted a chain of more or less automatic movements. Consciously directing attention to the finger movements did not improve the performance, on the contrary it made it quite impossible.

In preceding chapters we examined how information about the environment gets to the brain and is coded there; but none of this information would be of any value if the individual could not act on it. It is the movement of muscles which allows action, and the neuronal pathways which underlie this movement are the subject of this chapter. Practically all behavior, whether it is eating, making love, fighting, or learning, requires some movement of the muscles of the body; before we take up the more complicated behaviors, we should examine how some of the simpler movements are possible. Many of these movements, like tying a bow tie, seem almost automatic to a normal individual. But when parts of the brain are damaged—those parts which underlie motor activity—they become excruciatingly difficult, as they did to Professor Brodal. His unfortunate case, and others like it, remind us that the simple activities that we so often take for granted are based upon delicate and intricate activities in the nervous system—activities that are terribly vulnerable.

In this chapter, we will begin with a discussion of the muscles—what they look like, how they contract, and how they communicate with the nervous system. Then we will look at some of the *spinal reflexes*, the simplest kinds of muscular activity which can occur even in the absence of the brain.

Most motor activities, however, do require the brain, and the next sections will explore the pathways that the brain's information travels on its way to the muscles. We will also consider hypotheses about the structures in the brain which might be responsible for the initiation and control of movement.

Finally, we will look at some motor dysfunctions such as the one that Professor Brodal suffered because an understanding of these can help in determining the functions of various pathways during normal movements.

Muscle tissue is divided into two main types: **smooth muscle** and **striated muscle.** The striated type has regular transverse bands along the length of the muscle fibers, and the smooth type does not.

the muscles

Smooth muscle, such as that found in the gastrointestinal system, consists of long slender spindle-shaped cells with the nucleus located at the widest portion of the spindle. It typically appears as sheets of cells which are so closely packed that even with the light microscope it is difficult to see the individual cells. The smooth muscle looks very similar in all organs, but there are differences depending upon the function of the muscle. For example, the tissue of the digestive system resembles cardiac muscle because of its rhythmic activity. All smooth muscle activity, regardless of where it is, is controlled by the autonomic nervous system.

smooth muscle

There are two types of striated muscle. One is called **skeletal muscle,** because it is found on the bones, and the second is called **cardiac muscle,** because it is in the heart. Cardiac muscle beats regularly, and is

striated muscle

under the control of the autonomic nervous system, just like the smooth muscle. The nerves which produce activity in the cardiac muscle are the **pacemakers,** which are rhythmically active, and produce the heart's contractions.

The important muscles for our discussion are the skeletal muscles, because it is their activity which underlies movement of the body and behavior. The functional unit of skeletal muscle is the **muscle fiber,** which is a long cylindrical cell with several nuclei. Figure 9.1 shows the succeeding dissections of skeletal muscle tissue. The muscle fiber is made up of many smaller **myofibrils,** and these are composed of thin **actin myofilaments** and thick **myosin myofilaments.** When muscle tissue is contracted, it is the movement of the thin actin filaments past the myosin filaments which results in the shortening of the muscle. The myosin filaments remain stationary. How that event occurs, and how it is initiated by the activity of a neuron, is the subject of the next section.

Figure 9.1
Succeeding dissections of skeletal muscle. [From Bloom and Fawcett (1968).]

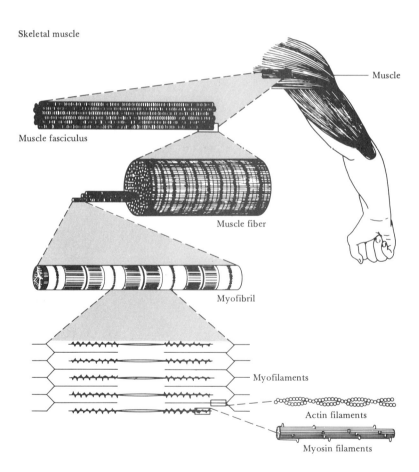

Skeletal muscle

Muscle

Muscle fasciculus

Muscle fiber

Myofibril

Myofilaments

Actin filaments

Myosin filaments

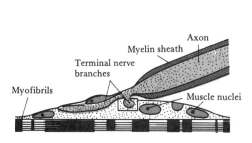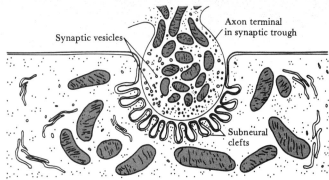

Figure 9.2
Schematic diagrams of the neuromuscular junction. [From Bloom and Fawcett (1968).]

The synaptic junction between the motor neuron and the muscle fiber is called the **motor endplate,** shown in Figure 9.2. It is a specialization of the muscle fiber that has an accumulation of nuclei. The motor axon loses its myelin sheath as it approaches the muscle fiber, and then the terminal branches occupy troughs in the endplate.

When the motor axon fires, its terminals release acetylcholine into the synaptic space. The neurotransmitter produces a large depolarization in the motor endplate, called an **endplate potential,** which is then propagated down the length of the muscle fiber as an action potential. During the action potential, the membrane of the muscle fiber becomes more permeable to many ions, including calcium (Ca^{2+}). The calcium ion plays a crucial role in producing a muscular contraction.

When calcium ions enter the fiber, they combine with a protein and then bind to the actin filaments. This allows the thin actin filaments to move past the thick myosin filaments, resulting in a contraction of the muscle. Figure 9.3 shows how these filaments move past one another

the neuromuscular junction and muscular contraction

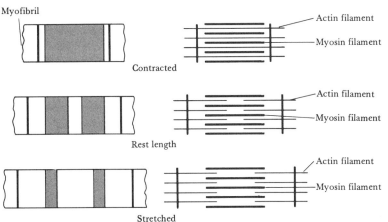

Figure 9.3
Schematic drawings of the appearance of contracted, rested, and stretched myofibril. [From Bloom and Fawcett (1968).]

and also demonstrates how the movement results in different appearances of the striated muscle during contraction, rest, and stretch. During these different states, the transverse bands on the striated muscle change width, and the changes can be explained by the movements of the actin and myosin filaments relative to one another.

Once the acetylcholine in the synaptic space is deactivated, the muscle fiber begins to relax. First the bound calcium–protein complex breaks apart and is released from the actin filaments, so they slide back to where they were. Then a **calcium pump** removes the accumulated calcium ion from the muscle fiber.

extrafusal and intrafusal muscle fibers Muscle fibers come in two different types. The **extrafusal muscle fiber** is the one we have been discussing, and is also the one that is responsible for the strong contractions of muscles. The **intrafusal muscle fiber** serves a different role. Both types are shown in Figure 9.4.

The extrafusal fibers are much more numerous and are served by the efferent **alpha motor neurons,** the ones which release acetylcholine from their terminals and trigger the muscular contractions. A single alpha motor neuron serves anywhere from a few dozen muscle fibers, in the eye muscles or fingers, to hundreds of muscle fibers in the thigh.

The intrafusal muscle fiber also contracts, but its contraction does

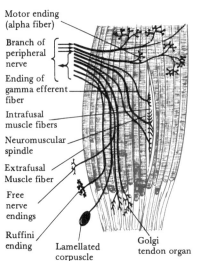

Motor ending (alpha fiber)
Branch of peripheral nerve
Ending of gamma efferent fiber
Intrafusal muscle fibers
Neuromuscular spindle
Extrafusal Muscle fiber
Free nerve endings
Ruffini ending
Lamellated corpuscle
Golgi tendon organ

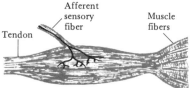

Afferent sensory fiber
Muscle fibers
Tendon

Figure 9.4
Schematic drawing of intrafusal and extrafusal muscle fibers, and associated structures. [From Gardner (1975).]

Figure 9.5
The tendon organ. [From Matthews (1974).]

not contribute to the force produced by the whole muscle. Its contraction is produced by activity in the **gamma motor neurons** which connect to the ends of the intrafusal fibers. The important function of this set of fibers is to relay information about muscular contraction back to the spinal cord. Each intrafusal fiber also has sensory endings which perform this function.

Several intrafusal fibers make up a **muscle spindle,** and it is the *sensory endings in muscles* activity of this spindle which is relayed back to the central nervous system. On the intrafusal fibers within the spindle are two types of afferent sensory endings which can relay information about both muscle length and the velocity of the change in length. Thus the spindle can provide information about both static and dynamic muscular activities.

Not only can the central nervous system make use of this information about muscle length and velocity of stretch by means of the information from the afferent sensory endings, but it can also modify the sensitivity of these afferent endings using the gamma motor neurons. Activity in these gamma neurons causes contractions in the muscle spindle, and the sensitivity of the afferent endings to stretch depends on how contracted the muscle spindle is relative to the rest of the muscle. If the muscle spindles are contracting faster than the rest of the muscle, then the afferent fibers will be very sensitive.

One of the important features of the gamma motor neuron and muscle spindle system is that activity in the muscle spindle afferents can produce an increase in activity of alpha motor neurons, and thus increase the contraction of the rest of the muscle. For example, if you contract a muscle, and then meet with resistance, the muscle spindle afferent fibers will send messages to the spinal cord, activating the alpha motor neurons, so that the muscular contraction can be increased. Activity in the gamma motor neurons can enhance the sensitivity of the muscle spindles, so that it is possible to rapidly correct the amount of muscular contraction needed. If you were walking around in a room with your eyes closed, you would need to be able to make rapid corrections of muscular contractions, just in case you walked off a step that you didn't know was there.

Apart from the sensory endings in the muscle spindles, there are also *the tendon organ* **tendon organs** which can relay afferent information about muscular activity. The tendon organ, shown in Figure 9.5, is found in the tendon, which attaches the muscle to the bone. These sensory endings have a relatively high threshold to muscular contraction, unlike the sensitive muscle spindles. When the tension on the muscle exceeds this threshold the tendon organ delivers an afferent volley of impulses which eventually reaches the spinal motor neurons. The volley has an inhibitory effect so that the muscle relaxes and the strain on the tendon organ subsides. The tendon organ thus provides a defensive mechanism to prevent damage to the muscle and is only activated when the muscle strain is fairly high.

clasp-knife reflex. An example of the activation of the tendon organ is the **clasp-knife reflex** exhibited by the decerebrate cat. When you try to bend the cat's knee, there is increasing resistance until the tendon organ is activated. Messages from this sensory ending go to the spinal cord where they synapse onto interneurons which inhibit the motor neurons and thus produce a relaxation in the muscles. At this point, the resistance suddenly disappears, and the cat's leg bends easily. The reflex is called "clasp-knife" because it resembles the closing of a pocket-knife.

Thus we can see that the activation of muscles is no simple matter. There are mechanisms which produce contraction and mechanisms which inhibit contraction. There are also ways to feed back information about the state of the muscles to the spinal cord and brain, and thus modify muscular activity. And there are also ways to prevent damage to the muscles.

---

summary
Muscles and Muscular Contraction

There are two types of muscles: *smooth* muscle which is found in the gastrointestinal system, around blood vessels, and elsewhere, and *striated muscle,* which has transverse bands, and which includes the *skeletal* muscle and the *cardiac muscle.* Skeletal muscle consists of long muscle fibers, each of which contains many smaller *myofibrils.* The myofibrils contain overlapping strands of *actin* and *myosin filaments.*

Neurons synapse upon muscle fibers at the neuromuscular junction on the *motor endplate* of the muscle fiber. When acetylocholine is released from the motor axon terminals, an *endplate potential* is produced in the motor endplate, which is propagated down the length of the muscle fiber as an action potential. The membrane of the muscle fiber becomes more permeable to calcium ions, which combine with a protein and then binds to the actin filaments. This triggers the sliding of the actin filaments past the myosin filaments—a movement which produces the contraction of the muscle.

Extrafusal muscle fibers are innervated by *alpha motor neurons;* these fibers are the ones responsible for the strong muscular contractions. *Intrafusal muscle fibers* are contained in the *muscle spindle.* The function of the spindle is to provide afferent sensory feedback about muscle length and the velocity of stretch in the muscle. The spindle also contains efferent endings called *gamma motor neurons* whose activity can indirectly modify the sensitivity of the afferent sensory endings. This arrangement permits efferent control over the kind of information about muscular activity which is relayed back to the brain. In some situations, the brain can "turn up the volume" of the information which it is receiving from the muscles.

Muscle spindles have a very low threshold to muscle stretch and thus can provide information about very minor changes in muscle length. The *tendon organs*, located in the tendon, have a much higher threshold, but fire when the muscle to which they are connected is straining heavily.

Activity in the tendon organ afferent fibers inhibits activity in the motor neurons at the spinal cord, so that the strained muscle relaxes.

Thus far we have stated that firing in the motor neurons causes contractions in the muscles, but we have not said what produces the firing. The cell bodies of these neurons are in the ventral horns, and they originate in the spinal cord. Literally hundreds, and in some cases thousands, of other cells have inputs to the motor neurons in the cord. Thus there are numerous paths by which a single motor neuron might be activated. We will discuss their activation by descending fibers from the brain in the succeeding sections. But in this section, we will examine how those neurons might be activated by pathways which begin in the sensory receptors of the body, travel to the cord, and then activate the motor neurons there. These pathways are called **reflex**, because they do not require any involvement of the brain, and can occur even in decerebrate animals. Some reflexes, even though they only involve the spinal cord, are quite complex, but we will concentrate on the simpler ones in this section.

Reflex arcs are often classified according to how many synapses occur in the path, and monosynaptic reflexes have but one synapse. A typical monosynaptic pathway is shown in Figure 9.6. The knee jerk is a good example of this kind of pathway. When the tendon of the knee is tapped, it produces a quick stretch in the muscle, and therefore produces a volley of impulses from the afferent sensory endings in the muscle spindle. This volley proceeds to the spinal cord where the afferent fibers synapse upon alpha motor neurons. The excitation of the motor neurons produces a quick contraction in the muscles of the leg, resulting in the knee jerk.

monosynaptic pathways

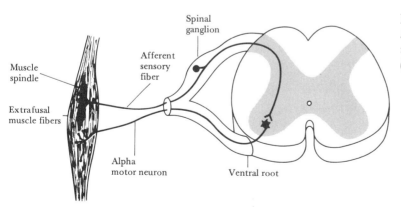

Figure 9.6
Schematic drawing of a monosynaptic reflex arc. [Adapted from Gardner (1975).]

Spinal ganglion

Afferent sensory fiber

Muscle spindle

Extrafusal muscle fibers

Alpha motor neuron

Ventral root

This is a very simplified example, because those neurons in the cord have many collaterals that branch off to affect activity in other motor neurons and in other ascending neurons. In order to jerk the leg, some muscles must contract (an event precipitated by the activation of the alpha motor neuron), but others must relax. The relaxation is produced by the inhibition of other alpha motor neurons by some of the collaterals within the cord. Nevertheless, this monosynaptic pathway is very simple compared to other events which might trigger firing in the motor neurons.

polysynaptic pathways Most reflexes involve more than two neurons, and hence more than one synapse. A disynaptic pathway, for example, involves a sensory afferent fiber, a motor neuron, and a short interneuron located within the cord. The clasp-knife reflex elicited by a large strain on the tendon organ is an example of a polysynaptic pathway with two synapses. The main neurons involved in this reflex are illustrated in Figure 9.7. When the tendon organ is stretched above its threshold, it fires a volley to the spinal cord, where its ending synapses onto the interneuron. The interneuron is activated, but it releases glycine, which presumably acts as an inhibitory transmitter substance—inhibiting the motor neuron on which it synapses. Thus the muscle fibers relax and the muscle is protected from damage.

reflex response to pain. Another example of a polysynaptic reflex is the one which occurs in response to a painful stimulus. If you burn your finger, for example, the impulses travel to the cord along the unmyelinated C fibers which mainly carry painful messages. These fibers synapse with many other neurons in the cord, some of which are interneurons. The interneurons excite motor neurons which lead back to the finger and produce contraction. This particular reflex is a very

Figure 9.7
Schematic drawing of a disynaptic pathway, involving one interneuron in the spinal cord. [Adapted from Gardner (1975).]

Ascending tract

Receptor
(eg., skin)

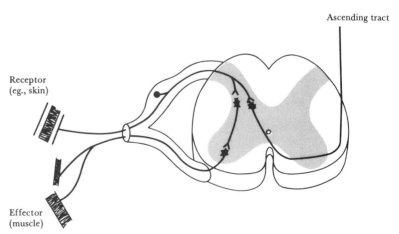

Effector
(muscle)

handy one to have because it means that the information does not have to travel all the way to the brain and back before the finger moves, only to the spinal cord. You may have noticed that your finger does move before you feel the pain.

collaterals in reflex pathways and recurrent inhibition. Again, it is important to keep in mind that the diagrams of reflex pathways are rather simplistic, and that every neuron which enters the cord has many collaterals and synapses and interacts with a great many neurons—not just the ones illustrated. Some neurons even provide input to themselves via an interneuron called the **Renshaw cell**. A collateral from an alpha motor neuron synapses with one of these Renshaw cells, and the Renshaw cell synapses with the same alpha motor neuron. The Renshaw cell is inhibitory, so it has the effect of slowing down the firing rate of the motor neuron. This phenomenon, called **recurrent inhibition**, means that when an alpha motor neuron fires, it is very soon inhibited by the Renshaw cell. This is another protective mechanism, so that a single muscle will not remain contracted for very long, and perhaps suffer damage.

If you have wondered why the doctor checked your knee jerk during a physical examination, it is because many reflexes are useful in diagnosing problems due to neurological disorders. If lower reflex arcs remain intact, then any motor problems are probably due to lesions in motor pathways in the brain, rather than in the spinal cord. This is true even if the person seems to be completely paralyzed and can initiate no motor activity on his own. *the use of reflexes in clinical diagnosis*

An examination of the reflexes can also help to pinpoint the location of a lesion in the spinal cord. For example, lesions involving a spinal nerve will result in motor and sensory losses in the area of the body served by that nerve. Any reflexes involving that body area would not be present. A lesion which is confined to the dorsal root will inhibit the transmission of sensory messages from that area of skin. Thus reflexes which are triggered by those sensory messages will not appear. But the patient will still have motor control over that area of the body because the ventral root is still intact and can still supply the area with motor messages.

Some muscular activity can occur via connections made in the spinal cord and do not involve the brain. These are called reflexes and can be either *monosynaptic pathways* or *polysynaptic*.

Monosynaptic reflexes involve only two neurons which synapse in the spinal cord. An example is the knee jerk. Information travels from the stretched muscle spindle to the spinal cord to the alpha motor neuron, which then produces contraction in the leg muscle.

One example of a polysynaptic

summary
Reflex Pathways

pathway is the *clasp-knife reflex*. When the tendon organ is activated, the information travels to an inhibitory interneuron in the cord, which inhibits the alpha motor neuron, thereby producing sudden relaxation in the muscle. Another example is the reflexive contraction of a muscle produced by a painful stimulus, which also involves an interneuron. All information traveling to and from the cord, however, is passed onto many neurons, not just one, so even the simplest reflexes involve a large number of cells. Some motor neurons even provide input to themselves via the *Renshaw*

interneuron. Since the Renshaw cell is inhibitory, it produces the phenomenon of *recurrent inhibition*, whereby the activity of an alpha motor neuron feeds back to reduce its own activity.

Reflexes are very useful in the clinical diagnosis of motor problems. For example, a lesion in a spinal nerve will produce both motor and sensory losses in one area of the body, and thus reflexes in that area will be lost. But if the spinal cord is intact, reflexes will still be intact and the problem is likely to be in higher parts of the nervous system.

efferent motor pathways

If a motor activity is not simply a reflex, it must be initiated in the brain, travel to the motor neurons, and out to the muscles. The pathways which this information travels are the subject of this section. We have already discussed the peripheral part of this pathway from the motor neuron to the muscle. This part is called the **final common pathway**, because it doesn't make any difference how those neurons are activated. If they are activated, they will produce muscular contraction. They might be activated via a reflex mechanism, or they might be activated by either the **pyramidal system** or **extrapyramidal system** which bring information from the brain.

pyramidal system

This system provides a direct path from the cortex to the brainstem and spinal cord. It consists of the descending axons of the **pyramidal tract** and the areas of cortex from which these axons arise. The system is shown in Figure 9.8.

The fibers which are shown in the figure arise from the pyramidal cells in the motor cortex, but other cortical areas, such as the premotor area, the somatosensory area, and the parietal lobe also contribute axons to the tract. From the cortex, the tract descends through the **internal capsule, basis pedunculi** in the midbrain, and the **longitudinal fascicles** of the pons. At the level of the medulla, about 80% of the fibers cross over to the other side of the brain. As the pyramidal fibers move toward the spinal cord, some fibers branch off to several of the cranial nerve motor nuclei. These fibers primarily control the activity of the face and tongue muscles.

The descending pyramidal fibers from the medulla form the **corticospinal tracts**, and are in the white matter of the cord. But as they descend to succeeding levels of the cord, some enter the gray matter to

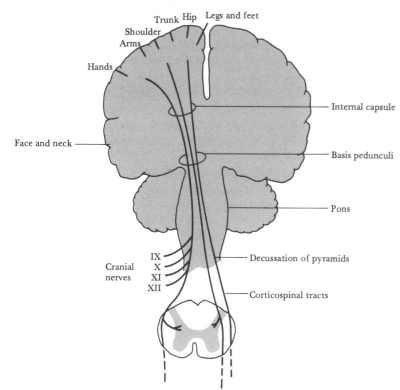

Trunk Hip Legs and feet
Shoulder
Arms
Hands
Face and neck

Internal capsule

Basis pedunculi

Pons

Cranial
nerves
IX
X
XI
XII

Decussation of pyramids

Corticospinal tracts

Figure 9.8
Schematic drawing of the pyramidal tract.

terminate on or near the spinal motor neurons. These pyramidal fibers are thought to be excitatory for the neurons on which they synapse, whether they are motor neurons or interneurons.

topographic organization. The topographic organization which was so prevalent in the sensory systems is also present in the pyramidal system. Figure 9.8 shows how the motor cortex is laid out with respect to its function. When a cell in the motor cortex is electrically stimulated, it results in a contraction of some muscle—which muscle depends on which part of the motor cortex was stimulated. As you might expect, those areas of the body which require very fine motor control, such as the mouth and hands, have the largest area of motor cortex devoted to them. This topographic organization is maintained throughout the pyramidal tract.

effects of damage in the pyramidal tract. When the pyramidal tract is sectioned at the medulla, the main impairment is a paresis of the muscles from the neck down over the contralateral half of the body. The lesion does not result in paralysis, like that which follows damage to the spinal motor neurons. However, the movement which remains lacks precision and fineness of adjustment. For example, the fine movements which are necessary to coordinate the opposing thumb and index finger are absent—this impairment was described by Professor Brodal.

This kind of paresis suggests that the spinal neurons can still be activated by descending fibers even though the pyramidal tract is sectioned, but that the control of fine movements and dexterity is now impossible. Heffner and Masterson (1975) emphasized the importance of the pyramidal system by showing a relationship between the termination locus of pyramidal fibers and the digital dexterity of 69 mammalian species. Those species whose pyramidal fibers terminated very close to motor neurons had very good digital dexterity; those species whose fibers terminated further away from the motor neurons had much less dexterity.

extrapyramidal system   The extrapyramidal, or supplementary motor system, is defined as all those nerve fibers mediating muscle activity which are not within the pyramidal system. This definition by exclusion says nothing of what is found within this system nor of the complexity of interconnections among its components. It does include cortical regions which lie both inside and outside the boundaries of the pyramidal system, and also includes a number of noncortical structures of which the basal ganglia and cerebellum are the more important. Also, the red nucleus, substantia nigra, and a number of brainstem nuclei are included.

Figure 9.9 schematizes some of the connections among the components of the extrapyramidal system. Both the cerebellum and the basal ganglia have their main output pathways directed toward the thala-

Figure 9.9
Some of the connections among the components of the extrapyramidal system.

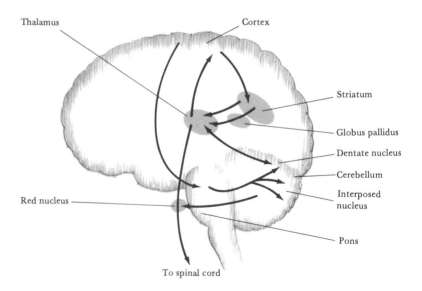

Thalamus

Cortex

Striatum

Globus pallidus

Dentate nucleus

Cerebellum

Interposed nucleus

Red nucleus

Pons

To spinal cord

mus, and fibers from the thalamus project to the cortex. Thus one major influence of both the cerebellum and the basal ganglia is upon the primary motor area of the cortex. These extrapyramidal structures have descending influences also—the cerebellum by way of the red nucleus and the basal ganglia by way of the nuclei in the midbrain tegmentum.

effects of damage to the extrapyramidal system. While damage to the pyramidal system often results in weakness of muscles and loss of fine motor control, damage to the extrapyramidal structures usually produces an abnormality of movement, rather than a reduction of movement. For example, disorders of the basal ganglia, such as the ones which are associated with Parkinson's disease and which we shall discuss again later, result in tremor and muscular rigidity. Motor dysfunctions seem more severe for slow movement rather than for fast. However, cerebellar damage produces a somewhat different picture. With a cerebellar disorder, tremor is most severe during voluntary movement and least marked when the muscles are at rest. In the next section we will see how different parts of the cerebellum are involved in motor activity, so damage to different parts is likely to produce different kinds of symptoms.

The three structures, motor cortex, basal ganglia, and cerebellum, function interdependently. The question is, How do they interact? What is the temporal order of their sequencing of motor acts? Recall the observation of Professor Brodal attempting to tie his bow tie: "his fingers did not know the next move." The automatic succession of movements has become disrupted. The way in which these brain structures interact to produce complicated sequences of movements is the subject of the next section.

The two major systems which bring information from the brain to the motor neurons in the spinal cord are the *pyramidal system* and the *extrapyramidal system.* The pyramidal system consists of the *pyramidal tract* and the areas of the cortex, particularly the motor cortex, from which the axons of the tract arise. The tract descends through the *internal capsule,* the *basis pedunculi,* and the *pons.* This system appears to control fine, dextrous movements.

The motor cortex and the pyramidal tract are arranged topographically. Areas of the body which are able to perform the finest movements, such as the lips, tongue, and fingers, have the most area of motor cortex devoted to them.

The extrapyramidal system is much more diffuse, and neurons from the motor cortex project to, and receive information from, several areas of the brain. The main structures involved in this system are the motor cortex, the basal ganglia, and the cerebellum. Damage to the extrapyramidal system often results in abnormal movements, rather than the weakness of muscles characteristic of pyramidal damage.

summary
Efferent Motor Pathways

central control of movement

We mentioned earlier that when certain areas of the motor cortex are stimulated electrically, the person will perform some limited movements. Electrical stimulation of one area, for example, might produce a movement in one of the fingers. Studies like these certainly shed some light on the brain areas involved in motor control, but they do not tell the whole story. The movements that are elicited are not finely controlled ones, and more important, they are not voluntary. The person being stimulated usually reports that they had no control over the movement and did not "will" it. In this section, we will discuss some studies that attempt to clarify the central motor control of natural movement.

Figure 9.10
A typical experimental set-up for studying single unit activity during movement. [From Evarts (1975). Reproduced by permission of the National Research Council of Canada.]

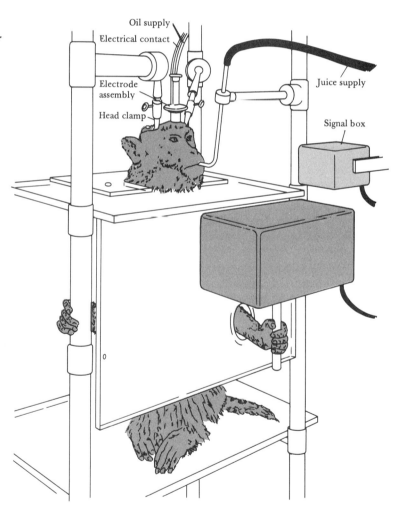

Oil supply

Electrical contact

Electrode assembly

Head clamp

Juice supply

Signal box

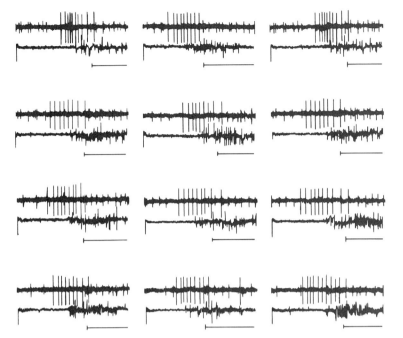

Figure 9.11
Top tracings: single unit activity in a motor cortex cell of a monkey. Bottom tracings: muscle activity. All the tracings begin when a light is flashed which signals for the monkey to move its wrist. [From Evarts (1975). Reproduced by permission of the National Research Council of Canada.]

The single unit studies that we discussed in the chapters on the sensory systems have also been applied to movement. Instead of flashing a light or sounding a noise while recording from a single cell, the stimulus is a learned movement. A typical experimental setting is shown in Figure 9.10. First, during long months of training, the monkey must be taught to perform some motor activity such as pressing a telegraph key or flexion and extension of the wrist. In the diagram, the monkey grips a vertical rod, and horizontally moves the rod either right or left by using the wrist joint. A light signal tells the monkey when to make the movement and also tells it what movement, right or left, to make. Juice is supplied as a reward when the monkey makes the correct choice. In this way, the experimenter can control the voluntary motor activity of the monkey's hand. During recording sessions the monkey's head must be held perfectly still with clasps to make sure that head movement does not dislodge the microelectrode.

Evarts (1966) performed a study like this in which the monkey was trained to press a telegraph key and release it in response to a light signal. He recorded from both single units in the motor cortex and from the muscles in the arm that was making the motor response. Figure 9.11 shows some of the responses of a single unit and the arm during 12 reaction time trials. The recording for each trial begins with the onset of the light stimulus. The results show that the activity in the

*single unit studies
in the motor cortex*

cortical neuron *precedes* the onset of the muscle response by an average of 50 msec. This result is not surprising. The motor cortex-pyramidal tract fibers are the major descending input to the spinal motor neurons. Evarts also reported that cells in the somatosensory cortex became active *after* the initiation of muscle activity. This study suggests that the sequence of information flow is from the motor cortex to the muscles to the somatosensory cortex, although there is undoubtedly information flow to and from other parts of the body and brain as well.

voluntary movement The sequence of information flow, which can partly be determined by timing studies like the one we just described, can tell us something about the areas that might initiate motor activity. The fact that the motor cortical cells fired before the motor activity does not necessarily mean that these cells initiated the movement. Judging from the wiring diagram (Figure 9.9) of the extrapyramidal system, other areas—particularly the thalamus, basal ganglia, and cerebellum—send input to the motor cortex, so it is possible that the motor cortex only fires after it receives information from other parts of the brain. Neurons in the cerebellum (Thach, 1970a,b), thalamus (Evarts, 1971), and basal ganglia (DeLong, 1974) do indeed become active *prior* to muscle activity, so it is possible that the motor cortex receives its information and instructions from other subcortical areas.

hierarchical command theory. Part of the cerebellum, called the **dentate nucleus**, sends input via the thalamus to the motor cortex, and another part, the **interposed nucleus**, receives input from the motor cortex. The **hierarchical command theory** of voluntary movement incorporates these anatomical relations by predicting that the flow of information would be as follows: first the dentate, then the motor cortex, then the interposed nucleus, and finally muscular activity. Thach (1978) made recordings from these four places during wrist movements of a monkey, using an experimental set-up similar to the one in Figure 9.10. Figure 9.12 shows when neurons in each area changed their firing rates in relation to the onset of motor activity.

On the average, most of the neurons in the dentate changed their firing rates first, followed by changes in the motor cortex, the interposed nucleus, and finally muscles. But there is also much overlap, particularly between the firing of the dentate and motor cortex neurons. In general, this study supports the hierarchical command theory, and it also illustrates that the search for timed sequences can be something like the problem of the chicken and the egg. But the question "Which came first?" is an intriguing one because it may lead to finding out how voluntary movements are first initiated. Once they are initiated, the pathway from motor cortex to basal ganglia, interposed cere-

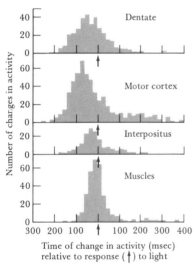

Figure 9.12
The relationship between changes in the activity of single units in the dentate, motor cortex, and interpositus, and the muscular response in a monkey's wrist to a light signal. The last graph shows when the muscular activity began relative to the light signal. [From Thach (1978).]

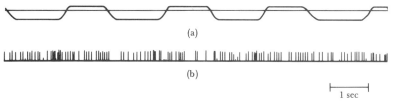

(a)

(b)

|—————| 1 sec

Figure 9.13
Responses of a single motor cortex cell during extension (top trace goes up) and flexion (top trace goes down) of the monkey's wrist. [From Schmidt et al. (1974).]

bellar nucleus, and finally the muscles is probably one way in which they are carried out.

anticipation of wrist movement. One way to get at the problem of what brain structures initiate movement is to use the idea of "set" or anticipation. Schmidt *et al.* (1974) trained monkeys to move a handle to one of two positions which required either flexion or extension of the wrist. The animal was supposed to alternate these responses, but it also had to hold the handle in one position for at least 500 msec before moving the handle to the other position. During this delay, the monkey was presumably anticipating the next movement. These scientists found that about 13% of the motor cortex cells they recorded from responded during this delay.

Figure 9.13 shows the responses of one such cell. This neuron increased its activity prior to an extension of the wrist (top trace) but did not show any increase prior to a flexion movement. The onset of the increased responding was about 250 msec before the muscle response, and the onset occurred before any of the pyramidal tract neurons began responding. This would suggest that these cells are "anticipating" the next movement—a wrist extension.

Thach (1978) found examples of "anticipatory neurons" in his study also. He trained the monkeys to move their wrist to three different positions, shown in Figure 9.14. The monkeys learned to move their wrist to the three different positions in the sequence ABCB-ABCBA, etc., against weights pulling in different directions. He predicted that some neurons would fire in relation to the kind of muscular activity which was necessary—either contraction of the extensor or flexor muscles. Others would fire in relation to the joint position—for example, some might fire most vigorously when the monkey's wrist was in the A position, regardless of which muscles were being used to hold it there. And he also predicted that some neurons would only change their firing rate when the direction of movement for the next move were the same, regardless of which muscles were going to be used and which joint position the wrist was in.

He found neurons in the motor cortex, the dentate nucleus, and the interposed nucleus which related to the muscle pattern required and to the joint position. He also found neurons which fired in relation to

initiation of movement

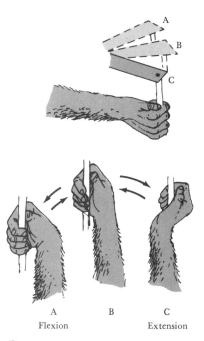

A   B   C
Flexion   Extension

Figure 9.14
Movement of a monkey's wrist during experiment described in text. [Adapted from Thach (1978).]

the direction of the next movement, but most of these were in the motor cortex or the dentate nucleus. These neurons tended to fire best when the directions of the next movement were the same, suggesting that they were anticipating the next movement. Neurons such as these are probably in the pathway that is responsible for initiating movement.

anticipation of reflex responses. Another kind of anticipatory cell in the motor cortex is one which might be able to inhibit spinal reflexes before the stimulus for the reflex occurs. Evarts and Tanji (1974) demonstrated that a tendon jerk reflex can be much reduced in size, or even eliminated, by prior instructions which change the set of the animal. They trained monkeys to grasp a handle and hold it in a certain position for 2 to 4 sec. At the end of the period, a movement of the handle would occur which would be either toward or away from the animal. But just before the handle moved, a light would come on in the signal box which would tell the animal to either push or pull the handle when it moved—red meant pull the handle (when it moved) and green meant push.

Whenever the handle moved away from the animal it should elicit a short jerk reflex in the biceps muscle of the arm holding the handle, followed by activity in the muscles which were required to perform either the push or the pull. This is a spinal reflex, one which should have occurred regardless of the animal's instructions. Figure 9.15 shows that it did not. On the left are the muscle responses during six trials in which the handle moved away, and the animal was supposed to pull the handle. The first "bleep" is the jerk reflex. Notice that it occurs every time, when the instructions were to "pull." On the right, however, are trials in which the handle moved away again, but the instructions were to "push" (a green light). In three of the trials the jerk reflex was entirely absent, and in the other three it was much reduced in size.

This study demonstrated that descending influences were able to "preset" the amplitude of the reflex. And Evarts and Tanji found cells in the motor cortex which might be doing the presetting. Some of these cortical neurons increased their activity about 200 msec following the onset of the light which gave the instructions. The time interval between the light and the movement of the handle which elicited the reflex varied between 600 and 1200 msec. This means that the motor cortex cells began firing at least 400 msec before the movement of the handle. This would be ample time for information from the motor cortex to reach the spinal cord and preset (perhaps by inhibiting) the neurons involved in the reflex.

initiation of movement and the frontal cortex. Initiation of movement is something that certainly involves higher areas of the brain, other than

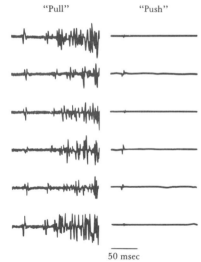

"Pull"   "Push"

50 msec

Figure 9.15

The effect of prior instructions on biceps tendon jerk. At the left are shown a series of biceps muscular responses to stretch when the prior instruction was "pull." At right are shown the responses from the same muscles to the same stretch, but with prior instructions to "push." [From Evarts and Tanji (1974).]

the motor cortex. A movement usually requires some kind of a decision, and it is unlikely that the motor cortex is making any complex decisions. One place to look for decision making for the initiation of movement is the frontal cortex.

Niki (1974a,b,c) and Niki and Watanabe (1976) have recorded single unit activity from the frontal cortex in the monkey during the performance of delayed alternation and delayed response tests. Both kinds of tests feature a temporal delay of 4 sec between the onset of the stimulus and when the animal is allowed to respond. These scientists found neurons which responded during this delay period and which showed a clear dependence on the direction of the impending response. For example, one neuron increased its activity during the delay whenever the animal was about to respond to the left side. Other neurons were active primarily before impending right-sided movements. The increase in response rate for neurons of this type occurred as much as several seconds prior to the response itself. Thus there would be plenty of time for these neurons of the frontal cortex to activate those "anticipatory" cells of the motor cortex well in advance of the actual motor response.

When areas of the motor cortex are stimulated electrically, the individual will perform some limited movement, although the movement is not voluntary. Voluntary movements, however, also involve activity in the motor cortex, activity which precedes the onset of the muscular activity. This implicates motor cortical activity in the sequence of brain events which leads to movement.

Cells in other areas of the brain, such as the thalamus, basal ganglia, and cerebellum, also show activity prior to movement. The *hierarchical command theory* predicts, based upon anatomical relations, that part of the sequence of neuronal activity which would precede a muscular contraction is cerebellar dentate nucleus, followed by motor cortical activity, followed by cerebellar interposed nucleus, and finally, muscular contraction. This sequence is generally borne out by timing the sequence of responses in neurons in these structures prior to the muscular activity.

The initiation of the hierarchical command sequence may involve "anticipatory" cells in the motor cortex and elsewhere. These cells begin firing before a movement occurs, provided the impending movement is in a particular direction. Thus they may anticipate movements and perhaps serve to program the sequence of neuronal events which will ultimately lead to the appropriate muscular activity.

Programming of the activity of the anticipatory cells may occur by means of the frontal cortex. Some cells in this brain area change their firing rate long before any movement begins, and only when the impending movement is in a specific direction.

summary
Central Control of Movement

motor dysfunctions

Motor dysfunctions in humans have provided a great deal of information about how the motor system works, and in this section we will discuss some of them. In the broadest sense, disorders of the motor system result in either some degree of paralysis or paresis, or in some type of tremor. But paralysis can range from a complete loss of movement to problems with muscle tone, and tremors can occur during directed activities or when the body is at rest. Furthermore, they might be restricted to specific muscle groups or they might occur in the whole body.

lesions in the motor pathway

We mentioned earlier that lesions in the pyramidal system usually result in some paresis and the loss of fine motor control, while lesions in the extrapyramidal system usually result in some abnormality of movement. Pyramidal lesions have different effects, however, depending upon whether they are *upper* or *lower motor lesions*.

Upper motor neuron lesions are generally associated with hemiparesis of the contralateral body part. This was a distinguishing symptom of Professor Brodal's stroke. The **lower motor lesions** usually result in a paresis or a complete paralysis of **specific muscle groups**. Muscular atrophy does not occur with the upper motor lesion because the spinal neurons are still intact, and the muscle cells receive some input from descending fibers of the extrapyramidal structures. The lower motor lesions, however, are often characterized by flaccid muscles that do atrophy. Once the spinal neurons are damaged, the muscles which they innervate have no input from any source.

cerebellar disorders

The most prominent features of disorders of the cerebellum involve difficulties in the timing and coordination of movements (described by Professor Brodal) and trouble with balance. The patient often exhibits jerky movements during some directed activity, particularly during the end of the movement. The cerebellum is intimately involved with several phases of movement control, as we discussed earlier, and may also be very important in the control of the stopping of a motor activity. The very late occurring responses of neurons in the interposed nucleus of the cerebellum may be related to the stopping, rather than starting, of some movement (Thach, 1978).

myasthenia gravis

Myasthenia gravis is characterized by fatigue of the muscular system. The essential symptom is a progressive weakness of the muscle which is marked even after very slight use (Wechsler, 1963). The patient has paresis or paralysis, but it is not accompanied by any other signs of central nervous system damage. The disease often affects the muscles of the head and neck first, although most of the body is eventually affected. Since the disease is progressive, the patient is finally bedridden and dies from exhaustion.

The cause of the disease is at the neuromuscular junction—the synapse between the motor neuron and the muscle fiber. The difficulty appears to lie with faulty acetylcholine metabolism; perhaps there is insufficient acetylcholine, or the neurotransmitter is broken down too rapidly. **Prostigmine**, a drug which inhibits the breakdown of acetylcholine, provides a marked improvement in muscle strength, so it is likely that the transmitter is broken down too fast.

Another progressive disease which begins slowly with a tremor in only one limb is **Parkinson's disease**. Over the years, the tremor spreads over the whole body. In the advanced stage, the head tends to bend forward, shoulders stoop, and the body flexes slightly at the knees, hips, neck, and elbows. Other symptoms include loss of associated movements such as swinging the arms while walking, and the loss of all facial expression. *Parkinson's disease*

Hornykiewicz (1966) reported that postmortem studies of Parkinsonian patients showed very low levels of brain dopamine which normally appears in very high concentrations in the basal ganglia. The level of **homovanillic acid**, the principle metabolite of dopamine, was only one-tenth the normal value. These findings suggested a treatment program in which patients are given the drug **L-dopa**, an immediate precursor of dopamine in the nervous system. When dopamine is injected it has no effect because it does not cross the blood-brain barrier. With the L-dopa treatment, about 80% of all patients show marked improvement, and this treatment is the most effective yet devised for Parkinson's disease patients.

The treatment is not exactly a perfect one for a number of reasons, however. For example, the dose has to be very high because the drug has to cross a number of barriers before it reaches the brain, and at each barrier, some of the L-dopa is broken down. This high dosage sometimes brings on some adverse side effects, such as rapid and unpredictable periods of involuntary movements.

In a follow-up study, Hornykiewicz (1970, Note 1) studied the brains of L-dopa-treated patients at the time of autopsy and found that their dopamine levels were only slightly higher than untreated patients. Even the treatments did not bring the dopamine up to normal levels. Thus the treated patients' brains were not accumulating dopamine, indicating that they were not storing it for some reason. Perhaps other treatments can be devised once the faulty metabolism of dopamine in these patients is better understood.

Huntington's chorea not only involves various motor abnormalities, such as involuntary movements, but also depression and mental deterioration. It is a progressive disease produced by a single dominant gene, which ultimately results in death. However, progress is being made concerning the causes of the disease and another neurotransmitter has been implicated.

Patients with this disease have abnormally low concentrations of the putative neurotransmitter GABA in substantia nigra, putamen-globus pallidus, and caudate nucleus (Perry *et al.*, 1973). This deficiency may result from a degeneration of GABA-containing neurons in these tracts. Since these tracts are involved in movement, the degeneration could account for the movement abnormalities.

recovery from neural damage The motor dysfunctions which we have discussed are of course only a few of the many that exist, but they serve to illustrate some of the things that can go wrong with the motor pathways. The difficulty may lie in a lesion produced by a wound or perhaps a stroke such as the one Professor Brodal suffered, or it may lie in some faulty brain chemistry, particularly some error in the metabolism of neurotransmitters. Some of these motor dysfunctions are not permanent—the brain can recover the functions that were lost. This chapter will conclude with a discussion of how neurons might be able to control movements even when some important pathways are damaged.

After a neurological injury, a patient is given therapy to help them recover the lost functions. Professor Brodal has some thoughts on what might be happening during this relearning phase, drawing upon the work of Raisman (1969) and Raisman and Field (1973).

When a given structure receives nerve afferents from two or more sources and one input is severed, then the remaining fibers "sprout" axon collaterals to innervate the membrane spaces left vacant by the degenerating terminals of the severed fibers. This phenomenon is called **axon sprouting**, and is diagrammed in Figure 9.16. In this example, the fiber with an inhibitory input (minus sign) is severed. The remaining excitatory fiber now sprouts a collateral which innervates the postsynaptic neuron.

In this case, two effects would result from the severing of the fiber. First, there would be a loss in the specificity of neuronal connections. Second, there would be an alteration in the delicate balance and interplay between excitatory and inhibitory influences in the system. In this case, there would be a net increase in excitation for the postsynaptic neuron, which would presumably lower the neuron's threshold for response.

As Professor Brodal comments:

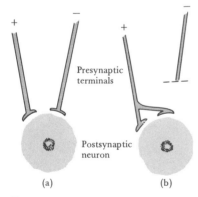

Figure 9.16
Schematic drawing of one possible mechanism (axon sprouting) underlying recovery from neural damage. (a) Normal connections. (b) What might happen if the inhibitory connection were severed.

Functionally there will presumably be confusion by establishing new patterns of neuronal connections. Even if such a mechanism were acting optimally, one could never expect complete reestablishment of the neuronal patterns which were present before, and scarcely, therefore, a complete functional recovery of the motor functions.

The way in which the nervous system can restore certain functions, which have been lost due to neurological injury is a very important question for researchers. It may be through axon collateral sprouting or perhaps other mechanisms such as redundant storage of motor control patterns. How it is accomplished, and how it might be speeded up or made to function more efficiently by physical therapies, are some of the goals sought by researchers working on the problems of the motor system.

The study of motor dysfunctions can help to shed light on the pathways and brain areas that are involved in certain types of movement. Cerebellar disorders, for example, usually produce difficulties in timing and coordination of motor sequences, particularly the stopping of these sequences. Thus this implicates the cerebellum in timing, coordination, and stopping of motor sequences.

Lesions in various parts of the motor system can tell us something about the roles of the structures involved also. Lesions in the pyramidal system usually result in paresis and loss of fine motor control, particularly with hemiparesis of the contralateral body part, while lower lesions in the spinal cord result in paralysis and muscular atrophy.

Extrapyramidal lesions usually result in some abnormality of movement, rather than paresis.

Diseases which affect motor control include *myasthenia gravis, Parkinson's disease*, and *Huntington's chorea*. These syndromes apparently have their effects by interfering with the metabolism of some neurotransmitters. Patients with myasthenia gravis, for example, have faulty metabolism of acetylcholine, the neurotransmitter which is used at the neuromuscular junction. Parkinson's disease patients have faulty metabolism of dopamine in the basal ganglia, while people with Huntington's chorea may have something wrong with the cells containing GABA, also in parts of the basal ganglia and substantia nigra.

summary
Motor Dysfunctions

---

paresis
smooth muscle
striated muscle
skeletal muscle
cardiac muscle
pacemakers
muscle fiber
myofibrils
actin myofilaments
myosin myofilaments

motor endplate
endplate potential
calcium pump
extrafusal muscle fiber
intrafusal muscle fiber
alpha motor neurons
gamma motor neurons
muscle spindle
tendon organs
clasp-knife reflex

KEY
TERMS

spinal reflex
Renshaw cell
recurrent inhibition
final common pathway
pyramidal system
extrapyramidal system
pyramidal tract
internal capsule
basis pedunculi
longitudinal fascicles
corticospinal tracts
dentate nucleus

interposed nucleus
hierarchical command theory
upper motor lesions
lower motor lesions
myasthenia gravis
prostigmine
Parkinson's disease
homovanillic acid
L-dopa
Huntington's chorea
axon sprouting

SUGGESTED READINGS

Brodal, A. (1973). Self observations and neuroanatomical considerations after a stroke. *Brain* **96,** 675–694.

Evarts, E. (1973). Brain mechanisms in movement. *Scientific American* **229,** 96–103.

Evarts, E. (1975). Changing concepts of central control of movement. *Canadian J. Physiol. Pharmacol.* **53,** 191–201.

10

emotions

REWARD AND MENTAL
ILLNESS

Schizophrenia
Depression and Manic-
Depression

SUMMARY: REWARD AND
MENTAL ILLNESS

KEY TERMS

SUGGESTED READINGS

introduction *The hair of the affrighted pedagogue rose upon his head with terror. What was to be done? To turn and fly was now too late, and besides, what chance was there of escaping ghost or goblin, if such it was, which could ride upon the wings of the wind? Summoning up, therefore, a show of courage, he demanded in stammering accents—"who are you?" He received no reply. . . . His heart began to sink within him; he endeavoured to resume his psalm tune, but his parched tongue clove to the roof of his mouth, and he could not utter a stave. . . . His terror rose to desperation; he rained a shower of kicks and blows upon Gunpowder, hoping, by a sudden movement, to give his companion the slip—but the spectre started full jump with him. Away, then, they dashed, through thick and thin; stones flying, and sparks flashing, at every bound. . . . (From* The Legend of Sleepy Hollow *by Washington Irving)*

The description of Ichabod Crane's fear as he tried to escape the headless horseman includes a number of physiological changes. In this chapter we will explore those physiological changes which occur during an emotional event, and examine how they might underlie the experience. We will see how important these changes are to the feelings of emotion which are described so vividly in much of our art and literature.

emotions and Scientists cannot study emotions directly, even though they have
emotional behavior emotions of their own. Instead, they study emotional behavior and assume that certain types of behavior are correlated with the presence of an emotion. For example, if a man has a rapidly beating heart, a snarling facial expression, and a sore foot from vigorous kicking of a garbage can, then scientists would presume that the emotion of anger is present. We could obtain further corroboration of this premise by asking the man how he feels. But even if the man states that he feels angry, we still have no direct evidence that the emotion of anger is

present. We must rely on measures of emotional behavior (including verbal and physiological measures) and hope that these correlate fairly well with the presence of the emotion.

The study of emotions in animals is also complicated by this problem. We can only speculate whether a dog behaving aggressively or affectionately is feeling some emotion. In Chapter 16, we will see that a few chimpanzees are learning American sign language, so eventually we may be able to ask them if they are feeling happy or sad. Nevertheless, even if we obtained an answer to this question, we would still be measuring emotional behavior rather than emotions.

In this chapter we will first examine the biological changes which occur during an emotional event and how these changes might result in illness if they go on for too long. Second, we will explore three theories of emotion, each of which attempts to explain how we can tell the difference between anger, fright, joy, sorrow, and the other emotions. There are many kinds of emotional behavior, but scientists have concentrated on the physiological bases to only a few. The next two sections of this chapter will examine the biological underpinnings to aggression and to reward. The final section of this chapter deals with hypotheses about the physiological problems underlying abnormal emotional behavior and psychosis.

the physiological signs of emotion

emotion and sympathetic arousal

In Chapter 4, we discussed the properties of the autonomic nervous system and mentioned its two divisions: the sympathetic and the parasympathetic. These two divisions play crucial roles in the physiological changes which occur during an emotional experience.

Figure 10.1 shows the organs which these two divisions innervate. For the most part, the parasympathetic and sympathetic divisions have opposite effects on these organs. For example, sympathetic arousal produces an increase in heart rate, and activation of the parasympathetic division produces a decrease. Working together, these two systems maintain the correct internal balance. The sympathetic division is activated when an arousing situation is encountered, and it prepares the body for some emergency action such as fighting or fleeing.

When the sympathetic system is activated, a number of physiological events take place, some of which were described by Washington Irving. Ichabod's hair stood on end, an event which scientists call **piloerection,** and which we have all observed in frightened cats if not affrighted pedagogues. His cardiovascular system showed marked changes and his mouth became dry. In addition, the activation of the sympathetic nervous system produces a number of other changes, including increased blood pressure, increased sweat gland activity, dilation of the pupils, and the shunting of blood away from the skin and

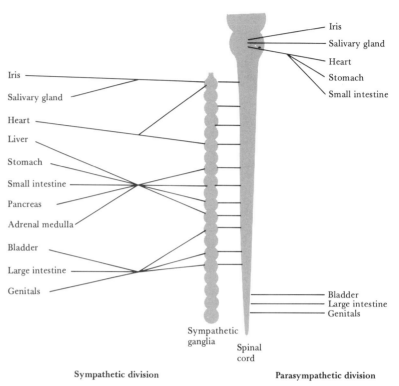

Iris
Salivary gland
Heart

Iris
Salivary gland
Heart
Liver
Stomach
Small intestine
Pancreas
Adrenal medulla
Bladder
Large intestine
Genitals

Stomach
Small intestine

Sympathetic
ganglia

Spinal
cord

Bladder
Large intestine
Genitals

Sympathetic division

Parasympathetic division

Figure 10.1
Organization of the sympathetic and parasympathetic divisions of the autonomic nervous system. (Diagram shows only one-half of each division—both divisions appear on both sides of the spinal cord.)

viscera and into the muscles, by the dilation and contraction of different blood vessels.

It is easy to see how some of these changes can prepare the body for an emergency. In fact, the constellation of changes is called the **fright–flight–fight syndrome,** because that is what it prepares the body to do. In particular, diverting blood away from the viscera and skin to the muscles would make the muscles more efficient and able to contract more strenuously. This event accounts for the expression "white with fear" and also accounts for unusual feats of strength. You may have read newspaper accounts of a frantic mother lifting the front end of her car off a child who has just been run over. Ordinarily she would not be capable of such a feat. But with the arousal of the sympathetic nervous system, and the shunting of the blood to the muscles, the mother (and in fact, all of us) are capable of such remarkable demonstrations of strength.

Irving alludes to the same phenomenon when he describes the behavior of Gunpowder, the horse:

As yet the panic of the steed had given his unskillful rider an apparent advantage in the chase. . . .

The adrenal glands, part of the endocrine system, play a critical role during an emotional experience. This pair of glands, located right above the kidneys, has two parts: an outer **adrenal cortex** and an inner **adrenal medulla.**

hormones from the adrenal medulla. As you can see in Figure 10.1, the adrenal medulla is innervated by the sympathetic nervous system. When the sympathetic system is activated, the adrenal medulla releases two hormones into the blood: epinephrine and norepinephrine. (These two substances are also called adrenaline and noradrenaline.) They mimic the effects of sympathetic activation and result in the release of energy stores and an increase in metabolism. They are chemically identical to the epinephrine and norepinephrine which act as neurotransmitters in the nervous system, but in the body, they also act as hormones.

hormones from the adrenal cortex. The adrenal cortex is activated by hormones from the pituitary gland, rather than by direct innervation from the sympathetic nervous system. When a stressful situation arises, the hypothalamus releases a substance called **corticotrophin releasing factor (CRF)** into the blood portal system that connects the hypothalamus to the pituitary. CRF causes the pituitary to release a hormone called **adrenocorticotrophic hormone (ACTH)** into the bloodstream. The ACTH then causes the adrenal cortex to release its hormones.

The hormones from the adrenal cortex are called **adrenocortical steroids,** and they are structurally related to cholesterol and to the sex hormones. The complicated arrangement by which an emotional event can trigger the release of adrenocortical steroids is diagrammed in Figure 10.2. As the adrenal cortex increases its output of adrenal hormones, the level of these hormones in the blood increases. This information feeds back to the pituitary and hypothalamus, which then shut off the production of ACTH and CRF. As the release of ACTH slows down, so does the release of adrenal hormones. Eventually, the level of circulating adrenal hormones drops back to normal.

Hormones from the adrenal cortex have wide-ranging effects on the body. In general, they also help to prepare for an emergency. They act to increase the metabolism of glucose, thereby providing additional energy. Some of them also inhibit inflammation by suppressing the formation of white blood cells. Inhibition of inflammation can be particularly important during an emotional event. It usually occurs when a small part of the body is damaged; the inflammation sets up a barricade between the toxic substance and the rest of the body and confines the irritant to a small location. But if the stress involves the whole body (as it would during psychological stress), then inflammation would be harmful rather than helpful.

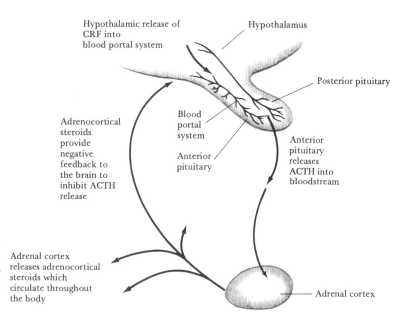

Hypothalamic release of CRF into blood portal system

Hypothalamus

Posterior pituitary

Adrenocortical steroids provide negative feedback to the brain to inhibit ACTH release

Blood portal system

Anterior pituitary

Anterior pituitary releases ACTH into bloodstream

Adrenal cortex releases adrenocortical steroids which circulate throughout the body

Adrenal cortex

Figure 10.2
Schematic diagram showing the role of the hypothalamus and the pituitary gland in the control of the release of hormones by the adrenal cortex.

Thus the physiological response during an arousing event is two-pronged: sympathetic fibers innervate and activate some organs, and the pituitary gland produces a hormonal activation of the adrenal cortex which results in the release of adrenocortical hormones.

the general adaptation syndrome
The changes which occur in the body during an emotional event are normally very adaptive. They permit unusual feats of strength, as we mentioned, and they prepare the organism for action. If these physiological changes go on for too long, because the emotional event lasts a long time, they can be very deleterious. Hans Selye (1976) has studied the effects of stress extensively and has coined the term **general adaptation syndrome (G.A.S.)** to describe the effects of long-term stress. Figure 10.3 diagrams the three main stages of this syndrome.

When a person first experiences a stressful event, whether it is the invasion of a toxic substance, or an emotional trauma, the body first displays the **alarm reaction.** During this period, the adrenals release large quantities of hormones and the sympathetic nervous system is active. This alarm reaction only lasts for a short period, and then the body enters the **resistance stage.** Adrenal hormones drop to near normal levels. If the stressful event continues, then the body will finally enter the **exhaustion stage.** Output of adrenal hormones goes back up and serious illness or death can result.

chronic stress and illness. It is clear that chronic stress can result in quite a number of seemingly unrelated illnesses. For example, Selye (1976)

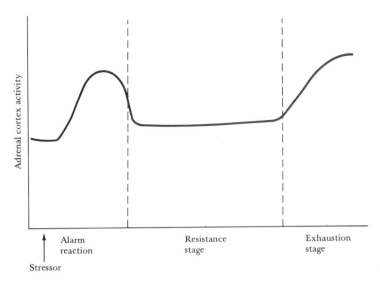

Alarm
reaction

Resistance
stage

Exhaustion
stage

Stressor

Figure 10.3
The three stages of the general adaptation syndrome.

describes the effects that increased output of adrenal hormones might have on the development of ulcers:

During World War II, veritable epidemics of "air-raid ulcers" occurred in people living in some of the heavily blitzed cities of Great Britain. Immediately after an intense bombardment, an unusual number of people would appear in hospital, with bleeding gastric or duodenal ulcers which developed virtually overnight. Many of the affected persons had not been physically hurt in any way during the attack but, of course, they suffered the great stress of extreme emotional excitement. (Selye, 1976, p. 260)

Selye's experiments showed that one reason why people developed ulcers of this kind has to do with the excessive release of adrenal hormones during stress. Normally, a person's digestive enzymes do not begin to digest the person's own stomach and intestines because this tissue is protected by an inflammatory barrier. When excessive amounts of anti-inflammatory adrenal hormones are released due to stress, the person's enzymes actually begin to irritate and digest the digestive tract.

Ulcers are not the only illnesses which can be produced or exacerbated by too much emotional strain. Diseases like hypertension (high blood pressure), colitis (an inflammatory disease of the colon), asthma, and headaches have also been related to stress.

Since so many physiological events occur during emotional excitement, it is possible to measure some of them to obtain an index of emotional excitement. For example, an experimenter can record **galvanic skin response (GSR)** to see changes in the resistance of the skin

monitoring the physiological signs of emotion

the physiological signs of emotion **247**

on the fingertips. During excitement, the sweat glands on the hands will be more active, and the electrodes can detect the changes in resistance.

Throughout history, people have often used the changes which accompany sympathetic arousal as an index of emotional excitement, particularly to detect lying. For example, the Chinese asked people who were suspected of some crime to try to swallow some rice crackers. If they could not do it in a reasonable amount of time, they were considered to be lying about their innocence. Recall that one of the effects of sympathetic arousal is a decrease in salivation, so the individual whose sympathetic system is active will have a "dry mouth" and would have difficulty swallowing the crackers. The unfortunate individual who was simply nervous because he was unjustly accused would have had little chance to pass the "test."

Modern polygraph tests take account of the fact that any person who is accused of a crime is likely to be anxious. Typically the instrument records at least three different measures of autonomic arousal, such as blood pressure, galvanic skin response, and respiration. The examiner asks several questions that are likely to produce sympathetic arousal in a truthful person, but probably not in an untruthful person who is more concerned about the questions concerning the crime.

Figure 10.4 shows part of a polygraph chart for an individual who was suspected of pickpocketing (Reid and Inbau, 1977). Questions 3

Figure 10.4
Polygraph records of a subject suspected of pickpocketing. Top traces: respiration. Bottom traces: blood pressure. The subject responded with respiration suppression and with increases in blood pressure at the relevant questions 3 and 5, which asked about the crime in question. [From Reid and Inbau (1977). Copyright © 1977, The Williams & Wilkins Co., Baltimore.]

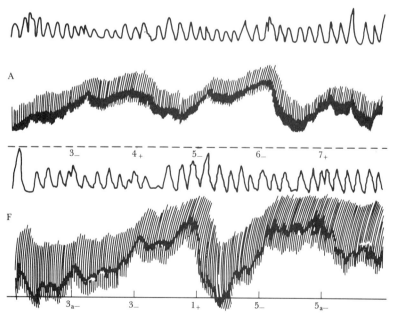

and 5 were related to the events of the pickpocketing, while the other questions were not. Notice the dramatic increase in blood pressure during and after the relevant questions, to which the subject later admitted that he lied.

Even though the polygraph technique has become more sophisticated, it is still not 100% accurate in detecting lies for a number of reasons. First, people vary a good deal in the amount of autonomic arousal they show under different circumstances. Some may show a GSR under most stressful situations, but others may show a heart rate increase sometimes, a respiration change at other times, and very little GSR changes at any time. This means that it is important to record as many physiological measures as possible in order to get an index of emotional excitement.

Second, any polygraph test relies on the basic assumption that the individual will show some autonomic arousal during lying. The instrument only records physiological changes, and if lying is not a stressful event, then there will be no changes. However, most people do find lying stressful, particularly if the stakes are high, as they are in criminal investigations. If you were simply asked to pick a number between one and five, and during the polygraph test you lied about which number you picked, you might very well show little or no change in any of the physiological measures being recorded. But if you had stolen some money, and you knew that you might go to jail if you were convicted, then the lies that you told during a test would likely result in some physiological change. Laboratory studies which try to assess the accuracy of the polygraph technique usually involve asking college students to "commit" a contrived crime and then lie about it during the polygraph test. The subjects are motivated by reward rather than by punishment, in that they are promised a monetary reward if they can beat the test. Raskin *et al.* (1978) report that the polygraph technique is about 90% accurate under these kinds of laboratory conditions.

Unfortunately, it is very difficult to determine how accurate the polygraph is in detecting lies in criminal settings because there is no sure way to find out if the decision made based on the polygraph test was accurate. For example, if the person is called "nondeceptive" and the charges are dropped, the investigators will never know whether or not the results of the test were accurate unless the crime is solved and someone else is convicted.

Traditionally, responses like heart rate, blood pressure, and GSR were not thought to be under voluntary control and this is one reason why they are so popular in polygraphy. But evidence has been accumulating that people are able to control these autonomic events at least part

controlling autonomic responses

of the time. Neal Miller (1969) found that even animals may be able to control some of these so-called involuntary responses.

instrumental conditioning of autonomic responses. Miller used a conventional instrumental conditioning technique to train rabbits to increase or decrease the blood flow in their ears. These experimenters simply provided rewarding brain stimulation (which we will discuss at greater length later in this chapter) to the rabbit every time the blood flow moved in the direction desired by the experimenters. Before long, the rabbit was showing blood flow changes of quite a significant size. The inevitable conclusion was that the rabbit had learned to control its blood pressure because it had been rewarded for doing so.

Miller used paralyzed animals during the initial studies in order to prevent the animal from using muscular movements to change blood flow. They administered the drug curare to the rabbits, which interferes with synaptic transmission at the neuromuscular junctions. The rabbits were awake but unable to control any of their skeletal muscles. They used this procedure in order to eliminate "cheating," that is, indirectly changing blood pressure by contracting muscle groups, or breathing faster. They subsequently found that it was difficult to replicate these studies with paralyzed animals, but this research led to a long series of studies in many laboratories on the control of "involuntary" responses. When the animal or human is not paralyzed, it can learn to control many of the physiological changes formerly thought to be involuntary.

biofeedback. The training technique which is used for humans is called **biofeedback**, because it provides the individual with feedback about their physiological responses. For example, when an individual is learning to control their galvanic skin responses, they usually watch a meter which tells them when they are making some response. No external reward is required. (Apparently humans consider the achievement of control to be reward enough.) The technique of biofeedback holds much promise for individuals who have tension headaches, high blood pressure, or other illnesses which may be partly due to overactivation of the sympathetic nervous system.

theories of emotion Many theorists have tried to explain why we feel a particular emotion. Some of these theories emphasize the physiological changes which occur during an emotional experience, and others emphasize changes which are presumed to occur in the brain. In this section, we will discuss the three most prominent theories.

James–Lange theory of emotion. William James, the famous American psychologist, and Carl Lange, a Danish physiologist, proposed that the physiological events which accompany an emotion *are* the emotion. If you hear a strange noise in your bedroom at night, your hands get clammy, your heart starts to race, and your blood pressure goes up. These and the other physiological events, according to the **James–Lange theory**, are the emotion of fear. Your heart does not start to race because you are afraid. You are afraid because your heart started to race. This theory equates the changes which occur in the body with the emotion.

Support for this theory comes from studies of quadriplegic and paraplegic individuals who receive little or no neural information from their bodies because their spinal cord is damaged (Hohmann, 1966). These patients reported that they felt less emotional than they used to, before the injury. This was particularly true of those patients whose spinal cord was damaged at higher levels, meaning that they received the least information from their body, compared to people with spinal damage at lower levels.

Figure 10.5 shows the change in the reported emotionality of these patients. Hohmann asked the patients to recall an emotional experience which occurred before the injury and to compare the intensity of the emotion. A score of zero meant that the emotion was just as intense as before the injury; a positive score meant that it was more intense; and a negative score meant that it was less intense. The labels on the horizontal axis represent the different groups of patients, each of which had a lesion which was at a different level. S1–3 for example, means that the spinal injury was very low, and the patient still received quite a bit of neural information from the body. C2–7 represents a group of patients with high lesions, who received little or no information from their bodily organs.

Notice that for both of the emotions of fear and anger, patients with lower injuries showed little change in reported emotional intensity. For successively higher injuries, the patients reported that the intensity of the emotions was less after the injury. Some of these patients described their emotions as rather "cold" or "mental" after the spinal damage:

Seems I get thinking mad, not shaking mad, and that's a lot different. I say I am afraid, like when I'm going into a real stiff exam at school, but I don't really feel afraid, not all tense and shaky, with that hollow feeling in my stomach, like I used to. (Hohmann, 1962, Note 2, cited in Schachter, 1971)

This study suggests that the peripheral events which accompany emotion are critically important in the perception of the emotion, as

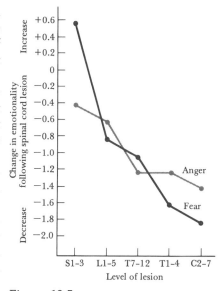

Figure 10.5
Changes in emotionality in patients with spinal cord damage at varying levels. [From Schachter (1971).]

the James–Lange theory suggests. However, this theory has some major flaws which were pointed out by Cannon (1927, 1929).

Cannon's theory of emotions. Cannon objected to the James–Lange theory on a number of grounds. For example, he pointed to the fact that people whose viscera were surgically separated from their central nervous system report at least some kinds of emotional experience. He also criticized the theory on the grounds that fairly similar physiological changes occur regardless of which emotion the individual is experiencing. For instance, someone who is angry and someone who is afraid will exhibit rapid heart rate, increased blood pressure, increased galvanic skin response, and many other similar physiological changes. This particular criticism is as valid now as it was in 1927. It is very difficult to tell what emotion an individual is experiencing by recording physiological changes. It is only clear that they are experiencing some emotion when their sympathetic system is aroused.

Cannon suggested that the experience of an emotion originates in the brain rather than in the viscera. He proposed that there are neural circuits which underlie various emotions in lower brain areas, and that these circuits activate the cortex and the viscera during the event. This theory depends more upon central events rather than peripheral ones to explain the experience of emotion.

As we shall see later in this chapter, certain emotions do indeed have underlying neural circuits in the brain. Manipulations of these circuits, such as by lesion or by drugs, can have drastic effects on emotional behavior.

cognitive–physiological theory of emotion. Stanley Schachter (1971) proposes that the experience of an emotion cannot be explained simply by the peripheral events which occur in the viscera. Nor can it be explained by the neural changes which accompany it in the brain. His theory of emotion hypothesizes that an emotional experience certainly includes the physiological changes induced by the sympathetic nervous system—but these changes are only part of the experience. The other part is a cognitive component that allows for the effects of the individual's interpretation of the situation.

Suppose a man is walking down a dark alley, and a mugger with a gun appears from the shadows. This event triggers sympathetic arousal. The state of arousal is then interpreted as "fear," rather than as joy, anger, or some other emotion, because the man's knowledge about dark alleys, guns, and muggers offers situational cues which direct the labeling of the arousal.

Schachter and Singer (1962) performed a very inventive study which explored the relationship between the physiological changes associated with sympathetic arousal and the person's cognitions about the situation during which the arousal occurs. They made use of the fact that the drug epinephrine has many of the same effects on bodily organs as the epinephrine which is released by the adrenal medulla during emotional excitement. The subject were told that they would all be given an injection of some fictitious drug which was being tested for its effects on vision. In reality, some of the subjects were given an injection of epinephrine, while the rest were given saline as a placebo.

In order to manipulate the subjects' ideas about what was producing the physiological arousal, the experimenters told the epinephrine injected subjects either that the drug had no side effects (epinephrine-ignorant group), that it had side effects which produced hand shaking, pounding of the heart, and a flushed face (epinephrine-informed group), or that it produced itching, numbness, and a slight headache (epinephrine-misinformed group). The subjects that received the placebo injection were told nothing about side effects. These instructions were designed to provide the correctly informed subjects with an appropriate explanation about what they would be feeling. The uninformed and misinformed subjects would have no explanation for their bodily feelings, and thus should tend to interpret their arousal in terms of the situation into which the experimenters placed them.

After the injections, all of the subjects were told that they had to wait a few minutes before taking the fictitious vision test. The experimenters then placed them into one of two different situations in order to "wait": one situation encouraged an "angry" emotion, and the other encouraged "euphoria." In the euphoria situation, the subject was placed in a room with a stooge who laughed a great deal, flew paper airplanes, and occasionally asked the subject to join in the euphoric behavior. Subjects who were exposed to the "anger" situation were asked to fill out an infuriatingly personal questionnaire that asked questions like "With how many men (other than your father) has your mother had extramarital relationships? 4 and under_____; 5–9_____; 10 and over_____." A stooge was also in the same room with the subject in the "anger" condition, and the stooge eventually showed irritation, ripped up the questionnaire, and stomped out.

Table 10.1 presents some of the results from this study. Notice that the epinephrine-informed group showed the lowest amount of activity and euphoric behavior, presumably because they had a valid explanation for their physiological arousal. The epinephrine-ignorant and epinephrine-misinformed groups showed the highest scores on this index of euphoric behavior, presumably because they felt arousal and attributed it to the "euphoric" situation. The experimenters saw the same pattern of results for the subjects who were placed into the "anger" situation. Those subjects with no rational explanation for their arousal level showed the most "angry" behavior, and also reported feeling angrier.

Table 10.1

Behavioral indications of emotional state in the euphoria and anger conditions[a]

Euphoria conditions			
Condition	N	Activity index	Mean number of acts initiated
Epinephrine-informed	25	12.72	0.20
Epinephrine-ignorant	25	18.28	0.56
Epinephrine-misinformed	25	22.56	0.84
Placebo	26	16.0	0.54

Anger conditions		
Condition	N	Anger index[b]
Epinephrine-informed	22	−0.18
Epinephrine-ignorant	23	+2.28
Placebo	22	+0.79

[a] From Schachter (1971).
[b] Positive scores indicate more angry behavior.

This study rather cleverly demonstrated that the experience of an emotion has both a physiological component and a cognitive component. An individual's emotion is based partly on the physiological changes which accompany sympathetic arousal and partly on the context of the situation. This cognitive component is also based upon neural events, of course, but the neural events are not likely to be simple circuits in lower parts of the brain. The lower neural circuits are certainly involved, but the cognitive component must also involve memories of past experiences and expectations, events about which we know very little.

---

summary
The Physiological Signs of Emotion

The internal balance of the body is partly maintained by the actions of the two divisions of the autonomic nervous system: the sympathetic and parasympathetic. The sympathetic nervous system becomes active during an emotional experience, producing such effects as increased heart rate and blood pressure, increased activity of the sweat glands, and a diversion of blood from the skin and viscera to the muscles. These effects prepare the body for an emergency, and the constellation of physiological changes is called the *fright–flight–fight syndrome*. The parasympathetic division innervates many of the same bodily organs and has mainly opposite effects. Once the stressful event is gone, the parasympathetic division serves to restore the body's internal balance.

The sympathetic division also innervates the inner part of the adrenal gland called the *adrenal*

electrical stimulation of the hypothalamus and found that 14 of their 15 cats attacked a rat during the stimulation. This very reliable attacking behavior may not seem too surprising in a cat until you realize that the vast majority of laboratory-reared cats do *not* attack rats spontaneously. The attack response was clearly controlled by the stimulation since it stopped abruptly whenever the electricity was turned off.

different neural substrates for fear-induced and predatory aggression. The cats in this study exhibited two different kinds of attack when they were being stimulated. One kind was called affective attack, which corresponds most closely to Moyer's fear-induced aggression. The cat would show a marked activation of sympathetic arousal responses, including piloerection, hissing and snarling, and deep breathing. Affective attack would often culminate with the cat springing on the rat with a high-pitched scream, and tearing at the rat with its claws.

The second form of attack behavior which they observed was called a stalking attack. This type had all the characteristics of a predator stalking its prey. The cat moved swiftly with its nose low to the ground and back arched. It went directly to the rat, and bit enthusiastically at its head and neck. Most of the sympathetic arousal signs seen in the affective attack were absent. For example, hissing and snarling were typically absent from this stalking form of attack.

Wasman and Flynn (1962) found that the areas in the hypothalamus which elicited the two kinds of attacks were for the most part different, suggesting that these two types of aggression are not mediated by the same pathways. Points which, when stimulated, elicited pure affective attack were typically more medial than the placements from which stalking was elicited, although some points elicited components of both types of attack. Kaada (1967) suggested that the hypothalamus is organized topographically for at least three different forms of aggression: stalking attack, affective attack, and flight responses. All of these responses fall under the term **agonistic behavior**, which includes fleeing and fear responses as well as fighting. Figure 10.6 shows the hypothalamic regions from which the various classes of agonistic behavior can be evoked. Predatory or stalking attack can be elicited primarily from the lateral hypothalamic area, affective attack and defensive reactions, which occur when there is no prey available, can be evoked from the medial areas, and flight responses can be evoked from the dorsal region. This topographic organization for various agonistic behaviors appears to be essentially the same for a number of animal species, such as the oppossum (Roberts *et al.*, 1967) and monkey (Delgado, 1969; Robinson *et al.*, 1969).

The fact that brain stimulation in a particular area of the hypothalamus can elicit agonistic responses does not tell us much about the role of that brain area in the response. That brain area might be responsible for organizing the motor sequences or for initiating activity in

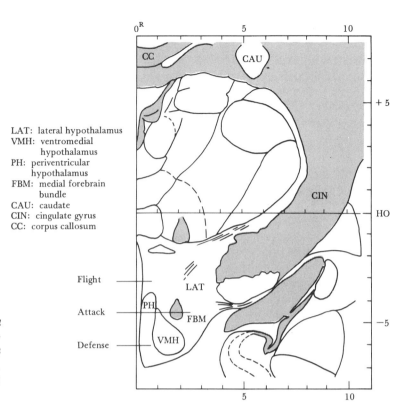

LAT: lateral hypothalamus
VMH: ventromedial
        hypothalamus
PH: periventricular
        hypothalamus
FBM: medial forebrain
        bundle
CAU: caudate
CIN: cingulate gyrus
CC: corpus callosum

Flight

Attack

Defense

Figure 10.6
Coronal section of the cat's brain showing points from which electrical stimulation elicits various classes of agonistic behavior. [From Jasper and Ajmone-Marsan (1961).]

other brain areas responsible for the organization of aggressive motor sequences. The stimulated area might also be involved in motivational components of aggression, rather than the actual motor sequences. To determine more precisely the role of these hypothalamic areas in the control of aggression, it is necessary to perform other types of studies. The next section explores some of the lesion experiments which have focused on aggressive behavior.

hypothalamic lesions and aggression
If stimulation of the hypothalamus produces aggression, one might expect lesions of the hypothalamus to reduce aggression; but this is not the case. In an early study by Wheatley (1944), discrete lesions of the medial and dorsal areas of the hypothalamus were lesioned, and the cats became extremely savage. These are the two areas now regarded as involved in defense and flight reactions, so the predatory attack region was left intact. One possible explanation for the increased aggressiveness is that the defensive regions of the hypothalamus normally act to inhibit the lateral attack regions. With the medial area removed, the lateral attack region went unchecked, resulting in

biting and clawing. It is clear that the medial and lateral areas of the hypothalamus are interdependent.

The medial and lateral areas of the hypothalamus are also intimately involved in the regulation of food intake, as we shall see in Chapter 11. Lesions in the ventromedial areas produce increased eating, to the point of obesity, while lesions in the lateral hypothalamic area produce a complete disregard for food. Lesions in the ventromedial areas may thus also destroy inhibitory input to the lateral areas, thus producing excessive activity in that part of the brain—and hence too much eating.

The fact that the same two areas of the brain are involved in both eating and predatory attack, and also the fact that the medial area seems to inhibit the lateral area for both types of behaviors, suggests that eating and attack behaviors are complementary. This is hardly a startling conclusion, since a cat normally hunts to eat. Although the neural circuits underlying the two behaviors overlap, they are probably not identical, since cats which attack rats in response to electrical stimulation usually do not eat their prey (Hutchinson and Renfrew, 1966).

Although the hypothalamus has received the most attention in the study of aggressive behavior, it is not the only structure involved. In fact, some forms of aggression can occur even when the hypothalamus has been surgically "isolated" from most of the rest of the brain. Ellison and Flynn (1968) disconnected the hypothalamus from its surrounding brain structures, except for its connection to the pituitary gland, with a specially designed set of surgical knives. These cats still showed predatory attack if they had done so before surgery, and midbrain electrical stimulation still was capable of producing various forms of aggression, although higher electrical currents were required. Their attacks were not quite so savage as before the surgery, but it is clear from this study that hypothalamic connections are not absolutely necessary for aggressive behavior to occur. They could not, therefore, be where the motor responses for aggression are organized, but must be involved in some other component of aggression, such as the initiation of the neural circuitry somewhere else in the brain, which does organize the motor responses.

A number of other areas in the brain have effects on aggressive behavior, particularly that which is elicited through hypothalamic stimulation. For example, stimulation of the ventral part of the hippocampus facilitates a predatory attack which is produced by stimulation in the hypothalamus (Siegel and Flynn, 1968). When this ventral area is lesioned, the predatory attack no longer can be elicited by hypothalamic stimulation. This suggests that the ventral region of the hippocampus has an excitatory influence on the hypothalamic mechanisms which are involved in predatory attack behavior. The thalamus, the amygdala, and certain midbrain areas are also known to be involved in various kinds of aggressive behavior in complex ways. Stimulation of some areas of the thalamus can produce predatory aggression and can also facilitate predatory aggression evoked by hypothalamic stimulation. But stimulation of other areas of the thalamus results in a complete suppression of the attack behavior which is normally elicited from hypothalamic stimulation.

The general conclusion from these lesion and electrical stimulation studies is that various kinds of aggressive behavior have different but overlapping neural circuitry underlying them. So far, it has been very difficult to delineate precisely what those neural circuitries might be. It is clear that the hypothalamus plays a critical role in most, if not all, kinds of aggressive behavior, but its activity interacts in complex ways with several other brain areas.

brain neurotransmitters and aggression Since behavior which can be called aggressive occurs in a wide variety of situations, and since many brain areas are known to be involved as a result of stimulation and lesion studies, it is likely that many transmitters are involved as well. This is what researchers have found. In this section we will examine the data for several neurotransmitters separately. For reference, Table 10.3 lists the neurotransmitters which we will discuss and a summary of their effects on the different types of aggressive behavior.

Table 10.3
Summary of neurochemical mediation of aggressive behavior

Transmitter	Changes in brain level	Behavioral concomitant
Norepinephrine	Decrease	Increase in affective or rage responses
		Inhibition of predatory aggression
Dopamine	Increase	Similar to norepinephrine but selective increase of dopamine following 6-OHDA appears to increase spontaneous aggression
Serotonin	Decrease	Increase in predatory aggression
	Increase	Blocks predatory aggression
Acetylcholine	Topical application in lateral hypothalamus	Facilitates predatory aggression

norepinephrine. A sham rage, which is related to the defensive reactions of affective attack, is associated with a drop in norepinephrine levels in the adrenergic nerve terminals (Reis and Gunne, 1965). Furthermore, the intensity of the rage is proportional to the amount of transmitter released (Reis and Fuxe, 1969), suggesting that this kind of aggression is closely related to the release of norepinephrine by the presynaptic terminals.

Norepinephrine has also been implicated in the control of shock-induced aggression. In this test for aggression, two animals are paired in a small enclosed area from which they cannot escape. The floor of the enclosure is wired so that shock can be applied to the animals' feet, and when this occurs, the animals attack each other in a series of "boxing" matches. Some studies suggest that when the level of norepinephrine goes down in the nerve terminals (when the terminal is releasing norepinephrine), the amount of shock-induced aggression goes up (Thoa *et al.,* 1972a,b).

The relationship between norepinephrine and shock-induced aggression is somewhat tenuous because the pharmacological evidence has been confusing. The drug 6-hydroxydopamine depletes both norepinephrine and dopamine. At lower doses, it depletes only the norepinephrine. At these lower doses, the drug facilitates shock-induced aggression. But other drugs which also interfere with the metabolism of norepinephrine have no effect on this kind of aggression (Goldstein, 1966). This bit of confusion will likely be resolved when more is known about all the actions of the drugs since each one is likely to have effects other than simply lowering norepinephrine levels. Pharmacological studies often result in apparently conflicting results, particularly because drugs are rarely as specific in their actions as experimenters might like.

While norepinephrine may be facilitating sham rage and possibly shock-induced aggression, there is reason to believe that it may inhibit predatory aggression. Typically, drugs which are effective in blocking mouse killing by the rat (amphetamine, for example), also facilitate the action of norepinephrine (Salama and Goldberg, 1970). It is of interest that amphetamine also decreases appetite. Perhaps the drug blocks mouse-killing because the rats aren't hungry.

dopamine. The confusion in the pharmacological studies on norepinephrine may be partly the result of the fact that most of these drugs also affect dopamine. This neurotransmitter may serve its own role in the control of aggression. Although any drug which depletes dopamine probably eventually depletes norepinephrine as well (since dopamine is a precursor for norepinephrine), there are drugs which will selectively increase the levels of dopamine after they have been lowered, without affecting norepinephrine levels. Eichelman and Thoa (1973) treated animals with 6-OHDA, the drug that depletes the levels of both neurotransmitters, and then injected either L-dopa, a precursor of dopamine, or **apomorphine**, a drug which stimulates the dopamine receptors. Both of these drugs should have the effect of reactivating the dopamine pathways without affecting the norepinephrine pathways. They found that there was an increase of a kind of aggression that they called spontaneous, which is closely related to the intermale aggression we discussed at the beginning of this section. The animals would much more readily attack one another after a period of isolation after the injections of L-dopa or apomorphine.

The spontaneous aggression looks on the surface to be very similar to shock-induced aggression also. Two animals spar and box, using species specific behavior postures. But the apomorphine injection did not facilitate any shock-induced aggression; it only increased spontaneous aggression (Thoa et al., 1972b). This would suggest that the dopamine pathways may be more specifically related to spontaneous or intermale aggression, rather than to shock-induced aggression. But the L-dopa injections increased both spontaneous aggression and shock-induced aggression as well. Perhaps L-dopa may be acting to raise norepinephrine levels in addition to dopamine levels. These pharmacological studies are often conflicting, but they are definitely pointing in the direction of different neural substrates for different types of aggression—thus confirming the results of the stimulation and lesion studies.

serotonin. The fact that stimulation and lesions in the midbrain areas have an effect on aggressive behavior led some workers to hypothesize that serotonin, which is contained in many of the fibers that pass through this brain area, may be important. But pharmacological studies have been difficult to evaluate. Raphe lesions facilitate mouse-killing behavior in rats, suggesting that depleted serotonin levels may be involved. Miczek et al. (1975) treated nonmouse killing rats with drugs which deplete serotonin (PCPA and *p*-chloroamphetamine) and compared their mouse-killing behavior and their serotonin depletion to saline-injected rats. Their results are shown in Figure 10.7. The shaded columns indicate percentage of serotonin depletion (note that the saline-injected rats had all of their serotonin intact), and the unshaded columns show the percentage of rats who showed mouse-killing after the injections (saline-injected rats showed no mouse-killing).

At first glance it might appear that the amount of serotonin depletion is related to the amount of mouse killing. But the difference in the amount of depletion between the high and low doses of PCPA is not very large, while the difference in mouse-killing behavior is. This clouds the issue somewhat, and the issue is further clouded by the fact that the high-dose PCPA mouse-killers killed their mouse in a very quick and frenzied way—different from the methodical and efficient mouse-killing behavior of most rats.

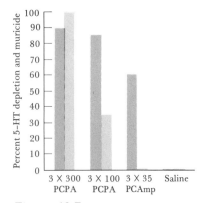

Figure 10.7
The effects of high and low doses of PCPA, p-chloroamphetamine, and saline on serotonin depletion and mouse-killing behavior in rats. [*From Miczek* et al. *(1975).*]

Many of the studies which examine the role of serotonin only test for mouse-killing, so these studies cannot tell us if serotonin pathways might be related to other kinds of aggression. The few that have tested other types of aggression lead us to believe that many forms are facilitated by serotonin depletion. For example, Miczek *et al.* (1975) found that their high-dose PCPA rats killed rat pups too; Yamamoto and Ueki (1977) found that their raphe-lesioned rats showed an increase in quite a variety of agonistic responses, ranging from mouse-killing to struggle and squeaking during capture, and flight responses.

Thus the role of serotonin is not very clear, although the evidence suggests that it may be involved in mouse-killing behavior in rats. This particular neurotransmitter is involved in other important behaviors as well, particularly sleep, as we shall see in Chapter 13.

acetylcholine. Although the research evidence related to the role of acetylcholine in aggressive behavior is not as large as the evidence about the other neurotransmitters, the techniques used to obtain the evidence are more precise. This is because researchers do not have to rely on drugs which deplete or facilitate a neurotransmitter throughout the body, such as PCPA or apomorphine. Instead, a tiny amount of cholinergic substance is applied to a particular brain region, and then the experimental animals are observed for aggressive response. This technique not only allows the researcher to learn something about the role of the neurotransmitter, but the role of the neurotransmitter in a particular brain area as well. Nothing about particular brain areas can be deduced when a drug is injected and distributed throughout the whole body.

Since electrical stimulation of the lateral hypothalamus elicits predatory aggression, the researcher can ask "Will the application of acetylcholine (or some cholinergic substance) directly to the lateral hypothalamus activate the neuronal system important for predatory attack?" This has been the approach of Bandler (1969) who found that direct stimulation of the lateral hypothalamus by **carbachol** (a cholinergic substance) facilitated predatory aggression in natural killer rats. He also showed that cholinergic stimulation in this area only facilitated aggression in natural killers—nonmouse-killers did not become killers when the carbachol was placed in the lateral hypothalamus. In this respect, cholinergic stimulation of the hypothalamus differs from electrical stimulation of the same region. Electrical stimulation of the lateral hypothalamus of the rat elicits predatory responses from nonmouse-killing rats as well as from the natural killers (King and Hoebel, 1968).

Bandler (1970) further reported that injection of a cholinesterase inhibitor, **neostigmine bromide**, facilitated predatory aggression, adding more weight to the argument that ACh is important. Neostigmine bromide inhibits the enzyme that breaks down acetylcholine, and thus there should be more neurotransmitter available at the synapse.

However, ACh synapses in the lateral hypothalamus are clearly not the only ones involved because **atropine**, a drug which blocks cholinergic synapses, only inhibits aggression when it is injected systemically—not when it is applied to the lateral hypothalamus. One of these other sites at which ACh synapses may be involved in aggression is in the thalamus, the place where direct electrical stimulation elicits predatory attack. Bandler (1971) found that application of carbachol to the thalamus facilitated attack, and application of atropine inhibited it.

Before concluding this section on the role of brain transmitters in aggression, we should point out that it is probably much too simplistic to think that a single neurotransmitter pathway may underlie a particular form of aggression. The confusion in the pharmacological studies might partly be the result of the fact that several neurotransmitters are involved in a particular form of aggression, and it is not the level of a single transmitter that is important, but the ratio between the levels of two or more. It is probably too optimistic to think that the control of many forms of aggression can be delineated by examining only one neurotransmitter at a time, so future research may have to become very sophisticated in the measurement of several neurotransmitters simultaneously, and their localization within the brain.

aggression and the human brain In a world filled with violence, it is small wonder that people might turn to neurophysiologists for some answers, rather than following the more difficult route of alleviating some of the environmental frustrations which may produce aggression. The animal studies which we have reviewed suggest that there may be some basis for believing that aggression is in part controlled by various pathways in the brain—at least in animals. The literature on brain control of aggression is extremely limited for human beings, because of the ethical problems involved in human experimentation. Nonetheless data have been collected, and in this section we will examine some of it, beginning with brain stimulation and lesion studies, and concluding with some remarks about the efficacy of psychosurgical intervention.

brain stimulation studies. Stimulation studies have mainly been conducted during operations for epilepsy, and thus the neurosurgeons have not been able to pick and choose the sites that they would like to stimulate. Most stimulation sites have been in and around the amygdala, a brain structure which can have either facilitatory or inhibitory effects on aggressive behavior in animals. It should not be surprising, then, that the results of amygdala stimulation in human beings have been contradictory.

Chapman (1958) found that some symptoms of temporal lobe epilepsy could be reproduced by electrical stimulation, but none of the patients ever showed any aggressive behavior. Kim and Umbach (1973), however, reported that amygdaloid stimulation could produce aggressive behavior in violent patients but not in the nonviolent ones. Sweet *et al.* (1969) reported a case in which stimulation of the amygdala elicited a violent attack from a patient:

Following the termination of the stimulus she relatively slowly over many seconds exhibited the progressively increasing electrical and clinical abnormalities with loss of response to the examiner as noted on the tracings, culminating in a directed attack against the wall, which she suddenly pounded furiously with her fists. . . . A similar kind of attack with the same electrical features was provoked by such stimulation of the most anterior electrode in the amygdala on the following day. This time she suddenly swung her guitar past the nose of her astonished psychiatrist, smashing the expensive instrument against the wall. . . .

Before concluding that the amygdala is an important area for the control of aggressive behavior in human beings, we should note that very few sites have been tested other than the amygdala. Valenstein (1976) points out that for patients who do exhibit aggression in response to electrical stimulation, it does not matter very much *where* in the amygdala the electrode is placed. This suggests that an individual may tend toward aggression as a "prepotent" response, and this prepotency may be a more important factor in eliciting aggression than the exact anatomical location of the electrode.

brain damage and aggression. An early case report by Alpers (1937) is in agreement with some of the results of the animal experiments in which ventromedial hypothalamic lesions resulted in rage behavior. This report describes a patient with a progressive development of uncontrollable rage episodes. At the time of the patient's death, an autopsy revealed a cyst in the wall of the third ventricle which distorted the surrounding hypothalamic tissue. A similar case of a hypothalamic tumor and rage behavior was described by Reeves and Plum (1969). But evidence from neuropathological reports is not always quite so consistent. Malamud (1967), for example, found that rage behavior could be associated with hypothalamic tumors, or amygdala tumors, or damage which involved both structures.

Some diseases, like herpes simplex or Wernicke's encephalitis, frequently result in damage to limbic structures, but aggressive behavior is rarely associated with these diseases. In summary, there are some types of pathology associated both with hypothalamic degeneration and aggression, but there can also be lesions in the hypothalamus without aggressive behavior. The control of aggressive behavior in human beings is far from clear.

psychosurgery. In spite of the confusion surrounding the brain control of aggressive behavior in human beings, some scientists have tried to alleviate uncontrollable aggression by means of psychosurgery, particularly of the temporal lobe and amygdala areas. Mark and Ervin (1970), for example, report cases in which they tried to localize the focus of what might be abnormal areas of brain tissue, by stimulating various areas and observing any aggressive behavior. When these areas were localized, they were destroyed. The results of operations like these are difficult to evaluate. Much of the time, the patients are not able to control their aggression until the amygdala nuclei in both sides of the brain have been destroyed, and there has been very little attempt to adequately assess the effects of such large lesions on behavior other than aggression.

Psychosurgery, particularly for aggressive behavior, is a very controversial topic at the moment. Some scientists claim that it is very effective and even use the technique on children, while others believe that not enough is known about the control of aggression in the human brain to resort to such an irreversible procedure, particularly when drugs are available which may alleviate the problem. Even those scientists who support the technique, however, admit that only a very small proportion of violent individuals become that way because of abnormalities in the brain. So even if psychosurgery were a valid remedy for relieving some kinds of brain damage, it would not be any panacea for violence in society.

summary
Aggression

Any organism which shows aggressive behavior usually shows more than one kind, some of which may be mediated by different neuronal substrates. The various kinds of aggression which have been studied include (1) predatory aggression, (2) fear-induced aggression, which overlaps with what some authors have called affective attack or defensive reactions (when no other animal is present), (3) irritable aggression, which overlaps with shock-induced aggression, and (4) intermale aggression, which overlaps with spontaneous aggression. Some authors have given similar types of aggression different labels, and others have listed other types, such as maternal aggression and territorial defense. The only way to tell how many neurologically separate types of aggression there actually are is to study the relationship between brain activity and aggressive responses.

Electrical stimulation of several areas of the brain, particularly the hypothalamus, can elicit different forms of aggression in animals. For example, stimulation of the lateral hypothalamus often elicits predatory aggression, stimulation of the medial areas often brings on affective attack or defensive reactions, while stimulation of the dorsal region sometimes brings on flight reactions. Lesions in the hypothalamus usually bring about an increase in aggression.

While the hypothalamus is probably the most important brain area in the control of aggressive behavior, other brain areas are involved. Both the hippocampus and the amygdala have inhibitory and excitatory actions on attack elicited by hypothalamic stimulation. It is also possible to elicit aggressive behavior by direct stimulation of midbrain areas and the thalamus.

The pathways that are involved in aggressive behavior apparently use one or more of the biogenic amines as the transmitter substance, since drugs which affect activity at these synapses also affect aggressive behavior. Sham rage (which is related to affective attack and fear-induced aggression) is associated with a drop in norepinephrine levels, while rises in the levels of this substance are related to increases in shock-induced aggression. An increase in the activity of dopamine pathways seems to be related to increases in spontaneous aggression. Serotonin levels are associated with mouse-killing by rats (a form of predatory aggression), and this kind of aggression was also facilitated by direct application of cholinergic substances to the lateral hypothalamus. These findings do not necessarily suggest that each neurochemical pathway controls a specific kind of aggression. It is likely that the pathways interact a good deal. They do suggest that different forms of aggression have at least partly different underlying neurochemical mechanisms.

The evidence for brain control of aggression in human beings is very sparse. A few neurosurgeons have found it possible to elicit violent behavior during electrical stimulation of parts of the amygdala and temporal cortex, but usually only in patients who were violent to begin with—not nonviolent individuals. The site of the electrode seems to be less important than whether the individual had shown a history of violence.

Hypothalamic tumors have often been found in patients who showed violent behavior, but they have also been found in nonviolent patients. Although some surgeons have suggested, and in fact performed, lesioning operations on the temporal lobes and amygdala to try to alleviate aggressive behavior, the confusion surrounding the brain control of aggression in human beings is such that psychosurgery of this type is questionable.

reward

The next kind of emotion we shall discuss is reward—an emotion which creates a situation that makes the animal or human perform the behaviors that led to the emotion again. Just as we had no way of telling if an animal was angered or afraid except from its agonistic behavior, we have no way of knowing when an animal feels good except from its behavior. The behavior that we use as a criterion for a rewarding experience is whether the animal or human performs the behaviors that immediately preceded the experience again. For example, if your dog finds a pat on the head rewarding, it will perform whatever behavior immediately preceded the pat on the head again.

The entire problem of the neural underpinnings of motivation and emotion is currently being rethought, and has changed dramatically during the last few years. A good deal of this rethinking has come about because of the studies on reward in the brain, particularly the ones dealing with rewarding electrical stimulation. Before we discuss more modern theories, however, we will examine the older concept, which placed very heavy emphasis on the familiar hypothalamus.

the hypothalamic drive model As we saw in the section on aggression, and as we shall see in the next chapter on hunger and thirst, different areas of the hypothalamus appear to have opposing effects on one another. For example, when lesions are placed in the ventromedial hypothalamus, obesity results. But if lesions are made in the lateral hypothalamus, the animal does not eat or drink, and if not force fed will eventually die. Studies like these led workers to believe that different parts of the hypothalamus acted like paired "centers" with opposing functions. For example, one nucleus might be a satiety center, and another might be a feeding center. Each of these centers were presumed to respond to blood glucose levels or some other index of body fuel. When the amount of body fuel fell, lateral hypothalamic neurons were activated to initiate feeding reflexes. But when the animal consumed food and blood glucose rose, the ventromedial hypothalamic neurons were excited to inhibit those in the lateral hypothalamic area.

The **hypothalamic drive model** viewed the hypothalamus as the site for drive reduction not only for eating behavior, but for other motivated behaviors as well. Research in the 1950s and 1960s lent credence to this hypothesis because it seemed that whenever a motivated behavior was mentioned, the hypothalamus soon drifted into the conversation. For example, lesions or electrical stimulation of discrete areas in the hypothalamus could affect aggressive behavior, drinking, sexual behavior, and sleep. The hypothalamus came to be thought of as a mosaic of mechanisms either exciting or inhibiting the various forms of motivated behavior and functionally organized to reduce tissue deficits.

brain self-stimulation The dramatic discovery of Olds and Milner (1954) initially supported this model of motivation. Olds and Milner were attempting to facilitate maze learning in rats with electrical stimulation of the brain, but they observed that some animals showed a tendency to return to the place in the maze where they had received the brain stimulation. Realizing the potential importance of this casual observation, these scientists placed the animal in a Skinner box and wired the electrical circuits in such a way that every bar press made by the animal delivered a brief pulse to the animal's brain; thus the rat could self-stimulate. The experimental set-up is shown in Figure 10.8.

When the electrodes were in the limbic structures, especially the hypothalamus, the animals self-stimulated with almost unbelievable persistence. An example of this is shown in Figure 10.9. These charts show typical cumulative lever-pressing records in which a chart moves across a pen recorder at a constant speed, and each time the animal presses the lever, the pen moves up one notch. When the pen reaches the top of the paper, it automatically drops back down to the bottom. Thus the slope of the lines indicates how fast the animal is lever pressing—a gentle slope indicates a slow rate, but the steep slopes in this chart (except during sleep) show that the rat is lever pressing almost constantly.

Studies which mapped the brain for the distribution of rewarding loci reported that the limbic structures yielded moderate rates of self-stimulation. The placements which typically yielded the highest rates of stimulation, and thereby thought to be the most rewarding, were along the **medial forebrain bundle** as it passed through the hypothalamus. This bundle is a complex, multisynaptic pathway which contains both ascending and descending axons, and extends from the

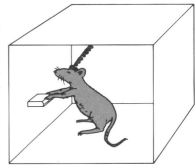

Figure 10.8
Experimental set-up for electrical self-stimulation of the brain.

48 Hours

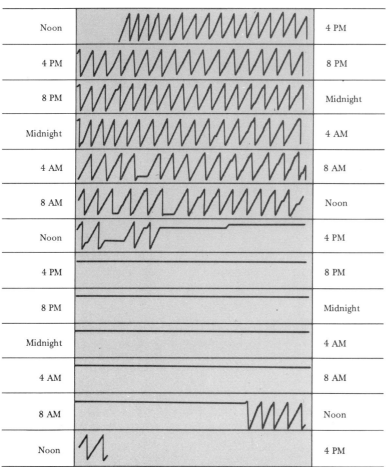

Figure 10.9
A cumulative bar-pressing record for a self-stimulating rat with an electrode in the anteroventral hypothalamus. Each sweep of the curve represents 500 responses. The rat responded almost continuously at about 2000 presses per hour for 24 hours and then slept most of the next day. [From Olds (1958). Copyright 1958 by the American Psychological Association. Reprinted by permission.]

olfactory bulbs to the mesencephalon. This pathway was viewed as the brain reward system, fitting nicely into the role the hypothalamus was supposed to play in the hypothalamic drive model.

Other placements in the brain were apparently aversive to the animal because it would learn to escape from such stimulation and would not lever press to stimulate itself. Such points, comprising a punishment pathway, typically lie medial to the rewarding loci (Olds, 1958).

comparison of brain stimulation reward and conventional rewards

Some of the earlier studies suggested that brain stimulation may have reward properties different from those of the more conventional rewards such as food or water. For example, an animal which has been taught to lever-press for food will keep pressing the lever for some time even though no food is being delivered. But animals trained to lever-press for brain stimulation stopped almost immediately once the current was turned off. Another difference was that animals trained to self-stimulate via a lever often did not go immediately back to the lever after they had been out of the box for a while, so there was a much larger decrement in performance after the long intertrial intervals. A third difference between the two kinds of rewards is that spaced trials lead to faster learning for conventional rewards, but the opposite is true for self-stimulation.

These differences between the two kinds of rewards were reconciled by a number of studies which emphasized the fact that brain stimulation reward comes immediately after a lever-press, but food pellet reward takes some time. The animal must first press the lever, then walk over to the food cup, pick it up, and eat it. Gibson *et al.* (1965) trained rats to press a lever in order to gain access to a water dipper—but when the rat licked the water dipper it received brain stimulation instead of water. These rats showed the same extinction rates as animals receiving water from the dipper, and they also maintained the lever pressing response during longer intertrial intervals. There is now general consensus that the same mechanisms underlie both kinds of reward (German and Bowden, 1974; Mogenson and Phillips, 1976).

catecholamine pathways and reward

The development of techniques which can trace and selectively destroy pathways which use the same neurotransmitters has shed new light on the problem of reward. In the process, the idea that there are "centers" in the brain which control motivated behavior has largely lost its appeal. Instead, researchers are now looking at pathways which traverse many areas of the brain. We saw this approach in the chapter on motor systems and again in the previous section on aggressive behavior. It is being applied to the study of all kinds of behaviors in physiological psychology.

The catecholamines, norepinephrine and dopamine, figure largely in the research on reward, and their pathways are shown in Figure 10.10. Panel (a) shows the ascending dopamine pathways. The cells of origin for most of the fibers lie in the substantia nigra, and their axons form the nigrostriatal pathway. This fiber system ascends within the medial forebrain bundle passing through the dorsolateral region of the hypothalamus. The fibers then distribute widely throughout the caudate and putamen.

Panel (b) shows the ascending noradrenergic pathways, whose fibers arise from a number of cell groups in the pons and brainstem. As the fibers go through the mesencephalon, they diverge, but then overlap again in the hypothalamus. The dorsal fiber bundle has its origin in the locus coeruleus and has widespread terminations in the

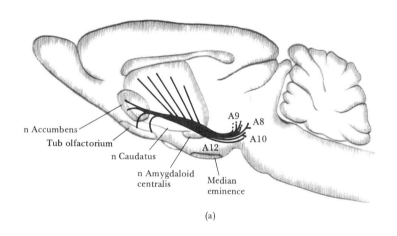

(a)

Figure 10.10
(a) The dopamine pathway of the rat brain. (b) The noradrenergic pathway of the rat brain. [From Ungerstedt (1971).]

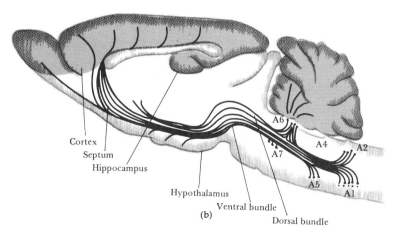

(b)

cerebral cortex and hippocampus. The ventral bundle begins in the other nuclei in the brainstem, and most of its fibers project to regions of the hypothalamus.

It is not an accident that the highest rates of self-stimulation come from electrode placements in the hypothalamic part of the medial forebrain bundle. This is the same region where the ascending catecholamine pathways are the most compact. An electrode placed in this area will activate more of these fibers than an electrode placed anywhere else. German and Bowden (1974) have reviewed the evidence that the ascending catecholamine pathways are involved in self-stimulation, and it is very convincing indeed. This evidence is summarized below.

self-stimulation sites and catecholamine fibers. We noted earlier that there are many sites which elicit self-stimulation that are outside the hypothalamus; this does not fit well with the hypothalamic drive model of self-stimulation. Some of those sites, for example, those in the locus coeruleus or the caudate putamen, are in the catecholamine pathway. Rewarding placements within these locations become readily understandable if the neural substrate for such behavior is the catecholamine systems rather than the hypothalamus. The cell bodies for the catecholamine neurons are in these structures, and almost without exception higher rates of self-stimulation were found in these nuclei of origin and in the fiber bundles rather than in the structures of termination of the catecholamine neurons. If one assumes that the reward value of the stimulation is somehow proportional to the number of cells in the system being stimulated, then higher rates of self-stimulation would be expected where the cell bodies are more compact, rather than where they diffusely terminate.

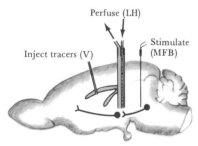

Figure 10.11
The push–pull cannula experimental set-up. [From Stein and Wise (1969). Copyright 1969 by the American Psychological Association. Reprinted by permission.]

release of catecholamine by rewarding brain stimulation. If rewarding brain stimulation depends on the excitation of catecholamine systems, then it follows that release of the transmitters should occur at the termination points of these systems. Stein and Wise (1969) used a **push–pull cannula** shown in Figure 10.11, to find out if catecholamines were being released. In this technique, a double cannula is inserted into the animal's brain in which fluid can be inserted and then removed. They introduced (pushed) fluid through one tube to bathe the brain region at its tip, and then withdrew (pulled) fluid from the other tube to analyze it for the presence of interesting neurochemicals. These authors demonstrated an increase of norepinephrine in the hypothalamus, amygdala, and hippocampus following periods of rewarding brain stimulation in the medial forebrain bundle. Thus it would appear that the release of norepinephrine is associated with self-stimulation.

chemical lesions and rewarding stimulation. Another technique which can provide still further evidence on the role of the catecholamine systems in reward is the use of 6-hydroxydopamine, which we discussed earlier in connection with aggression. This drug is taken up by catecholamine neurons and begins a degeneration process within the cells within an hour after injection (Sachs and Johnson, 1975). Stein and Wise (1971) reported a marked deficit in medial forebrain bundle self-stimulation following injections of 6-OHDA into the ventricle.

drugs which alter catecholamine transmission. Pharmacological studies have also produced a consistent series of results. Table 10.4 lists some drugs which alter transmission at the catecholamine synapses, but which do not cause any structural damage to the neurons. Those drugs which raise catecholamine levels or facilitate transmission also increase self-stimulation behavior, and those drugs which impede transmission reduce brain self-stimulation.

In summary, there is strong evidence that rewarding brain stimulation results from the excitation of the catecholamine fiber systems, so these neurons provide the physiological substrate for reward. However, it is not yet clear whether reward is mediated by noradrenergic fibers, dopamine fibers, or both at the same time.

One of the problems in trying to answer this question is that *reward—adrenergic* dopamine and norepinephrine have a common metabolic pathway, *or dopaminergic?* and hence drugs which interfere with one substance usually interfere with the other also. Furthermore, the systems are in close proximity, so traditional lesion techniques cannot differentiate between them. In any case, there is evidence that both pathways are involved.

Table 10.4

Effects of drugs that alter catecholamine levels

Drugs that lower catecholamines and reduce self-stimulation	
Drug	Mode of action
Reserpine	Depletes catecholamine stores
α-Methyl-*p*-tyrosine	Inhibits catecholamine synthesis
Drugs that raise catecholamines and increase self-stimulation	
Drug	Mode of action
Amphetamine	Potentiates the release of norepinephrine and dopamine from nerve terminals
Tranylcypromine	Blocks the action of monoamine oxidase

Stein and Wise (1971) proposed that norepinephrine is the major system underlying reward, partly because of their findings concerning the release of norepinephrine during brain stimulation, and because 6-OHDA reduces self-stimulation. They also found that **disulfiram**, a drug which inhibits dopamine-β-hyroxylase (the enzyme that converts dopamine to norepinephrine) suppressed self-stimulation behavior. Figure 10.12 shows the results from this experiment (Wise and Stein, 1969).

Panel (a) shows that self-stimulation abruptly ceased when disulfiram was injected, but was then reinstated when they injected norepinephrine. Panels (b) and (c) show that comparable injections of dopamine or serotonin failed to reinstate the self-stimulation behavior. This would suggest that norepinephrine pathways are more important than dopamine pathways for reward, but there is also evidence that dopamine pathways are involved.

Lippa *et al.* (1973) injected 6-OHDA at a dose which destroyed more noradrenergic fibers than dopaminergic fibers and found only a temporary loss of self-stimulation. After about 7 days, the self-stimulation returned. Wise and Stein only tested their animals for 6 days, so they had less opportunity to observe the recovery. Thus even with most of the norepinephrine pathways destroyed, the animals were able to return to stimulation of their own brains.

Other pharmacological studies have also implicated the dopaminergic pathways. For example, **haloperidol**, a drug which blocks dopamine receptors, reduced self-stimulation. Also rats will learn to lever press to receive a small quantity of apomorphine injected into their brains (Baxter *et al.*, 1974). This drug is considered to be a dopamine receptor stimulant, so the self-stimulation for the drug suggests that it is reinforcing.

Figure 10.12
Suppression of self-stimulation by disulfiram, and reversal of behavior suppression by intraventricular injections of 1-norepinephrine. Equivalent doses of d-norepinephrine, dopamine, or serotonin did not restore self-stimulation. [From Wise and Stein (1969). Copyright 1969 by the American Association for the Advancement of Science.]

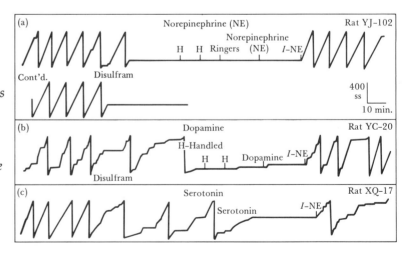

It is likely that rewarding mechanisms involve both systems. Belluzzi *et al.* (1975) have demonstrated that self-stimulation in the substantia nigra (origin of the nigrostriatal dopamine system) is dependent upon the intactness of norepinephrine fiber systems. They placed unilateral stimulating electrodes into the substantia nigra on one side of the brain, and then transected the noradrenergic fibers ventral to the structure on the same or the contralateral side of the stimulating electrode. When the norepinephrine fibers ware damaged on the same side as the stimulating electrode, self-stimulation was very much reduced. But when the norepinephrine fibers were damaged on the opposite side, self-stimulation rates were only slightly reduced, and they recovered quickly. Thus whatever rewarding effects are obtained by stimulating the dopamine pathway nearly disappear if the norepinephrine pathway is damaged.

In summary, it is clear the catecholamine fiber systems are the neural substrate for rewarding brain stimulation; it is not clear whether norepinephrine pathways, dopamine pathways, or both are involved. It is likely that both pathways act in concert to provide the neural processes for reward.

A quick glance at the catecholamine pathways in Figure 10.10 reveals that the hypothalamus is hardly the only structure involved. These systems have widespread influences throughout the brain, including the striatum and neocortex. With this in mind, it becomes less reasonable to adhere to the hypothalamic drive model, and other models for motivation need to be advanced.

brain stimulation and incentive motivation

One such model is that of **incentive motivation** (Bolles, 1972), which was developed within a learning theory context. This model emphasizes that organisms can in some sense come to expect reinforcement, and that in a learning situation, two expectancies are possible. One expectancy is that the animal learns that certain cues lead to biologically significant events, while the other is that the animal learns the consequences of its response to those biologically significant events. The catecholamine input to the striatum and cortex may provide the neural link between reward and the expectancies which occur during learning.

For example, the failure to eat or drink following lateral hypothalamic lesions or destruction of the dopamine pathways is now considered to be due to a kind of sensory neglect, wherein the animal ignores incentive stimuli which would initiate the motor responses required for feeding. It is not considered to be due to the destruction of any hypothetical feeding center. Presumably, the information about the incentive stimuli (odors, tastes, sight of food) reach the caudate and putamen via the dopamine pathways. In the previous chapter, we noted how current ideas of motor organization view the striatum as providing major input for sequencing the motor cortex. Perhaps the catecholamine fibers are also providing input to the cortex, providing the basis for the "expectancy" developed by the animal in the learning situation.

This model of course is only speculative, but it points out that the old conceptualizations of "centers" in the brain for various motivated behaviors are no longer appealing, and that a cognitive cast is now being added to the thinking of many physiological psychologists. The notion that there is a "pleasure center" in the brain which might be stimulated when we are in the doldrums is far too simplistic, but the notion of pathways which underlie many kinds of rewarding events is quite valid. In the next section, we will examine some psychoses whose etiology may involve some of the very same catecholamine pathways that mediate reward.

summary
Reward

The study of rewarding brain mechanisms began when it was discovered that an animal will learn a task in order to have certain parts of its brain stimulated by an implanted electrode. The electrode must have been exciting pathways in the brain which mediate a very pleasant emotional experience, and hence the stimulation was termed rewarding.

The most rewarding loci in the brain were mainly in the *medial forebrain bundle*, particularly as it passed through the hypothalamus. Other sites were also rewarding, particularly some in the midbrain and some in other limbic structures. Some electrode placements were clearly aversive, since the animal would learn a task to escape from stimulation. Brain stimulation appears to promote learning in exactly the same way that other kinds of reward (such as food or water) do. Thus the pathway is likely to be one that is involved in very basic reward, and is not simply some artifact of the brain stimulation laboratory.

The sites which are the most rewarding appear to be along the pathways that utilize the catecholamines, norepinephrine and dopamine. There is much evidence from pharmacological studies that the catecholamines are involved in the mediation of reward. For example, catecholamines are released in limbic structures during rewarding brain stimulation, and drugs which destroy catecholamine pathways also reduce self-stimulation by the rat. It is not clear yet whether the adrenergic synapses or the dopaminergic ones are more important, or whether both pathways are involved.

An earlier theory of motivation and emotion, the *hypothalamic drive model*, suggested that different centers in the brain, particularly in the hypothalamus, were responsible for exciting or inhibiting motivated behavior. But the studies on the catecholamine pathways indicate that many brain structures are involved, and that levels of neurochemicals (or ratios between the levels of two or more neurochemicals) along these pathways may be more important. One more recent theory of emotion and motivation suggests that the reward pathways actually provide incentive motivation to areas of the cortex. They carry information about incentive stimuli (such as the sight or odor of food) to other areas of the brain, which then organize the motor responses required for eating, or drinking, or some other motivated behavior. When these pathways are damaged or interrupted, the animal does not respond to incentive stimuli. This theory, termed *incentive motivation*, is still speculative, but it suggests that physiological psychologists are becoming more cognitive in their theorizing and are appreciating that higher organisms are not simple machines that respond to environmental events in a mechanical way. The organism also comes to expect and predict events which may lead to reward.

---

reward and mental illness

Before the 1950s the treatment of mentally ill patients largely was limited to confinement in a mental institution. These public facilities were overcrowded, suffered from lack of funding and staffing, and a patient's "treatment" consisted mainly of management, mostly because an effective treatment was nonexistent at the time. In the 1950s a series of antipsychotic drugs were developed which were very effective in relieving some of the patients' psychotic symptoms and thus allowed many of them to leave the hospital. The discovery of these drugs was something of a revolution because of the enormous impact it has had on the treatment of the mentally ill.

We do not mean to imply that these drugs cure any of the mental illnesses, but they often do relieve the symptoms which necessitated the confinement of the patient, such as severe depression, disordered thought processes, hallucinations, or withdrawal. Many people who would formerly have been confined can take their drugs and make use of outpatient clinics.

schizophrenia

The effectiveness of the antipsychotic drugs led scientists to hypothesize that these illnesses may in part be due to biochemical malfunctions in the brain. For example, drugs which relieve the symptoms of schizophrenia, which include hallucinations, blunted emotions, thought disorder, and withdrawal, generally have some effect on synaptic transmission. This had led scientists to hypothesize that something is wrong with synaptic transmission in these people. Exactly which synapses and which neurotransmitters are involved is far from clear, but the most popular hypothesis at present is the one which implicates dopamine.

the dopamine hypothesis of schizophrenia. One of the features that drugs which alleviate schizophrenic symptoms have in common is that the vast majority of them apparently decrease transmission at dopamine synapses (Carlsson, 1978). **Reserpine**, for example, is one of the earliest drugs used for the treatment of schizophrenia, and it is known to deplete monoamine stores in the brain and other tissues, including stores of dopamine. Drugs like **chlorpromazine** and **haloperidol**, which apparently block dopamine receptors, also have antipsychotic activity in schizophrenics.

Drugs which increase transmission at dopamine synapses often have the effect of increasing schizophrenic symptoms. For example, L-dopa, the immediate precursor of dopamine, induces psychotic symptoms in some patients being treated for Parkinson's disease (Goodwin and Murphy, 1974). The same drug has been reported to increase the severity of symptoms in schizophrenic patients (Barchas *et al.*, 1977).

An individual who takes a large dose of amphetamine, or one who uses the drug chronically over a long period of time, often develops **amphetamine psychosis**—a disorder that looks very much like classic paranoid schizophrenia. They rarely have the thought disorders or blunted affect of chronic schizophrenics, but since the drug users are often mistakenly diagnosed as schizophrenics, there is considerable overlap in the symptoms. Amphetamines have effects on the catecholamines; for example, they inhibit MAO (the enzyme which breaks down catecholamines intracellularly), they produce a release of catecholamines from the synapse, and they block the neuronal uptake mechanisms for the catecholamines (Patrick, 1977). All of these actions would have the effect of potentiating catecholamine (including dopamine) transmission. Amphetamines also have the peculiar effect of producing a rapid decrease in striatal dopamine synthesis, thus adding further weight to the argument that transmission at dopamine synapses is crucially important.

Most pharmacological studies have difficulty discriminating between dopamine activity and activity at other catecholamine synapses, as we have mentioned earlier. But Carlsson (1978) points out that the clinical potency of antipsychotic drugs is more closely related to their action on dopamine synapses, rather than synapses using other neurotransmitters. Nevertheless, the importance of other neurotransmitters has not been ruled out by any means.

dopamine levels in schizophrenic patients. Although the evidence that antipsychotics relieve schizophrenic symptoms because of their actions at the dopamine synapses is fairly strong, the evidence that schizophrenics have something wrong with their dopaminergic synapses is very weak. For example, Rimon *et al.* (1971) found no difference in the levels of **homovanillic acid** in the spinal fluid of schizophrenics and controls. Homovanillic acid is one of the metabolites of dopamine.

If schizophrenics have something wrong with their dopamine synapses, it might show up in autopsied brains. But with one exception the studies which have compared catecholamine enzyme levels in normal and schizophrenic brains have not found any significant differences. Wise *et al.* (1974) found that dopamine-β-hydroxylase activity (the enzyme that converts dopamine to norepinephrine) was from 30 to 50% lower in schizophrenic patients compared to controls. This is consistent with their hypothesis, which we shall discuss later in this section, that norepinephrine pathways rather than dopamine pathways are more important in the etiology of schizophrenia; but this finding has not been replicated (Wyatt *et al.*, 1975).

The failure to find any significant differences between the brains of schizophrenics and controls is frustrating but not very surprising. Many enzymes break down rapidly after death, and turnover rates may be more important than absolute levels anyway. Even when significant differences are found, the reason for the difference is always suspect because the lives of schizophrenics and normals are so different. The patients may have spent years in a hospital receiving little physical activity and huge quantities of drugs, so they are likely to differ from normals in a number of ways other than the obvious difference that they are mentally ill and the normals are not.

noradrenergic synapses and schizophrenia. Drawing upon the evidence that catecholamine fibers are the substrate for reward, and are clearly implicated in the effects of antipsychotic drugs, Stein and Wise (1971) proposed that schizophrenia might result from a progressive damage to a noradrenergic reward system in the brain. Although the dopamine hypothesis is more popular at the moment, this hypothesis certainly has validity because many of the pharmacological studies which implicate dopamine implicate the noradrenergic synapses as well.

They postulated that a series of biochemical events might lead to the gradual destruction of noradrenergic terminals in schizophrenic patients. In the normal situation, dopamine is converted to norepinephrine in the noradrenergic neuron, with the enzyme dopamine-β-hydroxylase as the catalyst. Both norepinephrine and dopamine-β-hydroxylase are released into the synaptic cleft during periods of neuronal activity. The noradrenergic neuron in the schizophrenic might be deficient in its ability to convert dopamine to norepinephrine, and thus both dopamine and norepinephrine are released. The released dopamine is converted to 6-OHDA, the drug that destroys catecholamine neurons. If this happens, the patient actually may be producing a chemical which destroys the neurons responsible for reward.

There is no clear evidence that this is happening, and the proposal has some weak points. For example, 6-OHDA, as we mentioned earlier, only produces a temporary suppression in rewarding self-stimulation, so it is not at all clear that norepinephrine pathways are the only ones involved in reward.

the development of schizophrenic symptoms. Other theories have been proposed to account for the etiology of schizophrenia. Most of the more recent ones implicate one or more of the catecholamine synapses primarily because the antipsychotic drugs act on these systems, and because these systems have been implicated in rewarding brain mechanisms. If the patient is deficient in rewarding mechanisms perhaps because of the destruction of norepinephrine pathways, then the blunted, flat affect so characteristic of schizophrenics would be understandable. If they are suffering from an increase in the activity of dopaminergic pathways, then the brain may be overactive. In this situation, the person may be overstimulated and subject to an overwhelming barrage of sensory input. Under these conditions it is possible that the person would withdraw from the overstimulation and then develop schizophrenic symptoms for protection.

Although the studies we have reviewed have certainly provided some insight into the roots of schizophrenia, they are far from conclusive. An ever present problem which plagues any studies in this area is that of diagnosis. Is schizophrenia a single, unitary disease, or is it the "garbage can" category of mental illnesses into which any mental disorder not obviously otherwise categorized is placed? If it is in fact many diseases, it is likely to have multiple causes, and thus the inconsistency and variability of patients' reactions to various drugs is quite understandable. Some patients may have no biochemical defects and their symptoms are produced by environmental stresses. Other patients may have one of several biochemical defects, some of which are produced by environmental stresses, others of which may have developed for genetic reasons. Heredity has very definitely been implicated in the etiology of schizophrenia, but no genetic pattern has emerged, and even an individual who has an identical twin diagnosed as schizophrenic may never develop the illness. It is likely that even schizophrenics who have inherited a tendency toward the disease may have inherited different biochemical errors.

In spite of the problems, during the last 25 years enormous strides have been made in the treatment of schizophrenic patients. It is likely that as subpopulations of schizophrenic patients are described and studied, we will learn much more about the roots of this illness (or illnesses).

depression and manic-depression Two other mental illnesses which have become amenable to treatment with drugs are depression and manic-depression. The drugs which alleviate symptoms for these illnesses also involve transmitter activity at the synapses. Just as in schizophrenia, there are still no clear-cut answers about the exact causes of the illnesses.

symptoms of depression and manic-depression. We all experience depression at one time or another, but it only is classified as a mental illness when the symptoms become severe and last for a long time. The individual suffering from psychotic depression has loss of motivation for living, sleep abnormalitities, loss of appetite, and often suicidal thoughts. Most of the patients are abnormally lethargic, but occasionally a depressed person will experience periods of agitation.

The persons suffering from chronic depression are called **unipolar** to distinguish their symptoms from persons who experience episodes of depression with intervals of manic behavior. This **bipolar** form of depression usually shows long periods of depression with an occasional episode of agitated, excited behavior. The two forms may have slightly different neurochemical substrates.

biogenic amine hypothesis of depression. Patients suffering from chronic depression have been treated with psychotherapy, electroconvulsive shock, and drugs, but the most effective method of treatment is usually some form of antidepressant drug which affects catecholamine transmission. The discovery and effectiveness of these antidepressants led scientists to the **biogenic amine hypothesis of depression,** which postulates that the biogenic amines (norepinephrine, dopamine, and serotonin) are involved in the disorder. In particular, an excess of catecholamines might lead to manic behavior, increased activity, and hostility, while a deficiency might produce depression and lassitude. This hypothesis fits in well with findings about the importance of the catecholamines in reward mechanisms.

evidence for the biogenic amine hypothesis. Several of the drugs which alleviate the clinical symptoms of depression also affect the catecholamines. For example, the **tricyclic antidepressant** drugs are thought to act by preventing the reuptake of the biogenic amines, thereby potentiating their activity at the synapse. Another antidepressant drug, **iproniazid,** is a potent inhibitor of monoamine oxidas (MAO) and therefore produces an increase in brain concentrations of norepinephrine and serotonin.

Reserpine, which was one of the drugs used for schizophrenia, depletes stores of biogenic amines in the brain and also produces symptoms of clinical depression in some patients receiving the drug (Berger and Barchas, 1977). Because of these findings, and particularly because some of the antidepressant drugs worked so well, scientists hypothesized that something was wrong with transmission at the biogenic amine synapses.

Unfortunately, as more drugs were tried and the hypothesis was further tested, problems arose. Many drugs affect catecholamine transmission, and when some of these were tried on depressed patients they showed no effect. Cocaine is one example: it is a potent inhibitor of neurotransmitter reuptake at the synapse, but it has no effect on the symptoms of chronic depression. **Lithium**, a drug which has multiple effects including the decrease of catecholamines at the synapse, is known to work well in manic patients. This fits well with the biogenic amine hypothesis, but the drug also alleviates depression, particularly in manic-depressive patients. The finding that it can alleviate both conditions is difficult to understand if the biogenic amine hypothesis is correct. The fact that lithium does not work very well for patients suffering from depression only suggests that the causes of manic-depression may be somewhat separate from the causes of simple depression.

Another problem with the hypothesis is that the drugs take weeks to have any effect on symptoms, but in the brain (at least of animals) they begin to affect transmitter activity within hours. Thus, although some of these drugs work extremely well, it is far from clear why they work. The biogenic amines are clearly involved, but exactly how is still debatable.

catecholamine levels in patients with depression. Studies which compare catecholamine metabolites in normals and depressive or manic-depressive patients have not been terribly rewarding. These studies usually examine metabolites in the urine, but tissues all over the body will contribute to these metabolites. It is not clear whether any differences which are found are due to differences in brain neurotransmitter activity.

Nevertheless, some promising approaches have been used. For example, several studies have examined the levels of **3-methoxy-4-hydroxyphenylglycol** (MHPG) in the urine of depressed patients (Schildkraut, 1974; Maas, 1975; Beckmann and Goodwin, 1975). MHPG is one of the metabolites of norepinephrine. Some of those patients had low levels of MHPG, while others had high levels. Interestingly, those patients with low baseline levels were later found to respond best to a drug called **imipramine,** which is a good inhibitor of noradrenergic reuptake. But those patients who had high baseline levels of the norepinephrine metabolite were found to respond better to treatment with another drug, **amitriptyline.** This drug inhibits reuptake at serotonergic synapses.

These studies are important because they demonstrate that norepinephrine levels may not be low in all depressed patients, only in some. MHPG levels in the urine may be a good predictor of whether the depression is related to lowered norepinephrine levels, and then drugs can be used which are better at affecting norepinephrine synapses. If the MHPG levels are high, it may mean that the individual's depression has little to do with activity at noradrenergic synapses, and hence a drug which affects serotonin or dopamine may be more effective. These studies also point out the importance of identifying subpopulations in a group of people who appear to have similar symptoms, but who may have different biochemical problems. This had already been done with patients who show only depression, and patients who show both depression and manic behavior. More sophisticated techniques, such as the measurement of MHPG levels in the urine, may be required to sort out the patients showing only depression.

side effects of the antipsychotic and antidepressant drugs. Many of the drugs which we have been discussing in connection with schizophrenia and depression are now widely prescribed, and some patients have been taking them for years. Some scientists say that they have been too widely prescribed, and that not enough attention has been paid to their potential side effects. The pharmacological revolution that brought about so many effective treatments for these previously intractable mental illnesses, probably also brought about an enthusiasm and an overprescribing of these drugs by many physicians. It has only been recently that some of their side effects have been noted, and physicians are likely to be less enthusiastic in the future. Table 10.5 lists

Table 10.5
Adverse effects of psychotropic drugs[a]

System	Effects	Drugs
Autonomic	Anticholinergic Dry mouth and skin Urinary retention Poor visual accommodation	Antipsychotics, tricyclics
	Excessive perspiration	Phenothiazines, tricyclics, benzodiazepines
Cardiac	ECG abnormalities and arrhythmias	Phenothiazines (esp. thioridazine), tricyclics
Cardiovascular	Hypotension	Phenothiazines, tricyclics, MAO inhibitors
	Hypertension	MAO inhibitors + adrenergic stimulators (e.g., tyramine, amphetamines, epinephrine, norepinephrine, and L-dopa)
Dermatological	Skin rash	All drugs
	Photosensitivity	Phenothiazines (esp. chlorpromazine)
	Pigmentation	Phenothiazines (esp. chlorpromazine)
Endocrinological	Amenorrhea	Antipsychotics
	Galactorrhea and gynecomastia	Antipsychotics

[a]From Sack (1977).   (continued)

Table 10.5 (Continued)

System	Effects	Drugs
Gastrointestinal	Nausea and vomiting	Antipsychotics
	Constipation	Phenothiazines and tricyclics
	Paralytic ileus	Phenothiazines + tricyclics + Antiparkinsonian agents
	Increased body weight	Antipsychotics, tricyclics
Hematological	Leukopenia and agranulocytosis	Antipsychotics
	Leukocyctosis	Lithium
Hepatic	Induction of metabolic enzymes	Barbiturates, haloperidol (possibly)
	Toxic reactions Cholestatis	Phenothiazines (esp. chlorpromazine), tricyclics
	Hepatotoxicity	MAO inihibitors
Neurological	Extrapyramidal reactions Parkinsonian syndrome Acute dystonias Akathisia	Antipsychotics
	Tardive dyskinesia	Antipsychotics
Ophthalmological	Lens Pigmentation	Phenothiazines (esp. chlorpromazine and thioridazine)
	Pigmentary Retinopathy	Thioridazine

some of the side effects which appear throughout the body of many patients treated with these drugs. The most interesting side effect for our purposes, however, is the one that deals with the motor systems.

In Chapter 9, we discussed the importance of the extrapyramidal system in the control of movement, and we also discussed how Parkinson's disease probably results from the degeneration of dopaminergic neurons in the brain pathways which control movement. It is hardly surprising, therefore, that antipsychotic drugs which also affect the dopamine synapses would produce movement disorders.

Weiss and Santelli (1978) found that primates exhibited motor disturbances after a few weeks of treatment with the antipsychotic drug haloperidol, a substance that blocks dopamine receptors and is widely prescribed for schizophrenics. After 10 weeks the monkeys began to show a wide variety of motor problems, including flailing of the arms, bizarre postures, limb tremors, and various motor abnormalities of the mouth and face. With further injections, more disturbances were seen. The monkeys showed rocking movements, vocalization, repetitive circling, and occasional periods of violent movements during which the animal crashed into the cage walls. With symptoms like these, it is easy to see why the motor disturbance side effects of the drugs were not detected earlier; they might often have been confused with the patient's own symptoms.

A wide variety of movement disorders have appeared in patients taking antipsychotic drugs, particularly a syndrome called **tardive dyskinesia** (Hollister, 1977). The patient with tardive dyskinesia shows involuntary movements of the mouth, lips, tongue, trunk, and extremities. In one survey (Fann *et al.*, 1972), tardive dyskinesia was diagnosed in 36% of the chronic mental hospital patients, so it is far from an unusual side reaction. Furthermore, movement disorders may appear within weeks of taking the drug, so it is not simply due to drug treatment administered over many years.

The cause for these motor disturbances is not completely clear. Many antipsychotic drugs block dopamine receptors and thus lower the activity of dopaminergic synapses. Presumably, lowered activity at dopaminergic synapses is also the cause of Parkinson's disease symptoms, so these motor disturbances are fairly easy to understand. But tardive dyskinesia, the most prevalent side effect of antipsychotic drugs, is thought to be due to *greater* activity at dopaminergic synapses, rather than reduced activity.

One hypothesis to explain this apparent contradiction is that the antipsychotic drugs are creating a condition of **dopaminergic hypersensitivity** (Hollister, 1977). Initially the drugs block dopamine receptors; but this might activate a feedback loop wherein there is an increase in the synthesis of dopamine and an increase in receptor formation and sensitivity. As a result, activity in the dopaminergic synapses of the nigrostriatal system may actually eventually be increased above normal levels, creating the tardive dyskinesia. One solution to this problem is to increase the dose of the drug, thereby blocking the new dopamine receptors which have been formed. This might temporarily relieve the motor disturbance, but as Hollister puts it, this solution is like "increasing one's bets in a losing game." No completely satisfactory solution to this problem is yet available.

---

summary
Reward and Mental Illness

The introduction of antipsychotic and antidepressant drugs in the 1950s produced an enormous impact on the treatment of the mentally ill. These drugs relieve the symptoms of schizophrenia, depression, and manic-depression in many cases. The way that the drugs act in the brain has led researchers to hypothesize about the causes of these mental illnesses.

Most of the drugs which alleviate

schizophrenic symptoms also have an effect on dopaminergic synapses. The *dopamine hypothesis* of schizophrenia suggests that the antipsychotic drugs act by decreasing activity at these synapses, and that the disease may be caused by overactivity. There is much evidence that the antipsychotics do indeed decrease dopamine activity, but the evidence that there is something wrong with dopamine transmission in schizophrenics is indirect. Since many of the antipsychotic drugs also effect norepinephrine synapses, the alleviation of schizophrenic symptoms may be due to the drug's action on this neurochemical as well.

The biogenic amines (norepinephrine, dopamine, and serotonin) have been implicated in chronic depression and manic-depression. Drugs which depress mood and create symptoms of depression tend to decrease activity at biogenic amine synapses; drugs which alleviate depression tend to increase activity. Because the antidepressant drugs, such as the *tricyclic antidepressants* and *iproniazid*, affect two or more of the biogenic amines at the same time, it is not clear whether one pathway is more important than another. These are the same pathways (particularly the catecholamine pathways) that are known to be involved in reward mechanisms in the brain; thus an individual suffering from one of these illnesses might have a defective reward mechanism.

One of the problems in trying to find the causes for these illnesses is that it is not clear whether the diagnoses are correct. Schizophrenic symptoms, for example, may be produced by environmental stresses or by a variety of biochemical errors, and this may explain why different drugs are effective in different cases and why no drugs are effective in others. Depression and manic-depression must also have somewhat separate causes, because different drugs are required to alleviate the symptoms of each. Thus it may be necessary to sort out subpopulations of patients. One promising approach along these lines uses baseline levels of a norepinephrine metabolite in the urine, and response to different drugs as the criterion. When norepinephrine metabolites are low, drugs which raise norepinephrine activity are the most effective—perhaps because the patient is suffering from a defect in this pathway.

The antipsychotic and antidepressant drugs have many side effects. This is easy to understand when you consider that these neurochemical pathways are involved in many behaviors. The most notable side effect of the antipsychotics is motor abnormalities, which makes sense in light of the importance of dopamine in the extrapyramidal system. These motor problems are only recently becoming known, and in the future physicians will probably be less enthusiastic in their prescribing habits than they have been in the past.

KEY TERMS

piloerection
fright-flight-fight syndrome
adrenal cortex
adrenal medulla
corticotrophin releasing factor
adrenocorticotrophic hormone (ACTH)
adrenocortical steroids

general adaptation syndrome (G.A.S.)
alarm reaction
resistance stage
exhaustion stage
galvanic skin response (GSR)
biofeedback
James–Lange theory

Cannon's theory
cognitive-physiological theory
agonistic behavior
apomorphine
carbachol
neostigmine bromide
atropine
hypothalamic drive model
medial forebrain bundle
push-pull cannula
disulfiram
incentive motivation
dopamine hypothesis of
    schizophrenia
reserpine
chlorpromazine

haloperidol
amphetamine psychosis
homovanillic acid
unipolar depression
bipolar depression
biogenic amine hypothesis of
    depression
tricyclic antidepressant
iproniazid
lithium
3-methoxy-4-hydroxyphenylglycol
imipramine
amitriptyline
tardive dyskinesia
dopaminergic hypersensitivity

SUGGESTED READINGS

Moyer, K. E. (1976). *Physiology of Aggression and Implications for Control: An Anthology of Readings.* Raven Press, New York. (A very wide-ranging collection of papers dealing with the physiological bases of aggression in humans and animals.)

Phillips, A. G., and Mogenson, G. J. (1978). Brain stimulation reward: current issues and future prospects. *Canad. J. Psychol./Rev. Canad. Psychol.* **32,** 124–128. (This review article, and the one that immediately precedes it in this issue, cover the high points of the rewarding brain stimulation literature.)

Schachter, S., and Singer, J. E. (1962). Cognitive, social, and physiological determinants of emotional state. *Psychol. Rev.* **69,** 379–399.

Schachter, S. (1971). *Emotion, Obesity, and Crime.* Academic Press, New York.

(The paper by Schachter and Singer is the classic experiment described in the text. Schachter's book presents a concise and easily readable version of his thoughts on emotions.)

Selye, H. (1976). *The Stress of Life,* revised ed. McGraw-Hill, New York. (A beautifully written book which covers the history and discovery of the G.A.S. and explains the relationship between stress and illness.)

11

hunger
and
thirst

In order to stay alive, animals have to fulfill two basic requirements: They must eat enough so that their energy expenditure does not exceed their food intake, and they must take in enough water so that their water loss does not exceed their water intake. Day-to-day variations in food and water intake can certainly occur without too many ill effects. For example, a one-day fast is probably not harmful; it only makes you hungry. But in the long run, a balance between food intake and energy expenditure, and one between water gain and loss, must be maintained. Too much food leads to obesity, and too much water leads to frequent trips to the bathroom and leached vitamins and minerals as well. Too little food or water, however, leads to death.

The subject of this chapter is how an organism maintains these balances, both by behavioral means, such as eating and drinking, and by physiological means, such as water conservation by the kidneys. Since the animal's very survival is at stake, the need to eat and drink is a very powerful motivating force. The physiological state which leads an animal or human to seek out and eat food is called hunger, while the physiological state which leads to water intake is called thirst. Although many animals do not have to drink because they get most or all of their water in their food, the regulation of food intake and water balance are physiologically separate, so we will consider them one at a time.

the regulation of food intake It often happens in science that theoretical positions move back and forth from one extreme position to another in the opposite direction—much like a pendulum of a clock. This is what has happened to the theories about the regulation of food intake. In the eighteenth and nineteenth centuries, the **peripheralist** viewpoint was most popular suggesting that hunger was due to peripheral sensations—particularly contractions of the stomach. A person felt satiated when the stomach was distended and the contractions ceased; the person felt hungry again when the stomach was empty and the contractions began again.

Gradually during the early twentieth century, evidence began to accumulate which did not support this extreme peripheralist viewpoint. For example, insulin produces stomach contractions, and the insulin-injected rat eats heartily. But these insulin-induced stomach contractions can be slowed down considerably by cutting the vagus nerve, one of the prime afferent pathways by which the brain receives information about the activity of the body's organs. Instead of eating less because their stomachs were no longer contracting, these insulin-injected, vagotomized rats actually ate more (Morgan and Morgan, 1940).

The importance of stomach contractions in hunger also lost ground when it became clear that even animals whose stomachs had been removed consumed food. These studies led scientists to explore the role of the brain in the mediation of hunger and to postulate more **centralist theories.** The centralist positions rested mainly on the fascinating role of the hypothalamus, and we will begin our story at the point when scientists began to explore the food-related functions of this structure. The pendulum swung from an extreme peripheralist view to an extreme centralist view, with the hypothalamus as the star performer. But, as we shall see later in this section, the pendulum is swinging back again and is now somewhere in the middle.

In the previous chapter we mentioned that earlier researchers had found two separate areas of the hypothalamus that apparently had opposite effects on food intake. Lesions in the **ventromedial** area resulted in **hyperphagia** (overeating) and obesity (Brobeck *et al.*, 1943). Lesions in the **lateral** area resulted in **aphagia** (no eating) and **adipsia** (no drinking), and eventually led to death if the animal was not force-fed (Anand and Brobeck, 1951). These two hypothalamic areas are shown in Figure 11.1. Though these effects have been studied extensively in the rat, they also appear in other species, such as the dog (Fonberg, 1969), and monkey (Hamilton and Brobeck, 1964).

the hypothalamus and food intake

Electrical stimulation of these two regions resulted in behaviors opposite to those produced by the lesions. Stimulation of the lateral hypothalamus (LH) led to eating, even in rats that had just eaten a full meal. And hungry animals stopped eating when they were stimulated in the ventromedial hypothalamus (VMH) (Robinson and Mishkin, 1968). Given these results, it is easy to see how the LH became known as the "feeding center," and the VMH as the "satiety center." But let us look at the effects of these lesions more closely.

the VMH syndrome. The sequence of postoperative changes in food intake and body weight which occur in a VMH-lesioned rat appear in Figure 11.2. There is an immediate drop in both weight and food intake after the operation. But after a week or so, the animal becomes a voracious eater and quickly gains weight. This period of rapid weight gain is called the **dynamic phase.** About 3 weeks after the operation, the animal's food intake drops off and then stabilizes, and the animal enters the **static phase.** During this phase, its food intake is only slightly higher than that of a normal rat—just enough to maintain its elevated body weight. If the obese rat is dieted down to a normal weight again, it will go through the hyperphagic dynamic phase again as soon as it has access to unlimited food.

Aside from eating more than a normal rat, these animals are different in many ways. For example, the VMH-lesioned rat eats more at a given meal (Teitelbaum and Campbell, 1958), and it is more likely to eat in a novel environment containing food (Sclafani, 1971). It is also

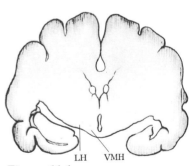

Figure 11.1
Coronal section of rat brain showing the positions of the lateral hypothalamic area (LH) and ventromedial hypothalamus (VMH). [From Keesey and Powley (1975).]

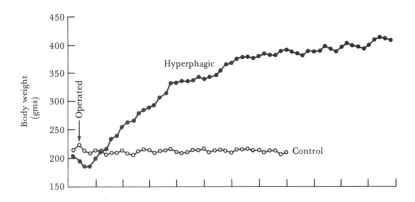

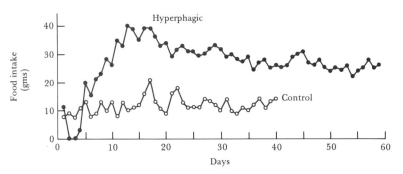

Figure 11.2
Postoperative body weight and daily food intake of a hyperphagic animal compared to that of a normal unoperated control animal. [From Teitelbaum (1955). Copyright 1955 by the American Psychological Association. Reprinted by permission.]

"finicky" in that it will overeat if the food tastes good, but it will *under-eat* if the food has been adulterated with some foul-tasting substance like quinine (Teitelbaum, 1955). It also does not like to work very hard for its food, and will lose weight if this becomes necessary. So a lesion in the VMH is not tantamount to being "more hungry."

If the VMH is a kind of satiety center, then it should have access to information about how much the animal has eaten. It might, for example, be monitoring the rate of glucose uptake by the cells. Glucose is the prime fuel for brain cells, so when blood levels are high, the cells would be utilizing glucose very quickly. Perhaps the VMH contains glucoreceptors that somehow monitor the rate of glucose utilization. When the rate is low, the animal would feel hungry, and when the rate is high, it would feel satiated. Brecher and Waxler (1949) found that injections of **gold thioglucose** (GTG), a drug that is taken up by cells which take up glucose, but which also destroys those cells, produced hyperphagia and obesity in mice. The GTG was found concentrated in the VMH. This suggested that the VMH might contain glucoreceptors, and it also strongly supported the notion that the VMH was a "satiety center."

Many of the effects of VMH lesions suggest that this area might be a satiety center, but many of them just raise more questions. For example, why doesn't the VMH rat just keep on eating until it explodes? Why does it enter a static phase? Why is the rat so finicky and lazy about food; if it were really hungry, wouldn't it eat anything and work harder? Even the studies using GTG which suggested the presence of glucoreceptors are open to question because this substance produces damage to the blood vessels and not just the cells. Furthermore, GTG apparently produces obesity only in mice. The studies on the lateral hypothalamic feeding center also raised questions, and we will examine them in the next section.

the LH syndrome. Lesions in this area lead to aphagia, adipsia, and eventual death. But Teitelbaum and Stellar (1954) found that these animals could make a partial recovery if they are tube-fed for a while. Figure 11.3 shows the course of recovery. On the tenth postoperative day the tube feeding began, and by the twentieth day, the animal would accept sweet palatable foods like moistened chocolate chip cookies. The animal would not accept dry, solid lab chow until nearly 2 months after surgery.

Figure 11.4 shows the four stages through which the recovering LH-lesioned rat passes (Teitelbaum and Epstein, 1962; Epstein, 1971). Notice that the "recovered" stage IV animal still has some residual deficits. For example, it only drinks during meals, apparently just to help swallow dry food. It also does not eat in response to depriving the cells of glucose, perhaps by some drug. The LH-lesioned rats are also "finicky" and will not accept food that tastes poorly.

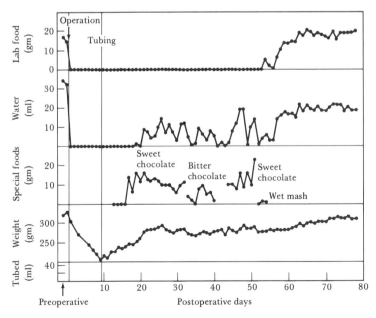

Figure 11.3
The production of both aphagia and adipsia by lateral hypothalamic lesions. Note the recovery of eating of palatable foods on day 16, the recovery of drinking on day 21, and the greatly delayed return to ordinary, dry food. The animal was kept alive by tube feeding during Stages I and II of the syndrome. [From Teitelbaum and Stellar (1954).]

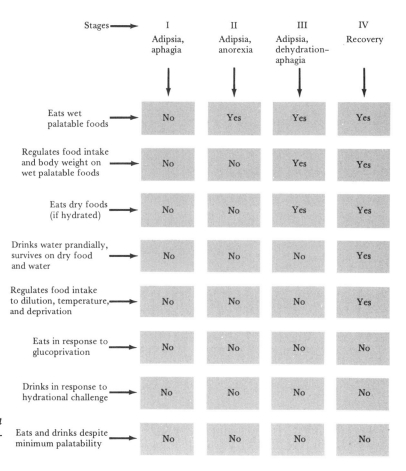

Stages →	I Adipsia, aphagia	II Adipsia, anorexia	III Adipsia, dehydration–aphagia	IV Recovery
Eats wet palatable foods	No	Yes	Yes	Yes
Regulates food intake and body weight on wet palatable foods	No	No	Yes	Yes
Eats dry foods (if hydrated)	No	No	Yes	Yes
Drinks water prandially, survives on dry food and water	No	No	No	Yes
Regulates food intake to dilution, temperature, and deprivation	No	No	No	Yes
Eats in response to glucoprivation	No	No	No	No
Drinks in response to hydrational challenge	No	No	No	No
Eats and drinks despite minimum palatability	No	No	No	No

Figure 11.4
The four stages of recovery from the lateral hypothalamic syndrome. [From Epstein (1971).]

While some of these effects support the view that the LH is a feeding center, many of them are puzzling. For example, why does the animal make *any* recovery? And why are both the LH and VMH rats so finicky? Even the brain stimulation studies, which have been a cornerstone of the theory that the LH and the VMH were feeding and satiety centers, were ambiguous. Valenstein *et al.* (1970) reported that LH stimulation elicited feeding when only food was present, but stimulation of the same sites could just as easily elicit gnawing or drinking if wood or water was present. Thus the LH could not be exclusively a feeding center.

Lesion studies are difficult to interpret because it is not clear whether the behavioral changes after the lesion are due to destruction of cell bodies or of axons which passed through the region. They are also difficult to interpret because it is never clear why the behavioral changes occurred. Did the lesion destroy a feeding center, or an area which organizes the motor responses necessary for feeding, or perhaps a pathway which activated other areas in the brain which organized the feeding motor sequence? In the case of the LH and VMH syndromes, many of these issues were clarified when scientists began to look at the role of the catecholamine pathways in food intake.

In recent years, the emphasis of research efforts has shifted away from the hypothalamus as a "center" for food intake control to the fiber systems that are passing through that region. These fiber systems are the same ones which we discussed in Chapter 10 in connection with reward, and we will see later that this is probably not just a coincidence. The main fiber systems include (1) the dopaminergic nigrostriatal pathway and (2) the ventral and (3) dorsal noradrenergic pathways.

the catecholamine pathways and food intake

dopaminergic nigrostriatal pathway. Lesions in the LH which result in aphagia and adipsia interrupt the ascending nigrostriatal fibers (Ungerstedt, 1971). Indeed, many lesions outside of the LH which produced aphagia also disrupted the dopamine pathway, suggesting that the aphagia was due not to LH lesions per se but to disruptions of this fiber system. Ungerstedt further demonstrated that injections of 6-OHDA, the drug that destroys catecholamine pathways, also produces aphagia and adipsia.

It soon became clear that the effects of LH lesions and the effects of injections of 6-OHDA were extremely similar. For example, both LH lesions and 6-OHDA injections result in depletion of brain catecholamines (Fibiger *et al.*, 1973; Ungerstedt, 1971). Another similarity is that the course of recovery after lesion or injections is very much the same. Figure 11.5 shows the food intake and body weight changes following 6-OHDA injections. A comparison of these charts with those in Figure 11.3 shows the striking similarity in the time course of the recovery process (Zigmond and Stricker, 1973).

The drug 6-OHDA does not specifically deplete dopamine; it also lowers norepinephrine levels. But injections of 6-OHDA plus **desmethylimipramine,** a drug which blocks amine uptake into norepinephrine terminals, prevent the 6-OHDA from getting into the noradrenergic cells. This procedure produces 95–99% depletion of dopamine, but less than 5% reduction of norepinephrine. It also produces prolonged aphagia and adipsia, indicating that it is the dopamine pathways, not the norepinephrine ones, that are crucial in the disruption of feeding.

If ingestive behaviors are dependent on the dopaminergic nigrostriatal fibers, then what is the functional role of this pathway? We have abandoned the notion that the LH is a "feeding center." It was

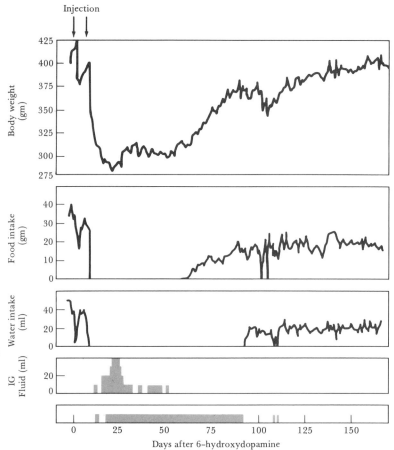

Figure 11.5
Food and water intakes and body weight of a rat given two intra-ventricular injections of 6-OHDA. The bottom graph represents access to highly palatable foods. [From Stricker and Zigmond (1976).]

apparently the destruction of this pathway that was responsible for most if not all of the feeding deficits. The next question to ask is what the dopamine pathway has to do with feeding.

functional role of the dopamine pathway. In the last chapter, catecholamine fiber systems were strongly implicated in the neural substrate for reward. The dopamine pathway is part of this putative reward system. Thus it is possible that the dopamine pathway is not simply a "feeding pathway" but part of a larger system that mediates motivation. Disruption of that system might produce a lack of attention toward stimuli that normally motivate the animal.

Ungerstedt (1974) suggests that the feeding deficits result from a disruption of just such attentional processes which should produce a response to sensory stimuli, a syndrome called **sensory neglect.** There is evidence that disruption of LH fibers produces just this kind of sensory neglect. Marshall *et al.* (1971) made unilateral lesions in the LH of rats, and then noticed that the animals did not orient well to various kinds of stimuli presented to the side of the body contralateral to the lesion. The stimuli were not just food-related, but included visual, olfactory, and somatosensory stimuli. Thus the animal was not paying much attention to stimuli opposite the lesion, stimuli that normally would have evoked some response.

dopamine and reward. The energizing function of the dopamine system may be closely related to stimuli that normally have some reward value to the animal. The behavioral deficits of the lesioned animal, which include aphagia, may occur because many kinds of stimuli which are normally rewarding, such as food, have lost their reward value. Wise and his colleagues (1978) attempted to test this hypothesis by treating some rats with **pimozide**, a drug used for schizophrenia which blocks dopamine receptors. The rats had previously been taught to lever press for food pellets, but after the injection their lever pressing slowly dropped off.

Figure 11.6 shows some of the results from this study. On the first day after the injection, the injected rats lever pressed normally, but by day 4, their lever pressing was way down. The control rats, injected with oil, continued to lever press normally. Panel (c) shows the lever pressing of uninjected rats who were not receiving any food from the pellet dispenser during the four test sessions. Notice that their lever pressing behavior was very similar to the pimozide injected rats over the four testing days, suggesting that pimozide treatment with food reward is similar to no drug without food reward.

Wise *et al.* (1978) also showed that the drop-off in lever pressing of the pimozide treated rats was not simply due to the cumulative effects of the drug, which might have been simply ruining their appetite. Their lack of eating was due to an interaction between their experience with food as a reward and their drug history. Panel (d) shows a group of rats which were injected with pimozide on day 1, but left in their home cage until day 4. They lever pressed at a high rate, unlike the drugged rats which had been tested for the three preceding days. This suggests that pimozide is not affecting hunger as much as it is affecting the rewarding quality of food. At first the rat simply lever presses and eats out of habit; but food is not rewarding enough to maintain the response, as it would be in the normal animal.

Figure 11.6
The interaction between the effects of pimozide and the availability of food reward for lever pressing on the lever pressing responses of rats. (a) Control (with reward). (b) Pimozide injected. (c) Control (no reward). (d) Pimozide injected (left in home cage until day 4). [Adapted from Wise et al. *(1978). Copyright 1978 by the American Association for the Advancement of Science.]*

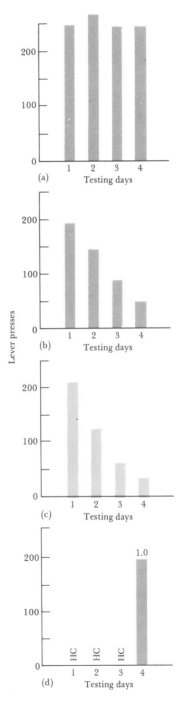

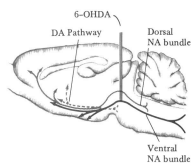

Figure 11.7
Side view of the rat brain showing the ventral and dorsal noradrenergic bundles, and the dopamine pathway. The introduction of 6-OHDA into the ventral bundle produced hyperphagia. [From Hoebel (1976).]

Wise *et al.* (1978) term this loss of reward value as **anhedonia** to distinguish it from lack of hunger. They suggest that drugs like pimozide, which disrupt the dopamine pathways, "take the pleasure out of normally rewarding brain stimulation, take the euphoria out of normally rewarding amphetamine, and take the 'goodness' out of normally rewarding food."

the ventral noradrenergic pathway and satiety. While the ascending dopaminergic fibers are apparently involved with stimulating the animal to start feeding, the ventral noradrenergic pathway may be involved with the cessation of feeding. The ventral bundle is the likely candidate for this function because it provides the noradrenergic input to the hypothalamus.

Ahlskog and Hoebel (1973) were able to selectively destroy the ventral noradrenergic bundle without damaging either the dorsal bundle or the dopamine pathway by introducing 6-OHDA through a cannula. Figure 11.7 shows these fiber systems, and where the cannula was placed. The 6-OHDA resulted in hyperphagia and obesity when introduced this way, very different from the aphagia which results from systemic injections. Figure 11.8 shows the comparison between the animals which had received the drug in the ventral versus the dorsal bundle on the percentage change in food intake. In a separate group of animals, the same fiber system was damaged by means of electrolytic lesions, and this also resulted in hyperphagia and obesity.

To make certain that the hyperphagia and obesity were in fact due to damage to norepinephrine-containing neurons by the 6-OHDA, Ahlskog and Hoebel (1973) also examined the effects of 6-OHDA plus desmethylimipramine. This drug, as you may recall, blocks the uptake of the 6-OHDA into noradrenergic neurons, so they should have remained intact. They did, and these rats did not become hyperphagic or obese. Thus the ventral noradrenergic system projecting into the hypothalamus is at least a component of the neural pathways mediating satiety.

other pathways involved in satiety. The ventral noradrenergic system is apparently not the only one involved in satiety because the hyperphagia resulting from VMH lesions and from chemical lesions of the ventral bundle are not exactly the same. For example, a chemically lesioned animal becomes even *more* hyperphagic when the VMH is lesioned electrolytically, so the effect of the two treatments are additive, not substitutive (Ahlskog *et al.*, 1975).

Another difference between the effects of the two treatments has to do with *when* the animals overeat. Normal rats sleep during the day and do most of their eating at night. VMH-lesioned rats, however, are hyperphagic during the day as well as the night; but rats made

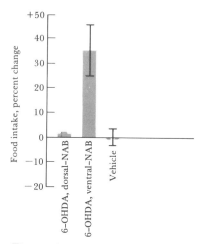

Figure 11.8
The change in food intake in rats which had received 6-OHDA in the dorsal or ventral noradrenergic bundle. Only the rats with destruction in the ventral bundle became hyperphagic. [From Hoebel (1976).]

hyperphagic with 6-OHDA are only hyperphagic at night (Ahlskog *et al.*, 1975). These eating patterns are shown in Figure 11.9.

These results indicate that the ventral noradrenergic bundle must be interacting with one or more other systems in satiety. One candidate for this other system is a pathway which uses serotonin as its transmitter. Breisch *et al* (1976) injected PCPA (the drug which depletes serotonin by inhibiting the enxymes tryptophan hydroxylase)into the ventricle of rats, and found that they became hyperphagic and obese.

The noradrenergic fibers are also implicated in the reward system, so damage or stimulation in these areas may also be somehow influencing general arousal and reward—they may not be specifically related to hunger. VMH lesions may make the animal *too* attentive to incentive stimuli, and *too* responsive to the taste of food. The "finickiness" of these animals supports such a view, but it is still speculative.

If the fiber systems running through the hypothalamus have more to do with general arousal and the reward value of various food stimuli, then we are back to our original question: What mediates hunger and satiety? Modifications of arousal and reward value might change the motivation of an animal toward eating, but there still must be some way to monitor the amount of food the animal eats relative to the energy it expends. Before we consider these proposed monitoring systems, we need to discuss what physiological events occur when an animal eats.

the digestive process. In simple terms, the digestive process (shown in Figure 11.10) is a long tube made up of several specialized portions. The cells of the body cannot absorb a chunk of steak; they can absorb small molecules like amino acids or glucose. Each specialized portion of the tube helps to break down whole chunks of food into large molecules and then into smaller ones.

The mouth and teeth begin the process. Chewing breaks the food into smaller particles; saliva moistens it and adds digestive enzymes. The food then moves down the esophagus into the stomach, where contractions churn up the food into **chyme.** The fluid chyme then passes into the small intestine, where the major portion of digestion and absorption occurs. Pancreatic enzymes have their largest effects on the food in the small intestine. By the time the material enters the large intestine, digestion is virtually complete.

The metabolism of food can be divided into two phases: the first, or **absorptive phase** is dominated by storage of nutrients, while the second, or **postabsorptive phase** is dominated by the breakdown and utilization of stored nutrients.

physiological mechanisms underlying hunger and satiety

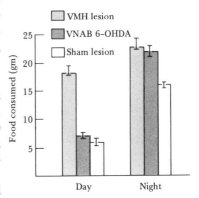

Figure 11.9

A comparison of the eating patterns of (1) rats made hyperphagic by VMH lesions, (2) rats made hyperphagic by 6-OHDA lesions in the ventral noradrenergic bundle, and (3) sham-lesioned rats. The VMH-lesioned rats overeat during both the day and night, but the drug-lesioned rats only overeat at night. [From Hoebel (1976).]

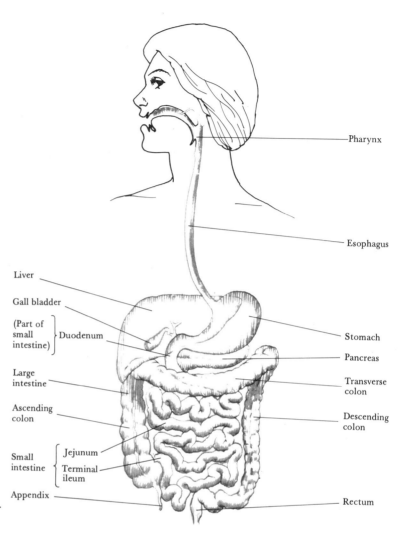

Pharynx

Esophagus

Liver

Gall bladder

(Part of small intestine) Duodenum

Large intestine

Ascending colon

Small intestine { Jejunum
Terminal ileum

Appendix

Stomach

Pancreas

Transverse colon

Descending colon

Rectum

Figure 11.10
The digestive tract. [From Grollman (1969).]

absorptive phase. As long as nutrients are still being absorbed from the small intestine, and blood glucose levels are high, the pancreas produces a hormone called **insulin.** Insulin facilitates the entrance of glucose into the cells of the body where it can be used as fuel. Extra glucose is changed into products that can be stored, particularly fat (stored in adipose tissue), and **glycogen** (stored in the liver). During the absorptive phase, amino acids are also being absorbed, and insulin facilitates their uptake by cells so that protein synthesis can occur.

Insulin is extremely important because the cells of the body, except for those in the brain and liver, cannot take up glucose without it. People with **diabetes mellitus** do not produce enough insulin so their blood glucose levels remain high and their body cells do not get enough fuel. This is why diabetics must inject insulin every day.

postabsorptive phase. When the nutrients have all been absorbed from the small intestine, blood glucose levels drop. This drop is the signal to the pancreas to lower its output of insulin, and insulin levels also drop. Low blood glucose is a stimulus for the pancreas to begin secreting another hormone, **glucagon.** Glucagon, and two other hormones (epinephrine from the adrenal medulla and growth hormone from the pituitary) participate in providing utilizable fuel from the stored nutrients. They stimulate the liver to convert stored nutrients back into glucose to be used as fuel, and they stimulate the breakdown of fats. The liver's conversion of stored nutrients, such as glycogen, back into glucose is also due to activity of sympathetic nerve fibers which innervate this organ. Thus the brain has a direct role in many parts of the postabsorptive phase.

It is during the postabsorptive phase that hunger begins, and it is during the absorptive phase that satiety ensues; it would make sense to search for "monitors" that were sensitive to one or more of the physiological events that occur during each phase.

receptors in the brain

The studies discussed earlier in this chapter led many scientists to believe that there were receptors in the LH and/or VMH which monitored some physiological signal which varied during the two phases of metabolism.

glucostatic theory. Mayer (1955) proposed that receptors existed which monitored the rate of glucose utilization. When it was high (during the absorptive phase) the animal would not feel hungry; when it was low (during the postabsorptive phase) hunger would be present. The studies using gold thioglucose, discussed earlier, seemed to support the notion that the VMH contained glucoreceptors. Recall that these studies were ambiguous because of the capillary damage produced by the drug. Thus far there is no clear evidence that there are any glucoreceptors anywhere in the brain.

lipostatic theory. Since extra nutrients are converted to fats, it is possible that there are receptors which monitor the amount of body fat. An animal certainly does regulate the amount of fat deposits over the long term. Liebelt *et al.* (1973) found that the tissue of a normal mouse rejected a transplanted graft of fat tissue from another mouse. But if the normal mouse first had a bit of its own fatty tissue removed, then it *would* accept the graft. Furthermore, animals made hyperphagic from gold thioglucose would also accept a graft of fat tissue. This means that the amount of body fat must be monitored somewhere, but as of yet, no receptors have been found in the brain which might be doing the monitoring.

peripheral control of hunger and satiety The failure to find any receptors in the brain which were sensitive to specific changes which occurred during metabolism has led many researchers back to the periphery. In this sense, the pendulum is swinging away from the notion of central control of feeding, back to more peripheral theories. But the newer theories do not simply state that it is stomach contractions which initiate feeding. Rather they suggest that the control of food intake is extraordinarily complex, and many factors are involved. As we shall see in this section, the brain still has an important role to play, but the liver has also assumed the role of a featured player.

the role of the mouth and head. It is clear that the taste, odor, sight, and texture of food plays at least a small role in the control of food intake. Animals eat more than usual if the food tastes very good, and less if it does not. Also, when an animal is surgically arranged so that its esophagus leads outside the skin instead of to the stomach, it will eat more than usual, but will stop eating eventually (Janowitz and Grossman, 1949). This means that sensations arising from the head during eating must have provided at least some negative feedback which caused the animal to stop eating. This feeling of satiety is short-lived, however, because the animal will quickly go back to eating.

role of the gastrointestinal tract. Smith and Gibbs (1976) suggested that a gastrointestinal hormone, **cholecystokinin (CCK)**, might be responsible for satiety. CCK is released when chyme passes from the stomach into the small intestine. Injections of this substance inhibit feeding in rats, apparently without causing any illness or pain.

The way that this hormone produces satiety is not at all clear. Peripheral injections of CCK induce satiety much better than intracranial injections (Nemeroff *et al.*, 1978), suggesting that it does not act on the brain very directly. But Pinget *et al.* (1978) found CCK in brain synaptosomes, suggesting that it does act in the brain, perhaps as a neurotransmitter. Regardless of how it works, it is clear that CCK is only one of the factors that mediate satiety. Mineka and Snowden (1978) found that repeated injections of CCK only inhibited eating for a short time. Within a few days, the rats were almost back to their normal food intake levels. Other signals can apparently override the CCK signal eventually.

the role of the liver. Russek (1971, 1975) performed a series of studies which focused attention on the liver as one of the important regulators of food intake. In one experiment using a dog, he injected glucose directly into the vein that carries blood from the intestines to the liver, the **hepatic portal vein**. This produced long lasting satiety, but a similar injection into the jugular vein did not produce satiety. Thus the amount of glucose available to the liver, rather than the brain, is apparently one of the crucial factors controlling food intake.

Friedman and Stricker (1976) argue that the brain is not a very good candidate to monitor fuel supply because its supply of fuel is held very constant by the body. During starvation, for example, the body will mobilize any fuels—fat tissue, muscle tissue—before the brain begins to lose its fuel supply. The liver, on the other hand, is in a good position to monitor fuel supply, not just of glucose, but of all body fuels.

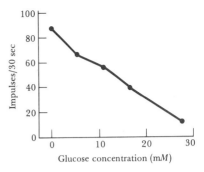

liver glucoreceptors. Niijima (1969) showed that the liver actually has receptors which monitor glucose levels, and which send their information to the brain. He showed that as the concentration of glucose in the liver goes up, the rate of firing in single vagal fibers goes down. This relationship is shown in Figure 11.11.

Novin and Vanderweele (1977) used a drug called **2-deoxyglucose (2-DG)** to demonstrate that the liver contains glucoreceptors. This drug is taken up by cells that utilize glucose, but it inhibits the utilization of endogenous glucose. They injected the drug directly into the hepatic portal vein of rabbits, or into their jugular veins. Figure 11.12 shows their results.

The rabbits with 2-DG in their portal vein immediately started eating and kept on eating. But the rabbits with 2-DG in their jugular vein did not eat at such high levels until 3 hours after the injection. It probably took this long for the 2-DG to make it down to the glucoreceptors

Figure 11.11
The relationship between impulses in the vagal nerve and the concentration of glucose in a perfusion through the liver. [From Niijima (1969).]

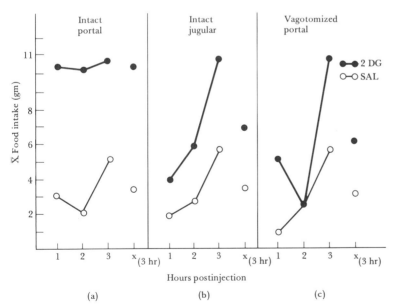

(a)   (b)   (c)

Figure 11.12
The effects of 2-DG injected into the (a) hepatic portal vein or the (b) jugular vein of rabbits on food intake. (c) The effects of 2-DG administered through the portal vein on rabbits which had been vagotomized. [From Novin and Vanderweele (1977).]

in the liver. Panel (c) shows the food intake of rabbits receiving 2-DG into their portal vein, but whose vagal nerve had been severed. Their food intake was attenuated suggesting that the liver could not pass on the information about lowered glucose utilization to the brain.

These glucoreceptors are probably sensitive not only to glucose obtained by eating, but also to the amount of fuel which has been stored by previous eating, particularly as glycogen. Infusions of glucose into the portal vein do not suppress feeding all the time, only in animals which have been starved. These animals have very little glycogen stored and thus the glucose is immediately utilized. But in free-feeding animals infusions of glucose into the portal vein do not suppress feeding, probably because the newly arrived glucose does not add very much to the fuel supplied by glycogen turnover (Novin and Vanderweele, 1977).

Infusions of glucose into the small intestine, however, only suppress feeding in animals which have been eating normally (and had high glycogen levels in the liver), not starved ones (Vanderweele and Sanderson, 1976). This glucose perhaps activated hormonal mechanisms (such as CCK) which inhibited feeding.

multiple controls over *food intake* It should be clear by now that there are many overlapping systems which regulate hunger and satiety. The liver plays a critically important role, but the mouth, the stomach, the small intestines, and the brain all have parts to play. Now that it is agreed that there is no central hunger "center" in the hypothalamus, more research is being devoted to analyzing the operation of the separate components. Stricker *et al.* (1977), for example, performed studies to separate the roles played by the brain and the liver in the control of food intake.

These scientists injected rats intravenously with insulin, a procedure which produces marked **hypoglycemia** (low blood sugar) because the insulin facilitates the entrance of blood glucose into the cells. This injection produced a sudden increase in food intake, as expected. But following the injection of insulin, they introduced various kinds of fuel into some of the rats. Some rats received glucose, others received fructose or mannose (two different types of sugars), while still others received ketone bodies. Fructose cannot cross the blood–brain barrier, but it is utilized by the liver as fuel; the ketone bodies are a fuel that can be used by the brain, but not the liver; mannose can be used by both the brain and liver.

The food intake of these groups of rats, and some other groups that were given injections of saline, are shown in Table 11.1. Notice that all the animals given some form of nutrient after the insulin injection showed a decline in food intake. Even the animals that had been given fructose, which could not have reached the brain, showed suppressed

Table 11.1
Food intake of insulin-injected rats after treatment with nutrients or saline[a]

Infusate	Food intake[b] (gm)
0.15M NaCl (10)	2.15 ± 0.28[c]
0.75M NaCl (9)	1.90 ± 0.25[c]
1.2M NaCl (10)	1.19 ± 0.43[c]
1.2M β-hydroxybutyrate (6) (Ketone bodies)	0.73 ± 0.24
1.2M glucose (8)	0.27 ± 0.19
1.2M mannose (10)	0.20 ± 0.13
1.2M fructose (9)	0.38 ± 0.14

[a] Adapted from Stricker *et al.* (1977). Copyright 1977 by the American Association for the Advancement of Science.
[b] All the animals receiving some type of fuel showed a decline in food intake.
[c] $P < 0.001$.

feeding. Thus the signals which monitor fuel supply, and increase food intake, are not in the brain—they must be in the periphery somewhere. We have suggested that they are in the liver. Some indeed are, but there must be others as well. The animals given the ketone bodies, which cannot be used as fuel by the liver, showed a moderate suppression of feeding. They did not eat as much as the animals given saline, but they did not eat as little as those rats given a nutrient which can be utilized by the liver.

Stricker and his colleagues also measured the output of epinephrine by these rats. Normally, when a rat is given insulin, the levels of epinephrine rise considerably. The epinephrine can then mobilize reserve sources of fuel. Figure 11.13 shows the levels of plasma catecholamine (which includes epinephrine) for the rats which were given each of the various nutrients. Notice that all of the animals which received a fuel which *can* be used by the brain showed a decreased output of epinephrine. Only those which received fructose, the fuel which does not pass the blood–brain barrier, kept their output of epinephrine high.

These studies demonstrate that the liver, and probably other sites as well, are monitoring fuel supply in the body and adjusting the level of food intake. These monitors must be sending their information to the brain, at least partly via the vagal nerve. But cells in the brain are also monitoring fuel supply. These monitors, however, do not send their information anywhere to adjust food intake. Instead their information about fuel supply is used to alter the rate of epinephrine output. When the brain is "hungry," it produces more epinephrine to mobilize reserve fuel supplies; but when the liver (or other peripheral site) is "hungry," it sends information to the brain to activate the motor pathways necessary for feeding.

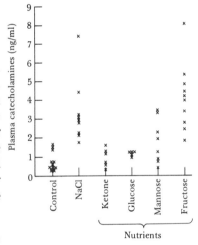

Figure 11.13
Plasma catecholamine levels of insulin-injected rats treated with various types of nutrients, with saline, or control rats which received no insulin or nutrients. [From Stricker et al. *(1977). Copyright 1977 by the American Association for the Advancement of Science.]*

activation of motor pathways The way that information about the level of body fuel which comes to the brain from the periphery can activate motor pathways necessary for feeding is not yet known; but some interesting speculations exist. One such speculation brings in the ideas about the importance of the catecholamine fibers as motivational pathways (Mogenson, 1976).

This fascinating model is diagrammed in Figure 11.14. The catecholamine pathways coming from the locus coeruleus and substantia nigra synapse onto interneurons which use the inhibitory neurotransmitter GABA. These interneurons synapse onto neurons in the striatum, cerebellum, and cerebral cortex which act as "motor tapes" for feeding reflexes, and presumably for other goal directed behaviors as well. Since the catecholamines are both probably inhibitory transmitters themselves, this arrangement would mean that neural activity in the catecholamine pathways would *disinhibit* the preprogrammed neural circuits responsible for the motor reflexes of feeding. (The interneurons would be inhibited, and they would not be able to inhibit the motor neurons.) This model fits in well with the fact that electrical stimulation of the catecholamine fibers acts as an "energizer" for goal-directed behaviors. The rat will eat if food is present, gnaw if wood is present, or drink if water is present. When objects are not present at all, the most frequently elicited behavior is locomotion, as if the animal were activated or energized for something. The model also fits in well with the fact that destruction of the catecholamine pathways result in aphagia, adipsia, and general lethargy.

human obesity The studies which trace the physiological bases of hunger in rats have been used to speculate on the reasons why so many people become overweight. These speculations may be able to give us clues about how people can learn to control their weight more effectively.

Figure 11.14
Neurons of the dorsal noradrenergic pathway (NA) and of the nigrostriatal dopaminergic pathway (DA) inhibit neurons in the cerebral cortex and striatum. These NA and DA neurons synapse on GABA inhibitory interneurons, which inhibit preprogrammed neural circuits ("motor tapes") represented in the cerebral cortex and striatum. The NA and DA thus disinhibit the preprogrammed circuits and feeding reflexes occur. [From Mogenson (1976).]

overeating and the tail pinch. Oddly enough, a mild pinch on the tail causes a rat to overeat. Rowland and Antelman (1976) report that such pinches caused the rat's intake to more than double. These tail

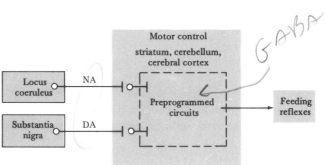

pinches are particularly effective in getting LH-lesioned animals to begin to eat, so scientists speculated that the tail pinch might be acting through the dopaminergic fibers. The mild stress produced by the pinch is apparently activating the motivational pathways that are important in various kinds of motivated behaviors.

The effects of this kind of mild stress on eating behavior suggest that stress may play an important role in human obesity. Many people overeat during stressful situations, and perhaps humans who become obese are particularly vulnerable to stress. The stress might produce an overactivation of the dopaminergic pathways, which then causes the person to pay too much attention to food stimuli.

Nemeroff *et al.* (1978) found that peripheral injections of CCK, the gastrointestinal hormone which produces satiety, inhibited the eating normally produced by a tail pinch. These scientists suggest that the hormone may be useful in controlling stress-induced eating by human beings. However, as we mentioned previously, there are clearly multiple controls over hunger and satiety, and any manipulation of one of them is likely to be overridden by another control mechanism. Also, repeated injections of CCK only inhibit eating for a short time in rats. Thus the substance probably will not be any panacea for human obesity.

obesity and external control. Schachter (1971) disagrees with the hypothesis that stress is a critical component in the overeating of obese humans. He and his colleagues (Schachter *et al.*, 1968) concocted an experiment in which they compared the number of crackers eaten by normal and obese subjects when they were experiencing various levels of stress. In this study, normal-weighted subjects tended to eat fewer crackers when they were led to believe that they would soon experience some painful shocks, compared to when they were told that the shocks would be insignificant. Obese subjects, on the other hand, ate about the same number of crackers regardless of whether they were calmly expecting mild shocks, or apprehensively fearful of strong ones. Figure 11.15 shows the results from this study.

It is possible that the stress produced by the fear of shocks is much more severe than the mild tail pinches which increased eating in rats. It may be that milder forms of stress do have some facilitating effect on eating behavior in obese people. But Schachter argues that the big difference between normal-weighted people and obese people is in their reliance on external cues for eating behavior, rather than on internal cues associated with hunger, stress, or anything else. Obese people may become obese because they pay little or no attention to physiological cues which are supposed to signal low body fuel levels. Instead their eating behavior is triggered by external cues, such as the sight, odor, and taste of food. Eating behavior in normal people is trig-

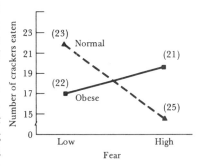

Figure 11.15
Effects of fear on the amounts eaten by normal and obese subject. Numbers in parentheses are numbers of subjects. [From Schachter (1971).]

gered by a combination of these external cues, and the internal changes which accompany the need for body fuel.

Quite a number of inventive studies have been performed to test this hypothesis. In one particularly clever study, Schachter and Gross (1968) manipulated the external cue of "clock time," to see if obese people relied more on the time of day to trigger eating, compared to normal-weighted people. Around the dinner hour, subjects were brought into the laboratory and told that they were participating in a study which was designed to relate physiological responses to personality. All the subjects had to do was sit still for about half an hour while the experimenters took the fictitious recordings. After the recordings, all the subjects were offered a box of crackers to munch on while they filled out some questionnaires.

Half the obese and half the normal subjects were in an experimental room with a "fast clock." These subjects were led to believe that the time was a few minutes past the dinner hour when the experimenter brought in the crackers. The other half of the subjects were led to believe that it was more than half an hour before the dinner hour when the crackers arrived. Table 11.2 shows the results from this study.

Notice that the obese subjects ate more crackers when the clock was running fast, when they thought that it was past the dinner hour. The normal-weighted subjects did exactly the opposite, suggesting that they relied more on internal cues. It is interesting that the obese subjects did not eat more crackers than the normal subjects overall. The only difference between the two groups was *when* they ate the crackers.

Other studies have shown that obese subjects eat more food than normals when it tastes good, but less than normals when the food is adulterated with quinine. Obese humans are less likely to work for food, but will eat heartily when the food is readily available. These and other findings suggest an uncanny parallel between the eating habits of obese humans and those of VMH-lesioned rats. As we discussed, the rat with lesions in the VMH is also finicky about the taste of food, nor will it work very hard to obtain it. If it is readily avail-

Table 11.2
Amount eaten (in grams) by subjects under four conditions[a]

Weight	"Clock time"	
	Slow	Fast
Obese	19.9	37.6
Normal	41.5	16.0

[a] From Schachter (1971).

able, it will eat huge quantities and gain weight rapidly. There is not evidence to suggest that obese humans have lesions in the VMH. At the moment, the most we can say is that the parallels are striking and it is possible that obese humans have functional abnormalities in the pathways that mediate satiety, or attentional processes related to food stimuli. Learning, no doubt, plays a key role, however, and there is not likely to be any simple solution to the problem of obesity.

In this section we have seen how the theoretical approach to the contol of hunger and satiety has shifted from an extreme *peripheralist* viewpoint, which emphasized the role of stomach contractions in hunger, to a *centralist* viewpoint, in which the hypothalamus played a key role. New findings, however, have now led researchers back to an emphasis of peripheral receptors which can monitor fuel supply and initiate feeding behavior.

Early research suggested that the *ventromedial* hypothalamus (VMH) was a "satiety center," because lesions in the VMH produced a host of symptoms including hyperphagia (overeating), "finickiness" about the taste of food, and very little willingness to work for food. Electrical stimulation of this area inhibited feeding. The *lateral* hypothalamus (LH) was considered to be a complementary "feeding center," primarily because lesions in this region produced *aphagia* (not eating) and *adipsia* (not drinking), and would eventually lead to death if the animal were not force-fed.

Newer techniques, however, enabled researchers to examine the role of the pathways which ran through these regions, and which were damaged during lesions. The dopaminergic nigrostriatal pathway produces symptoms almost identical to those produced by LH lesion. The LH lesion was therefore not destroying any hypothetical "feeding center," but was impairing the animal's dopaminergic system, the system which is so important in all kinds of motivation and reward. Chemical lesions of the

ventral noradrenergic bundle partly reproduce the symptoms of the VMH lesioned animal, so it is likely that many of the symptoms following VMH lesions were due to destruction of this pathway. Although the dopaminergic pathway probably serves an energizing and rewarding function which is critical if the animal is to continue eating, the role of the ventral noradrenergic bundle in satiety is not yet clear. The function of the dopamine pathway, however, is not limited to feeding behavior, but seems to operate in all motivated behaviors.

Since the VMH and LH were not the centers which both monitored fuel supply and initiated feeding behavior when fuel was low, researchers began to reexamine the role of peripheral structures. As food is taken into the mouth, it is slowly broken down by the organs along the digestive tract until it is in a form which can be absorbed by the small intestines. The period when food is still being absorbed from the digestive tract is called the *absorptive phase*, and the period when no food is being absorbed is called the *postabsorptive phase*. The absorptive phase is dominated by the storage of nutrients, while the postabsorptive phase is dominated by the utilization of stored nutrients.

Studies on the roles of peripheral structures in the control of food intake have revealed that there is no single feeding or satiety monitor—there are multiple controls. The mouth and head play a role in food intake; for example, humans and animals eat more when the food tastes good, but less when it tastes bad. When nutrients reach the small intestine, a gastrointestinal hormone called *cholecystokinin* (CCK) is released. The hormone produces satiety, since injections of it will inhibit feeding.

The liver is ideally suited to monitor the body's supply of nutrients and it probably plays the most important role in food intake. This organ contains receptors which monitor glucose utilization and which also monitor the amount of stored nutrients in some way. This information is then sent to the brain, probably via the vagus nerve.

When the body's fuel supply is low, a great many things happen. Fuel is mobilized from fat reserves, glycogen is converted back into glucose in the liver, and the organism also becomes hungry so that new nutrients can be obtained. While the liver contains the monitors which send messages to the brain to initiate feeding, the brain probably has its own monitors which control the release of epinephrine by the adrenal glands. This hormone is released to aid in the breakdown of stored fuel when the brain's monitors detect a reduction in fuel supply.

The control of food intake is therefore not the simple matter of stomach contractions that was once thought. Nor is it a simple matter of feeding or satiety centers in the brain which monitor fuel and initiate feeding. Current research emphasized the multiple controls over feeding and metabolism—by both peripheral structures, such as the liver, and by the brain. Current researchers are also speculating on the way that information about body fuel can activate motor pathways which control feeding reflexes. One such speculation suggests that the catecholamine fibers which act as general energizers inhibit interneurons that are themselves inhibitory. The interneurons are presumed to synapse onto preprogrammed neural circuits which control feeding reflexes and other goal-directed consummatory responses.

The complexity of food intake is such that it is no wonder that there are as yet no "miracle drugs" to cure obesity. But researchers ponder possible causes and cures for this common condition. Some scientists hypothesize that the physiological changes which occur during mild stress activate the dopaminergic pathways involved in incentive motivation for food stimuli. Perhaps stress plays a key role in the development of obesity. Other scientists emphasize that obese humans rely more on external cues to trigger eating (such as the taste, sight and odor of food), whereas normal-weighted people rely more on the internal changes accompanying low levels of body fuel. This kind of external control of eating behavior is remarkably similar to the behavior observed in VMH-lesioned rats, although there is no evidence suggesting that the parallel is more than coincidental.

---

the regulation of water balance   In order to survive, an animal must not only maintain an energy balance by means of food intake, it also must maintain a water balance. For the average adult, the daily water exchange is approximately 2500 ml. Water is lost through the lungs, the skin, and the kidneys, and it is gained through water intake, and the intake of foods containing water. Meat, for example, is actually about 70% water, and some fruits are nearly 100% water.

The water content of the body is generally from 50 to 60% of the total body weight; for a 150-lb person, over 75 lb would be water. This large volume of water is divided into two different body **compartments**—the **intracellular** and the **extracellular**.

The intracellular fluid compartment refers to the fluid which is contained within the cells of the body. The extracellular compartment refers to the fluid that is not in the cells, and is either in between the cells, called **interstitial fluid**, or fluid that is in the blood, called **plasma**. Because the cell membranes are not permeable to all ions, the concentration of ions is different for the intracellular and extracellular fluid. In particular, the concentration of sodium ions is very high in the extracellular fluid, but very low for the intracellular fluid. The concentration of potassium ions is the reverse; high inside the cell, low outside.

Although the ions have difficulty crossing the cell membranes, water does not. Under normal conditions, the water passes freely from one fluid compartment to another, but its movement is in part determined by ionic concentrations. Ions exert osmotic pressure; the more concentrated the ions are, the more the water will tend to move toward the compartment with this higher concentration of ions.

Figure 11.16 demonstrates this movement when the ionic concentrations of sodium are changed. Under normal conditions, the osmotic pressures inside the intracellular compartment and in the extracellular compartment are equal (even though the *kinds* of ions in the two compartments may differ), so there is no net water loss from either compartment. But if sodium ions are added to the extracellular compartment (perhaps because of an injection of sodium chloride), the osmotic pressure of the fluid within the extracellular compartment will increase. This will result in a movement of water from the cells of the body to the extracellular compartment to reestablish the osmotic balance between the two water compartments. As we shall see, the sudden loss of water from one of the fluid compartments, in this case the intracellular compartment, is a potent stimulus for drinking.

Loss of water from the intracellular compartment is called **cellular dehydration**, while loss of water from the extracellular compartment is called **hypovolemia**. These losses can occur independently of one another, or they may occur together. Each type of loss produces thirst and drinking.

The kind of drinking which results from loss of water from either one of the fluid compartments is called **primary drinking**. This kind of drinking is related to the water deficit, and the animal is drinking in order to restore water balance. Fitzsimons (1971) lists a number of

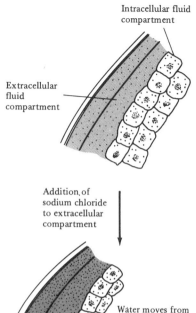

Intracellular fluid compartment

Extracellular fluid compartment

Addition of sodium chloride to extracellular compartment

Water moves from intracellular to extracellular compartment

Figure 11.16
An example of the effects of the osmotic pressure of ions.

events which would result in water loss and subsequent primary drinking. (See Table 11.3.) The table also lists which events produce water loss in the extracellular and intracellular compartments.

Because primary drinking results from loss of water from one or both of the two fluid compartments, researchers have formulated the **double depletion hypothesis** of thirst. This hypothesis has provided a very coherent framework for most of the findings related to primary drinking, and we will discuss the events which occur following loss of water from each of the body compartments in a moment. But the hypothesis does not attempt to account for the drinking behavior which occurs in the absence of water loss from the fluid compartments, called **secondary drinking**.

The table also lists a number of events, such as dry mouth, which often produce secondary drinking; but these events are not related to water loss. There are no apparent changes in the volume of water in either of the fluid compartments, but the animal nevertheless drinks. Later in the chapter we shall return to this topic, but for now, we shall

Table 11.3
The causes of drinking[a]

	Cellular volume	Extracellular volume
(a) Primary drinking		
Water deprivation	↓	↓
Injection of hypertonic solutions of substances which are excluded from the cells	↓	↑
Potassium depletion	↓	0
Hemorrhage	0	↓
Sodium depletion	0 or ↑	↓
Extracellular depletion by injection of hyperoncotic colloid	0	↓
Exercise	0	↓
(b) Secondary drinking		
Rhythmic	0	0
Gustatory	0	0
Dry mouth	0	0
Psychogenic	0	0
Direct stimulation of nervous centers	0	0
Pathological	?	?

[a] From Fitzsimons (1971).
Key: ↓ = decrease; ↑ = increase; 0 = no change.

simply state that most day-to-day drinking by an animal is of the secondary variety, rather than the primary. Most research on drinking behavior has emphasized the primary kind, which is usually related to emergency situations when a great deal of water is lost from one or both of the fluid compartments.

cellular dehydration

Figure 11.17 shows the events which occur during cellular dehydration. The left side shows the body's fluid compartments in the normal situation of water balance. The right side shows how the cells shrink as water is lost. This kind of water loss can occur from any of the events listed in Table 11.3, or it may occur from the increase in solute concentration of the plasma which results from postdigestive absorption from the gut. Drinking, which occurs during eating, helps to prevent solute concentration differences produced by this absorption.

When cellular dehydration occurs, two major events happen: the animal's pituitary releases **antidiuretic hormone (ADH)**, and the animal begins to drink. The ADH provides a signal to the water conservation mechanisms in the kidney to retain water. This retention aids in the reduction of the osmotic pressure of the extracellular fluid compartment. The new intake of water also reduces the osmotic pressure gradient, so water can be restored to the intracellular compartment.

cellular dehydration "monitors." The release of ADH by the pituitary, and the drinking behavior, can only occur if there is some mechanism which monitors the amount of cellular dehydration. This mechanism should have access to both the pituitary gland and to the neural pathways which initiate drinking.

These **osmoreceptors** are clearly located in or near the hypothalamus, but it is not yet certain exactly where. The **lateral preoptic area** is a very good candidate for the location of these receptors because rats with lesions in this area do not drink in response to intravenous sodium chloride injections, a procedure which produces cellular dehydration (Blass and Epstein, 1971). Blass and Epstein also demonstrated that intracranial application of hypertonic saline to the lateral preoptic region results in immediate drinking, even though the rats were otherwise in water balance. Intracranial application of hypertonic saline to other brain areas, such as the lateral hypothalamus, did not elicit drinking. Furthermore, when they applied distilled water to the lateral preoptic, they found that it reduced the amount of drinking in response to intravenous sodium chloride injections. These findings clearly suggested that the lateral preoptic region contains osmoreceptors which monitor cellular dehydration.

Peck and Novin (1971) came to a similar conclusion from their studies on the rabbit. They directly applied either hypertonic saline, su-

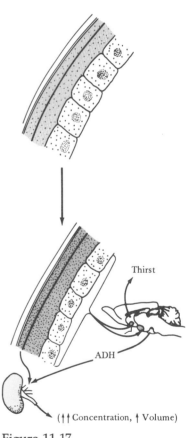

Thirst

ADH

($\uparrow\uparrow$ Concentration, $\uparrow$ Volume)

Figure 11.17
Simplified schema for the cellular dehydration control of thirst and ADH release. [From Epstein (1973).]

the regulation of water balance **313**

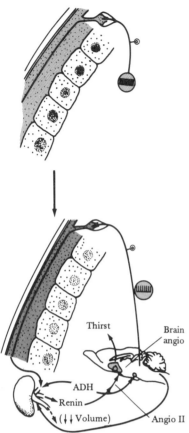

Figure 11.18
Simplified schema for the extra-
cellular control of thirst and ADH
release. [From Epstein (1973).]

crose, or urea to the lateral preoptic area by means of a chronic cannula. Both the saline and the sucrose are excluded from cells, and thus would produce cellular dehydration because of the increase in extracellular osmotic pressure; but the urea is not excluded, so it should not produce cellular dehydration. They found that a few placements of the cannula elicited drinking from the saline and sucrose, but not the urea. All of the placements were in the lateral preoptic region.

Unfortunately, this aesthetically pleasing and clear-cut picture of osmoreceptors in the lateral preoptic has become clouded by some recent findings. Coburn and Stricker (1978) demonstrated that rats with lesions in this area would increase their water intake following cellular dehydration produced by an injection of sodium chloride, if they were given some time. The rats also showed this kind of osmoregulation when the experimenters put the extra salt in their diet. This means that if the lateral preoptic does contain osmoreceptors, it is probably not the only place in the brain which monitors cellular dehydration; rats without the lateral preoptic can respond to osmoregulatory challenges if they are not too severe.

One spot which may also contain such osmoreceptors is the **periventricular area** of the hypothalamus. Lesions of this area also abolish drinking in response to injections of hypertonic saline (Buggy and Johnson, 1977). This area is also important as a monitor of water loss from the extracellular fluid compartment, as we shall see later.

The neurons of the lateral preoptic, and probably other areas as well, appear to be sensitive to cellular dehydration. They are the best candidates at the moment for the activation of neurons which control the motor responses involved in drinking behavior. Another set of neurons in the **nucleus circularis** may monitor cellular dehydration and adjust the output of ADH by the pituitary (Hatton, 1976). Lesions of this tiny area in the hypothalamus produce deficits in the release of ADH following cellular dehydration. Electrical stimulation of this area results in water retention by the kidneys. Since this nucleus sends fibers to the neurons in the hypothalamus which actually produce ADH, it is reasonable to suppose that these putative osmoreceptors are controlling the ADH response to cellular dehydration.

hypovolemia Figure 11.18 summarizes the events which occur during hypovolemia. These events are rather complicated and we will consider only the major ones, those which are more directly related to drinking behavior.

The diagram shows that in the normal state of affairs, when the animal is not hypovolemic, a mechanoreceptor which is responsive to pressure on the vascular walls is emitting a tonic rate of discharge. But when the extracellular compartment loses fluid, the pressure on the vascular walls declines and the rate of firing of this mechanoreceptor slows down. Some of these mechanoreceptors are located in the heart, where any changes in blood pressure would be immediately detectable. The signal which these neurons provide is relayed to the brain, where it initiates the following events.

ADH release. The signal from the mechanoreceptors results in the release of antidiuretic hormones from the posterior pituitary gland. The ADH then stimulates water retention in the kidney by increasing the permeability of the kidney tubules to water, thus allowing more water to be reabsorbed. Figure 11.19 summarizes the control of ADH release.

renin, angiotensin, and aldosterone.   The signal from the mechanoreceptors also results in sympathetic activation of cells in the kidney which secrete a hormone called **renin**. These **juxtaglomerular cells** release renin into the bloodstream, where a series of chemical reactions transforms the hormone into **angiotensin**. Angiotensin has a number of effects. First, it stimulates the adrenal cortex to release another hormone called **aldosterone**. This hormone acts on the kidneys, to stimulate the retention of sodium. This particular step in water con-

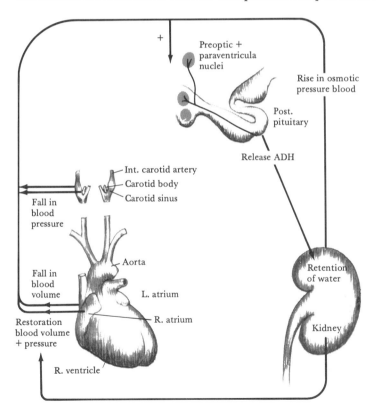

Figure 11.19
Summary of the control of release of ADH from the posterior pituitary gland. [From Clegg and Clegg (1968).]

servation is very important, because if an organism does not have enough sodium it cannot retain water. As you may recall from our discussion in the beginning of the chapter, water moves across membranes partly because of the osmotic pressure generated by sodium concentrations. If the sodium content of the kidneys is too low, then water will not be able to move down the concentration gradient back into the kidney tubules; it will be released into the urine. The renin–angiotensin–aldosterone system is summarized in Figure 11.20.

thirst. Another event which is precipitated by hypovolemia is thirst and drinking (if water is available). Thirst can probably be produced in several different ways, first by direct activation from the signals coming from the mechanoreceptors which monitor blood pressure. Fitzsimons (1971) tested this hypothesis by occluding the **vena cava** in rats. This vein brings blood back to the heart from the rest of the body, and its occlusion would result in immediate decline in blood pressure at the point where some of the mechanoreceptors are located. This procedure resulted in immediate drinking, even though the animals were not hypovolemic.

These rats might have begun drinking because the signals from the mechanoreceptors were going directly to the brain and initiating the motor responses there. But they might have begun drinking because the signals went to the kidney, which then released renin. The angiotensin which was produced from renin might have acted directly on the brain to initiate drinking. As it turns out, the rats probably began

Figure 11.20
The renin–angiotensin–aldosterone system.

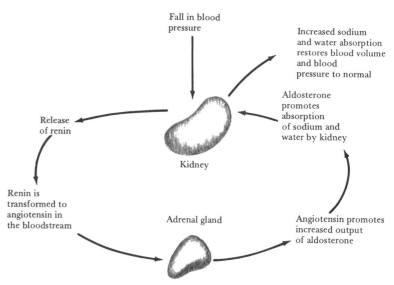

Fall in blood pressure

Increased sodium and water absorption restores blood volume and blood pressure to normal

Release of renin

Aldosterone promotes absorption of sodium and water by kidney

Kidney

Renin is transformed to angiotensin in the bloodstream

Adrenal gland

Angiotensin promotes increased output of aldosterone

drinking for *both* reasons. The body has more than one way to react to the loss of water.

Stricker (1973) demonstrated that the mechanoreceptors could initiate drinking directly by studying **nephrectomized** rats (animals whose kidneys had been removed). He injected a colloid into the intraperitoneal cavity of these animals, a procedure which results in hypovolemia. The fall in blood pressure which was precipitated by the loss of extracellular fluid produced drinking. This drinking could not have been mediated by the hormone from the kidneys, since the kindeys were gone. It probably was directly produced by the signals coming from the mechanoreceptors. The brain endpoint for those signals is not yet known.

angiotensin and thirst. Aside from changes in the activity of the mechanoreceptors, hypovolemia also causes the kidneys to release renin which is then transformed to angiotensin. Angiotensin causes the adrenal glands to release aldosterone; but it also can effect brain cells directly, and produce thirst. Epstein *et al.* (1970) injected angiotensin into the brains of rats and found that they immediately began drinking. The most effective sites in the brain included the septum, preoptic region, and anterior hypothalamus.

Since the angiotensin diffuses from the point of injection, it is not entirely clear at the moment exactly where these angiotensin receptors might be. A good candidate is the periventricular area of the hypothalamus, since lesions in and around this area abolish the drinking response to injections of angiotensin. This region also probably contains cells which are responsive to cellular dehydration, as you may recall from the previous section. But angiotensin receptors may be distributed through various areas and it may be impossible to pinpoint any "drinking center."

Recent findings suggest that angiotensin and angiotensin receptors may play only a minor role in the initiation of drinking (Stricker, 1978; Andersson, 1978). Many of the studies which demonstrated that injections of angiotensin produced increased water intake used rather large doses of the substance. The technique of radioimmunoassay has been able to show that these large blood and CSF levels of angiotensin probably never occur in the normal animal, even during water deprivation. Although angiotensin probably contributes to the initiation of drinking, it probably cannot account for all of the drinking which is observed following hypovolemia.

The research done on cellular dehydration and hypovolemia *secondary drinking* provides the framework for the double depletion hypothesis, and these studies are designed to account for primary drinking. Most of the drinking done by animals on a day-to-day basis is secondary in nature, in the sense that it is not a response to any water lost from one of the body's compartments. Animals drink in anticipation of their need for water, rather than in response to water loss. For example, 70% of the rat's 24-hour water intake is drunk just before, during, and immediately after meals (Fitzsimons and LeMagnen, 1969). Thus the rat anticipates a fluid deficit because most drinking will have occurred before the food is absorbed from the intestines.

learning. The anticipation of future water needs suggests that an animal learns to drink as much as it will need. Fitzsimons and LeMagnen (1969) demonstrated that learning plays a key role in drinking behavior by first maintaining rats on a carbohydrate diet. These rats consumed about an equal quantity of food and water. But when they were shifted to a high protein diet, which produces more hypovolemia and thus requires more water, the animals began to drink about one and a half times as much. At first, the rats drank the extra water *after* the meal, but within a few days they began to drink the extra water *during* the meal. This suggests that they had learned to anticipate a greater water deficit.

For some reason that is not quite clear, most animals have a tendency to drink more than they need. For example, Dicker and Nunn (1957) found that a rat usually drinks about 12 ml of water for each 100 gm of body weight. But when these experimenters restricted the rat's water intake to 7.5 ml per 100 gm of body weight, the animals accommodated with ease. There was no reduction in food intake or body weight, although there was a reduction in urine flow. Since overdrinking is not harmful, but underdrinking could have dire consequences, the animals may have learned to leave a safe margin for error in their anticipation of future water needs.

brain mechanisms for secondary drinking. Very little research has been conducted on the causes of secondary drinking, but one recent series of experiments suggests that the **zona incerta** may be involved in its control. This area is near the lateral hypothalamus and is often damaged when lesions are made in this region. Evered and Mogenson (1976), however, made lesions which were restricted to the zona incerta and found that the rats showed a permanent reduction in water intake of about 20 to 30%. Body weight and food intake were not affected by the lesion. The lesion also had no effect on the animal's ability to respond to hydrational challenges, produced by hypovolemia or cellular dehydration. Furthermore, the lesioned rats were able to increase their water intake when they were placed on a high protein diet. The lesions affected only the animal's secondary drinking behavior, not its primary drinking. This study is suggestive that the zona incerta may play a role in secondary drinking, but it is not conclusive.

In the previous section on the control of food intake, we noted that damage to the lateral hypothalamus resulted in aphagia and adipsia, and this syndrome is most likely related to a loss of attentional and motivational processes rather than to any loss of neural centers regulating food intake. The loss of drinking, therefore, can probably also be explained on the basis of inattention and lack of motivation. But the recovery from an LH lesion can tell us something about how these motivational processes are restored, and studies on the recovery of drinking shed light on this issue.

Figure 11.4 showed the four stages of recovery from an LH lesion; notice that the "recovered" animal still has some major deficits, particularly some related to drinking behavior. The rat does not respond to hydrational challenges. It will often "regress" when it is given some kind of challenge (such as an injection of hypertonic saline), and revert back to one of the earlier stages of recovery. But Stricker (1976) has found that the "recovered" animal is able to meet hydrational challenges if they are not too severe. For example, lesioned animals do not drink water during the first 3 hours after an injection of hypertonic saline, but Stricker recorded for 24 hours after a small injection, and found that the lesioned animals did drink.

Stricker (1976) suggests that the recovery of LH animals is partly due to recovery of the rewarding catecholamine systems. When the animal is first lesioned, catecholamine pathways are destroyed or severly damaged, so the animal does not eat or drink. But during recovery, there is an increased release of dopamine from the remaining intact fibers and also an increased efficiency of the neurotransmitter that is being released. This recovery of the dopamine pathways occurs slowly, and even in the "recovered" animal, the pathway is still impaired. Any intense stimulus (such as a large and sudden hydrational challenge) would increase the activity of the remaining dopamine pathways to such an extent that synthesis could not keep up with turnover. Then there would be a rapid drop in the dopamine levels and the animal would "regress" to an earlier stage of recovery. But if the hydrational challenge were slight, then the animal's dopamine pathways would be able to handle it—and the animal would drink.

the LH syndrome revisited— recovery of function

The regulation of water balance in an animal requires two basic things: first, the animal must have some way of monitoring water loss, and second, it must have the neural equipment which leads the animal to drink. For the first requirement, we find that an animal has monitors for different kinds of water loss, located both in the brain and in various places in the periphery. For the second requirement, we find that the motivation to drink is in part due to the activation of the rewarding catecholamine systems.

The body contains two fluid compartments, the *intracellular* and the *extracellular*, and there are two sets of monitors, which detect loss of

summary
The Regulation of Water Balance

water from each compartment. Water loss from the intracellular compartment can be produced by injections of hypertonic saline or potassium depletion (see Table 11.3). Regions of the hypothalamus are thought to contain *osmoreceptors* which are sensitive to cellular dehydration. The *nucleus circularis* in the hypothalamus may also monitor cellular dehydration in order to stimulate the pituitary gland to release *antidiuretic hormone* (ADH). This hormone aids in the retention of water by making the membranes of the kidney tubules more permeable to water and thus increases water conservation.

Water loss from the extracellular compartment is called *hypovolemia* and occurs during such events as hemorrhage, exercise, or sodium depletion. The major monitor for this type of water loss is located in the heart, and is actually keeping track of blood pressure. It is a neural monitor, and sends its signal to the brain via some as yet unknown pathway. When hypovolemia occurs, the pituitary releases ADH, and the kidney releases a hormone called *renin*. The renin is changed into *angiotensin*, which has two separate effects. First, it causes the adrenal glands to release *aldosterone*, a hormone which causes the kidneys to retain sodium. Second, it may act on angiotensin receptors in the brain, probably in the *periventricular area* of the hypothalmus, to initiate at least some drinking. Drinking behavior can also be initiated directly by the activity of the neural mechanoreceptors since hypovolemia produces drinking even in animals without kidneys. Thus the animal has two separate means

to regulate water balance, depending upon what type of water loss occurs. During water deprivation, water is lost from both compartments, so it is likely that all the mechanisms are brought into play to conserve water and to initiate drinking. However, these mechanisms are mainly reserved for emergency situations when a great deal of water is lost from one of the body compartments. This kind of drinking is called *primary drinking*, but most of the water consumed during the day is not in response to an emergency situation. The reasons why an animal engages in this *secondary drinking* are not clear, but learning to anticipate water deficits probably plays a major role.

The loss of water thus produces a number of effects which encourage the kidney's conservation of water, such as the release of ADH and aldosterone. Water loss also brings on drinking, to increase the amount of water in the body. The neural pathways which are activated as a result of any changes in activity of the "monitors" are not yet clear, but it is very likely that the rewarding catecholamine pathway is very much involved. Drinking is a motivated behavior, motivated by water loss, and the pathway seems to activate and direct the animal's attention toward stimuli which are appropriate to the motivation. There are probably other pathways more directly related to the motor responses required for drinking which are also activated during thirst. But when this major catecholamine pathway is damaged, it is difficult to get the animal to perform *any* motivated behavior, drinking included.

KEY TERMS

peripheralist theory	aphagia
centralist theory	adipsia
ventromedial hypothalamus	VMH syndrome
hyperphagia	dynamic phase
lateral hypothalamus	static phase

gold thioglucose
LH syndrome
desmethylimipramine
sensory neglect
pimozide
anhedonia
chyme
absorptive phase
postabsorptive phase
insulin
glycogen
diabetes mellitus
glucagon
glucostatic theory
lipostatic theory
cholecystokinin (CCK)
hepatic portal vein
2-deoxyglucose (2-DG)
hypoglycemia
intracellular fluid compartment

extracellular fluid compartment
interstitial fluid
plasma
cellular dehydration
hypovolemia
primary drinking
double depletion hypothesis
secondary drinking
antidiuretic hormone (ADH)
osmoreceptors
lateral preoptic area
periventricular area
nucleus circularis
renin
juxtaglomerular cells
angiotensin
aldosterone
vena cava
nephrectomy
zona incerta

SUGGESTED READINGS

Andersson, B. (1978). Regulation of water intake. *Physiological Reviews, 58*, 582–603.

Epstein, A. N. (1973). Epilogue: retrospect and prognosis. *In* The Neuropsychology of Thirst: New Findings and Advances in Concepts (A. N. Epstein *et al.*, eds.), pp. 315–332. Wiley, New York. (These two references provide additional detail on the regulation of water balance.)

Novin, D., Wyrwicka, W., and Bray, G. A., eds. (1976). *Hunger: Basic Mechanisms and Clinical Implications.* Raven Press, New York. (This book contains a collection of readings by scientists working in the area. The chapter by G. J. Mogenson is particularly readable.)

Schacter, S. (1971). *Emotion, Obesity, and Crime.* Academic Press, New York. (This book presents some of Schacter's studies and insights on the relationship between obesity and external control.)

12

*sexual
behavior*

introduction   The motivation to eat and drink is readily apparent in practically all animal species, but the motivation for sex may not be so obvious. Certainly animals can survive without sex as long as they consume food and water. Even so, the theory of evolution predicts that the motivation for sex is actually more important than that for food and water. If no members of the species engaged in sex the species would die out rather quickly; if only a few participated, the genes of these few would be very common in succeeding generations. Whatever genes had contributed to the motivation for sexual behavior would rapidly proliferate, and the result would be that practically all members of the species would possess them. The moth described in the beginning of Chapter 7 illustrates just how powerful the motivation for sexual behavior can be. The male only lives for a short time and does not waste any energy on finding food or water—it only searches for a mate (using olfactory cues).

While it may be true that nearly every member of the species has some motivation for sex, their sexual behavior is influenced by an enormous number of factors. In humans, for example, cultural standards invariably regulate sexual behavior. Our culture in the United States has traditionally frowned on premarital sex even though the motivation may be very strong. Practical matters may also have important effects: many people may feel more sexually aroused in the morning but because of the need to get up, get dressed, and get to work, the actual sex behavior may be put off until evening. Because this book deals with physiology and behavior we will discuss the biological factors that contribute to the control of sexual behavior. Nevertheless, it is important to keep in mind that sex behavior in humans (and animals, too) is influenced by many nonbiological factors as well.

Human beings basically come in two varieties: male and female. In the first section of this chapter we will discuss the obvious differences, those which are most closely related to sexual behavior. In the next section we will examine how those differences emerge during development in a process called **sexual differentiation.** In the last section we will examine the biological bases of adult sexual behavior, concentrating on hormonal, neural, and environmental effects, and the effects of drugs.

the differences between   It used to be a simple matter to tell the difference between adult men
males and females   and women. Now with "unisex" hairstyling and dress, it is no longer so simple. Without clothing, though, it is still very simple in most cases, because the distribution of body fat and body hair is different for both sexes, and of course the genitalia are different. But boys and girls who have not yet reached puberty and are not yet secreting adult levels of sex hormones are very similar in body size and shape, so the

only way to tell the difference is by checking the genitalia (or by asking, which is a somewhat more culturally acceptable method). In some animals, such as the dove, you cannot even discriminate between males and females by checking the external genitalia. The only way is to look for testes or ovaries during surgery. (Presumably, the doves can tell the difference without surgery.) Thus species vary a good deal in the amount of **sexual dimorphism,** or observable body differences between the sexes.

In this section we will explore the differences between the sexes. We begin with the genetic difference, the one that sets the stage for development of all the other differences. Then we will examine the morphological and physiological differences between males and females. And finally, we will examine some of the more controversial behavioral differences.

genetic difference between males and females

Normal human beings have 23 pairs of chromosomes in each nucleus of almost every body cell. The chromosomes contain the DNA which directs the formation of protein throughout the life of the organism. Twenty-two of these pairs are called **autosomes.** All human beings have these, although the genetic information on these chromosomes is not identical. In each pair of autosomes, the two chromosomes may not contain exactly the same bases in the DNA sequence, but the *function* of the information is the same. For example, if one member of a pair has a gene which codes for a particular protein which acts as a stomach enzyme, the other member of the chromosome pair has a gene in the same place which also codes for a protein with this function, although the actual constituents of the protein may not be identical.

The twenty-third pair of chromosomes are called **sex chromosomes** because they are different in males and females. Females have two X chromosomes, which contain homologous genes just like the autosomes. Males have only one X chromosome which has no homologous pair. Instead they have a much shorter Y chromosome. A female is therefore XX, while a male is XY. In some as yet unknown way, this genetic difference triggers different developmental patterns in the morphology and physiology of males and females.

morphological differences between males and females

The most obvious difference between adult males and females is in the morphology of the reproductive organs. Figure 12.1 diagrams the main components of these organs for males and females.

The primary reproductive organ for the male is the **testis,** and for the female it is the **ovary.** Generically these are known as **gonads,** and their presence determines the growth and development of the individual's **secondary sex characteristics.** Secondary sex characteristics in-

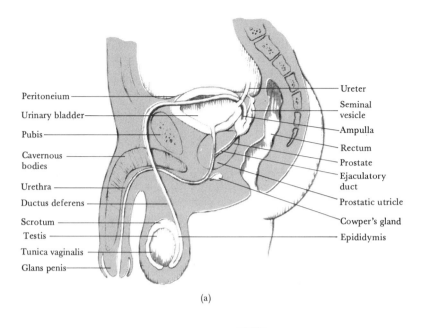

Peritoneium — Ureter

Urinary bladder — Seminal vesicle

Pubis — Ampulla

Cavernous bodies — Rectum

— Prostate

Urethra — Ejaculatory duct

Ductus deferens — Prostatic utricle

Scrotum — Cowper's gland

Testis — Epididymis

Tunica vaginalis

Glans penis

(a)

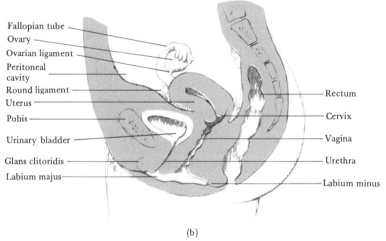

Fallopian tube
Ovary
Ovarian ligament
Peritoneal cavity
Round ligament — Rectum
Uterus
Pubis — Cervix
Urinary bladder — Vagina
Glans clitoridis — Urethra
Labium majus
— Labium minus

(b)

Figure 12.1
(a) Male reproductive anatomy.
(b) Female reproductive
anatomy. [Adapted from Turner
et al. (1971).]

clude the accessory organs and glands that are essential for successful reproduction, and the morphological features which differentiate the male and female of a species, such as body size, the pitch of the voice, and distribution of body hair and body fat.

male anatomy. In order for a man to successfully reproduce, he must produce sperm in a process called **spermatogenesis.** The testes, in which spermatogenesis occurs, hang in the **scrotal sac** outside the main body cavity. This is important because spermatogenesis requires a cooler environment, and the temperature of the scrotal sac is one degree cooler than that of the body. The sperm travels through a series of organs, including the **epididymis,** a highly coiled tube designed to store sperm from the tubules of the testes, the **ductus deferens,** and finally the **ejaculatory duct.** The ejaculatory duct joins the **urethra,** and sperm is pulsed out through this tube during ejaculation. In order to deliver sperm into the vaginal canal of the female, the penis must be erect. During sexual arousal, the cavernous bodies in the penis become filled with blood, producing erection. After ejaculation, the blood is released and the penis becomes flaccid.

The testes produce sperm, but they are also an endocrine gland which produces hormones called **androgens.** In human beings **testosterone** is the main androgen, and its release at puberty results in the development of the secondary sex characteristics, such as deeper voice, larger body size, and the distribution of body fat and body hair characteristic of the male. This hormone also has effects on the brain and behavior, as we shall see later in this chapter.

female anatomy. Panel (b) of Figure 12.1 shows the reproductive organs of the female which consist of ovaries, **oviducts, uterus, vagina,** and the external genitalia. Each ovary contains as many as 500,000 **follicles,** each of which contains a single immature egg cell. About every 28 days, one or more of these egg cells mature and is released by a ruptured follicle into the oviduct. This process is called **ovulation** and usually occurs during the middle part of the menstrual cycle. If the mature egg cell is fertilized by a sperm from the male, the egg will implant in the wall of the uterus and will develop into a fetus. If it is not fertilized, the egg cell will be discharged during menstruation, along with the blood and nutrients which had been built up in the uterine walls in order to receive a fertilized egg.

The ovaries are also endocrine glands which produce two hormones called **estrogen** and **progesterone.** These two hormones have widespread effects on secondary sexual characteristics at puberty, such as breast development and distribution of body hair and fat.

We mentioned that the primary gonads of males and females produce hormones, and hormonal differences are one of the main features that differentiate males and females. But males produce some estrogen and progesterone, and females produce some androgen so the hormonal difference between the two sexes is not a qualitative one, but rather a quantitative one. The ratio of androgens to estrogen and progesterone is much higher in males, and this ratio is reversed for females.

Figure 12.2 shows a summary of the metabolic events during the production of sex hormones in both sexes. The biosynthesis of all of

physiological differences between males and females

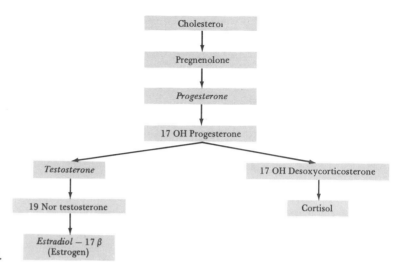

Figure 12.2
Biosynthesis of steroid hormones.

these steroid hormones follows a common route, so males are going to have some female hormones circulating in their blood, and females are going to have some androgens. Notice that the biosynthetic route for some adrenocortical hormones (e.g., cortisol) is related to the route for the production of sex hormones. This means that the adrenal glands as well as the gonads can be a source of sex hormones. Later in the chapter we will see how the adrenal glands can play an important role in the sexual behavior of females, and how their hormones can modify the development of some sexual characteristics.

Although both sexes produce all types of sex hormones, but in different ratios, the pattern of production is very different. In females the hormones are released cyclically. Across the menstrual cycle, the quantities of estrogen and progesterone that are released show marked fluctuations. Males produce hormones in a more tonic fashion without the marked fluctuations. The release of sex hormones by the gonads, in either a tonic or cyclic fashion, is controlled by hormones from the pituitary gland. The release of the pituitary gland's hormones is ultimately controlled by the hypothalamus; so it is actually the brain which is telling the gonads what to do and when to do it. This interesting arrangement is discussed in the next section.

hormones from the pituitary gland. The pituitary produces a number of protein hormones which have a variety of effects throughout the body. For example, it produces ACTH, which was mentioned in Chapter 10 in connection with its effects on the adrenal glands. It also produces **luteinizing hormone (LH), follicle-stimulating hormone (FSH),** and **prolactin,** all of which are involved in reproductive behavior. LH and FSH are called **gonadotrophins** because they directly control the output of steroid hormones from the gonads, while prolactin is involved in lactation.

In the adult male, the output of LH and FSH by the pituitary gland is relatively constant over time. FSH maintains spermatogenesis in the testes, and LH causes the production and secretion of testosterone.

In the female, the output of these two pituitary hormones changes dramatically over the menstrual cycle. Figure 12.3 diagrams the changes in output of LH and FSH across a 28-day cycle. During the first part of the cycle, when LH levels are low but FSH is high, the follicles in the ovary are being stimulated to mature by FSH (hence its name). The developing follicle is the source of estrogen, and when the follicle has reached maturity it releases a surge of this ovarian hormone. Right after the surge of estrogen the pituitary releases a surge of both its hormones, particularly LH.

The effect of the LH surge is to rupture the mature follicle so that ovulation occurs. The ruptured follicle, now called a **corpus luteum,** produces less estrogen so blood levels of estrogen drop; but it produces large amounts of progesterone, so progesterone levels rise. As

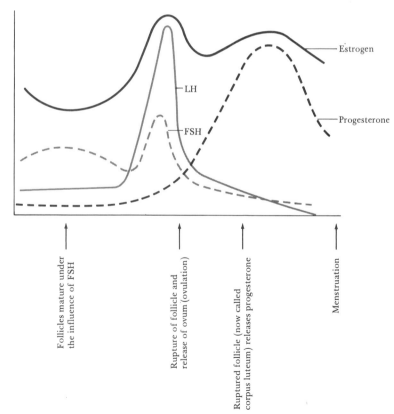

Figure 12.3
Major hormonal events during the menstrual cycle.

the differences between males and females **329**

the corpus luteum begins to degenerate during the final days of the cycle, the circulating levels of progesterone begin to drop also.

To summarize the cyclic hormonal production of females; the first part of the cycle is dominated by LH and rising estrogen levels, the middle, ovulational part is characterized by high estrogen levels and a sudden surge of both pituitary hormones (particularly LH), and the final part is dominated by low levels of both pituitary hormones, medium levels of estrogen, and high levels of progesterone. At this point, if the egg cells were not fertilized and implanted in the uterus, menstruation would commence.

the control of the pituitary by the hypothalamus. In the previous chapter we noted that cells within the hypothalamus, and cells which pass through it, play a key role in motivated behavior; sex behavior is no exception. The functions of these cells in sex behavior are diverse, and not yet entirely clear, but some of them are clearly involved in the control of hormone output by the pituitary gland.

Figure 12.4 diagrams the relationships between the hypothalamus and pituitary gland. Neurosecretory cells in the hypothalamus actually terminate in the posterior part of the pituitary. These cells release two hormones, called **oxytocin** and **vasopressin,** which are involved in the birth process and with water conservation by the kidney. Since they do not relate directly to sex behavior we pause only to mention them.

The connection between the hypothalamus and the anterior pituitary is not a neural one, but a blood connection. The hypothalamus releases a blood borne factor which affects the release of LH and FSH by the pituitary gland. One such blood borne factor is called **LH releasing factor (LH-RF)** because it results in increased output of LH by the pituitary gland.

It is not yet clear whether there is a separate releasing factor for FSH because LH-RF also has the ability to stimulate FSH release. There is some evidence that FSH may have a separate releasing factor because

Figure 12.4
Schematic diagram of the relationship between the hypothalamus and the pituitary gland. [*Adapted from Levine (1972).*]

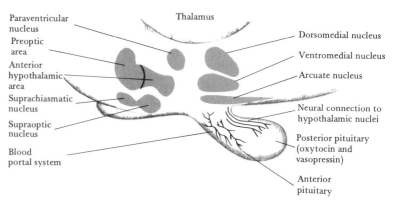

there appear to be separate hypothalamic areas which can stimulate the release of LH or FSH from the pituitary. Chappel and Barraclough (1976) electrically stimulated the medial preoptic area of the rat, and found a release of both FSH and LH. When they stimulated the dorsal anterior area of the hypothalamus, FSH secretion occurred alone. This suggests that these two different hypothalamic areas may synthesize separate releasing hormones. The FSH-RF molecule would be one which does not affect the release of LH, whereas the LH-RF molecule can affect the release of both pituitary hormones. Table 12.1 summarizes the events which occur in the hypothalamus, pituitary, and gonads, in both males and females.

The difference between the males and females which produces cyclicity in the female but not the male is in the hypothalamus, not in

Table 12.1
An overview of the reproductive hormones

Hypothalamic hormones

FSH-RH (follicle stimulating hormones—releasing factor)
LH-RH (luteinizing hormone—releasing factor)
↓

Pituitary gonadotrophins

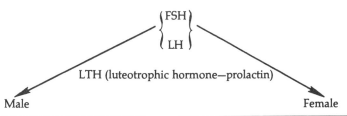

{ FSH }
{ LH }

LTH (luteotrophic hormone—prolactin)

Male

Female

Male	Female
FSH—development of the seminiferous tubules and maintenance of spermatogenesis	FSH—maintenance of ovarian follicles up to ovulation
LH—secretion of *testosterone*	*LH—ruptures mature follicle*
Secondary sex characteristics in males	Secondary sex characteristics in females
(a) growth and function of genitalia (b) increased hair growth (c) increased muscle mass (d) changes in fat distribution (e) deepening of voice	(a) growth and function of uterus (b) external genitalia (c) mammary glands (d) inhibit growth hormone secretion from pituitary resulting in smaller stature for females

the characteristics of the pituitary gland. For example, it is possible to take a pituitary from a male and transplant it into a female; this transplanted gland will now begin to release its hormones cyclically. The reverse procedure, in which a female pituitary is transplanted into the male, suggests the same thing: everyone's pituitary gland is about the same. The source of the cyclicity is in the hypothalamus, the structure which controls the release of hormones by the pituitary gland. Recently, some scientists have been able to detect very small morphological differences in the hypothalamus of males and females, some of which may be the source of sex difference in cyclicity. For example, the volume of the medial preoptic nucleus is much larger in male rats than it is in females (Gorski *et al.*, 1978). Because sex differences in the brain are so closely related to sexual differentiation we will discuss them again in the section on sexual development.

behavioral differences between males and females There are a very large number of behavioral differences between males and females, but the cause of these differences is in most cases still open to question. Some may be due to different rearing practices used for boys and girls, or to the effects of cultural role modeling. Others may be due to physiological factors, while still others may be due to an interaction between physiology and environment. Researchers have found sex differences in a huge variety of behaviors including verbal abilities, mathematical and spatial abilities, aggression, types of play behavior, suicide, drug use, and on and on, seemingly ad infinitum. The methods used in some of these studies are sometimes open to criticism. For example, a male experimenter may influence the performance of one sex more than another, and a female experimenter may do the same. In spite of these problems, many reliable sex differences in behavior have been repeatedly reported.

Any description of "male sex behavior" or "female sex behavior" for human beings is very difficult. It may be possible to make some generalizations, such as most people prefer to engage in sex with a member of the opposite sex. The actual body positions which are used for sex behavior are so varied that it is very difficult to make any firm generalizations about which sex behaviors characterize each sex. In contrast, we will see in a later section how the physiological responses during sexual arousal are remarkably similar in all humans, men and women.

In animals, the difference between male and female sex behavior is usually somewhat clearer. The essential features of the sex behavior of the male rat, for example, include **intromission,** or entry of the penis into the female's vagina, pelvic thrusting, and finally ejaculation. Before engaging in sex with a receptive female, the male rat usually sniffs and licks her genitals, mounts her from the rear in what is called the **dorsoventral position,** and achieves intromission. He may mount

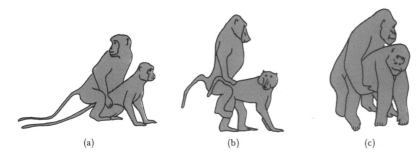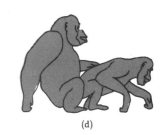

Figure 12.5
Some copulatory postures of nonhuman primates. (a) Adult male and female langurs. (b) Adult male and female anubis baboons. (c) Adult male and female gorillas. (d) Adult male and female chimpanzees. [From photos by Jay, Mcginnis, Sorby, and Bygott; found in Hanby (1977).]

several times before he actually ejaculates, but after ejaculation he shows a deep pelvic thrust and arches backward. He usually is not ready to engage in sex again for at least a few minutes.

The female rat's sex behavior occurs only during the receptive part of her cycle when she is ovulating. If she is receptive she will dart around, look backward toward the male, and wiggle her ears. She then arches her back and moves her tail to the side in a posture called **lordosis,** allowing the male to mount and achieve intromission.

In nonhuman primates, the sex behavior of males and females overlaps a good deal more than in rats, although the typical dorsoventral postures are shown in Figure 12.5. Female monkeys will often mount other monkeys, however, and males will mount other males. Mounting is probably a social as well as a sexual behavior. Even in animals it may be assuming too much to say that sex differences in sexual behavior primarily result from physiological differences. At least for lower animals like the rat, scientists have relied upon this assumption to find the neural and hormonal controls for the display of male and female sex behavior.

Human beings come in two basic varieties—male and female—and they have a number of differences. Genetically, females have two X chromosomes, while males have only one X and a nonhomologous Y chromosome. This basic difference between males and females triggers the sexual development of the individual toward the male or the female pattern.

Morphologically, males and females differ for a number of reasons. The reproductive system of the male is designed to produce sperm and to deliver it into the vagina of the

summary
Differences between Males and Females

female. This system includes a number of organs, such as the *testes*, where spermatogenesis occurs, the *epididymis*, a storage site for sperm, and a series of ducts which deliver the sperm to the outside. The testes also secrete *androgens*, the male sex hormones. *Testosterone* is the major androgen produced by human males, and it has a number of effects on the body. Its release at puberty results in the development of secondary sex characteristics such as deeper voice, larger body size, and the male-type distribution of body hair and body fat.

The reproductive system of the female is designed to produce eggs which can be fertilized by sperm and implanted into the uterus. The ovaries are the primary organ in which the development of *follicles*, which contain eggs, occurs. During the menstrual cycle, one or more follicles mature and rupture. The egg is released or *ovulated* and is passed into the uterus where it will implant if it has been fertilized.

The ovaries also secrete the hormones *estrogen* and *progesterone*. These hormones have widespread effects on the development of secondary sexual characteristics in the pubertal female.

The pituitary gland's hormones, *LH* and *FSH*, control the release of sex hormones by the testes and ovaries. In the female, LH and FSH are released cyclically, so that the production of estrogen and progesterone is cyclic across the menstrual cycle. In the male, the pituitary hormones are released more tonically, so the production of testosterone remains relatively constant over time. The output of pituitary hormones in both sexes is controlled by hormones which come from the hypothalamus. Cells in this part of the brain produce *releasing factors* which are carried to the pituitary gland by means of a blood portal system. These releasing factors direct the pituitary's output of LH and FSH, so it is actually the hypothalamus which ultimately directs the cyclic or tonic output of gonadal hormones in females and males.

The behavioral differences between males and females are widespread, but it is not clear whether they are due to physiological differences. In human sex behavior, aside from the slight differences in behavior required by different anatomies, there is tremendous similarity. In lower animals there is also much similarity. Male rats show more mounting, however, and they also show *intromission*, pelvic thrusting, and ejaculation. The typical female rat posture for sex behavior is called *lordosis*, and it consists of arching the back, raising the hind legs, and moving the tail to the side. Occasionally male rodents may also assume this posture.

The biological bases for many of these physiological and behavioral differences lie in the hormones which are secreted during prenatal life, or in some animals, perinatal life. The next section of this chapter deals with *sexual differentiation*, exploring how some of these sex differences come about.

sexual development The origin for many of the differences between males and females is in prenatal life. Even though some of the differences may not appear until puberty, the groundwork for the sex differences was laid when the organism was still in the uterus. The possession of an XY chromosome type results in the release of an androgen by the fetal testes in the male, and this substance begins to organize the male's nervous system and reproductive morphology in the male direction. The conventional wisdom states that the absence of this hormone, a condition resulting from the possession of two X chromosomes, organizes the female's nervous system and reproductive morphology in the female direction. (At the end of this section we will present another point of view which emphasizes the importance of low levels of estrogen in female sexual differentiation.)

In this section we will examine the effects of the presence or absence of the fetal androgen on a variety of systems. First we will see how the fetal hormone affects the development of the reproductive organs. Then we will turn to the hormone's effects on the brain. It has many effects including the masculinization of the hypothalamus so that it will direct the pituitary gland to release LH and FSH in the tonic, malelike fashion. The fetal androgen also has effects on later behavior, possibly even in humans.

Early in fetal life, the gonads look the same in males and females, but the sex chromosomes trigger them to begin their development into ovaries in the female and into testes in the male. Once the testes are partly developed, they begin to secrete androgen, and it is this hormone which results in the differentiation of the male reproductive organs. If the hormone is not present, the reproductive organs and accessory ducts characteristic of the female will develop. Thus it is the presence or absence of androgen which determines which reproductive organs will develop.

sexual differentiation of the reproductive organs

The reproductive organs of the female can be masculinized by early androgen treatment. In an early study, van Wagenen and Hamilton (1943) injected pregnant female rhesus monkeys with synthetic testosterone, and found that the genetically female offspring were **pseudohermaphroditic,** in that they had well-developed scrota, and a small male-type penis. The male offspring, which presumably would normally produce their own androgen during this gestational period anyway, were largely unaffected. Goy *et al.* (1977) report that female rhesus monkeys will show practically complete virilization in external morphology if the mother is given **testosterone propionate** (a synthetic androgen) every day between the 43rd and 105th day of gestation. Injections of lesser duration, smaller dose, or outside of this range result in less virilization. The period during which the reproductive organs of rhesus monkeys are sensitive to the masculinizing effects of androgen is thus within this period. This period of androgen sensitivity is different for each species; for example, in the rat, it extends even somewhat beyond birth.

In human beings, there is good reason to believe that prenatal androgenization of females also masculinizes the reproductive organs, although it is certainly impossible to perform experiments to prove it.

Certain "natural experiments," however, have provided interesting data on the effects of prenatal androgen on the genetic female. For example, in the 1950s, some mothers were given a synthetic form of progesterone *(progestin)* in order to prevent miscarriage. The female offspring were often pseudohermaphroditic—they had various degrees of masculinization in their external genitalia which ranged from an enlarged clitoris to a normal appearing penis. Another abnormal condition which results in this kind of pseudohermaphroditic female is the **adrenogenital syndrome.** The fetus's adrenal glands produce less corticosteroids and more androgens, resulting in malelike external genitalia. These human "experiments" have been studied extensively by Money and his colleagues (Money and Ehrhardt, 1972), and we will discuss them again later.

sexual differentiation—cyclic and tonic gonadotrophin release

Prenatal androgen secretion not only has an effect on the reproductive organs, but also on the nervous system. These central nervous system effects of hormones are called *organizing* because they do not show their dramatic consequences until after puberty, when the individual begins to secrete sex hormones in large quantities. They are distinguished from the *activating* influences of hormones which show their effects immediately.

Prenatal androgen has two different organizing effects on the nervous system. One organizing effect is on the brain cells which control the pituitary's release of LH and FSH. Prenatal androgen organizes the male's hypothalamus so that it will instruct the pituitary to release its hormones in a tonic fashion. The lack of prenatal androgen results in the cyclic surges of releasing hormones from the hypothalamus.

Pfeiffer demonstrated this kind of organizing influence in 1936, using rats. When male rats were castrated at birth, they would later accept a transplanted ovary; this ovary began to produce corpora lutea and to cycle normally. This meant that the secretion of LH and FSH must have been cyclic. Apparently the newborn male's hypothalamus was not completely differentiated in the tonic direction before the source of androgen was removed. Pfeiffer also implanted testicular tissue into newborn female rats and found that their ovaries showed no signs of cycling when they reached maturity. The testosterone from the transplanted testes organized the female's brain in a male direction so that LH and FSH output was not cyclic.

The sensitivity of nervous tissue to this kind of organizing effect of androgen occurs at a different time than the sensitivity of the tissue developing into reproductive organs (Goy *et al.*, 1962). Thus, depending upon when the androgen is administered, it is possible to produce a female with male genitalia but with cyclic gonadotrophin release, or a noncycling female with normal external genitalia. In the normal male fetus, the androgen is secreted by the testes long enough to cover both sensitive periods.

Several lines of evidence suggest that the area of the brain that is controlling gonadotrophin release, and which is organized differently for males and females by prenatal androgen, is the preoptic area. For example, the cyclicity of hormone release is abolished when the connections to the preoptic area are cut (Köves and Halász, 1970). Also, the neuronal cell bodies in this region show preferential uptake of radioactive estradiol, a synthetic estrogen (Pfaff, 1968; Stumpf, 1970). Therefore, this area probably contains estrogen receptors which can monitor the increase in estrogen levels and initiate a surge of gonadotrophin release.

Figure 12.6 summarizes the neural control of gonadotrophin release. The preoptic area, which is probably organized in prenatal life by androgen, acts on the **ventromedial arcuate nuclei** of the hypothalamus. The arcuate nuclei then control the output of releasing hormones, and discharge tonic levels of releasing hormones in these males. The pituitary then releases its hormones in a tonic fashion also. Interestingly, recent anatomical studies have found that the arcuate nucleus in newborn male and female rats is fairly immature and shows no sex differences (Walsh and Brawer, 1979). In both sexes this area contained a paucity of synapses, scant synaptic vesicles, and poorly developed pre- and post-synaptic specializations. Thus most of the sexual differentiation and organization of the arcuate nucleus is not accomplished prenatally (at least in the rat). Perhaps the arcuate nucleus is differentiated postnatally by hormones, or by the input from the preoptic area.

If the preoptic area is not subjected to prenatal androgen, it will affect the arcuate nuclei cyclically. The end result will be a cyclic release of gonadotrophins, typical of the female.

Although androgen is the prenatal hormone that is producing the organizing effect in the male "tonic" direction, it is not certain that it is doing so directly. Sutherland and Gorski (1970) found that infusion of estradiol into the hypothalamus of the neonatal female rat also suppressed cyclic ovulation in the adult animal. Furthermore, neonatal or prenatal injections of estrogens usually result in "androgenization" with respect to the cyclicity of gonadotrophin release. Since androgen is converted to estrogen in the neonatal rat brain, it is possible that androgen has its organizing effects only indirectly, through its conversion to estrogen. Females have an estrogen binding protein in the brain and blood which apparently blocks the effects of any estrogen produced by neonatal ovaries, but males lack this protein (Nunez *et al.*, 1971). Furthermore, the brains of neonatal rats contain receptors which bind estrogen (McEwen *et al.*, 1975). These studies suggest that androgen has its effects on the brain by means of its conversion to estrogen, a process which was diagrammed in Figure 12.2.

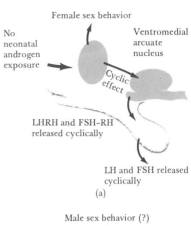

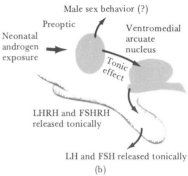

Figure 12.6
Summary of the control of gonadotrophin release, and the effects of neonatal androgen exposure. (a) Cyclic release of gonadotrophins is the result when neonatal androgen is not present. (b) Tonic release of gonadotrophins results when the hormone is present. [Adapted from Gorski (1973).]

sexual differentiation The presence of prenatal androgen also organizes the nervous system
of behavior so that the animal will display the appropriate kinds of sex behavior in
response to adult sex hormones. For example; the presence of androgen during the sensitive period ensures that the male rat will respond
with male-type sex behavior when his own testes begin secreting large
quantities of testosterone at puberty. The absence of androgen insures
that the female rat will respond with behaviors such as lordosis when
she begins to secrete estrogen and progesterone in a cyclic fashion.

Table 12.2 , taken from Whalen (1974), shows the kinds of behaviors seen in rats given normal or abnormal hormone treatments in
adulthood and neonatally. (The rats require injections of androgen or
estrogen and progesterone in adulthood because no sex behavior is
seen unless these hormones are present.)

The effects of pre- and postnatal androgen on the ability to perform
female sex behavior (i.e., lordosis) in response to estrogen and progesterone are very clear. If an animal has androgen circulating in its body
early in development, it cannot display this characteristic of normal
female sexual behavior, regardless of whether the rat is male or female. If androgens are not present, or if the male is castrated early,
then it can display this response. Thus, early exposure to androgen

Table 12.2

Relationships between hormonal conditions during development and sexual
responding of the rat in adulthood[a]

Hormonal condition during critical period	Hormonal condition during adulthood			
	Androgen			Estrogen and progesterone
	Mounts	Intromission responses	Ejaculation responses	Lordosis responses
Male				
Testes intact	+ + +	+ + +	+ + +	—
Castration at birth	+ + +	+	—	+ + +
Castration at birth + TP[b]	+ + +	+ + +	+ +	—
Female				
Ovaries intact	+ + +	+	—	+ + +
Ovariectomized at birth	+ + +	+	—	+ + +
TP at birth	+ + +	+ +	+	—
TP pre- and postnatally	+ + +	+ + +	+ + +	—

[a]From Whalen (1974).
[b]TP = Testosterone propionate

organizes the nervous system so that it cannot respond to later adult levels of estrogen and progesterone with lordosis.

The effects of early androgen on male sex behavior are less clear, although they suggest that the hormone organizes the nervous system so that it can later respond to androgen with mounts, intromissions, and ejaculaton responses. A complicating factor in these studies is that animals with little or no androgen during pre- and postnatal life develop very small penises, so their behavior may in part be influenced by feedback (or lack thereof) from their reproductive organs. This problem does not arise when studying lordosis because an animal can exhibit this posture regardless of the kind of reproductive organs it has.

primate studies. The behavioral differences between male and female primates are not so obvious as those between male and female rodents, but they nonetheless exist. For example, when male and female monkeys are infants and juveniles, the male plays more roughly, pursues other monkeys more frequently, and mounts other monkeys more often than do the females. Goy *et al.* (1977) have reported on the behavior of prenatally androgenized female monkeys, and found that their juvenile behavior resembles that of the male more than that of the normal female.

Figure 12.7, for example, shows a comparison of the mounting behavior of four groups of monkeys, during the first (run 1) and second (run 2) years of life. Notice that during run 2, the prenatally androgenized females (whose mothers had been injected with testoster-

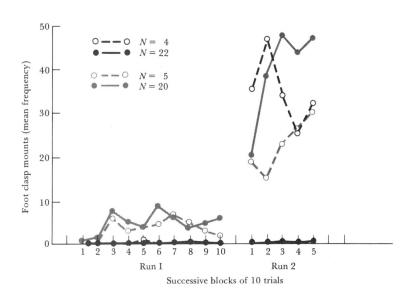

Figure 12.7
The overall frequency of mounting behavior during the first (run 1) and second (run 2) years of life by normal males (light solid circles), normal females (dark solid circles), prenatally androgenized females (dark open circles), and males whose mothers were injected with testosterone propionate during gestation (light open circles). [From Goy et al. *(1977).]*

one propionate) mounted about as often as the normal males and the prenatally androgenized males.

One interesting difference between the rat and monkey is that the behavioral differences appear in the monkey *before* adult levels of hormones begin circulating in the bloodstream. Thus the organizational effects of the androgen were not simply to make the animal more responsive to adult levels of testosterone or estrogen and progesterone. When the prenatally androgenized monkeys do become adult, they certainly are more responsive to testosterone than normal females. Eaton *et al.* (1973) ovariectomized these females, and injected them with testosterone. Compared to normal females which had been similarly ovariectomized and injected, the prenatally androgenized females were much more aggressive and showed more yawning, grooming, and sexual exploration toward other females. They also mounted other females more frequently.

Female rhesus monkeys don't usually reach puberty until about 2½ years of age. The onset of puberty is delayed by several months in androgenized females, but the females eventually begin to cycle. This indicates that their gonadotrophin release is more like that of normal females, even though their behavior is not. Thus the effects of early androgen are somewhat different in the monkey compared to the rat.

human studies. In human beings, early androgen has some effects remarkably similar to those observed in the monkeys. Money and Ehrhardt (1972) studied the behavior of a group of girls whose mothers had received progestin treatment during pregnancy, and another group which had the adrenogenital syndrome. Table 12.3 shows some of the differences they found between these girls and a matched control group.

The girls that had been exposed to early androgen were generally described by their mothers and themselves as more "tomboyish" and athletic, and generally tended to prefer male playmates. Figure 12.8 shows the results of another, similar study which compared females with adrenogenital syndrome to normal controls (Ehrhardt, 1977). The results were about the same: the prenatally androgenized females tended to be more active and to prefer boy playmates.

These studies do not suggest that "tomboyishness" or "preference for boy playmates" are biologically determined by any means. All of these behavioral traits have an enormous amount of learning involved. They do suggest that prenatal androgenization might predispose an individual to slightly more activity and higher energy expenditure; the other behavioral traits, such as athletic skill and preference for boys' clothes, might simply be correlated with the high activity level. None of the girls expressed any interest in lesbianism, suggesting that the presence of prenatal androgen has little to do with

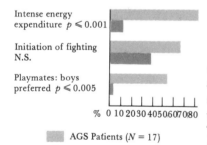

Intense energy
expenditure $p \leqslant 0.001$

Initiation of fighting
N.S.

Playmates: boys
preferred $p \leqslant 0.005$

% 0 10 20 30 40 50 60 70 80

▨ AGS Patients ($N = 17$)

▨ Unaffected sibs. ($N = 11$)

Figure 12.8
Comparison of female adrenogenital syndrome girls versus female siblings on activity and aggression. The bars represent the percentage of subjects from each group who were reported to exhibit the behavior specified by the category. [From Ehrhardt (1977).]

Table 12.3
Tomboyishness, energy expenditure, and clothing adornment perference in fetally androgenized girls versus their matched controls[a]

Behavioral signs	PI versus C	AGS versus C
Evidence of Tomboyism		
1. Known to self and mother as tomboy	$p \leq 0.05$	$p \leq 0.01$
2. Lack of satisfaction with female sex role	O	$p \leq 0.05$
Expenditure of energy in recreation and aggression		
3. Athletic interests and skills	$p \leq 0.05$	$p \leq 0.10$
4. Preference of male versus female playmates	$p \leq 0.05$	$p \leq 0.01$
5. Behavior in childhood fights	O	O
Preferred clothing and adornment		
6. Clothing preference, slacks versus dresses	$p \leq 0.05$	$p \leq 0.05$
7. Lacking interest in jewelry, perfume, and hair styling	O	O

Legend: PI = Progestin-induced hermaphroditism ($N = 10$), AGS = Adrenogenital syndrome ($N = 15$), C = Matched controls, O = No significant difference.
[a]From Money and Ehrhardt (1972).

the development of sexual identity or preference for a male or female sex partner.

Recently, a number of differences have been found in the brains of male and female rats. Some of these differences are known to depend upon the presence of pre- and postnatal androgen. These differences are located in and around the hypothalamus, particularly in structures which are known to be involved in adult sexual behavior. For example, the preoptic area of the male hamster contains a different pattern of dendrite branching compared to the female (Greenough *et al.*, 1977). Raisman (1974) found subtle, but significant, differences in the localization of synaptic terminals in the preoptic region, differences which depended upon the early hormonal environment. Gorski *et al.* (1978) found that the volume of the medial preoptic nucleus was larger in male and androgenized female rats when compared to normal females.

It is not yet clear whether any of these sex differences in the brain are related to the differences in sex behavior or in the gonadotrophin secretion pattern. Since they are in the area of the brain which is im-

sexual differentiation—brain structure

portant for both of these functions, the correlation is suggestive. Further study will perhaps tie in these fine structural differences to differences in behavior.

low estrogen levels and female sexual differentiation

Not all scientists agree that undifferentiated neural tissue is basically "female," and will differentiate in the female direction (with respect to gonadotrophin secretion and sex behavior) unless prenatal androgens are present. Döhler (1978) suggests that female sexual differentiation is dependent upon the presence of low estrogen levels during the early part of life. To support this point of view, he sites some findings which are perplexing if we accept the conventional wisdom about female sexual differentiation. For example, there are male mice and rats which are genetically insensitive to androgen and grow up to be pseudohermaphrodites because their body and brain tissue does not respond to the prenatal hormone. Döhler points out that these males would be indistinguishable from females if female sexual differentiation required no hormonal trigger. Instead, these males show neither female nor male sex behavior, and no cyclic release of gonadotrophins.

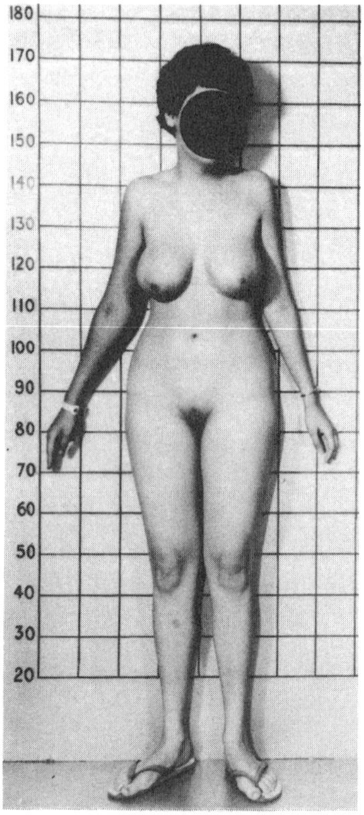

A similar kind of condition exists in human beings, called the **testicular feminization syndrome.** In this syndrome, an individual with the XY genotype grows up to look very much like a female, even though he (she?) has testes which secrete androgen. The normal target tissues of androgen are genetically incapable of utilizing the hormone. The individual who appears in Figure 12.9 has this syndrome, and shows well-developed breasts and external feminine characteristics. Nevertheless, the individual is different from the normal human female because she lacks pubic hair and has no internal female genitalia. (She does have undescended testes.) Furthermore, individuals with this syndrome do not menstruate or become fertile at puberty, suggesting that their gonadotrophin release is abnormal.

Christensen and Gorski (1978) suggest that the large amounts of circulating estrogen present in both male and female rats during the first few days of life may play a role in the differentiation of both sexes. In the male, the estrogen may synergize with the prenatal androgen. The female has estrogen binding proteins (which we discussed earlier) but there may nevertheless still be some unbound estrogen present. The circulating estrogen may act to partially masculinize the normal females. Christensen and Gorski cite a number of observations to support the view that the normal female rat shows some masculine traits. For example, normal females show a great deal of mounting behavior. Normal female rats also stop ovulating later in life, a process which may be due to the slight masculinization by prenatal estrogen. The differentiation of female traits may also be somewhat affected by exposure to unbound estrogen early in life. For

Figure 12.9
A patient with "testicular feminization." Well-developed breasts and external feminine characteristics but no pubic or auxiliary hair and infantile vulva. At laparotomy, no internal female genitalia, but undescended testes found. [From Money and Ehrhardt (1972).]

342 *physiological psychology*

example, small amounts of estrogen applied to the preoptic area in the newborn female rat produces an increase in receptive, female-like sex behaviors later. Also, female rats ovariectomized right after birth show less female sex behavior in response to estrogen treatments in adulthood, compared to female rats who are ovariectomized later (Toran-Allerand, 1976).

Whether or not low levels of estrogen are important in the differentiation of females is not yet known, but the evidence is suggestive. This issue is likely to receive a great deal of attention in the future.

---

summary
Sexual Development

This section explored the process of sexual differentiation by which males and females develop physiological and behavioral characteristics typical of their sex. The differentiation process begins in the uterus when the male's fetal testes begin to secrete androgen. Prenatal androgen is the organizing factor whose presence promotes the development of male characteristics. The absence of this hormone (or the presence of low levels of estrogen) allow the development of female characteristics.

One kind of sexual differentiation which occurs in response to the presence or absence of fetal androgen is the development of male or female reproductive organs. If genetically female organisms are androgenized by giving androgen to their mothers during pregnancy, their reproductive organs will be masculinized.

Another kind of differentiation involves the pattern of release of pituitary gonadotrophins. If fetal androgen is present, the pituitary will release LH and FSH in a tonic fashion at puberty. If fetal androgen is not present, the gonadotrophins will be released cyclically, resulting in the typical estrus or menstrual cycle of the female. The release of gonadotrophins is controlled by the hypothalamus and it is this part of the brain which is differentiated in response to the presence or absence of fetal androgen. The action of fetal androgen on the hypothalamus is called an *organizing action* because its effects are not seen until years later.

Males and females also behave differently, and there is reason to believe that fetal androgen may set the stage for some later behavioral differences. In rats, for example, fetal androgen organizes the animal's nervous system such that it does not respond to female sex hormones by displaying the female sexual posture, called *lordosis*. In cases where human females have been androgenized during prenatal life, the girls showed slightly more energy levels, and more athletic interests compared to a control group. These prenatally androgenized girls did not become lesbians, however, so there is no evidence thus far that prenatal hormones may be important in the etiology of homosexuality.

Although most scientists hypothesize that female sexual differentiation is accomplished in the absence of prenatal androgen, some suggest that low levels of estrogen are necessary. Support for this hypothesis comes from genetically male animals and humans with a genetic insensitivity to androgen (termed the *testicular feminization syndrome* in humans). These individuals do not grow up to be completely normal females (they are infertile and never menstruate), perhaps because the low levels of estrogen were not present.

---

the biological bases of adult sexual behavior

It seems almost an understatement to say that the patterns of sexual behavior in human beings are enormously diverse. Unlike the lower animals, humans have devised all sorts of methods to achieve sexual stimulation. An educational tour through any adult book store provides insight into this diversity and might also suggest that cultural factors, rather than biology, are affecting the patterns of sexual behavior in human beings.

Anthropologists have reported a great many variations in male and female sex behavior patterns, so it is simply not possible to say anything about which patterns are "normal" for our species. For example, the northern Irish in Inis Beag, an island off the coast of Ireland, consider sex behavior to be exclusively for the male. Female orgasm is unheard of, and nudity is absent except in infants (Messenger, 1971). In another culture, the Yolngu aborigine tribe in northern Australia, sexuality is less repressed. Sexual "practice" among juveniles is considered amusing rather than taboo as it is in our own culture (Money *et al.*, 1970).

Although the patterns of sexual behavior may be varied, the patterns of physiological responses to sexual stimulation are somewhat more regular. In the first part of this section, we will discuss these responses for both the male and female. Second, we will explore some of the physiological factors which affect sex behavior, including hormonal influences, neural controls, and the effects of drugs. Last, we will consider the stimulus control of sexual behavior.

physiological events accompanying sexual arousal

It has only been fairly recently that scientists have attempted to study the physiological events which occur during sexual arousal in human beings. Cultural taboos have undoubtedly contributed to this paucity of information. In our culture, sexual behavior is considered to be a private matter so it has been very difficult to study.

Despite these difficulties, Masters and Johnson (1966) have conducted some pioneering studies on the physiological events which occur in men and women during sexual arousal. They had to request volunteers to participate in sex behavior in the lab. It is entirely possible that the findings on these volunteers may not completely apply to the entire population, since the fact that they were uninhibited enough to volunteer in the first place makes them a somewhat biased sample. Many of the original participants were prostitutes. As their research projects progressed, however, a more diverse group of people were willing to participate, forming a sample that was more representative of the general population.

Masters and Johnson arbitrarily divide up a sexual response cycle into four phases: (1) the **excitement phase,** (2) the **plateau phase,** (3) the **orgasmic phase,** and (4) the **resolution phase.** The patterns of

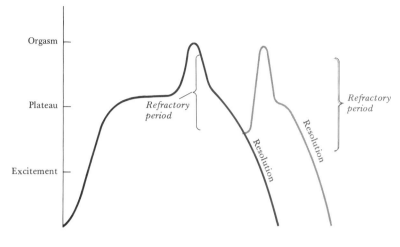

Figure 12.10
The sexual response cycle of the male. [From Masters and Johnson (1966). Copyright 1966 by Little, Brown and Company.]

these four phases are slightly different in men and women. They are diagrammed in Figures 12.10 and 12.11

The excitement phase can develop from any kind of physical or psychological stimulation which the individual perceives as sexually arousing. If the stimulation is sufficient, the cycle will move into the plateau phase. Sexual tensions are intensified and it is from this stage that the individual can move into the third phase—orgasm.

During orgasm, the sexual tensions which brought on vasoconcentration and muscle tension, particularly in the pelvic area, are released. Masters and Johnson found that the orgasmic reaction pattern of men showed less variability than that of women, and this is noted in their graphs. Men ordinarily have an involuntary refractory phase

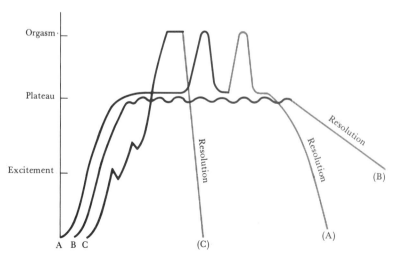

Figure 12.11
The sexual response cycle of the human female. [From Masters and Johnson (1966). Copyright 1966 by Little, Brown and Company.]

right after orgasm during which further sexual stimulation is not effective. Women, however, can return to the orgasmic phase from any point in the resolution phase, provided effective sexual stimulation is continued. Thus women have the potential for multiple-orgasmic experiences in a short period of time; the physiological ability of men to respond to continued stimulation is much lower.

The primary physiological responses to sexual stimulation in both men and women are (1) widespread vasocongestion and (2) **myotonia** (tonic muscle spasms). Tables 12.4 and 12.5 list some of the more specific physiological responses which occur in various parts of the body of men and women during the four phases.

Table 12.4
Physiological responses during the sexual response cycle in men[a]

Excitement phase
    Penis—with effective stimulation, penis becomes erect within about 3—8 seconds
    Scrotal sac—decreases in internal diameter; outer skin tenses and thickens; localized vasocongestion
    Testes—elevate toward perineum
    Sex flush—sometimes appears late in phase, but individuals vary widely
    Myotonia—both voluntary and involuntary muscle tension observed late in phase

Plateau phase
    Penis—increase in coronal area of glans due to increased vasocongestion; glans deepens in color in some men
    Testes—continue to increase in size until about 50% larger than in unstimulated state
    Myotonia—voluntary and involuntary tensions increase; pelvic thrusting becomes involuntary late in phase; total body reactions of male and female are quite similar

Orgasmic (ejaculatory) phase
    Penis—Ejaculatory contractions along entire length of penile urethra; expulsive contractions start at intervals of 0.8 second and after 3 or 4 seconds reduce in frequency and expulsive force
    Myotonia—loss of voluntary control; involuntary contractions and spasms

Resolution phase
    Penis—two stages: rapid reduction in size to about 50% larger than in unstimulated state and slower disappearance of remaining tumescence, especially if sexual stimulation continues to take place
    Scrotum—rapid or slow decongestion
    Testes—rapid or slow resolution
    Myotonia—as in female, rarely lasts more than 5 minutes, but not lost as rapidly as many of the signs of vasocongestion

---

[a] Adapted from DeLora and Warren (1977) and Masters and Johnson (1966).

Table 12.5

Physiological responses during the sexual response cycle in women[a]

Excitement phase

Vagina—lubrication within 10 to 30 seconds of effective stimulation; vaginal wall color changes to darker, purplish hue

Clitoris—shaft increases in diameter, through vasocongestion, and elongates in some women

Uterus—pulled slowly up and back if initially in normal anterior position

Sex flush—in some women a rash appears between the breastbone and navel late in this phase or early in the plateau phase

Plateau phase

Vagina—marked vasocongestion reduces central opening of the outer third by at least one-third; production of lubrication slows

Clitoris—retracts from normal position late in phase; withdraws; at least 50% overall reduction in length of total clitoral body by immediate preorgasmic period

Uterus—full elevation is reached

Sex flush—spreads over breasts in some women

Myotonia—overall increase extending from excitement phase; involuntary facial contractions, grimaces, clutching movements; involuntary pelvic thrusts late in phase near orgasm

Orgasmic phase

Vagina—strong, rhythmic contractions of orgasmic platform (3–15), beginning at intervals of 0.8 second and gradually diminishing in strength and duration

Uterus—contracts irregularly

Myotonia—muscle spasms and involuntary contraction throughout the body; loss of voluntary control

Resolution phase

Vagina—central opening of orgasmic platform rapidly increases in diameter by one-third; cervix and upper walls of vagina descend toward vaginal floor in 3 to 4 minutes; vaginal color returns to preexcitement state, usually in about 10 to 15 minutes

Clitoris—returned to preexcitement position within 5–15 seconds; vasocongestion usually disappears 5–10 minutes after orgasm

Sex flush—rapidly disappears from body sites in almost opposite sequence of appearance

[a] Adapted from DeLora and Warren (1977) and Masters and Johnson (1966).

Masters and Johnson pointed out that overall the sexual responses of men and women showed more similarities than differences. Even in orgasmic experience, where male and female anatomy might be expected to produce distinctly different experiences, the similarities were more striking. It is of course very difficult to tell if the orgasmic experience is different for men and women, but Vance and Wagner (1976) found that the verbal descriptions of orgasm varied very little between men and women. They asked students to write a paragraph which described what an orgasm felt like, and then had raters try to determine which were written by men and which by women. The raters were no more accurate than they would have been if they simply tossed a coin.

The descriptions which the students wrote were interesting because they often emphasized some of the physiological changes which were noted by Masters and Johnson. For example:

A sudden feeling of lightheadedness followed by an intense feeling of relief and elation. A rush. Intense muscular spasms of the whole body. Sense of euphoria followed by deep peace and relaxation. (female)

A tremendous release of built up tension all at once lasting around 5—10 seconds where a particular "pulsing" feeling is felt throughout my body along with a kind of tickling and tingling feeling. (male)

hormonal influences on sex behavior In the lower animals sex behavior is very much dependent upon adult levels of hormones. For example, a castrated male rat with no source of testosterone will very quickly cease mating, and will also show little interest in a receptive female. An overiectomized female rat will not cycle and will not become behaviorally receptive to the male. Her receptive behavior is dependent not just upon estrogen and progesterone, but upon the sequential production of these two hormones. In order to restore sex behavior in the male rat, one need only inject sufficient amounts of androgen. In order to restore the female's sex behavior, it is necessary to first prime her with estrogen for a few days, and then follow up with a single injection of progesterone.

activating effects of hormones in males. Men who have lost their testes for one reason or another may lose their sex behavior almost immediately, or it may show a gradual decline over the years (Money and Ehrhardt, 1972). As soon as testosterone replacement therapy begins these men return to their normal sex behavior.

For the lower animals, like the rat and rabbit, the amount of testosterone circulating in the bloodstream is correlated with the amount of sex behavior. If the male is given additional testosterone, over and above his normal levels, then his sex behavior will be increased. This increase shows up as a decrease in the amount of time to ejaculation, and an increase in the total number of ejaculations per unit time (Beach, 1942; Cheng and Casida, 1949). Sometimes the male will even attempt to mate with practically anything that remotely resembles a receptive female, such as a juvenile male, a nonreceptive female, or an anesthetized receptive female (the cad!).

In men, the relationship between amount of circulating testosterone and amount of sexual interest and behavior is not at all clear. Fox and co-workers (Fox *et al.*, 1972) studied a single subject over a period of months and found that testosterone levels increased shortly before and after intercourse. But it is not certain whether the increase in testosterone precipitated the interest in sex, or was precipitated by the sexual behavior. Testosterone levels are affected by various kinds of circumstances. For example, they increase in men watching a sex film, suggesting that sexual arousal actually leads to higher testosterone levels, and not that higher testosterone levels are leading to increased sexual arousal (Pirke *et al.*, 1974).

Testosterone levels are also affected by the anticipation of sex. Men who know they are soon to leave an isolated Arctic military base sometimes report that their beards start growing faster, a sign of increased testosterone production. In rhesus monkeys, the attainment of dominance can alter testosterone levels. Rose *et al.* (1975) found that the testosterone levels of monkeys which became dominant in a newly formed group went up by as much as 238%, while hormone levels in the subordinate monkeys went down. It is possible that dominance status (whatever that may mean in human beings) can also affect testosterone levels. It is likely that the sex behavior and related activities of men are influencing their testosterone levels, rather than the other way around.

The amount of sex behavior in males may also be influenced by genetic factors. Young and his colleagues (Riss and Young, 1953; Valenstein and Young, 1953; Riss *et al.*, 1955) found that males of different strains of guinea pigs showed different amounts and vigor of sex behavior. These differences were not dependent upon the amount of testosterone because when the males were castrated and injected with equal amounts of testosterone, the differences in sex behavior were still very apparent. Guinea pigs, and probably other mammals as well, are also sensitive to the kind of environment in which they are reared. If the males grow up in partly isolated environments, they show deficits in sex behavior when they are adult, deficits which are not dependent upon amount of circulating testosterone. It would appear that sex behavior in higher male animals requires a minimum amount of testosterone, but beyond that, the amount and vigor of the sex behavior which they show are determined by other things, such as situational factors, cultural factors, genetics, and early environment.

activating effects of hormones in females. The female rodent will likewise show no sex behavior if she is ovariectomized. In order to restore the lordosis response, the female needs not only estrogen and progesterone, but *sequential* injections of the hormones. She must be given priming injections of estrogen for a few days, followed by a single injection of progesterone; then she will come into heat a few hours later. This sequence approximates the hormonal events occurring in the female rodent around the time of ovulation—a time when sex behavior would most likely result in pregnancy.

In mammals with larger brains the influence of female hormones on sex behavior becomes less and less apparent. In both old and new world monkeys, for example, copulation is most likely to occur around the time of ovulation, but sexual behavior also occurs at other times (Rowell, 1972). In human beings, the time at which sexual behavior occurs is not clearly related to any portion of the menstrual cycle. Udry and Morris (1968) reported that even in humans, sexual intercourse was most likely to occur during midcycle, but other workers have not found this phenomenon.

Animals that show sex behavior around the time of ovulation, and at no other time, probably are strongly influenced by the female sex hormones. But since human females do not show this pattern, the female sex hormones probably do not play such an important role. Studies on monkeys and humans suggest that estrogen and progesterone are not critically important to the display of sex behavior in these higher mammals, but testosterone, surprisingly, is.

When ovariectomized female monkeys are given testosterone, they solicit mounting from males, and are more actively receptive (Trimble and Herbert, 1968). And if ovariectomized monkeys are also adrenalectomized, and hence have every possible source of endogenous testosterone removed, they become completely unreceptive (Everitt *et al.*, 1971). These poor females can be made fully receptive again if they are given testosterone injections.

Desire for sex in women also seems to depend upon testosterone rather than estrogen and progesterone. Ovariectomy or menopause does not seem to reduce a woman's "libido" (Kinsey *et al.*, 1953). Furthermore, women who receive injections of testosterone often report a heightened sexual desire (Salmon and Geist, 1943).

The female sex hormones may not have too much effect on the female's own desire for sex, but they do have an effect on her attractiveness to the male, at least in the monkey. When an ovariectomized female monkey is given injections of synthetic estrogen, the male becomes more eager to mate with her, initiates more sexual interaction, and more readily responds to the female's sexual invitations (Herbert, 1977). His increased interest is probably due partly to the effects of estrogen on the swelling of the sexual skin, and also on changes in the vaginal odors, which we shall mention again later in this section. When the ovariectomized female monkey is given progesterone, sexual activity declines (Herbert, 1974).

Herbert (1977) has suggested that the various hormonal influences on sexual receptivity and sexual attractiveness in female monkeys can account for the change in sexual behavior across the monkey's estrus cycle. During the earlier part of the cycle, the female is moderately receptive and attractive. This is when both estrogen and androgen levels are at midpoint. At midcycle, both hormone levels reach their maximum, and this is when receptivity and attractiveness are highest. After ovulation, progesterone levels begin to rise. This has the effect of decreasing the female's attractiveness and also decreasing androgen levels. Thus, in primates, sex behavior and sexual attractiveness are still at least partly dependent upon sex hormones, although the situation is more complicated than it is in the female rats.

The sex hormones are not only involved in sex behavior, but in a variety of other behaviors such as aggression, maternal behavior, hoarding behavior, and scent marking. In animals, these other behaviors are related to reproductive behavior in that they often make it easier to obtain a mate and facilitate the survival of the young. A more aggressive male, for example, may be more competitive in the reproductive game because he can obtain a larger territory and attract more females.

hormonal influences on behaviors other than sex

testosterone levels and aggression. The effects of the sex hormones on these kinds of behaviors in human beings are not clear at present. For example, many scientists who have been intrigued by the relationship between testosterone levels and aggression in male animals, have sought to find a similar relationship in men. Persky *et al.* (1971) found a significant correlation between testosterone levels and hostility as measured by a personality questionnaire (Buss–Durkee Hostility Inventory) in normal men between the ages of 22 and 28. But attempts to replicate these findings have largely failed (Meyer-Bahlburg *et al.*, 1974). Even men who have committed extreme acts of aggression do not show any differences in testosterone levels. Rada *et al.* (1976) studied 52 imprisoned rapists, and grouped them according to the amount of violence which was used during the crime. Although the most violent group had higher testosterone levels, the individual scores of the prisoners did not correlate with their testosterone levels.

Hays (1978) suggests that the studies on aggression and testosterone levels might lead to the hypothesis that testosterone levels are more important to the expression of aggression during adolescence than they are in adulthood. The neural tissues which influence aggressive behavior might be more sensitive to the hormone during those years when testosterone levels are first increased.

the effects of changing estrogen and progesterone levels. Estrogen and progesterone may be influencing certain kinds of behavior in women. Since the levels of these two hormones change during the menstrual cycle, then any behavior which also changes during the cycle might be influenced by the hormones. For example, many women experience a **premenstrual syndrome,** characterized by irritability, anxiety, and depression, which occurs shortly before and during the menses (Ivey and Bardwick, 1968). This syndrome has often been attributed to the effects of changing sex hormone levels, but correlation is not the same as causation. Beumont *et al.* (1975) compared the appearance of premenstrual syndrome in regularly cycling women to its appearance in women who cycle, but did not know when. These women had undergone hysterectomies, so they did not menstruate or know when their cycles occurred. The mood changes in the hysterectomized women were much less dramatic, suggesting that hormones may play only a small role in the premenstrual syndrome.

Estrogen is known to affect the sensitivity of some of the sensory systems, however. For example, the receptive fields of sensory neurons which lead away from the genital area of the female rat are enlarged when estrogen is present in the rat's body (Komisaruk *et al.*, 1972, Note 3). Thus when the rat is receptive, and estrogen levels are high, the genital area is very sensitive to touch. It is not just the genital area which becomes more sensitive, but other areas of the body as well. Bereiter and Barker (1975), for example, found that estrogen treatment increased the size of receptive fields for sensory neurons in the facial area of the rat.

The sex hormones probably have very diverse and widespread influences on many behavioral systems, but in human beings it is not yet clear how strong the impact of these hormones on behavior might be.

neural control of sex behavior Sex behavior is a very complicated phenomenon. It not only requires motivation for sex, but also motor sequences and sensory abilities. Even if an organism is motivated to engage in sex, and its motor and sensory equipment are intact, it may not do anything about it for a number of different reasons. Perhaps a competing motivation exists, such as fear of predation or, in humans, cultural taboos. Thus it is very difficult to pinpoint precise brain structures which play a role in the control of sexual behavior, and more difficult still to say exactly what that role is.

Despite these problems, studies on the lower animals have revealed that some brain structures are more critical than others and the hypothalamus once again plays a featured role. Lesion and stimulation studies have been able to identify which structures are most crucially involved, but they have not been able to clarify the nature of the involvement.

brain mechanisms in male sex behavior. Lesions or electrical stimulation of many parts of the central nervous system can affect male sex behavior. This is hardly surprising because male sex behavior involves a wide range of behaviors, including sensory abilities, motor abilities, motivation, and learning. But the area of the brain which has received the most attention, and which is clearly crucial to the performance of males, is the **medial preoptic area** of the hypothalamus. When this area is lesioned, the male will simply not show sex behavior, even though his testes are intact, and even though he may be given doses of testosterone.

Electrical and chemical stimulation studies have also emphasized the importance of this part of the brain for male sex behavior. Electrical stimulation potentiates copulation in male rats (Van Dis and Larsson, 1971). Also when very tiny amounts of testosterone are implanted directly into this area in the castrated male rat, the animal is more likely to engage in sex behavior than when the hormone is implanted elsewhere in the brain (Davidson, 1966).

Although these kinds of studies implicate the medial preoptic area in the control of male sex behavior, they cannot say anything about *how* it is implicated. Lesion studies are always problematical because sex behavior might disappear when any one of various types of behavior are impaired. The stimulation studies are also difficult to interpret because electrical stimulation does not reproduce the normal pattern of neuronal firing, and because implanted chemicals are likely to diffuse widely from the point of origin.

Caggiula and his colleagues (Szechtman *et al.*, 1978) have attempted to identify more precisely the role of this structure in male sex behavior by using tiny knife cuts. These cuts, in and around the preoptic area, are designed to sever some connections to the structure while leaving others intact.

When they made knife cuts which severed the preoptic area's lateral connections, but left the dorsal, anterior, and posterior ones intact, they found severe impairment of sexual behavior. The males were much less likely to copulate on any given test. When they did copulate, their behavior was erratic, although they nearly always ejaculated. Cuts which severed the dorsal connections produced an entirely different impairment. Rats with dorsal cuts were just as likely to copulate as normal rats, but they took more time and required more intromissions to achieve ejaculation. Anterior and posterior cuts had little effect on the performance of sexual behavior.

These scientists interpret their results in terms of the medial preoptic area's connections to the medial forebrain bundle (MFB), connections which would be severed by the lateral cuts. Animals with these cuts are not suffering from a lack of testosterone, since their hormone levels are normal. Nor are they suffering from an olfactory deficit, since they prefer the odors of receptive females compared to nonreceptive females, just like normal rats, but not castrated ones, do.

Also, they cannot be suffering from a motor deficit because they do copulate and ejaculate—but at a much lower frequency. Instead, they may be impaired in their ability to go from sexual arousal to copulation. The cues which elicit copulation in the normal rat do not seem to be sufficient for these rats. They need not only a receptive female, but one which is actively soliciting sex from them.

This hypothesis is interesting because it integrates the notions about the MFB (which we discussed in Chapter 10 in relation to motivation and reward) with the medial preoptic area, the structure which has so much to do with sex behavior. The medial preoptic area is sensitive to testosterone, but in order for copulation to occur normally, this area must connect with the MFB, the fiber system involved in many kinds of motivation.

brain mechanisms in female sex behavior. The preoptic area of the brain in a female is important for her display of *male* sex behavior, but not critical for female sex behavior. When this area is lesioned, her lordosis response is actually facilitated but her display of mounting is drastically reduced (Singer, 1968). Instead, lesions of the **anterior hypothalamic area** impair the lordosis response in female rats (Heimer and Larsson, 1966, 1967). A female rat with a lesion in this area will not respond to appropriate hormone treatments, as would a female which had simply been castrated.

Implants of estrogen into the brains of female rats have also emphasized the importance of the anterior hypothalamic area. Estrogen implants into this area produce lordosis in female rats (Lisk, 1962).

Female sexual behavior, however, normally requires two hormones: estrogen and progesterone. Although estrogen probably has its principal effect on lordosis by acting on the anterior hypothalamus, the site of action of progesterone is not yet known. The midbrain reticular formation has been implicated because progesterone implants there facilitate lordosis in estrogen-primed female rats (Rose *et al.*, 1971).

It is not surprising that male and female sexual behavior are influenced by slightly different areas of the brain, in view of the effects of perinatal hormones on brain structure. Most of these structural differences (size of medial preoptic area, dendritic branching in preoptic) have so far been found in or around the hypothalamus, but it is possible that structural differences will yet be found to exist elsewhere in the brain. The cortex, for example, appears to play a different role in male and female sex behavior, at least in rats. Large neocortical lesions in females facilitate lordosis, but the same lesions have a disruptive influence on male sex behavior (Larsson, 1964). The greater involvement of cortical tissue in males may be due to the male's more active motor sequences, and also his need to respond appropriately to complex sensory signals during sex behavior.

That hormones influence sex behavior in both male and female animals is definite. The way that they have their effect is not yet known. Since they must ultimately be influencing the pattern of firing in neuronal pathways, many scientists have hypothesized that they affect specific kinds of neurotransmitter activity. If this is the case, then it might be possible to modify sexual behavior by altering neurotransmitter activity with drugs, thereby circumventing the natural effects of the hormones.

Pharmacological studies like these have many pitfalls, as we have discussed in previous chapters. Nevertheless, many studies are beginning to implicate several of the neurotransmitters in the control of sex behavior.

neurotransmitters and female sex behavior. Studies which use drugs to modify serotonin activity have led scientists to believe that this neurotransmitter has a depressing effect on female sexual behavior. For example, **PCPA,** a drug which depletes serotonin, produces an increase in sexual activity in estrogen-primed female rats (Everitt *et al.,* 1975). The drug is given at about the time progesterone would be added to produce female sex behavior. This suggests that the inhibition of serotonin can be substituted for progesterone in the estrogen-primed female. Progesterone may thus produce female sex behavior partly by inhibiting serotonin.

PCPA can also increase sexual activity in estrogen-primed female rhesus monkeys which have been ovariectomized *and* adrenalectomized, suggesting that the drug is not simply encouraging adrenal progesterone release (Gradwell *et al.,* 1975). Carter and Davis (1977) report that a woman who was receiving PCPA as a treatment for Huntington's chorea showed an increase in sexual desire and sexual activity. Thus it is possible that the inhibition of serotonin is important for sexual behavior even in primates where androgens, rather than estrogen and progesterone, play a large role in female sexual behavior.

Although the studies on serotonin are highly suggestive, they are far from conclusive because the drugs used to alter serotonin levels are not very specific in their actions. They also usually affect catecholamine levels. Dopamine, in particular, has received attention. Drugs such as **pimozide,** which specifically block dopamine receptors, produce a marked increase in lordosis in estrogen-primed rats (Everitt *et al.,* 1974). Thus dopamine may also act like an inhibitor of sexual behavior in females. Although the evidence is only beginning to accumulate, it would appear that both dopamine and serotonin have an inhibitory influence on female sex behavior. Everitt (1977) points out that neither one can be substituted for estrogen, however. The ovariectomized female must first be primed with estrogen before any of the neurotransmitter inhibitors can facilitate sex behavior. Nevertheless, many drugs which affect these neurotransmitters can substitute for progesterone injections. Table 12.6 presents some of the drugs which have been used to increase sex behavior in estrogen-primed females, their action on various neurotransmitters, and their effects on sex behavior.

neurotransmitters and male sex behavior. Drugs which inhibit the activity of serotonin also facilitate sex behavior in males. For example, Shillito (1969) found that adult male rats treated with large doses of PCPA increased homosexual mounting in groups of all male rats. The serotonin inhibitor drugs also increase heterosexual behavior, particularly in "sexually sluggish" animals (Sjöerdsma *et al.*, 1970). Again, the drugs do not work unless testosterone is present in the animal's body (Everitt, 1977).

Dopamine has an opposite effect in males compared to females. For example, drugs like L-dopa which increase dopamine activity, also increase male sex behavior in rats (Benkert and Eversmann, 1972). L-dopa has also been reported to produce "hypersexuality" in men receiving the drug for Parkinson's disease (Goodwin, 1971).

Gossop *et al.* (1974) investigated the sexual behavior of men and women who used amphetamines regularly, and found that the men showed very little if any sexual dysfunction. Since amphetamines produce dopamine and norepinephrine release, this study supports the hypothesis that increased dopamine levels may be facilitating sex behavior in males. Many of the *women* who used amphetamines frequently showed severe sexual dysfunction. This would support the hypothesis that dopamine plays an opposite role in females, and that increased dopamine activity inhibits sex behavior in females.

Although these pharmacological studies are suggestive, they are difficult to interpret. In particular, they do not suggest how the hor-

Table 12.6

Drugs that affect lordosis in ovariectomized estrogen primed female animals[a]

Effects on Lordosis in	Rat	Hamster
Reserpine (decreases monoamine activity)	Increase	No effect
AMPT (catecholamine synthesis inhibitor)	Increase	No effect
PCPA (serotonin synthesis inhibitor)	Increase	Increase
Pimozide (blocks dopamine receptors)	Increase	No effect

[a] Adapted from Carter and Davis (1977).

mones may be affecting neurotransmitter levels, and they do not explain why certain hormones must be present in the body in order for neurotransmitter manipulations to have any effect. Hormones can affect the activity of neurons in a number of different ways. For example, they can act directly on the genome, modifying the production of RNA and hence protein synthesis. Or they might be affecting the function of enzymes more directly. Estrogen, for example, inhibits monoamine oxidase, one of the enzymes involved in the breakdown of the catecholamines (Luine *et al.*, 1975). There are many unanswered questions about hormones, neurotransmitters, and sex, but new techniques may provide clues to how these three systems are interacting.

Now that we have your attention . . . , we will mention some of the *sex and drugs* studies which have examined the effects of drugs on sexual behavior. Some of these studies have tried to find an **aphrodisiac,** or substance which promotes sexual arousal and performance.

Scientists (and interested laymen) have been searching for aphrodisiacs throughout the centuries, without too much success. Various substances have enjoyed notoriety as presumptive aphrodisiacs for a long time, but scientific testing usually reveals that their fame was probably due to a placebo effect. **Spanish fly,** for example, has long been thought to have aphrodisiacal properties. It is derived from insects (hence its name), and has an irritating action on the bladder which causes frequent urination and occasionally, persistent erections. Leavitt (1969) tested male rats with this toxic substance and found that it had no effect whatsoever on the sex behavior of those animals which survived the dose.

Testosterone and its derivatives have frequently been used to treat impotence, particularly after 1889 when a 72-year-old man administered extracts of dog testes to himself and reported an increase in sexual vigor. Unfortunately, most men who suffer from impotence have normally functioning testes and ample levels of testosterone. As we discussed earlier, the amount of circulating androgen in the body is not particularly correlated with the amount of sexual arousal or behavior. Nevertheless, testosterone treatments can be effective for the few men who suffer from impotence because of hypoactive gonads.

We mentioned earlier that L-dopa sometimes produces hypersexuality in men being treated for Parkinson's disease (Goodwin, 1971). Benkert *et al.* (1972) tested the drug on 10 impotent men, and found that they tended to show an increase in spontaneous erections during sleep. Unfortunately, the improvement did not extend to their sex lives. At the moment it would appear that the search for an aphrodisiac as a cure for impotence has not been very rewarding. It is more likely that most of the people who suffer from this disorder have psychological problems, rather than biological ones.

Nevertheless, the link between psychological problems and sexual dysfunction is probably at least partly biological. Animals under stress for long periods of time (e.g., by severe crowding) show an increase in the size of their adrenal glands, and a *decrease* in the size of their gonads. During a stressful situation, the pituitary gland releases large quantities of ACTH (discussed in Chapter 10) which activates the adrenals. Presumably, the pituitary is less able to release the appropriate quantities of LH and FSH during stress, and the gonads shrink. This may also be one reason why women experience irregular menstrual cycles when they are under stress.

stimulus control of sexual behavior Earlier in this section we mentioned that the excitement phase is brought on by any physiological or psychological stimulation that is perceived as sexually stimulating. This rather circular definition simply emphasized the point that stimuli which are perceived as erotic are by and large in the minds of the observer. The following examples of advertisements in the underground newspapers attest to the wide variety of stimuli which human beings find erotic:

TOY BALLOONS—BiWM (bisexual white male) professional with unique fetish—kid's balloons turn me on! If you have some or complementary turn-on would like to hear. . . .

MALE FEET—sought for adoration by attractive WM (white male) 35, can travel. (DeLora and Warren, 1977)

Most people, however, do not find balloons nearly as erotic as visual sexual imagery. Both males and females usually respond to sexually explicit movies by showing the first stages of sexual arousal, including penile erection and vaginal lubrication (Byrne, 1977).

pheromones. The olfactory system may also participate in the stimulus control of sex behavior. Some scientists have postulated that **pheromones,** which are chemical substances released by an organism which can affect the behavior or physiology of another member of the species, may be operating in human beings. (See Chapter 7.) They certainly have important effects on the sex behavior of some of the lower mammals.

The urine of mice, for example, contains some powerful pheromones. Female mice are strongly attracted to the urine of intact male mice, but not castrated ones (Scott and Pfaff, 1970). Male mice are attracted very strongly to the odor of female urine, provided the females are in estrus (Davies and Bellamy, 1974). Male rats are also attracted to the odor of estrus female rats (Le Magnen, 1952), and this attraction is dependent upon the male's prior sexual experience. If he is naive about sex, then he is not so interested in the odor. This suggests that learning probably plays an important role in the development of pheromonal attraction—a role that becomes more and more important in animals with more complex nervous systems and longer periods of development.

Michael and Keverne (Keverne, 1977; Michael and Keverne, 1970) have examined the role of pheromones of vaginal origin on the sex behavior of the rhesus monkey. They found that the odor from a receptive female attracted the male rhesus, and that he would press a lever hundreds of times to have access to such a female. When an unreceptive female was treated with this vaginal secretion, the male showed more sexual interest in her.

Keverne (1977) points out that the responses of the male to this odor are far from stereotyped, and that much variability is present. For example, some females treated with the odor do not receive additional sexual attention. Some males, instead of showing increased sexual attention toward the treated female may masturbate or may show more grooming behavior toward the female. This suggests that the odor is not strictly a pheromone, in that it does not reliably increase the male's sexual interest. Instead the odor may serve as one ingredient of female sexual attractiveness.

The female monkey's odors are not the only ingredient for sexual attractiveness, however, because anosmic males (who have lost their sense of smell) still show more interest in the female when she is in the early and middle part of her estrus cycle (Goldfoot *et al.*, 1978). The presence of this pheromone is not necessary for the male to show sexual interest in the female.

Whether these kinds of odors may be affecting sexual attractiveness in human beings is not yet known, although many scientists have speculated on the issue. Sexual arousal occurs at every phase of the menstrual cycle so the odors cannot be playing a terribly important role. If they are playing some role, then it may be due more to learning rather than to some intrinsic, biologically determined interest in a pheromone.

novelty. Normally, a male animal will repeatedly copulate with a receptive female until he is exhausted. But if a new receptive female is brought in, he will begin copulating with her almost as vigorously as he did during the first moments with the first female. This effect of novelty is very strong in animals like the ram and even appears in the primate.

Michael and Zumpe (1978) treated female rhesus monkeys with synthetic estrogen every day for several years so that they would be constantly receptive to the male. This constant receptivity approximates the sexual situation in human beings. Over this period, the sexual activity of the males gradually lessened,

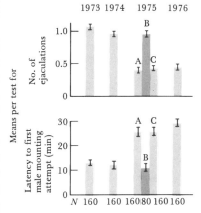

Figure 12.12
Sex behaviors of male rhesus monkeys tested regularly for several years with the same females. In 1975B, four new females were presented, and male potency abruptly increased. When the original females were reintroduced, there was an immediate deterioration in potency. N = number of tests. [From Michael and Zumpe (1978). Copyright 1978 by the American Association for the Advancement of Science.]

as shown in Figure 12.12. The number of ejaculations per test, for example, dropped to less than half of its initial level. In 1975, the experiments tested these males with new, estrogen treated females (B). The sexual activity of the males soared back to its original level. Figure 12.13 shows in detail the behavior of these males with the "old" females just prior to the entrance of the "new" ones. It also shows that the testosterone levels of the males increased, but not until several days *after* the introduction of the "new" females. Thus their increased sexual activity was not caused by a sudden jump in testosterone production. Rather their testosterone production was probably increased by the introduction of the "new" females.

Figure 12.13
Time course of behavioral and hormonal changes in the 8 weeks preceding, the 4 weeks during, and the 8 weeks following tests with "new" females. [From Michael and Zumpe (1978). Copyright 1978 by the American Association for the Advancement of Science.]

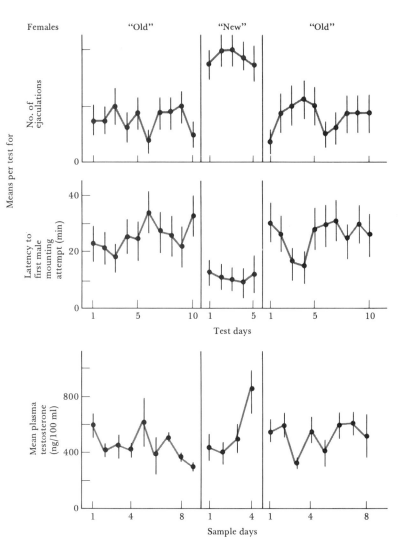

Michael and Zumpe (1978) speculate on the implications of these findings for human beings:

One can speculate that in societies with institutionalized monogamy, the uninterrupted sexual life of modern man—insulated as it is from exteroceptive seasonal factors—might provide conditions in which similar phenomena would be observed. Were this so, one would expect 1) a tendency to break and remake consort bonds (with new partners), 2) the use of cultural means for periodically changing one's stimulus properties (clothing, adornment, coiffure, and odor), and 3) an imposition of periodicity on sexual activity (menstrual and pregnancy taboos, Lent, safe periods, and so forth). Many of the prohibitions and customs surrounding sex in human societies are traditionally thought of as both protecting the sexes from each other and protecting the female from the constant sexual demands of the male. An alternative view is that they also function to maintain male potency. . . .

Human beings show an enormous diversity in their patterns of sexual behavior, but their physiological patterns of sexual response are somewhat less diverse. The pattern of response during a sexual cycle can be divided into four phases, all of which appear in both the man and woman. The stages include (1) the *excitement phase*, (2) the *plateau phase*, (3) the *orgasmic phase*, and (4) the *resolution phase*. The length of time each phase lasts varies between individuals, and for men and women. The main features of the first two phases are increased vasocongestion and *myotonia* followed by a relief of these tensions. During the resolution phase the muscular tension and vasocongestion subside.

This pattern of response is fairly uniform in men, but varies among women. Another difference which exists between men and women is that continued sexual stimulation after orgasm can often bring on another orgasmic phase in women, but not in men.

In lower animals, the sex hormones from the gonads play a large role in the control of sex behavior. Castration of either the male or female rat, for example, results in the complete disappearance of sex

behavior. In the higher animals, including human beings, the relationship between hormone levels and sex behavior is less straightforward. When a man loses his source of testosterone, he will slowly lose his sex drive and ability to perform, but it may take a period of years. When he is given exogenous androgen, his sex drive and behavior will return. In women, sex drive is not usually affected by ovariectomy, but it may be by adrenalectomy. This has led to the hypothesis that sex drive in women is more dependent upon adrenal androgens than it is upon ovarian hormones.

Many parts of the brain are involved in sex behavior because the display of sex behavior is a very complicated phenomenon. One of the areas that is chiefly involved, however, is the hypothalamus. In male rats, the *medial preoptic area* plays a critical role in sex. Lesions of this area eliminate sex behavior, despite the fact that the animal may have high testosterone levels. The role that this area plays, however, is not clear. It may act to stimulate other pathways, particularly the medial forebrain bundle, the pathway that is involved in reward and motivation.

The part of the hypothalamus that is

summary
Biological Bases of Adult Sexual Behavior

critical to female sex behavior is the *anterior hypothalamic area*. Stimulation of this area by electricity or by estrogen implants facilitates female sex behavior in rats. Lesions of this area eliminate female sex behavior.

Because the neural control of sex behavior must ultimately be linked to changes in neural firing patterns, scientists have begun to explore the effects of neurotransmitter manipulations on sex behavior. For example, drugs which deplete serotonin facilitate sex behavior in estrogen-primed female rats. This suggests that high serotonin levels may have a depressing effect on female sex behavior. Since the serotonin inhibitor can be used as a substitute for progesterone in producing estrus in estrogen-primed females, it is possible that progesterone actually acts by inhibiting serotonin. Dopamine is probably also involved, because dopamine blockers also facilitate sex behavior in estrogen-primed females.

Pharmacological studies suggest that serotonin also inhibits male sex behavior. Dopamine may be acting to increase male sex behavior rather than decrease it. For example, men who receive L-dopa as a treatment for Parkinson's disease sometimes exhibit "hypersexuality." Much more research on these systems is needed before anything definite can be said about how the neurotransmitter pathways are interacting in the control of sex behavior.

The search for an aphrodisiac, or substance which can enhance sexual arousal and performance, has not been rewarding. The toxic drug *Spanish fly* appears to have no influence on sex behavior, and testosterone appears to work only in men who suffer from impotence because of hypoactive gonadal function. The drug L-dopa may produce hypersexuality in patients treated for Parkinson's disease, but it does not cure impotence in otherwise normal men. Most sexual dysfunction appears to be due to psychological factors, which may trigger stress responses and reduce gonadal function.

Internal biological factors can only account for a small part of the control of sex behavior in human beings. Environmental stimuli probably play a much larger role. Sexually explicit visual imagery is usually arousing to both men and women, and may even have effects on testosterone levels. *Pheromones*, or chemical substances which are released by an organism which can affect the behavior or physiology of another member of the species, may also be an arousing stimulus. In lower animals, vaginal or urinary pheromones from an estrus female are highly attractive to the male, although in the higher animals, this response probably involves a great deal of learning. Novelty is also a powerful sexual stimulus. Male rhesus monkeys begin to show less and less interest in sex behavior over the years if they are only exposed to the same constantly receptive females. If new females are brought in, the males' interest increases considerably, and their testosterone levels soar.

In this chapter we have examined sex behavior from the standpoint of its physiology and its physiological controls. It is a motivated behavior, much like eating and drinking, and also like sleep (which we will discuss in the next chapter). As such, it seems to involve some of the same pathways in the brain. But sex is different from eating and drinking, and from sleep, in that it often involves two individuals who care about each other and who may feel needs and desires other than physiological release from sexual tension.

Some of the comments made by

respondents to a questionnaire dealing with sexual behavior in American women serve to illustrate this point:

Sex itself is not terribly important to me, but physical contact in the form of touching, hugs, embraces, caresses, etc., is most important. . . .

Closeness with another person is more important to me than orgasm (which I can have by myself, if necessary). If I had to choose between the two, I'd choose the touching. . . . (Hite, 1976)

The study of the physiological controls of sexual behavior can greatly enhance our understanding of our own sexual motivations, but in no other chapter in this book will it be as obvious that physiological psychology cannot answer all our questions.

SUGGESTED READINGS

Döhler, K. D. (1978). Is female sexual-differentiation hormone-mediated? *Trends in Neurosciences* **1**, 138–140.

Whalen, R. E. (1974). Gonadal hormones and the developing brain. In *Drugs and the Developing Brain* (A. Vernadakis and N. Weiner, eds.). Plenum Press, New York.

(The above two references provide more detail about the process of sexual differentiation. The Döhler article presents the point of view that female sexual differentiation is dependent upon the presence of low estrogen levels in early life.)

Money, J., and Ehrhardt, A. A. (1972). *Man and Woman, Boy and Girl.* Johns Hopkins University Press, Baltimore.

Bermant, G., and Davidson, J. M. (1974). *Biological Bases of Sexual Behavior.* Harper and Row, New York.

(The last two references are very easy to read, and provide more detail about a variety of subjects related to sexual behavior and its biological controls.)

13

*biological
rhythms
and
sleep*

introduction One of the most prominent characteristics of all living matter is change. Some changes are developmental in that they occur at particular stages in the lives of many individuals. Some changes are relatively permanent—some of the events which occur in the brain of an organism which has learned something tend to fall into this category. Others are very transient, such as the physiological and behavioral changes which occur in an organism under stress. The changes which we will discuss in this chapter are *rhythmic*. They may occur night after night, month after month, year after year, with such regularity that they may be easily overlooked by researchers interested in the physiological bases of behavior. But biological **rhythms** have some very important effects on our behavior.

Figure 13.1 diagrams a hypothetical rhythm which will be useful in explaining some of the terms used to discuss biological rhythms. Any event which changes from one point and eventually returns to that point can be thought of as a rhythm, regardless of how long it actually takes. The time which is required for the rhythm to complete a cycle is called the **period**. The **frequency** of the rhythm is the reciprocal of the period. For example, body temperature reaches a peak once every 24 hours. So the period is 24 hours, and the frequency for this rhythm is 1/24. The amount of change from the original starting point may also be important; the **amplitude** of a rhythm refers to this amount of change. For example, some people may only have body temperature fluctuations of 2 degrees during the 24-hour period, but others may have a cycle with a higher amplitude, perhaps 5 degrees. Also, individuals may differ in *when* their body temperatures peak. The term **phase** is used to locate the peak or trough of a cycle with reference to some external marker, such as a particular time of day. A person whose body temperature peaks at 4 P.M. would be "out of phase" with a person whose temperature peaks at 2 P.M.

The biological rhythms in humans which have received the most attention are the **circadian rhythms**, with a period of about 24 hours, and the female's 28-day menstrual cycle. Since we discussed the female's rhythm in the last chapter, we will concentrate on circadian rhythms in this one. In the first section, we will explore the changes which occur in the normal individual across the 24-hour cycle. Then we will examine the biological basis for this cycle, considering the evidence for the existence of an internal biological clock or **oscillator**. Do the circadian rhythms exist simply because the world turns at the rate of once per 24 hours? Or do we have a clock (or clocks) built into the nervous system which runs regardless of the social and visual cues associated with the day/night cycle? The last part of this section will examine what happens when the circadian rhythms are disrupted in various ways, and will lead us into discussions of "jet lag" and work shifts.

The second section of this chapter will deal with sleep, an altered

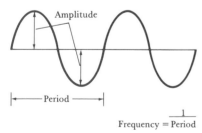

Figure 13.1
A hypothetical biological rhythm.

state of consciousness which is an integral part of the circadian rhythm. We will discuss the stages of sleep, and see how dreaming is a very unusual and puzzling kind of sleep. We will also discuss some sleep disorders, and what happens when a person is deprived of sleep for awhile. The deprivation studies can tell us something about why we sleep, and we will find that the intuitive answer, "to rest," is probably not the correct one. The third section of this chapter will deal with the brain mechanisms underlying sleep, dreaming, and waking.

It is becoming the rule, rather than the exception, to find rhythmic activity in physiological systems. Perhaps these rhythms were not as obvious before because it is necessary to take frequent measurements of some physiological variable over a period of several days to determine whether they show a circadian rhythm. As more data are collected, it is becoming clear that most systems do undergo daily, regular fluctuations.

circadian rhythms

physiological changes across the circadian cycle

Figure 13.2 shows where the average peaks are during the 24-hour activity-rest cycle for normal human beings for a variety of physiological measures. Notice that the peaks for the various measures are not at the same time, so they are out of phase. Nevertheless, the physiological systems are synchronized with one another within each individual since that person's peaks would tend to occur at the same time each day and remain in the same phase relation to the other peaks. Figure 13.3 shows how this synchrony would work for several days in a hypothetical case. The importance of this kind of synchrony will be seen later when we discuss the effects of phase shifts.

Individuals vary somewhat in where their peaks are for any physiological measure during the cycle. Some researchers have suggested that these individual differences in the timing of the circadian cycles may help determine whether a person is a "morning" or "evening" type (Horne and Östberg, 1977). "Morning" types usually describe themselves as "early to bed, early to rise," and generally say that they perform better earlier in the day compared to "evening" types. Figure 13.4 shows the daytime part of the body temperature cycles for these "morning" and "evening" types. The people who described themselves as "morning" types showed an average peak body temperature about 70 minutes earlier than the "evening" people (Horne and Östberg, 1977).

Although some of the physiological measures show cycles which resemble the hypothetical sine wave in Figure 13.1 many do not. They still show a circadian rhythm, but they may also increase or decrease in response to events which occur during the day. Figure 13.5, for example, shows a daily rhythm of ACTH and growth hormone. Both of

Human circadian system

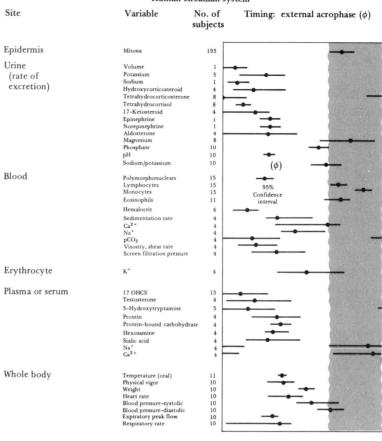

Site	Variable	No. of subjects	Timing: external acrophase (ϕ)
Epidermis	Mitosis	193	
Urine (rate of excretion)	Volume	1	
	Potassium	5	
	Sodium	1	
	Hydroxycorticosteroid	4	
	Tetrahydrocorticosterone	8	
	Tetrahydrocortisol	8	
	17-Ketosteroid	4	
	Epinephrine	1	
	Norepinephrine	1	
	Aldosterone	4	
	Magnesium	8	
	Phosphate	10	
	pH	10	
	Sodium/potassium	10	
Blood	Polymorphonuclears	15	
	Lymphocytes	15	
	Monocytes	15	
	Eosinophils	11	
	Hematocrit	4	
	Sedimentation rate	4	
	Ca^{2+}	4	
	Na^+	4	
	pCO_2	4	
	Visosity, shear rate	4	
	Screen filtration pressure	4	
Erythrocyte	K^+	4	
Plasma or serum	17 OHCS	13	
	Testosterone	4	
	5-Hydroxytryptamine	5	
	Protein	4	
	Protein-bound carbohydrate	4	
	Hexosamine	4	
	Sialic acid	4	
	Na^+	4	
	Ca^{2+}	4	
Whole body	Temperature (oral)	11	
	Physical vigor	10	
	Weight	10	
	Heart rate	10	
	Blood pressure–systolic	10	
	Blood pressure–diastolic	10	
	Expiratory peak flow	10	
	Respiratory rate	10	

24 hr = activity span   rest span

Figure 13.2
Peaks for a variety of biological rhythms in human beings. The horizontal lines represent a measure of variability. [From Luce (1970), Note 5.]

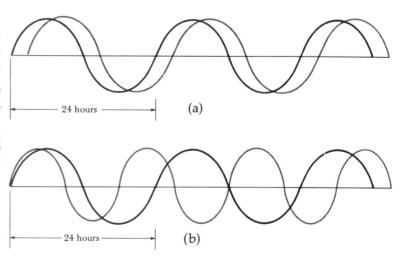

Figure 13.3
(a) Two biological rhythms which peak at different times during the day. Both have a period of 24 hours, however, so they are synchronized. (b) Two biological rhythms which peak at different times of day, most of the time. One rhythm has a period of 24 hours, but the other has a period of 18 hours, so they are not synchronized.

24 hours   (a)

24 hours   (b)

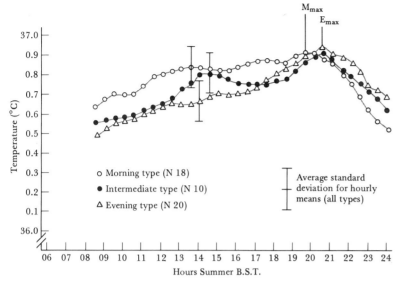

Figure 13.4
Mean daytime oral temperature curves for morning and evening types. [From Horne and Östberg (1977).]

these variables began rising just before waking in this individual, and reached their lowest point during the early part of sleep. They also showed rises during the day, rises which appear to be correlated with meals (Krieger, 1974). Thus a circadian rhythm may not be as obvious in physiological measures which are easily influenced by events which occur in the environment.

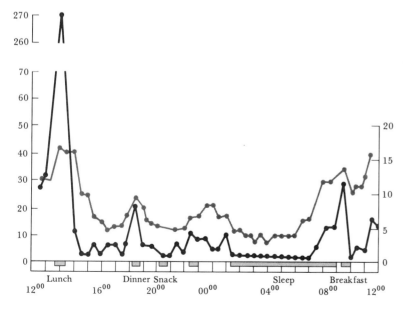

Figure 13.5
Circadian rhythms of growth hormone (light dots) and plasma ACTH (dark dots). [From Krieger (1974).]

behavioral changes across the circadian cycle Many physiological peaks occur during the day and it is reasonable to assume that performance on behavioral tasks will also be better during the day. This appears to be the case. Klein and his associates (1968) found that people tended to perform best at reaction time tests, mental ability tests, and complex psychomotor coordination tests between 2 and 4 P.M. The poorest performance was usually between 2 and 4 A.M. These peak and trough times correlate very well with the cycles of many physiological variables, particularly body temperature.

rhythmic response to drugs and stressors One of the most useful outcomes of the research on circadian rhythms deals with predicting responses to drugs and stressors. One of the authors recalls that during graduate school, Mongolian gerbils in the laboratory were very resistant to anesthetics after lunch, so all operations had to be conducted between 7 and 11 A.M. This was very difficult for a confirmed "evening" type.

Apart from causing disruptions in the lives of nocturnal graduate students, circadian rhythms can be useful in timing drug doses for illnesses. Halberg (1976) reports a doubling in the cure rate of leukemic rodents by timing the treatment with an anticancer drug according to the circadian rhythm. The drug is given eight times per day, but the size of each dose varies depending upon the animal's toxic response. Higher doses are given when the animal is least susceptible to toxic side effects, and lower doses when the animal is most susceptible. This way, the animal can receive a much higher overall amount of drug without adverse reactions, compared to more traditional treatments in which each of the eight doses is the same size.

Klein and his colleagues (1968) noted that response to various stressors which may occur during air travel varied during the circadian cycle. One such stressor is the lack of oxygen (this is quite stressful!). It is very important for pilots to remain conscious for as long as possible during such a situation. One of the pilots in the study was almost 50% more resistant to this kind of stressor at 3 A.M. than he was at 3 P.M.

A final example of the effects of circadian rhythms on the response to drugs and stressors deals with pain and morphine. It is hardly surprising that a mouse will jump if it is placed on a hotplate at 52°C, but it may be somewhat surprising that the mouse will jump sooner at certain times of day (Frederickson *et al.*, 1977). Furthermore, the effects of pain killers, such as morphine, vary in the way that they inhibit the mouse from jumping, again depending upon the time of day. Frederickson and his colleagues (1977) treated different groups of mice with the same dose of morphine at different times of day and

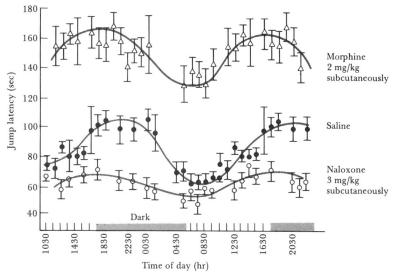

Figure 13.6
Circadian changes in latencies to the jump response on the mouse hotplate. Mice treated with saline (●), mice treated with naloxone (○), mice treated with morphine (△). [From Frederickson et al. (1977). Copyright 1977 by the American Association for the Advancement of Science.]

compared their "jump latencies" at various times of day to animals which were treated with saline. Figure 13.6 shows their results.

The morphine was most effective in producing analgesia during the early hours of the dark part of the cycle, which is when mice are normally most active. This was the same period that the animal had the longest jump latency without any drugs (middle trace). This suggests that morphine was being added to a naturally occurring analgesia which is released cyclically. The time that the morphine was the most effective may be the time when the endogenous analgesic was highest.

In Chapter 8 we discussed a candidate for this endogenous analgesic called enkephalin. This substance is a morphine-like compound which is produced in the brain and which inhibits the perception of pain under many different circumstances. To determine whether this naturally produced analgesic shows a circadian rhythm, Frederickson and his co-workers also examined the effects of naloxone across the day. This drug is an antagonist of morphine, and of morphine-like compounds. If the endogenous pain killers show a circadian rhythm, then the effects of naloxone should also. Naloxone should be least effective in decreasing the jump latencies about the same time that the mouse is most resistant to pain naturally. The bottom trace of Figure 13.6 shows that this is exactly what they found. These results suggest that it may be very important to consider circadian rhythms when timing painkiller treatments. Indeed, the studies so far suggest that treatment with many drugs may be more effective if circadian rhythms are taken into account, and that not taking them into account can result in drug overdose as well as ineffective treatments.

circadian rhythms **371**

what produces the
circadian rhythms?

The timing of most of the circadian rhythms we have discussed might suggest that they are due to the external influence of the day/night cycle, and not to an inherent "clock" which exists inside the body. But studies in which the day/night cycle are altered, or in which individuals have no cues to tell them when it is dark or light outside, suggest that an internal clock (or clocks) exists.

Several studies have been conducted on human beings in environments which are essentially free of time cues. These studies all suggest that a rhythm is maintained under these conditions, but it differs in some respects from the normal circadian rhythm. Webb and Agnew (1974a), for example, studied seven male subjects, aged 18–29 years old. These volunteers were kept isolated between 10 and 14 days in rooms designed to eliminate all cues to the time of day. The sound levels were kept constant by an air conditioner and the subjects could request food through a communication system anytime during the experiment. To counteract the effects of boredom, each room was equipped with books and a stereo system; it was also

Figure 13.7
Sleep wakefulness patterns of eight subjects in an environment free of cues to time of day. Upper graphs are for subjects who did not exercise strenuously, lower graphs are for subjects who did. [From Webb and Agnew (1974a).]

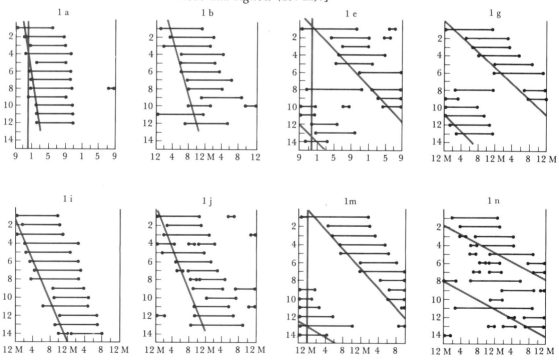

equipped with microphones and a closed-circuit TV in order to monitor the subject.

Figure 13.7 shows the sleeping–waking patterns for several subjects during the experiment. The lines across each day represent when the subject slept. Subject 1a showed a typical pattern: each "day" he went to bed slightly later than the "day" before, and also slept later. The patterns for the other subjects were essentially the same, although slightly more irregular. Subject 1m's pattern was such that by the end of the first week he was sleeping during the actual daytime and staying awake during the night. Subject 1n showed a similar, but more erratic pattern. He tended to nap a great deal.

Webb and Agnew (1974a) calculate that all of their subjects had **free-running rhythms** (which exist in the absence of external cues) which were longer than 24 hours. Subject 1a, for example, showed a rhythm which was 24 hours, 21 minutes in period length, while another subject showed a rhythm which was 27 hours and 26 minutes.

It is possible that the subjects in this study continued on their "circadian" rhythms because they had been used to the 24-hour cycle for so many years. In conjunction with the animal studies, however, these studies on humans suggest that the circadian rhythm is very persistent, and not simply dependent on external time cues. Some internal neurological clock (or clocks) appears to exist which is capable of free-running on its own, but which entrains to the normal 24-hour day/night cycle. Left to its own devices it will continue to produce a "circadian" rhythm, albeit at its own speed, which varies between individuals. The source of this timing mechanism is still a mystery in human beings, but we have some clues to its location in animals.

Since time cues about the day/night cycle are transmitted to an animal through the eyes by means of the alterations in light and dark, it makes intuitive sense to search for an alleged clock in some structure which is capable of receiving fairly direct input from the eyes. The **suprachiasmatic nucleus (SCN)**, in the medial part of the hypothalamus, is one such structure, and it has received the most attention in the research on biological clocks.

neural mechanisms underlying circadian rhythms

Lesions of the SCN disrupt a variety of physiological and behavioral circadian rhythms in rats. For example, Stephan and Zucker (1972b) showed that circadian rhythms of drinking and wheel-running behavior were disrupted after these lesions; adrenal corticosterone rhythms are also disrupted (Moore and Eichler, 1972). These physiological and behavioral systems normally show a free-running pattern in the absence of a day/night cycle, but the free-running rhythms are disrupted when the SCN is lesioned. Figure 13.8 shows drinking activity of a rat

Dark   Light

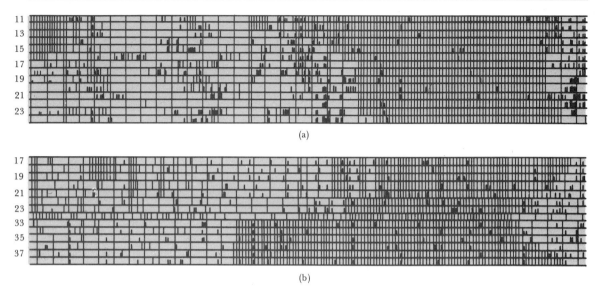

(a)

(b)

Figure 13.8
(a) Drinking activity of a sham-lesioned rat. (b) Drinking activity of a rat with a lesion in the SCN. [From Zucker et al. (1976).]

with a sham-lesion [panel (a)], and a rat with a lesion in the SCN [panel (b)].

the SCN and circadian rhythms in the hamster. The laboratory rat is not the best subject to use in studies of biological rhythms because its activity is not especially confined to one time of day. It gets up many times and runs around, although it is mainly nocturnal. This is easily seen in the activity patterns of the sham-lesioned rat in Figure 13.8. The hamster is an excellent choice for an experimental subject because its activity is much more confined to the nighttime.

Figure 13.9
Distribution of wheel-running of an unoperated control hamster under various illumination conditions. [From Zucker et al. (1976).]

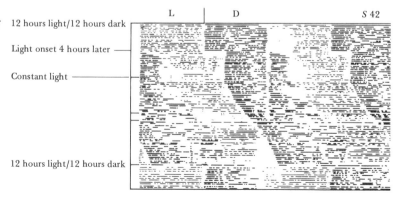

12 hours light/12 hours dark

Light onset 4 hours later

Constant light

12 hours light/12 hours dark

Figure 13.9 shows the activity patterns of an intact hamster (Zucker *et al.*, 1976). When the animal is exposed to 12 hours of light and 12 hours of darkness, its wheel running begins very shortly after the onset of the dark. In the second phase of the experiment, the light period began 4 hours later than usual, and the hamster quickly adapted its activity schedules to this new light onset time. After it had adapted, the experimenters changed the lighting schedule to constant light, and the hamster began to free run, using its own biological circadian clock, which evidently had a period of slightly more than 24 hours. When the light/dark cycles are reinstated, the hamster quickly resets its clock and goes back to a circadian rhythm with a period of 24 hours, again confining its activity to the dark part of the cycle.

Figure 13.10 shows the activity records from a hamster that had a lesion in the SCN (Zucker *et al.*, 1976). This animal showed an irregular activity cycle when the light and dark cycle were present, and when the light onset time was changed, its activity continued to be erratic. This is very different from the intact animal which easily adapted to the 4-hour delay in the onset of the lights.

During the constant light conditions, this lesioned hamster was completely unable to establish a free running rhythm. When the light/dark cycle was reinstated, it was similarly incapable of responding in the normal way by confining its activity to the dark part of the cycle.

Zucker *et al.* (1976) concluded that damage to the SCN not only abolishes the animal's ability to establish a free-running circadian rhythm, but also "loosens" the animal's ability to entrain to a stable light/dark cycle. Whether this structure is actually the clock or whether it is simply connected to some other clock or clocks is not yet clear. Lesions of the SCN may only "unplug" the clock from the input from the eyes. It is possible that the SCN is simply in the pathway from the eyes to some other brain structure which is responsible for the maintenance of circadian rhythms.

12 hours light/12 hours dark

Light onset 4 hours later

Constant light

12 hours light/12 hours dark

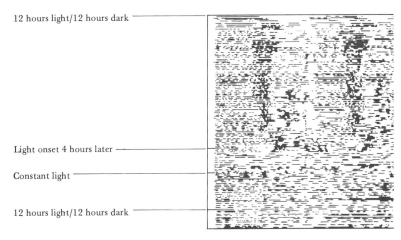

Figure 13.10
Distribution of wheel-running for a hamster with a lesion in the suprachiasmatic nucleus. [From Zucker et al. (1976).]

the SCN and control of three separate biological rhythms. Stetson and Watson-Whitmyre (1976) argue that the SCN in the hamster is a primary oscillator itself rather than simply a structure along the pathway. They found that lesions in this area of the hamster not only disrupt the activity circadian rhythm, but also estrus cyclicity and sensitivity to the length of the day. It may seem odd that estrus cyclicity and sensitivity to day length are related to circadian rhythms, but they actually are. In the case of the estrus cycle, which is 4 days in length, the hamster's pituitary gland releases a surge of LH (luteinizing hormone) on the afternoon of the day of ovulation. Since a female with a constantly high estrogen level releases this surge every day at the same time, there is strong reason to believe that the release is somehow triggered by a signal from the circadian clock. In the normal animal, this signal would be ignored unless high levels of estrogen were present, as would be the case on the day of ovulation.

Sensitivity to day length also appears to be connected to a circadian clock. Hamsters breed seasonally, so that their gonads regress when the days are short and become functional when the days are long. They have a period of photosensitivity which begins about the same time as when they become active at night. If light is present during this photosensitive phase they perceive a "long day" and their gonads begin to grow. To restate this phenomenon in anthropomorphic terms, the hamster becomes active at the same time every night. If the days are long, and the light is impinging on the active part of the hamster's life, the animal will realize that spring is coming and it is time to think about breeding. Thus the activity cycle, which is clearly determined by the clock, serves as a marker for the sensitivity to the day length.

The hamsters with lesions in the SCN were unable to show any of these rhythms. When exposed to continuous darkness, the lesioned females showed persistent estrus and were unable to cycle. The control females continued to cycle although their cycle length was determined by the period of their internal biological clock—it was 4 "days" long. Males with lesions did not show gonadal regression under constant darkness, as the control animals did.

Thus destruction of the SCN in hamsters results in the loss of a number of seemingly unrelated circadian rhythms: corticosterone secretion, locomotor activity, estrus cyclicity, and photoperiodic sensitivity. Stetson and Watson-Whitmyre (1976) contend that the SCN is indeed a primary clock and it is not simply a structure which is coupled to another clock located elsewhere in the brain.

circadian activity in the SCN. Further support for the hypothesis that the SCN is a biological clock in the rat comes from a recent study which examined the activity of the cells in this structure across the cycle (Schwartz and Gainer, 1977). These scientists injected female rats at 9 A.M. or at 9 P.M. with [14C]deoxyglucose, a radioactively labeled glucose which is taken up by nervous tissue in proportion to the rate of glucose consumption. About 45 minutes after the injection, the amount of radioactivity found in various areas of the brain would be correlated with the amount of glucose consumption and general metabolic activity in that area. High amounts of radioactivity indicate high activity; low amounts indicate low activity.

The rats injected at 9 A.M. were 3 hours into the light part of their cycle (the inactive portion, since rats are fairly nocturnal creatures). These rats showed high incorporation of the radioactively labeled glucose in the SCN, suggesting that this area of the brain was metabolically active during this portion of the cycle. The rats injected at 9 P.M. (3 hours into the dark part of the cycle) showed almost no incorporation in the SCN, suggesting that the SCN was inactive during the dark (and active) portion of the cycle. Other areas of the brain certainly incorporated radioactivity since they consumed glucose, but no other area showed any difference in incorporation dependent upon the time of injection. This study rather strongly suggests that metabolic activity in the SCN shows a circadian rhythm.

If the SCN is the primary clock, it must be reset every day in order to continue driving the circadian rhythms in time with the dark/light cycle. Light must be the major factor in the resetting, and the SCN is in an excellent location to receive this light input from the eyes. How this is accomplished is completely unknown. The clock is notoriously insensitive to pharmacological manipulations, although alcohol can slow it down somewhat (Zucker et al., 1976). Drugs which affect neurotransmitters seem to have little if any effect. It certainly appears that this clock exists, at least in the rat and hamster, but how it oscillates and how it is reset remains a mystery.

At one time, before there was so much research on biological rhythms, people generally received complaints about "jet lag" and work shifts with a certain amount of skepticism. Most people thought that these complaints were simply psychological in origin. More recently a number of scientists, particularly those associated with the aviation field, have examined the problem of circadian rhythm disruptions more closely. *disruptions of circadian rhythms*

effects of phase shifts. One way in which a circadian rhythm might be disrupted is by a **phase shift**. In this case, a person might wake up normally in the morning, go about business as usual, but instead of going to bed at midnight, the person might stay up until 6 A.M. then try to sleep from 6 A.M. to 2 P.M. This would constitute a delay in the onset of "light" (until 2 P.M.). The other kind of phase shift is when the onset of the "light" period is advanced, rather than delayed.

These phase shifts are becoming more and more typical in our modern world. For example, people are employed in jobs which re-

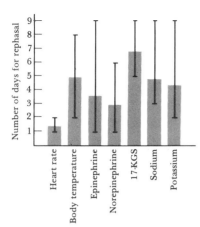

Figure 13.11
Average number of days to rephasal for human subjects undergoing a 12-hour phase shift. (Vertical lines represent range.) [From Higgins et al. (1975), Note 4.]

quire shift work. For three days they work the 7 A.M. to 3 P.M. shift; for the next three, they work 3 to 11 P.M.; and for the last three they work 11 P.M. to 7 A.M. Air travel across time zones also results in phase shifts. Persons traveling from New York to London might leave at 6 P.M. Six hours later they arrive in London. If the travelers are on New York time, their circadian rhythms are at midnight. But London time is 5 A.M., so they must begin a new "day" in only a couple of hours. The disruption in the travelers' circadian rhythms may be only a minor inconvenience. If the pilot is also suffering from this "jet lag," it becomes much more important to determine exactly what kinds of physiological and behavioral problems result from phase shifts.

Higgins *et al.* (1975, Note 4), of the Civil Aeromedical Institute, performed some studies on 15 men, aged 20 to 28, to determine the effects of a 12-hour phase shift on various physiological and behavioral measures. The subjects slept nights and worked days during the first four days of the experiment, but on the fifth day, they went to bed at 9 P.M., and woke up again at midnight—thus beginning their 12-hour phase shift. For the next 10 days, they slept between 10:30 A.M. and 6 P.M.

Figure 13.11 shows the average number of days required by the subjects before each of the physiological parameters moved their peak by 12 hours, or *rephased* to the shift. Several physiological responses adapted very quickly in most of the subjects, particularly those which normally change during a stressful situation. These rapidly adapting physiological responses included heart rate, and norepinephrine and epinephrine levels in the urine. Other physiological parameters took several more days to adapt to a new peak, notably internal body temperature and urinary levels of 17-ketogenic steroids (17-KGS).

The critical feature about the phase shift is not so much that it takes a few days to adapt, but that during the adaptation the physiological rhythms of all of these measures were out of synchrony. For example, body temperature normally peaks about the same time as many physiological functions. Perhaps this facilitates the formation of enzymes which are needed at certain times of day. During the adaptation process body temperature is out of synchrony with the other physiological variables. Stomach enzyme production might be peaking during sleep instead of around midday. It would be a strange feeling indeed to wake up in the middle of the night and have the desire to hunt for an all-night restaurant.

Figure 13.11 also shows the range for each of the physiological measures (the vertical lines). Some subjects adapted to the phase shift very quickly. Others showed complete adaptation during the 10 days for some of the parameters, but no adaptation at all for others. Thus there is a good deal of variability both among and within individuals in the ability to adapt to a phase shift.

Behavioral performance also took some time to adapt to the phase shift. Figure 13.12 shows the performance scores on the Multiple Task Performance Battery. The general conclusions from these data are (1) before the shift, performance scores show a circadian rhythm, with peak performance in the late afternoon, (2) performance deteriorates immediately after the shift (probably because of the loss of sleep), (3) performance gradually goes back up after the shift, but the circadian rhythm does not reappear for some time because subjects are performing poorly late in their new "afternoon" (Higgins *et al.*, 1975, Note 4).

phase shifts and the menstrual cycle. The suprachiasmatic nucleus, which is probably the circadian oscillator in the hamster, is responsible not only for the daily activity cycle but also the estrus cycle. Although we have no evidence that a circadian oscillator operates similarly in human females, there is evidence to suggest that frequent phase shifts disrupt not only the circadian rhythm, but also may be associated with irregular menstrual cycles. Preston *et al.* (1973) issued log books to airline stewardesses on BOAC who were going to be taking many transmeridian flights, so they could record their menstrual cycles. These women had more irregular cycle lengths than the normal popu-

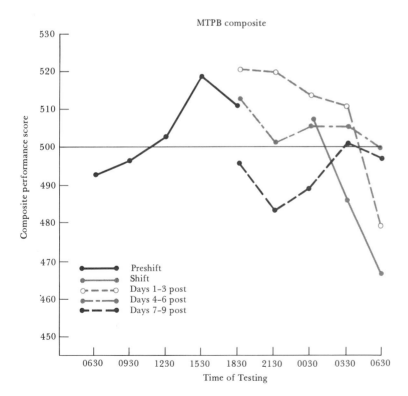

Figure 13.12
Multiple Task Performance Battery mean composite performance scores as a function of time of testing (n = 15).

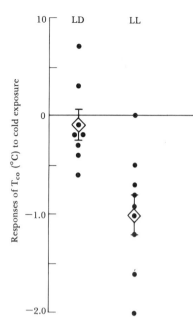

Figure 13.13
Maximum fall in body temperatures for animals in a 12-hour light/12-hour dark environment (LD), and animals maintained in an environment free of external time cues (LL). [From Fuller et al. (1978). Copyright 1978 by the American Assoiation for the Advancement of Science.]

lation. This study is not conclusive, but it does hint that circadian rhythm disruptions may have more widespread effects than a minor case of "jet lag."

effects of constant lighting conditions. Another way in which circadian rhythms might be disrupted is through constant light or darkness. Earlier in the chapter, we mentioned that many animals will begin to free-run in such an environment. The endogenous clock may not be sufficient to maintain normal physiological and behavioral rhythms, however, and some deleterious effects may results.

Fuller *et al.* (1978) placed squirrel monkeys in just such a time-free environment, in which lighting and temperature were maintained at constant levels. These monkeys showed a free-running body temperature rhythm which was about 25.2 hours in length. But the amplitude of the change in temperature across the "day" was smaller than the control animals. The control animals on a 12-hour light/12-hour dark cycle showed temperature variations of about 1.9 degrees, while the animals in the time-free environment only showed a range of about 1 degree. This change in amplitude may not seem terribly important, but the animals in the time-free environment were also deficient in their ability to maintain their own body temperature when they were subjected to cold stress. Figure 13.13 shows the fall in body temperature during cold stress for the control animals (LD) and for the animals in the time-free environment (LL). The control animals only showed a fraction of a degree drop in temperature on the average, but the experimental animals averaged more than a 1-degree drop.

Fuller *et al.* (1978) attribute this failure in thermoregulation to an uncoupling of the circadian clocks in the monkey during exposure to the time-free environments. Although body temperature is still showing a rhythm while the monkeys were in the constant environment, the rhythm was probably not in synchrony with the other physiological rhythms. They may have been all free-running at their own pace, producing an organism that cannot cope as effectively with stresses from the environment.

A constant lighting environment may also be detrimental to the reproductive system. For example, girls who are blind from birth, or became blind shortly thereafter, come into puberty earlier than girls with sight (Zacharias and Wurtman, 1969). In infancy, constant light may have important effects on the release of gonadotrophins. Dacou-Voutetakis *et al.* (1978) studied infants who were receiving three continuous days of intense light therapy for jaundice, and found that their LH production showed marked fluctuations relative to control infants. Figure 13.14 shows their results. Whether these changes have any effect on the maturation of the reproductive or nervous system is not yet known.

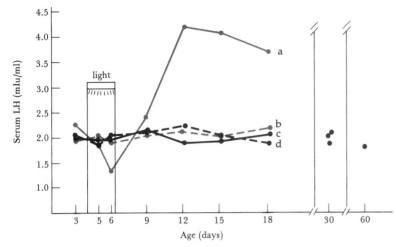

Figure 13.14
Mean concentrations of LH in the serum of newborns under phototherapy for jaundice and in various control groups. Jaundiced babies under phototherapy (a), jaundiced babies without phototherapy (b), jaundiced babies with covered eyes without phototherapy (d), healthy babies (c). [From Dacou-Voutetakis et al. (1978). Copyright 1978 by the American Association for the Advancement of Science.]

manic depression and circadian rhythms. One other, rather speculative, example of a circadian rhythm disruption deals with the mental illness manic depression. This illness is characterized by shifts from hyperactivity to depression, and in some individuals the shift occurs regularly. Halberg (1968) proposed that an uncoupling of the circadian oscillators within the human body may be one of the contributing factors to the cycling of manic depressives. If some of the physiological rhythms of the patients are free-running while others are synchronized to the normal 24-hour day, the person will be out of synchrony much of the time. Figure 13.15 shows how this might work. Rhythm A is synchronized with the 24-hour cycle, but rhythm B is free-running slightly faster. Around the seventh and the fourteenth days, both rhythms are fairly synchronized. But around the fourth, tenth, and sixteenth days, the rhythms are very much out of phase.

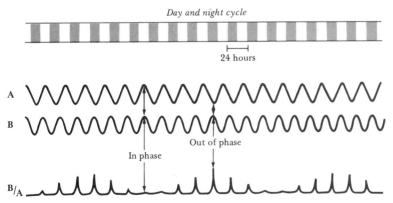

Figure 13.15
This hypothetical model shows two circadian rhythms. Rhythm A is synchronized to the day–night cycle, but B free runs slightly faster. When A and B are the most out of phase, the ratio B/A may become very high. This ratio indicates the cyclic beat phenomenon which occurs every few days. [From Kripke et al. (1978).]

circadian rhythms **381**

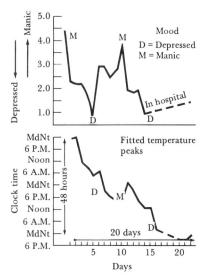

Figure 13.16
Self-rated mood of a manic depressive patient over a period of 20 days (top graph). The bottom graph shows the patients peak temperatures for each of the 20 days. [From Kripke et al. *(1978).]*

Kripke *et al.* (1978) studied a sample of manic depressive patients who cycled rapidly to determine whether there might be any support for this hypothesis. Various physiological and behavioral measures were taken several times a day. Figure 13.16 shows some of the results for one of the patients, a 41-year-old woman who suffered from a cycle of mania and depression which was about 10 days in length. The top graph represents her own reported mood for the 20 days of the experiment. (She was admitted to the hospital toward the end of the experiment.) The bottom graph shows at what time of day her body temperature peaked. Her mood cycles were about 10 days in length, as expected. But across the 20 days of the experiment, her peak temperature kept coming later and later in the day. A person with a more regular circadian rhythm on temperature would have been peaking about the same time each day.

Based on the 10-day cycle length in mood swings, these scientists estimated that the patient had a free-running rhythm of 21.8 hours, which was superimposed over the normal 24-hour rhythm. Then the person would find herself most out of phase about every 5 days, when the mood shift occurred. Several other patients' physiological rhythms were also abnormal, suggesting that there might be some validity to the hypothesis that disruptions in circadian rhythms might underlie some forms of manic depression. These data are only speculative, and more research is needed before anything more definite can be said.

summary
Circadian Rhythms

The most prominent of our biological rhythms is the one which has a cycle length of one day. A wide variety of physiological systems go through a cycle of this length. These systems include body temperature, heart rate, various urine metabolites, adrenal corticosterone, and ACTH. They do not all peak at the same time of day, but they remain in phase with one another provided the individual continues on a regular cycle of activity and rest. Individuals tend to vary in their peak times for various functions. For example, "morning" people tend to show a peak body temperature around 70 minutes earlier than "evening" people. Behavioral performance on simple and complex tasks also shows a circadian rhythm. Most people tend to perform best in the late afternoon, and worst in the early morning hours.

Organisms also show circadian rhythms in their response to drugs and stressors. For example, mice are least sensitive to pain during the early part of the dark cycle, and this is also when morphine is most effective in further reducing the response to painful stimuli. Apparently the mouse's naturally produced enkephalins also show a circadian rhythm because the effects of naloxone, an opiate antagonist, follow a similar circadian rhythm.

Although the circadian rhythms are entrained to the dark/light cycle, they are not a "passive" system in the sense that individuals appear to have their own internal biological clocks. When people are placed in environments free of time cues, they show activity/rest cycles which are clearly "circadian," except that the length of the "day" is longer than 24 hours.

The best candidate for the location of the internal biological clock is the *suprachiasmatic nucleus* in the hypothalamus. Lesions of this structure abolish various circadian rhythms in the rat and hamster and also eliminate the free-running rhythms in constant environmental conditions. Since the structure receives input from the eyes, it is in a good location to "reset" the clock when there are clear light/dark cycles present in the environment.

Scientists have recently begun studying the effects of circadian rhythm disruptions, and have found that they may be quite widespread. One kind of disruption, the *phase shift*, occurs when the onset of the light period is advanced or delayed. Many physiological systems begin to adapt to the new rhythm rather quickly, particularly those systems which show the fastest response to stress (e.g., heart rate and epinephrine and norepinephrine levels in the urine). But others may take several days or even weeks to adapt. Phase shifts are becoming more and more frequent as air travel across time zones and work shifts become commonplace. During the period of adaptation, the most important factor which produces changes in physiological systems and in behavioral performance is probably the desynchronization of the physiological systems.

Another kind of circadian rhythm disruption which may have deleterious effects is constant lighting conditions. Although an animal 's internal biological clock or clocks will begin to free-run, recent studies suggest that thermoregulation may be deleteriously affected, and the organism's reproductive system may also be changed in subtle ways.

Circadian rhythm disruptions may also be partly responsible for the rapid mood swings of manic-depressive patients. Some of these patients show abnormal circadian rhythms, and it is possible that their shifts from one extreme mood to another may be occurring when their own free-running biological rhythms are most out of phase with the 24-hour light/dark cycle.

Although the research on circadian rhythms is only beginning, it is becoming clear that it will yield some very important contributions to our understanding of the physiological bases of behavior. As we study eating behavior, thermoregulation, emotional behavior, or the effects of drugs, we must now take into account possible circadian rhythm effects, because they are likely to interact with all of these other behavioral systems.

***

sleep

Human beings spend about one-third of each circadian cycle in sleep, so sleep constitutes an important part of the circadian rhythms. Despite the fact that we spend so much time sleeping, research on sleep (its functions, its causes, even its description) has not been terrribly vigorous until recently. There are still many unanswered questions about sleep.

In this section we will first explore the nature of sleep. Electroencephalograms have played a particularly important role in establishing the characteristics of this period in our lives, and we will see that sleep has its own rhythms which are easily observed in the EEG. Next we will look at some of the more common sleep disorders, such as narcolepsy and insomnia. And finally we will examine some of the hypotheses about the function of sleep. It is interesting that no one is quite sure *why* we sleep, even though we spend so much time doing it.

the nature of sleep *eeg and the sleep stages.* When a person enters the altered state of consciousness known as sleep, it is hardly surprising that the records of their EEG begin to show some dramatic changes. Figure 13.17 shows the four stages through which a person who is falling asleep passes, as well as a typical pattern during wakefulness. The distinction between the four stages is not altogether clear-cut, but as the stages progress, the person falls into deeper and deeper sleep. Stage 1 contains **alpha waves** (8–12 cycles per second), and the deeper stages contain more and more **delta waves** (1–4 cycles per second). In contrast, the EEG during wakefulness usually contains a great deal of **beta-wave** activity (very high frequency, low voltage waves). Thus as a person falls asleep the electrical activity of the brain becomes more and more synchronized.

Occasionally during sleep, a person will show a highly desynchronized EEG which looks very similar to the beta activity common to wakefulness. But the person is clearly asleep. During these periods, the person shows a number of phasic events, including **rapid eye movements (REMs)**, which look as though the person is darting his or her eyes back and forth. These REMs may occur singly, but more usually occur in clusters in both eyes. In animals (and probably in humans as well although no one has ever recorded them), the REMs are accompanied by another phasic event: rapid spiking activity in the pons,

Figure 13.17
EEG records typical of wakefulness (W) and the various sleep stages. [From Rechtschoffen and Kales (1968).]

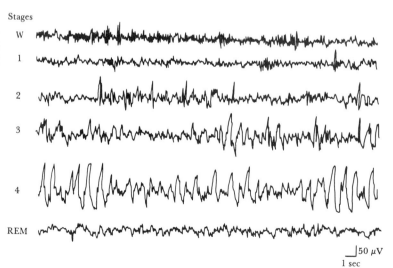

geniculate bodies (in the thalamus), and occipital cortex, called **PGO waves**.

Males usually have erections during these periods of highly desynchronized EEG activity, and there is a complete loss of muscle tonus in the antigravity muscles (e.g., in the neck). The person appears paralyzed, except for the movement in the eyes. Since this kind of sleep is so different from the sleep present in stages 1 through 4, and since the EEG resembles waking, this period is sometimes called "paradoxical sleep." In this chapter we will refer to the sleep in stages 1 through 4 as **S-sleep** (for synchronized, or slow-wave), and the sleep with REMs as **D-sleep** (for desynchronized).

neural activity during sleep. Although one might think that sleep is a period of "rest" for neurons, this is clearly not the case. Single cell recording during sleep and waking has revealed that average neuronal firing rates may decrease during S-sleep, but are actually higher during D-sleep than they are during waking. The pattern of firing may also be different. For example, pyramidal tract neurons usually show a uniform spiking rate, but during sleep, they fire in bursts followed by long silent periods.

The changes in neural activity are accompanied by changes in cerebral blood flow. During D-sleep, blood flow to the brain might increase as much as 80% relative to the blood flow during S-sleep (Reivich *et al.*, 1968). Figure 13.18 shows the changes in cerebral blood flow in the cat during S- and D-sleep relative to an awake control. Virtually all parts of the brain showed increased flow during D-sleep. It is clear that D-sleep in particular is anything but a "restful" period for the neurons in the brain.

cycles within sleep. Sleep is a part of a circadian rhythm, but it also contains its own rhythms. Figure 13.19 shows the movement of an individual through the various stages of sleep during a single night. About every 90 minutes or so the person moves through all or most of the stages, including D-sleep. The cycles are not exactly identical to one another, however. It is typical for most of the Stage 4 sleep to occur during the early part of the night; most of the D-sleep episodes occur later.

D-sleep and dreaming. The REMs characteristic of D-sleep, as well as the desynchronized EEG, have led researchers to hypothesize that these are periods of dreaming. This hypothesis is for the most part true. When subjects are awakened during D-sleep, they report that they have been dreaming about 80% of the time. When they are awakened during S-sleep, they report dreaming only about 20% of the time, in spite of the fact that most sleep is of the S-type (Hartmann, 1967). Freemon (1972) found that the relationship between D-sleep

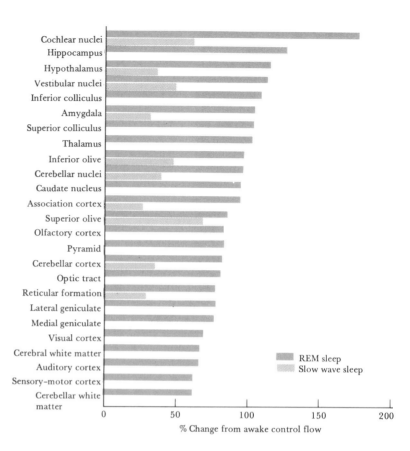

Figure 13.18
Blood flow in various cerebral regions of the cat during REM sleep and slow wave sleep. [From Reivich et al. (1968).]

and dreaming depends in part on how one defines a dream from the verbal report of the awakened subject. When researchers defined a dream as some kind of narration or progression of events, rather than simply any mental content or imagery, then dreams were even more heavily confined to D-sleep.

It is clear from the laboratory studies that everyone dreams, even though they may not be able to recall their dreams in the morning. Some people will say that they never dream, but the studies show that if they are awakened during D-sleep, the chances are that they will report a dream. These "nondreamers" may simply be "nonrecallers."

An interesting question which has been raised about the relationship between D-sleep and dreaming is whether the eye movements, which occur in phasic bursts, bear any relationship to the content of the dream. Roffwarg *et al.* (1962) performed an inventive experiment to test this hypothesis. They recorded the REMs of sleeping subjects who were awakened during D-sleep periods to report their dreams. Judges looked at the reports only (not the records of REMs) and tried to guess what the eye movements should look like if the person were

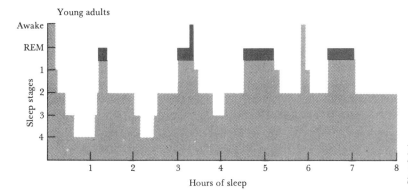

Figure 13.19
The cycles within sleep during a typical night. [From Berger (1969).]

actually watching the events in the dream. These guesses came very close to the REMs recorded from the subjects, suggesting that the nature of the REMs is somehow related to the content of the dream.

dream content. Many people (scientists included) wonder whether the content of one's dreams has any significance. Even though Freudian dream analysis has gone out of fashion, some people believe that the content of their dreams can tell them something about their subconscious motives and anxieties. This is a very difficult question to answer, particularly from a physiological standpoint, but there are several studies which suggest that dreams are not, at least, simply random thoughts. Their content seems to reflect, or at least be related to, many of the events which happen during waking life. For example, Breger *et al.* (1971) found that the dreams of patients who were about to undergo an operation often contained symbolism about the cutting off or cutting out of objects. Cartwright (1970) found that sexually arousing stimuli tended to be followed eventually by more dreams with sexual content, although the dreams were highly symbolic. Some waking activities seem to be followed by dreams with less of the activity, rather than more of it. For example, Hauri (1970) asked subjects to participate in 6 hours of physical exercise, and found that their dreams contained less physical activity. And Wood (1962) reported that after social isolation, dreams contain more social interaction. Some studies, however, have found no relationship between the events of waking life and the content of dreams. Dement and Wolpert (1958), for example, found that depriving subjects of fluid for 24 hours was not followed by more thirst-related dreams.

Although we cannot say for certain that the content of dreams has any significance, we can say what it is that most people dream about. Hall (1951) classified an enormous number of dream reports and found that about 34% of them involved movement of some kind, such as walking, swimming, running, and so forth. The next most common activities were talking, sitting, watching, and socializing. Hall also mentions that we rarely do anything very boring in dreams, which is what we might be doing for most of the day, such as typing or housework. In general, dreams seem to relate to a person's stressful problems.

These problems seem to be fairly unique to the individual because it is not difficult to tell the difference between the dreams of one person and another. Kramer and his colleagues (1976) asked three judges to sort out dream reports from five normal and five schizophrenic subjects, each of whom had contributed between 13 and 15 dreams. The judges were able to identify which dreams belonged to the normals and which belonged to the schizophrenics with a fair degree of accuracy. They were also fairly good at sorting the dreams according to which person each belonged to, and even which dreams came from the same night. This study supports the view that dream content is affected not only by the stable traits of the individual, but also by the transient events which occur in the person's life on any particular day.

Dream content may also be partly dependent upon what kinds of external stimuli are present while the dreamer is dreaming. Dement and Wolpert (1958) tried presenting a variety of stimuli, such as a tone, flashing lights, and a spray of cold water, to try to find out if these events would be somehow incorporated into the dream. The water was the most effective in these experiments. One subject, for example, dreamed that he was in a meadow with his girlfriend and that a rain shower started which made them run into the woods.

individual differences in sleep patterns Although popular mythology would suggest that 8 hours of sleep per night is "normal," studies on individual differences have revealed that there is wide variation in the amount that people sleep, and in sleeping patterns. For example, the country in which you live has some effect. Our culture tends to regard sleep as basically a nighttime activity, while other cultures regard the daytime nap as "normal."

The sleep logs of a sample of 89 college students reveal some interesting variations in both total sleep time and in sleep patterns (reported in Webb, 1975). The average sleep amount per 24 hours, including naps, was 8 hours and 5 minutes. The shortest sleeper slept only about 6 hours and 5 minutes, while the longest slept 9 hours and 55 minutes per night. Only 51% of the subjects averaged between 7 and 8 hours per night, the so-called "norm."

changes in sleep during development. One of the most striking changes during the development of the individual from birth to old age is in sleep patterns. In infants, the total sleep time is about 16.3 hours per 24-hour period, but infants also show wide variations in sleep amount (Parmalee *et al.*, 1961). During this early developmental period, the infant spends a huge amount (50–80%) of its sleeping time in a state which resembles D-sleep. In the uterus, the fetus may spend nearly all of its sleep time in D-sleep.

As people get older they spend less time sleeping and tend to confine more of their sleep to the nighttime. Also, the proportion of D-sleep declines. Figure 13.20 shows some of the changes which take place across the life span. The largest changes occur during infancy, childhood, and adolescence. Toward old age, people tend to spend much more time awake, and they usually have many more awakenings during the night compared to the young adult. In general, the older person tends to spend more time in the lighter stages of sleep. These trends are only averages, however, and individuals show wide variability. Webb (1975) is often asked by anxious parents how long their children should sleep. He gives general advice based on his extensive research on sleeping patterns: wake the child up at the same time every morning and watch the child at night. Only the child can tell a parent how long it should sleep.

sleep disorders

There are many physiological and behavioral problems which can disrupt sleep as one of their symptoms, but in this section we will only consider disorders that have sleep problems as their major symptom.

drug-dependent insomnia. At one time, a patient who complained of insomnia was given a prescription for one of the sedative-hypnotic drugs which was supposed to aid in sleeping. But this "cure" for insomnia turned out to be worse than the disease, primarily because an individual becomes tolerant to their sleep-promoting effects after us-

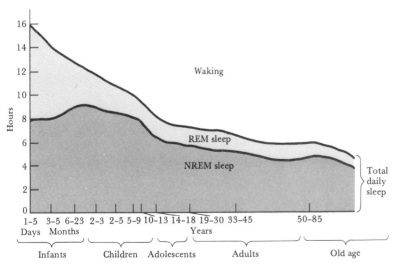

Figure 13.20
Changes in the total amount of daily sleep, D-sleep, and S-sleep as a function of age. [Adapted from Houston et al. (1979).]

ing them for awhile. The person must continue to increase his dosage until dangerously high levels are required to obtain a "decent night's sleep." Furthermore, most of the sedatives are addictive.

The sedatives have a large impact on the proportions of the stages of sleep, particularly when the doses are higher. For example, **flurazepam**, which is a widely prescribed sleeping pill, suppresses both Stage 4 and D-sleep. Figure 13.21 shows the proportion of total sleep time spent in the various stages of sleep of four subjects during baseline, drug treatment, and withdrawal conditions (Feinberg *et al.*, 1977).

During withdrawal from the sedatives, D-sleep shows a very pronounced increase, or **rebound effect**. This rebound is often accompanied by vivid dreaming, nightmares, and generally disturbed sleep. Thus the individual is tempted to get more sleeping pills from the doctor and the cycle goes on and on. Dement and Zarcone (1977) suggest that perhaps 50% of insomniacs have drug-induced insomnia as at least part of their problem. They suggest that the withdrawal of an individual who is taking drugs for sleep can be extremely difficult for three reasons:

1. *The patient strongly believes in the necessity of the drug and in the fact that he has insomnia.*

Figure 13.21
Percent of total sleep time spent in the different sleep stages for baseline, flurazepam treatment, and withdrawal conditions. [Redrawn from the data from Feinberg et al. (1977).]

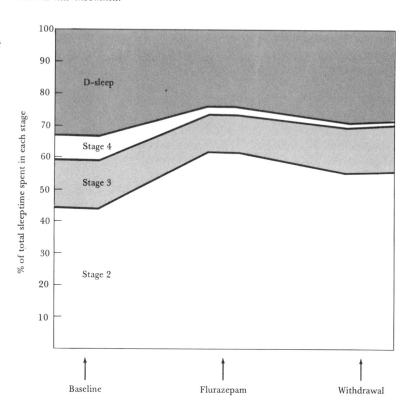

2. The actual drug ingestion often involves multiple drugs and very inconsistent schedules of self-administration.
3. The most effective program of withdrawal involves a very demanding interaction between physician and patient and the use of behavior change contracts. (Dement and Zarcone, 1977)

Withdrawal from the sedatives is made even more difficult by the fact that sudden withdrawal might result in life-threatening convulsions. Even after complete withdrawal, the sleep disruptions may linger for weeks or months, so this kind of insomnia is extremely difficult to treat. It is unfortunate that more research was not conducted on the relationship between the sedatives and sleep before they were so widely prescribed.

central sleep apnea. Some of the people who suffer from insomnia wake up frequently during the night because they cannot breathe. These periods of **central sleep apnea** involve a loss of contraction of the diaphragm, and hundreds of them during the night would result in extremely disturbed sleep (Guilleminault *et al.*, 1973). Dement and Zarcone (1977) suggest that insomniacs who snore might be suffering from sleep apnea, and that these people, in particular, should not take any sedatives. Sedatives act as a respiratory depressant and the combination of sleep apnea and this kind of drug might be fatal. Unfortunately, there is no good treatment yet available for this syndrome.

A number of investigators believe that central sleep apnea may be present in some infants, and may actually cause their deaths. Once in a while, a parent may place an apparently healthy infant in the crib to go to sleep and find it dead in the morning. This terrible phenomenon is called **sudden infant death syndrome (SIDS)** or simply crib death. It is possible that the infant had a low grade infection which combined with an immature nervous system to produce a fatal episode of apnea.

narcolepsy. One of the more common kinds of hypersomnia, as opposed to insomnia, is **narcolepsy**. Yoss and Daly (1957) described the criteria for the diagnosis of narcolepsy as follows: (1) recurring brief episodes of sleep (sleep attacks), (2) sudden loss of muscle tone without a clouding of consciousness, induced by laughter, anger, or startling stimuli, (3) sleep paralysis (brief episodes of inability to perform voluntary movements) while falling asleep or awakening, and (4) hallucinations while falling asleep or waking up.

Some of these symptoms would suggest that D-sleep is intruding at times when it normally should not. The sleep paralysis, for example, is associated with D-sleep. In the narcoleptic it occurs too early—right after sleep onset rather than after an hour or more of S-sleep. The hallucinations may also represent the intrusion of D-sleep at inappropriate times, particularly when falling asleep or just when awakening.

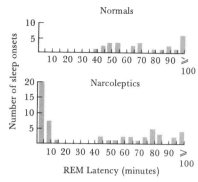

Figure 13.22
Latency to enter D-sleep (REM) for normal and narcoleptic subjects. [From Montplaisir et al. (1978).]

The sudden loss of muscle tone during the day could also be a D-sleep intrusion.

The hypothesis of D-sleep intrusion at inappropriate times as a cause of narcolepsy is supported by studies of the sleep of narcoleptics in the laboratory. Figure 13.22 shows the latency of D-sleep onset in a group of narcoleptics and control subjects (Montplaisir *et al.*, 1978). Notice that the narcoleptic patients tended to go right into D-sleep—very different from the control group who did not show D-sleep until 40 to 100 minutes after sleep onset. Montplaisir and his colleagues (1978) also found that narcoleptics tended to have very "fragmented" sleep, in the sense that they had frequent awakenings, more and shorter periods of D-sleep, and large amounts of body movement. Figure 13.23 shows a summary of a polygraphic record of a narcoleptic patient during the night. A comparison of this pattern with the one of the normal individual in Figure 13.20 shows how fragmented their sleep actually is.

Although it is likely that the intrusion of D-sleep at inappropriate times is the cause of narcolepsy, there is no good treatment for the disorder. Amphetamines are often prescribed, but the individual develops tolerance to this drug rather quickly.

sleep deprivation Although most of us may have been warned by our parents about the harmful effects of "not getting a good night's sleep," the experimental studies suggest that sleep deprivation is not so harmful as some might believe. There are several types of sleep deprivation which we shall discuss, including total sleep deprivation, partial but chronic sleep deprivation, and selective deprivation of D- or S-sleep.

total sleep deprivation. Kleitman (1963) kept subjects awake for several days, although he had to keep them busy in order to keep them awake. He found (not surprisingly) that this tended to make the subjects very sleepy. After two days, the sleepiness tended to plateau and the subjects became as sleepy as they were going to get. He also found

Figure 13.23
The cycles of the sleep stages in a typical narcoleptic patient. [From Montplaisir et al. (1978).]

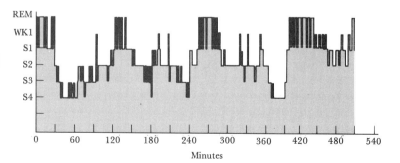

that they were most sleepy during the night, when they would ordinarily be sleeping; during the day they functioned nearly normally, especially on short tasks, even though they were totally sleep deprived. This probably reflects the effects of the circadian rhythms of various physiological functions. Webb and Cartwright (1978) summarize a large variety of studies which attempted to measure the effects of total sleep deprivation:

Sleepiness . . . (is) . . . the prime consequence of sleep deprivation. Beyond that it is quite clear that performance decrements are task determined and relatively limited. While hallucinations or illusions do occur, these are rare and never before 60 hours of deprivation.

It would appear that if you miss a night's sleep you will not turn into a pumpkin, contrary to what your parents may have told you.

partial but chronic sleep deprivation. Webb and Agnew (1975) call attention to the fact that most people sleep longer on weekends when their jobs or class schedules do not require them to get up so early. This might suggest that most of us are chronically sleep-deprived during the week. These scientists placed 14 subjects in an environment free of time cues and, as expected, the subjects began to free-run on their own circadian clocks. Surprisingly, all of the 14 subjects slept more during the 14-day experiment than they would have if they had been getting their self-reported average of $7\frac{1}{2}$ hours per night. They slept an average of 120 hours in the 14 days, which is about 8.6 hours per night. Webb and Agnew (1975) do not consider the possibility of this chronic sleep deprivation to be very much of a problem, however, especially since the effects of sleep deprivation are not so dramatic as we had once thought they might be. To quote their speculations:

Perhaps as in the case of eating, given unlimited amounts of food, we will eat more than we need. Our regular sleep diets may be simply and sensibly keeping us from being "sleep fat." (Webb and Agnew, 1975)

Thus it is possible that most of us are suffering from a minor amount of chronic sleep deprivation, but not all scientists agree that this is totally without harm. Taub (1977) compared male college students who regularly slept $7\frac{1}{2}$ to 8 hours per night to those who got $9\frac{1}{2}$ to 10 hours of sleep per night. There were a wide variety of differences between the two groups, some of which are shown in Figure 13.24. Both groups showed an increase in body temperature during the day, but overall, the long sleepers' body temperature was higher. Long sleepers also had shorter reaction times and did better on tests which required vigilance.

The mood of the long sleepers was also better. On self-report personality inventories, the long sleepers scored higher on cheerfulness, energy, and general activation, and lower on hostility and depression.

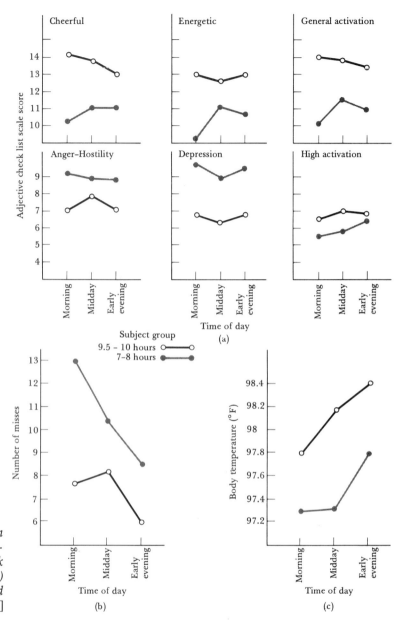

Figure 13.24
(a) Subjectively rated mood in long and short sleepers. (b) Number of misses on a vigilance task in long and short sleepers. (c) Body temperature in long and short sleepers. [From Taub (1977).]

Since this study is correlational, it does not show that the differences in sleep length were actually responsible for the performance or personality differences.

Webb and Agnew (1974b) performed an experiment to determine if chronic limitation of sleep length might result in poorer performance. They put 15 volunteers on a schedule which permitted only 5½ hours of sleep per night for a period of 60 days. They found that this kind of schedule tended to result in a sleep which had less D-sleep, but about the same amount of S-sleep. The authors reported that the chronicallly sleep-limited subjects did not show any serious changes in performance or in personality. Thus the question of whether we can exist and prosper on less sleep still remains open. (Personally, we would feel grouchy on 5½ hours of sleep . . . unless scientists were observing.)

selective deprivation of stage 4 sleep. It is possible to deprive an organism of D-sleep. It is not possible to deprive one of all kinds of S-sleep because S-sleep precedes D-sleep. Deprivations of Stage 4 sleep by itself can be accomplished by waking the organism up each time the EEG shows pronounced delta waves. This procedure does not produce very remarkable changes in the performance or behavior of an individual. Apart from sleepiness resulting from the frequent awakenings, the individual may suffer from some depression (Agnew *et al.*, 1967). After Stage 4 deprivation, the individual shows a rebound effect in that the next night's sleep contains more Stage 4 than is usual.

selective deprivation of D-sleep. A human being can be deprived of D-sleep by simply waking him up whenever his brain waves signal high-frequency low-voltage activity. An animal can be deprived of this kind of sleep by taking advantage of the fact that the neck muscles lose their tonus when the animal enters this kind of sleep. If the animal is sleeping on a platform surrounded by water, it will drop its head into the water when it enters D-sleep, and abruptly wake up. (This allows the sleep researcher to get a full night's sleep while the subject is deprived.)

Studies on the effects of D-sleep deprivation are contradictory. Webb (1974) contends that the studies have not yet shown that D-sleep deprivation results in any psychological harm. Animals and humans have been deprived of D-sleep for long periods of time without any obvious behavioral deficits.

Some scientists have found very subtle effects on memory processes in animals and humans deprived of D-sleep. For example, rats which are able to explore a maze beforehand are very quick at learning to find food in the same maze later on. Apparently the rats remembered some of the details of the maze during their explorations, even though they were not rewarded in any way (at least by the experimenter). Rats deprived of D-sleep are very poor at this kind of "latent learning," and although they can learn to find food in the maze, it takes them as long as when they have never done any previous explorations (Pearlman, 1971).

In human beings, D-sleep deprivation may also affect memory processes in subtle ways. For example, Tilley and Empson (1978) asked subjects to memorize two stories in the laboratory before going to sleep. Half of the subjects were then deprived of Stage 4 sleep while the other half were deprived of D-sleep. The D-sleep-deprived subjects were much less able to recall the stories in the morning, compared to the Stage-4-deprived subjects.

One factor which may contribute to the controversy surrounding the effects of D-sleep deprivation on memory is that it may be impossible to completely deprive an organism of D-sleep. If the experimenter tries to wake up the organism each time the brain waves signal D-sleep, then some of the components of D-sleep begin to intrude at other times during the night, or even during waking. For example, the PGO waves characteristic of D-sleep in animals begin to appear during S-sleep and even during waking in animals that are deprived of D-sleep (Dement *et al.*, 1969). Penile erections, which normally accompany D-sleep, also begin to appear in S-sleep (Fisher, 1966). Thus whatever functions D-sleep serve which are related to memory may be moved to S-sleep or waking if the animal is deprived of D-sleep.

functions of sleep In spite of all the research on sleep it is still not at all clear why we sleep. The answer that makes the most intuitive sense is that sleep serves a restorative function. Perhaps somehow our bodily functions become "worn down" during the day and require sleep in order to recuperate. The evidence for this hypothesis is very weak. Neurons do not become worn down during the day, and during sleep (particularly D-sleep) at least some neurons are at least as active as they are during wakefulness. Also, the sleep-deprivation experiments which we discussed in the last section do not point to any enormous deterioration of bodily functions when sleep is not possible. If sleep is not necessary for restoration, then why do we sleep?

nonresponding hypothesis. One hypothesis to explain our desire for sleep, if not our need for it, is that sleep is a behavior which has evolved that keeps the organism from being active during times when it might be dangerous or at least maladaptive to be up and around (Webb, 1974; Webb and Cartwright, 1978). Sleep is the system that permits the necessary periods of inactivity or "nonresponding," which keep an animal out of sight (and out of danger) for part of the time.

This theory finds support in a comparison of the sleeping patterns of various animals. Grazing animals such as cows, sheep, and deer sleep very little and then only in short bursts which are distributed throughout the 24-hour day. For these animals, long sleeping periods might be maladaptive because they are constantly in danger from predators. In addition, they can find food at any time of day because they eat off the land.

Gorillas sleep about 14 hours per 24, and this pattern also fits in with the "nonresponding" hypothesis. They have no need to fear predators, and their food supply is continuous and concentrated, so they have no need to forage for long hours like the grazing animals. In human beings, the sleeping pattern may have evolved in conjunction with the same kinds of ecological considerations.

Whether or not the "nonresponding" hypothesis is correct, it is still possible that sleep serves other functions as well. The most popular recent hypothesis concerning the function of sleep, D-sleep in particular, is that it has some role in memory processes.

D-sleep and memory consolidation. The studies which we reviewed earlier on D-sleep deprivation suggested that D-sleep had some role in memory consolidation, but exactly what that role might be is still in question. D-sleep deprivation does not always result in poorer recall, only when the memory to be recalled involves something unusual or emotional. For example, in Tilley and Empson's experiment (1978), the material to be recalled were stories such as "The War of the Ghosts." In contrast, experiments which have found no effect on D-sleep deprivation on memory have used more unstructured, less emotional material, such as paired associates.

Perhaps D-sleep is important in integrating emotional or unusual material which has been learned during the day. This hypothesis is supported by studies which find more D-sleep after learning experiences. For example, animals living in enriched environments with lots of toys and playmates showed more D-sleep compared to animals living in sterile environments (McGinty, 1969). Also, some scientists have found that animals which have learned a task during the day engage in more D-sleep during the night (Lucero, 1970). These studies suggest that D-sleep may play a role in memory, particularly memory for unusual or emotional events, but there is much research yet to do to establish exactly what that role might be.

D-sleep and sensory and motor "practice." Another hypothesis about the function of dreaming emphasizes its importance in maturation. Young animals and humans spend a great deal of time in D-sleep and some scientists have suggested that D-sleep may be a way to provide the CNS with endogenous stimulation at a period in life when exogenous stimulation is not very abundant, particularly in the uterus (Roffwarg *et al.*, 1966). The D-sleep may serve to provide "practice" to key sensory and motor areas of the nervous system during maturation. The fact that we spend so much of our dream time in motor activities would tend to support this view.

One kind of practice which D-sleep may be providing has to do with binocular vision. Berger (1969) suggested that D-sleep and the rapid eye movements which accompany it serve to stimulate the oculomotor system and to coordinate binocular eye movements. Support for this hypothesis comes from studies which have found that a person's depth perception is better right after D-sleep than it is right before D-sleep (Lewis *et al.*, 1978).

Jouvet (1975) suggests that D-sleep is not simply providing practice to key motor and sensory pathways of the brain, but is actually doing some programming. Many of the instinctive behaviors which higher animals possess occur in response to particular environmental or developmental events. For example, a song bird does not sing at just any time, it sings when the environmental conditions are right, when the season is right, and when its hormonal conditions and age are right. Jouvet suggests that D-sleep serves to organize and program the integration of these various events with the motor pathways which will subserve the instinctive behavior. When this kind of integration is difficult the organism will require more D-sleep. For example, one instinctive behavior of chicks is to imprint on a moving object during the first day of life. They then follow that particular moving stimulus around as if it were their mother (usually it *is* their mother). Jouvet (1975) suggests that one test of his hypothesis would be to find out if suppression of D-sleep *in utero* or immediately after birth would alter the appearance and timing of this imprinting phenomenon. If it did, it would be possible that the D-sleep were indeed functioning as some kind of an integration mechanism between genetically programmed instinctive behavior, and the environmental and developmental events which affect the display of this kind of behavior. This study has not yet been done, however, so we do not yet know for certain whether D-sleep may be functioning in this way. Indeed, despite all the hypotheses concerning the functions of D-sleep, or of sleep in general, we still do not really know why we sleep.

---

summary
Sleep

Sleep is a very complicated and active process which can be described by the patterns on the EEG. *S-sleep* (synchronized or slow wave) consists of four stages, during which the EEG shows more and more waves of low frequency and higher amplitude. The fastest waves, which are common during waking, are called *beta*. The waves characteristic of relaxation are called *alpha* (8–12 per second). And the slowest waves, characteristic of stage 4 sleep, are called *delta* waves (1–4 per second).

About four or five times per night, the individual enters *D-sleep* (desynchronized), which is characterized by fast, low-voltage waves that look very much like the beta waves present during waking. This period also shows phasic events such as *rapid eye movements* (REMs), and *PGO waves*. Also during this period, muscle tonus is lost. Neural activity is highest during D-sleep, and it is likely that the rapid eye movements correspond to the mental activity taking place in the dream. Dream content seems to depend at least partly on the stressful problems which are facing an individual at any particular time, and they may also depend upon the external stimuli which are impinging upon the individual during the dream.

Although most people display fairly

typical sleep cycles in which they move through the four stages of S-sleep and then show a period of D-sleep several times per night, individuals vary widely in their total sleep time and sleeping patterns. Younger animals show the most sleep, and spend much more time in D-sleep than adults. Sleep logs of college age adults show that normal people may sleep anywhere from about 6 hours per night to well over 9 hours.

Some common sleep disorders include *drug-dependent insomnia, central sleep apnea,* and *narcolepsy.* Drug-dependent insomnia is probably the most common form of sleep disorder and results from taking too many sedative hypnotic drugs over too long a time. These drugs generally reduce the amount of D-sleep, and when they are withdrawn the person may suffer from nightmares and generally disturbed sleep. Sleep apnea occurs in individuals who wake up frequently during the night because they cannot breathe. It involves a loss of contraction of the diaphragm, and may be one of the causes of the *sudden infant death syndrome.* Narcolepsy has a number of symptoms, including frequent daytime sleep attacks, sudden loss of muscle tone during emotionally arousing events, and attacks of paralysis and hallucinations while falling asleep or waking up. The most likely hypothesis to explain these symptoms is that some of the events which occur during D-sleep are intruding at inappropriate times.

The effects of sleep deprivation are not yet entirely clear. Total sleep deprivation makes an individual very sleepy, but performance and personality are not severely affected unless the person has gone without sleep for some time. Partial but chronic sleep deprivation may have subtle effects: people who normally get 9–10 hours of sleep per night tend to have healthier personalities, and to perform better on simple tasks compared to people who get only 7–8 hours of sleep. But experiments which have tested the effects of chronic sleep limitation have not found any severely deleterious effects.

Selective deprivation of D-sleep apparently affects memory consolidation, particularly when the task which was learned required some emotional or unusual material. These findings have led scientists to hypothesize that one of the functions of D-sleep is to aid in memory consolidation for emotional material. D-sleep may also serve as a period of sensory and motor "practice," particularly for binocular vision. Young animals have the most D-sleep, and they need the most practice; D-sleep would be a suitable time for this kind of neural "practice" since the muscles are still. One additional hypothesis about the function of sleep is that it is a behavior which has evolved because members of the species which did not respond at certain times of the day would be better adapted to the environment. Thus sleep may simply by an evolved period of "nonresponding."

It is curious that despite all the research on sleep, it is still not clear why we sleep. Further studies on the nature of sleep, particularly D-sleep, may provide more answers in the future.

Even though we cannot answer the question of why we sleep on a functional level, we can begin to answer it at the neural level. The traditional arsenal of the physiological psychologist of lesion, stimulation, and electrical recording studies, as well as pharmacological stud-

neural mechanisms of sleep and waking

ies, have been applied to the study of sleep. These studies have revealed that sleep is clearly an active process; there are brain mechanisms which put the animal to sleep. There are also separate but interacting brain mechanisms which are involved in the change from S- to D-sleep. And there are also brain mechanisms which wake the animal up. In this section we will examine some of the brain structures which play major roles in the processes of sleeping, dreaming, and arousal.

the reticular formation and arousal Early in the study of sleep, Bremer (1935) found that transection of the cat's brain at the level of the midbrain produced an animal which appeared to be sleeping constantly. This transection (A) is shown in Figure 13.25. The cat's brain showed an EEG pattern which was synchronized and remained that way for some time. This experiment suggested that there was a brain structure (or structures) *beneath* the level of the transection which is somehow responsible for arousal, and that when it was disconnected from the forebrain the animal would not be aroused.

This structure appears to be the **reticular formation**, which runs throughout the medial core of the brainstem, and rostrally into the midbrain. Moruzzi and Magoun (1949) showed that electrical stimulation of the reticular formation produced immediate and widespread desynchronization of the entire brain. Lindsley *et al.* (1949, 1950) showed that this kind of stimulation produced behavioral arousal as well. Lindsley and his colleagues performed their studies on monkeys and found that if the animal were awake at the time of the stimulation, the monkey became quite alert and aroused. If the animal were asleep, the stimulation woke it up.

Lesion studies also support the view that the reticular formation

Figure 13.25
Transection at A produces a cat which is constantly sleeping. Transection at B produces a cat which shows constant EEG activation. [From Akert (1965).]

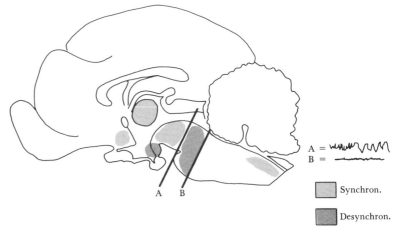

A = 〰〰〰
B = ———

▢ Synchron.

▩ Desynchron.

functions as an arousal mechanism. Large lesions produce permanent sleep—in fact, they produce coma and eventual death. Smaller lesions, or lesions which are performed in stages, result in an EEG with large delta waves, but the animal usually can show some recovery.

The reticular formation is a large network of cells which receives input from many sensory channels, and stimulation of the peripheral sensory system produces neural activity in this structure. The reticular formation not only mediates arousal directly, but it is also the important link in the chain from sensory input to arousal. Thus an animal will wake up when there is a loud noise. The reticular formation may also mediate a change from simple arousal to a highly alert state. Fuster (1958) implanted stimulating electrodes in the reticular formation of monkeys, and trained them to discriminate between two objects on a tray. If the monkey reached for the correct object it received a reward. The objects were only lighted up for a brief second, however, so the monkey had to make its decision very quickly. The monkeys which received reticular stimulation during the task performed better in two ways. First, their reaction time was faster. Second, they made more correct choices than the unstimulated monkeys. These results suggest that activity in the reticular formation is not just important for arousal, but also for attention and alertness.

The reticular formation is not the end of the story, however, because many other brain regions appear to be involved in the sleeping-waking cycle. Figure 13.25 shows shaded areas where electrical stimulation can produce cortical desynchronization or synchronization, and these structures are located in many parts of the forebrain, midbrain, and brainstem. Recent studies are emphasizing the roles of several brainstem structures in sleep.

One of the brain areas which has received a great deal of attention is the **raphe**, a series of nuclei which run through the core of the brainstem from the medulla to the back of the midbrain (shown in Figure 13.26). Jouvet and Renault (1966) lesioned large sections of the raphe in cats and found that they would not go to sleep for days. Eventually the animals would go back to sleep, but even then they only showed S-sleep for a few hours a day (very different from the normal cat which sleeps 60–70% of the time).

the raphe, serotonin, and sleep

These nuclei in the raphe are very rich in serotonin, so it is possible that it is this neurotransmitter pathway which is involved in sleep. Indeed, the huge raphe lesions severely depressed the amount of serotonin in the animals' brains.

The importance of these serotonin-containing nuclei is further emphasized by studies in which the serotonin depleting drug PCPA is injected. Jouvet (1974) reports that a single injection of PCPA had no effects on the cat's sleeping-waking cycle for the first day after injec-

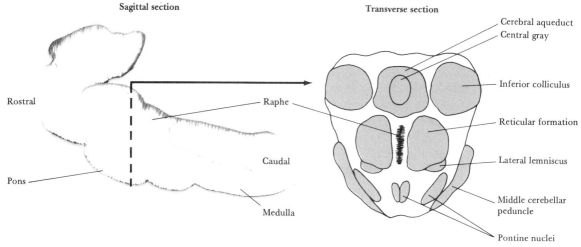

Figure 13.26
The raphe. [*From Carlson (1977).*]

tion. But then the cat suffered a period of wakefulness which lasted up to 40 hours. The delayed onset of the wakefulness corresponded in time to the fall in serotonin levels which was precipitated by the PCPA injection. And the return to the normal sleep cycle, which occurred about 200 hours after the injection, corresponded to the return of normal brain levels of serotonin.

PCPA inhibits the synthesis of serotonin by blocking trytophan hydroxylase, the enzyme which converts tryptophan into 5-HTP, as shown in Figure 13.27. So if an animal whose serotonin is depleted by PCPA is injected with 5-HTP, its serotonin levels should go right up. An injection of 5-HTP into an animal which has received PCPA immediately reverses the insomnia.

These studies support the view that the raphe's serotonin-containing neurons are intimately involved with sleep, but unfortunately the picture is not all that clear. Chronic administration of PCPA depletes serotonin by about 90% and keeps it that way, but cats receiving this kind of chronic administration eventually begin to sleep again (Dement *et al.*, 1972). Thus there must be other mechanisms involved in sleep as well.

the locus coeruleus, One of the pathways which appears to be involved in the waking
norepinephrine, and waking process is the dorsal noradrenergic bundle, which arises from the **locus coeruleus** and which contains norepinephrine. Lesions in this bundle result in an animal which sleeps much more than normal (Jones *et al.*, 1969). Also, stimulation of this area produces arousal (Moruzzi and Magoun, 1949).

The role of this pathway in waking can also be tested pharmacologically, with the drug **alpha-methyl-*p*-tyrosine**, or AMPT for short. This drug inhibits catecholamine synthesis, and it also suppresses both behavioral and EEG arousal.

Pujol *et al.* (1973) transected the ascending dorsal noradrenergic bundle, and found that this procedure produced increased activity in the raphe nuclei. These cats showed a significant increase in both S- and D-sleep which accompanied the increase in raphe activity. Thus the transection might have been shutting off the effect of the dorsal noradrenergic "waking pathway" on the cortex, and increasing the activity of the raphe nuclei.

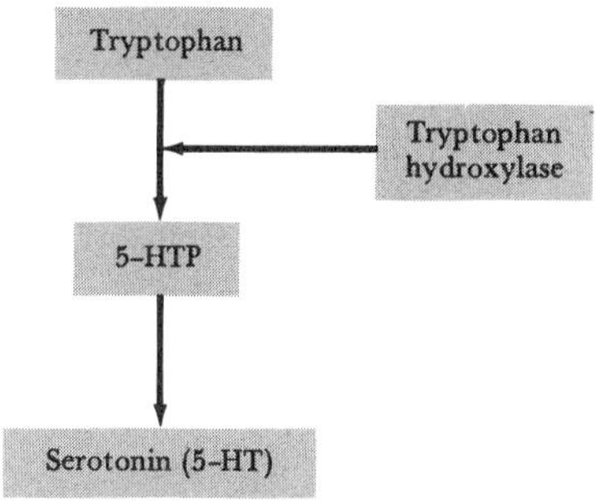

These two pathways seem to be critically involved in the sleeping-waking cycle, but other brain areas must be involved as well. For example, electrical stimulation of the **nucleus of the solitary tract** in the brain stem, which we will mention again later in the chapter, produces cortical synchronization (Magnes *et al.*, 1961). The hypothalamus probably plays a role of its own since manipulations of its activity can also affect the sleeping-waking cycle. For example, stimulation of the preoptic area produces cortical synchronization (Sterman and Clemente, 1962), and lesions of the posterior part of the hypothalamus produce long-lasting somnolence (Naquet *et al.*, 1966). Certainly more research is needed to find out how the suprachiasmatic nucleus in the hypothalamus, which is critical to the circadian rhythm, might be tied into the mechanisms which underlie the sleeping-waking cycle. There are as yet many unanswered questions about sleep and waking. But much progress has been made on the mechanisms underlying the cycles within sleep: the change from D-sleep to S-sleep and back again.

Figure 13.27

Synthesis of serotonin. PCPA blocks the enzyme tryptophan hydroxylase, and thus blocks the synthesis of serotonin. Administration of 5-HTP, however, reverses the effects of PCPA.

D-sleep is apparently so important to organisms which display it that it has brain mechanisms all its own. These mechanisms appear to be located in the pons, particularly in the **gigantocellular tegmental field (FTG)** ("giant cells of the tegmentum"). Large lesions of this area abolish D-sleep altogether, although the animal may still show S-sleep. Smaller lesions in and around this area may abolish the muscular inhibition which is normally present during D-sleep, although the animal seems to be still dreaming. After such lesions, a cat displays "pseudohallucinatory" behavior at the times when it would ordinarily be entering D-sleep. Jouvet (1975) describes this kind of behavior:

the FTG and D-sleep

They suddenly stand up, leap and either display some aggressive behavior or play with their front paws as they might play with a mouse, or they show a rage behavior or a defense reaction against a larger predator.... During these episodes the animals do not react to visual stimuli and they often collide with the walls of the observation cage. Normally, these episodes last for 4 to 5 minutes (which is the average time of a PS [D-sleep] episode). At the end, the animals either suddenly awaken ... or return to a posture of quiet sleep.

Hobson and his colleagues (McCarley and Hobson, 1971; Hobson *et al.*, 1975) have studied the electrophysiological activity of the cells in the FTG during sleep and dreaming, and have further supported the view that the FTG is critically involved in D-sleep. The axonal processes of these cells extend throughout large areas of the brain. Their cell bodies, however, are located in the pons. During D-sleep in cats, they show dramatic increases in firing rate. They also show a smaller increase about 5 minutes before the onset of D-sleep. Furthermore, the FTG cells often show a phasic burst of firing which precedes the rapid eye movements by 250 milliseconds. Neurons around the FTG also show some of these properties during and immediately before D-sleep, but in diminishing degrees. These findings have led Hobson and his colleagues to suggest that the FTG may be a critical part of the executive system for D-sleep.

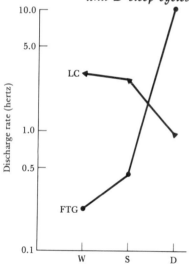

the FTG, the locus coeruleus, and D-sleep cycles

If the FTG is responsible for triggering the D-sleep episodes, what triggers the neurons of the FTG? Hobson *et al.* (1975) found that the FTG and the locus coeruleus were working together, inhibiting one another, to produce the cyclic changes from S-sleep to D-sleep and back again.

Figure 13.28 shows the discharge rates for cells in the locus coeruleus and FTG during waking, S-sleep, and D-sleep. Notice that when the FTG cells are firing slowly, the locus coeruleus cells are firing fast (waking and S-sleep). This situation reversed during D-sleep. Figure 13.29 shows the discharge rates (as a percentage of the total number of firings) during the 2 minutes immediately preceding the onset of D-sleep, and the 1 minute after its onset. During the 2 minutes prior to D-sleep onset, the locus coeruleus cells are firing very fast (the line on the graph is ascending very steeply). When D-sleep has begun, they slow down considerably (the line is ascending only very slowly). The FTG cells do exactly the opposite. In fact, their firing rates are the mirror image of the firing rates of the locus coeruleus cells.

Since the cells of these two areas send neurons to one another, it makes sense to hypothesize that they are interacting in a reciprocal fashion. Rapid firing in one group inhibits firing rates in the other. Each group would become dominant in turn as the animal moved through the cycles of D-sleep and S-sleep during the night. While the FTG, the locus coeruleus, and the raphe are very important in the control of sleep, they are not the only mechanisms which can affect sleep, dreaming, or arousal. Multiple controls are usually the rule for important motivated behaviors such as eating, fighting, and sex behavior, and sleep behavior also apparently has multiple controls.

Figure 13.28
The discharge rates for cells in the locus coeruleus (LC) and gigantocellular tegmental field (FTG) during waking (W), S-sleep (S), and D-sleep (D). [From Hobson et al. (1975). Copyright 1975 by the American Association for the Advancement of Science.]

404 *physiological psychology*

An animal that has just eaten often goes to sleep. Hungry animals are generally more active, which makes sense if they must go out and look for food in order to stay alive. This simple and intuitively obvious principle must have some physiological mechanism underlying it, and the evidence is pointing to intestinal movements during digestion.

Kukorelli and Juhász (1977) studied the role of eating and of electrical stimulation of the intestines and found, as expected, that satiated cats do indeed sleep more than starved ones. They also found that electrical stimulation of the small intestine, at a very low frequency and intensity (1 Hz, 2–6V), made the cats sleep for even longer periods. Figure 13.30 shows their results. The white columns show the percentage of time spent in waking, drowsiness, S-sleep, and D-sleep (as measured by an EEG) by starved and satiated cats without the intestinal stimulation, while the shaded columns show the times spent by intestinally stimulated cats.

These scientists suggest that satiated animals probably sleep longer because of the naturally occurring rhythmic afferent impulses generated by the rhythmic intestinal movements during digestion. This in-

sleep-inducing
intestinal stimulation

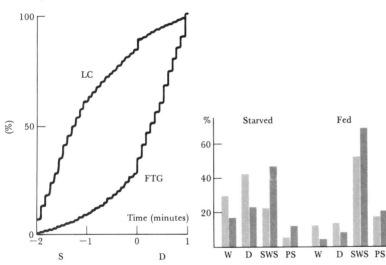

Figure 13.29
Discharge rates (expressed as percentage of total firing during the 3-minute period) of single units in the LC and FTG during the 2 minutes preceding the onset of D-sleep, and the 1 minute following its onset. [From Hobson et al. (1975). Copyright 1975 by the American Association for the Advancement of Science.]

Figure 13.30
Distribution of total recording time in the wakefulness stage (W), drowsiness (D), S-sleep (SWS), and D-sleep (PS), before (light columns) and during (dark columns) intestinal stimulation. [From Kukorelli and Juhász (1977).]

formation from the intestinal movements may be producing sleep by means of the neural structures which we discussed earlier in this section. One area of the brain which receives information from internal organs is the nucleus of the solitary tract in the medulla, and this structure is known to have modulating influences on the reticular formation. For example, low frequency electrical stimulation of this region produces EEG synchrony (Magnes *et al.*, 1961), and lesions, produced by cooling, result in arousal (Berlucchi *et al.*, 1964). Perhaps the intestinal movements are sending low frequency, steady afferent impulses to the nucleus of the solitary tract, which then inhibit the activity of the reticular formation, producing drowsiness and sleep.

A full stomach may be producing drowsiness and sleep in more than one way. In Chapter 11, we mentioned that when food enters the small intestine, a gastrointestinal hormone called CCK is released. Injections of this substance produce satiety, in some as yet unknown way; they also promote sleep (Rubinstein and Sonnenschein, 1971), even in animals whose gastrointestinal tract has been denervated. These animals could not have been receiving afferent impulses from their intestines, so the CCK must have been promoting sleep in some independent way.

sleep-inducing chemicals The role of chemicals other than CCK in sleep has been studied for some time, but the results are not at all clear. Early scientists believed that sleep might occur because during the day some hypnogenic chemical built up in the body to a level which eventually became high enough to induce sleep. A simple test of this hypothesis is to deprive an animal of sleep for awhile and then inject some·of its blood (or other bodily chemical) into a nondeprived animal. Legendre and Piéron attempted to do this back in 1913; then injected dogs with blood or serum from sleep deprived and from undeprived dogs. Both injections resulted in sleep. Perhaps the stress of the injection made the dogs tired.

Experiments in which cerebrospinal fluid (CSF) is transferred have been much more successful, however. Legendre and Piéron (1913) found that CSF from sleep-deprived dogs produced a state of sleep lasting several hours when it was injected into the nondeprived dogs. Control CSF from nondeprived dogs did not have this effect. More recently, CSF from deprived goats has been tested for its sleep-promoting properties in a variety of animals (Fencl *et al.*, 1971). This substance produces cortical synchrony and sleep in cats and rats, while CSF from nondeprived goats does not. Furthermore, the amount of sleep deprivation in the donor goat has an effect on the amount of sleep which is produced in the recipient. Two days of deprivation results in the most sleep in the recipient, but then the effectiveness of this sleep-promoting substance levels off. Biochemical studies suggest that the sleep factor is a peptide, with a molecular weight between 350 and 700.

Unfortunately, no one knows where this peptide comes from, or where it acts to promote sleep. Since it is in the CSF, and not the blood, it is likely that it comes from neural tissue (or glial cells), but more research is needed before anything definite can be said about this sleep factor.

The areas of the brain which affect the sleeping-waking cycle are widespread, and there is clearly no "sleep center" anywhere in the brain. Some of the important structures include the *reticular formation*, the *raphe*, the *FTG*, and the *locus coeruleus*.

The reticular formation, which runs through the medial core of the brain stem, is clearly involved in arousal. Lesions here produce sleep or coma, and electrical stimulation produces arousal if the animal is asleep, and alertness if the animal is already awake.

The raphe, which runs through the middle of the brain stem to the back of the midbrain, appears to be involved in sleep. Lesions of this structure produce insomnia. These raphe nuclei contain serotonin, and it is possible that this serotonergic pathway mediates sleep, perhaps by inhibiting the reticular formation. Drugs which inhibit the synthesis of serotonin also produce insomnia.

The locus coeruleus, which contains norepinephrine, appears to be involved in both waking and in the change from S-sleep to D-sleep. The dorsal noradrenergic bundle arises from the locus coeruleus, and there is evidence that this pathway is involved in arousal. Transection of this pathway produces increased sleep and increases in the activity in the raphe nuclei, emphasizing the importance of interactions between all of the brain structures involved in sleep and waking.

The locus coeruleus also interacts with the FTG to produce the changes from S-sleep to D-sleep and back again during the sleep cycle. The cells of the FTG (*gigantocellular tegmental field*) are important in D-sleep, since lesions of this area produce an animal with no D-sleep. As the FTG cells begin to fire faster, the cells of the locus coeruleus fire more slowly; at this point the animal moves into D-sleep. When the local coeruleus cells speed up, the FTG cells slow down, and the animal moves back into S-sleep.

Important motivated behaviors usually have many controls, and sleep probably has multiple controls as well. For example, intestinal stimulation at low frequencies produces sleep. This stimulation may be mimicking the afferent impulses which occur during the intestinal movements of digestion, and may explain why people feel sleepy after a big meal. Afferents from many internal organs reach a structure in the medulla called the *nucleus of the solitary tract*, and this structure has modulating influences on the reticular formation.

Another possible controlling mechanism which may be involved in sleep is a chemical which is produced in the cerebrospinal fluid. Fluid from sleep-deprived animals produces sleep in nondeprived animals, but unfortunately not very much is known about how this chemical may work.

The study of the neural mechanisms

summary

Neural Mechanisms of Sleep and Waking

underlying sleep has revealed once again that the brain is extraordinarily complex, and that many brain structures interact in subtle ways to produce behavior. We have no "sleep center" just as we have no "eating," "sex," or "fighting" center. Instead, we are finding that important behaviors have multiple controls, and that some pathways serve multiple functions.

In these last few chapters, we have examined behaviors which are in general common to most living species. Not surprisingly, we found that it was the lower brain structures which played the major roles, although the cortex probably has some modulating influences. In the last chapters, we will tackle the physiological processes which underlie the most advanced behaviors which a nervous system can perform. These include learning, remembering, developing, thinking, and speaking. They can be summed up in one word: *changing*. The story of how our nervous system can change, throughout development and through experience, will emphasize the most advanced and most recently evolved parts of our brains.

KEY TERMS

rhythms
period
frequency
amplitude
phase
circadian rhythms
oscillator
free-running rhythm
suprachiasmatic nucleus (SCN)
[^{14}C]deoxyglucose
phase shift
alpha waves
delta waves
beta waves
rapid eye movements (REMs)
PGO waves

S-sleep
D-sleep
drug-dependent insomnia
flurazepam
rebound effect
central sleep apnea
sudden infant death syndrome (SIDS)
narcolepsy
reticular formation
raphe
locus coeruleus
alpha-methyl-*p*-tyrosine (AMPT)
nucleus of the solitary tract
gigantocellular tegmental field (FTG)

SUGGESTED READINGS

Dement, W. C. (1974). *Some Must Watch While Some Must Sleep.* W. H. Freeman, San Francisco, pp. 243–259.

Webb, W. B. (1975). *Sleep: The Gentle Tyrant.* Prentice-Hall, Englewood Cliffs, New Jersey.

Cartwright, R. D. (1977). *Night Life: Explorations in Dreaming.* Prentice-Hall, Englewood Cliffs, New Jersey.

(These three paperbacks provide interesting reading on the topics of sleep and dreaming. The references listed below provide more information on the topics of biological rhythms, the suprachiasmatic nucleus, and sleep disorders.)

Rusak, B., and Zucker, I. (1975). Biological rhythms and animal behavior. *Annual Review of Psychology* **26**, 137–171.

Stetson, M. H., and Watson-Whitmyre, M. (1976). Nucleus suprachiasmaticus: the biological clock in the hamster? *Science* **191**, 197–199.

Dement, W. C., and Zarcone, V. (1977). Pharmacological treatment of sleep disorders. In *Psychopharmacology: From Theory to Practice* (J. D. Barchas *et al.*, eds.). Oxford Univ. Press, New York.

14

*plasticity
in the
nervous
system:
development*

introduction In this chapter, and in Chapter 15, we will discuss the concept of plasticity in the nervous system. One of the remarkable features of our
nervous system is not simply that it changes from day to day, as we
discussed in the last chapter, but that it can change in response to both
internal and external events. For example, the nervous system (and
behavior) can change in response to the sex hormones, as we discussed in Chapter 12. It also shows changes in response to stress, sensory deprivation, or environmental enrichment. More complex
nervous systems can show a tremendous amount of learning, and
since learning and memory must involve changes in the nervous system, then this too is an example of plasticity.

The period during which an organism is most plastic, and most susceptible to modification by internal and external events, is the period
of development. During this time the organism is growing along lines
which were laid down by its genes; but internal and external events
can, and do, change the way that the genetic information unfolds. We
will first examine the developing brain—how it changes and grows
throughout the formative years. Then we will consider the role the
genes play in the developmental process. The next sections will take
up hormones and nutrition, and the way that each can modify the
nervous system of the developing organism. Finally we will examine
the large role that the environment plays in the development of an
individual, particularly the roles of stress, brain damage, sensory deprivation, and environmental enrichment.

the developing Every human being begins life as a single fertilized ovum.
nervous system Within the short space of nine months, it grows and develops
into a perfectly operating system of organs, glands, and nervous
system, delicately woven into a unique person. The process
whereby the single fertilized ovum is turned into a living,
breathing human being involves cell **proliferation, growth, differentiation,** and **integration**. The ovum, which is a single cell,
certainly is not enough for an entire human being, and it must
divide many times through mitosis. Mitosis ensures that each
daughter cell contains the same complement of DNA as the
original cell, and it is with these many divisions that cellular
proliferation takes place. Accompanying the process of proliferation is an increase in mass, a change called growth. The mass
of individual cells increases because cells take up metabolites
from the environment and transform them into the proteins,
fats, carbohydrates, nucleic acids, and other materials which
make up the cells.

One of the most interesting features of development is that the dividing cells do not remain like the mother cells—they differentiate.
One set of cells may specialize to form the kidney and another set may

become the brain, even though they all have the same DNA in the nucleus. For reasons not yet fully understood, only parts of the DNA are activated in each cell. In different cells, different parts may be activated, resulting in the production of different proteins. It is these different proteins, and their consequences, which make the cells different. If differentiation is to subdivide the cells of the embryo into various parts, then the remaining feature of development, integration, is to see that the parts work in unison. The brain of the organism is one of the key features of the process of integration, and the development of the brain follows some standard guidelines.

Figure 14.1 shows a side view of the human brain at various stages of development, from 10 to 41 weeks after conception. The major sulci begin to appear at 22 weeks, and as they become deeper, the minor sulci begin to form. The lateral fissure is initially wide open in the 19-week-old fetus. But because of the growth of the frontal, temporal, and parietal lobes, the fissure gradually closes by the time of birth.

the developing brain

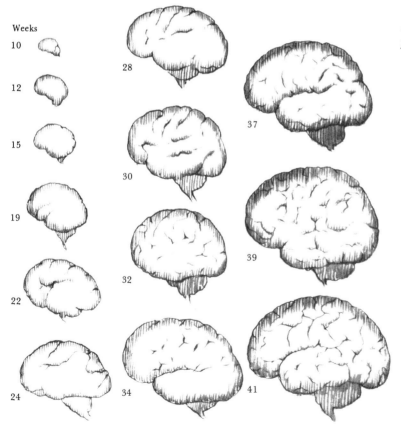

Weeks
10
12
15
19
22
24
28
30
32
34
37
39
41

Figure 14.1
Development of the brain during fetal life. [From Larroche (1966).]

The cells of the embryo which will eventually differentiate into the nervous system begin as a tube, called the **neural tube.** The anterior parts of the tube become the fore-, mid-, and hindbrains, and the rest becomes the spinal cord. The inside of the tube, after much bending and folding, becomes the ventricles of the brain and the **central canal** of the spinal cord. Even in an embryo only 3 mm long the major divisions of the brain can already be seen, and these gradually grow and differentiate into the structures described in Chapter 4. By the age of 3 months, the embryo's brain has assumed the general shape of the adult's, but the cortex appears smooth.

the developing neurons Although the major structures and interconnections of the brain are completed very early, differentiation of the fine structure of the nervous system takes much longer, and may continue throughout life. The larger neurons, such as the pyramidal cells in the cortex, are formed first. These large neurons, called **Class I,** are different from the smaller **Class II** neurons. The Class I cells are formed earlier, and they make up the major connections of the brain. The Class II cells are the short-axoned neurons which make connections within a given brain structure.

Jacobson (1974) has proposed that the two types of cells provide a basis for the interaction between the effects of genes and environment on the developing nervous system. The formation of the Class I cells is predetermined and proceeds with very little variability in all human beings. They are formed under the strict control of the genes and provide a general framework for the nervous system. The Class II cells, formed later in development and sometimes even after birth, provide a basis for the effects of the environment upon the developing nervous system. Their structures are much more variable between individuals, and they can be affected by subtle changes in the environment such as in diet, sensory input, and hormonal levels.

By the time of birth, most of the cells of the nervous system are formed. But the cellular processes continue to change, growing dendrites, making more synaptic endings, probably throughout life. It was originally believed that all of the neurons were formed by the time of birth, but Altman (1967) has described some cells in the brain of the rat which continue to divide postnatally. In some areas of the brain like the hippocampus, this **neurogenesis** may continue indefinitely. The dividing cells were mainly of the Class II type—the short-axoned neurons which are probably concerned with the modulation and refinement of neural information in various brain areas.

In most brain areas, however, neurogenesis stops abruptly. The time at which it stops is often correlated with the development of a behavior with which the area is involved. For example, Altman points out that in many mammalian species the time at which neurogenesis ceases in the cerebellum is correlated with the time that the animal first shows refined adult body movements, particularly walking. The guinea pig is very mature at birth and can walk fairly well, and its cerebellar neurogenesis has virtually ceased at this time. Children cannot walk very well until they are about two years old, and neurogenesis continues in their cerebellum until that time. Other mammals show a similar pattern.

The gross structure of the human brain might suggest that our brains are alike—that we all have the same basic nervous equipment to work with. But finer studies of brain tissue show that this is not the case. Male and female animals show slight differences in some structures of the brain, for example. And since each of us have different genes (except for identical twins), then the genes which are playing such a large role in the developing nervous system are slightly different. In the next section, we will examine the role that the genes play, and how they might contribute to individual differences in the development of behavior.

---

summary
The Developing Nervous System

The process of development involves four different kinds of changes: (1) *cell proliferation*, (2) *cell growth*, (3) *differentiation*, and (4) *integration*. Cells divide, become larger, and eventually differentiate into liver cells, neurons, muscle cells, and so on. Finally, the organs and glands which make up a living system must communicate with one another and integrate in order that the whole organism can work in unison. The nervous system is the primary integrative organ.

The nervous system begins as the *neural tube*. The top of the tube differentiates into the fore-, mid-, and hindbrain, and the rest becomes the spinal cord. The center of the tube becomes the ventricles of the brain and the central canal of the spinal cord. The cells which make up the developing nervous system can be divided into *Class I* and *Class II* cells. Class I cells are large neurons, formed early in development, which make up the major connections in the brain. Class II cells are smaller, and make connections within a given brain structure. The Class II cells are probably more susceptible to environmental effects, and are more plastic.

The process of *neurogenesis* (nerve cell division) continues after birth in some brain areas, but is usually complete long before the organism reaches maturity. But neurons do not stop changing in other ways, as we shall see in later sections.

In some ways, the stages of life are like the different movements of a symphony, although many times one movement will merge into the next with little break for the musicians to catch their breath. The notes of the symphony are relatively invariant, written by the DNA in our genes. But the way the notes are played by the various instruments, and the way the DNA unfolds throughout development, are all af-

the genetic contribution to development

fected by the environment. Two symphonies, even though they are using the same "notes," may sound quite different. For example, the notes may dictate a lot of brass in the second movement; but the orchestra playing the notes may have only one cornet, and the brass notes will be overpowered by the violins.

Analogies usually break down if they are scrutinized too closely, and this one is no exception. But it does serve to illustrate two points. First, an individual is a product of the interaction between heredity and environment, just as the symphony is an interaction between the written notes and the way they are played. There can be no person unless both heredity and environment are present, and there can be no symphony without both a score and an orchestra. Second, it illustrates the point that the DNA plays a role throughout our lives. All the notes of the symphony are not played at the same time—they provide a blueprint for the entire duration of the symphony. The same is true of our genes. The genes that we inherit from our parents are the ones which dictate whether a cell is to become a liver cell or a neuron, and also the ones which might predispose us to baldness, alcoholism, or heart disease later in life.

the gene The strands of DNA which are present in the nucleus of the cell are made up of sequences of four bases: **adenine, thymine, guanine,** and **cytosine.** The DNA (shown in Figure 14.2) forms the genetic code. A sequence of three bases along a strand is a "code" for one of the 20 amino acids, such as leucine or serine. For example, the **triplet** adenine–adenine–thymine codes for leucine. A series of many such triplets would code for a series of amino acids, which will be linked together by the RNA in the cytoplasm to form a particular protein. This series of triplets, which codes for a single protein with a specific function, is called a **gene.** The sequence may be long or short depending upon the number of amino acids needed to form the protein. The protein which is formed might then be used as an enzyme or to initiate or control the reactions needed to produce the substances needed in the body.

genes and protein synthesis. Proteins are formed in the cytoplasm, but the DNA never leaves the nucleus. If the gene is to produce a protein, then it must transmit the message to the cytoplasm. To do this, **messenger RNA (mRNA)** is used. The sequence of bases on the DNA acts as a template for the formation of another analagous sequence of bases on the mRNA. The RNA then moves to the polysomes of the cytoplasm and there, with the help of **transfer RNA (tRNA),** amino acids are linked together to form a protein (diagrammed in Figure 14.3).

genes and chromosomes. The genes are arranged on **chromosomes,** and the human being has 46 of these. We inherit 23 from our mother and 23 from our father. Twenty-two of these pairs of chromosomes are **homologous.** Although the sequence of bases of the two members of a pair may not be identical, the genes on both members of 22 of the pairs are homologous in that each one codes for a protein which has the same function. These homologous genes are called **alleles.**

homozygotes and heterozygotes. If two alleles are identical and the protein which is produced by each is the same, then the individual is a **homozygote** for that gene. But if the two alleles are different, the individual is called a **heterozygote.** Sometimes, even though the individual is heterozygous for a particular pair of alleles, only one of the alleles will produce most of the protein, and the other allele will remain relatively silent. This active allele is called **dominant,** at least in its relationship to the other **recessive** allele. For example, there are several alleles in the population which control blood type. An individual who is type A certainly has the gene for type A blood as one of its alleles, but the other one may either be another allele for type A, or the allele for Type O blood, which is recessive. The individual's **genotype,** which expresses which alleles are present on the two homologous chromosomes, may thus be either AA or AO. If the person has type B blood, then the same situation applies: the person's genotype may be BB or BO, and the **phenotype,** which is the observable trait, is simply Type B.

The blood groups can illustrate another relationship which can exist between the alleles on the two chromosomes, that of **codominance.** If a person's blood type is AB, then the person has the A allele on one chromosome, and the B allele on the other. Both alleles are making a contribution to the individual's phenotype, so that the two alleles are codominant. To summarize, A and B are both dominant to O, but neither A nor B is dominant over the other.

The reason why two alleles differ from one another and thus produce different proteins is very simple. The sequence of bases in the DNA is different. Usually there is not very much difference in the sequence and it may even be restricted to a single base. For example, the DNA sequence which consists of AAT–AGT would produce a hypothetical protein (an absurdly short one) which consisted of leucine and serine. But if the first base of the DNA sequence were changed through an accident in division so that the sequence now read CAT–AGT, then the protein would be valine–serine. It might perform better or worse, or the same as, the leucine–serine sequence. This single base change is called a **mutation,** and although mutations are usually detrimental to the organism, they occasionally produce a protein which does a better job than the original in the environment in

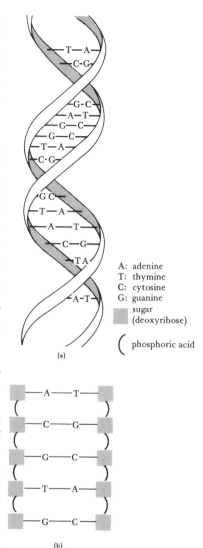

A: adenine
T: thymine
C: cytosine
G: guanine
sugar (deoxyribose)
phosphoric acid

(a)

(b)

Figure 14.2
(a) Schematic diagram of the double helix structure of DNA. (b) The structure of DNA.

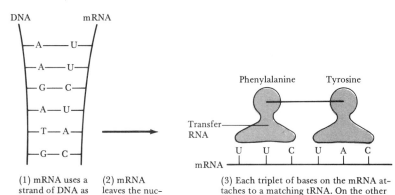

DNA   mRNA

A —— U
A —— U
G —— C
A —— U
T —— A
G —— C

Phenylalanine   Tyrosine

Transfer—
RNA

U   U   C   U   A   C

mRNA

Figure 14.3
Schematic illustration of how DNA codes for protein.

(1) mRNA uses a strand of DNA as a template, using uracil instead of thymine

(2) mRNA leaves the nucleus of the cell.

(3) Each triplet of bases on the mRNA attaches to a matching tRNA. On the other end of the tRNA is the amino acid which is coded by the triplet. The amino acids are linked together to form a protein

which the organism lives. In any case, they certainly contribute to the genetic variability characteristic of all populations.

Only 22 of the 23 pairs of chromosomes are homologous. The last pair consists of the sex chromosomes, and although they are homologous in the female, they are not in the male. The females sex chromosomes are XX, but the male only has one X chromosome, and another smaller chromosome called Y.

regulation of genes As the organism develops, each cell is not using all of its DNA to produce thousands of proteins all the time. Some cells may only use a very small part of their total amount of DNA, while others may use more, but at different times. The cell may wait many years before using certain parts of its DNA to produce proteins. For example, Huntington's chorea, a disease which produces loss of motor control and a progressive deterioration of the nervous system, usually does not show up until age 40 or older. The disease is genetic and controlled by a single dominant allele, but nevertheless the DNA responsible apparently remains inactive until many years have gone by.

The factors that control the DNA's production of protein are not understood completely but they must involve some kind of regulation. Jacob and Monod (1961) proposed an **operon model** to account for gene regulation (diagrammed in Figure 14.4). Some genes are called **structural genes** because they code for specific proteins, but there are other genes called **regulator** and **operator genes** whose functions are not so clear. These genes which do not code for proteins may work together to control the activity of the structural genes. The internal environment of the organism plays a crucial role in gene regulation. For example, although a woman may inherit genes which predispose her to become bald, her hormonal environment may limit the expression of the trait in some fashion.

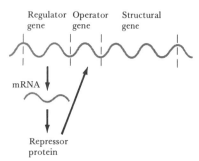

Regulator Operator Structural
gene   gene   gene

mRNA

Repressor
protein

Figure 14.4
A simplified diagram of the operon model. The regulator gene produces mRNA which produces a repressor protein. The repressor protein combines with the operator gene, and inhibits the structural gene from producing its own mRNA.

416 *physiological psychology*

But if the genes only code for proteins, how might they influence the behavior of the organism? In the simplest case, a child might be born who possesses a single aberrant gene which produces a drastically altered protein. If the protein is important in an array of metabolic processes, the child's behavior as well as much of his physical development may be severely changed.

single gene effects on behavior

phenylketonuria (PKU). There are many conditions known which result in behavioral and physical abnormalities, and which have been related to the action of a single gene, usually a recessive one. **Phenylketonuria (PKU),** which results in mental retardation and light pigmentation of the skin and hair, is due to a single recessive gene, for which the affected individual must be homozygous. The abnormal genes are supposed to code for an enzyme which catalyzes the conversion of phenylalanine to tyrosine, but because the PKU genes either produce no enzyme, or an inactive one, the reaction is inhibited. Thus the products of other conversions of phenylalanine build up in the nervous system and retard its development.

PKU is a good example of the way in which genes and environment can interact. The diet of the PKU baby is crucial in preventing some of the worst effects of the genetic defect. Although the enzyme itself cannot be given to the PKU child, it is possible to lower the amount of phenylalanine in the diet so that the metabolites do not build up to such toxic levels. Thus although the gene results in mental retardation in one kind of an environment, one with the usual amount of phenylalanine, it has only mild effects in another environment which has very low amounts of the amino acid.

PTC tasting. Another single gene which affects behavior is one which determines whether or not an individual can taste a substance called **phenylthiocarbamide (PTC).** The allele which provides the ability to taste the substance is dominant over the nontasting allele, so that heterozygotes are able to taste the substance, and the homozygous recessives are the nontasters. Since a few people have taste sensitivity to PTC which falls somewhere between the two extremes, it is probable that there are other genes present which also affect sensitivity to this substance. This demonstrates another way in which the environment —genetic rather than nutritional—can affect the unfolding of the DNA score.

polygenic studies

If a behavorial trait is influenced by genes, then it most probably involves many genes rather than one or two, and it is not generally possible to trace a pathway from the behavior back to a single gene as it is with PKU. Nevertheless it is possible to estimate how much of the variation in the population is due to genetic variation and how much is due to the environmental variation and the interactions between genes and environment. For example, it is theoretically possible to estimate how much variation there would be in IQ if every one were raised in identical environments. This would be an estimate of how much genetic variation contributes to the variability of a particular behavioral trait. This is very different from saying that we can estimate how much genes contribute to behavior in an individual. It is impossible to do that because the answer would be "none" and "all" at the same time. An individual cannot exist without both genes and environment.

research techniques. The major techniques for studying the relationship between genes and complex behavioral traits include **twin studies** and **adoption studies.** In the twin study the correlation between **dizygotic (DZ)** twins is compared to the correlation between **monozygotic (MZ)** twins. If the correlation between MZ twins is higher then it is quite possible that the reason is that MZ twins have 100% of their genes in common, while the DZ twins have only about 50% in common, since they are only as genetically alike as siblings. If one assumes that the environment in which DZ twins are reared is as similar as the environment in which MZ twins are reared, then any difference between the correlations can be attributed to the difference in their genetic relatedness. This assumption has not been immune to criticism (Lewontin, 1975), but in general, the findings from these studies often agree with the findings from adoption studies. In an adoption study, the behavior of adopted children is compared to the behavior of their biological parents and their adoptive parents. If the children's behavior is closer to their biological parents, who had little or no environmental influence on the children, then there is reason to suspect a genetic involvement in the behavior.

heredity and performance on intelligence tests. The behavioral studies that have received the most attention, and also the most controversy, are those that deal with performance on intelligence tests. Not only is intelligence difficult to measure (some say impossible), but it seems reasonable to assume that environmental factors will play a very important role in the development of intelligence. Many studies have been performed, however, and Erlenmeyer-Kimling and Jarvik (1963) have summarized some of the findings, shown in Figure 14.5.

Some interesting comparisons reveal that genetic variation in the population may be very important in contributing to the variation in intelligence test performance. Unrelated persons reared together, for example, are much less alike (have a lower correlation) than monozygotic twins reared apart. The correlation between like sex dizygotic twins is lower than that for monozygotic twins reared together, or apart. Estimates for the amount of variation in test perform-

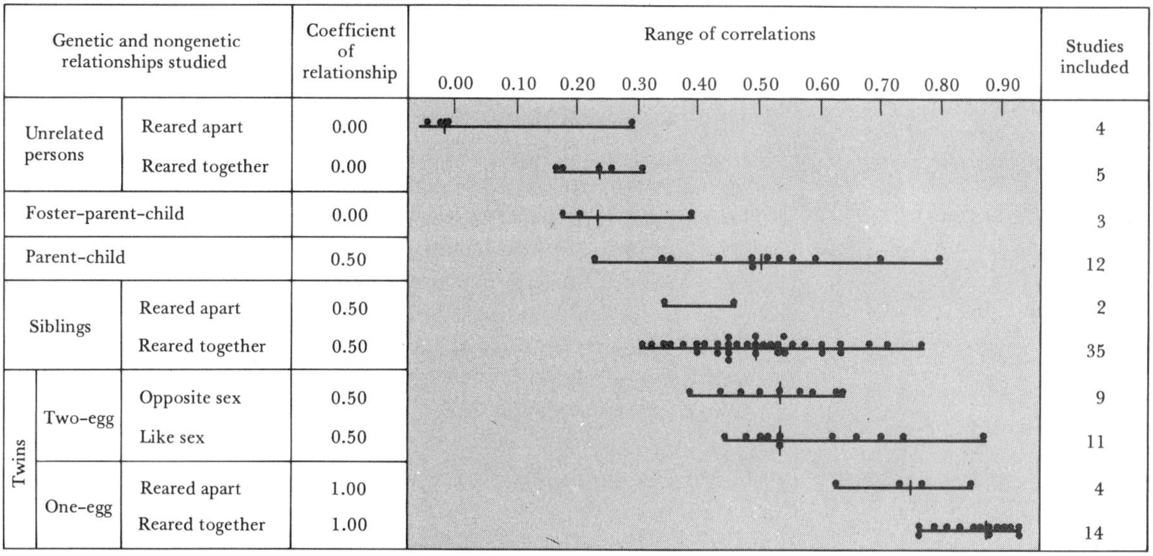

Genetic and nongenetic relationships studied		Coefficient of relationship	Range of correlations	Studies included
Unrelated persons	Reared apart	0.00		4
	Reared together	0.00		5
Foster-parent-child		0.00		3
Parent-child		0.50		12
Siblings	Reared apart	0.50		2
	Reared together	0.50		35
Twins — Two-egg	Opposite sex	0.50		9
	Like sex	0.50		11
Twins — One-egg	Reared apart	1.00		4
	Reared together	1.00		14

Figure 14.5
A summary of the correlation coefficients and their ranges for pairs of individuals with various degrees of genetic and environmental relationship. [From McClearn (1973).]

ance which is attributable to genetic variation are fairly high, suggesting that if we had all been reared in exactly the same environment, we would still perform differently on these tests, because we have different genes. But this conclusion must remain tentative at best, because most of the studies have a number of limitations. For example, heritability estimates are only valid for the population which is actually studied. These populations rarely include very many children who come from extremely deprived environments. Studies on animals suggest that such extreme environments may have much more impact on behavior; it is possible that heritability estimates would be lower (because the extreme environments are having more effect) in children from deprived environments.

A rather unusual way to approach the question of the importance of heredity in the development of intelligence is to study the progressive development of mental abilities in MZ and DZ twins. R. S. Wilson (1978) gave standard mental abilities tests to pairs of twins many times during the first 6 years of life. Figure 14.6 shows the changes in mental development scores for a number of twin pairs. Notice that over the years, the lags and spurts in mental development tended to coincide in the MZ twins, but not in the DZ twins. This suggests that the rate of development of mental abilities is also affected by genes.

the genetic contribution to development **419**

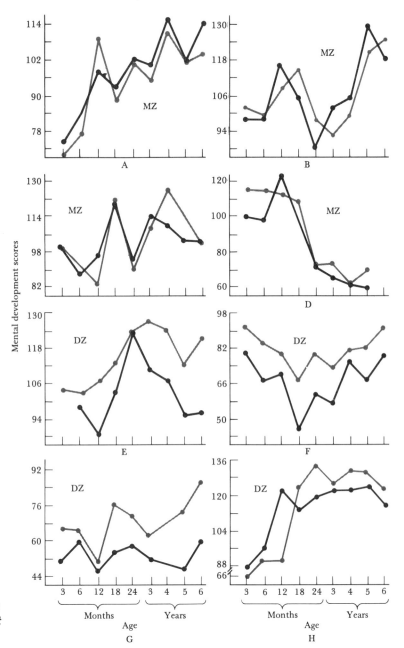

Figure 14.6
Mental development curves for pairs of MZ and DZ twins. [From R. S. Wilson (1978). Copyright 1978 by the American Association for the Advancement of Science.]

heredity and schizophrenia. Studies on the genetic contribution to mental illness have also been prevalent. Schizophrenia, in particular, has received attention and the findings have pointed toward the possibility of inheriting a predisposition to become schizophrenic. Table 14.1 shows the results of an adoption study in which the experimental

Table 14.1.

Characteristics of individuals born to schizophrenic mothers and reared in adoptive or foster homes (experimental) and of individuals born to normal mothers and similarly reared[a]

Item	Control	Experimental	Exact Probability (Fisher's Test)
Number of subjects	50	47	
Number of males	33	30	
Age, mean (years)	36.3	35.8	
Number adopted	19	22	
MHSRS, means[b]	80.1	65.2	0.0006
Number with schizophrenia	0	5	0.024
Number with mental deficiency (I.Q. 70)[c]	0	4	0.052
Number with antisocial personalities	2	9	0.017
Number with neurotic personality disorder[d]	7	13	0.052
Number spending more than 1 year in penal or psychiatric institution	2	11	0.006
Total years incarcerated	15	112	
Number of felons	2	7	0.054
Number serving in armed forces	17	21	
Number discharged from armed forces on psychiatric or behavioral grounds	1	8	0.021
Social group, first home, mean[e]	4.2	4.5	
Social group, present, mean[e]	4.7	5.4	
IQ, mean	103.7	94.0	
Years in school, mean	12.4	11.6	
Number of children, total	84	71	
Number of divorces, total	7	6	
Number never married, >30 years of age	4	9	

[a]From Heston (1970). Copyright 1970 by the American Association for the Advancement of Science.
[b]The MHSRS is a global rating of psychopathology moving from 0 to 100 with decreasing psychopathology. Total group mean, 72.8; S.D., 18.4
[c]One mental defective was also schizophrenic; another had antisocial personality.
[d]Considerable duplication occurs in the entries under "neurotic personality disorder"; this designation includes subjects diagnosed as having various types of personality disorder and neurosis whose psychiatric disability was judged to be a significant handicap.
[e]Group 1, highest social class: group 7, lowest.

children had biological mothers who were schizophrenic, but were adopted into normal homes. The control children had normal biological mothers, and were also adopted into normal homes. Not only do more of the experimental children develop schizophrenia, but they also show more abnormal behavior in general.

heredity and alcoholism. Evidence for a predisposition to alcoholism comes from several sources, particularly a study by Schuckit, Goodwin, and Winokur (1972). They found that the frequency of alcoholism in half-sisters or half-brothers with an alcoholic parent and who also lived with that parent was 46%. If the child did not live with the alcoholic parent, the incidence was still high—50%. In contrast, if a child who had normal parents lived with an alcoholic stepparent, the incidence of alcoholism in the children was only 14%. The incidence of alcoholism for children of normal parents who lived with nonalcoholic stepparents was only 8%.

Goodwin and his colleagues (Goodwin, 1979) performed an extensive study on the now grown-up children of alcoholic parents in Denmark, some of whom had been adopted into normal homes, and control children born to nonalcoholic parents who were also adopted. They used rather strict criteria to categorize the drinking behavior of the subjects in the study (shown in Table 14.2).

Table 14.2
Criteria for drinking categories in Danish adoption studies[a]

Category	Criteria
Moderate drinker	Neither a teetotaler nor a heavy drinker
Heavy drinker	For at least 1 year drank daily and had 6 or more drinks at least 2 or 3 times a month; or drank 6 or more drinks at least 1 time a week for over 1 year, but reported no problems
Problem drinker	Meets criteria for heavy drinker; had problems from drinking but insufficient to meet alcoholism criteria
Alcoholic	Meets criteria for heavy drinker. Must have had alcohol problems in at least 3 of the following groups: (1) Social disapproval by friends, parents; marital problems (2) Job trouble, traffic arrests, other police trouble (3) Frequent blackouts, tremor, withdrawal hallucinations, withdrawal convulsions, delirium tremens (4) Loss of control, morning drinking

[a]From Goodwin (1979).

The major conclusions from this study implicate heredity as a predisposing factor in the development of alcoholism. Children of alcoholics were more vulnerable to alcoholism, regardless of whether they were reared by their alcoholic parents or by nonalcoholic foster parents. Sons of alcoholics were particularly vulnerable—they were four times more likely to become alcoholic compared to sons of nonalcoholic parents, even if they were reared in nonalcoholic homes. It is of interest that these children were not any more vulnerable to other behavioral problems, such as drug abuse or mental illness. They were only at greater risk to become alcoholic.

Many other behavioral traits have been studied with these techniques to find underlying genetic predispositions. Although the problems of these studies have been enormous, fraught with sampling bias, diagnostic problems, and disagreements over definitions, they in general point to the conclusion that genes play a much larger role in some of our behavior than had been suspected. The idea that human beings are a "tabula rasa" or a blank slate at birth is no longer tenable. But does this mean that it doesn't matter very much what kind of an environment we provide for our children—that they will tend to develop along their own predispositions anyway? Emphatically, no. Rather these studies suggest that the environments that we are providing *now* do not have as much impact as we had thought on the behavioral development of children, not that environments in general don't affect behavior very much. Twenty years ago, the environments which were provided for PKU children had little effect on the children's development, but with more knowledge about the roots of the disease, a much better environment was developed—one which lowered the crucial phenylalanine levels. The development of intelligence in children at the moment would appear to be limited to a range determined by their genes. But this may simply mean that we don't know very much about what kinds of environments can have a large impact on the development of intelligence.

It is impossible to say that any particular behavior is genetic—all behavior is a product of both heredity and environment. The genes can only code for proteins, not for behavior. But the possession of certain combinations of proteins may predispose an individual toward behaving in certain ways, provided the environment fosters the behavior.

A gene is composed of a strand of DNA. The DNA strands consist of bases (*adenine, guanine, cytosine* and *thymine*), and a series of three bases (*triplet*) codes for a single amino acid. (The sequence adenine–adenine–thymine, for example, codes for leucine.) Proteins are synthesized in the cytoplasm, however, and not the nucleus where the DNA is. *Messenger RNA* uses a strand of DNA as a template, and carries the information out to the cytoplasm where protein synthesis can ensue.

Genes are located on *chromosomes*, of which humans have 46. They are

summary
The Genetic Contribution to Development

arranged in 23 pairs, with one member of the pair carrying one allele of a gene, and the other member carrying another *allele* (except for the sex chromosomes in the male). If the alleles are identical, the individual is said to be *homozygous* for the trait for which the genes are coding. If they are different, the individual is *heterozygous*. If one allele codes for most of the protein, then that allele is *dominant* to the other *recessive* allele. A person's *genotype* expresses which alleles are present on the homologous chromosomes. The *phenotype* tells which trait is expressed.

The DNA does not code for proteins all the time. Only parts of the DNA are active at any one time. One theory which explains "the turning on and off" of genes is the *operon model*. In this model, *structural genes* actually code for proteins, but other genes present on the chromosome (*regulator* and *operator* genes) may work to determine when the structural gene is active.

Sometimes the effects of a single gene can be so overwhelming that drastically modified development can result. *Phenylketonuria* (PKU) is one example. This form of mental retardation is due to the presence of a homozygous recessive gene which affects the conversion of phenylalanine to tyrosine. New diets, low in phenylalanine, have partly alleviated the effects of this condition.

Most behaviors are affected by many genes, however, and it is not generally possible to trace the presence of a particular behavior back to the effects of a single gene. Instead, scientists rely mainly on *twin studies* and *adoption studies* to estimate the importance of genetic variation in the population in determining the amount of variability in a given trait. Studies like these have suggested that the genetic variability of a group contributes to behavioral variability in such traits as performance on intelligence tests, rates of mental development, some forms of mental illness, and alcoholism.

Although the contribution which our genes make to our development is not plastic, the expression of those genes is. Our heredity sets ranges within which the internal and external environments can have their effect. On some traits, those ranges are very large, and environmental factors will have a great deal to do with the final expression of the trait. For other traits, the range might be quite small. The size of those hypothetical "ranges" probably varies between the individuals and between generations.

nutritional contributions to development The importance of nutrition to the developing nervous system is very clear in the case of PKU children, but nutrition also plays a vitally important role in the development of normal children. Particularly during the early part of life when the central nervous system is developing rapidly, nutrition can mean the difference between a normal, healthy youngster and an apathetic, mentally retarded one. Figure 14.7 shows the time, for a variety of species, during which the fastest growth is occurring, the Class II neurons are laying down their connections, and the glial cells are forming. This period of rapid development of the nervous system, called the **brain growth spurt,** has attracted much attention because it may be the time when the individual is most vulnerable to nutritional and environmental effects.

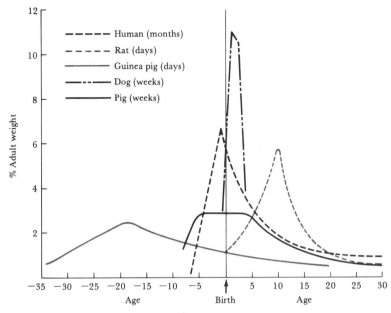

Figure 14.7
Brain growth spurts in several different species. [From Coursin (1975).]

An organism can be malnourished because it does not get enough calories, or because its caloric intake does not include an appropriate balance of the required substances. In humans, the first type of deficit results in **marasmus,** while the second, where protein is selectively depleted, results in **kwashiorkor.** The clinical picture for these severely debilitating conditions is seen in Figure 14.8.

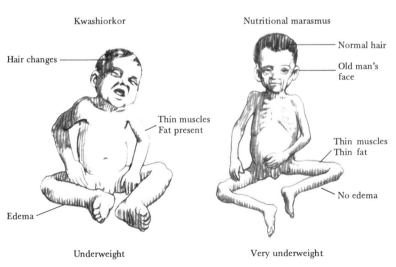

Figure 14.8
The clinical picture for two types of malnutrition: marasmus (deficient calories), and kwashiorkor (deficient protein). [From Vahlquist (1975).]

nutritional contributions to development **425**

malnutrition and brain development If malnutrition occurs during the time when brain cells are dividing, then the cells will not divide as much and the individual will be left with fewer brain cells (Winick and Rosso, 1975). Since cells in different areas of the brain continue to divide for different lengths of time after birth, the effects of malnutrition will be very much dependent upon when the malnutrition occurs. For example in the rat, cerebral cells cease dividing at birth, but cerebellar cells continue for at least 17 days. Postnatal malnutrition, therefore, affects cell number in the cerebellum, but has little effect on cell number in the cerebrum. In the human being, cells in the cerebrum and cerebellum continue to divide for many months after birth and postnatal malnutrition will affect cell number in all the areas which are still dividing (Winick and Rosso, 1975).

The importance of these findings lies in the fact that a reduction in cell size is largely reversible if the organism is later given proper nutrition, although there is some uncertainty as to whether neurons will later form the same connections that would have formed at the normal time in development. Reductions in cell number, however, are probably not reversible. If cell division is retarded by malnutrition, it can only be speeded up again if the organism is given the right diet when the brain cells are still proliferating (Winick, Fish, and Rosso, 1968). If cellular proliferation has ended before nutritional rehabilitation begins, that brain area will have an irreversible reduction in cell number. There are many such sensitive periods in the development of the organism, during which the effects of internal and external events are particularly important.

The effects of malnutrition on cell size and number are not the only ones which have been found. Malnutrition retards the formation of myelin (Dobbing and Widdowson, 1965), and also affects the formation of neuronal processes (Salas *et al.*, 1974). The ability of the neurons to function properly is also no doubt affected, and electrophysiological studies have reported delays in the development of normal electrical activity. The top half of Table 14.3 shows a number of anatomical and electrophysiological effects of malnutrition which have been observed in the rat. Myelin losses are not extensively reversed by later nutritional rehabilitation. The degree to which other deficits can be reversed varies.

behavioral effects of malnutrition Table 14.3 also lists some of the behavioral effects of malnutrition in the rat. It would seem reasonable to predict that the changes in the nervous system which occur as a result of malnutrition would be related to behavioral changes. But it is not always so easy to conclude this, especially for human beings, because malnourished children are usually deprived in other ways also. They usually have poorer educa-

Table 14.3
Effects of early malnutrition in the rat

Reference	Effect
Anatomical	
Cragg (1972)	Reduced brain weight; loss of axon terminals in cortex
Bass *et al.* (1970)	Delayed myelination
Davison and Dobbing (1966)	Delayed myelination
Eayrs and Horn (1955)	Loss of axon terminals
Salas *et al.* (1974)	Reduction of dendritic spines
Electrophysiological	
Mourek *et al.* (1967)	Delays maturation of visual evoked responses
Salas and Cintra (1973)	Delayed development of evoked responses
Bronzino *et al.* (1975)	Delays maturation of visual evoked responses
Behavioral	
Altman *et al.* (1970)	Delayed locomotor patterns
Salas (1972)	Delayed maturation of swimming
Levitsky and Barnes (1972)	Increased fighting
Frankova (1973)	Increased fighting
Whatson *et al.* (1974)	Increased fighting
Howard *et al.* (1976)	No effect on adult active avoidance learning

tion, fewer cultural advantages, and less than satisfactory sanitation. Nevertheless, malnutrition is certainly correlated with mental and behavioral abnormalities, although it may or may not be the single cause.

Monckeberg (1975) studied 500 preschool children from Santiago who belonged to different social levels. Children from middle-class families were compared with those from low socioeconomic families. One group of low socioeconomic children was typically malnourished; children in another group, however, had participated in a diet supplement program for 10 years and their nutritional status was good. Only 3% of the children in the middle class and well-nourished poor groups had IQs below 80; but 40% of the children in the malnourished poor group had subnormal IQs. Even in this study, it is not entirely clear that malnutrition was the sole source of the difference in IQ scores. It is possible that the parents of the well-nourished poor youngsters were reacting to the improvement in nutrition, and providing a better environment for their children. Or the children themselves, because they were healthier and more active with the improved nutrition, might have precipitated a more positive relationship in the home. Even in rats, a mother rearing malnourished offspring behaves differently from other rat mothers: they especially spend more time with the pups (Wiener *et al.*, 1977). The direct effects of malnutrition are probably only the beginning. They may initiate a snowball effect, influencing many areas of the organism's development.

---

summary
Nutritional Contributions to Development

The most devastating effects of malnutrition are seen when the lack of food occurs during the sensitive period of development. This varies between brain areas and between species, but is the time when the cells are growing and dividing rapidly (the *brain growth spurt*). Brain areas in which cells are dividing during a period of malnutrition will suffer an irreversible reduction in cell number. Malnutrition at other times may cause a reduction in cell size, but this is much more amenable to recovery. Malnutrition also retards the formation of myelin and the elaboration of neuronal processes.

Malnutrition can occur because the organism does not get enough calories, which results in *marasmus*, or because there is not enough protein in the diet, which results in *kwashiorkor*. In human beings malnutrition probably affects behavior, since malnourished youngsters generally do poorly on a variety of performance tasks, compared to their well-nourished counterparts. Unfortunately, children who do not receive the proper nourishment often do not receive some of the other advantages of life as well. So it is difficult to say precisely what the behavioral effects of malnourishment are on the human being. In animals, however, malnutrition is known to produce a variety of behavioral effects, such as delayed locomotor patterns, increased fighting, and delayed maturation of neuronal functions.

---

hormonal contributions to development

The endocrine system consists of a number of glands which produce substances called hormones, and release them into the circulatory system. Sawin's (1969) description of a hormone is that it is secreted by living cells in trace amounts and is transported by the blood to a specific site of action. It is not used as a source of energy, or to initiate reactions, but rather to regulate reactions in order to bring about an appropriate response by the organism. There are three main classes of hormones designated by their chemical structure: amines, steroids, and peptides. Different classes of hormones probably have distinct methods of regulating reactions in the cells of the target organs, although the method of regulation is not completely understood. Some hormones appear to act via receptors in cell membranes, others may act somewhat like enzymes, and still others may act directly on the genes in the cell (Rasmussen, 1974).

Most of the endocrine glands are shown in Figure 14.9. Table 14.4 lists some of the hormones which the body produces, where they are

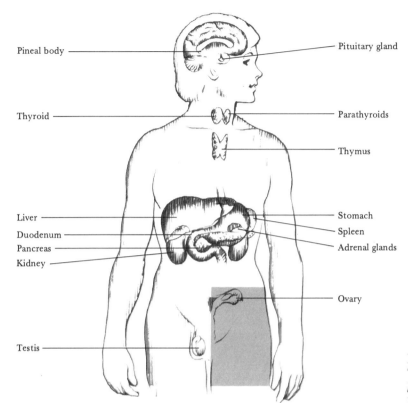

Pineal body

Pituitary gland

Thyroid

Parathyroids

Thymus

Liver

Stomach

Duodenum

Spleen

Pancreas

Adrenal glands

Kidney

Ovary

Testis

Figure 14.9
The endocrine glands of the human being. [From Turner and Bagnara (1971).]

synthesized, and their principal actions. The most interesting hormones to psychologists include the sex hormones (androgens, estrogens, and progestogens), the hormones from the adrenal glands (for example, the adrenocortical steroids, mentioned in Chapter 10), and **thyroxine** (from the thyroid).

The *pituitary gland* is called the master endocrine gland because it produces a number of hormones which have other endocrine glands as their targets. It is composed of two parts: the **anterior** and the **posterior pituitary.** The hormones from these two parts are listed in Table 14.5.

Hormones exert an extremely diverse array of effects in many animals. For example, thyroxine is important for growth, metabolic rate, and glucose absorption in mammals, growth of antlers in deer, color in bird feathers, and migration in fish. This enormous range of effects would suggest that one hormone can act in different ways.

On a metabolic level, hormones must affect the processes

how do hormones modify the nervous system?

Table 14.4

Hormones other than those of the pituitary[a]

Hormones	Cellular Source	Principal Actions
Thyroxine; triiodothyronine	Thyroid	Growth; amphibian metamorphosis; molting; metabolic rate in birds and mammals
Parathyroid hormone (PTH)	Parathyroids	Elevates blood calcium; lowers blood phosphate
Epinephrine	Adrenal medulla	Mobilization of glycogen; increased blood flow through skeletal muscle; increased oxygen consumption; heart rate
Norepinephrine	Adrenal medulla; adrenergic neurons	Adrenergic neurotransmitter; elevation of blood pressure; constricts arterioles and venules
Insulin	Pancreatic islets (β-Cells)	Lowers blood glucose; increases utilization of glucose, and synthesis of protein and fat
Glucagon	Pancreatic islets (α-cells)	Increases blood glucose; stimulates catabolism of protein and fat
Androgens (e.g., testosterone)	Testis; adrenal cortex; ovary	Male sexual characteristics
Estrogens (e.g., estradiol)	Ovary; placenta; testis; adrenal cortex	Female sexual characteristics
Progestogens (e.g., progesterone)	Ovary; placenta; adrenal cortex	Maintenance of pregnancy; inhibition of reproductive cycles
Relaxin	Ovary; uterus; placenta	Enlargement of birth canal by relaxation of uterine cervix and pelvic ligaments
Glucocorticoids (e.g., cortisol, corticosterone)	Adrenal cortex	Promote synthesis of carbohydrate; protein breakdown; anti-inflammatory and antiallergic actions
Mineralocorticoids (e.g., aldosterone)	Adrenal cortex	Sodium retention and potassium loss through kidneys

[a]From Turner and Bagnara (1971).

occurring inside the cell in some way, and Sutherland (1972) have proposed the **second messenger hypothesis** to account for the action of some of the hormones. In this model, the hormone would form a complex with a receptor in the cell's membrane, and this complex would then activate a reaction inside the cell which eventually results in the production of **cyclic AMP**. The cyclic AMP is the "second messenger," because it has a regulatory role in intracellular processes, either increasing or decreasing the rates of reactions.

Another method by which hormones may act involves the DNA in

Table 14.5
Hormones of the pituitary gland

Hormone	Principal Action
From anterior pituitary	
Somatotrophin (STH) (growth hormone)	Promotes growth of bone and muscle and protein synthesis
Adrenocorticotrophin (ACTH)	Stimulates release of adreno-cortical steroids
Thyrotrophin (TSH)	Stimulates thyroid for release of thyroid hormone
Gonadotrophins	
(a) Luteinizing hormone (LH)	Ovary—formation of corpora lutea Testis—promotes secretion of androgen
(b) Follicle-stimulating hormone (FSH)	Ovary—growth of follicles Testis—promotes spermatogenesis
(c) Prolactin	Initiation of milk secretion
From posterior pituitary	
Vasopressin (ADH)	Elevates blood pressure. Promotes retention of body water
Oxytocin	Promotes contraction of uterus; postpartum ejection of milk from mammary gland

the nucleus of the cell. Steroid hormones, particularly estrogen, may bind with an intracellular receptor which moves directly into the nucleus of the cell. This complex may act as a regulator of DNA activity, turning some genes on or others off, thereby controlling the protein synthesis of the cell. Steroids have been shown to stimulate RNA synthesis in liver cells (Kenney *et al.*, 1965) and nerve cells in culture (Vernadakis, 1973). Steroid hormones may also act in other ways, for example by binding with membranes, or by affecting the cytoplasmic messenger RNA.

Although it is not yet clear how hormones might be modifying the development of the brain on a cellular level, it is clear that they are. The changes which the hormones can produce in protein synthesis or in RNA production could easily modify the growth and activity of nerve cells, and perhaps this is the way that they have their effects.

In Chapter 12, we have already seen how some hormones can modify the developing nervous system. The release of androgen by the male's fetal testes determine not only what reproductive organs will grow and elaborate, but also how the brain will be "organized." If the pre-

sex hormones in development

hormonal contributions to development **431**

natal androgen is present, the organism will develop a hypothalamus which will later direct the pituitary gland to release gonadotrophins in a tonic fashion. If the prenatal hormone is absent, the hypothalamus will direct the pituitary to release its hormones cyclically.

The sex hormones thus affect the nervous system during development by altering the pattern of the release of gonodotrophins. In the male, the pattern is tonic. In the female, the pattern is cyclic so that the levels of gonadotrophins rise and fall with each estrus (or menstrual) cycle.

The prenatal androgen is also apparently affecting the parts of the brain which are involved in sex behavior. Female rats which are prenatally androgenized display more malelike sex behavior, and the same is true of certain female primates. In human beings, the prenatal androgens may also be organizing the brains of males and females differently. Girls who accidentally were androgenized tend to engage in more energetic activities than normal girls. But they certainly don't think of themselves as boys, or become homosexuals, so it is clear that the modifying influence of the sex hormones during development is limited in human beings. Although prenatal androgen can affect reproductive morphology, and perhaps energy expenditure, it doesn't seem to affect sexual identity or sexual preference. These are probably much more influenced by environmental factors.

thyroid hormones in development If a young animal is thyroidectomized it will show a lowered metabolic rate, poor growth, and retardation of central nervous system development (Sawin, 1969). The effects are reversible, provided the hormone replacement therapy is given early enough, before too much damage occurs, suggesting the presence of a sensitive period for the effects of thyroxine. Furthermore, the time at which the thyroid is removed correlates very well with subsequent learning deficits: the earlier the removal, the worse the animal performs in a maze test (Eayrs, 1960).

Excessive thyroid hormones during development can also create problems. If neonatal rats are given injections of thyroxine, they show an advanced maturation of the electrical activity of the brain, an accelerated formation of dendritic spines, and deficits in learning abilities as an adult (Eayrs, 1968). The sensitive period for these effects is restricted to the early life of the animal, lasting until the rat is about 14 days old.

Studies on thyroidectomized animals have contributed to an understanding of how thyroxine acts on the brain cells. Removal of the thyroid results in decreased protein synthesis in the brain, but RNA synthesis is not affected (Balazs, Cocks, Eayrs, and Kovacs, 1971), suggesting that the hormone acts by enhancing the translation of genetic material into protein.

The other hormones also affect development, but their effects are not so directly linked to behavior as the effects of the sex hormones and of the thyroid hormone. The hormones from the adrenal glands play a particularly interesting role, but since that story is closely related to the effects of environmental stress, we will discuss it in the next section.

Hormonal Contributions to Development

Throughout development, the endocrine glands are secreting hormones which can have widespread effects on the organism. The hormones which have some of the largest effects on later behavior include androgen (secreted prenatally by the fetal testes in the male), and *thyroxine*, the thyroid hormone.

Prenatal androgen has effects on several developmental processes. First, it modifies the development of the reproductive system, so that in the male, the immature gonads develop into testes, penis, vas deferens, and the other male structures. In the absence of this hormone, the gonads develop into the female reproductive system. The fetal hormone also has effects on the developing brain. In the male, the hormone organizes the hypothalamic structures, so that it later directs the pituitary gland to release its gonadotrophins in a tonic fashion. In the female, the absence of the hormone organizes the hypothalamus so that it directs the pituitary in a cyclic fashion. The hormone also has effects on the way that the nervous system later mediates sexually dimorphic behaviors, such as the amount of energy expenditure.

Thyroxine is also important during the developmental period. Thyroidectomy in young animals produces lowered metabolic rate, poor growth, and mental retardation. Excessive thyroxine during development can produce premature development of neural activity and structures.

Probably in the natural world, baby rats have to endure a number of different stresses during their development, but in the laboratory they can grow up virtually undisturbed. Their mother only has to walk a few inches to obtain food, water, and nesting material, so they have little opportunity to get cold or wet, or suffer the trauma of separation from their mother.

environmental contributions to development

beneficial effects of stress during development. Intuitively it might seem that early stresses would be detrimental to the animal's growth, but Levine (1960) and his co-workers found that early stress could be beneficial in some respects. They compared rats that had been stressed during infancy by shock or simply by human handling, to rats that had been left undisturbed. As adults, the stressed rats explored novel environments more, while the undisturbed rats would crouch timidly in an open field and defecate and urinate more. The stressed rats matured earlier also. For example, they opened their eyes earlier, achieved motor coordination sooner, and they tended to be heavier at weaning.

the effects of stress

The stressed animals seem better able to cope with stressful situations as adults than their undisturbed counterparts, especially with respect to their physiological responses. When an animal is stressed, the sympathetic nervous system will respond very quickly, as discussed in Chapter 10. In addition, the animal's endocrine system will react in order to mobilize the animal's energy resources and provide it with the ability to respond to the stress adaptively. The pituitary gland releases ACTH, which in turn directs the cortex of the adrenal glands to release their steroid hormones. The animals that had been stimulated in infancy show a faster response to stress as measured by their output of adrenal steroids, and also a faster decline in the blood level of the hormones. The unstimulated rats were slower to respond with increased adrenal hormones, and their blood levels remained higher for a longer period of time. The infant stimulation also hastened the development of this stress response. Normally, the release of ACTH and steroids in response to stress does not come about until the rat is about 16 days old. But the stimulated pups began to show increases in steroid output by 12 days old.

How early stimulation produces these effects is not yet clear, although it may represent an example of the way in which the environment can "fine tune" the nervous and endocrine responses of an organism. An early environment which contains some stress may help the development of a neuroendocrine system which is better able to cope with stresses later in life. However, it is also true that the mothers of handled pups behave differently toward them (Villescas, Bell, Wright and Kufner, 1977), just as do the mothers of malnourished pups. The change in the behavior of the pups when they are adults may be only partially a result of the handling per se; the different rearing pattern may also play a role.

detrimental effects of stress. Although some kinds of stressors may be beneficial, others may be quite detrimental. In particular, removing the infant from its mother too early, and for a long period of time, may be risky. For example, Ackerman, Hofer, and Weiner (1978) compared adult rats which had been removed from their mothers at 15 days of age to adults which had been removed at 22 days, and found several differences. The rats removed early showed a very high risk of gastric ulcers later in life, compared to the rats removed later. The rats removed earlier also had difficulty in regulating their body temperature, which was probably the cause of the increased risk for gastric ulcers.

Early maternal separation can also have effects on the synthesis of enzymes in the developing rat. For example, Butler, Suskind, and Schanberg (1978) examined **ornithine decarboxylase** activity, an enzyme important in brain development, in rat pups removed from their mothers. They found that activity of this enzyme declined by as much as 50% when the pups were removed for only an hour. Interestingly, the decline in activity could not be attributed to any loss of nutrition, or to a change in body temperature. They also ruled out the possibility that the early separation produced a change in adrenal activity, and that adrenal hormones might have affected enzyme activity deleteriously. They concluded that the only possible reason for the decline in enzyme activity was the loss of maternal care.

In primates, early maternal separation can have disastrous consequences. Harry Harlow's pioneering work on the mother–infant relationship in the rhesus monkey has shown that a developing monkey must have a mother, or at the very least, some playmates, in order to grow up normally. Infant monkeys who have been raised with an inanimate surrogate mother show a "sociopathic" syndrome in adulthood which includes infantile sexual behavior, absence of grooming, exaggerated aggression, and a lack of cooperation with other monkeys. The females show little if any mothering of their own offspring (if they can ever become pregnant). Harlow's description of these females is worth quoting:

Combining our human and male-monkey talents, we are winning the good fight and imparting to naive and even resistant female monkeys the priceless gift of motherhood. Possibly it is a Pyrrhic victory . . . female monkeys that never knew a real mother, themselves become mothers—helpless, hopeless, heartless mothers devoid, or almost devoid of any maternal feeling (Harlow, 1962).

These studies suggest that stress can have an important impact on the way an organism develops. But different stressors have different consequences, and the effects of stress may vary between species and between individuals. It is clear, however, that even mild stresses, such as handling of rat pups in infancy, can have consequences which reach far into adulthood.

Perhaps the most stressful "stressor" which could be applied to a developing organism is brain damage. This may seem to be a rather unusual occurrence, and indeed it is. But we are discussing it at this point because the developing organism's response to brain damage can tell us something about the plasticity of the nervous system. The way that the brain recovers from a lesion, making new connections, forming new dendrites and axon endings, may shed light on the question of how the nervous system can make plastic changes.

the effects of brain damage

Typically, a young animal is much better able to recover behavioral functions after a brain lesion than an older one. For example, a large lesion in the motor cortex might cause permanent paralysis in an adult animal, but the same lesion in a developing animal might only result in transient difficulties. The developing animal's brain is clearly more plastic in this sense.

axon "sprouting." Probably the most important reason for this enhanced plasticity is that the young animal is better able to make new synaptic connections. Recent studies have demonstrated that the axons in the developing organism's brain can quickly "sprout" new collateral branches when old ones have been severed.

Lynch and his colleagues (Lynch, Deadwyler, and Cotman, 1973; Lynch, Stanfield, and Cotman, 1973) have studied this sprouting phenomenon in the hippocampus of the young rat. The normal pattern of connections to the **dentate gyrus** (part of the hippocampus) are shown in Figure 14.10. This nucleus receives three major inputs: (1) from the pyramidal cells in other parts of the hippocampus on the same side of the brain; (2) from the pyramidal cells in the contralateral hippocampus; and (3) from a posterior cortical area called the **entorhinal cortex.** Notice that the pyramidal cells' inputs to the dentate gyrus are re-

Figure 14.10
(a) The hippocampal formation, consisting of two layers of cell bodies which are seen here as heavily stained elements forming two "C's." The larger, right-handed "C" is the hippocampus proper and is composed of the pyramidal neurons. The smaller, left-handed C is composed of the granule cells which form the dentate gyrus. The dentate gyrus receives three massive inputs: (1) from the pyramidal cells of the ipsilateral side (Assoc.); (2) from the pyramidal cells of the contralateral side (Comm.); and (3) from the entorhinal cortex (Entor.). (b) The disposition of the three major afferents as they contact two typical granule cells. [From Lynch and Wells (1978).]

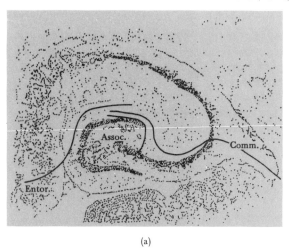

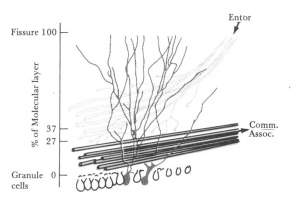

(a)

(b)

stricted to the bottom portion of the dendritic trees. The inputs from the entorhinal cortex fill the remainder of the dendritic trees.

These scientists removed the fibers coming into the dentate gyrus from the entorhinal cortex in rats of varying ages in order to observe the way that new connections might be formed. Figure 14.11 shows their results. The axon endings from the entorhinal cortex degenerated, as expected. But this region of the tree was not left without any input. After the operation, the axons from the pyramidal cells in the ipsilateral and contralateral hippocampus gradually "sprouted" new branches. These branches grew into the parts of the tree originally occupied by the axons from the entorhinal cortex. This growth was quite large in the animals which suffered the lesion early in life, but there was also growth in the animals which suffered the lesion in adulthood.

recovery from brain damage in primates. This kind of plasticity also exists in the primate brain. Goldman (1978) removed a portion of the left frontal lobe of fetal rhesus monkeys 6 weeks before birth. (She did this by removing the fetus from the uterus, returning it, and subsequently delivering it around term.) On the fifth postnatal day, she injected the right side of the monkey's brain with radioactively labeled proline and leucine. Control monkeys received the injection, but not the removal of part of the frontal lobe. The experimental arrangement is shown in Fig. 14.12.

The radioactivity was carried, via axonal transport, to all the places in the brains of the monkeys where the injected axons went. By tracing the radioactivity, it was possible to determine the paths of those axons.

In the brains without the lesions, these axons extended to the ipsilateral caudate nucleus, and a very few of them went to the contralateral caudate nucleus. But in the lesioned monkeys, a huge amount of radioactivity was found in the contralateral caudate nucleus. This means that the axons that originally would have sent only a few terminals to the opposite side of the brain, now sent a large number. Nor-

Figure 14.11

This illustrates the "sprouting" which takes place in the dentate gyrus following removal of the afferents originating in the entorhinal cortex: the extreme left panel again summarizes the distribution of the three major afferents of the granule cells in the normal, adult rat. The next panel (0–14 days) illustrates the distribution of the commissural and associational projections if the entorhinal projections are destroyed in rats from birth to 2 weeks of age. As shown, the projections to the inner portion of the dendrite extend outwards to occupy essentially the entire dendritic tree. If, however, the lesion of the entorhinal cortex is performed at 3 weeks postnatal, then the two afferents appear to generate a less dense network in the denervated outer dendritic segments. Finally, as shown in the extreme right-hand panel, removal of the entorhinal cortex in adults results in a growth response by the commissural and associational inputs which does not extend nearly as far into the outer zones as found after similar lesions in young rats.

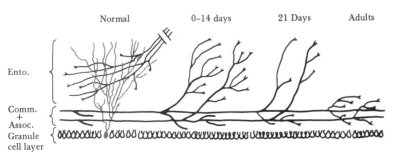

Normal   0–14 days   21 Days   Adults

Ento.

Comm. + Assoc.

Granule cell layer

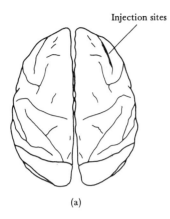

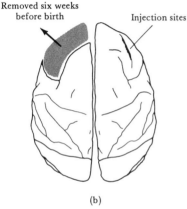

Removed six weeks
before birth   Injection sites

(b)

Figure 14.12
*Injection sites in control monkey
(a), and the monkey whose left
hemisphere was resected before
birth (b). Both monkeys were
injected with radioactively
labeled proline and leucine after
birth. [From Goldman (1978).
Copyright 1978 by the American
Association for the Advancement
of Science.]*

mally, that contralateral caudate nucleus would have received projections from the left frontal lobe. But since that part of the brain was removed, the caudate was left without very much input. The axons from the right frontal lobe apparently took over the job, and sent input to the left caudate nucleus.

This kind of plasticity is remarkable indeed. Previously, most people assumed that neurons were fairly immutable once they were laid down. And most people believed that this occurred prior to birth in the human being. It is now becoming clear that dramatic alterations in synaptic connections can be made, particularly in the developing organism.

brain grafts following brain damage. If axons can sprout new connections, particularly in the developing organism, then it is not into the realm of science fiction to suppose that **brain grafts** from young animals could be used to sprout new connections in the brains of adults. Das and Hallas (1978) transplanted cortical tissue from the brains of young rats into the cerebellum and forebrain of adult rats. As far as they could tell, the transplanted tissue was accepted by the host brains without any problems. After several weeks, the tissue from the young rats differentiated into tissue that looked exactly like normal tissue in the adult rat's cerebellum and forebrain. The adult rats with the brain grafts behaved normally, and some of them grew to the ripe old age of 2 years.

Perlow and his colleagues (Perlow, Freed, Hoffer, Seiger, Olson, and Wyatt, 1979) found that these brain grafts from young animals would also be accepted by brain damaged adults. They injected adult rats with the drug 6-OHDA on one side of their brains. The drug destroyed the dopamine system on the injected side. This drug-induced lesion is normally followed by a kind of dopamine hypersensitivity, which we discussed in Chapter 10. The striatal neurons develop increased sensitivity to dopamine by virtue of an increased number of dopamine receptor sites, presumably as a reaction to the loss of most of the neurotransmitter and the cells which use it. When the rats are subsequently injected with apomorphine, a drug which facilitates activity at dopamine synapses, they show strange circling motor abnormalities. This is probably because the dopamine pathway, which is involved in movement, is hypersensitive and overstimulated by the apomorphine. Perlow and his co-workers hypothesized that brain grafts might be able to reinnervate the dopamine system, and reduce the motor abnormalities seen following apomorphine injections.

They grafted pieces of fetal ventral mesencephalon (containing the substantia nigra, the locus of origin for the dopamine pathway) into the brains of adult rats treated with 6-OHDA. Control rats received grafts from the peripheral nervous system. The grafting procedure was simple: they injected the embryonic tissue into the lateral ventricle of the adult, on the same side of the brain as the drug lesion.

While the grafts from the peripheral nervous system degenerated, the grafts from the fetal substantia nigra survived and flourished. They apparently became integrated into the dopamine system of the host brain. Rats with the substantia nigra grafts showed reduced circling behavior in response to an injection of apomorphine, compared to rats with the peripheral nervous system graft, or rats without grafts. This study suggests that it is not only possible for a host brain to accept grafts from the fetal central nervous system; it is also possible for the graft to elicit an alteration in the behavior of the recipient animal consistent with the normal function of the grafted tissue.

This finding may have some important clinical uses in the treatment of Parkinson's disease, which is characterized by reduced function in the dopaminergic pathways. The usual treatment is peripheral administration of L-dopa, a precursor of dopamine. But this treatment is not always very effective, perhaps because of untoward side effects or because the drug is only a precursor of the transmitter, not the transmitter itself. If these patients could be given local sources of dopamine, supplied by a brain graft, then the treatment might be much more effective. Clearly the brain, and particularly the developing brain, is incredibly plastic. Not only can it change its synaptic connections in response to brain damage and local brain environment, it can change its connections in response to experience, as we shall see in the following sections.

Some of the most amazing examples of plasticity come from studies in which the visual environment of a developing animal is changed in *the effects of sensory deprivation* some way. For example, Hubel and Wiesel (1963) studied the changes which occur in the visual pathway of kittens deprived of vision in one eye. Normally, visual cortex cells are binocular in the sense that images from either eye will produce responses in the same cell. A single cell might respond more vigorously to stimulation from one eye, but around 80% of the cells will respond to both eyes. Most of the cells in the kittens deprived of vision in one eye were monocular; they would only respond to stimulation from the nondeprived eye. This phenomenon is called **ocular dominance shift.**

Figure 14.13 shows the ocular dominance distributions for a normal kitten (a) and for a kitten deprived of vision in one eye (b). The normal kitten has some cells which respond best to left eye stimulation, and others that respond best to the right eye. Most of the cells are binocular, though they often have a "preference." The kitten deprived of vision in the right eye between day 10 and day 31 showed many more cells that could only be driven by stimulation of the left (nondeprived) eye.

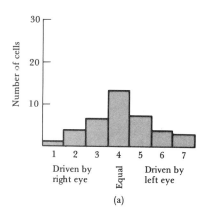

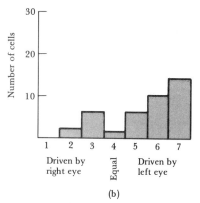

Figure 14.13
Ocular dominance distribution of a normal, nondeprived kitten (a), and a kitten deprived of vision in the right eye from 10 to 31 days old (b). Definition of ocular dominance groups along horizontal axis: (1) cells driven only by the contralateral eye; (2) marked dominance for the contralateral eye; (3) slight dominance; (4) no obvious difference between the two eyes; (5) ipsilateral eye dominated slightly; (6) marked dominance for ipsilateral eye; and (7) only driven by the ipsilateral eye. [From Hubel and Wiesel (1970).]

Monocular deprivation not only results in an ocular dominance shift. It also results in anatomical changes in the lateral geniculate body of the thalamus, which is in the afferent visual pathway. Wiesel and Hubel (1963) found that after 3 months of monocular deprivation, the geniculate layers receiving input from the deprived eye were thinner and the cell bodies appeared shrunken. These scientists suggest that the monocular deprivation retarded the growth of the geniculate cells which should have been receiving input from the deprived eye, and probably caused some atrophy as well.

partial sensory deprivation of pattern vision. The visual deprivation does not have to be total in order to have effects on the cells in the visual cortex. Hirsch and Spinelli (1971) fitted kittens with special goggles which allowed the kitten to only see certain shapes out of each eye (shown in Figure 14.14). One eye saw only vertical lines while the other saw only horizontal lines. When they were not wearing goggles, the kittens were left in the dark, so the lines were the only visual stimulation which the kittens received.

After about three months of this partial sensory deprivation, Hirsch and Spinelli examined the properties of the visual cortical cells in the cats. The cells, which responded to light presented to the eye which saw vertical lines, had receptive fields which were vertically oriented. The cells which responded to the eye which saw only horizontal lines had horizontally oriented receptive fields. Since normal cats have many different types of cells, some which respond to horizontal bars, others to vertical bars, diagonal bars, or moving bars, these cats were clearly abnormal. Their restricted visual environment had clearly affected the properties of the feature detectors in their visual cortex.

deprivation of movement in the visual field. It is not only the pattern of stimulation which can affect development, but visual movements as well. Chalupa and Rhoades (1978) reared some hamsters in the dark, others in a normal 12-hour light/12-hour dark environment, and still others in a "strobe" environment designed to eliminate the visual experience of movement. Each day these hamsters saw only brief light flashes (4 microsecond flashes every $\frac{1}{2}$ second), so that the light was never on long enough for the animals to see anything move. Discos often use this kind of stroboscopic lighting and the "stop action" effect is quite striking.

When the animals reached adulthood, Chalupa and Rhoades examined the properties of their superior colliculus cells (cells which are in the visual pathway). Figure 14.15 shows the properties of some of the cells they found.

Both the dark reared hamsters, and the hamsters reared in a normal day/night cycle, showed many directional cells which responded best when the stimulus was moving in a particular direction. Panels (b) and

(c) are examples of these kinds of cells. The cell in panel (c), for example, showed sharp directional sensitivity—it only responded when the stimulus moved down and to the right. But the "strobe" reared hamsters had very few of these directionally sensitive cells. Most of their cells were more like the one in panel (a).

Figure 14.14
A kitten wearing goggles which limit the sensory experience during development.

sensitive periods for sensory deprivation. Sensory deprivation studies performed on adult animals yield completely different results. It is possible, for example, to deprive one eye of an adult cat for more than a year without altering the way the neurons in the visual cortex respond to binocular stimulation. Thus the period of development is a sensitive one for the effects of sensory deprivation.

Sensitive periods for various effects, however, are not always within the same time period. In Chapter 12, for example, we saw that the sensitive period for the effects of prenatal androgen on the reproductive organs comes earlier than the sensitive period for the effects of this prenatal hormone on the brain. The same independence of sensitive periods appears to hold true for some of the visual cortex cells in cats.

Daw, Berman, and Ariel (1978) placed kittens in a drum which rotated in one direction with one eye open from the time the kittens were $2\frac{1}{2}$ to 5 weeks old. Between 5 weeks and 12 weeks, they placed the kittens in the same drum. But now the drum moved in the opposite direction, and the opposite eye was open. They later tested the properties of the visual cortex, and found first that most of the cells responded to stimulation in the eye that was open *second*. This meant that the sensitive period for establishing ocular dominance was after 5 weeks of age.

They also tested to see what direction of movement would be preferred by most of the cortical cells. Many of them preferred the direction that the drum moved *first*, rather than second. This meant that the sensitive period for establishing a preference for the direction of movement was before 5 weeks of age.

plastic changes after more normal kinds of experience. The experiments we have discussed so far all involve some kind of deprivation. They show that deprivation can affect the properties of the visual cortical cells, but this kind of experience is fairly extreme and unlikely to occur in normal animals and humans. Spinelli and Jensen (1979) wondered if cells in the brain would change their response properties after a more normal kind of experience. This is an important question which we will discuss further in the next chapter. Scientists assume that some brain changes must occur during normal experience, but those changes have been very difficult to pin down.

Spinelli and Jensen (1979) allowed kittens to develop without any kind of visual deprivation. Instead, some of the kittens received 8

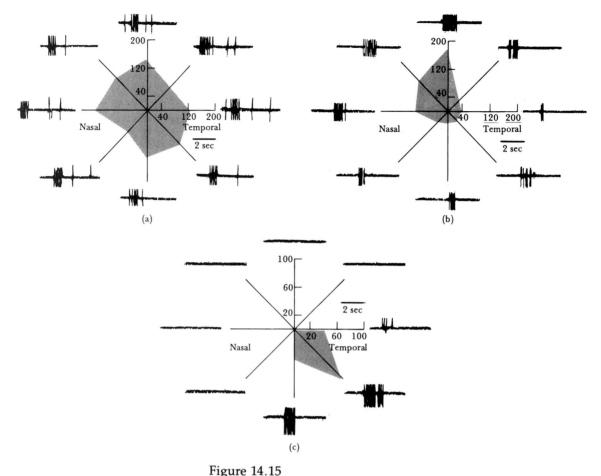

Figure 14.15
(a) Responses of a visual cortical cell that showed no directional sensitivity. (b) Responses of a cell that showed a preference for stimuli moving in an upward and nasal direction. (c) Responses of a cell that showed extreme preference for stimuli moving in a downward and temporal direction. [From Chalupa and Rhoades (1978). Copyright 1978 by the American Association for the Advancement of Science.]

minutes of training on a visual-motor task every day for about 10 weeks. The task was avoidance training: the kitten was suspended in a sling and each foreleg was attached by a string to a switch which the kitten could activate by bending its leg. The kitten was also fitted with goggles, like the kind we described earlier, so the experimenters could present each eye with horizontal or vertical lines during the avoidance training. When the kitten extended its leg, it received a mild shock on its leg, and vertical lines were presented to one eye. When it bent its leg it received no shock and horizontal lines to the other eye. (Other kittens received variations of this stimulus combination.) All the kittens had to learn was that bending its leg was associated with safety as far as the shock was concerned, and vertical lines presented to one eye. They learned this task quickly, and performed well during the 10 weeks.

The kittens showed a variety of changes in electrophysiological responses, compared to kittens that had not been trained. For instance, there was a shift toward ocular dominance, meaning that many more cells were monocular, rather than binocular. For the binocular cells, Spinelli and Jensen found some which had different orientation sensitivities depending on which eye was stimulated. For example, a single cell might respond best to vertical lines coming from the right eye, but horizontal ones coming from the left.

The changes were not limited to the visual cortex. The area of the somatosensory cortex which processed input coming from the shocked foreleg was much larger. (This area would be contralateral to the shocked leg.) This "trained" side of the brain also had more polymodal cells which would respond not only to touch on the foreleg, but visual stimulation as well.

The size of the changes is rather surprising given that the kittens only spent 8 minutes a day on the task, but whether the changes are permanent or temporary is not yet known. These findings nevertheless suggest that normal kinds of experience (or at least relatively normal, compared to sensory deprivation) can modify the properties of the visual and somatosensory cortex cells.

experiential modifications of visual cortex in human beings. It is difficult to study the development of the visual neurons in humans, because single cell analysis is impossible. But there is some information that suggests that the visual environment can modify the properties of cells in the human cortex.

Most people see horizontal and vertical lines with greater acuity than oblique lines, and Annis and Frost (1973) proposed that this effect may be due to few experiences with oblique lines early in life. The Cree Indians, however, grow up around many diagonal lines because their houses are conical. Annis and Frost found that the Cree Indians saw oblique lines with as much acuity as the horizontal and vertical lines. Perhaps these people have more cells which respond best to the oblique angle.

More evidence for the effects of the environment on the properties of the visual cortex comes from studies on people who have an **astigmatism**. These people have a visual defect that causes lines of a particular orientation to look blurred, but has no effect on the clarity of other lines. Mitchell, Freeman, Millodot, and Haegerstrom (1973) found that even when this defect was optically corrected, these people still saw the affected orientation with less acuity. These results suggest that the problem is not simply at the level of the eye, where the astigmatism is; it might be due to a defect in the way those lines are being coded by the visual cortex.

To test this hypothesis, Freeman and Pettigrew (1973) reared kittens with masks which only blurred lines in a particular orientation, to simulate astigmatism. The cortical neurons of these kittens responded best when they were presented with lines which were in an orientation which was not blurred by the masks. It is possible that if a person were born with an astigmatism, or developed one very early, the cortical cells would be less responsive to lines in the orientation which was blurred by the defect. Later correction with glasses would have no effect on the way the cortex is processing those lines.

plasticity in the visual cortex. These studies all point to the importance of the visual environment in shaping the way that our brains perceive the world. Especially during development, the brain is very plastic, and the environment has an effect on the direction of the changes which are made. The response properties of neurons must be determined by synaptic connections, so it is clear that the environment must be having some kind of an effect on those connections.

The kind of effect the environment is having, however, is not yet known. Hubel and Wiesel propose that an animal is born with the neural connections necessary for normal responses in the cortex, but these connections break down if there is abnormal visual stimulation during the sensitive early part of life. In this scheme, the connections in the visual cortex would tend to be plastic only in the sense that they are vulnerable to abnormal environments. As long as the environments were normal, the cortical cells would maintain their responses.

Other scientists propose that the brain only possesses a rough outline for responding to visual stimulation. The characteristics of the visual environment are responsible for putting down the final connections. In this scheme, the environment would play a much more active role in shaping the responses of the developing neurons. A third hypothesis proposes that neural connections are multipotential in the newborn. During development, some connections drop out and others become stronger as a result of experience. Regardless of which hypothesis is correct, it is clear that the visual environment, and perhaps the whole of our sensory world, plays an important part in development.

the effects of complex environments If sensory deprivation can produce such dramatic plastic changes in the nervous system, then what about sensory enrichment? Is it possible that the nervous system can change in response to an environment that provides ample opportunity for learning, social interaction, and plain fun?

Although no one really knows what constitutes an "enriched" environment for any animal, it is certainly possible to provide developing animals with a more complex environment and compare their brains and behavior to those animals reared in the standard laboratory cage. Rosenzweig, Bennett, and their colleagues (e.g., Bennett *et al.*, 1964; Rosenzweig, 1970) placed rats after weaning in either an "enriched environment" (a large cage containing 12 rats and many frequently changed toys), or individually in an impoverished environment (the standard boring lab cage, with ample food and water, but not much else). As adults, the "enriched" rats had a heavier cerebral cortex, greater thickness of cortical tissue, larger nerve cell bodies, and more glial cells. The brain chemistry of the rats reared in the complex environments was also different. There was a higher ratio of RNA to DNA, suggesting increased metabolic activity, and a change in several enzymes which are related to brain function.

changes in synaptic connections. The "enriched" rats also show changes in synaptic connections. Greenough and his colleagues (Volkmar and Greenough, 1972; Greenough, 1975) studied the dendritic branching patterns in the occipital cortex in rats reared in three different kinds of environments. One group was reared in the complex environment described earlier, a second was reared in the impoverished lab cage, and a third was reared in a social environment which contained pairs of rats but no toys.

Figure 14.16 shows a typical pyramidal neuron from the occipital cortex of the rat. This shows how these neurons have a long **apical dendritic shaft**, and also many **basal dendrites** protruding from the cell body. Figure 14.17 shows how the branching of the dendrites can be labeled in terms of their order. A branch which comes right off the apical dendrite would be a first-order branch (1) while a branch which protrudes from another branch of the apical dendrite would be a second-order branch.

Figure 14.18 shows how the branching of these apical and basal dendrites differed in the enriched rats (EC), the socially reared rats (SC), and the impoverished rats. The enriched rats showed more lower order branching off the apical shaft, and more higher order branching of basal dendrites.

The enriched rearing produces many changes in the pattern of synaptic connections. For example, the synapses of these animals are generally larger, and there are more of them, at least in certain parts of the brain (Møllgaard *et al.*, 1971). These findings all point to a more complex brain—one with the potential for making more synaptic connections.

Presumably, some of these structural changes in the brains of the enriched rats underlie changes in behavior. The enriched rats respond to novel environments with much the same aplomb as the rats which had been stimulated in infancy by handling. They are also less emo-

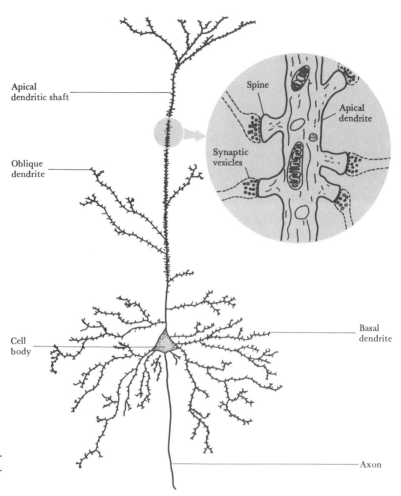

Figure 14.16
An idealized drawing of a pyramidal neuron from the occipital cortex. [From Greenough (1975).]

Apical dendritic shaft

Oblique dendrite

Cell body

Spine

Apical dendrite

Synaptic vesicles

Basal dendrite

Axon

tionally reactive and aggressive than the impoverished rats, and they adapt to testing situations much more quickly. Although it is tempting to assume that they are more capable learners, this hypothesis has been difficult to test because the impoverished animals are so emotional. Enriched rats do perform better on many learning tasks, particularly the more complex ones (Brown, 1968), but it is not yet clear whether they are more intelligent, or just more relaxed.

what parts of the complex environment produce the brain changes? The complex environment is just that—complex. It is possible that certain components of this environment are more critical than others in producing the "enriched" brain. The social rearing does not seem to be the critical factor, since the socially reared animals had brains similar to the impoverished ones, as we discussed earlier. Visual stimulation also

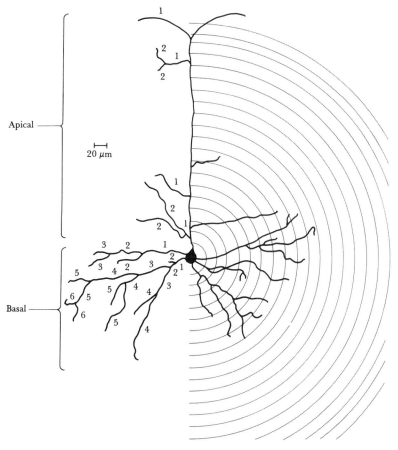

Figure 14.17
The ordering of dendritic branch-es. [From Greenough (1975).]

does not seem to be critical, because blinded rats show almost the same brain changes after enrichment as sighted animals (Rosenzweig *et al.*, 1969). The frequency of toy changes is also not the whole answer because rats reared by themselves in a complex environment do not show the typical brain changes.

However, rats which actively participate in the complex environment, even if they are by themselves, do show the critical brain changes (Rosenzweig and Bennett, 1972). Ordinarily if they are by themselves, they will take little interest in the toys. But if they are placed into the cage during the dark part of their day, or after receiving amphetamines, they will make use of the toys and their brains will subsequently resemble those of the enriched rats. This suggests that at least one of the relevant features of enrichment is the active participation in a varied physical environment, which can be the result of drugs, darkness, or social grouping.

Human beings who have been reared in institutions generally show a behavioral pattern which includes emotional apathy, lack of interest

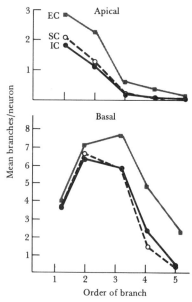

Figure 14.18
The average number of branches at each order for apical and basal dendrites of Layer 4 pyramidal neurons. Environmental complexity (EC) rats have more higher order branches than rats from social (SC) or isolation (IC) conditions, particularly in the basal region. SC rats had more branches than ICs in some types of neurons. [After Greenough (1976).]

in the environment, and mental retardation. But it is not known whether the brains of human beings reared in these impoverished settings are in any way different from those of people reared in more normal environments. Nevertheless, it is quite likely that brain differences are present. The human brain probably shows even more plasticity in the face of environmental enrichment or impoverishment than that of the rodent.

sensitive periods for environmental effects. Many of the effects of malnutrition are most devastating if they occur during cell growth and division. But the effects of the complex environment on brain structure are in some ways more subtle, and more reversible. For example, a rat which has been impoverished during early life, and is then placed into a complex environment as an adult, shows many of the same brain changes as the rat which had a complex environment from weaning. The changes are smaller, but they nevertheless occur. Even an "elderly" rat can benefit from enrichment (Riege, 1971). Early life may be a sensitive period for the impact of enriched and impoverished environments on the brain, but most scientists flatly deny that it is a critical period. The brain apparently maintains a great deal of plasticity throughout the life of the organism.

Behavior patterns also show this plasticity throughout life. For example, even though culturally impoverished children develop more slowly than more enriched children, many of the detrimental effects of early impoverishment on behavior are reversible if the child is later given a more complex physical and social environment.

interactions between environment, sex, genes, and nutrition. The effects of the environment on brain structure and on behavior interact with a number of other factors during the development of an organism. Two animals, even though reared in the same environment, may not show the same kind or amount of changes in the brain and in behavior for a number of different reasons. For example, male rats are more vulnerable to the effects of impoverishment on brain development, while females are more buffered. Male monkeys also are more vulnerable to the harshest effects of isolation on later social behavior. The nervous systems of male and female monkeys develop at different rates, so that the isolation is affecting the animals at different stages of their development, even though they may be the same age. If the impact of the environment has a sensitive period, then it is possible that since the females are developmentally "older," they are less vulnerable.

The environment in which an organism is reared also interacts with the organism's genes. For example, when rats are used as subjects, the researchers always assign some members of each litter to each of the rearing conditions, in order to partially control for the effects of genetic variation on brain development. The environment interacts with nutrition, also, and enriched environments can partially ameliorate some of the worst effects of malnutrition during early life. Furthermore, there are always some animals which suffer very little from impoverished environments, suggesting that some as yet unknown factors are interacting with the animal's rearing condition, which somehow provide the animal with a degree of insulation.

The studies on the effects of enrichment and impoverishment suggest that there is a great deal yet to be learned about how the environment affects development. Many environments which we believe are enriched, might not be as enriching as we had thought. Furthermore, we may be missing important components of enrichment. The studies on rats point to the importance of active participation in the environment on brain development. Studies on monkeys suggest that movement and body contact may be an important component of enrichment. Monkeys reared with a Clorox bottle covered with fur showed the typical behavioral pattern of isolation rearing. But if the bottle was suspended so that it would swing to and fro, the monkeys showed fewer abnormalities. They were less timid in novel environments, and they showed little if any stereotyped rocking behavior (Mason, 1968). As we learn more about how environments influence the development of brain and behavior, we should be able to expand the range of behavior that is set for us by our genes.

---

summary
Environmental Contributions to Development

In this section we discussed studies which clearly demonstrated that the environment plays a major role in changing the nervous system during development. Several different kinds of environmental manipulations were examined, including the effects of (1) stress, (2) brain damage, (3) sensory deprivation, and (4) enrichment and impoverishment.

Stress can be either beneficial or detrimental to the growing organism. Minor stresses, such as handling of rat pups during infancy, seem to benefit the rat pup in that the rats are later better able to cope with environmental stresses in adulthood. They are less emotional and show faster maturation of the nervous system. But more severe stresses, such as long-term separation from the mother, can have disastrous consequences. Mother-infant separation can produce difficulties in thermoregulation, enzyme production, and can also produce an increased risk for gastric ulcers later in life. Monkeys separated from their mothers early in life develop a "sociopathic syndrome"; they are hyperemotional, hyperaggressive, and the females make very poor mothers themselves, if they can be induced to become pregnant.

Brain damage is a very severe stressor, but it is clear that the developing organism can handle this stress much better than the adult. Young animals typically show much more recovery of function after lesions than adults. The changes in the nervous system which result from brain damage can tell us something about how the nervous system can make plastic changes.

When an area of brain is deafferented (the cells which provide input to that area are cut or destroyed), other brain areas begin to "sprout" new collateral branches on their axons. These new branches then grow into the deafferented area, and form new synaptic connections. It had previously been known that dendrites continue to grow during development, and new synapses might be formed by this plastic process. But it may be possible that the axons in the undamaged brain might also be growing—and sprouting new collateral branches which can make new connections.

The plasticity of the brain tissue in the developing organism has made it possible to transplant brain tissue from young animals into the brains of adults. These *brain grafts* survive, and appear to function in the behavior of the host animal.

Sensory deprivation is another form of environmental effect which can produce changes in the properties of the developing nervous system. Visual deprivation of one eye, for example, produces an *ocular dominance shift* in which most of the cells in the visual cortex are monocular rather than binocular, and respond only to input from the nondeprived eye. Monocular deprivation also produces anatomical changes in the lateral geniculate cells which receive input from the deprived eye.

Even less drastic sensory deprivation can affect the properties of visual cortical cells. Kittens reared with goggles, such that they only saw vertical or horizontal stripes, tended to develop a visual cortex which contained an overabundance of cells which had vertical or horizontal receptive fields. Deprivation of movement vision (by rearing the animal in a "stroboscopic" environment) produces a striking decrease in the number of cells which subsequently respond to moving stimuli. The plasticity of the visual cortical cells to these kinds of effects is restricted to a sensitive period during the early part of development. Sensory deprivation in adulthood has little effect on the properties of these brain areas. The sensitive periods for different kinds of cells in the visual cortex may be slightly different, however, even though they all occur during the early part of development.

Changes in the response properties of visual cortical cells occur with normal kinds of experience, in addition to sensory deprivation. Kittens trained on a visual–motor task for 10 weeks showed an ocular dominance shift, and also showed more polymodal sensory cells in the somatosensory cortex.

The visual cortical cells in human beings may also be plastic in the face of sensory deprivation. For example, people who are born with astigmatism may be able to correct the optical defect later. But their visual cortical cells may continue to be relatively insensitive to lines in the orientation which was blurred by the astigmatism.

The studies on sensory deprivation show that the environment can produce plastic changes in the properties of visual cortical cells. But the environment may be playing an active, or a more passive role. Some scientists hypothesize that the newborn kitten's visual cortical cells are already functionally active, and can respond to normal kinds of visual stimulation. Sensory deprivation or an abnormal sensory environment may cause an attrition of these properties. Other scientists propose that the environment actually shapes the responsiveness of the cortical cells to different kinds of stimulation.

The effects of enriched and impoverished environments also demonstrate that the kind of environment in which an organism is reared changes the properties of the growing nervous system. Rats reared in more complex environments (with other rats and with frequently changed toys) show a heavier cerebral cortex, greater thickness of cortical tissue, larger nerve cell bodies, and more glial cells. They also show more dendritic branching and more and larger synapses. These brain changes probably underlie profound behavioral changes as well. For example, the "enriched" rats are less emotional, less aggressive, and generally do better at complex learning tasks. Thus the complex environment produced some very remarkable changes in the brains of these rats. The component of the complex environment which has the most effect on the nervous system is the active participation in a physically changing environment. Rats which do not participate actively in the complex environment show few changes in their brains.

The effects of environmental enrichment, sex, genes, nutrition, and perhaps all kinds of internal and external events, interact during development. For example, female rats show fewer benefits from enrichment, and fewer changes from impoverishment as well. Perhaps the internal events (hormones) are interacting with the external events (enrichment) in complex ways, about which we know very little. Also, the worst effects of malnutrition can be partly overcome by rearing an animal in an enriched environment. Clearly, the DNA is not unfolding in a vacuum, and all the events which can affect it are interacting with one another.

The effects of enrichment and impoverishment also show a sensitive period—younger, developing organisms are more susceptible to these kinds of environmental influences. But even very old rats show at least some brain changes in response to enrichment. This suggests that these kinds of brain changes might underlie plasticity throughout life. Perhaps these changes, and those which occur in response to stress, sensory deprivation, brain damage, and other kinds of internal and external events, might be similar to the plasticity of the nervous system in adulthood. In the next chapter, we will discuss plasticity in adulthood— the kind of plasticity our nervous systems use to learn and to remember.

kwashiorkor
thyroxine
anterior pituitary gland
posterior pituitary gland
second messenger hypothesis
cyclic AMP
ornithine decarboxylase
axon "sprouting"

dentate gyrus
entorhinal cortex
brain grafts
ocular dominance shift
astigmatism
apical dendritic shaft
basal dendrites

SUGGESTED READINGS

Riesen, A. H., ed. (1975). *The Developmental Neuropsychology of Sensory Depriva-tion.* Academic Press, New York.

Greenough, W. T. (1975). Experiential modification of the developing brain. *American Scientist,* **63,** 37–46.

Rosenzweig, M. R., Bennett, E. L., and Diamond, M. C. (1972). Brain changes in response to experience. *Scientific American,* **226,** 22–29.

Levine, S. (1976). Stress and behavior. In *Progress in Psychobiology* (Thompson, R. F., ed.). W. H. Freeman, San Francisco.

Lynch, G., and Wells, J. (1978). Neuroanatomical plasticity and behavioral adaptability. In *Brain and Learning* (Teyler, T., ed.). Greylock Publishers, Stamford, Connecticut.

(The first three references deal with the effects of the environment on the developing brain. The fourth one provides more detail on the phenomenon of axon sprouting.)

McClearn, G. E. (1970). Behavioral genetics. *Ann. Rev. Genetics,* **4,** 437–468.

Prescott, J. W., Read, M. S., and Coursin, D. B., eds. (1975). *Brain Function and Malnutrition.* John Wiley, New York.

(These last two references provide more information about the genetic contribution to development and the effects of malnutrition on the developing brain.)

15

plasticity in the nervous system: learning and memory

introduction Perhaps the most frustrating problem in the entire field of physiological psychology is the search for the "engram"—the biological basis for the memory trace. After years of studying the processes underlying learning and memory, the famous psychologist Karl Lashley remarked:

I sometimes feel, in reviewing the evidence on the localization of the memory trace, that the necessary conclusion is that learning is just not possible (Lashley, 1950).

The situation has not improved very much since 1950. Out of frustration, Rozin (1976) fancifully proposed that we return to the homunculus, or "little man in the head," as an explanation for learning and memory. He admitted that this might just put the problem off, since we would then have to study how the little man could learn and remember. But he states that he might just have found empirical evidence that such a little man exists:

The first positive evidence . . . is shown in (Figure 15.1), which is an electron micrograph of a synapse from the brain. The large central body on the picture is a presynaptic ending, abutting, on its lower right hand side, on the surface of the postsynaptic neuron. Note within the presynaptic ending two clusters of round structures, one of five circles, the other of four. A moment's perusal will make it obvious that these are footprints. . . . There is a little man in the head. He just moves around a lot and is very, very small (Rozin, 1976).

One of the important reasons why progress in this area has been so slow is because the definitions of the phenomena are vague. The definitions were derived from behavioral observations, but they may have little relevance to the biological substrates which underlie them. In the first section of this chapter we will discuss these definitions, along with some other conceptual issues that plague scientists in this area.

conceptual issues
the problem of definitions Learning is extremely difficult to define, although when we see it we can usually recognize it. The broadest definition would simply state that learning is the modification of behavior as a result of experience. Closer scrutiny of this definition reveals some pitfalls. For example, if you injured your foot by falling down the stairs, you would probably limp for a few days. Thus your behavior is being modified by your experience. But could you call this kind of modification "learning?"

More restricted definitions of learning tend to categorize different types of behavioral changes which result from experience. The categories to which we will refer throughout this chapter include **habituation, sensitization**, and **associative learning**. But as we shall see, this category system has some weaknesses.

habituation. If you live inside a city, you can easily go to sleep at night despite the honking of horns and the general brouhaha. You have become habituated to the noise, and your responsiveness to it has decreased. Habituation refers to a decrement in behavioral response which occurs with repeated stimulus presentations (Teyler and Alger, 1978). Habituation is different from fatigue in that the decline in behavioral responsiveness is specific to the stimulus. The muscles involved in the response will still show responses to a different stimulus.

Thompson and Spencer (1966) have listed several criteria for habituation. Among these are (1) depression of response after repeated stimulus presentations, (2) recovery of responsiveness after an absence of stimulus presentations, (3) greater decrement for weaker stimuli and faster rates of stimulus presentation, (4) delayed recovery with prolonged periods of stimulation, (5) dishabituation with the presentation of a strong stimulus, and (6) generalization of the habituation to other similar stimuli. Thus the definition of habituation is fairly clear-cut and a phenomenon must pass these tests and others as well before it can be called habituation.

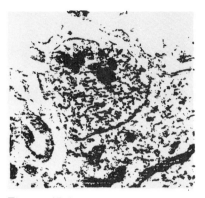

Figure 15.1
Sketch of an electron micrograph of a synapse. [Adapted from Rozin (1976).]

sensitization. Another kind of behavioral modification is an increase in behavioral responsiveness with repeated presentation, or sensitization. The Chinese water torture apparently relied on this kind of phenomenon to extract confessions from suspects. Tiny drops of water would repeatedly strike the forehead, and initially they would seem harmless. But after awhile, the unfortunate recipient would become sensitized, and each drop probably felt like a sledge hammer.

associative learning. The kind of learning which is most easily recognized as learning is the associative type. This category includes situations where the organism learns to associate two events, because they consistently occur together in time or in some other predictable relationship. Associative learning can be subdivided into **classical conditioning** and **instrumental conditioning**.

Classical conditioning (or Pavlovian conditioning) occurs when two environmental events occur in rapid succession, and when the second event automatically produces a reflex response in the organism. The first event initially produces no response, that is, it is neutral. But the organism eventually learns to associate the first event with the second, so that the first event comes to elicit the reflex response when it is presented by itself.

Traditionally, the first event is termed the **conditioned stimulus** (CS) and the second event which initially elicits the response is the **unconditioned stimulus** (UCS). At first, the response is called the **unconditioned response** (UCR). But as learning progresses, and the CS comes to elicit the response, it is called the **conditioned response** (CR). In Pavlov's experiments, for example, the UCS was meat powder put in the mouth, and the dog reflexively salivated to it; salivation was the UCR. A bell which immediately preceded the presentation of the meat was the CS. After many pairings, the dog came to salivate to the sound of the bell alone. This salivation was the CR. The experimental arrangement is shown in Figure 15.2.

This kind of learning does not occur unless the CS and the UCS are paired, and the CS comes first in time. When they are not paired, but they are both nevertheless presented, a kind of sensitization might occur which is called **pseudoconditioning**. For example, if the bell is rung at odd intervals and the meat is presented without any connection with the bell, the dog may still salivate more to the sound of the bell than it normally might.

When one of the events to be associated with another is a response by the organism, rather than an external event, then instrumental conditioning is occurring. In this situation, the animal learns that a particular response is followed by an external event. If the event is rewarding in some way, the animal will increase the frequency of the response. If the event is painful or even just not rewarding, then the animal decreases the frequency of the response. A typical example of this kind of learning which we will discuss later in this chapter is called **passive avoidance** (shown in Figure 15.3). Rodents generally prefer the dark, so if they are put into the lighted side of a two-chambered box, they will usually move into the dark side right away. But if this response is followed by a shock, then the next time they are placed into the lighted side, they will stay there. Thus they have decreased the frequency of a response which was followed by a painful event.

Although these definitions seem fairly straightforward, they have produced much confusion in the search for the biological bases of learning and memory. Not all scientists have agreed that habituation and sensitization are actually forms of learning. But others consider them to be very simple types of learning. Furthermore, the distinction between classical conditioning and instrumental conditioning is more semantic than real. For example, the rat in the passive avoidance situa-

Figure 15.2
Experimental setup to study classical conditioning.

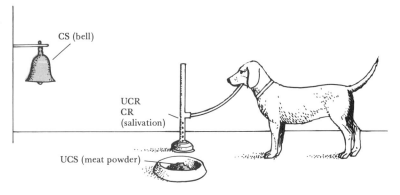

CS (bell)

UCR
CR
(salivation)

UCS (meat powder)

tion was also being classically conditioned. It learned to associate darkness, and the other stimuli present in the dark side of the chamber, with shock.

These definitions were derived from behavioral observations, rather than from biological ones. They categorize behavioral events very well, but there is no assurance that these behavioral events will be mediated by distinct biological events. Thus the brain substrates for habituation and instrumental conditioning may be very similar. Furthermore, it may turn out that there are many different kinds of instrumental conditioning, at least biologically speaking. The processes which underlie passive avoidance may be quite different from those which underlie an increase in frequency of a response due to its rewarding consequences. This point becomes even more salient when we consider that the principles of learning an instrumentally conditioned task vary somewhat between species and also for different learning tasks in the same animal.

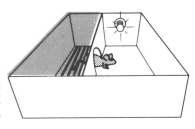

Figure 15.3
Two-chambered box used to study passive avoidance. The rat learns to avoid the dark side of the box because the floor grid produces a shock.

At one time there was a clear distinction between instinctive behavior and learned behavior. The behavior of insects and other lower animals was thought to be primarily instinctual in that the information contained in their genes dictated their behavioral repertoire. Their behavior is not easily modified by experience, and although they can learn some things, the range of learning is restricted. *biological predispositions and learning*

Learned behavior was the province of the higher animals with more complex nervous systems. The principles of learning were thought to be universal and the higher animals were thought to learn tasks in basically the same way. Indeed, most of the principles of learning were derived from studies on a single animal (the white rat) in a single learning situation (instrumental conditioning in the Skinner box). If the principles of learning are universal, then it hardly makes any difference what species or what paradigm is used. One might as well take advantage of the fact that the rat is convenient, and that its lever pressing behavior is easily recorded in a Skinner box.

Unfortunately, animals have never been known to cooperate with scientists and bear out their assumptions. Although some of the features of learning appear to be universal, some are unique to the species which is being studied. Animals have clearly demonstrated that they possess biological predispositions to learn certain tasks, and extreme stubbornness to learn others.

the taste aversion studies. The studies on the way that animals come to avoid certain tastes dethroned some of the long held assumptions about the principles of learning. For example, the universal principles assumed that it didn't matter what kind of stimulus was paired with what kind of consequence. But the taste aversion studies, which we discussed in Chapter 7, demonstrated that many animals preferentially learn to pair a taste with subsequent sickness. Pairing a taste with a shock, or a visual stimulus with a sickness, proved to be much more difficult for the animal. Also, the principles of learning established in classical conditioning studies indicated that the optimum time between a stimulus and its consequence should be extremely short for maximum learning—less than a second. For most learning tasks this is true, but animals can make the taste—sickness association and subsequently avoid that taste, even when the time interval between the taste and the consequence is hours long.

Many other more ethologically oriented experiments have confirmed the view that animals (and perhaps human beings as well) possess biological predispositions to learn certain tasks, but not other ones. The kinds of tasks which they are predisposed to learn are likely to be those which have some adaptive value. Rats find their food by smell and taste, and must rely on these sensory cues to avoid poisons. But many birds find their food by sight, so they possess predispositions to pair a visual stimulus with sickness.

These studies carry with them the implication that there are yet other types of learning, which we did not mention in the first part of this section. Seligman and Hager (1972) suggest that we should be studying the biological bases of "prepared" and "unprepared" learning tasks. The "prepared" tasks would be those for which the animal possesses some predisposition to learn; the "unprepared" tasks would claim no such predisposition. Manning (1976) argues (or rather hopes) that the basic mechanisms underlying learning of the "prepared" or "unprepared" variety may be very similar. Most and perhaps all learning is based on the plasticity of the nervous system. And this plasticity itself is programmed by the DNA in our genes. No clear dichotomy exists between instinct and learning, and the study of instinct and of animal learning are moving closer together.

learning in the developing organism   Another kind of behavioral change which may emerge as a slightly different form of learning is the process of learning in the developing organism. In the last chapter, we saw that the developmental process could be drastically altered by experience. Rats reared in complex environments, for example, showed many behavioral and physiological changes compared to rats reared in isolated environments. But the developmental process may be influencing learning and memory in subtle ways also. Young animals are learning many things very rapidly, but they also apparently forget some of them faster. Humans display infantile amnesia—we have practically no recall at all of specific events that occurred during the first few years of life (Campbell and Coulter, 1976). Nonetheless many of these events (such as brief handling or maternal separation) may have profound influences on later behavior, as we saw in the last chapter. The learning that goes on in the developing organism may be slightly different from the learning that goes on in the adult.

As a result of these disputes about what constitutes learning, and about how many different varieties of learning there may be, many scientists have opted for a more unifying theme—plasticity. Scientists voice much less concern over whether a particular model reflects the biological mechanisms of learning and memory. Instead they are studying all forms of plasticity in the nervous system. Rather than trying to restrict the definition of learning to a small number of behaviorally derived pigeon hole categories, they have moved to the study of a phenomenon which is even broader than the psychologically defined term "learning." *plasticity in the nervous system*

As we saw in the last chapter, and as we shall see in later sections of this one, plasticity can take many forms. There may be changes in synaptic connections by virtue of modifications of dendrites or axonal branching patterns. Or synapses may become functional or nonfunctional. These changes may be limited to small numbers of cells or they may encompass the entire brain. The possibilities stretch the imagination, and as new techniques are developed, new plastic mechanisms may be discovered.

The hope that someone, someday, will discover *the* biological mechanism underlying learning and memory is fading. But in its place is emerging a discipline which examines its assumptions and definitions critically, and discards them if the behavior or physiology of the animal does not conform.

Perhaps partly because of the problem with definitions, this area has been plagued with methodological problems as well. The seemingly simple task of comparing the changes in an animal which has learned to one which has not does not reveal very much about the physiological bases of learning or memory. *methodological issues*

For example, one might compare an animal that has learned to avoid a shock by pressing a lever when a light comes on, to an animal that has not learned this task. The "learned" animal will probably show a number of changes in its brain compared to the "unlearned" animal. But there is no assurance that these changes have anything at all to do with learning or memory. They might reflect changes due to the increase in stress, or to sensory stimulation, motivation, or motor activity, or any number of other nonspecific factors associated with the learning task.

One way to control for these extraneous experiences which occur during learning is to use the "yoked" control. The "unlearned" animal is placed in the box, is shocked, and the lights are turned on and off. But the unfortunate rat cannot learn to avoid the shock by pressing a lever because the lever is "unplugged." Thus the yoked controls are receiving the same amount of sensory stimulation, shock, and perhaps stress, but they are not learning the experimenter's task. But the yoked controls are doing a great deal of "unauthorized" learning. They are, for one thing, learning that they *cannot* avoid a shock in the box (Greenough, 1978).

With designs like these, it may not be possible to separate the effects of stress or other nonspecific factors from the effects of learning on the brain. But this separation may not be very valuable anyway. Stress, sensory stimulation, and motivation may actually be integral parts of the learning process, so that trying to eliminate them may be a little like throwing the baby out with the bathwater.

In this chapter, we will see a number of different approaches to the study of plasticity in the nervous system. First we will discuss several model systems, in which scientists study the process of learning in invertebrates or in limited areas of the vertebrate nervous system. Learning in the marine mollusk or in the cat's pupillary reflex system may not seem very closely connected with the kinds of complex learning that human beings can do. But these systems have a number of advantages. The neuronal pathways can often be mapped with startling detail, and the input and output can be rigidly controlled. The plasticity that these simple neuronal pathways can show may reveal the foundation for the incredibly complex plasticity of the human brain.

Second, we will examine studies which have used intact, behaving animals. These are necessarily "dirtier," and so far they have only been able to provide answers about the correlates of learning and memory, rather than the nature of the memory trace. But these studies are important for two reasons. First, they help to assuage the nagging doubts that the events which occur in the model systems during learning are decidedly dissimilar to those which occur in the intact animal. Second, they are comfortably closer to the goal which we all share— understanding the basis of learning and memory in the human being.

---

summary
Conceptual Issues The study of the biological bases for learning and memory has been hampered by a variety of problems, some of which stem from the definition of what constitutes learning and memory. The broad definition of learning states that it is behavioral modification as a result of experience. But this definition is so broad that it tends to be of little value. As a result of behavioral observations over the years, scientists have generally divided the definition of learning into various categories. These categories include *habituation, sensitization,* and *associative learning.* Associative learning can be further subdivided into *classical conditioning* and *instrumental conditioning.* Unfortunately, it is not at

all clear whether these categories represent discrete kinds of plasticity in the nervous system, even though they can be distinguished behaviorally.

Another difficulty which arises from this category system is that various subtypes of learning may be overlooked. For example, organisms appear to be biologically predisposed to learn certain tasks, particularly those which enhance adaptation. The biological substrates for these kinds of tasks may be somewhat different. Also, learning during development may represent a special kind of plasticity. To alleviate some of these problems with definitions and categorization, scientists have turned to a more general term—plasticity. Researchers are exploring all the ways in which an organism can show plastic changes in the nervous system, without worrying so much about whether their particular design reflects associative learning, habituation, or developmental changes superimposed over learning phenomena.

Aside from the problem with definitions, the field has been plagued with methodological difficulties. These stem mainly from the near impossibility of isolating the effects of learning from the effects of other variables which invariably accompany it, such as stress, motivation, and sensory stimulation. There may be no way to compare the brain of an animal which has learned a task to one which has not and expect the differences to represent the substrate of learning and memory. But as we shall see later in this chapter, this difficulty may be less of a problem than we originally believed, because it highlights the importance of motivation, emotion, sensory stimulation, stress, and motor activity, in the process of learning.

Because the conceptual problems surrounding the study of learning and memory in the behaving animal have been so overwhelming, many scientists have begun to use model systems to understand the basis for neural plasticity. These systems are varied, but they have in common the fact that the stimuli which impinge on the animal can be carefully controlled, and the response of the animal is easily recorded and measured. The next section explores some of these model systems.

The use of model systems to study learning and memory is growing widely. Scientists who tell their friends that they are studying learning and memory in the marine mollusk might be greeted with gales of laughter. But these simple organisms have yielded some remarkable data about the basis for plasticity in neural tissue. In this section we will discuss experiments with one of these sea creatures—*Aplysia.* We will also examine some model systems which make use of the vertebrate nervous system.

model systems

These hardy sea creatures (shown in Figure 15.4) are herbivores that feed on seaweed around the shoreline. Their central nervous system contains only five ganglia. But they are capable of at least some plasticity in behavior, although much of their behavior is fixed. Kandel and his associates (Kandel, 1976) have made careful studies of the

aplysia

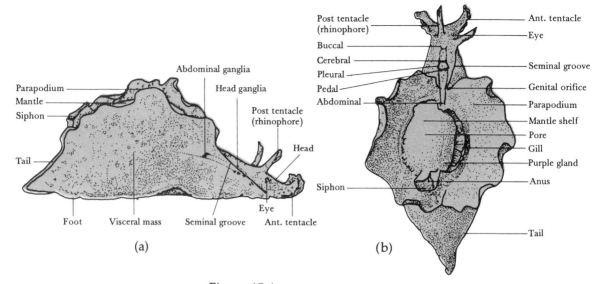

Figure 15.4
Side (a) and dorsal (b) view of **Aplysia.** *[From Kandel (1976).
Copyright 1976 by W. H. Freeman and Company.]*

kinds of plasticity of which this animal is capable. They first studied plasticity at the level of the neuron, and then of behavior.

posttetanic facilitation. One kind of neural plasticity which they studied was **posttetanic facilitation**. A neuron is repetitively stimulated for a few seconds, and the activity of the next neuron in the pathway is recorded. This second neuron fires faster not just during the stimulation (or **tetanization**), but for a few minutes afterward. This simple kind of plasticity may not seem like much compared with the changes which must underlie memories which last for years; but it may underlie very short-term behavioral plasticity.

Figure 15.5 shows the experimental setup for studying posttetanic facilitation. The right connective is stimulated electrically, and the EPSP is measured in cell R-15, which receives input from the axons of the right connective. Panel (b) shows the amplitude of the EPSPs at various times after the stimulation. Notice that even 10 minutes afterward, cell R-15 is still showing slightly higher EPSPs compared to unstimulated control periods.

This kind of plasticity also occurs in vertebrates, and the mechanism which underlies it is at the synapse. Liley (1956) found that there was an increase in the amount of neurotransmitter released by the presynaptic nerve terminal in the rat nerve-muscle junction. Thus this facilitation is not due to a change in the receptor surface of the post-

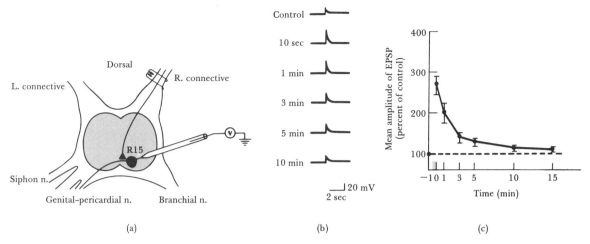

Figure 15.5
Posttetanic facilitation of a monosynaptic EPSP in the abdominal ganglion of **Aplysia.** *[From Schwartz, Castellucci, and Kandel (1971).] (a) Experimental setup for intracellular recording from cell R15, which was hyperpolarized to prevent firing. The EPSP is elicited by stimulating the right connective. (b) Sample records from a single experiment. The right connective was first stimulated every 10 seconds to obtain a control value of the EPSP amplitude. A brief tetanus (5/second for 30 seconds) was then applied to the right connective. Following tetanization the EPSP was again evoked at the control rate of one every 10 seconds. The EPSP remained facilitated for more than 10 minutes. (c) Graph based on an average of 10 experiments described in (b). In each experiment the control value (100% in the graph) was taken from the mean of about 10 pretetanic EPSPs. The hatched bar at the bottom of the graph indicates tetanization; zero time indicates the end of tetanization. [From Kandel (1976). Copyright 1976 by W. H. Freeman and Company.]*

synaptic membrane, but rather due to a change in the amount of neurotransmitter released.

habituation. Aplysia also exhibts habituation, and Figure 15.6 shows the experimental setup which Kandel and his associates used to study the phenomenon. When the creature's siphon is physically stimulated, it makes a defensive reaction—withdrawing its gill. But after many stimulations the behavior gradually subsides, and becomes habituated to the touch. The gill-withdrawal reflex returns immediately however, if a novel stimulus is presented.

Figure 15.7 shows the neural pathways which participate in this habituation, and also shows how much easier it is to study the neural

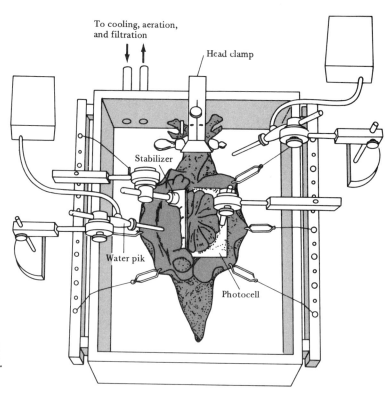

Figure 15.6
*Experimental setup for studying
habituation of the gill-
withdrawal reflex in* **Aplysia.**
*The siphon is stimulated with
the Water-pik, and the photocell
measures the response in the gill.*
*[From Kandel (1976). Copyright
1976 by W. H. Freeman and
Company.]*

phenomenon in simple animals. The numbers on the figure indicate
where the possible loci of plasticity might be. These nine points are as
follows: (1) adaptation of the receptor (siphon); (2) neuromuscular depression; (3) muscle fatigue in the gill; (4) buildup of postsynaptic inhibition on the motor neuron; (5) inhibition of the excitatory
interneuron; (6) presynaptic inhibition of the sensory neuron; (7) a
decrease in the resistance of the motor neuron's membrane; (8) synaptic depression of the connection between the excitatory interneuron
and the motorneuron; and (9) synaptic depression between the sensory neuron and the motor neuron.

Any one of these events could account for habituation, and it was
possible to test most of them, one by one. For example, to eliminate
the first two possibilities, Kandel and his colleagues directly stimulated the motor neurons to the gill. The gill contracted and the response did not habituate despite repeated stimulations. To eliminate
the possibility of receptor adaptation, they stimulated the siphon
while recording from the sensory neuron which leads from the siphon
to the motor neurons and interneurons. The response of the sensory
neuron did not change despite repeated stimulations.

Since the habituation did not occur in either the gill or the siphon, it must have occurred in the central nervous system. During habituation the motor neurons begin firing slower and slower to each stimulation. By recording from various sites during stimulation, they were able to narrow down the possibilities until they were left primarily with the synapse between the sensory neurons and the motor neurons (point 9). The potential change across the motor neuron membrane was decreased during habituation, indicating that the efficacy of the synapse had declined. The decline in the EPSP in L7 motor neuron is due to the decrease in the amount of neurotransmitter released by the presynaptic cells. It was not due to any change in the sensitivity of the motor neuron's membrane.

These studies of habituation and of posttetanic facilitation demonstrate the enormous value of using tiny invertebrates to study plasticity. It is extremely difficult, and often impossible, to obtain such detailed maps of the input and output network of neurons in the higher mammals. To complicate things still further, the output of higher animals often varies. For example, a rat pressing a lever in a Skinner box does not always use the same muscles and motor neurons. Thus we are very far away from pinpointing the locus of plasticity in the nervous system of higher animals.

Marine mollusks may only be able to show limited kinds of plasticity. But recent evidence suggests that they can show more than we expected. Mpitsos, Collins, and McClellan (1978) have recently demonstrated what seems to be instrumental conditioning in *Pleurobranchea*, another marine mollusk. This close relative of *Aplysia* is a carnivore which feeds on other marine animals (including its relative). Mpitsos *et al.* (1978) describe studies in which the animal receives a shock immediately after "bite–striking" for a piece of food. Figure 15.8 shows the latency to strike for food after several trials in which the shock was contingent upon the animal's response.

After 10 trials, the instrumentally conditioned animals showed a much longer latency to strike compared to the controls which received shock not contingent upon their behavior. The response also extinguished over a period of hours, as shown in Figure 15.9. This model system of instrumental conditioning may prove very valuable since the neurons mediating the "bite–strike" response can be mapped. Mpitsos and his colleagues suggest that these marine mollusks may be able to perform many kinds of associative learning provided that the response to be learned fits into the genetically programmed behavioral repertoire of the animal. They may simply be restricted in the range of associations which they can make. Their biological predispositions may consist of more rigidly determined preexisting connections compared to higher animals. But they may nevertheless be capable of making many plastic changes.

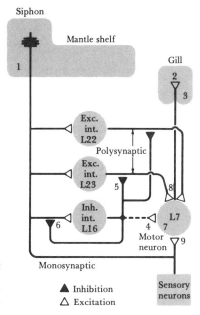

Figure 15.7
Schematic diagram showing the possible loci of plasticity in the mediation of habituation of the gill-withdrawal reflex in **Aplysia.** [*From Kandel (1976). Copyright 1976 by W. H. Freeman and Company.*]

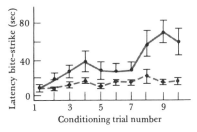

Figure 15.8
Bite–strike latencies of conditioned (solid lines) and control (dashed lines) animals. Experimental animals were given 10 conditioning trials with a 1-hour intertrial interval. [From Mpitsos, Collins, and McClellan (1978). Copyright 1978 by the American Association for the Advancement of Science.]

Moving somewhat closer to the complex human brain, Weinberger and his colleagues (Oleson, Westenberg, and Weinberger, 1972) have been studying the pupil dilation in the cat paralyzed by drugs. They present an auditory stimulus to the ear, which can be rigidly controlled, and pair it with an electric shock to the paw. The shock produces immediate dilation of the pupils, and eventually the sound does too. The size of the dilation response is measured by an infrared pupilometer.

Figure 15.10 shows the amplitude of the pupil response during habituation, sensitization, and conditioning. The upward vertical lines represent seconds, and the downward lines are the sounds and the shock. Panel (a) shows the pupillary response to the sound, and panel (b) shows the response after the sound has been presented alone for many trials. The response has clearly habituated, and no longer occurs to the sound.

The response also shows sensitization. After the cat was habituated to the tone, the experimenters began to present both the tone and the shock. For these trials, the two stimuli were alternated, not paired, so that classical conditioning did not occur. Panel (c) shows that the response to the sound pips returned during the early sensitization trials. After several sensitization trials, however, the response diminished again (panel (d)).

Following sensitization, the experimenters began to pair the two stimuli. The sounds began about $1\frac{1}{2}$ seconds before the $\frac{1}{2}$-second shock was presented. Panel (e) shows the pupillary response during early conditioning trials. Notice that the response does not begin until the shock is presented. But in later conditioning trials (panel (f)), the response begins after the onset of the sound.

This kind of plasticity is not mediated by the receptors in the ear. Ashe, Cassady, and Weinberger (1976) recorded the amplitude of the cochlear microphonic (the potential generated in the cochlea as a result of sound) and found that it failed to show consistent changes which correlated with the changes in pupil dilation during training. This is reminiscent of the lack of adaptation shown by the *Aplysia's* siphon. The plastic changes must be occurring in the central nervous system of the cat.

Oleson, Ashe, and Weinberger (1975) recorded multiple unit responses at various places in the central nervous system during discrimination training. For these trials, a tactile stimulus and a sound were used as the conditioned stimuli. The animal learned that one stimulus predicted the onset of the shock (CS +), while the other one was not followed by anthing aversive (CS −). The responses in the auditory cortex, the somatosensory cortex, and the cochlear nucleus all became larger to the CS +, and smaller to the CS − during training. But since the changes observed in these places did not clearly precede the changes in pupil dilation, they probably were not necessary for the

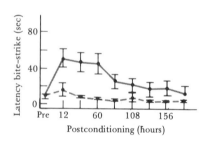

Figure 15.9
Bite–strike latencies of conditioned (solid lines) and control (dashed lines) animals during extinction trials. During these trials, the food (homogenized squid) was presented but was not paired with shock. [From Mpitsos, Collins, and McClellan (1978). Copyright 1978 by the American Association for the Advancement of Science.]

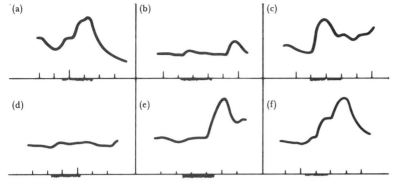

Figure 15.10
Pupillary dilation responses to white noise pips for a single cat before habituation (a), after habituation (b), during early sensitization trials (c), after repeated sensitization trials (d), early in conditioning trials (e), and after acquisition (f). Upward vertical lines indicate one second marker, downward vertical lines indicate auditory pips and shock. [From Oleson, Westenberger, and Weinberger (1972).]

acquisition of the response. They might have reflected some aspects of sensory coding, orientation, or motor activity.

This model system has a number of advantages. For example, it utilizes the intact, though paralyzed mammal. The CS and the UCS can both be rigidly controlled, and the response can be easily measured. Once the pathway which innervates the muscles which control pupil dilation are mapped precisely, it will be possible to backtrack from the motor neurons to the brain and to the receptor to find the loci of plasticity. The model can never be as elegant as the *Aplysia* model because it will be impossible to locate every neuron and synapse which participates in the learning process. But the principles are much the same.

classical conditioning of the rabbit's nictitating membrane

Another model system which shares the same advantages as the cat's pupillary response involves the somewhat esoteric nictitating membrane of the rabbit. Thompson, Berger, Patterson, and their colleagues have been exploring the potential of this model system for learning and memory studies (Thompson, 1976; Thompson, Patterson, and Berger, 1978). The model system, originally worked out by Gormezano and his co-workers (Gormezano, 1966) has one other advantage: the rabbit is immobilized, but does not need to be drugged. This is important because drugs may alter the neuronal events which accompany learning.

In this model, the experimenters use an air puff to the cornea as the UCS, and a tone for the CS. The response of the nictitating membrane (NM) to the air puff, or to the tone after conditioning, can be measured by suturing a small plastic loop to the membrane and connecting it to a recording device.

These experimenters first determined that the activity in the **abducens nucleus** (the sixth cranial nerve) is almost perfectly correlated with the amplitude of the NM response. This means that the activity in this motor nucleus is the final common pathway for the NM reflex. Figure 15.11 shows the relationship between the NM response and the multiple unit activity in the abducens nucleus, using standard scores. (Standard scores reflect the amplitude of each measure as a function of the distance from the measure's own mean.) Panel (a) shows the two responses during the 250 msec prior to the onset of the CS (pre-CS period). Panel (b) shows the responses for the 250 msec right after the onset of the CS, during training. And panel (c) shows the responses for the 250 msec after the onset of the air puff (UCS).

Notice that prior to the CS, there is very little activity in either the abducens nucleus or the NM. During the CS period, there is increasing activity in both as training proceeds. Not surprisingly, there is a great deal of activity in both as soon as the air puff is presented.

The fact that the amplitude of the two measures correlates so well is very important. It means that the activity in the abducens nucleus is contolling the NM response, and that this nucleus is the final common pathway for the response. It is somewhat analogous to the recordings taken in the motor neuron of *Aplysia*, and thus is getting a little closer to the kind of mapping which is needed to identify various loci of plasticity. The closely correlated activity in the abducens nucleus also suggests that the site of plasticity is not in the nerve—muscle junction between the axons from this nucleus and the muscles in the membrane. This was also true for the gill-withdrawal reflex in *Aplysia*.

Figure 15.11
Comparison of the development of neuronal activity in the abducens nucleus (dots) and the nictitating membrane response (bars) during conditioning. Data are computed over successive eight-trial blocks separately for (a) the pre-CS period (250 msec prior to onset of tone CS), (b) the CS period (250 msec from tone onset to air puff UCS onset), and (c) the UCS period (250 msec after UCS onset). [From Thompson (1976).]

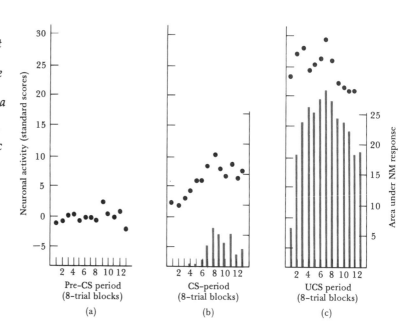

The next logical step would have been to study the responses in the nerves which feed into the abducens nucleus. Unfortunately, this pathway has not yet been mapped. So Thompson and his colleagues are working on this mapping problem, but in the meantime have decided to take a "flyer" (in their own words) and record from brain structures rather far removed from the final common pathway.

The structure which they are studying is the hippocampus, because this area has been implicated in learning and memory for some time. For example, lesions in this area produce severe deficits in long-term memory in human beings. But as we shall see later in the chapter, the precise role of this structure is still obscure.

Figure 15.12 shows the responses of the NM and the multiple unit activity in the hippocampus (area CA1) during conditioning (Berger, Alger, and Thompson, 1976). Panel (a) shows the first eight trials, and panel (b) shows the last eight trials, after conditioning had occurred.

First, notice that in panel (a) there is a very large increase in hippocampal activity after the onset of the UCS. It correlates well with the amplitude of the NM response. Second, the hippocampal activity precedes the NM response by about 30 msec. During the later trials (panel (b)), the hippocampal activity still precedes the onset of the NM response—both have moved forward in time so that they begin before the onset of the air puff.

Panel (c) shows that the NM response can occur without any activity in the hippocampus. For these trials, the air puff was presented, but no tone was used as a CS. Thus the hippocampal activity could not have been the result of motor activity. This hypothesis was unlikely anyway in view of the fact that the brain activity preceded the NM response. Panel (d) shows the later trials during which only the air puff was presented. The NM response is still occurring, and there is still no change in hippocampal activity.

Panels (e) and (f) show the first and last series of trials during which only the CS (tone) was presented. During these trials, there was no NM response and no hippocampal activity. This means that the hippocampal activity seen in the conditioned animals could not have simply been the result of sensory stimulation.

So the hippocampal activity is not the result of motor activity alone, and it is also not the result of just sensory stimulation. It develops as a result of the pairing of the two stimuli—that is, conditioning. Since it precedes the NM response by many milliseconds, there is every possibility that this brain area is involved in the beginnings of the formation of the memory trace. Since these scientists have not yet studied other brain areas, it is possible that several other areas will show similar kinds of activity as well. This model system is well on its way to providing some very valuable information about classical conditioning in the intact nervous system.

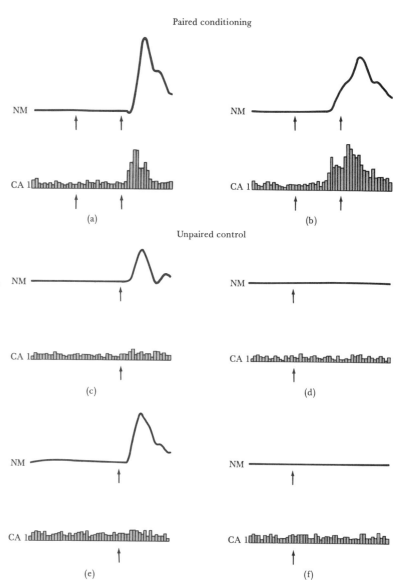

Figure 15.12
Upper trace: Average nictitating membrane (NM) response for one block of eight trials. Lower trace: Hippocampal unit poststimulus histogram (15-msec bins) for one block of eight trials. (a) First block of eight paired conditioning trials, day 1. (b) Last block of eight paired conditioning trials, day 1, after conditioning has occurred. First cursor indicates tone onset; second cursor indicates air puff onset. (c) First block of eight unpaired UCS-alone trials, day 1. (e) Last block of eight unpaired UCS-alone trials, day 2. Cursor indicates air puff onset. (d) First block of eight unpaired CS-alone trials, day 1. (f) Last block of eight unpaired CS-alone trials, day 2. Cursor indicates tone onset. Total trace length is 750 msec. [From Berger, Alger, and Thompson (1977). Copyright 1977 by the American Association for the Advancement of Science.]

learning in the isolated hippocampus Since the hippocampus seems so closely tied to learning, some scientists have taken out slices of it, put them in a medium which keeps them alive, and tried to find out if the slices could learn by themselves. This seemingly preposterous model system has provided some remarkable information about plasticity in isolated brain tissue. For example, Bliss and Lømo (1973) found that electrical stimulation of some synapses in one section of the hippocampus of the rabbit could produce an increase in excitability in cells in another section—an increase that lasted from 30 minutes to 10 hours. Following upon this work, Teyler and his colleagues (Teyler and Alger, 1976, 1978) found that a slice of hippocampus can display several types of plasticity.

Figure 15.13 shows the hippocampus in the rodent brain and the various cellular layers within the structure. Teyler and Alger stimulated a section of the slice electrically, and then recorded spike activity and EPSP amplitude in the same section.

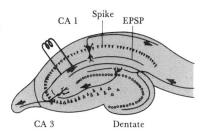

habituation. Repeated stimulation of the cells in the dentate produced habituation. The spiking and EPSP activity gradually declined. But repeated stimulation of CA1 or CA3 produced only potentiation—the amplitudes of the responses grew larger. Thus perhaps it is only part of the hippocampus, the dentate, which shows plastic changes similar to those seen in habituation.

long-term potentiation. The cells in the slice also show another plastic phenomenon—**long-term potentiation**. After a series of low frequency stimuli, the spike and EPSP activity increase, and remain high for hours. Figure 15.14 (top) shows the increase for the cells in the dentate, CA1 and CA3. These increases in activity lasted as long as the slice did, about 6 hours. It is interesting that the dentate cells exhibited this long-term potentiation in spite of the fact that they also showed habituation during the stimulus train. Figure 15.14 (bottom) shows the changes in cell responses after each stimulus in a stimulus train which results in potentiation. Notice that the cells in CA1 and CA3 are showing increases in activity, but that those in the dentate are showing habituation. The significance of this dual kind of plasticity in the dentate cells is not clear yet.

This kind of long-term potentiation may very well be involved in long-term memory. Although the cellular basis for this phenomenon is not understood, there are suggestions that a brief stimulus train, such as the kind which produces long-term potentiation, can produce changes in the size of synapses. Van Harreveld and Fifkova (1975) found that the neurotransmitter glutamate was released from some active nerve endings. Glutamate can cause a swelling in the dendritic spine, thereby reducing resistance to electric current. If the resistance between synapse and dendrite is reduced, the entire synapse may become more efficient, and the same amount of neurotransmitter coming from the presynaptic cell would be capable of producing a larger EPSP in the dendrite. This is only a hypothesis at the moment, since it is not certain that glutamate is used as a transmitter in the hippocampus, or that it can produce postsynaptic swelling there. However, Van Harreveld and Fifkova (1975) have presented evidence that hippocampal spines do become enlarged following hippocampal stimulation of the type which produces long-term potentiation.

The slice technique has several advantages over some of the other

Figure 15.13
Schematic diagram of a hippocampal lamella showing the dentate, CA3 and CA1 subdivisions. Also shown is a stimulating electrode in the Schaffer collaterals and recording electrodes in the cell body layer of CA1 (to record extracellular population spikes) and in the dendritic layer of CA1 (to record extracellular population EPSPs.) Arrows indicate direction of normal impulse travel in axon tracts. [From Teyler and Alger (1978).]

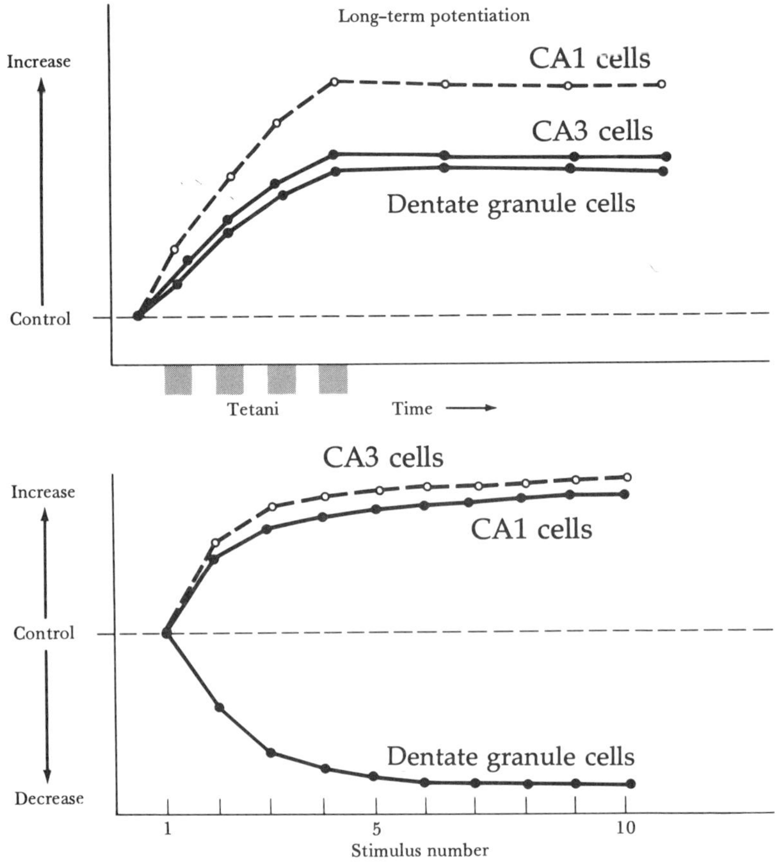

Figure 15.14
(Top) Summary figure showing increased response amplitude following a series of tetanic stimulations. This long-term potentiation has been shown to remain for long periods of time and is seen at all three fields of the hippocampus. (Bottom) Summary figure showing the response of the hippocampal subfields to repetitive stimuli similar to those used to establish LTP. During the repetitive stimulation, the dentate gyrus cells show a response decrement whereas the CA3 and CA1 cells show a potentiation. [From Teyler and Alger (1978).]

model systems (and also some disadvantages). For example, there is no contamination from drugs, since the experimenters don't use any. Also it is possible to run new experiments on each new slice from the brain of a single animal. The slices are genetically identical, but the effects of experience are not built up. Each new slice is "naive." The amount of control which can be effected in this *in vitro* technique is truly mind boggling compared to that which is common in intact animals. But of course this technique cannot study actual behavior, only neuronal activity in isolation.

---

summary
Model Systems

The use of model systems to study learning and memory is increasing rapidly. They have the advantage of better control over stimuli and clearer measurement of responses. Because they lack many of the complicating variables of intact, behaving animals (such as varying motor sequences), they are better able to isolate the factors mediating the simpler forms of plasticity. It is likely (or at least hoped) that complex learning is based on some of these simple forms of plasticity.

In this section we discussed four different model systems. These included plastic changes in *Aplysia*, the cat's pupillary reflex, the rabbit's nictitating membrane, and the isolated hippocampus.

The marine mollusk *Aplysia* can show several forms of plasticity at the neural level and at the behavioral level. One kind of neural plasticity is called *posttetanic facilitation*. When the animal's connective is electrically stimulated, the cell which receives monosynaptic input from the stimulated axons begins to fire faster. It continues to fire faster for several minutes after the stimulation, thus showing a plastic change. The animal also shows habituation of a behavior—the gill-withdrawal reflex. When the siphon is repeatedly stimulated tactually, the gill-withdrawal reflex gradually declines. Since the neurons which mediate this sensory motor pathway have been mapped, it was possible to isolate the loci of the plastic changes. Various sites were eliminated, such as fatigue in the gill muscle, and sensory adaptation in the siphon. The plastic changes occur mainly at the synapse between the sensory neuron and the motor neuron.

The paralyzed cat's pupillary reflex is another good model used to study various forms of plasticity. A shock to the paw elicits pupil dilation, and this response can be rapidly conditioned to a stimulus such as a tone. As in *Aplysia*, the site of plasticity is not at the level of the receptor. The amplitude of the cochlear microphonic failed to show any consistent increases or decreases even though the cat's pupillary response was gradually becoming larger to the tone during training.

Classical conditioning in the rabbit's nictitating membrane (NM) is a good model system for a number of reasons. The rabbits do not have to be drugged, and the final common pathway which mediates the response has been worked out. An air puff to the cornea serves as the UCS, a tone is the CS, and the flicking of the membrane is the response. Multiple unit activity in the *abducens nucleus* is almost perfectly correlated with the amplitude of the response, so that this nucleus represents the final common pathway for the membrane response. Multiple unit activity in the hippocampus precedes the activity in the NM response by many milliseconds, suggesting that this structure is intimately involved in the initial formation of the memory trace. Since the hippocampal activity does not appear when only the tone is presented, or when only the air puff is presented, the activity is clearly not the result of motor or sensory activity alone. It is a correlate of pairing the two stimuli during conditioning.

Plastic phenomena can also be studied in a slice of the isolated hippocampus. Repeated electrical stimulation of the dentate cells produces habituation in spiking activity and in the amplitude of population EPSPs. This habituation does not appear in the cells of CA1 or CA3. The cells of all three areas display *long-term potentiation*, however. When a brief train of low-frequency electrical stimulation is applied to the cells, they continue to show increased activity for several hours. This model has the advantage of rigid control over many variables, and also offers the possibility of finely detailed mapping.

These are only a few of the model systems which are being used to study plasticity. In general, they all lean heavily on the simpler forms of behavioral modification with experience. But the types of plasticity seen in these systems probably form the foundation for the complex plastic responses in the human brain.

learning and memory in the intact, behaving animal It would be more rewarding for all of us if we could arrange this section of the chapter into various brain areas, and mention the role that each plays in the process of learning and memory, much like we did for the sensory systems. But this area has not advanced to that point yet. Instead we will present basic questions which scientists ask about learning and memory, and discuss the approaches which are being used to answer them. These questions are:

(1) Where are memories located?
(2) What changes in the brain are correlated with learning?
(3) What events can disrupt the formation of memories?
(4) What events can modulate memory formation?

where are memories located? This was one of the very first questions which scientists asked about memory, and it still does not have a definite answer. Two opposing hypotheses are (1) that memories are stored diffusely throughout the entire brain, and (2) that memories are stored in discrete neural networks within sensory or other areas which contributed to the coding of the sensory events which were important in the learning process.

The application of the lesion technique might seem eminently capable of deciding whether one of these two hypotheses is correct, or whether the answer lies in some compromise between the two. But after many years of performing lesion studies, Lashley made the comment that appears at the beginning of this chapter. Based on his findings, he formulated two principles: the **principle of equipotentiality**, and the **principle of mass action**. Both of them still make sense some 30 years later.

the principle of equipotentiality. Lashley trained rats to make a visual discrimination between a lighted and a dark alley. The rats were rewarded for running down the lighted alley, and punished with shock for running toward the dark. Then he made lesions in various parts of the rats' brains.

He found that the only lesion which seriously disrupted their later performance on this task was one in the visual cortex. This was the only part of the brain that was necessary for the retention of the task. Removal of a part of the visual cortex did not seriously disrupt retention. Which part of this area of the brain was removed did not seem to matter.

Thus Lashley concluded that the neurons within a given sensory area are all capable of participating in memory formation for a task which uses that sensory system. All the neurons in that area show equipotentiality in the sense that they all contribute to the retention of the task. For tasks learned in another sensory modality, the neurons which participate would be located in the area of cortex devoted to that sensory system.

Lashley's lesion studies would appear to support the view that memories are discretely located within a sensory area of the brain (although diffusely spread around within that area). But lesioning the visual cortex of the rat's brain might have simply interfered with the rat's ability to perceive the visual stimulus, so that the rat could just not perform the discrimination anymore. It might not have destroyed the memory itself. The memories might have been diffusely represented throughout the brain, including the visual cortex. Thus, although Lashley's studies certainly provide proof for the principle of equipotentiality, they do not allow us to decide between the two hypotheses mentioned at the beginning of this section.

the principle of mass action. Lashley also trained rats on complex maze tasks in which the rat can utilize information from many different sensory modalities. It can use visual cues, somatosensory cues, kinesthetic cues, and perhaps even auditory cues. After the rats were trained, he lesioned some part of the rats' brains. His conclusion from these studies was that the *amount* of cortex which remained was more important than the location of the lesion. Rats which had a great deal of cortex removed performed poorly on retention tests compared to rats which had only a small amount removed, regardless of where the lesions were placed.

Superficially this study might suggest that memories are stored diffusely throughout the brain. But it is also possible that the different sensory elements of the task were stored individually in the different sensory areas. When any one of these elements was removed by the lesion, the rat was left with fewer cues to perform the task correctly. Larger lesions would destroy more of these memories.

cross-modal transfer of information. One kind of study which can help to settle this issue is a study involving **cross-modal transfer of information**. (See Figure 15.15.) It is possible for humans and some higher primates to learn a task originally using visual cues, but to perform well on a retention task which provides only somatosensory cues. For example, if you learn that there is a piece of candy under a circle, but not under a square, then you will visually choose the circle to obtain the reward. You will still choose the circle even when you are only allowed to feel the shapes of the circle and square with your fingers. This means that the learning which you accomplished with visual cues can be retrieved using somatosensory cues. Animals with less complex nervous systems cannot usually do this.

If memories are stored diffusely in the brains of all animals, then why can't the rat perform a task like this? One reason why they cannot may be that memories are not stored diffusely, at least not memories for simple tasks using only one sensory modality. Rats may not be able to recall the visually acquired task using somatosensory cues be-

Figure 15.15
Cross-modal transfer of information. A human being who learns to select a circle over a square using visual cues, can easily perform the task later using somatosensory cues.

learning and memory in the intact, behaving animal **475**

cause they have very few fiber connections between their sensory areas. Humans and higher primates have many of these fiber connections, so cross-modal transfer of information is much less difficult (Geschwind, 1965).

These cross-modal transfer studies suggest that memories are not stored diffusely in the entire brain. But the truth is we really have no adequate method to determine where memories are located. The use of lesion studies has some disadvantages and some scientists believe that the technique will never be able to provide any valuable information relative to this question (Isaacson, 1976; Lynch, 1976). For example, the behavior which is measured after the lesion reflects performance, not necessarily memory. An animal might seem to "forget" the shock experience in the dark side of the box for a number of reasons. Perhaps it has become much more sensitive to light as a result of the lesion, so its motivational and sensory systems have been altered. Or it might seem to remember the task even better because its motor activity has slowed down. On tasks which involve a food reward, lesions which affect the incentive value of the food might easily influence later performance. Thus it is extremely difficult to separate loss of memory from some change in motivation, sensory coding, emotionality, or motor activity.

Lynch (1976) points out that the lesion studies have yet one other problem in interpretation. Judging from the results of their axon "sprouting" experiments, which we discussed in the last chapter, a lesion in one part of the brain is likely to produce altered connections and abnormal activity in other, nonlesioned, parts. Thus any change in performance may have little to do with the structure which was lesioned.

A last problem with these studies is that it is not easy to tell the difference beween a loss of memory and a loss in the ability to retrieve that memory. Some studies have shown that brain lesions which are followed by performance deficits in learning tasks are related to retrieval. For instance, Meyer, Horel, and Meyer (1963) ablated the striate areas in cats, and the lesion produced a loss in the ability to perform a visually guided placement task. Months later, the animals were given amphetamines, and their memory miraculously returned. Perhaps the amphetamines facilitated the retrieval of a memory that had become difficult to retrieve because of the lesion.

We are left with a perplexing and important question which we are not yet able to answer. At least some of the evidence which we have discussed suggests that memories are diffusely stored within a particular sensory region, but discretely stored between sensory regions. Memories in one sensory area are available to the other sensory areas by means of the fiber connections between them, at least in the higher primates.

Even though we can't say for certain where memories are stored, we can certainly begin to isolate the brain areas which play critical roles in the process of their formation. The sensory areas which perceive the input relevant to the learning task will play a large role. But the hippocampus apparently plays a unique role in the formation of different kinds of memories which are formed through the use of all the sensory systems.

the role of the hippocampus. Interest in the involvement of the hippocampus in learning and memory was spurred by an individual called H.M. This now historical figure in the annals of neuroscience had severe epilepsy. When drugs failed to provide relief, he underwent a radical bilateral medial temporal lobe resection, which included the hippocampus. The operation was successful in that it drastically reduced the frequency of convulsions. But H.M. was left with a remarkable deficit in memory (Milner, 1970).

H.M. can carry on conversations, so there is nothing wrong with his short-term memory. He can do arithmetic problems, remember a span of digits for a few minutes, and can even repeat them backward. He also can remember events which occurred before the operation. But he has been unable to learn anything new since the surgery.

Psychologists have long made the distinction between short-term memory (STM) and long-term memory (LTM). At a party, for example, you might be introduced to someone and be able to remember the person's name during a brief conversation. But later on in the evening, you could easily forget the name. The information was not retained in LTM. Many scientists hypothesize that the physiological substrates for STM and LTM are different. Possibly, as Hebb (1949) proposed, STM involves changes in neural firing patterns, but LTM must involve some physical changes in the patterns of connections between neurons.

Several other patients had been given the same kind of surgery, and they exhibited the profound memory deficit only when the lesion included the hippocampus. Thus this structure began to interest quite a number of scientists. In the last section, we saw how activity in this area might be the first to change during classical conditioning of the rabbit's nictitating membrane.

One would expect that hippocampal lesions in animals would produce striking memory problems as well, but this does not appear to be the case. These lesioned animals are typically able to acquire a variety of new habits—something H.M. could not do. But hippocampal lesions in animals do produce some deficits, particularly on spatial problems.

For example, Jarrard (1978) used a circular maze which had eight different food wells located in various places to test spatial abilities of rats with hippocampal lesions. Some animals received the lesions after they had been trained, and some were lesioned before they underwent training in this spatial task.

Figure 15.16 shows a comparison of the control animals trained before or after a sham lesion, and the lesioned rats (panels (a) and (b)). The hippocampal lesioned animals performed poorly regardless of whether they had learned the task before or after the operation. This suggests that the lesion produced deficits in both the ability to perform tasks learned before the lesion, as well as deficits in the ability to acquire new tasks. This experiment alone would not be able to say

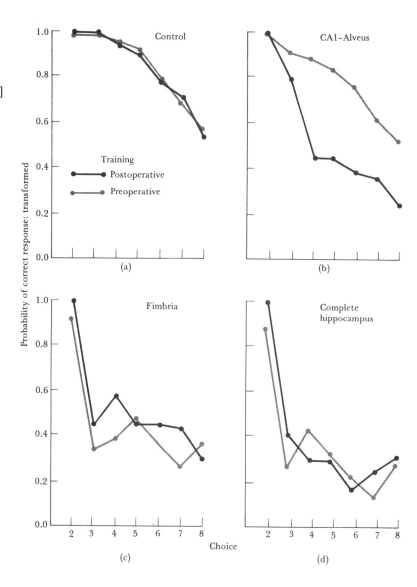

Figure 15.16
Probability of correct response on choices 2–8 for groups after preoperative and postoperative training. [From Jarrard (1978).]

very much about the role of the hippocampus in animals, however, because the animals may simply have been incapacitated in some way, and thus could not perform much of anything after the operation. But Jarrard also lesioned the CA1 and alveus alone in some animals which had been trained either before or after the operation. This lesion interrupted connections between the hippocampus and the entorhinal cortex.

Figure 15.16 shows the performance of these animals on their retention test. They had difficulty performing in this maze if they were first exposed to it after the lesion. But if they had learned the task before the lesion, then they performed about as well as the control animals. Thus the lesion did not interfere with any behavioral capacity to perform in the maze. Nor did it interfere with memories stored before the lesion. It apparently interfered with the ability to acquire new memories.

Some scientists propose that the hippocampus serves different functions in animals and humans, so that the study of animals with hippocampal lesions will not tell us very much about its role in human learning and memory. One difference between animals and humans is of course language, so this hypothesis is quite possible. But in any case, we must conclude that the role of the hippocampus, in animals, or in humans, is simply not clear yet. Researchers are convinced that the structure is involved in some way—it keeps coming up again and again in many different kinds of studies. We saw in the last section that activity in the hippocampus preceded the NM response during classical conditioning in the rabbit. The isolated hippocampus can even show some forms of plasticity when it is lying in a dish. In the next section, we will see that it undergoes many biochemical changes after learning experiences. Much more research, using novel approaches, will have to be done before we will have a clear picture of the role of this important structure.

what changes in the brain are correlated with learning?

In the section on model systems, we saw that a variety of electrophysiological changes occur during learning. During pupillary conditioning in the cat, for example, a large number of brain areas showed increased firing patterns. In the rabbit, CS-related activity in the hippocampus increased just before the nictitating membrane response appeared. These model systems hold the best hope for mapping the electrophysiological changes which occur during learning, partly because the animal is immobilized, and partly because it is possible to map the neurons which mediate the response (final common pathway) and those which mediate the stimulus input.

In this section we will explore the neurochemical changes which occur after an animal has learned. Some of these changes may have something to do with the structural changes which are believed to occur when a long-term memory is formed. But many of them may simply be related to the stress of learning, or perhaps to motivational or emotional differences between an animal that has learned and one that has not. Thus this section will not be able to nail down precisely which changes are due to learning per se. But as we discussed earlier in the chapter, this distinction may turn out not to be crucially important.

changes in RNA and protein synthesis. A wide variety of studies have found changes in both qualitative and quantitative measures of RNA and protein synthesis in animals which have learned a task. For example, Hydén and his colleagues (Hydén and Egyházi, 1962) trained rats to walk on a tightrope, and compared their brains to animals that had had vestibular stimulation in an apparatus which mechanically altered their orientation. The trained rats showed an increase in the amount of RNA in brain cell nuclei.

In another series of studies, Hydén (1973) explored protein synthesis activity in the brains of rats. These rats were trained on a "transfer of handedness" task in which they were forced to use their nonpreferred paw to reach for food. At different times during the acquisition of this task, they injected radioactively labeled leucine (an amino acid) into the rats. By looking at the amount of radioactivity which was incorporated into the protein fractions of brain tissue in different areas, they were able to estimate the amount of protein synthesis which was going on in various brain areas at different times during the learning process. The interesting conclusion from this study was that during the acquisition of the task, the labeled leucine was incorporated more and more in the cortex. But in the hippocampus, the amount of incorporation dropped steadily during acquisition. This study suggests that the rate of protein synthesis is highest in the hippocampus during the early stages of learning. But as the task is learned, and the animals become proficient, the rate of protein synthesis is faster in the cortex. It is very tempting to use these kinds of results to support the view that the hippocampus is somehow involved in the transfer of STM to LTM, and that it plays its role during the early phases of learning.

Glassman and his colleagues (Rees *et al.*, 1974) have also found changes in RNA and proteins after training. They used a task in which the animals were trained to avoid a shock when a buzzer comes on by jumping onto a platform. Controls for this learning experience included animals that remained in their home cage, and animals that were exposed to the shock, buzzer, and apparatus, but which were not allowed to learn to avoid the shock by jumping onto a platform. Thirty minutes before the 15-minute training period, the animals were injected with either radioactively labeled uridine (a precursor for RNA), or labeled lysine (a precursor for protein).

Examination of the brains of the animals at various times after training revealed that the amount of uridine incorporation decreased with time, suggesting that the rate of RNA synthesis was declining after training. But the amount of lysine incorporation increased. Since RNA codes for protein, this timing makes sense. Perhaps the new RNA was coding for the new protein synthesis.

neurochemical correlates of learning in developing animals. As we discussed in the last chapter, the period of development is a time of rapid learning. Although the brain changes which occur during this period may partly reflect the ontogenetic process, they may also tell us something about what happens during learning. Rose and his colleagues (Rose, Hambley, and Haywood, 1976) make the point that the biochemical changes categorized as developmental plasticity are probably similar to those involved in learning. One advantage to studying plasticity resulting from experience in the developing organism is that those biochemical changes are likely to be larger, and thus easier to detect.

The rats reared in enriched environments (and which undoubtedly learned more) showed a number of biochemical differences compared to those reared in isolated environments. In particular, they showed a higher RNA/DNA ratio, which probably indicated that the enriched rats were synthesizing more RNA, at least during the early stages of enriched rearing (Bennett, 1976). Increases in the total amount of RNA was seen even after only 4 days of enriched rearing. The enriched rats also showed increases in total acetylcholinesterase activity.

Since the enriched rats differed from the isolated ones in many ways, other than the fact that the enriched rats probably learned more, it is not possible to say that these brain changes are due to learning. But this is true of virtually all the studies which we have described. It is possible that any animal that learns something experiences more stress than one that does not learn, simply because the task of learning is stressful. Greenough (1976) argues that the study of animals which have been reared in complex environments can tell us something about the enduring effects of differential experience, not just the transient changes in biochemistry or electrophysiology that accompany and immediately follow the acquisition process. Since the changes in synaptic connectivity are likely to be too small to detect after a single learning experience, then large amounts of differential experience may be necessary to show the structural changes which are presumed to underlie learning and memory.

Bateson, Rose, and their colleagues (Rose, Hambley, and Haywood, 1976) have been studying the imprinting phenomenon (shown in Figure 15.17) in chicks as a means to determine the biochemical changes which accompany and immediately follow learning. Since these chicks are very young and growing rapidly, the changes resulting from the imprinting experience are superimposed over biochemical changes associated with development. But they too have found that

Figure 15.17
During the first few days of life, the chick can be imprinted onto any stimulus which is moving, such as a model of its mother, a moving football, a human being. It can also be imprinted onto a flashing light.

alterations in RNA and protein synthesis are typically associated with this form of learning.

In one set of studies (Bateson, Rose, and Horn, 1973) they exposed different groups of chicks to an imprinting stimulus which consisted of a flashing light. Normally chicks will learn to follow whatever they see moving during a sensitive period of development which occurs during the first few days of life. This moving stimulus is usually the mother, which is why baby chicks are often observed walking in a row behind the mother. But the chicks can also be imprinted onto a flashing light (or a moving football, or a human being).

On day 1, some chicks were exposed to 20 minutes of flashing lights, others to 60, and still others to 120 or 240 minutes. On day 2, all of these chicks were injected with radioactively labeled uracil (a precursor for RNA), and then exposed to a flashing light for 60 minutes. The experimenters reasoned that the chicks which had been exposed to the shortest periods on day 1, would have the most to learn on day 2, and that they would show the largest amount of incorporation. The chicks which had been exposed for several hours on day 1 would not have very much to learn on day 2; they should show less incorporation, which would reflect less RNA synthesis.

This is exactly what they found. The fact that all of the chicks received identical sensory stimulation on day 2 suggests that the difference in uracil incorporation was not due to a difference in the amount of sensory stimulation. Rather it was a function of how much the chicks learned during the 1-hour exposure on day 2. It is an interesting sidelight that the highest incorporation occurred in the forebrain roof, a structure which contains the hippocampus.

methodological problems. Neurochemical studies are not immune from methodological problems. The behavioral controls, for example, are not able to clearly isolate learning from other variables. Many, or perhaps most of the biochemical changes may be due to factors other than learning, particularly the stress of learning. But biochemical studies labor under other difficulties as well. For example, when a radioactively labeled precursor is injected into an animal, it is probably not distributed as evenly over the nervous sytem as one might hope. So the labeled precursor may accumulate in particular areas of the brain, or in particular cellular compartments. Increased incorporation may thus be reflecting more about where the labeled precursor accumulates, than where there is the most RNA or protein synthesis.

Despite these problems, the weight of the evidence clearly suggests that learning is accompanied by increases in RNA and protein synthesis. The significance of these findings is the subject of the next section.

the significance of neurochemical changes. Most scientists agree that memory involves changes in synaptic connectivity. It is possible that synapses are selectively made more efficient, or less efficient. It is also possible that new synapses are formed, or old ones lost. In the process, dendrites might be growing or regressing, and axons might be sprouting or losing some of their previously formed sprouts. Presumably neurochemical events which accompany learning are responsible for these changes in connectivity. Certainly changes in synaptic connectivity would require proteins, and perhaps this is where the new protein synthesis comes in. Other scientists have proposed that the changes in RNA and protein synthesis have quite a different function however.

Dunn (1976) hypothesizes that the neurochemical events which have thus far been associated with learning reflect the stress of learning, rather than the formation of memory. He points out that the changes which have been observed are extremely widespread, and that they might thus be facilitating synaptic connectivity changes practically everywhere in the brain. He has become particularly interested in the role that ACTH might play, the pituitary hormone that activates the adrenal glands. This hormone is known to increase RNA and protein synthesis, and perhaps the increases seen in learning animals are due to ACTH. Support for this view comes from studies of learning in animals which have had their pituitary glands removed. These animals display poor learning performance, but if they are injected with ACTH, their performance improves (deWied, 1974).

Dunn proposes that the novelty of a new experience is a stressful event, and that the entire brain shows metabolic changes in response. These neurochemical events are not without their value however. They produce a neural environment in which plastic changes might occur more readily. Presumably, the plastic changes would occur in those areas in which the electrophysiological changes are occurring—enhanced by the neurochemical events which accompanied the stress.

Another hypothesis to explain the significance of the neurochemical events, which is almost the polar opposite of Dunn's, is that the macromolecules which are formed not only facilitate memory, but actually *are* the memory. In an extreme viewpoint, this might mean that a separate and distinct kind of RNA or protein is formed for each and every experience that produces a memory. Ungar (1970) proposed a variety of this kind of theory on the basis of his "transfer of memory" studies.

One example of this kind of study used mice which had been trained in the passive avoidance shuttlebox. The animals initially ran into the dark side of the box, but after receiving shocks for doing so, they began to remain on the lighted side. Extracts of brain tissue from the trained and untrained donor mice were injected into naive mice. The behavior of these recipient mice in the shuttlebox was then observed.

Figure 15.18 shows the results from this study. Notice that the ex-

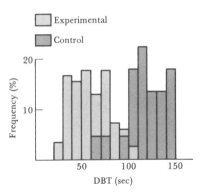

Figure 15.18
Distribution of activity in 110 rat brain extracts. Abscissa, time in dark box (DBT) in seconds; ordinate, frequency in percent, among groups of mice injected with 84 extracts from trained rats (dark columns) and 26 extracts from untrained rats (lighter columns). [From Ungar (1970).]

perimental mice (those injected with extracts from trained mice) spent much less time in the dark side of the box compared to the control mice, even though they had never been trained. This study suggests that some chemical factor which was produced in the brains of the trained mice was transferred to the untrained mice.

Using the amount of time spent in the lighted side of the compartment as a bioassay, Ungar and his associates were able to isolate the active chemical ingredient in the brain extract. The substance is a polypeptide composed of 15 amino acids. Ungar coined the term **scotophobin** for this substance (from the Greek words for "dark" and "fear").

Ungar's theory of how memories might be coded in the brain proposes that the brain is composed of functionally different neural pathways, many of which are genetically programmed and laid down very early in development. Each of these pathways would have a specific and unique protein which would be synthesized during use. When two pathways were simultaneously stimulated by experience, such as might happen during classical conditioning of a tone and a shock, the synaptic junctions between the two pathways would be strengthened, and a new pathway would be formed—one which reflected the combination of the two environmental events and hence the learning. At the newly created junction, the two unique proteins from each of the pathways would combine to form another "connector molecule," which would encode the connection between the two pathways. Presumably, it is this connector molecule that is being transferred from the brains of trained animals into naive ones.

Although the transfer of memory paradigm holds promise, there has been a great deal of dispute over the results from these studies (Gaito, 1974). Sometimes the effect is obtained, and other times it is not, so the nature of the chemical transfer is still obscure. The studies have been criticized on a variety of grounds. For example, the recipient mice in the previous experiment might have done better on the task simply because they were less sensitive to light, not because they had received an injection of a substance which was able to form new and specific connections between previously existing pathways. Also, the trained mice probably produced chemicals that were related to stress (such as ACTH) and these are known to improve learning performance.

Despite these difficulties in interpretation, Gaito (1974) concludes that the effect is genuine. But it is still too early to say exactly what the effect is, or how it promotes learning.

what events can disrupt the formation of memories? Assuming that the formation of memories takes a little time and, as a student, you are probably well aware of this fact, then it should be possible to disrupt that formation. The events that can disrupt it can tell us two things about memory formation. First, they can shed light on the question of how much time is required for STM to transform into LTM. Second, the kinds of events which are capable of disrupting memory formation can tell us something about which events are important for the process. Two of the amnestic agents which are most commonly used are **electroconvulsive shock** (ECS) and drugs which inhibit protein synthesis.

ECS and retrograde amnesia. ECS was first used as a treatment for severe mental illness. Although no one knew quite why the treatment worked, it seemed to promote rational behavior in some patients. But many of them seemed to exhibit a loss of memory after the treatment —not just for the treatment itself, but often for events which immediately preceded the ECS. This kind of memory loss is called **retrograde amnesia**. ECS is now much less used in the treatment of mental illness since further research showed that it is really only effective for severe depression, and since drugs are now available which are less dramatic but more effective. But ECS has become an important tool in the study of memory consolidation.

A typical kind of experiment using ECS would involve training an animal in some task, and then administering the ECS. There are several ways to do this, but one might be to attach electrodes to the animal's ears and administer electrical current until the animal has a convulsive seizure. Later, when the animal is tested on the task, it performs as if it had never experienced it before.

An early study which used ECS to investigate retrograde amnesia varied the time interval between the end of training and the application of the shock. Duncan (1949) trained rats to avoid a shock by running from the dark side of a compartment to the lighted side. The rats were given a single trial in the box each day for 18 days, and after each trial they were given ECS. But in this study the amount of time which elapsed between the end of training each day and the application of the ECS varied between 20 seconds and 14 hours.

Figure 15.19 shows the results. Those animals that received the ECS immediately after training did not learn very much each day. They continued to remain in the dark side of the box. But those animals which received the ECS an hour or more after the training experience performed quite well.

From this study it would be tempting to conclude that the memory consolidation process is only vulnerable to disruption during the first hour after training. After that, it does not matter whether the firing patterns in the brain are radically altered, presumably because the new synaptic conditions have already been formed. But more recent work with ECS has demonstrated that the amount of retrograde amnesia very much depends upon the intensity of the shock, and the area of the brain which is stimulated.

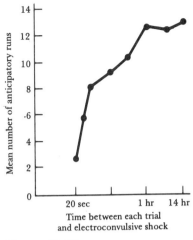

Figure 15.19
The behavior of rats trained to run from the dark side to the lighted side of a two-chambered box, but which received ECS at varying intervals after training. [*From Duncan (1949).*]

Gold, Macri, and McGaugh (1973) trained rats on a simple passive avoidance task and then administered one of two shock levels to one of two different areas of the brain. Figure 15.20 shows their results. The vertical axis is the difference between the rat's latency score on the first test, and on the second test (after the shock). The lower the difference score, the less the rats remembered.

The rats which received the 2 mA shock to the frontal cortex only showed retrograde amnesia when the shock was applied immediately after the training. If the experimenters waited only 5 seconds, the rats showed excellent memory for the task. The higher shock level (4 mA) produced retrograde amnesia even if the experimenters waited 30 seconds after training. The second graph shows that direct electrical stimulation of the posterior cortex is effective in producing retrograde anmnesia even when it is applied several minutes after training. A third group in this study received a 1 mA shock to either the frontal or posterior cortex, and none of these animals showed any retrograde amnesia, presumably because the current wasn't high enough.

This study clearly demonstrates that retrograde amnesia is quite a relative matter. It depends upon the amount of current which is used to stimulate the brain and also on where the brain is stimulated. Thus it is impossible to conclude that memory consolidation takes a specified amount of time (e.g., 1 hour), after which it is over. But it is clear that the process of memory consolidation is time dependent, and that the process can be disrupted by drastically altering the firing patterns in the brain.

protein synthesis inhibitors and retrograde amnesia. The studies which use protein synthesis inhibitor drugs to produce retrograde amnesia have basically come to the same conclusion about the time dependency of memory consolidation. Retrograde amnesia produced by these kinds of drugs is partly dependent upon the dose, and also on the amount of time which elapses between the end of training and the injection. For example, Ungerer (1973) trained mice to press a lever for a food re-

Figure 15.20
Median retention scores for crossing into a shock compartment after training on a one-trial inhibitory (passive) avoidance task and then receiving either frontal or posterior cortex stimulation at various intensities and training-treatment intervals. The retention scores are based on the difference between latencies to cross on the training and test trials. Note that the lengths of the RA gradients vary directly with the intensity of the stimulation. [From Gold et al. (1973). Copyright 1973 by the American Association for the Advancement of Science.]

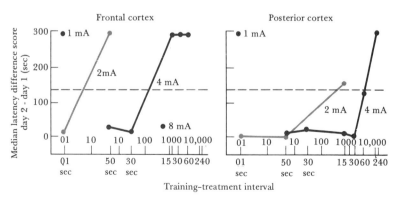

ward, and then injected them with **acetoxycycloheximide (AXM)**, a protein synthesis inhibitor, 3, 30, 60, or 180 minutes after training. Figure 15.21 shows the results.

When the drug was injected 3 minutes after training, there was a substantial reduction in the animals' performance when tested 6 days later. But when the drug was administered later after training, then the animals performed much better on their retention test.

Studies such as this suggest that protein synthesis is involved in the formation of LTM. However, one of the problems with studies which use drugs to inhibit various steps in metabolism is that they generally produce illness or general debilitation as well. Quartermain and his colleagues (Quartermain and Botwinick, 1975; Quartermain, 1976) have devised a good experimental paradigm to control for these illness effects. They first inject the animals with the drug (or saline for control groups), and then train them 30 minutes later. In their studies the task consists of training the animals to go to either the right side or the left side of a maze to avoid shock, or to obtain food. During one kind of retention test, the animals are retrained to go to the same side. Animals which have retained the information learned during the first training session can relearn the task quite quickly. But animals which learn more slowly on the retention test might simply be sick. So these scientists then test them on another maze, in which the correct choice is the opposite one from the one that they learned first. For this reversal test, prior learning (and remembering) is detrimental. Thus animals which remember the task from the first training session do worse because their previous learning is a source of proactive interference. If the drugged animals do better, it shows that (1) they do not remember the first training session, and (2) they are not so sick that they can't learn or perform much of anything.

Using the protein synthesis inhibitor **cycloheximide**, they found that the injection was indeed producing a true amnesia. Table 15.1 shows the results (as the mean number of trials to criterion) for the cycloheximide-injected and saline-injected animals.

Studies using protein synthesis inhibitors thus show that memory consolidation is time dependent, and they suggest that protein synthesis is important for the formation of memories. By themselves, they would not be able to tell us whether protein synthesis is absolutely necessary for the formation of memories, however; for example, amnestic agents (ECS as well) might be affecting the ability to retrieve the memory, rather than the ability to store it in the first place. Also, drugs rarely have only one specific effect. The protein synthesis inhibitors usually have a number of side effects on metabolism, any one of which might be playing a critical role in retrograde amnesia. But since other kinds of approaches to the study of plasticity have emphasized the importance of protein synthesis, these studies martial further support for the hypothesis. It now becomes important to determine what

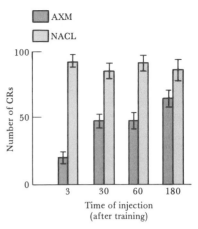

Figure 15.21
Effect of acetoxycycloheximide (AXM) on retention for a food-rewarded lever-pressing task in mice. AXM significantly impaired retention when administered 3 min after training but not when administered 30, 60, or 180 min after training. [From Ungerer (1973).]

Table 15.1

Mean trials to criterion for initial discrimination and reversal in mice treated with cycloheximide or saline[a,b]

| | N | Mean trials to criterion | | |
		Initial discrimination	Retest, same side	Retest, reversal
Shock avoidance, Y maze, brightness discrimination				
Cyclo	12	8.8	9.9	7.6
Saline	12	9.5	8.0	10.7
Appetitive incentive, T maze, spatial discrimination				
Cyclo	10	28.7	29.1	26.2
Saline	11	28.3	27.2	30.2

[a]From Quartermain (1976).

[b]Mice were trained to a criterion of 4 correct avoidances or escapes, or 17 correct appetitive discriminations. Cyclo or saline was injected 30 minutes before the initial discrimination, and animals were reversed 24 hours after initial training. Typical scores for mice retested to the side reinforced during the initial discrimination are given for comparison.

kinds of proteins are being synthesized, and how they might contribute to the plastic changes in synaptic connectivity. Research on this subject is progressing, but because the amount of new proteins produced after a learning experience is likely to be minute, the task is an arduous one.

what can modulate the formation of memories? Since it has proven so difficult to determine exactly what the biological mechanisms are which underlie the storage of memories, many scientists have begun to look at the events which can modulate information storage. McGaugh and Gold (1976), for example, prefer to view the studies on amnestic agents as clues to the events which modulate memory storage, rather than as clues to the process of memory storage itself. This viewpoint seems quite appropriate, and avoids many of the disputes over which events are actually involved in the storage of memory. It also addresses the issue of the separation of effects. For example, if the physiological changes associated with stress or motivation can be shown to modulate the formation of memory, then it becomes less useful to try to separate the effects of these so-called "extraneous variables" from the learning process. As we have discussed before, the problem of separating these effects in learning studies has always been a major one.

In this section we will examine some of the events which can modulate memory formation. The amnestic agents could certainly fall into this category, and we will see that a number of other physiological factors do also.

the role of physiological changes associated with stress. The physiological changes which accompany stressful events apparently play quite a large role in memory formation. Dunn (1976) proposed that these events were critical for the formation of memory, as we discussed earlier. This hypothesis may or may not be correct, but it is clear that these changes can have at the very least a modulating influence on memory formation.

For example, animals which have been trained in a passive avoidance task which uses footshock as the punisher will show much better retention when the shock is strong. Gold and his colleagues (Gold and McGaugh, 1978; Gold and VanBuskirk, 1975) reasoned that this effect might be due to some of the physiological changes associated with higher stress levels, and which might be able to modulate the process of memory formation. To test this hypothesis, they trained animals to avoid running into the dark side of a shuttlebox by giving them a weak footshock. Immediately after training, the animals were injected with either epinephrine, a hormone from the adrenal glands which is normally released during stress, or saline. Figure 15.22 shows their results using several different doses of epinephrine. The vertical axis measures the latency to go back into the side of the box in which they were shocked. Low retention latencies mean that the animals did not remember very much from the first experience.

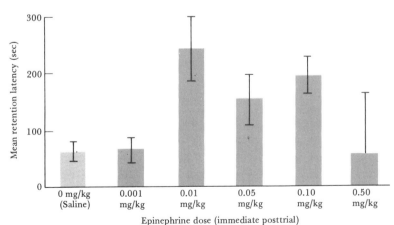

Figure 15.22
Effects of posttrial epinephrine injections on retention of an inhibitory (passive) avoidance response. At intermediate doses (0.01–0.1 mg/kg), a single performance as measured 24 hours after training + treatment. [From Gold and van Buskirk (1975).]

First, notice that the saline-injected animals did not remember the task very well, since the footshock was weak. The animals which received either very low or very high doses of epinephrine also did not remember very much. But those which received the intermediate doses after the weak footshock performed quite well on the retention test.

These scientists suggest that the hormone injections (at intermediate doses) were mimicking a memory modulating event that is normally available to the animals during stressful situations. It makes intuitive sense that it is valuable and adaptive for an animal to do a great deal of learning during a stressful situation. Too much stress, however, might inhibit learning. Indeed high doses of epinephrine act like an amnestic agent when the footshock is weak. Furthermore, while a single intermediate dose of epinephrine will enhance retention when the footshock is weak, the same dose will produce retrograde amnesia if the footshock is strong.

The way that epinephrine might be acting as a memory modulator probably has something to do with its action on the central nervous system. Gold and VanBuskirk (1978) suggest that epinephrine may be altering the activity of the central noradrenergic synapses. They found that the levels of brain norepinephrine showed a transient decrease in animals trained with strong footshock, and those trained with weak footshock plus an intermediate dose of epinephrine. They did not find the transient decrease in animals trained with low footshock, or those whose low footshock was followed by a very small dose of epinephrine.

To find out more about the role of these central noradrenergic synapses in mediating the effects of epinephrine, Gold and VanBuskirk pretreated some rats with saline, others with **propanolol** (a β-adrenergic blocking agent), and still others with **phenoxybenzamine** (an α-adrenergic blocking agent). Then half the rats were trained in a passive avoidance task using a low footshock, and the other half were trained with a high footshock. Half of each pretreatment drug group was treated with epinephrine, and the other half with saline.

Figure 15.23 shows the results when the animals were receiving a low footshock during training. First, notice that the animals which were pretreated with saline, and then given another dose of saline after training, did not perform very well on the retention test. They ran right back into the black compartment in which they had been shocked six days before. This confirms the results of the previous study in which low footshock was not very effective as a punisher. Second, notice that the animals pretreated with saline, but given a dose of epinephrine after training, showed quite good retention. The epinephrine, under low footshock training, enhanced the retention of the task.

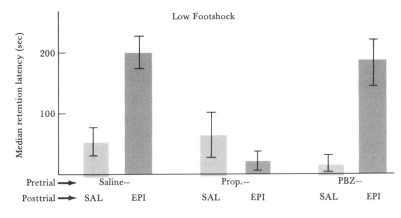

Figure 15.23
Effects of propranolol and phenoxybenzamine pretreatment on posttrial epinephrine enhancement of retention performance. Note that after training with low footshock, propranolol but not phenoxybenzamine attenuated the effect of epinephrine on retention. [From Gold and van Buskirk (1978).]

Pretreating the animals with PBZ (phenoxybenzamine) had no substantial effect on the animals' memory. But pretreatment with propranolol did. It blocked epinephrine's enhancing effects on retention. This suggests that epinephrine may be enhancing the formation of memory by acting at the β-adrenergic synapses in the central nervous system.

Figure 15.24 shows the other part of the study in which the animals were trained with a strong footshock. This time, the animals treated with saline before and after training showed quite good retention. Apparently the shock was strong enough so that the rats produced ample epinephrine of their own, and remembered the event quite well. An exogenous dose of epinephrine after training actually inhibited retention. Thus for the high footshock condition, epinephrine injections act like an amnestic agent.

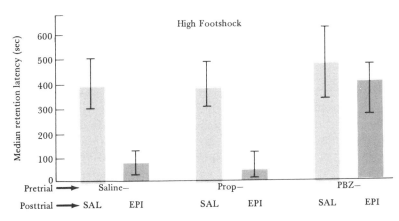

Figure 15.24
Effects of propranolol and phenoxybenzamine pretreatment on posttrial epinephrine retrograde amnesia. After training with high footshock, phenoxybenzamine but not propranolol attenuated the amnesia produced by a posttrial epinephrine injection. [From Gold and van Buskirk (1978).]

Propanolol, under these circumstances, had no effect on the pattern of results. But PBZ did. Animals pretreated with PBZ were protected from the amnestic effects of epinephrine. This suggests that epinephrine can act like an amnestic agent by acting on the α-adrenergic synapses. Thus it is possible that epinephrine (and by inference, stress) can enhance or inhibit retention of a task, depending upon the combined amount which is present in the nervous system from exogenous and endogenous sources. The enhancement appears to be due to its action on β-adrenergic synapses, and the inhibition may be due to its action on the α-adrenergic synapses.

a common mechanism underlying many amnestic agents. One of the things that many amnestic agents, such as ECS and protein synthesis inhibitors, have in common is that they all produce a great deal of stress in the organism. Gold and Sternberg (1978) reasoned that this stress might be the basis for their amnestic effects. To obtain information about this, they trained rats and mice in a passive avoidance task using a high footshock. Under these circumstances, an exogenous dose of epinephrine acts very much like other amnestic agents. But this effect can be prevented by pretreating the animals with PBZ, as we just discussed.

Gold and Sternberg pretreated the animals with either PBZ or saline, trained them, and then administered one of five different amnestic agents. These included (1) ECS directly to the cortex, (2) electrical stimulation to the amygdala which did not produce seizures, but which is still capable of producing retrograde amnesia, (3) cycloheximide (a protein synthesis inhibitor), (4) DDC (a drug which blocks the synthesis of norepinephrine and which is also known to produce retrograde amnesia, and (5) PTZ (a convulsant drug).

Table 15.2 presents the results from this study. As expected, the animals pretreated with saline, and then given one of the amnestic agents, performed poorly on their retention test. But all of the groups which were pretreated with PBZ showed excellent retention. They were protected from the effects of the amnestic agents. This suggests that these amnestic agents all share a common biological mechanism with epinephrine.

Perhaps all of these amnestic agents are acting on α-adrenergic synapses. But as is usual with drug studies, the interpretations can never be as clear cut as we might like. PBZ has a number of effects, other than blockade of α-adrenergic synapses. For example, it impairs postganglionic sympathetic transmission, and also increases the activity of tyrosine hydroxylase (Dunn and Bondy, 1974). But these findings clearly point the way for future research which emphasizes the modulating influences of stress and its neuroendocrine concomitants on memory formation.

Table 15.2
Retention performance of rats and mice in a one-trial inhibitory avoidance task[a, b]

Pretraining injection		Posttraining treatment (all are amnestic agents)	Median latency (seconds)	Animals at maximum latency (%)
Saline	(rats)	Cortical stimulation	56	27
PBZ		Cortical stimulation	180	79
Saline	(rats)	PTZ	44	27
PBZ		PTZ	180	90
Saline	(rats)	DDC	52	30
PBZ		DDC	180	70
Saline	(rats)	Amygdala stimulation	15	20
PBZ		Amygdala stimulation	180	90
Saline	(mice)	Cycloheximide	150	10
PBZ		Cycloheximide	300	90

[a] Adapted from Gold and Sternberg (1978).
[b] The latency to enter the shock compartment was used as the measure of retention (the longer the latency, the less the retention). Cutoff latency for rats was 180 seconds and for mice it was 300 seconds.

state-dependent learning. Stress may be just one factor which modifies the process of memory formation. Another factor which affects the recall process (if not the actual formation of memories) is the state in which the animal is in when it learns the material. Producing the same state during retention tests usually facilitates performance. This phenomenon is called **state-dependent learning** (Overton, 1964).

For example, Swanson and Kinsbourne (1976) studied the effects of stimulant drugs on hyperactive children. The children were given two paired associate tasks on day 1. For one set of paired associates, they were under the influence of the stimulant *Ritalin*, which is a commonly prescribed drug for hyperactivity. For the other set they were in an undrugged state. On day 2, the paired associates' lists were presented again. But this time, half the items which the children learned in the drugged state were presented after the children were again drugged. The other half were presented when the children were undrugged. The experimenters also split up the items which the children learned in the undrugged state on day 1. Thus the children's performance scores on day 2 would reflect the following experimental conditions:

(1) items learned and relearned in same state (drugged);

(2) items learned and relearned in same state (undrugged);

(3) items learned and relearned in different states (drug then placebo);

(4) items learned and relearned in different states (placebo then drug).

The state-dependent learning hypothesis would predict that the children would make fewer errors for the items learned in the same state in which they were trying to relearn them. This is exactly what they found. The children performed well when they were relearning under the drug, since stimulants generally improve learning performance in hyperactive children. (This sounds like a contradiction, but it works.) But they performed best when they were relearning the items which they had learned in the same state.

State-dependent learning effects have been found for a variety of drugs, such as alcohol and marijuana, and other centrally acting substances. Why they occur has not yet been answered. It is possible that the animal's physiological condition at the time of learning provides some important cues for the learning process, much like the stimuli in the external environment. For example, a rat might be learning to turn left toward a light, and the experimenter may think that the light is the only stimulus which the animal can use to recall the task. But clearly other stimuli are present as well. The color of the maze, the temperature of the room, the texture of the alleyway may all be significant cues when the animal tries to perform the task later. If the rat is placed in another maze, in a different room, it probably will not perform as well even if the light is still directing the way to the correct choice. State-dependent learning phenomena suggest that the internal state of the animal is also important for providing cues which can modulate the retrieval of the memory.

the role of other factors in memory modulation. So many manipulations are known to influence learning and memory that it is impossible to list them all in this section. But a few examples will highlight the range of effects.

For instance, hormones other than those which are associated with stress may be modulating learning and memory. Some workers have found that learning proceeds more readily during certain parts of the estrous cycle in rats (Sfikakis, Spyraki, Sitaris, and Varonos, 1978), so perhaps the gonadal hormones have memory modulating influences. Another example of a memory modulator is the enkephalins, which we discussed in connection with pain in Chapter 8. These substances are endogenous morphine-like compounds which produce analgesia. Rigter (1978) found that some of these substances can attenuate the effects of CO_2, which is another amnestic agent. Animals which were pretreated with one of the enkephalins were trained on a passive avoidance task, and then given CO_2. They performed better on retention tests than animals which were pretreated with saline.

The list of substances which are known to affect the learning and memory process is long. But it is not yet clear why any of them are having their effects. Some may be affecting the stress responses of the animal during or immediately after learning (like epinephrine and PBZ). Others may be affecting motivation in subtle ways. Still others may be affecting the sensory processes which are needed to learn and remember. The study of these memory modulators underscores the point that learning simply does not proceed at all without some stress, motivation and sensory stimulation. It may not be possible to isolate the events which occur during memory formation from those which occur in response to these other kinds of experiences. But it may be possible to find out how these experiences interact in the central nervous system to produce a memory of an experience.

Studies which use intact, behaving animals, and more complicated learning tasks, are necessarily "dirtier" than those which use a model system. But they have been able to provide tantalizing partial answers to some important questions which cannot be answered by the model systems. The questions which we discussed in this section included: (1) where are memories located? (2) what changes in the brain are correlated with learning? (3) what events can disrupt the formation of memories? and (4) what events can modulate memory formation?

The question of where memories are located has been a difficult one to answer. Leison studies have led to the principle of *equipotentiality*, which states that a memory for a simple task is stored diffusely throughout the sensory area which was used to process the input for the task. For example, a visual discrimination would be stored diffusely throughout the visual cortex. Lesion studies have also led to the formulation of the principle of *mass action*. For complex tasks, the amount of cortex which remains after the lesion is more important in retention than the actual placement of the lesions.

Partly because we are only able to measure performance, and not memory directly, these studies are equivocal. The weight of the evidence suggests that memories are stored diffusely throughout the particular sensory area that was used to form the memory. The various elements of a complex task which requires several sensory modalities would be stored in the different sensory areas. Cross-modal transfer studies suggest that in the higher primates and in human beings, an individual can have access to visual memories through another sensory modality by virtue of the fiber connections between the sensory association areas. We will need to use approaches other than the lesion method to provide an answer to this question. In the next chapter, we will see how evoked potentials can provide some evidence in support of the theory that the sensory areas which are used to acquire a task participate the most in the memory for the task.

The question of what changes are correlated with learning is also a difficult one, because it is not clear whether the changes are due to stress, or some other nonspecific change during the learning process.

summary
Learning and Memory in the Intact, Behaving Animal

Nevertheless, these studies point to changes in the rate of synthesis of both RNA and proteins. The new proteins may be involved in the structural changes which are assumed to underlie long-term memory, or they may reflect more general features of all types of learning, such as stress. An alternative hypothesis proposes that new and unique proteins are formed during a learning experience, which actually encode the features of the task, by producing modifications in the structural connections in the nervous system.

The study of events which can disrupt the formation of memory after training can yield information about the timing of memory consolidation, and may also tell us which biological events are crucial for the retention of a task. Amnestic agents, such as ECS and protein synthesis inhibitor drugs, can inhibit the retention of a task provided they are administered soon after training. If they are administered some time after training, the animals usually retain the memory for the task quite well. These studies show that the process of memory consolidation is time dependent. They suggest that particular firing patterns and protein synthesis are involved in the formation of memories. Presumably, the animal requires a certain kind of neural firing pattern as well as protein synthesis in order to transfer a short-term memory into a long-term one.

Because the interpretations of studies which use protein synthesis inhibitors or ECS are difficult, some workers have preferred to address the question of what events can modulate memory, rather than what events are critical for memory formation. Epinephrine, which is normally released in response to stressful events, appears to be one of the major modulators of memory formation. Too little or too much epinephrine inhibits the formation of a memory, regardless of whether the substance is released endogenously or injected. Moderate amounts of epinephrine in the organism during training enhance the retention of a task. This substance may be acting by means of the central noradrenergic synapses, and there is evidence that other amnestic agents (such as ECS and protein synthesis inhibitors) may be acting on some of these synapses as well.

Other than epinephrine, a variety of manipulations are known to modulate memory formation, such as gonadal hormones and the enkephalins. The state which an animal was in when it learned the task also has some effect on the retrieval of the memory, if not its formation. It is easier for an animal to retrieve a memory when it is in the same state as when it learned the task in the first place. This phenomenon is called *state-dependent learning*, and is known to occur for a variety of states, particularly those produced by centrally acting drugs.

These memory modulating events highlight the point that it may be very difficult, even futile, to try to separate the effects of learning on the brain, from the effects of nonspecific factors, such as stress, motivation, and sensory stimulation. It appears likely that the formation of memories during learning is very much related to these nonspecific factors, and cannot occur without them.

KEY TERMS	habituation sensitization associative learning classical conditioning	instrumental conditioning conditioned stimulus unconditioned stimulus unconditioned response

conditioned response
pseudoconditioning
passive avoidance
Aplysia
posttetanic facilitation
tetanization
abducens nucleus
long-term potentiation
principle of equipotentiality
principle of mass action

cross-modal transfer of information
scotophobin
electroconvulsive shock
retrograde amnesia
acetoxycycloheximide (AXM)
cycloheximide
propanolol
phenoxybenzamine
state-dependent learning

SUGGESTED READINGS

Kandel, E. R. (1976). *The Cellular Basis of Behavior.* Freeman, San Francisco. (This reference provides a rich source of information on the *Aplysia* model system.)

Teyler, T. (1978). *Brain and Learning.* Greylock Publishers, Stamford, Connecticut.

Rosenzweig, M. R., and Bennett, E. L., eds. (1976). *Neural Mechanisms of Learning and Memory.* MIT Press, Cambridge, Massachusetts.

(Both of these edited books contain a wealth of information about the physiological bases of learning and memory. Teyler's book is very easy to read and follow, and Rosenzweig and Bennett's collection is more detailed and complete.)

16

*higher
processes*

introduction Perhaps the greatest task lying ahead of the scientists involved in physiological psychology is the study of higher processes. Questions about how events in the nervous system can underlie "knowing," "understanding," or "thinking" are much more difficult compared to those about how we move a finger or code a painful stimulus. Model systems, like the one which uses the marine mollusk to study plastic phenomena, won't be of much help. Even the higher animals can only give us limited information. For much of our information we must rely on the human being, even though the kinds of experiments we can do are severely limited.

Intensive research on the higher processes is in its infancy, partly because some of the more sophisticated tools which are needed to study them were not previously available; but this is also because the scientific "climate" wasn't quite right. In 1874, Wundt stated that the central problem of physiological psychology was the study of the events underlying consciousness and subjective experience. But during the early twentieth century the scientific climate was dominated by the behaviorist movement, particularly in the United States. Scientists emphasized the study of overt behavior, and subjective experience did not qualify. "Knowing," "understanding," and "thinking" were not suitable behaviors for scientific inquiry (John and Schwartz, 1978).

More recently, the study of such phenomena as thinking has become quite reputable. New techniques have been developed which can trace some of the neural events which occur during different kinds of thinking, even though the person may not be performing any overt behavior. In this chapter, we will explore some of the techniques and discuss what they have found out about the higher processes so far.

Not surprisingly, the cortex plays a major role in the higher processes. We will begin by discussing the association cortical areas and the studies which have tried to determine their functions. The lesion technique has been used most extensively, but supporting studies come from single unit recordings as well. Second, we will discuss a technique called **averaged evoked potentials**, which holds much promise in the study of the higher processes. It can be noninvasive, so normal intact human beings can participate without danger.

The third technique, called the **split-brain**, has also revealed a great deal of important information about the way that the two hemispheres perform higher processing. Originally, studies on asymmetrical functions were performed on patients who had had their corpus callosum severed (to relieve epilepsy), and thus had "two brains in one." But more recently, it has been possible to use less dramatic techniques to study the hemispheric lateralization of function in intact brains.

Last, we will discuss not an approach, but the very special higher process called language. The study of language has combined a variety of approaches, but for the most part it has had to rely on information from brain damaged human beings.

Nearly three-fourths of the human cortex is made up of association areas. These large expanses of the brain, shown in Figure 16.1, are often called "silent" because the cells within them often show responses that bear very unclear relationships to sensory stimulation or motor activity. Presumably these are the areas that subserve higher processes like "knowing," "thinking," and "understanding." Phylogenetically, as you can see in Figure 16.1, human beings have by far the most association cortex compared to the other members of the animal kingdom. It seems an inescapable conclusion that these areas are thus very important for the higher processes at which human beings are so proficient.

Most of the information we have about the importance of the association areas for various types of higher processes comes from lesion studies in monkeys and from brain damaged human beings. But there is also supporting work from electrophysiological recordings. In this section, we will examine the association cortex of the frontal, temporal, and parietal lobes separately.

the frontal association cortex

The most obvious deficit which is seen following removal of the frontal lobes is a difficulty in **delayed response** performance. In this kind of test, the monkey is shown a tray with two food wells, and one of them is baited with something tasty while the monkey watches. Then an opaque screen is drawn down so that the monkey can't see the tray, and the experimenter puts two identical objects over the wells. When the screen is pulled up after a short delay, the monkey can push away one of the objects and get the food. To get the problem right, all the monkey has to do is to remember which food well was baited. Normal monkeys can easily bridge a delay up to 2 minutes, but animals with damage in the frontal lobes have trouble even if the delay is only 1 second long.

areas within the frontal association cortex. Thus the frontal association cortex is clearly involved with delayed response performance. But this task requires quite a number of potentially separate higher processes. For example, the delay feature of the task introduces the question of memory. Perhaps the monkeys were having difficulty remembering what they had just seen. The fact that there were two food wells, one on the right and one on the left, introduces a spatial factor into the task. Perhaps they could remember what they had seen, but they had difficulty orienting in space. On an even more subtle level, response

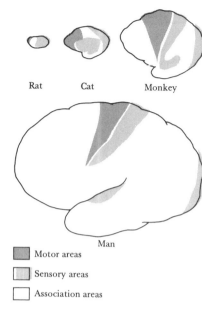

Rat   Cat   Monkey

Man

- ■ Motor areas
- ▨ Sensory areas
- □ Association areas

Figure 16.1
Approximate scale drawings of the cerebral hemispheres of four mammals. Note both the increase in size and relative increase in amount of "association" cortex. [From Thompson (1967).]

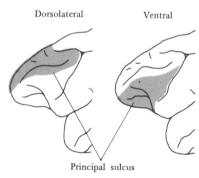

Dorsolateral   Ventral

Principal sulcus

Figure 16.2
Diagrammatical illustration of the dorsolateral and ventral portions of the frontal cortex. [From Goldman (1972).]

persistence might have been altered. If the lesion made the monkeys more persistent, they might have been less able to change their response in accord with what they saw the experimenter do.

In order to try to separate out some of these effects, Mishkin and his colleagues (1966, 1969) made more refined lesions in various places in the frontal cortex, and then tested the monkeys on a variety of tasks. They lesioned either the **dorsolateral** part of the frontal cortex, or the **ventral** part, as shown in Figure 16.2. The tasks that they gave the monkeys were alternation tasks. In the **object alternation** test, the monkey had to remember which object (between a cube and a pyramid, for example) had food underneath it on the last trial, because on the next trial the other object will have the food under it. Whether the correct object is on the left or right makes no difference for the correct solution (thus eliminating the need for spatial abilities). In the **spatial alternation task**, the food wells are covered by identical objects. This time the monkey has to remember which side was baited with food, because the object on the other side will be baited the next time. This task requires the ability to remember spatial features of the task, and to use the memory to orient in space in the present.

Figure 16.3 shows the results from this study. The animals with the dorsolateral lesions were impaired on only the spatial alteration problem. But the animals with the ventral lesion in the frontal cortex were impaired on both tasks. These results suggest that the dorsolateral part of the frontal cortex is critically involved in the spatial aspects of the task; lesions in this area do not appear to affect a visual discrimination between two objects.

Further studies using even more refined lesions and more elaborate testing devices have been able to identify the functions of various parts of the frontal lobes even more precisely. For example, the **principal sulcus** in the dorsolateral part of the frontal cortex plays a large role in tasks which require the monkey to integrate previous spatial cues with its present response (Goldman and Rosvold, 1970). When there is only a delay factor but no need for spatial abilities, or when only spatial abilities are required, the principal sulcus is less important.

electrical recording studies and delayed response. Some scientists have recorded from single units within the part of the thalamus which projects to the frontal association cortex and from cells within the cortex itself during delayed response tasks. These studies reveal that single units respond during particular parts of the task, and some even respond in a fashion that looks as if they are anticipating the monkey's decision.

Figure 16.4 shows six different types of single units which Fuster and Alexander (1973) found in the thalamus. Some neurons increased firing rate with either the raising or lowering of the screen during the

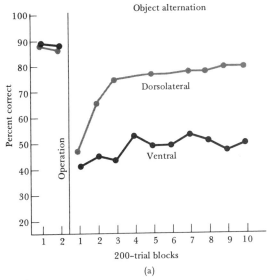

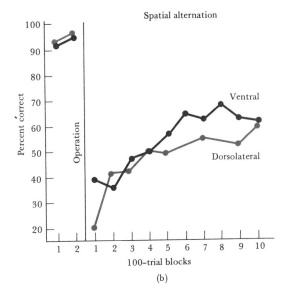

Figure 16.3
The performance of monkeys with dorsolateral and ventral lesions in the frontal cortex on a test of (a) object alternation and (b) spatial alternation. [From Mishkin et al. (1969).]

delayed response test (type A), or with sustained increases in firing whenever the screen was up (type B). Type C cells showed a sustained increase throughout the cue (baiting the food well) and delay phases of the trial. Type D showed increases during the delay, but decreases during the cue and response periods. And type I cells showed inhibition during the cue and response periods.

Many cortical units showed similar patterns, particularly in the principal sulcus (the area that appears to mediate spatial memories). Niki (1974a,b,c) found a different kind of cell in the frontal cortex that appeared to be anticipating the motor response of the monkey. Of 198 cells that showed some change in firing during a delayed alternation task, 26 showed increases during the delay period that corresponded to whether or not the next response would be to the left or to the right. Perhaps these units represent a code for the correct spatial choice, and thus were coding spatial memory. The fact that the differential responding of these units disappeared when the animal was switched to a simple visual discrimination problem suggests that the cells were not simply related to the motor activity of choosing left or right.

frontal lobe damage in humans. People with damage to the frontal lobes may experience any one of a number of symptoms, some of which resemble the defects seen in the monkeys. For example, Milner (1963)

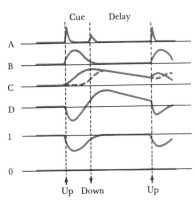

Figure 16.4
Types of units according to firing frequency changes in delayed response behavior. Arrows mark the movements of the opaque screen interposed between the animal and the test field. [From Fuster and Alexander (1973).]

found that some of the patients exhibited a response persistence type of disorder. She asked the subjects to sort cards according to either color, form, or number. These patients had difficulty in shifting from one sorting principle to another. They tended to continue sorting the cards by the same attribute, e.g., color. They also showed deficits in some spatial tasks, such as the ability to find an object embedded in a group of dissimilar objects. Thus this area in humans appears to involve some of the same functions as it does in monkeys.

inferotemporal cortex The most dramatic changes which are seen following lesions in this area of cortex are deficits in visual discrimination. Originally, interest in this area began when Klüver and Bucy (1937, 1938) published their findings on the effects of lesions which included this area. Their monkeys showed a remarkable array of symptoms, an array which is now known as the **Klüver-Bucy syndrome**. The main features of this disorder include **psychic blindness**, a term coined to express the monkey's tendency to approach animate and inanimate objects without hesitation. They would even pick up rubber snakes, which ordinarily cause quite an emotional reaction. The monkeys with these large lesions also showed a tendency to put small objects in their mouths, and they also showed hypersexuality and an absence of emotional expression.

Further studies revealed that the problems with psychic blindness were due to the lesion in the inferotemporal cortex. Most of the other problems (hypersexuality, lack of emotional expression) were due to the lesions in the subcortical areas which were included in the original operations. Thus scientists began to think of the inferotemporal cortex as part of the visual system—perhaps an area where visual associations are made.

areas within the inferotemporal cortex. The most critical areas for the performance of a visual discrimination task lie in the posterior part of the inferotemporal cortex and also on the borderline between the inferotemporal cortex and the prestriate area. Twai and Mishkin (1969) divided the inferotemporal cortex into six 5-mm strips (shown in Figure 16.5) and lesioned small groups of monkeys in one of the strips. Three other groups of monkeys received lesions in control areas (superior temporal gyrus, prestriate cortex, and fusiform gyrus on the ventral surface of the temporal lobe).

Figure 16.5 shows the performance of these nine groups on a visual pattern discrimination. None of the control groups showed any deficits. They all reached criterion in less than 50 trials. But all of the animals lesioned in the posterior part of the inferotemporal cortex showed deficits.

Using different tasks, it has been possible to at least speculate on the

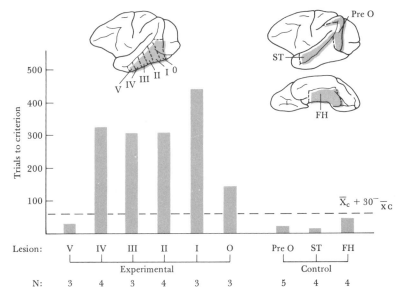

Figure 16.5
Performance of nine groups of monkeys on a visual pattern discrimination task, each of which received lesions in one of the locations diagrammed above the graph. [From Mishkin (1972).]

separate functions served by the area between the posterior inferotemporal cortex and the prestriate area—functions which are all included in the visual discrimination task. Lesions in part of the prestriate cortex appear to impair visual attention. Animals with lesions in this area are impaired whenever irrelevant background cues are added to a pattern discrimination (Gross, Cowey, and Manning, 1971). Animals with posterior inferotemporal lesions are impaired in another way. They do poorly when the task involves a large number of associations. For example, if several different pairs of visual stimuli are presented, a normal animal can learn to respond to the correct one of each pair during a testing session. But the posterior inferotemporal lesions produce severe impairments in this ability. This has led to the suggestion that part of the prestriate cortex subserves visual attention, while the inferotemporal cortex subserves the ability to make visual associations.

electrophysiological studies in the inferotemporal cortex. Studies of single units agree with the conclusion that this area is important for the higher processing of visual information. For example, many of these cells respond to visual stimuli, but not to auditory or somesthetic stimuli (Gross, Rocha-Miranda, and Bender, 1972). The cells in this area are different from those in the visual cortex in that they have very large receptive fields, which always include the fovea. Figure 16.6 shows some of those receptive fields for cells which were sampled during a single pass of the electrode through the inferotemporal cortex.

Figure 16.6
The receptive fields of single units which were sampled during a pass of the electrode through the part of the inferotemporal cortex indicated by an arrow. All receptive fields included the fovea. (The receptive field of a neuron refers to that area in the visual field within which a stimulus can produce a change in the firing pattern.) la, lateral fissure; ot, occipitotemporal sulcus; ts, superior temporal sulcus; cd, caudate nucleus; H, hippocampus; Pl, pulvinar; TA, TE, TF, TH, and A refer to cytoarchitectonic areas. [From Gross et al. (1972).]

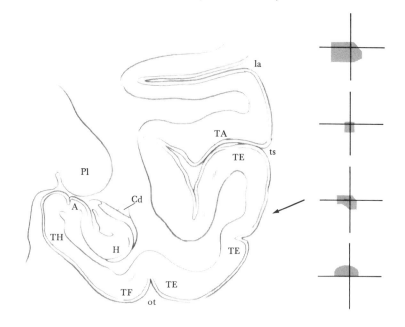

These large receptive fields would suggest that stimuli which fall on widely separate parts of the retina can activate the same neurons in the inferotemporal cortex, so it is clear that the cells must have some very complex properties. Some of them showed some remarkably specific preference for their best response. For example, one cell responded best to an outline of a monkey's hand, while another responded best to the shape of a bottle brush (Gross *et al.*, 1972). These cells may be so preferential that it will be impossible to find out which stimuli are most effective in producing a response. These very specific preferences indicate that the inferotemporal cortex is indeed serving some very high-level processing function for vision. The most likely hypothesis is that it is involved in visual associations.

inferotemporal damage in humans. If a human being suffers damage to the left inferotemporal area, difficulties in language are likely to result. This is because some of the language areas (which we will discuss later in this chapter) overlap this area of cortex. Milner (1954) studied patients with right inferotemporal damage and found many consistencies with the results of the lesion studies in monkeys. The patients showed great difficulty with visual discriminations, particularly when there were irrelevant background designs present.

Studies on the parietal lobe have been few in number, and also have not been able to unify our notions about what it is that this area does. But a discussion of this area serves to illustrate the point that the cortex is incredibly complex, and many regions serve more than one function. Even simple terms like "motor cortex" or "sensory cortex," which refer to the so-called nonassociation areas, are no longer completely valid. The motor cortex also serves somatosensory functions, and the sensory cortex also serves nonsensory functions, and probably some associative functions as well.

Human beings who have damage to the posterior part of the parietal cortex exhibit a striking deficit called **sensory neglect**. They ignore the contralateral visual field, even though they can see quite well. For example, if they are asked to bisect a straight horizontal line, they only bisect one-half of it, so that the line is divided into three-quarter and one-quarter segments. They also neglect their contralateral body parts, and may go out into cold weather wearing only one glove. Some scientists have suggested that the parietal areas are important in the association and higher analysis of visual, somatosensory, and behavioral information. This is a tall order for one brain area; it probably reflects more about the fact that we don't know very much about this part of the brain.

the parietal lobes and spatial orientation. One kind of association which might be made between visual and somatosensory information is orientation in space. Pohl (1973) suggests that there are two kinds of spatial orientation: **egocentric**, which refers to identifying the position of an object by reference to the position of the observer, and **allocentric**, which refers to identifying the position of an object by reference to another object. He found that parietal lobe lesions caused an impairment in the allocentric variety of spatial orientation, but not in the egocentric variety.

He lesioned monkeys in one of three places: the temporal lobe, the parietal lobe, or the frontal lobe. Then he tested them on three different tasks. In the **landmark reversal task**, two identical squares were placed over the two food wells, but near one was a cylinder (shown in Figure 16.7). The monkey first had to learn to choose the food well near the cylinder. Once it had learned that task, the experimenter began to only reward responses to the food well farthest from the cylinder. This test was designed to measure allocentric spatial orientation. In the **object reversal task** the monkey first learned to respond to only one object (cylinder or cube). Once it had learned that, the experi-

parietal association cortex

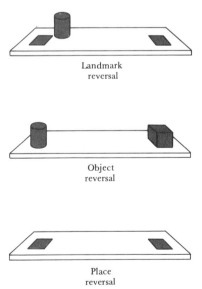

Landmark
reversal

Object
reversal

Place
reversal

Figure 16.7
Three types of reversal tasks (see text for explanation). [From Mishkin (1972).]

higher processes in the association cortex **507**

menter rewarded the other object. And in the **place reversal task**, the monkey first learned to respond to either the left or the right object. Then the experimenters reversed the rewarded place to the other side. This task was designed to measure the egocentric variety of spatial orientation.

Figure 16.8 shows the number of errors each group of lesioned monkeys made during the reversal tests. Notice that the parietal lesioned group had great difficulty with the landmark reversal, but not with any of the other tests. The temporal lesioned animals had most difficulty with the object reversal, which was probably due to their deficit in visual discriminations. The frontal lobe animals had difficulty on the place reversal, which supports the view that they show deficits in spatial memory.

electrophysiological studies of parietal cortex. Studies which have recorded the activity of single units in the parietal cortex have clearly emphasized that the functions of this area are not at all simple. Many cells in

Figure 16.8
The performance of three groups of animals with lesions in the parietal cortex (P), frontal cortex (F), or temporal lobes (T) on three different types of reversal tasks. [From Mishkin (1972).]

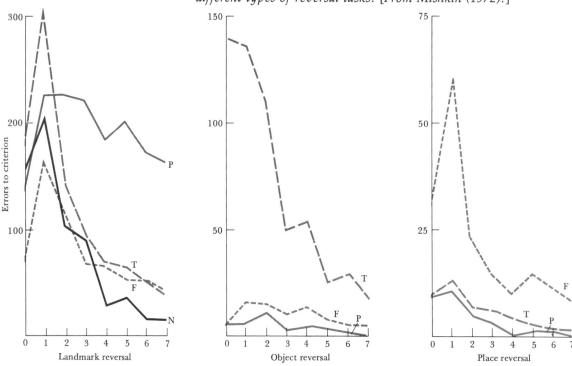

this area respond to visual stimulation, but some of them seem to be more connected to motor activity. Mountcastle and his colleagues (1975), for example, described cells which fired in association with eye and hand movements during visually guided reaching tasks. They postulated that these cells served a "command" function for hand and eye movements during exploration of the visual and somatosensory environment.

But Robinson and his colleagues (Robinson, Goldberg, and Stanton, 1978) suggest that many of these cells are performing sensory functions. They found cells which respond to sensory stimulation in the absence of hand or eye movements, although the cells responded best when the visual stimulus was a target for movement. They suggest that neurons in this area are associating information from the visual and somatosensory environment with internal data, and generally fall into the broad category of visual attention.

In this section we discussed some of the higher processes which are subserved by the association cortical areas. These included the ability to perform such tasks as delayed response, delayed alternation, visual attention and association, and association between visual and somatosensory information. Some of these may not seem like such "high processes" compared to the kinds of things a human being can do. But the study of higher processes must walk before it can run, and it is likely that the more complex higher processes, such as daydreaming, decision making, and mathematical ability, are based on some of these simpler forms.

The frontal association cortex is involved in the ability to perform delayed response tasks. Lesions in this area in monkeys produce severe deficits in this ability. The *dorsolateral* portion of the frontal cortex appears to be involved in the spatial aspects of the task, while the *ventral* portion appears to involve both the delay feature (which necessitates memory) and the spatial aspects of the task. Within the dorsolateral portion, the principal sulcus seems to mediate spatial memories. Single units in the frontal cortex respond to particular

portions of a delayed response task. Some even respond differentially to the decision which the monkeys make as to whether to reach right or left.

The inferotemporal cortex has been most associated with visual discrimination and association. Monkeys with lesions in this area display a part of the *Klüver-Bucy syndrome* which includes *psychic blindness*. They can see objects, but they do not respond to them in any discriminative way. The most important part of the inferotemporal cortex for visual associations appears to be the posterior area. The adjacent prestriate cortex is involved in visual attention. Electrophysiological studies confirm the view that this area is involved with higher order processing and association of visual information.

Studies of parietal cortex have not been able to provide any clear-cut answers to the question of what functions this area subserves. Unilateral lesions in this area produce *sensory neglect* for the contralateral visual and somatosensory field. Studies of single units suggest that it is involved with associations between visual and so-

summary
Higher Processes in the Association Cortex

matosensory information and with orientation in space.

Most of the studies we reviewed in this section used the lesion method although the technique is not without its drawbacks. However, other approaches have generally supported the general notions which have been derived from the lesion studies. It is important to remember that the cells within any one area of association cortex are likely to subserve multiple functions, and no strict correlation between structure and function is possible.

averaged evoked potentials

Another approach to the study of higher processes involves the use of averaged evoked potentials, which can be obtained from the EEG records of animal or human subjects. When a stimulus (such as a flash of light or a tone) is presented to the subject, the EEG record looks very similar to the records which came before the stimulus. But within that EEG record are some tiny changes which can be recovered by averaging. The stimulus is presented to the subject repeatedly and the EEG waves which are recorded for a few hundred milliseconds immediately after the onset of the stimulus are averaged. All of the random events which occur in the EEG, and which are not related to the stimulus, eventually average to zero. But the tiny changes which are time dependent upon the stimulus remain, because they occur repeatedly with each stimulus presentation. Figure 16.9 shows how the averaged evoked potential (AEP) emerges after averaging many raw EEG records.

Figure 16.9
The emergence of an AEP from raw EEG records.

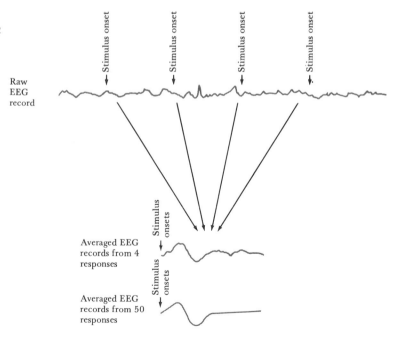

By means of studies like the ones which we will discuss, it is becoming clear that the shape of the AEP depends partly upon the characteristics of the physical stimulus, but also upon the meaning of that stimulus to the individual. The shape of the AEP is different when different kinds of higher processes are going on in the subject's brain. Thus the AEP can be a powerful tool to study the physiological correlates of higher processing.

One kind of higher processing which has been studied with this technique is attention. When a man says to his son, "I didn't hear you back the car over the lawnmower, I wasn't paying attention," what exactly does he mean? We know from some of the studies reviewed in the last chapter that short-term plasticity is probably not mediated at the level of the receptor. The person who wasn't paying attention was probably not temporarily deaf to the clatter (although he may wish he had been).

the AEP and attention

The AEP can be used to study the process of selective attention. Hillyard and his colleagues (Hillyard, Hink, Schwent, and Picton, 1973) presented tone pips through headphones to both ears of human subjects, but they asked the people to only pay attention to the pips in one ear. The tone pips occasionally included a pip of a higher frequency and the subject was asked to count these irregular pips which were presented to the "attended" ear. During the presentations, the experimenters recorded the EEG.

Figure 16.10 shows the AEPs for the right ear stimulus when they were attending to the right ear (solid line) and when they were attending to the left (dashed line). Panel (b) shows the AEPs for the left ear stimulus under "attend left" and "attend right" conditions. Notice that for all three subjects, the amplitude of the AEP for the attended stimulus is larger, regardless of the ear to which the subject is attending.

The human auditory AEP normally contains two clearly observable peaks. One is called N_1, and it peaks between 80 and 110 msec after the onset of the stimulus. (N stands for negative—the polarity of the records is reversed on these figures, so high peaks are negative, and low peaks are positive.) A second component is called P_2 (positive or downward peak), and it occurs between 160 and 200 msec after the stimulus onset. The results from this study suggest that the major change in the AEP which occurs with selective attention and nonattention is in the N_1 portion of the waveform. The very early portions (which do not reflect attention) are correlated with the physical properties of the stimulus. The N_1 portion is correlated with whether or not the subject is attending to the stimulus.

Hillyard and his colleagues suggest that a later component, called P_3, is correlated with another aspect of attention. They averaged the records for those "signal" pips presented to the attended ear which the

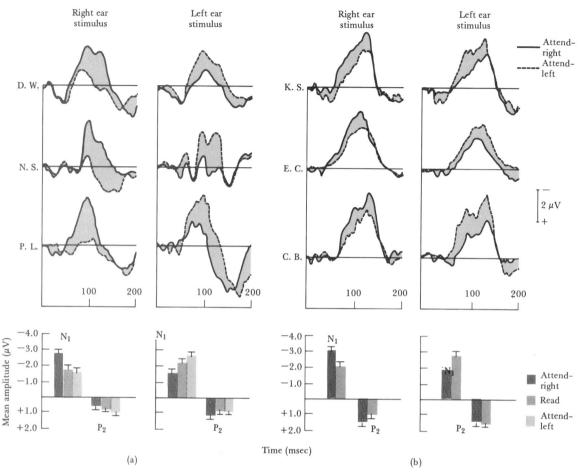

Figure 16.10
AEPs from three subjects under attend right (solid lines) and attend left (dashed lines) conditions. [From Hillyard, Hink, Schwent, and Picton (1973). Copyright 1973 by the American Association for the Advancement of Science.]

subject was supposed to be counting. Figure 16.11 shows a comparison of the signal AEPs and the AEPs to the standard pips presented between the signals.

The largest difference between the signal AEP and the standard AEP appeared quite a while after the pip had actually been presented. This late positive component peaked between 250 and 400 msec after the tone onsets. This P_3 component was quite large for the signal tones, but virtually nonexistent for the standard tones.

Hillyard and his colleagues (1973) suggest that the N_1 component corresponds to a "stimulus set" mode of attention, while the P_3 corresponds to a "response set" mode of attention. The stimulus set would

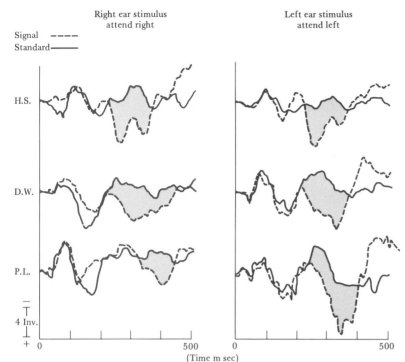

Signal ----
Standard ——

Right ear stimulus
attend right

Left ear stimulus
attend left

H.S.

D.W.

P.L.

4 Inv.

0   500   0   500
(Time m sec)

Figure 16.11
The P_3 component (shaded area) evoked by signal tone pips in the attended ear. The P_3 is absent in the AEPs to the standard tone pips (solid tracings). [From Hillyard, Hink, Schwent, and Picton (1973). Copyright 1973 by the American Association for the Advancement of Science.]

preferentially admit signals to an attended channel of sensory input (the attended ear), while blocking input to an unattended channel (the unattended ear). This kind of attentional process occurs very early in the analysis, which was why the differences in the N_1 occurred early in the AEPs. The "response set" is another kind of attention which compares incoming sensory stimuli (filtered through the "stimulus set" mode) against a memorized template. For the tones, the signal pip input would be compared against the memorized template of the standard tones. When the signal input did not match, then the late appearing P_3 would result.

single unit studies of selective attention. Benson and Hienz (1978) were able to teach a selective attention task very similar to the one we just described to a group of monkeys, so that the behavior of single units could be studied. They fitted the monkeys with headphones, and presented tones randomly to the left or right ear. When the monkey was supposed to attend to the left ear, the experimenters lit a response key on the left. When they were supposed to attend to the right ear, the response key on the right came on. The monkeys received a reward when they made a response to a tone in the ear which was supposed to be attended, but no reward if they made a response to a tone in the other ear. This seemingly simple task took the monkeys about 3 months to learn, which makes it clear why studies of selective attention are easier to do in humans.

After the monkeys had been trained, the experimenters began to record from single units in the auditory cortex. Of the 77 single units they observed, 14 showed increased responding for tones entering the attended ear, regardless of whether the attended ear was the right or the left. Figure 16.12 shows the behavior of two of these cells during the attend and nonattend trials.

The cell shown in panel (a) showed a higher firing rate in the first 300 msec after the onset of the attended tone. The behavior of the cell

Figure 16.12
The responses of two single units immediately after the presentation of an auditory stimulus (auditory cortex). Both units showed increased activity dependent upon whether or not the monkey was attending to the auditory stimulus. [From Benson and Hienz (1978).]

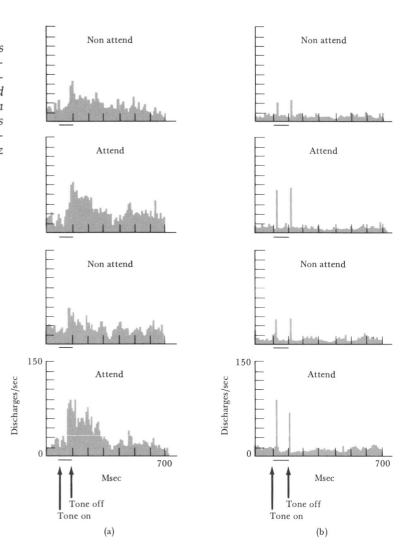

in panel (b) showed quite a different pattern of firing, but still the major difference between the attend and nonattend conditions occurred soon after the onset of the tones. This cell showed increases both at the onset and offset of the tones to both ears, but the activity was greater for the attended tones.

It is not yet possible to correlate the behavior of single units to the changes which are seen in the AEP during selective attention. Too few single units have been studied and the activity of a huge number of cells contributes to the waveform of the AEP. But it is interesting that single units show changes almost immediately after the onset of a tone, and that the changes depend upon whether the animal is attending to the stimulus or not. The N_1 early component of the AEP also showed this same property.

You may recall from Chapter 15 that cells in the auditory cortex of the cat behaved differently depending on whether the stimulus was one that the cat had learned was followed by shock. The response to the CS + (e.g., a sound) became larger as the cats learned that it was followed by a shock. The response from the same cell became smaller to the other CS − (e.g., a touch) because it was not followed by anything aversive (Oleson, Ashe, and Weinberger, 1975). The learning experience may have caused the cat to attend to one of the stimuli (because it was followed by shock) but not to the other one. The process of learning contains an element of attention. The attentional component appears in both the studies using AEPs and the studies on learning in the cat's pupillary reflex system.

Another higher process which can be studied with AEPs is behavioral set. Part of what determines how we perceive a stimulus is how we expect to see it. For example, if you were reading the row of numbers in Figure 16.13a, you would read the fourth figure as "13." But if you were reading the row of letters in (b), then you would read the fourth one as "B." The numbers or letters which preceded the ambiguous stimulus had established a behavioral set in your mind, and this would affect the way that you perceived the fourth stimulus.

Begleiter and his colleagues (Begleiter, Porjesz, Yerre, and Kissin, 1973) studied the effects of behavioral set on the AEP using a very ingenious design. They instructed the people to press one button when they saw a bright flash of light on a screen and to press a different button when they saw a dim light. They also told the subjects that each flash of light would be preceded by either a high tone or low tone which would tell them whether the upcoming flash was going to be bright or dim. Thus the tones established a behavioral set in the minds of the subjects, which might affect how they reacted to the flashes.

Figure 16.14a shows the AEPs for the bright flash (top trace) and the

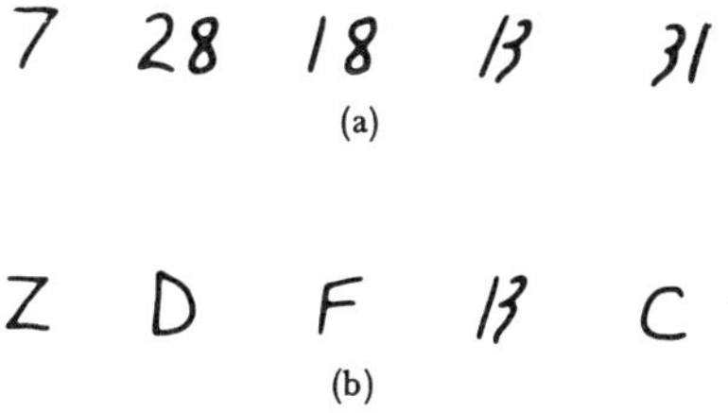

the AEP and behavioral set

7 28 18 13 31

(a)

Z D F 13 C

(b)

Figure 16.13
The effects of behavioral set on perception. (a) Fourth stimulus is read as "13". (b) Fourth stimulus is read as "B."

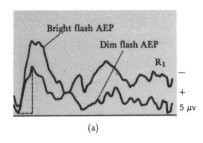

Bright flash AEP

Dim flash AEP

R_1

−
+

5 μv

(a)

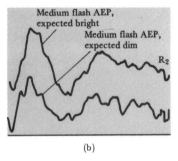

Medium flash AEP, expected bright

Medium flash AEP, expected dim

R_2

(b)

Figure 16.14
The effects of expectations on the AEP. The AEP for a medium flash is larger when the subjects expect the flash to be bright compared to the AEP when they expect the flash to be dim. [From Begleiter, Porjesz, Yerre, and Kissin (1973). Copyright 1973 by the American Association for the Advancement of Science.]

dim flash (bottom trace). The amplitude differences between the two traces are quite large. But this might have been because the two stimuli to which the subjects were responding were quite different. So in the next series of trials, the experimenters gave the subjects a slightly different set of instructions. This time they said that there would be two bright flashes and two dim flashes. Both bright flashes would be preceded by the same tone which preceded the bright flash in the first experiment, and both dim flashes would be preceded by the other tone. But in actuality, the experimenters only presented three different flashes: one bright, one dim, and one medium flash. Sometimes the medium flash was preceded by a tone that indicated a bright flash was coming next, and other times it was preceded by the tone that indicated a dim flash was coming. Thus the experimenters were able to establish two different behavioral sets for the same physical stimulus. Any difference in the traces could not be due to the properties of the physical stimulus.

Figure 16.14b shows the results for the medium flash preceded by a tone that indicated a bright flash (top trace), and for the same medium flash preceded by the "dim flash tone" (bottom trace). Notice that the top trace looks very much like the AEPs to the bright flash. The bottom trace looks very much like the AEPs to the dim flash. Thus the expectations of the subjects had some very interesting effects on the shape of the AEP waveform.

One very interesting feature of this experiment was that the difference in amplitude for the two expectation conditions did not appear in the AEPs recorded from the occipital cortex. It only appeared at the vertex. The experimenters suggest that the processing at the occipital lobes is devoted mainly to the physical properties of the stimulus, and that is why the two waveforms looked so much alike—the physical stimulus was identical for both expectation conditions.

the AEP and decision making The AEP waveform also reveals some interesting correlations with the decision-making process. Begleiter and Porjesz (1975) instructed their subjects that a series of flashes would be presented on a screen, and that some would be dim and some bright. This time, no tone preceded the flashes. The subjects simply were to press one button if they saw a bright flash, and another button if they saw a dim one. As expected, the AEP waveforms for the dim and bright flashes were quite different.

For the next series of trials, the experimenters told the subjects that the task was going to be the same, but that it might be a little more difficult. For every flash that the subjects got right, they would receive a nickel; but for every mistake, 20 cents would be deducted. This added a little incentive to an otherwise boring task. Since it is necessary to present each kind of stimulus many times in order to have enough records to average, then the experimenters may run into the problem of large delta waves appearing in their EEG records (ZZZZ ...).

Instead of presenting only bright and dim flashes, the experimenters presented bright, dim, and medium flashes. Sometimes the subjects would press the "bright" button for a medium flash, and sometimes they would press the "dim" button. Thus the EEG records for the same physical stimulus could be averaged depending upon the decision which the subjects made about it.

Figure 16.15 shows the results for three subjects. The top trace in each panel shows the AEP for the medium flashes when the subjects decided it was bright (M_b), and the bottom trace shows the AEP for the medium flashes which the subjects thought were dim (M_d). The amplitude of the traces is larger when the subjects made the decision that the medium flash was bright.

These amplitude differences could not have been due to any differences in the physical properties of the stimulus—they were all medium flashes. And they could not have been due to differences in behavioral set, since no tones were presented to establish any expectations. But they might have been due to the different motor responses (pressing one button or another) which were required for each decision. Begleiter and Porjesz also examined the AEPs for subjects which were asked to simply look at a visual stimulus, and then press one or another button. There was no decision involved—the subjects just pressed whichever button they felt like. The AEP which followed a stimulus for which the subjects pressed one button were compared with those for which the subjects pressed the other button. There were no differences between the two, suggesting that the different motor responses required for the decisions were not important. Thus the amplitude differences appeared to reflect the perceived brightness of the stimulus.

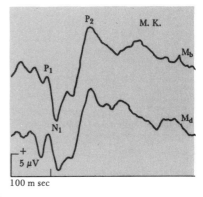

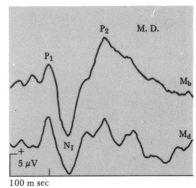

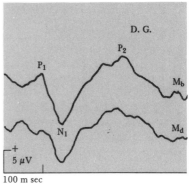

Figure 16.15
AEPs recorded at the vertex, for three typical subjects in response to identical stimuli of medium intensity that resulted in different behavioral decisions. The top trace in each panel is the average for those flashes the subject decided were bright (M_b). The bottom trace is the average for those flashes the subject decided were dim (M_d). [From Begleiter and Porjesz (1975). Copyright 1975 by the American Association for the Advancement of Science.]

averaged evoked potentials **517**

the AEP and localization of memories

John and his colleagues (Bartlett and John, 1973; John and Schwartz, 1978) have been using the AEPs recorded in animals to study higher processes. They have obtained similar changes in the AEP waveform dependent upon various kinds of higher processing, and have also concluded that part of the waveform is due to the input of the stimulus, and another part is due to higher processes which are going on in the animal's brain. These two processes are termed **exogenous influences** and **endogenous influences.**

In one very intricate study they trained cats to discriminate between lights flickering at two different speeds, and then presented the cats with a light which flickered at an intermediate speed. This situation could hypothetically produce quite a number of different waveforms, depending upon what the cats decided to do. For any of the three stimuli, the cat could make one of two responses, one of which would be correct. Through a number of algebraic manipulations, these scientists were able to compute correlations which would reflect the similarity between two situations which hypothetically released the same exogenous or endogenous process. The higher the correlations, then the more confident the experimenters were that the waveforms contained elements of the hypothetical exogenous or endogenous influences.

These correlations were very high, particularly for records obtained from certain regions of the brain. Figure 16.16 plots the correlations for endogenous influences against the correlations for exogenous influences for different brain areas. Notice that the correlations for both exogenous and endogenous influences are high for those areas of the brain which are intimately involved in sensory processing of visual stimulation. The lateral geniculate and the visual cortex showed the highest correlations for both endogeneous and exogenous processes.

Bartlett and John (1973) interpret this to mean that the representation of an experience, or memory, is widely distributed throughout the brain. But the amount that any particular anatomical region participates in that representation is logarithmically proportional to the impact of those sensory events which are used to retrieve the memory upon that region. To phrase this another way, the more effect that a sensory event has upon a region, then the more that region participates in the endogenous processes (memory) related to the event.

This may explain why it is so difficult to find out where memories are located, as we discussed in the last chapter. The endogenous processes related to a memory are probably going on in many areas of the brain. But they are strongest in the areas that deal with the sensory input used to learn the task. It also helps to explain why the only lesions which seem to obliterate the memory for a particular event are those in the sensory cortex, lesions that also obliterate the coding of the sensory information. The new AEP approach may help to recon-

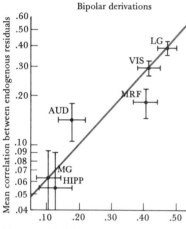

Figure 16.16
Mean correlation coefficients between exogenous residuals plotted against those between endogenous residuals for different brain regions: AUD, auditory cortex; HIPP, hippocampus; LG, lateral geniculate; VIS, visual cortex; MG, medial geniculate; MRF, mesencephalic reticular formation. [From Bartlett and John (1973). Copyright 1973 by the American Association for the Advancement of Science.]

cile the theories about where memories are stored. It also is pointing up the integral relationship between memory and sensory processes.

This approach offers many advantages, not the least of which is the ability to use normal human subjects without danger. EEG records are taken during the presentation of visual or auditory stimuli, and the records are averaged. The remaining averaged evoked potential (AEP) represents the consistent changes in brain activity which are linked to the stimulus onset. It has been used successfully to study attention, behavioral set, and decision making.

Auditory AEPs are different depending upon whether or not the subject is attending to the stimulus. An early component (N_1) of the AEP shows differences which are correlated with attention, which probably reflects stimulus filtering. A later component (P_3) shows differences also—particularly to auditory pips which act as signals against a series of background pips. This component probably represents a different kind of attentional process. Single units in the auditory cortex in monkeys also show differences in response patterns dependent upon whether or not the monkey is attending to the stimulus.

Behavioral set can also influence the shape and size of the AEP. Subjects showed larger AEPs to a flash of light they expected to be bright compared to their AEP to the same flash when they expected it to be dim. Also, in experiments where the subjects had no expectations about the brightness of the next flash, they showed different AEPs depending upon whether they decided it was bright or dim. Thus the AEP also reflects the decision-making process.

In animals, the AEPs from different areas of the brain also correlate with certain higher processes. When a cat is performing a task, the areas that show the greatest change are the same ones which are involved in the sensory processing needed for the task. This suggests that the neural activity for coding memory for a task is widely distributed throughout the brain, but is strongest in those areas which do the sensory processing.

summary
Averaged Evoked Potentials

An approach which has been able to tell us a great deal about asymmetrical functional systems in the nervous system which subserve the higher processes is the split-brain technique. Quite literally, the brain is split into two halves, the right and the left, by surgically severing the major fiber connections between them. This procedure can be done in animals, but in humans it is only a last ditch effort to control life-threatening epileptic seizures. Sperry and his colleagues (e.g., Sperry, 1974) have made extensive studies of the behavior of human beings who have undergone this kind of surgery. Superficially these people appear quite normal. But more sophisticated tests reveal that they actually have two brains in one, each with its own strengths and weaknesses.

asymmetry in the nervous system: the split-brain

In order to determine what kind of specializations each side of the brain possesses, it was necessary to design tests in which information would only reach one side. For tactual input, this is quite simple. The left side of the brain receives input from the right hand, and the right side from the left hand. Visually, the problem is more complicated because some of the fibers from each retina cross at the optic chiasm. This means that information delivered to the left or right eye will reach both hemispheres. But information presented to the left or right visual field will only reach one hemisphere. Sperry and his colleagues designed a testing situation with two screens which would permit the presentation of information to only one of the visual fields, and thus to only one of the hemispheres. Figure 16.17 schematically shows this experimental setup.

Immediately it became obvious that the left hemisphere dominated in virtually all kinds of verbal tasks. When they presented a written word to the right visual field, so that the input reached the person's left hemisphere, the individual could easily read it out loud, and write it with the right hand. The same word presented to the right hemisphere resulted in no response. The person reported that he saw nothing, or that he only saw a flash of light. At first it seemed as though the right hemisphere was an idiot. It couldn't talk about what it saw, read what it saw, or write anything. Some surmised that consciousness itself was located in the left hemisphere and that the right side was just going along for the ride. But further testing revealed that the right hemisphere had thoughts and feelings too.

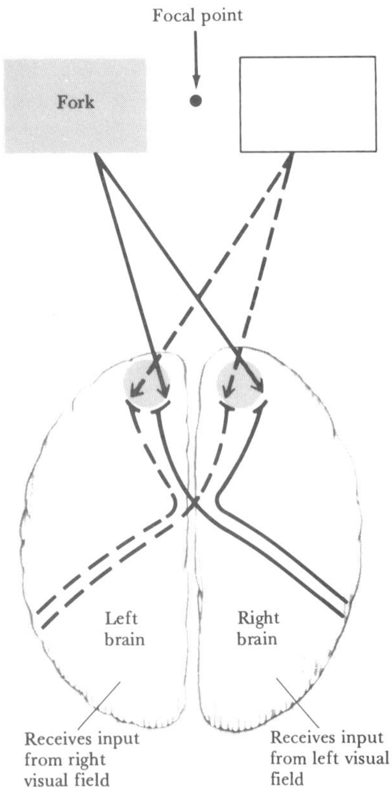

When a simple noun is flashed to the left visual field, the right hemisphere can read it. It just can't talk about what it saw. But if the experimenters provide a tray full of objects, the person's left hand will quickly point to the object whose name was flashed to the right hemisphere (even though verbally the person is reporting that he didn't see anything). For example, if the word "fork" is presented to the right hemisphere, the person can point to a fork, and can pick out a fork from a bag full of objects without looking.

These experiments show that the left hemisphere is dominant for verbal abilities. This is true for the vast majority of right-handed people, and most lefties as well, as we shall see later. This is no surprise, since the effects of brain damage in the left hemisphere have long been known to affect language much more severely than similar damage on the right side. The left hemisphere is also better at mathematical tasks. It required quite a bit of ingenuity to find tests at which the right hemisphere might excel. The right hemisphere has only limited ability to read, and virtually no speech, but it has marvelous spatial abilities.

For example, the split-brained patient's left hand (controlled by the right brain) is much better at arranging colored blocks so that they form a specific pattern. This is true, even though the person may be

Focal point

Fork

Left brain

Right brain

Receives input from right visual field

Receives input from left visual field

Figure 16.17
The experimental setup for transmitting visual input to either the left or the right hemisphere.

right-handed. The left hand is also better at drawing. Figure 16.18 shows some drawings done with the right and left hands of a split-brain patient who is right-handed. Although the right brain only has a limited vocabulary (mostly nouns), and does not speak, it is far from being an idiot.

cross-cuing in split-brain patients. Even though these patients appear normal in most social situations, they do have certain defects. These defects are due to the lateralization of certain functions in the human brain—verbal and spatial abilities in particular. But these people show a remarkable ability to adapt to their defects, and to overcome them in clever ways.

Gazzaniga (1967) describes how one patient showed some communication between the left and right hemispheres, even though the traditional mode of communication (the corpus callosum) was severed. The experimenters flashed a red or a green light to the right hemisphere to find out if the person would respond. At first the patient merely guessed, because although the right brain knew what color the flash was, the left hemisphere was doing the talking. Thus

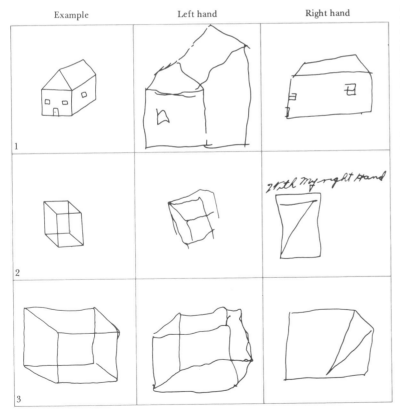

| Example | Left hand | Right hand |

Figure 16.18
Drawings made by split-brained patients using the right hand and the left hand. The left-hand drawings are clearly superior to the right-hand ones for all three patients (who were all right-handed!). These drawings illustrate the superiority of the right hemisphere in spatial or visual-constructional tasks. [Courtesy, Michael S. Gazzaniga.]

the patient was scoring at chance levels. Eventually the patient began to score much higher provided he was allowed to guess a second time. The strategy he was using was to allow the left hemisphere to make a guess, to just say "green." If the guess was wrong, and the light was red, the patient would frown and shake his head. The left hemisphere took this cue from the right, and then said "oh no, I meant red."

implications of hemispheric specialization of function. The split-brain research suggests that there are two separate spheres of consciousness within the brain. These normally communicate with one another, and integrate their functions. But when communication is impossible, the individual may actually become two separate brains, each with its own thoughts, emotions, and goals. Many scientists hypothesize that the two hemispheres use different approaches in perceiving and reacting to the environment. The left hemisphere uses a more analytical, verbal, and logical approach, while the right uses a gestalt, intuitive approach—one that emphasizes the spatial qualities of the environment.

anatomical asymmetries in the brain Even though it has been known for some time that language abilities reside mainly in the left side of the brain, very few anatomical differences were noted between the two hemispheres which might underlie these functional differences until recently. With more sophisticated techniques, a number of differences have been found, some of which may account for the hemispheric lateralization of functions (Galaburda, LeMay, Kemper, and Geschwind, 1978).

The most striking asymmetry in the cortex is in the upper surface of the temporal lobe. Geschwind and his colleagues found that the **planum temporale** in this area was larger on the left side in 65% of the 100 adult brains they examined, approximately equal in 24%, and larger on the right in only 11% of the cases. This anatomical asymmetry could easily be related to the specialization for language which the left hemisphere possesses, since damage to this area on the left side often results in language disturbances.

The two hemispheres also show cytoarchitectonic asymmetries. Figure 16.19 shows the left and right sides of a human brain and demonstrates that certain cell areas in the auditory cortex are much larger in the left than they are on the right. In particular, the **temporoparietal cortex** showed this difference. It was approximately seven times larger on the left compared to the right (Galaburda *et al.*, 1978).

How these and other anatomical asymmetries might correlate with hemispheric specialization of function is not yet known. It would be very interesting to know, for example, whether patients who show persistent aphasia (loss of speech) after left brain damage have highly asymmetrical brains in these temporal areas. Individuals who make some recovery might show less asymmetry, and thus might have larger areas in the nondominant hemisphere for speech which could take over some of the functions. Galaburda *et al.* (1978) reported that one man whose brain they were able to study had developmental dyslexia (reading problems). The planum was smaller than normal on both sides of the brain. It is tempting to conclude that these anatomical asymmetries in the brain form the basis for the lateralization of function. But the data are not yet conclusive.

asymmetries in the body

The most obvious asymmetry in the human body is handedness. Right- and left-handedness relates in a very subtle way to cerebral dominance for language. Right-handed people tend to have language subserved by the left hemisphere. But left-handed people tend to be more variable. Most show left brain dominance, but many show right brain dominance or bilateral language abilities.

The face also shows asymmetry, at least in the way that it expresses emotion. Sackheim, Gur, and Saucy (1978) took photographs of actors' faces when they were showing some emotion, such as disgust, happiness, or surprise. Then they cut the photographs in half, and made left face composites and right face composites. An example of these composites is shown in Figure 16.20.

They presented the composites to subjects, and asked them to rate the intensity of the emotion on a scale from 1 to 7. These subjects rated the left face composites as "more intense" than the right face composites. This shows that emotions are expressed more intensely on the left side of the face compared to the right. Anatomically, the left side of the face receives more contralateral projections from the right brain, particularly in the lower part of the face. Thus the right brain may be more involved in the display of emotion by the face.

the origins of asymmetry

It is possible that the asymmetries in the nervous system and the body develop as a result of environmental influences. Because of the preponderance of right-handed people, the world is generally arranged for right-handers. Scissors, school desks, and office equipment are but a few of the annoyances which left-handed people must face. At one time, schools and parents discouraged children from using their left hand to write. During this period, the frequency of left-handed writing was only 2.1% of the population in the United States. But after the push for right-handedness subsided, and people began to allow children to use whichever hand they preferred, the frequency of left-handedness rose to 11% by 1972 (Levy, 1977). It is clear that the environment can have a substantial impact on asymmetries, at least in handwriting.

But the evidence for genetic factors, or maternal intrauterine influ-

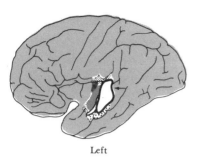

Left

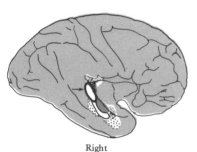

Right

Figure 16.19
*Diagram of cytoarchitectonic
areas of the human auditory
cortex in the left and right side
of the human brain. The white
area (marked by arrows) is very
asymmetrical and is the
temporoparietal cortex. [From
Galaburda et al. (1978).
Copyright 1978 by the American
Association for the Advancement
of Science.]*

ences, on asymmetrical development is very strong. This is particularly true for brain development. Asymmetries in the brain are present in the fetus, suggesting that they are at least beginning to develop long before cultural factors can have any effect.

Some sex related factor, such as prenatal sex hormones, may also be influencing the process of lateralization. Witelson (1976) found that right hemisphere abilities were more developed in boys; for the most part, left brain abilities (particularly verbal skills) are more developed in girls (Maccoby and Jacklin, 1974). Reid (cited in Levy and Levy, 1978) found that the right hemisphere of boys was more highly developed compared to girls of the same age. It is possible that the different hemispheres were developing at different rates in boys and girls because of the impact of environmental factors. Perhaps boys are given more experience with "right-brained" tasks, while girls might be rewarded for verbal abilities.

It would be very difficult to explain sex differences in anatomical asymmetry of foot size by resorting to environmental influences. Levy and Levy (1978) compared the sizes of the left and right feet in 150 individuals who came into a shoe store. Table 16.1 presents their data for right- and left-handed males and females.

Notice that most of the right-handed males tended to have larger right feet; most of the right-handed females tended to have larger left feet. For the left-handed people, the pattern was reversed. These findings also applied to children under 6, suggesting that the pubertal release of sex hormones could not be the cause. This sex difference in asymmetry of foot size may be due to the actions of prenatal sex hormones, or to some other sex related factor.

Figure 16.20
(a) Left-side composite, (b) original, and (c) right-side composite of the same face. [From Sackheim, Gur, and Saucy (1978). Copyright 1978 by the American Association for the Advancement of Science.]

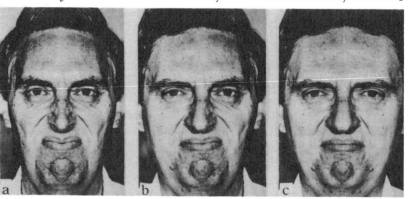

Table 16.1
Distribution of right-handed and nonright-handed male and female subjects with respect to relative foot size[a]

Relative Foot Size	Right-handed		Nonright-handed	
	Males	Females	Males	Females
Left > right	2	55	6	0
Equal	10	18	6	2
Right > left	28	14	0	9
Total	40	87	12	11

[a]Levy and Levy (1978).

A third approach to the study of higher processes involves the *split-brain technique*. This operation surgically severs the hemispheres, so that it is possible to determine which higher processes are subserved by each hemisphere.

The left side of the brain is specialized for language functions, at least for the vast majority of right-handed people, and most left-handed people as well. The right side is better at spatial tasks. The left hemisphere apparently takes a more analytical, logical, and verbal approach, while the right takes a more intuitive and spatial approach to the perception of the environment.

Humans also show anatomical asymmetries, particularly in the temporal lobes. In the human body, hand preference is strongly asymmetrical, and so is the intensity of emotion which is expressed on the left and right sides of the face. Although environmental factors can have some impact on the direction of handedness, most of the asymmetry develops very early and is probably due to genetic or other prenatal factors.

summary
Asymmetry in the Nervous System

Many animals communicate with one another in various ways. Ants use chemical signals, some South American fish use electrical impulses, birds use songs, and bees use dances on the walls of their hives. But of all the animals, humans are unique in that they acquire and use language. They may not be unique in the ability to acquire language (as we shall see later in this section), but they are the only species which acquires it naturally. This means that the study of the physiological basis to this very special higher process must be limited to the study of human beings. We cannot do lesion experiments, or electrical stimulation on normal brains, or anatomical studies except after natural death. Despite these limitations, scientists have learned a great deal about the neurological substrates for language.

In this section we will discuss the brain structures which are criti-

language

cally involved with language, and which have been identified mainly by studying brain damaged humans. First we will see that the brain areas subserving language are strongly lateralized, mostly in the left hemisphere as we saw in the last section. Second, we will look at the specific brain structures within the left hemisphere which play crucial roles in language. Third, we will examine the way that these critical areas interact with one another and with the sensory systems by means of fiber connections. In order to speak, read, write, and understand spoken and written language, it is not enough merely to have the speech areas of the brain intact. These areas must communicate with the auditory and visual cortex, as well as with the motor systems which control the jaws, mouth, and tongue.

Last, we will discuss the contributions that animals have made in the study of language. This may seem like a contradiction since we just said that humans are the only ones who naturally acquire language. But it seems clear that some nonhuman primates at least possess some ability for language, and they also may possess some forerunners of the speech areas which are present in the brains of human beings.

hemispheric lateralization
of language function

The studies which we described in the last section on split brain patients should have convinced you that language functions are strongly lateralized in the human brain. But the patient with a split brain is not normal. In this section we will discuss several other approaches which have also reached this conclusion, many of which use normal people with intact brains.

The Wada test. This approach involves injecting a barbiturate, usually sodium amytal, into one of the carotid arteries (Wada, 1949). It produces an immediate contralateral paralysis as the barbiturate depresses neuronal activity on one side of the brain. When the injection is made so that the hemisphere which is dominant for speech is depressed, the patient shows several language difficulties. For example, they misname objects, and they have difficulty in repeating a well-known series, such as the days of the week. Depression of the nondominant hemisphere still produces the same contralateral paralysis, but no language problems. Milner, Branch, and Rasmussen (1966) studied 212 patients with this technique; their results appear in Table 16.2.

Ninety-two percent of the right-handed people had speech represented in the left hemisphere. But the left-handed people showed a good deal more variability. Some of them had bilateral representation of speech. These individuals showed some interesting differences in defects depending upon which hemisphere was depressed. Some made mistakes in repeating the days of the week and counting for-

Table 16.2[a]

		Speech representation		
Handedness	Number	Left	Bilateral	Right
Right	95	87 (92%)	1 (1%)	7 (7%)
Left or ambidextrous without early damage	74	51 (69%)	10 (13%)	13 (18%)
Left or ambidextrous with early damage	43	13 (30%)	7 (16%)	23 (54%)

[a]From Milner, Branch, and Rasmussen (1966).

ward and backward after depression of the right hemisphere. After left-side depression, they made mistakes in naming objects, but none in series. For others this pattern was reversed. Thus it is possible that some left-handed people develop separate kinds of speech functions in their two hemispheres.

averaged evoked potentials. AEPs have also been used to study hemispheric lateralization of language functions. For example, Buchsbaum and Fedio (1970) found that the dominant hemisphere for speech showed a larger AEP compared to the nondominant hemisphere when verbal stimuli were presented.

Thatcher (1977) has been using AEPs in a number of different studies designed to investigate the higher processes. In one study, he presented subjects with a series of stimuli, some of which were simple random dot displays (controls), and others of which were words which provided the same amount of retinal stimulation. Figure 16.21 shows three typical series.

The first few stimuli were random dot displays. But the subject did not know how many displays they would see so that they would not be able to predict when the word was coming. The first word was then presented followed by another variable number of random dot dis-

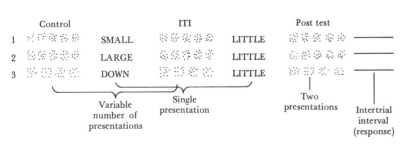

Figure 16.21
Trial sequences and experimental design. Within a session of trials the total number of illuminated dots and the average retinal area subtended were the same for all display conditions. Displays were 20 msec in duration and were presented at 1 Hz. [From Thatcher (1977).]

plays. Finally, the second word was presented, which was either a synonym of the first word, an antonym, or a neutral word that had no apparent connection to the first word. Last, another series of random dot displays was presented. The only response that was required of the subject was to press a lever after the second word to indicate whether the word was a synonym, an antonym, or a neutral. During all of these presentations, the experimenter recorded raw EEG from several locations on both hemispheres.

Figure 16.22 shows some of their AEPs. Thatcher provided some very detailed statistical analyses of the results, but we will hit only some of the main points. First note that the AEPs to the words were strikingly different from those to the random dot displays presented before the first word. Presumably, the presentation of a word releases quite a different pattern of neural firing compared to a random dot display. The word has meaning and associations, and the display does not. Second, the AEPs to the first word were smaller, and less widely distributed across the brain, compared to the AEPs to the second word. This might be explained by the fact that the higher processes going on during presentation of the second word are more involved. The subject not only has to extract the meaning of the second word, but has to compare it to the memory of the first word in order to determine whether it is a synonym, antonym, or neutral.

The AEPs from the left hemisphere and from the right hemisphere were also different for the words. Figure 16.23 shows a comparison of

Figure 16.22
AEPs to the first word, random dot displays [before first word, and after second word, and to the second word (synonym and antonym)]. [From Thatcher (1977).]

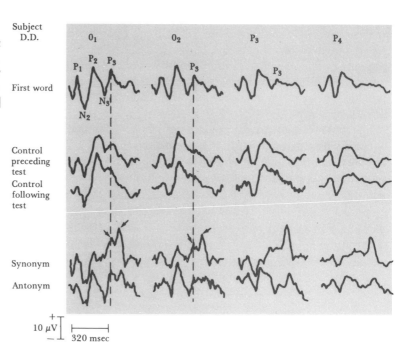

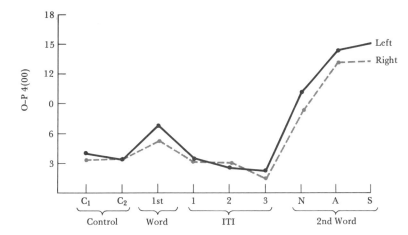

Figure 16.23
Mean baseline to P-4(00) amplitude for left and right electrode sites for the various conditions of the experiment.

the size of the late positive component P-4(00) for left and right hemispheres. During the first control random dot displays, the size of this component did not differ between the hemispheres. But during the first word, a difference emerged, with the left hemisphere showing the larger amplitude. The difference disappeared again during the middle series of random dot displays, but emerged again for the second word, regardless of whether it was a neutral, synonym, or antonym. Again, the AEPs for the second word showed a larger P-4(00) component compared to those for the first word.

This technique has some remarkable potential, in that it is completely harmless to the subjects. Thatcher's sophisticated way of using the AEP promises to provide some very valuable information about brain areas which subserve language and thinking.

studies of brain damaged human beings. Without a doubt, the vast majority of our knowledge about the neurological basis for language comes from the study of people who have experienced some kind of brain damage, particularly a stroke. A stroke is the common term for an occlusion or rupture of one of the brain's blood vessels.

In humans there are four large conducting arteries to the brain: the two **internal carotid** and the two **vertebral arteries**. Each cerebral hemisphere is supplied by the three main branches of the carotid arteries. These are shown in Figure 16.24. The vertebral arteries supply blood to the medulla, pons, and cerebellum.

Venous drainage of the brain occurs by means of both superficial and deep cerebral veins. Figure 16.25 shows the major veins which subserve the cerebral hemispheres. It is easy to see how a rupture of any of these blood vessels would do widespread damage.

Studies of stroke victims confirm the view that in most people, language functions are strongly lateralized. For example, damage to the

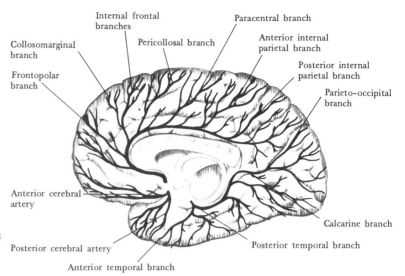

Figure 16.24
The anterior and posterior cerebral arteries are seen on the medial aspect of the brain. Long segments of these conducting arteries lie deep within the various sulci and fissures. Many branches seem to end abruptly as they bend to penetrate the underlying cortex. [From Crosby et al. (1962).]

left hemisphere is much more likely to result in language disturbances, particularly for right-handed people.

Stroke victims, and the symptoms which they display, have also been our major source of information concerning the brain structures within the left hemisphere which are important for language. These structures are the topic of the next section.

brain structures involved in language The major brain areas which are involved in language include **Broca's area, Wernicke's area**, part of the motor cortex, and the thalamus. The first three are shown in Figure 16.26. In this section we will outline what happens when each of these areas is damaged, or electrically

Figure 16.25
Superficial cerebral veins drain into the dural venous sinuses. Frequently flow is in two directions since there is extensive anastomosis between the venous channels. Venous drainage is best described as regional. [From Crosby et al. (1962).]

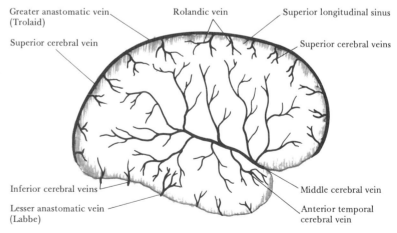

stimulated, and in the next section we will consider some hypotheses about how the various structures communicate with one another and with the rest of the brain.

Broca's area. Broca (1824–1880) retains a place in the history of neuroscience because he was the first to link **aphasia**, a language disorder resulting from brain damage, to specific lesions, and also to show that these lesions were for the most part in the left hemisphere. Broca and his colleagues had collected 20 cases of aphasia, all having pathological changes in the left hemisphere. Nineteen of these cases had the lesion in the third frontal convolution, an area which is now known as Broca's area.

People with lesions in this area characteristically exhibit little speech, which is emitted slowly with great effort. They also articulate very poorly. They have more than just a difficulty in enunciating the correct sounds—they also fail to produce correct sentences. Typically, they omit the small grammatical words and endings. However, the patient understands both spoken and written language. Musical ability is strangely not affected—the patient is usually able to sing familiar songs without problems in articulation.

This kind of language disturbance is grossly termed an **expressive aphasia**, because the deficit is in expression, not in understanding. Varieties of this syndrome include **dysarthria** (difficulty in timing, intonation, and loudness) and **anarthria** (complete loss in the ability to speak). Patients may also be able to say just one word. One of Broca's patients was called "Tan" because that was the only word which he uttered.

Wernicke's area. Wernicke (1848–1905) described patients who had quite a different kind of aphasia. They were able to speak quite fluently, but their speech was generally devoid of content. People with damage to Wernicke's area (which includes the planum temporale) generally produce speech effortlessly and rapidly, but there is relatively little informational content. There are also many errors in word usage.

This kind of aphasia falls into the general category of **receptive aphasia**, because there is apparently a deficit in the appreciation of the meanings of both spoken and written words. The patients may use words that they apparently have made up, or substitute a word of the right class (such as lawyer for doctor), or a general term when they mean a specific term (such as ladies for nurses). Damage to Wernicke's area results in longer lasting aphasia compared to damage to the other speech areas. This would suggest that Wernicke's area is the most critical area for language.

motor cortex. The motor areas which subserve the lips, jaw, and tongue in both the nondominant and dominant hemispheres also play an im-

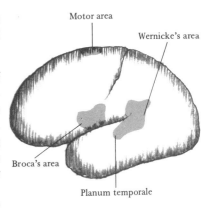

Figure 16.26
Approximate location of the "speech" areas in the human brain.

portant role in language, or at least in the production of speech. Damage to these areas results in a transient aphasia, but the patient usually recovers much sooner than when Broca's or Wernicke's areas are damaged. Penfield and Rasmussen (1950) electrically stimulated parts of the motor cortex and found that the patient produced a long drawn vowel sound. They were unable to stop the sound until they were out of breath. After taking a breath, the patient helplessly resumed the vowel sound. It would appear that this part of the motor cortex is involved with the production of speech, but not with the higher process of language.

thalamus. Although the thalamus is not traditionally associated with language functions, brain damage in this area does sometimes affect speech in strange ways. Penfield and Roberts (1959) describe one patient who had a lesion in the pulvinar nucleus of the thalamus. This patient misnamed objects; for example, he called a pair of scissors "a subscriber." When he was asked if he knew how to use the object he said "no," but then he picked up the scissors and used them appropriately.

Another patient with thalamic damage exhibited incoherent, repetitious speech (Mohr, Watters, and Duncan, 1975). A conversation with this person went like this:

Doctor: How are things going?
Patient: I thinks, a, going fine and . . . I can say, s'quit alright, si sings say rou, rup . . .
Doctor: What happened?
Patient: Well . . . See up chup a lupdup. Cheche den, etc., and, a She is quite please at that (Mohr, Watters, and Duncan, 1975).

Electrical stimulation studies on the thalamus reveal that the language functions of this structure may also be lateralized. Fedio and Van Buren (1975) stimulated the left or right pulvinar nucleus while they presented slides which showed an object that was easily named, or slides with spatial designs which could not be so easily verbalized. Left pulvinar stimulation interfered with naming of objects and also interfered with the recall of objects which had been presented a few seconds before. Right pulvinar stimulation did not produce these deficits. But stimulation of the right thalamus did produce a defect on the nonverbal spatial designs. During stimulation of the right pulvinar, the patients were frequently unable to recognize a complex pattern which had been correctly perceived a few seconds earlier. Thus the thalamus shows asymmetries which are analagous to those seen in the cerebral cortex. Unfortunately, although it appears that the thalamus is involved in language function, it is not clear how it is involved.

The language areas of the brain are connected to each other and to sensory and motor areas by fiber bundles which run between them. Figure 16.27 shows some of the major connnections within a hemisphere and between the hemispheres. The major connections which we will discuss include the association bundles between the visual cortex and the **angular gyrus** (a visual-auditory association area) in the parietal lobe, the fibers between the angular gyrus and Wernicke's area, and the **arcuate fasciculus** which connects Wernicke's area to Broca's area.

Wernicke was the first to postulate the importance of cortical connections in language. In doing so, he made a substantial contribution because he provided a theoretical model for the aphasias which went beyond the mere specification of the syndromes. Wernicke theorized (summarized by Geschwind, 1970) that Broca's area, because of its proximity to the motor cortex, incorporates programs for the complex coordination of the muscles for speech. Broca's area guides the motor cortex. This makes sense in view of the fact that damage to Broca's area results in an expressive aphasia.

Wernicke's area, on the other hand, lies next to the sensory cortex for hearing, and hence is important for comprehending spoken language. But since patients with damage in Wernicke's area have difficulty communicating as well, Wernicke postulated that the act of speaking initiates, in some manner, the auditory form of the words in the intact Wernicke's area. When this area is damaged, there is an absence of appropriate excitatory input from Wernicke's area to Broca's area.

cortical connections between language areas

Figure 16.27
Major connections between the speech areas in the human brain. [Modified from Geschwind (1965).]

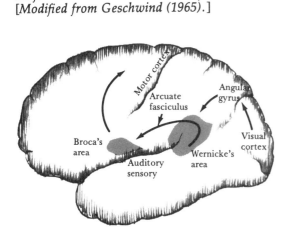
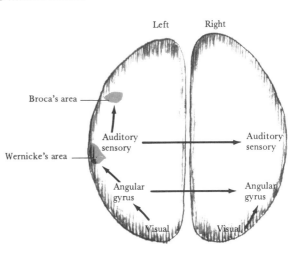

Wernicke and his students extended the model to incorporate other features of language disturbances. For example, the understanding of written language would require that sensory information in the visual cortex reach Wernicke's area, which it does by means of the angular gyrus. Damage to Wernicke's area therefore affects the comprehension of both spoken and written language. Also, since language functions reside in the left hemisphere, any visual messages received by the right hemisphere will have to be conveyed to Wernicke's area in the left. These messages must arrive by means of the callosal connections between the angular gyrus in each hemisphere.

The model of cortical connections which appears in Figure 16.27 can explain several interesting varieties of language disorder. Geschwind (1970) calls these **disconnection syndromes**, and they provide some strong supporting evidence for Wernicke's theory. The examples we will give serve to illustrate the importance of the cortico–cortical connections.

word deafness. This disconnection syndrome presents a remarkable array of symptoms. Liepmann and Storch (1902, summarized by Geschwind, 1965) described a patient with normal hearing levels who could express himself normally both in speaking and writing. The patient could read, but could not understand spoken language. The lesion in this patient spared both Broca's and Wernicke's area, but the direct auditory pathway to the auditory cortex was destroyed on the left side. In addition, the callosal fibers from the auditory area on the right side were also lost. The patient's speech was normal because both Wernicke's and Broca's areas were normal, as were the connections between Broca's area and the motor cortex. The patient could comprehend written language because there was nothing wrong with the connections between the visual cortex and Wernicke's area. But auditory input from the left ear could not reach Wernicke's area, and input from the right ear could not get to the left hemisphere. This interesting and very unusual case illustrates how important it is for auditory input to reach Wernicke's area in order to understand spoken language.

alexia without agraphia. In 1892, Dejerine (cited by Geschwind, 1965) described a patient who suddenly lost the ability to read (**alexia**) and along with it, the ability to see in the right visual field. The patient was still able to write (**agraphia** refers to the lack of ability to write) but could not read what he had just written. A postmortem examination (see Figure 16.28) revealed that the stroke damaged the left visual cortex, which accounted for the loss of vision in the right visual field. The posterior part of the corpus callosum was also destroyed. This part normally conveys messages from the right visual cortex to the left hemisphere. Thus the patient could not read because visual messages

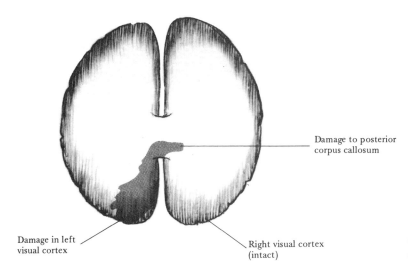

Damage to posterior
corpus callosum

Damage in left
visual cortex

Right visual cortex
(intact)

Figure 16.28
*The pattern of cerebral damage in
a patient who had alexia without
agraphia.*

which were received by the remaining visual cortex in the right hemisphere could not be conveyed to Wernicke's area in the left.

These disconnection syndromes are extremely rare cases, and most
of the time a stroke will affect overlapping fibers and structures. It is
very unusual for a clear pattern of speech deficits to emerge. But because of these "pure" cases, it has become possible to identify the
roles of the structures and connecting pathways involved in language
and to predict the effects of various lesions.

There is no doubt that animals can communicate with each other and
even with human beings on fairly sophisticated levels. One of your
authors has a dog who makes her request for food quite plain by pick-
ing up her food dish in her teeth and dropping it in her owner's lap.
But whether or not animals possess language is quite another matter.

Scientists have attempted to teach chimpanzees, who are our closest
relatives, to talk; they have failed miserably. Apparently the chimp's
vocal apparatus is simply not suited to speech. But some scientists
have been able to teach chimps to communicate with sign language of
various kinds. Their results suggest that chimps are certainly capable
of the rudiments of language.

Gardner and Gardner (1971) trained a chimp named Washoe to use
American Sign Language by rearing her in an environment in which
everyone around her used this mode of communication. They constantly "talked" with her, rewarded her for her use of sign language
and found her to be an extremely receptive language learner. She
learned over 100 signs and strung them together to form phrases such
as "Roger you tickle," "go out," "key open food." She showed the

language in animals?

language **535**

ability to generalize, an important component of language. For example, she generalized the use of the sign for "more" to "more food," "more tickle," "more drink," and so on. She also was productive in the sense that she invented signs. She called ducks "water birds," and watermelon "candy-fruit-drink," all signs that no one had ever used in her presence.

Other scientists have taught chimps to communicate with plastic symbols (Premack, 1970) or with computerized push buttons which contain visual designs (Rumbaugh, 1977). Savage-Rumbaugh, Rumbaugh, and Boysen (1978) report that their chimpanzees even communicate with each other by means of the computer operated push buttons. First they trained Sherman and Austin to request a hidden food by pressing the correct button on the panel. Once both the chimps were proficient on this task, the experimenter took one of the chimps into the next room. There it observed the baiting of a container with 1 of 11 different foods. When it was brought back, the experimenter asked the chimp (by symbols) what the food was. It responded, and then the other chimp (who had not seen the food) was allowed to request that particular food. The chimps learned this task very quickly. One chimp would communicate the contents of the hidden container in the other room to the other chimp, who would then request it.

In another series, the experimenters tested whether or not a chimp could symbolically ask for a piece of food from another chimp. The experimenters gave one chimp a variety of food and allowed the other one to watch through a window. The observing animal spontaneously requested food through the keyboard, and the experimenters encouraged the other chimp to comply with the request. Eventually the chimp with the food complied on his own, although occasionally he would ignore the request. These scientists point out that the "errors" on this task were quite revealing:

Errors on the part of the recipient (of the request) most often occurred when a highly preferred food was requested. The recipient appeared either to ignore the request or to act as though he hadn't understood but would be quite willing to offer a piece of chow instead of a piece of chocolate . . . (Savage-Rumbaugh, Rumbaugh, and Boysen, 1978).

hemispheric specialization in animals. Whether or not the chimps and other nonhuman primates possess the forerunners of the speech areas which are seen in human beings is not yet clear. But they do show some anatomical hemispheric differences. LeMay and Geschwind (1975) found that part of the temporal lobe was larger on the left side in some of the great apes. This is the same area that is larger on the left in most human beings and corresponds roughly to Wernicke's area.

The nonhuman primates may also possess some lateralization of function for communication. Petersen and his colleagues (Petersen, Beecher, Zoloth, Moody, and Stebbins, 1978) trained Japanese macaques and five other monkeys of different species to discriminate between two parts of a species-specific call made by wild Japanese macaques. The two sounds were similar but they communicated different things to the Japanese macaques. One sound is produced primarily by estrous females soliciting male consorts, and the other is emitted by both males and nonestrous females. The experimenters reasoned that since these sounds function in communication for the Japanese macaque, then the macaques should be processing them in the left hemisphere if they have any hemispheric specializations. But since these sounds have no communication value for the other species of monkeys, then they should be processed equally by both hemispheres.

To test this hypothesis, they presented a series of one of the sounds, and intermittently inserted the other sound. The monkeys were trained to respond as soon as they heard the second sound inserted. Petersen and his colleagues found that the Japanese macaques did better on this task when the sounds were presented to the right ear, compared to their performance with the left ear. Input from the right ear is transmitted mainly to the left hemisphere. But the other species of monkeys generally showed no difference in their performance with their left or right ears. This study suggests that sounds which are relevant to communication are processed more effectively by the left hemisphere in the Japanese macaque. It could also mean that the forerunners of hemispheric specialization for language function are present in some of the nonhuman primates.

---

summary
Language

The natural tendency to acquire language is unique to human beings, and it is one of the very highest "higher processes." Approaches other than the split-brain technique have clearly demonstrated that language ability is strongly lateralized. For example, the *Wada test*, which involves depression of one of the hemispheres with an injection of a barbiturate, has shown that depression of the left hemisphere usually affects language very deleteriously. Depression of the right hemisphere only has minimal effects on language for most people. The vast majority of right-handed people have their language functions in the left hemisphere, but left-handed people are more variable, and occasionally have bilateral language functions.

AEPs have also revealed strong lateralization. AEPs to words are larger than AEPs to random dot displays, particularly on the left side of the brain. Brain damage in the left hemisphere usually results in language disturbances; but brain damage in the right hemisphere rarely does.

The four areas which are most important for language include *Broca's area*, *Wernicke's area*, part of the motor cortex, and the thalamus. Damage to Broca's area results in *expressive aphasia*, suggesting that this area provides guidance to the motor areas for speech. Damage to Wernicke's area results in *receptive aphasia*—the patient speaks fluently but makes no sense. Usually, damage to this area also results in the loss of the ability to understand language as well. Thus Wernicke's area is probably the most important, and most intimately involved in the higher process of language. The motor cortex (on both sides of the brain) controls the muscles in the jaw, tongue, and lips. Although damage to the thalamus sometimes produces language disturbances, the role of this structure is still obscure.

Studies on patients with *disconnection syndromes* have revealed that the fiber bundles which connect the speech areas to one another and to the sensory and motor systems are critically important. In order to understand spoken language for example, input from the auditory cortex must reach Wernicke's area. In order to read, input from the visual cortex must reach Wernicke's area. And in order to speak, the connections between Wernicke's area and Broca's area, as well as the connections between Broca's area and the motor cortex subserving the mouth areas, must be intact.

Studies on primates show that humans may not be the only species which is able to acquire language. Chimps have shown astounding abilities to communicate through the use of symbols. They even "talk" to each other using these symbols. Some primates also show left hemisphere lateralization for communication sounds used in their species-specific repertoire. The forerunners of language appear to be present in some of the primates, both anatomically and functionally.

The varieties of approaches and the ingenious tasks which have been designed to study the physiological basis for the higher processes create an atmosphere of optimism about what we can learn about the brain. Admittedly, we do not know very much about the neural basis of "thinking," "knowing," or "understanding"—at least not yet. The human brain is the most complicated piece of machinery on Earth, and it doesn't relinquish its mysteries easily. It is in many ways the "last frontier," and it is ironic that our ultimate tool to study it is our own brain.

KEY TERMS

average evoked potentials
split-brain technique
delayed response
object alternation task
spatial alternation task
principal sulcus
Klüver-Bucy syndrome
psychic blindness
sensory neglect
egocentric orientation
allocentric orientation
landmark reversal task
object reversal task
place reversal task
exogenous influences
endogenous influences

planum temporale
temporoparietal cortex
Wada test
internal carotid arteries
vertebral arteries
Broca's area
Wernicke's area
expressive aphasia
dysarthria
anarthria
receptive aphasia
angular gyrus
arcuate fasciculus
disconnection syndromes
word deafness
alexia without agraphia

Geschwind, N. (1970). The organization of language and the brain. *Science* **27**, 54–58.

Premack, D. (1970). The education of Sarah, *Psychology Today* **4**, 54–58.

Rumbaugh, D. M., ed. (1977). *Language Learning by a Chimpanzee: The Lana Project*. Academic Press, New York.

(These three references all deal with language. The first one concerns itself with language and its brain substrates in humans; the next two present interesting reading about language abilities in chimpanzees.)

Galaburda, A. M., LeMay, M., Kemper, T. L., and Geschwind, N. (1978). Right-left asymmetries in the brain. *Science* **199**, 852–856.

Harnad, S., Doty, R. W., Goldstein, L., Jaynes, J., and Krauthamer, G., eds. (1977). *Lateralization in the Nervous System*. Academic Press, New York.

(Both of these references are rich in information about both anatomical and functional lateralization in the nervous system.)

*appendix:
human
brain
atlas*

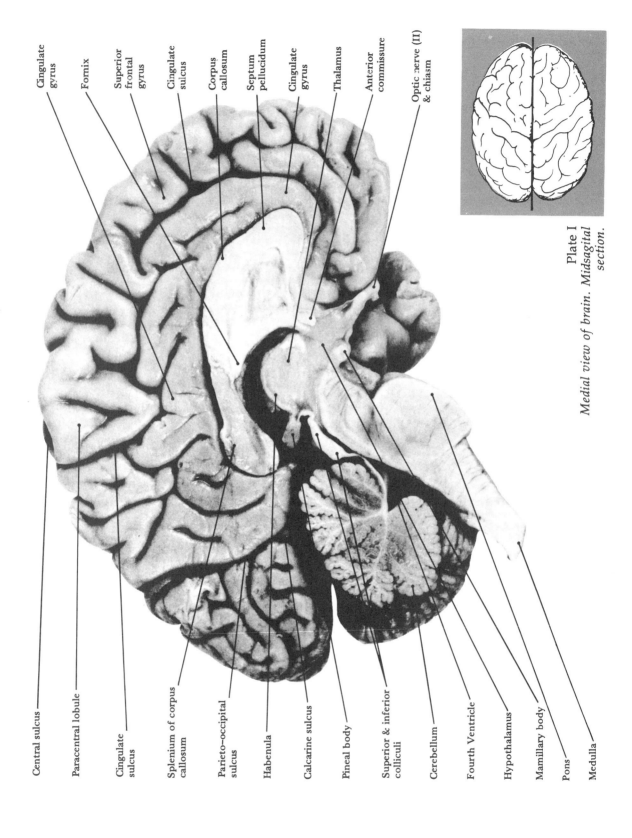

Cingulate gyrus

Fornix

Superior frontal gyrus

Cingulate sulcus

Corpus callosum

Septum pellucidum

Cingulate gyrus

Thalamus

Anterior commissure

Optic nerve (II) & chiasm

Central sulcus

Paracentral lobule

Cingulate sulcus

Splenium of corpus callosum

Parieto-occipital sulcus

Habenula

Calcarine sulcus

Pineal body

Superior & inferior colliculi

Cerebellum

Fourth Ventricle

Hypothalamus

Mamillary body

Pons

Medulla

Plate I

Medial view of brain. Midsagital section.

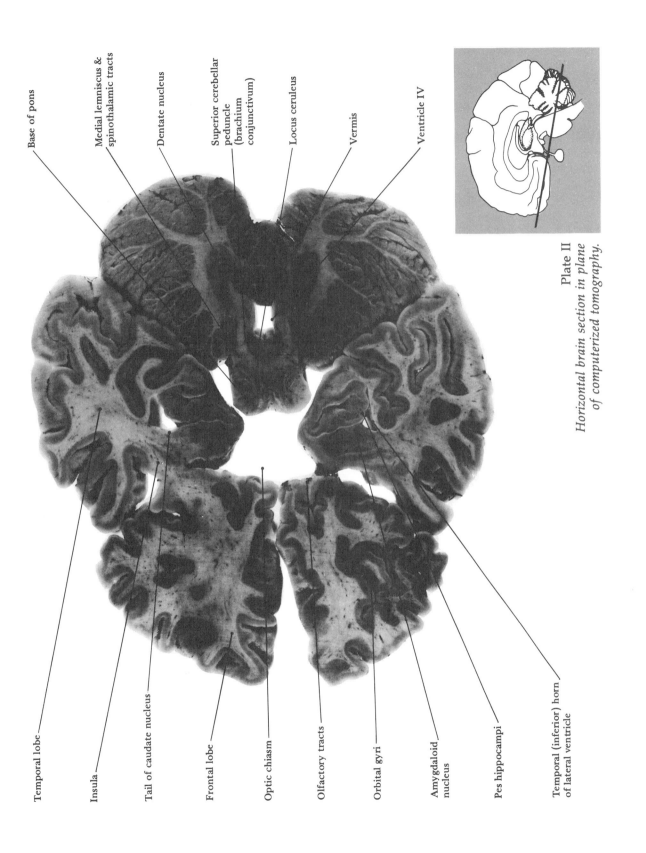

Base of pons

Medial lemniscus &
spinothalamic tracts

Dentate nucleus

Superior cerebellar
peduncle
(brachium
conjunctivum)

Locus ceruleus

Vermis

Ventricle IV

Temporal lobe

Insula

Tail of caudate nucleus

Frontal lobe

Optic chiasm

Olfactory tracts

Orbital gyri

Amygdaloid
nucleus

Pes hippocampi

Temporal (inferior) horn
of lateral ventricle

Plate II

*Horizontal brain section in plane
of computerized tomography.*

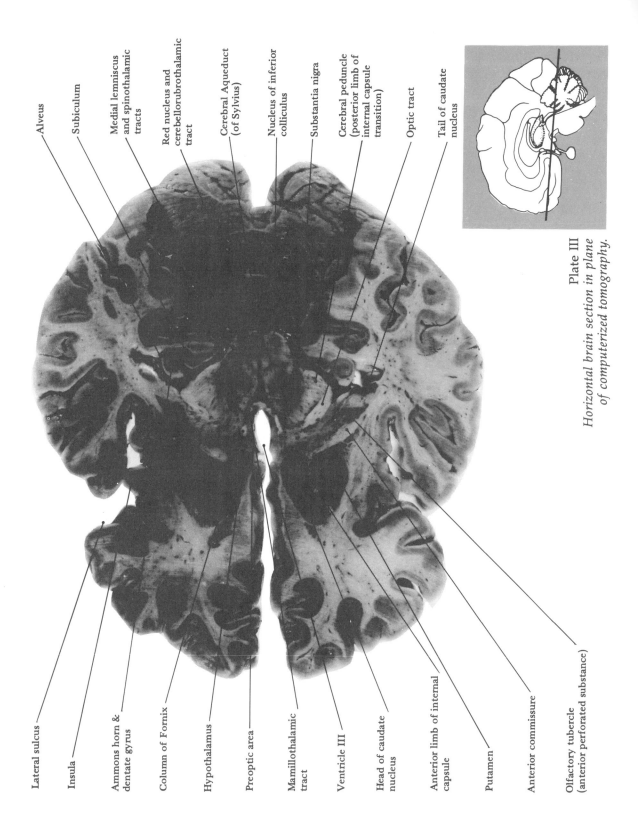

Alveus

Subiculum

Medial lemniscus and spinothalamic tracts

Red nucleus and cerebellorubrothalamic tract

Cerebral Aqueduct (of Sylvius)

Nucleus of inferior colliculus

Substantia nigra

Cerebral peduncle (posterior limb of internal capsule transition)

Optic tract

Tail of caudate nucleus

Lateral sulcus

Insula

Ammons horn & dentate gyrus

Column of Fornix

Hypothalamus

Preoptic area

Mamillothalamic tract

Ventricle III

Head of caudate nucleus

Anterior limb of internal capsule

Putamen

Anterior commissure

Olfactory tubercle (anterior perforated substance)

Plate III

Horizontal brain section in plane of computerized tomography.

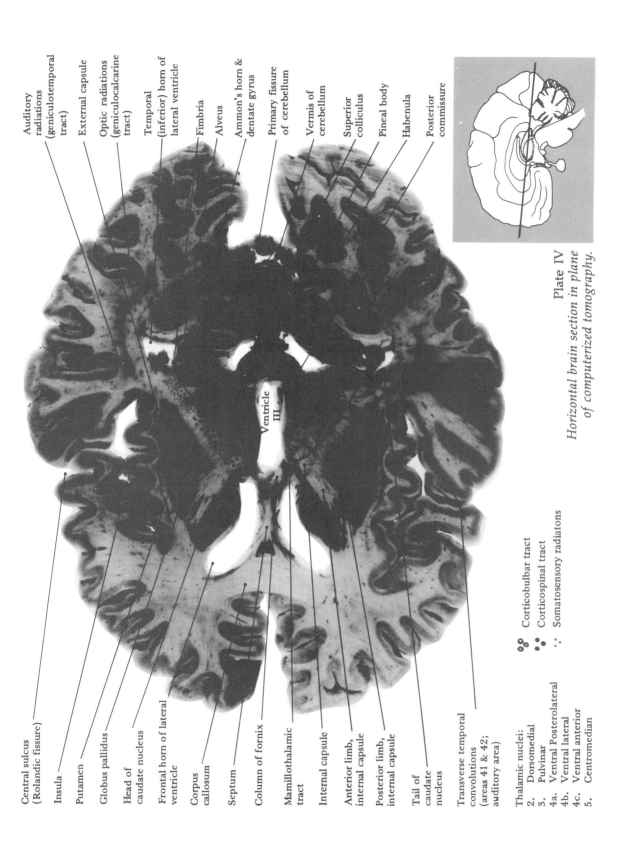

Central sulcus (Rolandic fissure)

Insula

Putamen

Globus pallidus

Head of caudate nucleus

Frontal horn of lateral ventricle

Corpus callosum

Septum

Column of fornix

Mamillothalamic tract

Internal capsule

Anterior limb, internal capsule

Posterior limb, internal capsule

Tail of caudate nucleus

Transverse temporal convolutions (areas 41 & 42; auditory area)

Thalamic nuclei:
2. Dorsomedial
3. Pulvinar
4a. Ventral Posterolateral
4b. Ventral lateral
4c. Ventral anterior
5. Centromedian

Auditory radiations (geniculotemporal tract)

External capsule

Optic radiations (geniculocalcarine tract)

Temporal (inferior) horn of lateral ventricle

Fimbria

Alveus

Ammon's horn & dentate gyrus

Primary fissure of cerebellum

Vermis of cerebellum

Superior colliculus

Pineal body

Habenula

Posterior commissure

Ventricle III

Corticobulbar tract

Corticospinal tract

Somatosensory radiatons

Plate IV

Horizontal brain section in plane of computerized tomography.

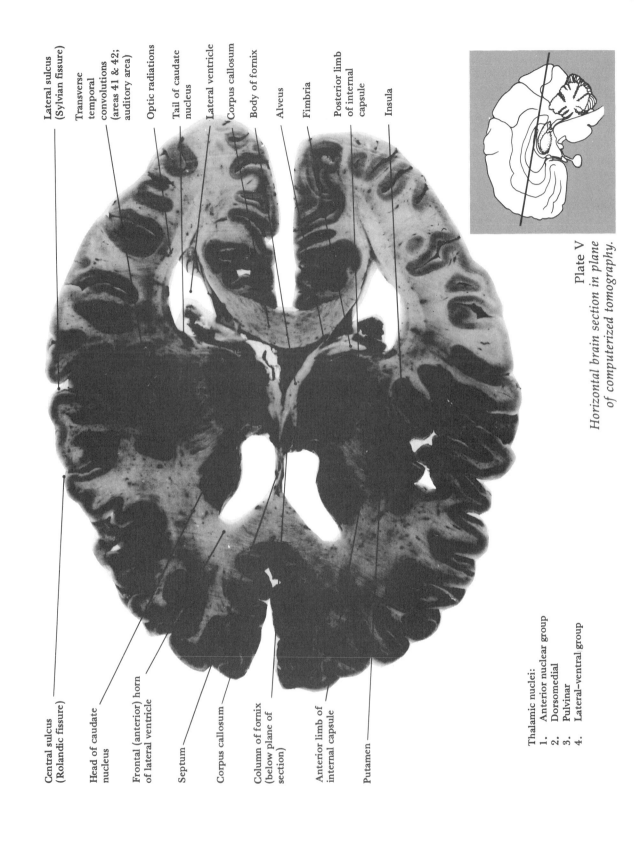

Central sulcus
(Rolandic fissure)

Head of caudate
nucleus

Frontal (anterior) horn
of lateral ventricle

Septum

Corpus callosum

Column of fornix
(below plane of
section)

Anterior limb of
internal capsule

Putamen

Lateral sulcus
(Sylvian fissure)

Transverse
temporal
convolutions
(areas 41 & 42;
auditory area)

Optic radiations

Tail of caudate
nucleus

Lateral ventricle

Corpus callosum

Body of fornix

Alveus

Fimbria

Posterior limb
of internal
capsule

Insula

Thalamic nuclei:
1.   Anterior nuclear group
2.   Dorsomedial
3.   Pulvinar
4.   Lateral–ventral group

Plate V

Horizontal brain section in plane
of computerized tomography.

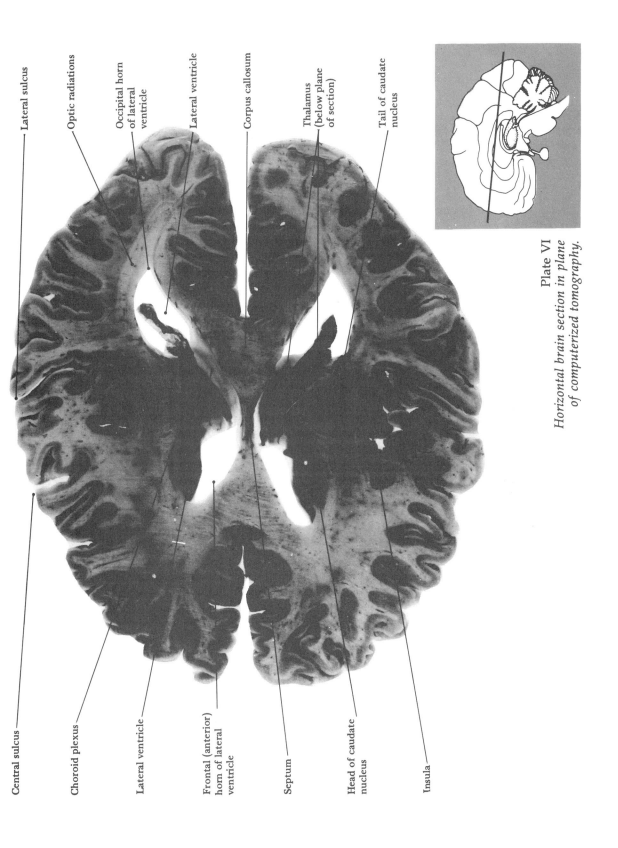

Central sulcus

Lateral sulcus

Optic radiations

Occipital horn of lateral ventricle

Lateral ventricle

Corpus callosum

Thalamus (below plane of section)

Tail of caudate nucleus

Choroid plexus

Lateral ventricle

Frontal (anterior) horn of lateral ventricle

Septum

Head of caudate nucleus

Insula

Plate VI

Horizontal brain section in plane of computerized tomography.

BRAIN ATLAS CREDITS

Abducens nucleus The nucleus of the sixth cranial nerve.

Absorptive phase That portion of the metabolic cycle that is marked by the storage of nutrients.

Accessory olive One nucleus of the olivary complex that receives input from both ears. It is the first place in the auditory system where binaural interaction can occur. See Figure 6.9.

Accessory structures Features of the sense organ or receptor cell which modify the physical stimulus energy. For example, the lens mechanism of the eye, or the bulb of the Pacinian corpuscle.

Accommodation The name for the process of the change in the shape of the lens of the eye when a person looks from a distant object to a near object. The lens thickens in this situation. With age the lens gradually loses the ability to accommodate sufficiently. When this occurs many individuals who wear eyeglasses switch to "bifocals."

Acetoxycycloheximide (AXM) A drug that inhibits protein synthesis.

Acetylcholine (ACh) The neurotransmitter that is used by the neurons which terminate on muscle cells at the neuromuscular junction. This transmitter is also found in the brain, the spinal cord, and in the autonomic nervous system.

Acetylcholinesterase (AChE) The enzyme which catalyses the reaction that breaks apart the acetylcholine molecule. This reaction thereby stops the effect of ACh on the postsynaptic cell. See Figure 3.8.

ACh See acetylcholine.

AChE See acetylcholinesterase.

Across-neuron response pattern A proposal that taste stimulus information is coded by the pattern of nerve activity across many separate fibers. There would, therefore, be a distinct pattern for each stimulus. Patterns that are similar presum-ably would elicit similar taste sensations. See Figure 7.6.

ACTH See adrenocorticotrophic hormone.

Actin myofilaments When a skeletal muscle contracts, the thin actin myofilaments slide past the thicker myosin myofilaments. See Figures 9.1 and 9.3.

Action potential The nerve impulse. Also referred to sometimes as the spike potential. The rapid fluctuation of the permeability of the neuron's membrane to sodium and potassium ions. This change is signaled by a series of electrical changes in potential across the nerve cell membrane. These changes are also propagated down the length of the cell.

Adaptation A decrease in response that is the result of repeated or prolonged stimulation.

A-delta fibers A class of nociceptors that have thinly myelinated axons and convey information regarding sharp pain.

Adenine One of the nucleotide bases of the DNA molecule. See Figure 14.2.

Adequate stimulus The form of physical energy that has the lowest threshold for excitation of the receptor cells in a given sense organ.

ADH See antidiuretic hormone.

Adipsia A cessation of drinking. Can result from destruction of the lateral hypothalamus.

Adoption studies A major technique for studying the relationship between genes and complex behavioral traits. The behavior of adopted children is compared to the behavior of their biological parents and their adoptive parents.

Adrenal cortex The outer portion of the adrenal gland. It is activated by ACTH from the pituitary gland. The cortex releases hormones called adrenocortical steroids when stimulated by ACTH. See Figure 10.2.

Adrenal glands Part of the endocrine system. A pair of small glands located directly above the kidneys. The gland has two parts: an outer adrenal cortex, and an inner adrenal medulla.

Adrenal medulla The inner core of the adrenal gland. It is innervated by sympathetic fibers. The medulla releases two hormones into the blood: epinephrine and norepinephrine. They mimic the effects of sympathetic activation, and result in the release of energy stores and an increase in metabolism.

Adrenalin See epinephrine.

Adrenocortical steroids The hormones released by the adrenal cortex in response to ACTH. These hormones have wide-ranging effects on the body. In general they prepare the body for emergency; for example, they act to increase the metabolism of glucose.

Adrenocorticotrophic hormone (ACTH) A hormone produced in and released by cells in the anterior pituitary gland. This hormone stimulates cells of the adrenal cortex to release the hormones known as adrenocortical steroids. See Figure 10.2.

Adrenogenital syndrome The adrenal glands of a female fetus produce less corticosteroids and more androgens, resulting in malelike external genitalia.

Adsorption The attachment of molecules of taste and olfactory stimuli onto the membranes of the respective receptor cells.

AEP See averaged evoked potential.

Afferent Nerve fiber pathways that proceed toward the brain, or toward a given part of the brain.

Agonistic behavior Combative behavior. A general term that includes behaviors such as fighting, fleeing, and predatory stalking as well as fear responses.

Agraphia Inability to write.

Alarm reaction The first stage of the general adaptation syndrome. It occurs at the first experience of a stressful event. During this period, the adrenals release large quantities of hormones and the sympathetic nervous system is active. See Figure 10.3.

Aldosterone A hormone released from the adrenal cortex that acts on the kidneys to stimulate the retention of sodium.

Alexia Inability to read.

Alleles Homologous genes.

Allocentric A spatial orientation that identifies the position of an object in space by reference to another object.

All-or-none principle The nerve impulse is the largest possible response that the neuron can make. This impulse is conducted along the entire length of the axon without decrement in the size of the impulse.

Alpha-methyl-para-tyrosine (AMPT) This substance inhibits the activity of tyrosine hydroxylase, and therefore prevents catecholamine synthesis.

Alpha motor neuron The axons of these neurons synapse onto the extrafusal fibers of the skeletal muscles. Activity of the alpha motor neurons results in muscle contraction.

Alpha waves Rhythmic brain wave activity that ranges from 8 to 12 Hz. Generally associated with an awake but relaxed individual.

Amacrine cells A type of retinal cell that forms part of the synaptic connections that occur between bipolar and ganglion cells. Amacrine cells spread neural activity laterally across the retina. See Figure 5.6.

Amitripyline A drug that inhibits the re-uptake of serotonin at the synapse.

Amphetamine A drug which blocks the re-uptake mechanisms at both noradrenergic and dopaminergic synapses. This results in a potentiation of the transmitter effects, and then eventual depletion of the transmitter.

Amphetamine psychosis A disorder that looks very much like classic paranoid schizophrenia. Can result from a very large dose of amphetamine, or from its chronic use over a period of time.

Amplitude The amplitude of a wave refers to the height of a wave, that is, the difference between the peak and the trough of the wave. With respect to sound waves the amplitude of wave equals its intensity and corresponds to our perception of loudness.

AMPT See alpha-methyl-para-tyrosine.

Ampullae Enlargements on each semicircular canal, that contain the receptor cells. These cells have hairs or cilia (see Figure 8.14). The cells respond whenever there is a shearing force on the cilia resulting from movement, rotation, or acceleration of the head.

Amygdala A part of the limbic system which is found in the medial aspect of the temporal lobe and anterior to the hippocampus. See Figure 4.11. This structure appears important in the control of emotional expression.

Analog code In the nervous system, it refers to the transmission of information across synapses where amount of released neurotransmitter codes the rate of action potentials arriving at an axonal terminal.

Anarthria Complete loss of the ability to speak.

Androgen Male sex hormone produced by the testes.

Angiotensin It is a protein in the blood. It results from the action of renin on angiotensinogen. Promotes the release of aldosterone from the adrenal cortex. See Figure 11.20.

Angular gyrus A region of visual-auditory association cortex in the parietal lobe. See Figure 16.27.

Anhedonia An absence of reward value or pleasure.

Anterior Toward the front. Similar to rostral. See Figures 4.1 and 4.2.

Anterior hypothalamic area Lesions in this area of the hypothalamus have been shown to disrupt sexual behavior in the female rat. It no longer shows lordosis behavior.

Anterior olfactory nucleus A cluster of neurons in the posterior portion of the olfactory bulb. These neurons receive synaptic input from the axons in the lateral olfactory tract.

Anterior pituitary gland Also called the adenohypophysis. It releases trophic hormones in response to stimulation from the hypothalamic hormones. See Table 14.5 for the homones of the anterior pituitary.

Anterior thalamus The nuclei in the anterior thalamus that receive nerve fibers from the mammillary bodies in the posterior hypothalamus. The neurons in these nuclei in turn send axons to the cingulate gyrus. These nuclei are therefore considered to be part of the limbic system.

Antidiuretic hormone (ADH) A hormone released from the posterior pituitary gland. This hormone causes the kidneys to retain water, and thus a more concentrated urine is excreted.

Antidromic invasion If an axon is electrically stimulated along its length, a nerve impulse will be conducted in both directions, i.e., from the point of stimulation to the synaptic terminals, and also from the point of stimulation back to the cell body. An antidromic spike refers to this method of recording an action potential at the cell body following stimulation to the axon. In the normal situation axonal conduction is one way from the initial segment or hillock to the axon terminals.

Aphagia A cessation of eating. Can result from destruction of the lateral hypothalamus.

Aphasia A general term meaning a language dysfunction. It could be either in the expression of language or in the comprehension of language.

Aphrodisiac A drug or substance believed to promote sexual arousal and performance.

Apical dendritic shaft The long dendritic extension of cortical pyramidal neurons that reaches the surface layer of the cortex. See Figure 14.16.

Aplysia A small marine gastropod (see Figure 15.4). It serves as a model system for the study of plasticity in a simple nervous system.

Apomorphine A drug that is relatively specific as a dopamine receptor stimulant.

Arcuate fasciculus A fiber bundle that connects Wernicke's area and Broca's area. See Figure 16.27.

Ascending Nerve fiber pathways that proceed from lower to higher levels in the central nervous system. For example, from the spinal cord to the thalamus.

Association nuclei These are nuclei within the thalamus. The neurons within these nuclei send axons to the areas of association cortex. For example, nucleus medialis dorsalis projects to the frontal association cortex, the pulvinar nucleus to the temporal lobe.

Associative learning The organism learns to associate two events, because they consistently occur together in time or in some other predictable relationship.

Astigmatism An uneven curvature in the lens or cornea of the eye. It causes lines of some orientation to appear blurred, but has no effect on the clarity of others.

Astrocytes A class of glial cells that surround the blood capillaries. These cells therefore control the materials which are transported back and forth between the neurons and the circulatory system.

Atropa belladonna A herb that is the source for the drug atropine.

Atropine A drug which blocks the effects of acetylcholine at synapses with muscarinic receptors. Atropine acts like a false transmitter by blocking receptors but not stimulating them.

Audiogram The record of an individual's hearing level or threshold over a range of frequencies. See Figure 6.3.

Audiometry The measurement for the human's threshold of hearing over a range of frequencies.

Auditory canal The tube through which the sound waves travel to reach the tympanic membrane and middle ear. See Figure 6.4.

Autonomic nerves The nerves of the peripheral nervous system which innervate the smooth muscles of the internal organs of the body, such as the stomach, liver, sweat glands of the skin, and so on. These nerves form the autonomic nervous system which has two divisions, the sympathetic and the parasympathetic. See Figure 4.19.

Autoradiography A technique for tracing anatomical pathways with the use of radioactive molecules, such as radioactive protein or glucose. It is possible to visualize the cells which have taken up the labeled molecule.

Autosomes Any chromosome that is not a sex chromosome.

Averaged evoked potentials The average of electrical brain changes that are time dependent upon the onset of a stimulus. This potential gradually emerges from EEG recording across a series of stimulus presentations as random EEG changes average to zero. See Figure 16.9.

AXM See acetoxycycloheximide.

Axo-axonic contacts This occurs when an axon terminal makes synaptic contact on another axon.

Axo-dendritic contacts This occurs when an axon terminal makes synaptic contact on the dendrite of another nerve cell.

Axon The protoplasmic extension of a neuron that conducts nerve action potentials from the individual segment or hillock to the axon or synaptic terminals.

Axon hillock The initial unmyelinated segment of the axon. It is here that the nerve action potential originates. It also has the lowest threshold of excitation within the neuron.

Axon sprouting This phenomenon is diagramed in Figure 9.16. When nerve fibers are cut and their axon terminals degenerate, surrounding intact fibers sprout new collaterals to fill the space and form new synaptic connections.

Axonal conduction The movement of a nerve action potential along the axon without decrement in size of the potential.

Axoplasm The cytoplasm that is found within the axon.

Axoplasmic transport The movement of molecules along the length of the axon. It can occur in both directions, i.e., from cell body to synaptic terminals and the reverse.

Axo-somatic contacts These occur whenever an axon terminal makes synaptic contact on the membrane of the neuron's cell body.

Basal cells A type of cell in the olfactory epithelium. These cells provide the sheath system for the receptor cell axons leaving the epithelium. These cells also are a source for new receptors, since the receptor cells are continually renewed. See Figure 7.8.

Basal dendrites Dendrite extensions from the base of the pyramidal-shaped neurons in the cortex. See Figure 14.16.

Basal ganglia A term that is synonomous with the corpus striatum. See Figure 4.7 and Table 4.1.

Basement membrane The membrane which marks the bottom of the taste bud. Nerve fibers to the bud penetrate this membrane.

Basilar membrane The membrane which separates the scala media from the scala tympani. The organ of Corti sits on top of the basilar membrane. The membrane is set into vibratory motion whenever pressure waves travel through the cochlea. See Figures 6.6 and 6.7.

Basis pedunculi The ventral portion of the mesencephalon. It contains the cerebral peduncles, large fiber bundles from the motor cortex to the spinal cord. The substantia nigra is also within the basis pedunculi.

Benzotropine A drug which blocks the re-uptake of dopamine into the synaptic terminal.

Best frequency The frequency with the lowest intensity threshold that elicits a response from a neuron in the afferent auditory system.

Beta waves Brain wave activity 15–30 Hz that is generally associated with arousal.

Biofeedback A training technique by which an individual can learn to control many of his or her physiological responses such as blood pressure or galvanic skin response.

Biogenic amine hypothesis of depression This hypothesis postulates that an excess of catecholamines might lead to manic behavior, increased activity, and hostility. A deficiency, however, might produce depression and lassitude.

Bipolar cell A type of retinal cell that receives synapses from rods and cones and then in turn makes synaptic connections with ganglion cells. See Figure 5.6.

Bipolar depression Long periods of depression which has intervals of manic behavior.

Blood–brain barrier A barrier which prevents many substances from passing from the blood to the neurons of the brain. The barrier is most likely composed of the walls of the blood capillaries as well as the astrocytes (glial cells) which surround the capillaries.

Bony ossicles Three small bones in the middle ear cavity. They are the malleus, the incus, and the stapes. The ossicles amplify the sound pressure waves at the oval window. See Figures 6.4 and 6.5.

Brain grafts A recent technique that transplants embryonic brain tissue into an adult brain. The grafted tissue grows and forms synaptic connections with the host brain. Some of these connections appear to be functional.

Brain growth spurt A period of rapid growth of the nervous system during the prenatal or early postnatal development. See Figure 14.7.

Broca's area A motor speech area at the base of the left precentral gyrus in the human brain. Damage to the area results in an expressive aphasia. See Figure 16.26.

Calcium pump A metabolic process that removes calcium from the muscle cell. It is probably similar to the sodium pump that is present in nerve cells.

Cannon's theory of emotion The hypothesis that the experience of an emotion originates in the brain rather than in the viscera. Cannon proposed that there are neural circuits which underlie various emotions in lower brain areas, and that these circuits activate the cortex and the viscera during the event.

Carbachol A potent cholinomimetic. That is, it imitates the interaction between endogenously released acetylcholine and its postsynaptic receptors.

Cardiac muscle A special type of striated muscle that is the muscle tissue for the heart. Cardiac muscle shares some of the characteristics of both skeletal and smooth muscle.

Catecholamine A general term for compounds which contain the catechol nucleus (a chemical term that means a benzene ring with two adjacent hydroxyl groups), and an amine group (NH_2). Dopamine, norepinephrine, and epinephrine are the three most important catecholamines in the brain.

Catechol-O-methyltransferase (COMT) An enzyme located on or near the postsynaptic membrane which inactivates the catecholamine neurotransmitters, dopamine and norepinephrine.

Caudal Toward the tail. Similar to posterior. See Figures 4.1 and 4.2.

Caudate nucleus A component of the corpus striatum. See Figure 4.10. In the primate brain the caudate nucleus has a large head that is located in the frontal lobe and a long arcing tail that sweeps around the thalamus and into the temporal lobe. See appendix of cross sections.

CCK See cholecystokinin.

Cell body The portion of the neuron that contains the nucleus and other cytoplasmic organelles. Also called the soma.

Cell membrane A bilayer of lipids and proteins that forms the cellular boundary between the cell's cytoplasm and the extracellular fluid environment.

Cell proliferation In embryonic development, cell proliferation refers to the increase in the number of cells by the cycles of cellular division.

Cellular dehydration The loss of water from the intracellular fluid compartment. See Figure 11.17.

Central canal A continuation of the brain's ventricular system down the center of the spinal cord.

Central fissure A major landmark of the cerebral hemisphere. It runs along the dorsal-ventral side of the brain. It is the boundary between the frontal and parietal lobes. It also divides the motor and somatosensory cortical areas. It is also known as the fissure of Rolando. See Figure 4.7.

Central gray A region in the central core of the brainstem which, when stimulated electrically, results in an attenuation of the pain from a noxious stimulus.

Central nervous system The brain and spinal cord. That is, all the neuronal cell bodies and fibers that are contained within the cranial cavity and vertebral column.

Central sleep apnea A sleep disorder characterized by respiratory disturbances. For reasons not yet known, there is a loss of contraction of the diaphragm muscles with the onset of S-sleep.

Centralist theory of hunger and thirst The theory that postulates hunger and thirst to be mediated by activities in the brain, especially in the hypothalamus.

Cerebellum A large convoluted mass of brain tissue on the dorsal aspect of the brainstem. It has hemispheres, lobe, cortex, and subcortical structures, hence the label "little brain." Its functional importance is the regulation and coordination of movement.

Cerebral cortex The outermost layer of brain tissue. It is referred to as gray matter since it is mostly neuron cell bodies. The cerebral cortex has many functional areas, for example, there are sensory areas for each modality. There are also areas for the control of movement as well as association areas.

Cerebral peduncles Large fiber bundles that pass along the ventral surface of the mesencephalon. These fibers are, for the most part, fibers from the neocortex to the pons and spinal cord.

Cerebrospinal fluid (CSF) The fluid that fills the ventricles of the brain, subarachnoid space, and the central canal of the spinal cord. The brain floats in the CSF and is protected from bumping against the skull during sudden jerks and movements.

C fibers A class of nociceptors that are unmyelinated and convey information that correlates with the sensation of ache.

Chlorpromazine An antipsychotic drug which blocks dopamine receptors.

Cholecystokinin (CCK) A gastrointestinal hormone that is released when chyme passes from the stomach to the small intestine. Injections of this substance inhibit feeding in rats.

Choline A principal component of the neurotransmitter acetylcholine. Its metabolic source is from a group of phospholipids, the phosphotides.

Choline acetylase See choline acetyltransferase.

Choline acetyltransferase The enzyme which catalyzes the reaction between acetyl coenzyme A and choline which produces the neurotransmitter acetylcholine. Choline acetyltransferase is found in high concentration in the cytoplasm of cholinergic nerve endings. Sometimes this enzyme is referred to as choline acetylase.

Cholinergic synapse A synapse that has acetylcholine as the neurotransmitter.

Chorda tympani A branch of the VII cranial nerve (facial) that innervates the taste buds on the anterior two-thirds of the tongue.

Chromosomes Rod shaped bodies in

the nucleus of a cell that contain that cell's genetic information in the form of its DNA.

Chyme The semifluid mass of partly digested food that passes from the stomach to the small intestine.

Cingulate cyrus This region of cortex lies along the midline of the brain. It runs in an antero-posterior direction, and is above the corpus callosum. See Figure 4.11.

Circadian rhythms Biological rhythms that have a 24-hour period. For example, the normal sleep-waking cycle in humans.

Clasp-knife reflex This reflex can be demonstrated in a decerebrate animal such as a cat. When you try to bend the cat's knee, there is increasing resistance until the tendon organ is activated. Sensory information from the tendon organ results in an inhibition of the alpha motor neurons, and therefore a relaxation in the muscles. Then the resistance to bending the knee suddenly disappears and the leg bends easily. This reflex is called "clasp-knife" because it resembles the closing of a pocket-knife.

Class 1 cells One of the two types of cells in the dorsal horn of the spinal cord that respond to painful stimulation. These cells respond only to noxious stimulation, in contrast to the Class 2 cells.

Class 2 cells One of the two types of cells in the dorsal horn of the spinal cord that respond to painful stimulation. Class 2 cells respond to other somatosensory modalities in addition to pain. In this respect they differ from Class 1 cells.

Class I cells The neurons with long axons which comprise the major fiber tracts for making connections between brain structures.

Class II cells The neurons with short axons that make connections within a given structure of the brain.

Classical conditioning A form of associative learning. Two stimuli are presented to an organism. One is neutral, the other elicits a reflex response. With the pairing or association the initially neutral stimulus acquires the property of eliciting the response by itself.

Cochlea The spiral-shaped structure in the inner ear that contains the receptor cells for hearing. The cochlea is divided into three tubes or canals: the scala vestibuli, scala media, and the scala tympani. See Figure 6.6.

Cochlear microphonic An electrical waveform recorded from the cochlea that faithfully follows the auditory stimulus. It is a candidate for the receptor potential.

Code Patterns of nerve action potentials that occur within and between afferent nerve fibers form the neural code that conveys information to the brain. This information is the neural representation of the information that is in the environment. See Table 5.1.

Codominant This occurs when both alleles make a contribution to an individual's phenotype.

Coenzyme A (CoA) Coenzyme A is a substance which takes part in many reactions in the body. When combined with the acetate ion, CoA is involved in the formation of the neurotransmitter acetylcholine.

Cognitive-physiological theory of emotion The hypothesis that an emotional experience includes both the physiological changes induced by the sympathetic nervous system and also a cognitive component that is the individual's interpretation of the situation.

Cold fibers A class of thermoreceptors that have a static response which falls off as the temperature goes above 43°C and which cease firing as temperatures fall below 5°C. See Figure 8.5.

Commissures A nerve fiber bundle that interconnects the two halves of the brain. The largest of the brain's commissures is the corpus callosum. Others are the anterior and the posterior commissures.

Complex cells One of the classes of visual cortical cells described by Hubel and Wiesel. These cells responded most vigorously to a line, in a specific orientation, and moving. See also simple and hypercomplex cells.

Compression A less than one-to-one ratio of change in the stimulus to a change in neural response. For example, if one sound is twice as loud as another, a responding neuron will increase its rate of firing, but will not double its rate.

COMT See catechol-O-methyltransferase.

Condensation An increase in density of the molecules in the air, so that the pressure of that area increases above the normal atmospheric pressure. The opposite of rarefaction. See Figure 6.1.

Conditioned response (CR) The response that is elicited by the conditioned stimulus (CS) alone after it has been paired with the unconditioned stimulus.

Conditioned stimulus (CS) The originally neutral stimulus in classical conditioning that produces a conditioned response only after it has been paired with an unconditioned stimulus.

Conductive hearing loss An elevation of an individual's hearing threshold that is due to damage to the parts of the ear that transmit the airborne sound waves to the receptor cells and nerves.

Cones The class of photosensitive receptor cells that code color information. The cones contain iodopsin as the photosensitive pigment. They have their highest density at the fovea.

Contralateral The side opposite to that of a given point of reference.

Convergence In neural pathways whenever there are fewer fibers leading away from a synapse than are leading to it, it is called convergence.

Cornea The transparent protective covering over the outside of the front of the eyeball. See Figure 5.5.

Coronal plane A section through the brain that cuts across the brain from left to right and is perpendicular to the horizontal plane. Also called frontal plane or transverse plane. See Figure 4.3.

Corpus callosum The largest of the brain's commissures. It interconnects the cortical areas of the cerebral hemispheres, as well as some crossing cortical to subcortical fibers. See Figure 4.11.

Corpus luteum The ruptured follicle after ovulation. It secretes progesterone to maintain pregnancy.

Corpus striatum Literally it means striped body. This name derives from the large fiber tract, the internal capsule which passes between large clusters of neurons. These neuronal masses are also known as the basal ganglia. They are the caudate nucleus, the globus pallidus and the putamen. The corpus striatum is found within the frontal lobe but beneath the surface of the cerebral cortex.

Corticospinal tracts Fiber bundles that originate in the cerebral cortex and end in the spinal cord. The pyramidal tract is one such fiber bundle.

Corticotrophin releasing factor (CRF) A substance released by neurons in the hypothalamus which stimulates cells in the anterior pituitary to release ACTH. See Figure 10.2.

CR See conditioned response.

Cranial nerves Fiber bundles that enter and leave the brain at irregular intervals along the brainstem. There are 12 cranial nerves. See Table 4.1 and Figure 4.13.

CRF See corticotrophin releasing factor.

Cross-adaptation Prolonged stimulation with a given taste quality, e.g., sodium chloride to elicit the salty taste, results in a reduced response to other salty stimuli, but not to stimuli of other taste qualities.

Cross-modal transfer of information The learning of a task with the use of one sensory modality and test for retention of the task by means of another sense modality. See Figure 15.15.

CS See conditioned stimulus.

CSF See cerebrospinal fluid.

Cycle As it pertains to sound wave motion, cycle refers to the displacement of the sound source or vibrating body from its stationary position to the maximum movement, first in one direction and then in the other. Each cycle, therefore, includes one condensation and one rarefaction. See Figure 6.1.

Cyclic AMP The "second messenger" in the interaction of hormones and cells. It has a regulatory role in the metabolic processes of many types of cells.

Cycloheximide A drug that inhibits protein synthesis.

Cytosine One of the four nucleotide bases of the DNA molecules. See Figure 14.2.

Dark adaptation The increase in sensitivity of the eye as time in the dark increases after being exposed to light. The curve for this increase is shown in Figure 5.9.

Dark current The partial depolarization of the photoreceptor cell membrane that occurs in the dark and the continuous release of neurotransmitter substance that accompanies the depolarization. The depolarization in the dark is due to an increase in sodium conductance through the membrane. Light energy reduces this conductance.

Decibel scale A physical scale of sound intensity. This scale is a comparison between the sound intensity in question and the widely used standard physical pressure of 0.0002 dyne/cm^2. The comparison is expressed as a logarithmic scale. See Table 6.1.

Delayed response A behavioral task in which a stimulus cue is presented that signals the spatial location of a reward. A temporal delay occurs between the presentation of the cue and when the organism is allowed to respond. The stimulus cue is not present during the delay nor at the time the response is made.

Delta waves Large, slow rhythmic brain waves ranging from 1 to 4 Hz. This type of brain wave is generally associated with slow wave sleep (also called S-sleep).

Dendrites The array of protoplasmic extensions from the cell body which have a treelike appearance. The dendrites are thought of as the receptive surface of a neuron. See Figure 2.6.

Dendritic spines Small buds or outgrowths along the dendritic surface. See Figure 2.6. The spines are sites of synaptic contact. The spines also increase the dendritic surface area and thereby allow for greater neuronal connectivity.

Dendritic trees See dendrites. See also Figure 2.6.

Dendro-dendritic contacts These are functional synaptic contacts between dendrites of adjacent neurons.

Dentate gyrus Part of the hippocampal formation of the brain. It, along with the fibers from the entorhinal cortex, have been extensively investigated in the study of axon

Dentate nucleus One of the major subcortical nuclei in the cerebellum. It receives information from the cerebellar cortex and sends information to the red nucleus in the midbrain and also to the thalamus.

2-Deoxyglucose (2-DG) A radioactively labeled glucose that is taken up by nervous tissue in proportion to the rate of glucose consumption.

Depolarization A change in the value of the membrane potential so that the inside of the cell is less negative, for example −65 mV instead of −70 mV. Depolarization of the neuron usually means excitation because the value of the membrane potential moves toward the threshold for a nerve action potential.

Dermatome The area of body surface that sends somatosensory information to the spinal cord by means of one dorsal root.

Dermis The inner layer of skin that lies below the epidermis. This layer varies in thickness between 1 and 2 mm. The dermis contains glands, blood vessels, hair follicles, free nerve endings, and nerve endings with a variety of encapsulated end organs. See Figure 8.1.

Descending Nerve fiber pathways that proceed from higher to lower levels in the central nervous system. For example, from the cortex to the spinal cord.

Desmethylimipramine A drug which blocks amine uptake at NE nerve terminals, but not at dopamine terminals. The use of this drug can therefore produce a selective depletion of dopamine content in the brain.

2-DG See 2-deoxyglucose.

Diabetes mellitus A disease that results from a failure of the pancreas to release sufficient insulin so that cells can take up glucose from the blood stream. As a result, blood glucose levels remain high and cells are deprived of glucose.

Diencephalon The posterior portion of the forebrain that includes the thalamus and hypothalamus. See Figure 4.10.

Differentiation The process in embryonic development that includes the formation of specialized tissues and organs from the cells that have arisen originally from the single fertilized egg cell or ovum.

Diffuse ganglion cell A retinal ganglion cell that receives synaptic inputs from many rods and cones. See Figure 5.6.

Digital code In the nervous system, it refers to the pattern of nerve action potentials transmitted along the axon of a neuron.

Disconnection syndromes Types of language disorders that occur when one or more of the brain areas important for language are separated (i.e., disconnected by fiber transections) from one another.

Disparity detectors A class of visual cortical cells that respond most strongly when the stimulus is presented to both eyes, but also when the stimulus is a specified distance away. This suggests that these cells are coding depth. See Figure 5.16.

Disulfiram A drug that inhibits the enzyme dopamine-beta-hydroxylase (this enzyme converts dopamine to norepinephrine). The use of this drug suppresses self-stimulation behavior. See Figure 10.12.

Dizygotic twins (DZ) Twins that developed from two zygotes. They thus have only 50 percent of their genes in common. Also called fraternal twins. They are only as genetically alike as siblings.

Dominant The allele that determines the physical characteristics of expression of the gene whether or not a recessive allele is present.

Dopamine A catecholamine which is a brain neurotransmitter. Its highest concentration in the brain is found in the basal ganglia. It has been implicated in Parkinson's disease and also schizophrenia.

Dopamine hypothesis of schizophrenia This hypothesis suggests that dopamine pathways are involved in schizophrenia. It is based on the evidence that drugs which block dopamine receptors reduce schizophrenic symptoms.

Dopaminergic hypersensitivity An increased response to dopamine and dopamine receptor stimulants following a period of reduced activity such as may occur with the chronic use of dopamine receptor blocking agents.

Dopaminergic synapses Synapses which have dopamine as the transmitter substance.

Dorsal Pertaining to the back or top of an animal. See Figures 4.1 and 4.2.

Dorsal and ventral bundles The dorsal and ventral fiber systems which arise in the brainstem and ascend to the forebrain. These bundles were mapped by histochemical flourescence, and use norepinephrine as the neurotransmitter. See Figure 4.16.

Dorsal and ventral cochlear nuclei Clusters of neurons in the brainstem that receive axonal terminations of the auditory sensory nerve fibers. See Figure 6.9.

Dorsal and ventral horns A cross section of the spinal cord shows a central gray area (cell bodies) and lateral regions containing fiber tracts (white area). The central gray area has a configuration approximating that of an "H." See Figure 4.18. The dorsal and ventral extensions of the H are called horns. The dorsal horns are sensory in function and the ventral horns are motor. See also dorsal and ventral roots.

Dorsal and ventral roots The points

of entry and exit of nerve fibers to and from the spinal cord. The afferent sensory fibers enter the cord by means of the dorsal roots. These fibers terminate in the dorsal horns. The efferent motor fibers leave by means of the ventral roots. The cell bodies of these axons are in the ventral horns of the cord. See dorsal and ventral horns.

Dorsal and ventral tegmental pathways Two pathways which are cholinergic. The dorsal pathway starts in the reticular formation and projects to the midbrain tectum, thalamus, and other brain structures. The ventral pathway arises from the ventral tegmentum in the midbrain and projects to the basal forebrain and neocortex.

Dorsal column nucleus The place in the medulla where the somatosensory axons in the dorsal columns terminate. Neurons in these nuclei send axons which cross the midline to form the medial lemniscus. See Figure 8.3.

Dorsal columns A part of the lemniscal somatosensory pathway. Axons entering the spinal cord ascend to the medulla in the fiber bundles, known as the dorsal columns. These fiber tracts maintain a topographic organization of the body surface. See Figure 4.18.

Dorsal root ganglia The cell bodies of the dorsal root sensory fibers are located in the dorsal root ganglia just outside the spinal cord. See Figure 4.18.

Dorsolateral frontal cortex The cortical area that covers the dorsal and lateral extent of the frontal lobe and includes the banks and depth of the principal sulcus. See Figure 16.2.

Dorso-ventral position The position adopted by rats during copulation. It is similar to some typical positions used by nonhuman primates. See Figure 12.5.

Double depletion hypothesis The

hypothesis that thirst and the ensuing drinking behavior result from a loss of water from one or both of the two fluid compartments. The hypothesis does not account for secondary drinking.

Drug-dependent insomnia A sleep disorder that results from chronic use of sleeping pills. As the body builds up tolerance for the pills, they become ineffective and produce insomnia rather than sleep.

D-sleep Desynchronized sleep. Associated with REMs, PGO waves, and recall of dreams.

Dualistic position The philosophical position that the nature of the human person is composed of two elements: one is material, physical, and occupies space—the body; the other is nonmaterial, nonphysical, and does not occupy space—the soul or psyche.

Ductus deferens The excretory duct of the testis. Sperm pass from the testis to the seminal vesicle and ejactory duct by means of the ductus deferens. See Figure 12.1a.

Dynamic phase The period of rapid weight gain following a lesion in the ventromedial hypothalamus. Usually lasts for about three weeks. See Figure 11.2.

Dyne The unit of measure for pressure. For example, normal atmospheric pressure is about one million dynes per square centimeter. One dyne is the force which will increase the velocity of a mass of one gram one centimeter per second every second.

Dysarthria A disturbance in speaking that is characterized by difficulty in timing, intonation, and loudness.

DZ See dizygotic twins.

ECS See electroconvulsive shock.

Efferent Nerve fiber pathways that proceed away from the brain, or away from a given part of the brain.

Egocentric A spatial orientation that identifies the position of an object in space by reference to the position of the observer.

Ejaculatory duct This duct joins the urethra, and sperm is pulsed out through this tube during ejaculation. See Figure 12.1a.

Electroconvulsive shock (ECS) An electrical stimulation of the entire brain that results in electrical seizures and convulsions.

Electro-olfactogram A measure of the electrical activity of a large population of olfactory cells, and its general waveform reflects the intensity of the stimulus. See Figure 7.13.

Electrostatic gradient The distribution of ions across a semipermeable membrane is partly due to electrostatic forces; like charges tend to repel each other, unlike charges tend to attract.

Endogenous Produced from within. With respect to AEPs, it refers to that portion of the potential that is due to higher processes which are going on in the brain. See Figure 16.16.

Endolymph The fluid that fills the scala media and the semicircular canals. The endolymph has a high concentration of potassium ions.

Endplate potential (EPP) The potential setup in a motor endplate as a result of nerve activity and the accompanying release of the neurotransmitter. The endplate potential is therefore analogous to the postsynaptic potentials recorded from neurons.

Enkephalins Short chained peptide molecules that have recently been isolated in the brain. These molecules have analgesic properties similar to morphine. They are the brain's own form of analgesic.

Entorhinal cortex A region of cortex next to the hippocampus. It sends fibers to the hippocampal formation. These nerve connections have received extensive study in the investigation of axon sprouting in rats of various ages. See Figures 14.10 and 14.11.

Epidermis The outer layer of the skin. It forms the protective sheathing for the organism. Cells of the epidermis are being continually sloughed off at the surface of the body. New epidermal cells are continually formed in the deeper regions of the epidermis. See Figure 8.1.

Epididymus A highly coiled tube attached to the posterior surface of the testis. It is part of the spermatic duct system and is designed to store sperm from the tubules of the testes. See Figure 12.1.

Epinephrine A hormone released from the medulla of the adrenal gland. It produces effects similar to those of the sympathetic fibers of the autonomic nervous system. It is also found in low concentrations in the brain, but its function there is not known.

EPP See endplate potential.

EPSP See excitatory postsynaptic potential.

Estrogen Female sex hormone produced by the ovary. It causes maturation of the secondary sex characteristics of the female.

Eustachian tube An air channel that connects the middle ear cavity with the oral cavity. This tube reflexively opens whenever you swallow. Thus you are able to equalize air pressure on both sides of the tympanic membrane.

Excitatory postsynaptic potential A partial depolarization of the membrane potential of the postsynaptic cell. If this depolarization reaches threshold it can result in a nerve impulse being conducted along the axon of the postsynaptic neuron.

Excitement phase The first phase of the sexual response cycle. It can develop from any kind of physical or psychological stimulation which the individual perceives as sexually arousing. See Figures 12.10 and 12.11 and Tables 12.4 and 12.5.

Exhaustion stage The final stage of the general adaptation syndrome resulting from chronic stress. Adreno-cortical activity once again increases and serious illness or death can result. See Figure 10.3.

Exocytosis The fusion of the synaptic vesicle with the membrane of the axon terminal and the release of the neurotransmitter molecules. See Figure 3.2.

Exogenous Derived from external causes. With respect to AEPs it refers to that portion of the potential that is due to stimulus input. See Figure 16.16.

Expressive aphasia The type of language disturbance that is a deficit in expression, and not in understanding.

Extracellular fluid compartment The portion of the body water that is outside of the body's cells. It is divided into the interstitial fluid and the plasma. See Figure 11.16.

Extra-fusal muscle fiber These are the fibers that are responsible for the strong contractions of the skeletal muscles. See Figure 9.4.

Extralemniscal pathways A part of the afferent somatosensory pathway that is more diffuse than the lemniscal component. This pathway provides information about pain. See spinothalamic tract.

Extra-pyramidal system A complex system of interconnections among many structures of the brain that have a functional role in the organization of muscular activity, and therefore motor behavior. But these nerve fibers are not within the pyramidal system and the pyramidal tract. See Figure 9.9.

Facial nerve One of the three cranial nerves that provide somatosensory information about the head and face. See Table 4.2.

False transmitter A drug which can fill a receptor site, but does not change the membrane potential of the postsynaptic cell.

Feature detection Some neurons (such as those in the visual cortex) respond only to very specific stimulus characteristics. For example, a neuron may give its best response to a black bar in a particular orientation. Neurons with such specific stimulus preferences are called "feature detectors."

Fenestration A surgical technique which creates a new window to the inner ear. This is done in an attempt to bypass a completely immobile stapes.

Final common pathway That portion of the efferent motor pathways in the brain that goes from the motor neurons in the ventral horn of the cord to the muscles.

Fissures Major invaginations of the cortex. The two most important are the central and lateral fissures. See Figure 4.7.

Flavor aversion An organism tends to avoid a taste which is followed by sickness.

Flurazepam A widely prescribed sleeping pill that suppresses both stage 4 of S-sleep and also D-sleep.

Flutter-vibration The types of sensations that are reported when a mechanical vibrator that can be adjusted to different frequencies is applied to the human skin. At low frequencies, 5–40 Hz, the human being reports that the sensation feels like a flutter. At higher frequencies, 60–80 Hz, the sensation is more like a vibration or a hum.

Follicle stimulating hormone (FSH) A hormone from the anterior pituitary that acts on the gonads. In the male it maintains spermatogenesis. In the female it develops and maintains a follicle up to ovulation.

Follicles Formations in the ovaries that produce the egg cells or ova.

Forebrain A major division of the brain which includes the telencephalon and diencephalon. See Table 4.1.

Fornix A fiber tract which goes from the hippocampus to the mammillary bodies in the posterior hypothalamus. The fibers of the fornix pass through much of the hypothalamus before reaching the mammillary bodies.

Fovea The portion of the retina that yields the best visual acuity during daylight vision. The light focusing mechanisms of the eye, the cornea and lens, bring the rays of light into focus at the fovea. See Figure 5.5.

Free nerve endings Nerve fibers that branch out into layers of the skin without any encapsulations. See Figure 8.1.

Free-running rhythm A rhythm that continues in the absence of external cues.

Frequency As the term applied to sound waves, frequency is the number of cycles which pass a given point per unit of time.

Fright-flight-fight syndrome An activation of the sympathetic nervous system. The cluster of physiological changes that occur within the body to prepare it for an emergency. These include increased blood pressure, increased sweat gland activity, dilation of the pupils, and the movement of blood to the muscles and away from the skin and viscera.

Frontal lobe The anterior portion of the cerebral hemisphere. Its posterior border is the central fissure and its ventral border is the lateral fissure. The cortex of the frontal lobe contains the motor area and a large area of association cortex. See Figure 4.7.

FSH See follicle stimulating hormone.

FTG See gigantocellular tegmental field.

GABA See gamma-aminobutyric acid.

Galvanic skin response (GSR) A measure of the sweat gland activity due to activity of the sympathetic nervous system. The change is a change in the electrical resistance of the skin on the fingertips.

Gamma-aminobutyric acid (GABA) A substance found in the brain and spinal cord and almost nowhere else in the body. Its highest concentration in the brain is in the substantia nigra, globus pallidus, and hypothalamus. It is thought to be an inhibitory neurotransmitter.

Gamma motor neurons Neurons which synapse onto the intrafusal fibers of the skeletal muscles.

Ganglion cells The axons of these cells form the optic nerve which exits from the eye at the optic disc and proceeds along the base of the skull to terminate in the brain.

Gap junctions A place of contact between two nerve cells. The distance between the membranes of the two cells is only about 20 angstroms. Synaptic transmission across gap junctions is thought to be electrical rather than chemical.

Gate control theory A hypothesis to account for the transmission of pain through the spinal cord. The theory is schematized in Figure 8.9.

Gene The functional unit in the chromosomes that codes for a protein.

General adaptation syndrome A term introduced by Hans Selye to describe the effects of long-term stress. It has three main stages: the alarm reaction, the resistance stage, and the exhaustion stage. See Figure 10.3.

Generator potential The change in the membrane potential of a receptor cell that can result in a change in the rate of nerve impulses in that cell. This occurs in receptor cells that have their own axon. See Figure 5.1.

Genotype This expresses which alleles are present on the two homologous chromosomes.

Gigantocellular tegmental field (FTG) A rather small cluster of very large neurons in the brainstem tegmentum. Lesions of this region abolish D-sleep. These cells increase their firing rates during periods of D-sleep. See Figures 13.28 and 13.29.

Glabrous skin This type of skin is found only on the palms of the hands and soles of the feet. It is thick, and deeply furrowed. Glabrous skin provides good gripping qualities to the manipulative surfaces of the body.

Glial cells Cells within the brain and spinal cord that are not neurons. They presumably have supporting and nutritive functions. See also astrocytes and oligodendroglia.

Globus pallidus A component of the corpus striatum. It lies lateral to the internal capsule. It is part of the extrapyramidal motor system. See Figure 4.10 and appendix.

Glomeruli The site within the olfactory bulb where the axon terminals of the receptor cells synapse onto the dendrites of the mitral and tufted cells. See Figure 7.9.

Glucagon A hormone released from the pancreas that converts liver glycogen to glucose.

Glucostatic theory Theory that the brain has receptors that monitor the rate of glucose utilization. When the glucose levels are high during the absorptive phase, the animal will not feel hungry; but it will feel hungry when the levels of glucose are low during the postabsorptive phase.

Glutamic acid Believed to function as a neurotransmitter because of its high concentration in brain tissue.

Glycogen Extra glucose is stored in the liver as glycogen. The hormone glucagon converts stored glycogen back into glucose so that it can be utilized during the postabsorptive phase.

Gold thioglucose (GTG) A drug that

becomes concentrated in the VMH when injected into mice. This causes destruction of the VMH and results in hyperphagia.

Gonads The generic term for the primary reproductive organs for males (testis) and female (ovary). They produce reproductive cells and sex hormones.

Gonadotrophins Hormones from the anterior pituitary gland that act on the gonads, for example, luteinizing hormone and follicle stimulating hormone.

Granule cell A cell type in the olfactory bulb. It makes connnections within the bulb. It is analogous to the amacrine cells in the retina.

Gray matter Portions of the nervous system that are made up almost entirely of cell bodies and short axoned neurons. See also white matter.

Growth Growth is a developmental increase in mass. The size of each cell in development increases because cells take up metabolites from the surrounding fluids and transform them into fats, carbohydrates, and proteins.

GTG See gold thioglucose.

Guanine One of the nucleotide bases of the DNA molecule. See Figure 14.2.

Gyrus (plural gyri) The ridges of cortical tissue that lie between two sulci.

Habituation The decrement in behavioral or neural response that occurs with repeated stimulus presentations.

Hair cells The receptor cells in the auditory system (Fig. 6.8) and in the vestibular system (Fig. 8.14).

Haloperidol A drug which blocks dopamine receptors. It is used clinically in the treatment of schizophrenia.

Hepatic portal vein The vein that carries blood from the intestines to the liver.

Hertz The term used to designate cycles per second.

Heterozygote When two alleles are different and the proteins which are produced by each allele are different, the individual is a heterozygote for that gene.

Hierarchical command theory A theory proposed to account for the sequential organization within the brain for voluntary movement. It predicts that the flow of information among brain structures would be something like the following: dentate nucleus, then motor cortex, then interposed nucleus, and then muscle activity.

Hindbrain A major division of the brain that includes the metencephalon and the myelencephalon. See Table 4.1.

Hippocampus A part of the limbic system that lies in an antero-posterior direction in the medial aspect of the temporal lobe. See Figure 4.11. It has important functions in human memory processes.

Histochemical fluorescence An anatomical technique that permits the visualization of nerve pathways that have a specific neurotransmitter, e.g., norepinephrine, or dopamine, or serotonin. The visualization is possible because cells which contain the neurotransmitter emit a specific glow, e.g., green, when exposed to certain chemicals.

Homologous Chromosomes are homologous when the genes on both members code for a protein that has the same function, even though the sequence of bases may not be identical.

Homovanillic acid The principal metabolite of dopamine. It was found to be on one-tenth the normal level in patients with Parkinson's disease. This suggested that the disease may be due to an insufficient level of dopamine in the brain. Giving such patients L-dopa, the immediate precursor to dopa-

mine, attenuates the symptoms of Parkinson's disease.

Homozygote When two alleles are identical and the proteins which are produced are the same, the individual is a homozygote for that gene.

Horizontal cells A type of cell in the retina that spreads neural activity laterally. Horizontal cells form part of the synaptic connections that occur between the photoreceptors, rods and cones, and bipolar cells. See Figure 5.6.

Horizontal plane A section through the brain that is parallel to the ground. See Figure 4.3.

5-HT See serotonin.

Huntington's chorea A degenerative brain disease of genetic origin. Patients with this disease have abnormally low concentrations of the neurotransmitter GABA in the substantia nigra and corpus striatum.

Hydrophilic Having an affinity for or capable of dissolving in water; water seeking. See phospholipids.

Hydrophobic A tendency to repel water. See phospholipids.

5-Hydroxytryptamine See serotonin.

Hypercomplex cells One of the classes of visual cortical cells described by Hubel and Wiesel. These cells responded most vigorously to a bar-shaped stimulus, which was not only in a particular orientation and moving, but was of a specified length. See also simple and complex cells.

Hyperphagia An excessive intake of food well above normal levels. This can occur as a result of either lesions in the ventromedial nucleus of the hypothalamus or from transection of ventral NE bundle.

Hyperpolarization An increase in the negativity of the membrane potential relative to the resting level. For example, the membrane potential is -75 mV instead of the resting value of -70 mV. Hyperpolarization of the membrane potential typically means the cell is inhibited because the potential has moved away from the threshold value.

Hypoglycemia A significantly low blood sugar level.

Hypothalamic drive model This model viewed the hypothalamus as the site for drive reduction for each type of motivated behavior. It is functionally organized to reduce tissue deficits.

Hypothalamus A small volume of tissue located beneath the thalamus and surrounding the third ventricle. See Figure 4.12. The hypothalamus contains a number of nuclei. Some of these secrete the hypothalamic hormones that act on the pituitary gland which is situated just below the hypothalamus.

Hypovolemia The loss of water from the extracellular fluid compartment. See Figure 11.18.

Imipramine A drug which inhibits the re-uptake of norepinephrine at the synapse.

Inactivation by enzymes One of two mechanisms to terminate the effect of the neurotransmitter on the postsynaptic cell. Enzymes located on or near the postsynaptic membrane break down the transmission molecule so that the parts of the molecule are no longer capable of interacting with the receptor sites. See also re-uptake.

Incentive motivation The hypothesis that emphasizes that organisms learn to expect reinforcement, that is, that certain cues lead to biologically significant events.

Incus One of the three ossicles of the middle ear cavity. It is situated between the malleus and stapes. See Figure 6.5.

Inferior Toward the bottom. Similar to ventral. See Figures 4.1 and 4.2.

Inferior colliculi A part of the midbrain tectum. These structures lie ventral to the superior colliculi. The inferior colliculi are part of the auditory system. The neurons in the inferior colliculi send axons to the medial geniculate nucleus in the thalamus which is the thalamic relay nucleus for audition.

Inferotemporal cortex A cortical area in the primate brain that appears to be important for complex processing of visual information. Neurons in this area receive synaptic inputs from neurons in the prestriate cortex.

Information processing The mechanisms by which the nervous system receives messages from the environment, encodes them, and transmits the encoded messages within the nervous system and also to effector systems.

Infrared Wavelengths of light which are just longer than what we see as red.

Inhibitory postsynaptic potential A change in the membrane potential of the postsynaptic cell in the direction of increased negativity. This means the membrane potential is moving away from the threshold of excitation. Therefore the postsynaptic neuron is less likely to conduct a nerve impulse along its axon.

Inner ear A fluid chamber within the temporal bone of the skull that contains the cochlea and the semicircular canals.

Instrumental conditioning A form of associative learning. The response of the organism determines the presence or absence of the reinforcement.

Insular-temporal cortex A cortical area that appears to function as auditory association cortex. Removal of this tissue impairs auditory pattern discrimination.

Insulin A hormone released from the pancreas. It facilitates the entry of glucose into the cells of the body where it can be used as fuel.

Integration The summation of synaptic inputs, both excitatory and inhibitory, that determines the firing rate of a neuron. With respect to embryonic development, integration refers to the production of a unified working organism.

Intensity The energy transferred by a wave per unit time across a unit area.

Internal capsule The main avenue for ascending and descending fiber bundles between the neocortex and subcortical structures. It is the band of fibers that gives the name to the corpus striatum. The fibers of the pyramidal system pass from cortex to spinal cord in the internal capsule.

Internal carotid artery A main arterial blood supply to the brain. Its branches include the anterior and middle cerebral arteries which provide the blood for large areas of the cerebral hemisphere.

Interposed nucleus A subcortical nucleus of the cerebellum that receives input from the motor cortex.

Interstitial fluid The portion of the extracellular fluid that lies between the cells of the body.

Intracellular fluid compartment That portion of the body water that is within the cells of the body. See Figure 11.16.

Intrafusal muscle fibers Small numbers of intrafusal fibers form the muscle spindles. The intrafusal fibers have sensory endings which send information to the central nervous system pertaining to the stretch forces that may be acting on the muscles. See Figure 9.4.

Intromission The entry of the penis into the vagina.

Iodopsin The type of photopigment molecule that is found in the cone photoreceptor cells. In some species, such as man, there are three separate iodopsins for the three types of photosensitive cones. It is these three classes of cone receptors that provide the basis for color vision.

Iproniazid A drug that is a potent inhibitor of monamine oxidase, and therefore produces an increase in brain concentrations of norepinephrine and serotonin.

Ipsilateral The same side as a given point of reference.

IPSP See inhibitory postsynaptic potential.

Iris The muscle structure that regulates the size of the pupil, thus regulating the amount of light entering the eye. The iris also gives the eye its color.

James-Lange theory of emotion The hypothesis that the physiological events which accompany an emotion *are* the emotion. For instance, your heart does not start to race because you are afraid. You are afraid because your heart started to race.

Joint receptors Sensory receptors located at each joint in the body. These receptors provide the main source of information for the kinesthetic sense. Some joint receptors adapt slowly and are able to provide precise information regarding the angle that the joint is held in. See Figure 8.12.

Juxtaglomerular cells The cells in the kidney which release the hormone renin when there is a fall in blood pressure. See Figure 11.20.

Kanamycin An antibiotic drug that has ototoxic side effects. It destroys the outer hair cells.

Kinesthetic sense Provides information about the position of the body from receptors in the joints, tendons, and muscles.

Klüver–Bucy syndrome A complex of behavioral changes that result from the bilateral removal of the temporal lobe including the amygdala and hippocampus. Initially described in the monkey. These lesions produce a complete lack of emotional expression, as well as changes in visual discrimination, dietary preferences, and sexual behavior. Symptoms similar to these have been described in humans following bilateral temporal lobe damage.

Krause end-bulb A type of encapsulated end organ found in the skin. See Figure 8.1.

Kwashiorkor A condition of malnutrition that results from severe protein deprivation. See Figure 14.8.

Landmark reversal task Measures allocentric spatial orientation. The organism, usually a monkey, learns to choose one of two spatially separated food wells, the one that has an object (the landmark) near it. Then the animal must learn to respond to the food well away from the landmark. See Figure 16.7.

Lateral Toward the side. The opposite of medial.

Lateral fissure A major landmark of the cerebral hemispheres which runs in an antero-posterior direction along the side of the brain. See Figure 4.7. It sets off the temporal lobe of the cerebral hemisphere. It is also known as the Sylvian fissure.

Lateral geniculate bodies An example of a relay nucleus in the thalamus. These neuron clusters receive fibers from each eye, and send axons to the primary sensory cortex for vision which is located in the occipital lobe.

Lateral geniculate nucleus The thalamic nucleus that receives the axons of the retinal ganglion cells. See Figure 5.7.

Lateral hypothalamus (LH) The lateral region of the hypothalamus that contains neurons as well as diffuse fiber systems that pass through it (see Figure 11.1). Lesions of this area produce aphagia and adipsia.

Lateral interaction The activity of one receptor cell and its connections have an effect on the activity in the connections of nearby receptor cells, regardless of whether any physical energy is hitting those nearby receptors.

Lateral lemniscus A fiber pathway that ascends through the brainstem and mesencephalon. It contains afferent auditory fibers that eventually terminate in the medial geniculate nucleus of the thalamus. See Figure 6.9.

Lateral olfactory tract The nerve pathway from the olfactory bulb to the brain. The axons in this tract terminate in the anterior olfactory nucleus, the olfactory tubercle, the prepyriform cortex, and the medial parts of the amygdala.

Lateral preoptic area A brain region just anterior to the hypothalamus. Lesions of this area in the rat result in an animal that does not drink in response to cellular dehydration.

L-dopa The chemical 3,4 dihydroxyphenylalanine or levodopa. It is the metabolic precursor of the neurotransmitter dopamine. Used in treating Parkinson's disease. See also homovanillic acid.

Learned specific hunger The increase in intake of a diet that contains a previously missing dietary nutrient.

Lemniscal pathway A part of the afferent somatosensory system. It is a fiber tract in the brainstem that ascends to the somatosensory nuclei of the thalamus. This pathway carries primarily information about touch, particularly its precise localization. See medial lemniscus. See Figure 8.3.

Lens Part of the focusing mechanisms of the eye. It is located behind the pupil and changes its curvature or shape as the individual fixates on near or far objects. See Figure 5.5.

LH See lateral hypothalamus. See luteinizing hormone.

LH releasing factor (LH-RF) A hormone released by the hypothalamus that results in an increased output of LH by the pituitary gland.

LH-RF See LH-releasing factor.

LH syndrome The complex and sequential changes in food and water intake that occur as a result of a lesion in the lateral hypothalamus. See Figures 11.3 and 11.4.

Limbic system A group of interconnected brain structures that are found in the tel- and diencephalon. They are found close to the midline of the brain and the medial aspect of the temporal lobe. The structures form a ring around the thalamus. The limbic system includes the amygdala, hippocampus, septal area, cingulate gyrus, and parts of the thalamus. See Figure 4.11.

Lipostatic theory The theory that hunger and satiety are mediated by the levels of body fat stores, and that these levels are monitored by lipid receptors.

Lithium A drug which has multiple effects, including a decrease of catecholamines at the synapse. Thus it tends to alleviate symptoms in manic patients.

Localization of function The hypothesis that different areas of the brain subserve different kinds of behavior.

Locus coeruleus A neuron cluster in the brainstem that has norepinephrine-containing cell bodies. It appears to be important in the regulation of sleep.

Longitudinal fascicles Portions of the pyramidal motor system that are found in the pons.

Long-term potentiation A type of enhanced responsiveness following a series of low frequency stimuli. This potentiation was observed in a slice of hippocampus tissue and lasted for several hours. See Figures 15.13 and 15.14.

Lordosis A species-specific posture adopted by the female rat that allows the male rat to achieve intromission.

Luteinizing hormone (LH) A hormone from the anterior pituitary gland that acts on the gonads. It stimulates the secretion of testosterone in the male, and development of the follicle into a corpus luteum.

Mach band An interesting visual illusion that is probably due to the lateral interaction that occurs among cells in the retina. An example of the illusion appears in Figure 5.13.

Magnification An increase in the number of nerve fibers or cells that are sensitive to certain stimulus properties. For example, in the cortex there is magnification of information from the fingertips in primates, from the whiskers of a mouse, and from the snout of a pig.

Malleus One of the three ossicles of the middle ear. It is attached to the inner side of the tympanic membrane. It is set into motion by the vibrations of the membrane. The movement of the malleus sets the incus into motion. See Figure 6.5.

Mammillary bodies Nuclei on the ventral surface of the brain that mark the posterior extent of the hypothalamus. The neurons in these nuclei project across axons to the anterior thalamic nuclei. These axons form the mammillo-thalamic tract.

MAO See monoamine oxidase.

Marasmus A condition of malnutrition that results from insufficient calories. See Figure 14.8.

Medial Toward the midline.

Medial forebrain bundle (MFB) A fiber bundle which extends in an antero-posterior direction through the basal forebrain and also through the lateral hypothalamus. The MFB has complex anatomical connections, and a corresponding functional complexity. It is thought to be an important part of the brain's reward system.

Medial geniculate body The thalamic relay nucleus for the sense of hearing.

Medial lemniscus The axons of the neurons of the dorsal column nuclei. These axons project to the somatosensory thalamic relay nuclei. See Figure 8.3. See also lemniscal pathway.

Medulla The most caudal part of the brainstem. See myelencephalon.

Membrane potential All cells have an electrical charge which exists across their membrane. The inside of the cell is electrically negative with respect to the outside. The charge is due to the ionic concentrations that are found inside the cell as well as those outside.

Meninges The three layers of connective tissue that cover the brain and spinal cord. From the outside in they are the dura mater, the arachnoid, and the pia mater.

Merkel cell A type of sensory receptor in the skin. Electron micrographs present evidence for a synapse between the Merkel cell and a nerve fiber.

Mesencephalon The middle portion of the brain, or more simply, the midbrain. It has three principal components: the tectum, the tegmentum, and the basis pedunculi.

Messenger RNA The molecule which carries the genetic information from the DNA in the cell nucleus to the ribosomes in the cytoplasm where protein synthesis occurs. See Figure 14.3.

Metencephalon The portion of the hindbrain that contains the cerebellum and pons. See Table 4.1, and Figure 4.12.

3-Methoxy-4-hydroxyphenyglycol (MHPG) A metabolite of norepiphrine. It can be assayed from urine samples and thus used as an index of activity at noradrenergic synapses.

MFB See medial forebrain bundle.

MHPG See 3-methoxy-4-hydroxyphenyglycol.

Microspectrophotometry A technique used to measure the wavelengths of light that a single photoreceptor cell absorbs. This technique has demonstrated that photoreceptor cells code color information as proposed by the trichromatic theory. See Figure 5.17.

Midbrain A major division of the brain that corresponds to the mesencephalon. See Table 4.1.

Middle ear A small air filled cavity in the skull that is between the tympanic membrane and the inner ear. The middle ear contains the three bony ossicles, the malleus, the incus, and the stapes. The function of the middle ear is to amplify the sound pressure waves.

Middle ear reflex A reflex contraction of muscles in the middle ear to very loud sounds. The contraction tends to dampen or restrict the movement of the bony ossicles. This reflex is a defensive response to prevent damage to the inner ear by intense sounds.

Midget ganglion cell A retinal ganglion that receives synaptic inputs from a few cone receptor cells. See Figure 5.6.

Mind-body problem A restatement of the dualistic position that man is composed of two elements: a physical one (body) and a nonphysical one (mind).

Minimum audible pressure On the average, human beings can hear a 1000 Hz tone when the intensity is only 0.0002 dyne/cm². The auditory threshold, or minimum audible pressure, changes as a function of the frequency of the sound. Figure 6.2 plots this relationship.

Mitral cells Neurons in the olfactory bulb that receive synaptic input from the olfactory receptor cells. The axons of the mitral cells form the lateral olfactory tract.

Monoamine oxidase (MAO) An enzyme which breaks down the catecholamines, dopamine and norepinephrine. Monoamine oxidase is found within the presynaptic axon terminal, on the outer membrane of the mitochondria.

Monozygotic twins Twins that developed from a single zygote. They thus have 100 percent of their genes in common. Also called identical twins.

Motor endplate It is the specialization that occurs in muscle tissue at those places where a nerve axon terminal makes synaptic contact. See Figure 9.2.

Muscarine A drug which can be extracted from poisonous mushrooms. It stimulates cholinergic receptors in smooth muscles. The symptoms of mushroom poisoning include profound sweating, increased sweating, pupillary constriction, and slowing of heart rate.

Muscarinic receptors One of the two types of ACh receptors. The others are nicotinic receptors. Internal organs which receive cholinergic parasympathetic fibers have muscarinic receptors. The organs can be stimulated by acetylcoline or muscarine, but not by nicotine. Atropine blocks muscarinic, but not nicotinic receptors.

Muscle fiber The functional unit of skeletal muscle is the fiber. It is a long cylindrical cell with several nuclei. See Figure 9.1. Composed of myofibrils.

Muscle spindle A group of intrafusal muscle fibers. The muscle spindle has sensory endings which provide the central nervous system with information about muscle length and the velocity of the change in length.

Mutation A change in the gene, i.e.,

in the sequence of bases. This results in the coding of a different protein, and most likely a change in the phenotype.

Myasthenia gravis A debilitating disease which produces extremely weak muscles. Probable cause is a deficiency of acetylcholine at the neuromuscular junction.

Myelencephalon It is the medulla, and is actually a continuation of the spinal cord. It contains all of the ascending and descending fiber tracts connecting the brain and spinal cord.

Myelin A fatty sheath that insulates the nerve axon from surrounding tissue and fluids.

Myofibrils Threadlike strands that run the length of the muscle fiber. The fibril is the contractile mechanism of the muscle cell. The myofibril contains the actin- and myosin-myofilaments. See Figure 9.1.

Myosin myofilaments The thicker of the two myofilaments within a myofibril. When a muscle contracts, the myosin myofilaments remain stationary and the thinner actin myofilaments slide past. See Figures 9.1 and 9.3.

Myotonia Tonic muscle spasms.

MZ See monozygotic twins.

Naloxone A drug which blocks the analgesic effects of morphine, and also partially blocks the analgesic effects of stimulation of the central gray and the raphe nucleus.

Narcolepsy The sleep disorder that is characterized by the sudden and rapid transition from the waking state into D-sleep.

Nature versus nurture The issue whether human behavior is the result of genes (nature) or the environment (nurture). The issue will most likely be resolved in favor of a complex interaction between both nature and nurture—an interaction that is only beginning to be understood.

Neostigmine bromide A drug that inhibits the enzyme that breaks down acetylcholine, and thus there should be more neurotransmitter available at the synapse.

Nephrectomy Removal of the kidney.

Neural tube Nervous system development begins with an infolding of the neural plate into a tube. The lumen of the tube becomes the ventricular system of the brain and spinal cord.

Neurogenesis The process by which cells in the neural epithelium become differentiated into neurons.

Neuromodulator The neuromodulators are molecules which amplify or dampen neuronal activity, but they are not neurotransmitters; that is, they are not released at synaptic junctions.

Neuromuscular junction The synapse that is formed between the axon terminal of a neuron and the membrane of a muscle cell.

Neurotransmitter Molecules released from an axon terminal. These molecules act to excite or inhibit the nerve, muscle, and gland cells.

Neurotubules Long tubular elements (200–300 Å in diameter) are found in the axon, dendrites, and cell body. They have a smooth contour and vary in length. They are considered to be important in the transport of molecular material from the cell body to distant parts of the neuron, e.g., to the synaptic terminals.

NGC See nucleus gigantocellularis.

Nicotine A drug which can be extracted from tobacco. It stimulates cholinergic receptors in skeletal muscles.

Nicotinic receptors One of the two types of ACh receptors. The others are muscarinic receptors. Cholinergic receptors at the neuromuscular junction can be stimulated by acetylcholine and nicotine, but not by muscarine. Atropine has no effect on nicotinic receptors.

Nociceptors These are the receptors and fibers in the skin which transmit painful information to the spinal cord. There are at least two types—A-delta and C fibers. See Figure 8.8.

Nodes of ranvier Small gaps in the myelin sheath. At these junctions the membrane of the axon is exposed to extracellular fluid. See Figure 2.5.

Nonspecific nuclei These are nuclei within the thalamus. As the name implies, these nuclei have widespread connections with the cortex. As a result they have also widespread influences on the electrical activity of the cortex.

Noradrenalin See norepinephrine.

Noradrenergic synapses Synapses which have norepinephrine as the transmitter substance. Synapses of this type are found throughout the brain, and in the sympathetic portion of the autonomic nervous system.

Norepinephrine (NE) A brain neurotransmitter. It is synthesized from another transmitter, dopamine. Norepinephrine is thought to be important in mood and motivation. Also called noradrenalin.

Nucleus circularis Lesions of this small nucleus of the hypothalamus produce deficits in the release of ADH. Electrical stimulation of this area results in water retention by the kidneys.

Nucleus gigantocellularis (NGC) A nucleus in the reticular formation that receives information from both the A-delta and the C fibers regarding pain stimuli.

Nucleus of the solitary tract A nucleus in the medulla that is the site of termination of the nerve fibers coming from the taste buds. Electrical stimulation of this nucleus results in synchronization of the electrical activity of the neocortex.

Nucleus raphé magnus A region in the brainstem that, when stimulated electrically, results in an attentuation of the pain from a noxious stimulus.

Nurture (See nature versus nurture.) The total number of environmental influences and conditions acting on an organism.

Object alternation This behavioral task is similar to spatial alternation, but the organism must alternate its responses to two small objects independent of where they are spatially. See Figure 16.3.

Object reversal task The animal initially learns to respond to one of two distinct objects, e.g., a small cylinder. Then the animal must learn to reverse, i.e., to respond to the other object, e.g., a small cube. See Figure 16.17.

Occipital lobe The most posterior portion of the cerebral hemisphere. It contains the primary sensory cortex for vision.

Ocular dominance columns The visual striate cortex is organized in a way that columns of cells alternate between fiber terminations which are bringing information from the left, with those from the right eye. This anatomical separation of information from each eye provides the basis for binocular vision by means of neuronal connections between the columns.

Ocular dominance shift In the normal cat, cells in the visual cortex are binocular. That is, the cells respond to visual stimuli in either eye. Most of the cells in kittens deprived of vision in one eye were monocular; they would only respond to stimulation from the nondeprived eye. See Figure 14.13.

Off-center A descriptive label for a class of ganglion cells in the retina. The response properties of these cells are such that the cells increase their firing rate to the offset of a spot of light in the center of its receptive field. See also on-center.

Olfactory bulb The place of termination of the axons of olfactory receptor cells. Neurons within the olfactory bulbs give rise to the olfactory tract.

Olfactory cilia Fine finger-like extensions of the olfactory receptor cell. These cilia fan out over the surface of the olfactory epithelium. It is on the cilia where odorous molecules probably interact with the receptor cell.

Olfactory epithelium The area of epithelial tissue within the nasal cavity that contains the receptor cells for the sense of smell. In addition to receptor cells, the olfactory epithelium also has supporting cells and basal cells. See Figure 7.8.

Olfactory nerve The first cranial nerve. It is composed of the axons of the olfactory receptor cells. It terminates in the olfactory bulb.

Olfactory rod The portion of the olfactory receptor cell that is between the cell nucleus and the olfactory cilia. See Figure 7.8.

Olfactory tubercle A region of the ventral surface of the forebrain that receives synaptic input from the axons of the lateral olfactory tract.

Oligodendroglia A class of glial cells that form the myelin sheaths for the axons of the neurons in the central nervous system.

Olivary complex A cluster of nuclei that receive synaptic inputs from axons from both ventral cochlear nuclei. See Figure 6.9.

Olivo-cochlear bundle A nerve fiber bundle that arises in the olivary complex and projects to the base of the hair cells in the cochlea. See Figure 6.19.

Ommatidia The photoreceptor cells of the horseshoe crab, *Limulus*. See Figure 5.12.

On-center A descriptive label for a class of ganglion cells in the retina.

The response properties of these cells are such that the cells increase their firing rate to the onset of a spot of light in the center of its receptive field. See also off-center.

Operator gene A component of the operon model of gene regulation. Operator genes combine with the repressor protein (derived from the regulator gene) to suppress the activity of the structural gene. See Figure 14.4.

Operon model A model proposed for the regulation of genes. It includes structural, regulator, and operator genes. The model is diagramed in Figure 14.4.

Opponent process theory A theory of color vision which states that color vision is mediated by cells which change their firing rates in response to different wavelengths in an opponent manner. For example, red light might produce an increase in firing, but green would produce a decrease in firing in the same cell. This theory proposes three types of cells: red-green, blue-yellow, and black-white.

Opsin The complex protein that forms part of the photopigment molecule in the rods and cones. The opsin portion of the photosensitive molecule is specific for each photopigment. See also retinal.

Optic chiasm The place in the afferent visual pathway where the axons of the two optic nerves come together. The axons from the nasal half of each retina cross the midline at the chiasm. The axons from the temporal half of each retina remain uncrossed. This means that after the chiasm the axons which have come from the right half of each retina go to the right hemisphere of the brain, and fibers from the left half of each retina go to the left hemisphere. See Figure 5.7.

Optic nerve The second cranial nerve. It is composed of the axons of the ganglion cells which are in the retina. There is a partial mixing

of the axons from each eye at the optic chiasm. After the chiasm, these axons are known as the optic tract.

Organ of Corti A complex cellular structure that rests on top of the basilar membrane. The organ of Corti contains the hair cells, the receptor cells for the sense of hearing. See Figures 6.6 and 6.8.

Orgasmic phase The third phase of the sexual response cycle, the achievement of an orgasm. See Figures 12.10 and 12.11 and Tables 12.4 and 12.5.

Ornithine decarboxylase An enzyme that removes the carboxyl group from the amino acid ornithine. This amino acid is part of the metabolic pathway of urea synthesis.

Oscillator A presumed internal biological clock.

Osmoreceptors Receptors, presumably in or near the hypothalamus, that monitor the amount of cellular dehydration. These receptors stimulate the release of ADH and the neural pathways to initiate drinking.

Osmotic gradient The force which moves ions through a semipermeable membrane down their concentration gradients, i.e., from high to low concentration.

Otitis media A transient form of middle ear dysfunction which is an inflammation of the middle ear tissue. The Eustachian tube becomes infected and closes up, preventing the passage of air into the middle ear cavity.

Otoconia The fine layer of calcium salts in the utricule and saccule. The cilia of the receptor cells are embedded in this layer. Shifts of the otoconia resulting from steady movement produce a shearing action on the cilia of the receptor cells and therefore initiate the transduction processes in the utricule and/or saccule.

Otosclerosis A bony growth around the stapes which restricts its movement, and therefore brings about a conductive hearing loss.

Outer ear One portion of the ear. It consists of the pinna and the auditory canal. Its function is to collect the waves of sound energy.

Outer segment That part of the photoreceptor cell that contains the photopigment molecules. See Figure 5.8.

Oval window A membrane that separates the inner ear from the middle ear. The stapes fits up against the middle ear side of this membrane.

Ovaries The female gonads. They produce egg cells and the hormones estrogen and progesterone.

Oviduct A tube through which egg cells (ova) travel from the ovary to the uterus. In mammals the oviduct is called the Fallopian tube. See Figure 12.1b.

Ovulation The maturation and release of an egg cell into the Fallopian tube.

Oxytocin A hormone from the posterior pituitary gland. It contracts smooth muscles and is involved in the secretion of milk.

Pacemakers The nerves in the cardiac muscle of the heart. They are rhythmically active and produce the heart's contractions.

Pacinian corpuscle An encapsulated nerve fiber that functions as a pressure receptor. These corpuscles are found throughout the skin. See Figure 8.1.

Papillae The tiny projections on the dorsal surface and sides of the tongue which contain the cell clusters known as taste buds.

Parabrachial nucleus A small nucleus in the pons that receives taste sensory information from the nucleus of the solitary tract. Neurons in the parabrachial nucleus send axons to the thalamic relay nucleus for taste. See Figure 7.2.

Para-chlorophenylalanine (PCPA) A drug which blocks the enzyme tryptophan hydroxylase and thereby prevents the synthesis of the neurotransmitter serotonin.

Parasympathetic division Fibers of the autonomic nervous system which generally have effects opposite to those of the sympathetic division. For example, activation of parasympathetic fibers results in a slowing of heart rate, pupils contract, and sweat gland activity slows down.

Paresis A weakness of the muscles usually following some type of stroke. There is some ability to move the muscles, so therefore paresis differs from paralysis.

Parietal lobe This lobe is bounded by the central and lateral fissures and the parieto-occipital sulcus. It contains the primary somato-sensory cortex. See Figure 4.7.

Parieto-occipital sulcus This sulcus serves as the major dividing line between the parietal and occipital lobes. See Figure 4.7.

Parkinson's disease Named after the English physician, James Parkinson who first described the course and severity of the disease. It is characterized by tremors and other disorders of movement. The disease appears due to a metabolic dysfunction of dopamine in the basal ganglia. Treating patients with the dopamine precursor, L-dopa, attenuates the symptoms.

Passive avoidance The organism learns to refrain from making a specified response in order to avoid a noxious stimulus.

PCPA See para-chlorophenylalanine.

Perilymph The fluid in portions of the cochlea. The perilymph is similar in composition to the cerebrospinal fluid.

Period As the term pertains to sound waves or to any rhythmic activity, the period of the wave is the time required for one cycle to occur.

Peripheralist theory of hunger and thirst An older theory that hunger and thirst were due to peripheral sensations. For example, hunger was due to stomach contractions and thirst to a dry throat.

Peripheral nervous system All the neuronal cell bodies and fibers that lie outside of the cranial cavity and vertebral column.

Periventricular area A region of the hypothalamus that may contain osmoreceptors. Lesions in this result in deficits in drinking in response to cellular dehydration and hypovolemia.

PGO waves Rapid spiking activity that occurs in the pons, lateral geniculate nucleus, and occipital cortex. These waves occur in conjunction with rapid eye movements during D-sleep.

Phase A term used to locate the peak or trough of a cycle with reference to some external marker, such as a particular time of day.

Phase difference detectors Some neurons in the inferior colliculus respond only to particular phase differences between auditory inputs to the two ears. See Figure 6.15.

Phase locking When a neuron fires preferentially during a certain portion of the cycle of a sound wave, it is called "phase locking." See Figure 6.14. The same phenomenon occurs in the responses of some joint receptors that respond in the same phase of the cycle of movement.

Phase shift A change in the onset of a part of the daily circadian rhythm. For example, an individual who normally goes to sleep at 10 P.M. may delay the onset of sleep until 2 A.M.

Phenotype The observable trait of the underlying genotype.

Phenoxybenzamine A drug that blocks alpha-adrenergic receptors.

Phenylketonuria (PKU) A genetic

abnormality in the metabolism of the amino acid phenylalanine. The individual lacks the enzyme for converting phenylalanine to tyrosine. The condition results in mental retardation, but can be prevented if the infant is given a low phenylalanine diet.

Phenylthiocarbamide (PTC) A substance which some individuals cannot taste. The insensitivity to the taste of PTC is genetically determined. The absence of taste is the phenotype for a homozygous recessive genotype.

Pheromones Olfactory cues that are produced by one individual that convey information to other individuals of the same species.

Phospholipids A principal part of all cellular membranes. The phospholipids consist of a phosphate group that is hydrophilic (water seeking), and a fatty acid tail that is hydrophobic (water repelling).

Photopigment Light sensitive molecules that are contained in the rods and cones. These molecules react to light energy and as a result the process of visual transduction is initiated. The photopigment molecule has two parts: retinal and opsin.

Phrenology The practice that the examination of bumps on the cranium would reveal deficits and strengths in the personality of the individual.

Physostigmine A drug which inhibits the enzyme acetylcholinesterase. Such inhibition results in a buildup of ACh at the synapse to act on the postsynaptic membrane.

Piloerection A raising or bristling of the hair, usually due to cold, shock, or fright.

Pimozide A drug which blocks dopamine receptors.

Pinna The fleshy structure on each side of the head that is commonly called the ear. See Figure 6.4.

PKU See phenylketonuria.

Place reversal task The animal initially learns to respond to one place, i.e., the left of two food wells. Then the animal must learn to reverse, i.e., to respond to the right. See Figure 16.17.

Planum temporale The upper surface of the temporal lobe, most of which is hidden in the lateral fissure. See Figure 16.19.

Plasma The portion of the extracellular body water that is in the blood.

Plateau phase The second phase of the sexual response cycle. Sufficient stimulation moves the response to a higher degree of intensity. See Figures 12.10 and 12.11 and Tables 12.4 and 12.5.

Pons The anterior or rostral part of the hindbrain. It has a dorsal pontine tegmentum which contains part of the reticular formation and nuclei of several cranial nerves. The ventral portion of the pons contains the pontine nuclei as well as large bundles of nerve fibers.

Postabsorptive phase The portion of the metabolic cycle that is dominated by the breakdown and utilization of stored nutrients.

Posterior Toward the back. Similar to caudal. See Figures 4.1 and 4.2.

Posterior nuclear group These are neurons in the thalamus that receive projections from the spinothalamic tract. These neurons have very large receptive fields. Some even respond to touch anywhere on the body surface.

Posterior pituitary gland Also called the neurohypophysis. It releases the hormones oxytoxin and vasopressin (ADH) in response to neural input from the hypothalamus.

Postsynaptic cell The cell that receives inputs from the terminals of the presynaptic cell. See Figure 3.1.

Postsynaptic membrane The membrane of the postsynaptic cell which lies across from the presynaptic terminal has specialized features. In the electron micro-

scope the membrane appears more opaque, which indicates a thickening of the membrane. See Figure 3.1. This membrane contains the receptor sites for the neurotransmitter molecules released from the synaptic terminals.

Postsynaptic potential A change in the membrane potential of the postsynaptic cell as a result of the action of the neurotransmitter released from the synaptic terminals of the presynaptic cell.

Posttetanic facilitation Enhanced responsiveness in a postsynaptic neuron following tetanization of the presynaptic nerve fibers. See Figure 15.5.

Premenstrual syndrome An experience common to many women that occurs shortly before and during the menses. It is characterized by irritability, anxiety, and depression.

Prepyriform cortex The sensory cortex for olfaction. It receives input from the olfactory bulb by means of the lateral olfactory tract. In the higher primates, including man, this area is located on the anterior medial surface of the temporal lobe.

Prestriate cortex An area of cortex that lies immediately anterior to the striate cortex. It is considered to be visual association cortex. Neurons in the prestriate cortex receive synaptic inputs from neurons in the striate cortex.

Presynaptic cell The neuron that makes synaptic contact onto another neuron. The nerve cell which releases the neurotransmitter molecules that act on the membrane of the postsynaptic cell.

Presynaptic facilitation A hyperpolarization of the synaptic terminal through an axo-axonic synapse. This results in an increased amount of neurotransmitter being released when a nerve action potential arrives at the terminal.

Presynaptic inhibition A reduced

amount of neurotransmitter being released as a result of axo-axonic contacts that alter the membrane potential of the synaptic terminal. See Figure 3.6.

Primary drinking Drinking which results from the loss of water from either one of the body's fluid compartments.

Primary qualities The basic essential attributes of a sensory modality that cannot be reduced to simpler components. For example, the basic taste qualities or the primary hues in the visual modality.

Principal sulcus A major sulcus that extends in an antero-posterior direction in the dorsolateral frontal cortex of the brain of the monkey. See Figure 16.2.

Principle of equipotentiality The principle that a memory for a simple task is stored diffusely throughout the sensory area which was used to process the input for the task.

Principle of mass action The principle that for complex learning tasks that amount of cortex removed is more important than the location.

Progesterone A hormone produced in the ovary that prepares the female reproductive organs for pregnancy.

Prolactin A hormone from the anterior pituitary gland that is important for the secretion of milk from the mammary glands.

Propanolol A drug that blocks beta-adrenergic receptors.

Proprioceptive The type of sensory information that comes from stimuli internal to the body, as contrasted with stimuli from the external environment.

Prostigmine A drug which inhibits the breakdown of acetylcholine provides a marked improvement in muscle strength for individuals with myasthenia gravis.

Pseudoconditioning A type of sensitization that may occur when the

CS and UCS are presented to an organism but are never paired together in a predictable relationship.

Pseudohermaphrodite A genetic female that has a well-developed scrotum and a small male-type penis. This condition can occur as a result of the presence of testosterone during the fetal development of the female.

Psychic blindness One component of the Klüver-Bucy syndrome. It refers to the monkey's tendency to approach animate and inanimate objects without hesitation.

PTC See phenylthiocarbamide.

Pupil The opening in the iris of the eye through which light energy passes to reach the photosensitive cells in the retina.

Push-pull cannula A technique used for obtaining brain fluid samples for analysis. It consists of a double cannula. A fluid is pushed through one cannula to bathe a brain region at its tip. Other fluids can then be withdrawn through the other cannula and analyzed. See Figure 10.11.

Putamen A component of the corpus striatum. It lies lateral to the globus pallidus, and is a part of the extrapyramidal motor system. See Figure 4.10 and the Appendix.

Pyramidal neuron Neurons whose cell body has the general shape of a pyramid. Such neurons are typically found in the neocortex and hippocampus. Their axons go to other parts of the brain.

Pyramidal system The motor system of the brain that arises from the neurons in the motor cortex. The axons of the neurons pass through the internal capsule, form the pyramidal tract in the brainstem, and terminate on the motor neurons in the ventral horn of the spinal cord. See Figure 9.8.

Pyramidal tract The axons which form the pyramidal shaped tract along the ventral surface of the

brainstem. Most of the axons cross at the decussation of the pyramids in the medulla. It is the major motor pathway in the brain. See Figure 9.8.

Rapid eye movements (REMs) Eye movements that usually occur during periods of D-sleep.

Rapidly adapting mechanoreceptor This describes a functional property of the Pacinian corpuscle. The nerve fiber within the corpuscle responds to the onset of a touch stimulus, and also to the offset, but does maintain a discharge throughout the duration of the stimulus. See Figure 8.2. See also Pacinian corpuscle.

Raphé A series of nuclei that extend through the core of the brainstem. Lesions in the raphé produce a state of chronic wakefulness in cats. Most of the serotonin content of the brain is found within the neurons of the raphé. See Figure 13.26.

Rarefaction A decrease in the density of the molecules in the air which results in a decrease in the air pressure below the normal value. The opposite of condensation. See Figure 6.1.

RAS See reticular activating system.

Rebound effect The increase in the amount of time spent in D-sleep following a period of D-sleep suppression that can occur with the use of sleeping pills.

Receptive aphasia A language dysfunction that is characterized by a deficit in the appreciation of the meanings of both spoken and written words.

Receptive field The area in space within which a stimulus can produce a response of some kind in a particular neuron along the sensory pathway. See Figure 5.2. In the auditory system, receptive field usually refers to a range of frequencies to which a neuron is maximally sensitive.

Receptor potential The change in the membrane potential of a sensory receptor cell as a result of stimulus energy. This is a slow-graded response which results in a change in the amount of neurotransmitter released by the receptor cell. See Figure 5.1.

Receptor sites A portion of a cell membrane that can interact with neurotransmitters, hormones, or other molecules. Receptor sites are considered to be molecules on or within the membrane of the cell. The binding of the transmitter molecule with the receptor brings about changes in the membrane or within the cell itself.

Recessive An allele that gives the physical characteristic or expression of a gene only when it is paired with another recessive allele, i.e., when an individual is a homozygote for the recessive allele.

Recurrent inhibition As the alpha motor neuron increases its firing rate, it activates the Renshaw cells via axon collaterals. When the Renshaw cells become active they tend to inhibit the motor neurons that activated them. See also Renshaw cell.

Refractory period The period following an action potential when a neuron is less responsive. This is divided into an absolute refractory period during which the neuron will not respond regardless of the intensity of the stimulus. There follows a relative refractory period during which a neuron can respond but only to a much stronger stimulus than usual.

Regulator gene A component of the operon model of gene regulation. Regulator genes produce messenger RNA for a repressor protein. See Figure 14.4.

Releaser A type of pheromone that elicits a specific behavioral response.

REMs See rapid eye movements.

Renin A hormone released by the kidneys. It converts angiotensinogen in the blood to angiotensin which in turn stimulates the release of aldosterone from the adrenal cortex. Aldosterone promotes the absorption of sodium by the kidney. See Figure 11.20.

Renshaw cell A small interneuron in the ventral horn of the spinal cord. It receives an axon collateral from the alpha motor neuron. The Renshaw cell in turn synapses back onto the motor neuron. The motor neuron synapse onto the Renshaw cell is excitatory, but the synapse from the Renshaw cell to the motor neuron is inhibitory. This synaptic arrangement produces the phenomenon of recurrent inhibition.

Reserpine A drug that prevents the storage of catecholamines within the synaptic terminal. As a result the transmitters are broken down by monoamine oxidase.

Resistance stage The second stage of the general adaptation syndrome. During this stage adrenocortical activity returns to a level just above normal. See Figure 10.3.

Resolution phase The final phase of the sexual response cycle. The return to quiescence. See Figures 12.10 and 12.11 and Tables 12.4 and 12.5.

Resting potential The potential that exists across the membrane of a neuron when it is at rest. That is, when it is not conducting a nerve action potential. Though there is variation among types of nerve cells, a value of -70 mV is typically used to describe the resting membrane potential of a neuron. When at rest the neuron is considered to be polarized. The inside is negative with respect to the outside.

Reticular activating system (RAS) A portion of the reticular formation which sends axons to the neocortex. Stimulation of the RAS wakens the sleeping animal and produces an electrocortical record of arousal. The RAS is a functional label as opposed to the reticular formation, which is an anatomical term.

Reticular formation The name applies to the medial core of the brainstem from the caudal part of the medulla up to the mesencephalon. The reticular formation derives its name (from Latin meaning "net") from the apparent random crisscrossing of nerve fibers and cell bodies which make it look like a net. See also reticular activating system.

Retina The layer of tissue within the eyeball that contains the light sensitive photoreceptor cells as well as other neurons including the axons that form the optic nerve.

Retinal One part of the photopigment molecule found in the rods and cones of the eye. This part of the molecule is unstable and when it is exposed to light it changes shape, i.e., it becomes isomerized. See also opsin.

Retinal disparity The difference between the images produced on the retinas of the two eyes. Each eye sees a slightly different picture of the object. This difference becomes smaller as the distance between the eyes and the object increases.

Retrograde amnesia Amnesia for events that precede a trauma to the brain, such as a head injury or an electroconvulsive shock.

Re-uptake The molecules of the neurotransmitter are taken back up directly into the synaptic terminal. See also inactivation by enzymes.

Rhodopsin The photopigment molecule that is found in the rod receptor cells.

Rhythm Any event which changes from one point and eventually returns to that point can be considered a rhythm.

Rods One of the two types of receptor cells for vision. They are found throughout the retina except for the central part of the fovea. The rods are sensitive at low levels of light energy, e.g., nighttime. They do not code color stimulus information. Rods contain rhodopsin as the photosensitive pigment.

Rostral Toward the snout. Similar to anterior. See Figures 4.1 and 4.2.

Round window A membrane that lies just below the oval window. It is at the end of the scala tympani. The round window provides a pressure relief point, so that whenever the stapes pushes in on the oval window, the increased pressure within the cochlea is transmitted through the cochlea to the round window. See Figure 6.7.

Ruffini endings A type of sensory receptor found in the skin. See Figure 8.1.

Saccule One of the five sensory mechanisms of the vestibular system that are found in the inner ear. The saccule is thought to function in a complementary way to the utricle in that they are situated at right angles to each other. See utricule. See Figure 8.13.

Sagittal plane A plane passing along the anterior-posterior axis that is perpendicular to the coronal plane and to the horizontal plane. See Figure 4.3.

Saltatory conduction Proceeding by leaps, hops, or abrupt movements. Saltatory conduction in nerve fibers refers to those axons which are covered with myelin. In such fibers the nerve impulse "jumps" from one node of Ranvier to the next. Ionic exchanges through the membrane can occur only at the nodes because of the myelin covering.

Scala media A tube of the cochlea which is entirely sealed off from the scala vestibuli and the scala tympani. The scala media is filled with endolymph. The scala media contains the organ of Corti which houses the receptor cells for the sense of hearing. See Figures 6.6 and 6.7.

Scala tympani The largest of the tubes of the cochlea. It joins the scala vestibuli at the very apex of the cochlea and ends at the round window. See Figures 6.6 and 6.7.

Scala vestibuli This tube of the cochlea begins at the vestibule opposite the oval window. Fluid pressure waves from the oval window travel up the scala vestibuli toward the apex of the cochlea. See Figures 6.6 and 6.7.

SCN See suprachiasmatic nucleus.

Scotophobin A polypeptide composed of 15 amino acids that has been extracted from the brains of rats and mice that have been trained to avoid a dark compartment. See Figure 15.18.

Scrotal sac The scrotal sac or scrotum hangs outside the main body cavity, and contains the primary male reproductive organ—the testes. See Figure 12.1a.

Second messenger hypothesis Proposed to account for the action of some of the hormones. It proposes that the hormone forms a complex with a receptor in the cell's membrane to initiate a "second messenger," cyclic AMP, that has a regulatory role in intracellular processes.

Secondary drinking Drinking which occurs in the absence of water loss from the body's fluid compartments.

Secondary sex characteristics These include the accessory organs and glands that are essential for successful reproduction, and the morphological features that may occur between the male and female of the species, such as body size, pitch of the voice, and so on.

Semicircular canals Located above and behind the vestibule, the semicircular canals contain the cells for the vestibular sensory system. These cells transduce changes in head movements into neural messages. See Figures 6.4 and 8.13.

Sensitization An increase in behavioral responsiveness with repeated stimulus presentations.

Sensory neglect A neglect or inattention to sensory stimuli from some regions of the body surface. For example, humans with damage to the posterior parietal cortex neglect body parts contralateral to the damage. Rats with unilateral lesions in the lateral hypothalamus do not respond to stimuli presented to the contralateral side of the body.

Sensory-neural hearing loss An elevation in an individual's hearing threshold that is due to damage to the nervous system.

Sensory neuron The neuron which receives synaptic inputs from sensory receptor cells.

Septal area A part of the limbic system which lies along the midline of the brain and anterior to the thalamus. See Figure 4.11. It is interconnected with both the amygdala and the hippocampus.

Septal rage A behavioral change that results from the destruction of the septal area in the rat. It is a pronounced increase in aggressive behavior.

Serotonin A brain neurotransmitter. Its highest concentration in the brain is found in the raphé nuclei in the brainstem. It is synthesized from the amino acid, tryptophan. Serotonin is also known as 5-HT and 5-hydroxytryptamine.

Serotonergic synapses Synapses which have serotonin as the transmitter substance.

Sex chromosomes The chromosomes that determine the sex of the organism. Females have two X chromosomes. Males have an X and Y chromosome pair.

Sexual differentiation The development of primary sexual organs and tissues in the fetus.

Sexual dimorphism Observable body differences between the male and female of the same species. For example, in many mammalian forms, the males are, on the average, heavier than the females.

SIDS See sudden infant death syndrome.

Simple cells One of the classes of visual cortical cells described by Hubel and Wiesel. These cells responded most vigorously to a straight line or bar oriented at a particular angle. See also complex and hypercomplex cells.

Skeletal muscle The type of muscle tied to the bones of the skeleton. It is also called striated muscle because of the pronounced striations or bands that are seen in the tissue. See Figure 9.1.

Skin senses The receptor mechanisms that are spread throughout the body surface, both within and just below the skin. These include receptors for touch, temperature change, and pain.

Smooth muscle The type of muscle around the internal organs of the body. It consists of long slender spindle-shaped cells that are closely packed together in sheets of tissue.

Sodium-potassium pump A metabolic process which moves ions against their concentration gradients. It moves sodium from inside the neuron to the outside, and it transports potassium ions from outside the neuron to the inside.

Soma See cell body.

Somatic nerves Nerves of the peripheral nervous system. The somatic nerves are the 31 pairs of spinal nerves that contain sensory information from specialized receptors and also fibers to the skeletal muscles. See Figure 4.18.

Somatosensory cortex The region of cortex that receives the sensory information that originated on the surface of the body. This cortical area is the postcentral gyrus. It maintains a topographic representation of the body surface. See Figure 8.4.

Spanish fly A drug derived from insects. It has an irritating action on the bladder which causes frequent urination and sometimes persistent erections.

Spatial alternation The behavioral task in which the organism must learn to alternate responses to two partially separate places that may contain a reward. The outcome of the previous trial is the cue the organism must use for success on any given trial. See Figure 16.3.

Spatial summation The process whereby EPSPs and IPSPs arriving simultaneously at the axon hillock are algebraically summed; if the result reaches threshold, an action potential will be triggered.

Specific anosmia The condition in which a person of otherwise normal olfactory acuity cannot perceive a particular compound at a concentration such that its odor is obvious to most other people. See Table 7.1 and also Figure 7.10.

Specific hunger An increased taste preference for and consumption of specific nutrients based upon a physiological deficit.

Specific nerve energies A theory initially proposed by Johannes Müller in 1826. His principle implies that the modality of sensation depends upon what sense organ or nerve fiber is stimulated and not upon the energy that provided the stimulus.

Spectral opponent cells Neurons in the lateral geniculate nucleus of the monkey which apparently code color information as proposed by the opponent process theory of color vision. For example, a cell is inhibited by green light, but stimulated by red light. See Figure 5.18.

Spermatogenesis The production of sperm cells in the testes of the male.

Spinal reflexes Simplest form of muscular activity. Spinal reflexes do not require the involvement of any part of the brain. Everything occurs within the spinal cord.

Spinothalamic tract A somatosensory tract that carries information concerning pain, temperature, and diffuse touch sensitivity. These fibers synapse in the dorsal horn of the spinal cord. Other axons then cross the midline in the cord and ascend to the thalamus as the spinothalamic tract.

Spiral ganglion Lies in the midst of the cochlea. The spiral ganglion contains the cell bodies of the sensory afferent neurons. The axons of these neurons form the auditory component of the VIII cranial nerve.

Split-brain technique A surgical procedure that transects the commissures which interconnect the two cerebral hemispheres.

S-sleep Slow wave sleep. Characterized by large delta waves.

Stapes One of the three ossicles of the middle ear. It lies between the incus and the oval window. Movement of the incus pushes the stapes in and out against the oval window.

Stapes mobilization A surgical technique in which the bony growth around the stapes is removed. The ossicle is thereby free to move again against the oval window.

State-dependent learning When learning occurs in a certain biological state, e.g., a drugged state, retention is best when tested in the same biological state.

Static phase During this phase of the VMH syndrome, the animal's food intake stabilizes and levels off a little above the normal level. It is sufficient to maintain the animal's elevated body weight. See Figure 11.2

Stereopsis The fusion of the two retinal images into a single three-dimensional image.

Striate cortex The area of cortex that receives axons from the neurons in the lateral geniculate nucleus. See Figure 5.7.

Striated muscle See skeletal muscle.

Structural gene A component of the operon model of gene regulation. Structural genes code for specific proteins. See Figure 14.4.

Substantia nigra A cluster of neurons in the mesencephalon just dorsal to the cerebral peduncles. Many cells contain melanin which gives the nucleus a dark appearance in fresh brain tissue, hence its name. Many neurons in the substantia nigra send axons to the corpus striatum. These axons thus form the nigro-striatal bundle. This pathway is important in the onset and symptoms of Parkinson's disease.

Sudden infant death syndrome (SIDS) Sometimes called crib death. The death overnight or even during a nap of an apparently healthy infant during a period of sleep. The cause of this is not yet known.

Sulcus (plural sulci) An invagination or infolding of the cerebral cortex. See Figures 4.7 and 4.10.

Superior Toward the top. Similar to dorsal. See Figures 4.1 and 4.2.

Superior colliculi Located in the tectum of the midbrain. The superior colliculi are a part of the visual system. The neurons receive fibers from both the retina and the visual cortex. The neurons in the superior colliculi send axons to a number of other parts of the brain; one is the oculomotor nuclei which control the movements of the eyes.

Support cells A type of cell in the olfactory epithelium. See Figure 7.8.

Suprachiasmatic nucleus (SCN) A nucleus in the hypothalamus that, as its name implies, lies just above the optic chiasm. Lesions of the SCN disrupt a variety of physiological and behavioral rhythms in rats and other animals.

Sustained ganglion cell Ganglion cells in the retina that increase or decrease the rate of nerve impulses throughout the duration of a visual stimulus. This type of cell is contrasted with the transient ganglion cell that changes its rate of firing only at the onset and at the offset of a visual stimulus. See Figure 5.10.

Sympathetic division That portion of the autonomic nervous system that prepares the bodily organs for arousal and stress. For example, activation of the sympathetic fibers results in increased heart rate, dilation of the pupils, and contraction of some arteries.

Sympathetic ganglia Fibers of the sympathetic division have their cell bodies in the spinal cord. The fibers terminate in the sympathetic ganglia on the cell bodies of the postganglionic fibers. The sympathetic ganglia form a chain of ganglia running along the outside of the spinal cord. See Figure 4.19.

Synapse The place of functional contact between neurons. It consists of a presynaptic neuron, a synaptic space or cleft, and a postsynaptic nerve cell. Most synapses have a chemical transmitter mediating the activity between the two cells. An exception to this is the gap junction where transmission is thought to be electrical. See Figure 3.1.

Synaptic cleft The space between the membranes of the presynaptic and postsynaptic neurons. This distance ranges from 120 to 200 angstroms for chemical synapses. See Figure 3.1.

Synaptic terminals The swellings or knobs at the end of the axon's delodendria. These terminals contain the transmitter molecules that are released by the arrival of nerve impulses.

Synaptic transmission The transfer of information from one neuron to another. Such transmission usually involves the release of a chemical transmitter from the presynaptic neuron to act on the membrane of the postsynaptic neuron.

Synaptic vesicles Small membrane bound globules that are found within the synaptic terminals. The vesicles are sites where the transmitter molecules are stored. As a result of nerve activity, the vesicles fuse with the terminal membrane to release the transmitter molecules into the synaptic cleft.

Synaptic web Molecular material that is found within the synaptic cleft. See Figure 3.1. It appears to bind the membranes of the two cells, but its functional significance is not yet understood fully.

Tardive dyskinesia One of the side effects of antipsychotic drugs. Symptoms include motor abnormalities, such as involuntary movements of the mouth, lips, tongue, trunk, and extremities.

Taste buds A cluster of cells within certain papillae on the surface of the tongue. The taste buds contain the taste receptor cells. See Figure 7.1.

Taste pore A small opening at the top of a taste bud. It is through this pore that taste stimuli can come into contact with the taste receptor cells within the bud. See Figure 7.1.

Tectorial membrane A membrane that covers the tips of the cilia of the auditory hair cells. The vibratory motion of the basilar membrane results in a shearing force from the tectorial membrane on the hairs of the auditory receptors. The shearing force bends the hairs and initiates the process of auditory transduction.

Tectum The tectum is the roof of the midbrain. The tectum contains four clusters of neurons, the superior and inferior colliculi. The superior colliculi are important in the coordination of eye movements.

The inferior colliculi are part of the afferent auditory pathway.

Tegmentum The portion of the midbrain that is between the tectum and the basis pedunculi. Many ascending and descending fiber tracts pass through the tegmentum. The large red nucleus, part of the brain's extra pyramidal motor system, is within the midbrain tegmentum.

Telencephalon The most dorsal or anterior portion of the brain. It includes the cerebral cortex, corpus striatum, and a number of structures of the limbic system. See Table 4.1.

Temporal lobe The portion of the cerebral hemisphere which is ventral to or below the lateral fissure. It contains the primary sensory cortex for hearing. It also contains large expanses of association cortex. See Figure 4.7.

Temporal summation If a single input to a neuron is activated two or more times in rapid succession, the response of the cell can reach threshold, whereas if the inputs had come slower in time the cell would not have produced an action potential.

Temporoparietal cortex An area of cortex just outside the primary auditory cortex. It has been shown that this region is much larger in the left cerebral hemisphere of the human brain than it is in the right side. See Figure 16.19.

Tendon organ Another sensory ending, found in the tendons which attach the muscles to the bones. Tendon organs have a high threshold. But when there is too much tension in the muscle, the organ is activated. The sensory information from the tendon organ produces an inhibition in the alpha motor neurons that innervate the given muscle, and relaxation of the muscle follows on the motor neuron inhibition. See Figure 9.5.

Testes The male gonads. They produce sperm and hormones called androgens.

Testicular feminization syndrome An individual who is an XY genotype (a genetic male) grows up to look very much like a female (see Figure 12.9). The individual has testes which secrete androgen but the normal target tissues are incapable of utilizing the hormone.

Testosterone The principal androgen in men. Its release at puberty results in the development of secondary sex characteristics.

Testosterone propionate A synthetic androgen.

Tetanization A period of high-frequency stimulation of a single nerve fiber or fiber bundle.

Thalamus Largest structure within the diencephalon. The thalamus consists of many clusters of neuronal cell bodies that form individual nuclei. Each nucleus sends axons to a region of the cortex. In this sense the thalamus can be considered the antechamber of the cerebral cortex. See Figure 4.10 and the Appendix.

Threshold of the axon The value that the membrane potential must reach in order for the axon hillock to trigger on action potential.

Thymine One of the nucleotide bases of the DNA molecule. See Figure 14.2.

Thyroxine The hormone secreted from the thyroid gland. It affects the metabolic rate of the cells of the body.

Tonotopic organization The systematic spatial organization of the auditory receptor cells along the length of the basilar membrane for representation of frequencies. Low frequencies are located at the apex of the cochlea. High frequencies are found toward the base of the cochlea near the oval window. A spatial arrangement is maintained

among auditory fibers throughout the afferent auditory system.

Topographic organization The spatial organization or mosaic of receptor cells across the surface of a sense organ is maintained throughout the afferent sensory pathway by the spatial organization of nerve fibers which project from the sense organ.

Transduction The process by which the sense organ transforms the physical stimulus energy into a neural signal.

Transfer RNA A form of RNA in the cytoplasm that assembles the amino acids in sequence along the messenger RNA template. See Figure 14.3.

Transient ganglion cell A type of ganglion cell in the retina that changes its rate of nerve impulses at the onset of a light stimulus and also at the offset of the stimulus. This cell is to be contrasted with the sustained ganglion cell which shows a change in nerve impulses throughout the duration of the stimulus. See Figure 5.10.

Trichromatic theory A theory of color vision which states that color vision is mediated by three separate types of receptors. All of the three types are cones, and each of which is most sensitive to a particular range of wavelengths.

Tricyclic antidepressants A group of drugs, of which imipramine is the best known, that blocks the re-uptake of catecholamines and thus potentiate their effects. These drugs are used clinically to treat depression.

Trigeminal nerve One of the three cranial nerves that provide somatosensory information about the head and face. See Figure 8.3 and also Table 4.2.

Triplet A sequence of three nucleotide bases is the code for one amino acid in the synthesis of proteins. See Figure 14.3.

Tufted cells neurons within the olfactory bulb that receive synaptic input from the olfactory receptor cells. The axons of the tufted cells enter the lateral olfactory tract. See Figure 7.9.

Tuning curves A plot of the responses of neurons in the afferent auditory system as a function of frequency and intensity. See Figure 6.13.

Twin studies A major technique for studying the relationship between genes and complex behavioral traits. The focus is to examine the correlation between dizygotic twins compared to that of monozygotic twins for a given behavior.

Tympanic membrane Commonly known as the ear drum. It is a rather taut membrane that is stretched across the medial end of the auditory canal. The tympanic membrane separates the outer and middle portions of the ear. The membrane vibrates in response to sound pressure waves.

Tyrosine hydroxylase The enzyme that catalyzes the conversion of the amino acid tyrosine to dopa, the initial step in the metabolic synthesis of dopamine and norepinephrine. Tyrosine hydroxylase is found throughout the brain but in small quantities. Its activity is considered to be the rate-limiting factor in catecholamine synthesis.

UCR See unconditioned response.

UCS See unconditioned stimulus.

Ultraviolet Ultra plus violet; beyond the violet. It refers to light energy having a wavelength just shorter than what we see as violet or purple. See Figure 5.4.

Unconditioned response (UCR) The response that is elicited by the unconditioned stimulus.

Unconditioned stimulus (UCS) The stimulus in classical conditioning that reliably elicits the unconditioned response.

Unipolar depression Chronic depression without periods or episodes of manic, agitated behavior.

Upper and lower motor lesions Interruption of connections between the cortex or subcortical levels and the motor neurons in the cranial nerve nuclei or ventral horn of the cord are upper motor lesions. Lower motor lesions are the destruction of the motor neurons or their axons. Upper lesions are generally associated with a hemiparesis of the contralateral body part. Lower motor lesions generally result in a flaccid paralysis. These designations of upper and lower lesions are usually only with reference to the pyramidal system.

Urethra The tube or canal through which urine from the bladder is excreted. In the male it also serves as the canal for the passage of sperm cells to the female. See Figure 12.1a.

Uterus The part of the reproductive system that receives the fertilized egg cell or ovum and provides for the development of the embryo. See Figure 12.1b.

Utricule One of the five sensory mechanisms of the vestibular system that are found in the inner ear. The utricule and saccule are designed for detecting steady movement. The receptor cells have cilia, similar to those in the semicircular canals. The cilia are embedded in a fine layer of calcium salts, the otoconia. Steady movement of the head produces a shearing force on the cilia.

Vagina The muscular tube that leads to the uterus. This tube receives the male penis during copulation for the transfer of sperm cells.

Vagus nerve One of the three cranial nerves that provide somatosensory information about the head and face. See Table 4.2.

Vasopressin A hormone from the posterior pituitary that constricts blood vessels and thereby increases blood pressure.

Vena cava The main venous drainage from the body to the right atrium.

Ventral Toward the belly or bottom of an animal. See Figures 4.1 and 4.2.

Ventral cochlear nucleus One of the two sensory nuclei of the acoustical branch of the statoacoustical nerve. See dorsal cochlear nucleus.

Ventral frontal cortex The cortex on the ventral surface of the frontal lobe. Also sometimes called the orbital cortex because it lies above the orbit of the eye. See Figure 16.2.

Ventricles of the brain The hollow spaces or cavities in the interior of the brain. There are four in number, although the first two are called the lateral ventricles. They are the ventricles of the cerebral hemispheres. The third ventrical is in the diencephalon and the fourth ventrical is in the hindbrain. See Figure 4.6.

Ventromedial arcuate nucleus It controls the output of releasing factors from the hypothalamus. See Figure 12.6.

Ventromedial hypothalamus (VMH) Large nuclei in the ventral region of the hypothalamus close to the walls of the third ventricle. Destruction of this region has produced hyperphagia. See Figure 11.1.

Vertebral arteries The blood supply for the posterior portion of the brain and spinal cord.

Vestibular ganglion The cell bodies of the sensory axons for the vestibular receptor cells are located in this ganglion which is in the medulla. See Figure 8.15.

Vestibular nuclei Four separate nuclei in the medulla that receive the axonal terminations of the sensory fibers coming from the vestibular receptors in the inner ear. See Figure 8.15.

Vestibular system The sensory system that provides us with information about the orientation and movement of the head, and therefore is very useful in the maintenance of balance.

Vestibule A fluid filled cavity of the inner ear which is directly behind the oval window.

Visible spectrum That portion of the entire range of wavelengths of electromagnetic radiation that are visible to the human eye. This portion ranges from 380 to 760 nanometers. See Figure 5.4.

Vitreous humor The transparent jelly-like substance that fills the major portion of the eyeball. See Figure 5.5.

VMH See ventromedial hypothalamus.

VMH syndrome The postoperative course of body weight and food intake following VMH lesions are plotted in Figure 11.2. It shows both a dynamic phase (first three postoperative weeks) and a static phase. In addition to the hyperphagia, animals with VMH lesions become "finicky" with respect to food preferences.

Wada test A test to determine hemispheric localization of language. It does this by selectively depressing the cortical functions in one hemisphere and then the other while subject is being tested for language capabilities. The depression of function is done by injecting a drug into each internal carotid artery.

Warm fibers A class of thermoreceptors that have a limited range of the temperatures they respond to. They show a maximal response around 45–47°C, and their firing rates rapidly fall off when the temperature goes above or below that range. See Figure 8.5.

Wavelength The distance between two points of corresponding phase in consecutive cycles of a periodic wave. See Figure 5.3.

Wernicke's area A region in the posterior of the left temporal and parietal lobes surrounding the auditory cortex. It is important for the understanding of language. See Figure 16.26.

White matter Portions of the nervous system that are made up almost entirely of myelinated axons.

Word deafness A type of disconnection syndrome in which the patient could speak and write. The patient could also read but could not understand spoken language. Lesions which produced these symptoms included damage to the direct auditory pathway on the left side plus loss of fibers in the corpus callosum from the auditory area on the right side.

Zona incerta Recent research showed that this region of the brain (near the lateral hypothalamus) may be involved in the regulation of secondary drinking.

Abeles, M., & Goldstein, M. Responses of single units in the primary auditory cortex of the cat to tones and to tone pairs. *Brain Research*, 1972, *42*, 337–352.

Ackerman, S.H., Hofer, M.A., & Weiner, H. Early maternal separation increases gastric ulcer risk in rats by producing a latent thermoregulatory disturbance. *Science*, 1978, *201*, 373–376.

Agnew, H.W., Webb, W.B., & Williams, R.I. Comparison of stage four and 1–REM sleep deprivation. *Perceptual and Motor Skills*, 1967, *24*, 851–858.

Ahlskog, J.E., & Hoebel, B.G. Overeating and obesity from damage to a noradrenergic system in the brain. *Science*, 1973, *182*, 166–169.

Ahlskog, J.E., Randall, P.K., & Hoebel, B.G. Hypothalamic hyperphagia: Dissociation from hyperphagia following destruction of noradrenergic neurons. *Science*, 1975, *190*, 339–401.

Akaike, N., & Sato, M. Role of cations and anions in frog taste cell stimulation. *Comparative Biochemistry and Physiology, A*, 1976, *55*, 383.

Akert, K. The anatomical substrate of sleep. *Progress in Brain Research*, 1965, *18*, 9–19.

Akil, H., & Mayer, D.J. Antagonism of stimulation-produced analgesia by PCPA, a serotonin synthesis inhibitor. *Brain Research*, 1972, *44*, 692–697.

Akil, H., Mayer, D.J., & Liebeskind, J.C. Antagonism of stimulation-produced analgesia by naloxone, a narcotic antagonist. *Science*, 1976, *191*, 961–962.

Alpers, B.J. Relation of the hypothalamus to disorders of personality: Report of a case. *Archives of Neurology and Psychiatry*, 1937, *38*, 291–303.

Altman, J. Postnatal growth and differentiation of the mammalian brain, with implications for a morphological theory of memory. In G.C. Quarton, T. Melnechuk, & F.O. Schmitt (Eds.), *The neurosciences: A study program.* New York: Rockefeller University Press, 1967.

Altman, J., Sudarshan, K., Das, G.D., McCormick, N., & Barnes, D. The influence of nutrition on neural and behavioral development. III. Development of some motor, particularly locomotor patterns during infancy. *Developmental Psychobiology*, 1970, *4*, 97–144.

Amoore, J.E. The stereochemical specificities of human olfactory receptors. *Perfumery and Essential Oil Record*, 1952, *43*, 321–323, 330.

Amoore, J.E. Specific anosmias and the concept of primary odors. *Chemical Senses and Flavor*, 1977, *2*, 267–281.

Anand, B.K., & Brobeck, J.R. Hypothalamic control of food intake in rats and cats. *Yale Journal of Biology and Medicine*, 1951, *24*, 123–140.

Andersson, B. Regulation of water intake. *Physiological Reviews*, 1978, *58*, 582–603.

Annis, R.C., & Frost, B. Human visual ecology and orientation anistropies in acuity. *Science*, 1973, *182*, 729–731.

Ashe, J.H., Cassady, J.M., & Weinberger, N.M. The relationship of the cochlear microphonic potential to the acquisition of a classically conditioned pupillary dilation response. *Behavioral Biology*, 1976, *16*, 45–62.

Balazs, R., Cocks, W.A., Eayrs, J.T., & Kovacs, S. Biochemical effects of thyroid hormones on the developing brain. In M. Hamburg & J.W. Barrington (Eds.), *Hormones in development.* New York: Appleton, 1971.

Bandler, R.J. Facilitation of aggressive behavior in rat by direct cholinergic stimulation of the hypothalamus. *Nature (London)*, 1969, *224*, 1035–1036.

Bandler, R.J. Cholinergic synapses in the lateral hypothalamus for the control of predatory aggression in the rat. *Brain Research,* 1970, *20,* 409–424.

Bandler, R.J. Direct chemical stimulation of the thalamus: Effects on aggressive behavior in the rat. *Brain Research,* 1971, *26,* 81–93.

Barash, D.P. *Sociobiology and behavior.* New York: American Elsevier, 1977.

Barchas, J.D., Elliott, G.R., & Berger, P.A. Biogenic amine hypothesis of schizophrenia. In J.D. Barchas, P.A. Berger, R.D. Ciaranello, & G.R. Elliott (Eds.), *Psychopharmacology: From theory to practice.* London & New York: Oxford University Press, 1977.

Barker, J.L., Neale, J.H., Smith, T.G., Jr., & MacDonald, R.L. Opiate peptide modulation of amino acid responses suggests novel form of neuronal communication. *Science,* 1978, *199,* 1451–1453.

Barlow, H.B., Blakemore, C., & Pettigrew, J.D. The neural mechanism of binocular depth discrimination. *Journal of Physiology (London),* 1967, *193,* 327–342.

Bartlett, F., & John, E.R. Equipotentiality quantified: The anatomical distribution of the engram. *Science,* 1973, *181,* 764–767.

Basbaum, A.I., Marley, N., and O'Keefe, J. Effects of spinal cord lesions on the analgesic properties of electrical stimulation. In J.J. Bonica & D. Albe-Fessard (Eds.), *Recent advances in pain research and therapy: Proceedings of the First World Congress on Pain.* New York: Raven Press, 1976.

Bass, N.H., Netsky, M.E., & Young, E. Effect of neonatal malnutrition on developing cerebrum. I. Microchemical and histologic study of cellular differentiation in the rat. *Archives of Neurology (Chicago),* 1970, *23,* 289–302.

Bateson, P.P.G., Rose, S.P.R., & Horn, G. Imprinting: Lasting effects on uracil incorporation into chick brain. *Science,* 1973, *181,* 256–258.

Baxter, L., Gluckman, M.I., Stein, K., & Scerni, A. Self-injection of apomorphine in the rat: Positive reinforcement by a dopamine receptor stimulant. *Pharmacology, Biochemistry and Behavior,* 1974, *2,* 387–391.

Beach, F.A. Effects of testosterone propionate upon the copulatory behavior of sexually inexperienced male rats. *Journal of Comparative Psychology,* 1942, 227–247a.

Bealer, S.L. Intensity coding in the transient portion of the rat chorda tympani response. *Journal of Comparative and Physiological Psychology,* 1978, *92,* 185–195.

Beckmann, H., & Goodwin, F.K. Antidepressant response to tricyclics and urinary MHPG in unipolar patients: clinical response to impipramine or amitriptyline. *Archives of General Psychiatry,* 1975, *32,* 17–21.

Begleiter, H., & Porjesz, B. Evoked brain potentials as indicators of decision-making. *Science,* 1975, *187,* 754–755.

Begleiter, H., Porjesz, B., Yerre, C., & Kissin, B. Evoked potential correlates of expected stimulus intensity. *Science,* 1973, *179,* 814–816.

Beidler, L.M. Properties of chemoreceptors of tongue of rat. *Journal of Neurophysiology,* 1953, *16,* 595–607.

Beidler, L.M. A theory of taste stimulation. *Journal of General Physiology,* 1954, *38,* 133–139.

Beidler, L.M. Innervation of rat fungiform papilla. In C. Pfaffman (Ed.), *Olfaction and taste III.* New York: Rockefeller University Press, 1969.

Belluzzi, J.D., Ritter, S., Wise, C.D., & Stein, L. Substantia nigra self-stimulation: Dependence on norodrenergic reward pathways. *Behavioral Biology*, 1975, *13*, 103–111.

Benkert, O., Crombach, G., & Kockott, G. Effect of L-Dopa on sexually impotent patients. *Psychopharmacologia*, 1972, *23*, 91–95.

Benkert, O., & Eversmann, T. Importance of anti-serotonin effect for mounting behavior in rats. *Experientia*, 1972, *28*, 532–533.

Bennett, E.L. Cerebral effects of differential experience and training. In M.R. Rosenzweig & E.L. Bennett (Eds.), *Neural mechanisms of learning and memory*. Cambridge, Mass.: MIT Press, 1976.

Bennett, E.L., Diamond, M.D., Krech, D., & Rosenzweig, M.R. Chemical and anatomical plasticity of brain. *Science*, 1964, *146*, 610–619.

Benson, D.A., & Hienz, R.D. Single-unit activity in the auditory cortex of monkeys selectively attending left vs. right ear stimuli. *Brain Research*, 1978, *159*, 307–320.

Bereiter, D.A., & Barker, D.J. Facial receptive fields of trigeminal neurons: Increased size following estrogen treatment in female rats. *Neuroendocrinology*, 1975, *18*, 115–124.

Berger, P.A., & Barchas, J.D. Biochemical hypotheses of affective disorders. In J.D. Barchas *et al.* (Eds.), *Psychopharmacology: From theory to practice*. London & New York: Oxford University Press, 1977.

Berger, R.J. Oculomotor control: A possible function of REM sleep. *Psychological Review*, 1969, *76*, 144–164.

Berger, T.W., Alger, B.E., & Thompson, R.F. Neuronal substrates of classical conditioning in the hippocampus. *Science*, 1976, *192*, 483–485.

Berlucchi, G., Maffei, E., Moruzzi, G., & Strata, P. EEG and behavioral effects elicited by cooling of medulla and pons. *Archives Italiennes de Biologie*, 1964, *102*, 372–392.

Beumont, P.J.V., Richards, D.H., & Gelder, M.G. A study of minor psychiatric and physical symptoms during the menstrual cycle. *British Journal of Psychiatry*, 1975, *126*, 431–434.

Blass, E.M., & Epstein, A.N. A lateral preoptic osmosensitive zone for thirst in the rat. *Journal of Comparative and Physiological Psychology*, 1971, *76*, 378–394.

Bliss, T.V.P., & Lmo, T. Long-lasting potentiation of synaptic transmission in the dentate area of the anesthetized rabbit following stimulation of the perforant path. *Journal of Physiology (London)*, 1973, *232*, 331–356.

Bloom, W., & Fawcett, D. W. Muscular tissue. *Textbook of histology* (9th ed.). Philadelphia, Pa.: Saunders, 1968.

Bolch, J. Biorhythms: A key to your ups and downs. *Readers Digest*, 1977, *111*, 63–67.

Bolles, R.C. Reinforcement, expectancy and learning. *Psychological Review*, 1972, *79*, 394–409.

Brecher, G., & Waxler, S. Obesity in albino mice due to single injections of goldthioglucose. *Proceedings of the Society for Experimental Biology and Medicine*, 1949, *70*, 498.

Breger, L., Hunter, I., & Lane, R. The effect of stress on dreams. *Psychological Issues*, 1971, *7* (Monograph 27).

Breisch, S.T., Zemlan, F.P., & Hoebel, B.G. Hyperphagia and obesity following serotonin depletion by intraventricular p-chlorophenylalanine. *Science*, 1976, *192*, 382–385.

Bremer, F. Cerveau "isolé" et physiologie du sommeil. *Comptes Rendus des Seances de la Societe de Biologie et de Ses Filiales*, 1935, *122*, 460–463.

Brobeck, J.R., Tepperman, J., & Long, C.N.H. Experimental hypothalamic hyperphagia in the albino rat. *Yale Journal of Biology and Medicine*, 1943, *15*, 831–853.

Brodal, A. Self observations and neuroanatomical considerations after a stroke. *Brain*, 1973, *96*, 675–694.

Bronzino, J.D., Morgane, P.J., Forbes, W.B., Stern, W.C., & Resnick, O. Ontogeny of visual evoked responses in rats protein-malnourished during development. *Biological Psychiatry*, 1975, *10*, 175–184.

Brown, R.T. Early experience and problem-solving ability. *Journal of Comparative and Physiological Psychology*, 1968, *65*, 433–440.

Bruce, H.M. An exteroceptive block to pregnancy in the mouse. *Nature (London)*, 1959, *184*, 105.

Bruce, H.M. Further observations on pregnancy block in mice caused by proximity of strange males. *Journal of Reproduction and Fertility*, 1960 *1*, 311–312.

Buchsbaum, M., & Fedio, P. Hemispheric differences in evoked potentials to verbal and nonverbal stimuli in the left and right visual fields. *Physiology and Behavior*, 1970, *5*, 207–210.

Buggy, J., & Johnson, A.K. Preoptic hypothalamic periventricular lesions: Thirst deficits and hypernatremia. *American Journal of Physiology*, 1977, *233*, R44–R52.

Burgess, P.R., & Perl, E.R. Cutaneous mechanoreceptors and hociceptors. In A. Iggo (Ed.), *Handbook of Sensory Physiology* (Vol. II). Berlin & New York: Springger-Verlag, 1973.

Burton, H., & Benjamin, R.M. Central projections of the gustatory system. In L.M. Beidler (Ed.), *Handbook of Sensory Physiology* (Vol. IV, Part 2). Berlin & New York: Springer-Verlag, 1971.

Butler, S.R., Suskind, M.R., & Schanberg, S.M. Maternal behavior as a regulator of polyamine biosynthesis in brain and heart of the developing rat pup. *Science*, 1978, *199*, 445–446.

Byrne, D. The imagery of sex. In J. Money & H. Musaph (Eds.), *Handbook of sexology* (Vol. 1). Amsterdam: Excerpta Med. Found., 1977.

Campbell, B.A., & Coulter, X. The ontogenesis of learning and memory. In M.R. Rosenzweig & E.L. Bennett (Eds.), *Neural mechanisms of learning and memory*. Cambridge, Mass.: MIT Press, 1976.

Cannon, W.B. The James-Lange theory of emotions: A critical examination and an alternative. *American Journal of Psychology*, 1927, *39*, 106–124.

Cannon, W.B. *Bodily changes in pain, hunger, fear and rage* (2nd ed.). New York: Appleton, 1929.

Carlson, N.R. *Physiology of behavior*. Boston: Allyn and Bacon, 1977.

Carlsson, A. Antipsychotic drugs, neurotransmitters, and schizophrenia. *American Journal of Psychiatry*, 1978, *135*, 164–172.

Carter, C.S., & Davis, J.M. Biogenic amines, reproductive hormones and female sexual behavior: A review. *Biobehavioral Reviews*, 1977, *1*, 213–224.

Cartwright, R. The relation of daytime events to the dreams that follow. In E. Hartmann (Ed.), *Sleep and dreaming*. Boston: Little, Brown, 1970.

Casey, K.L. Somatosensory responses of bulbo-reticular units in awake cats: Relation to escape producing stimuli. *Science*, 1971, *173*, 77–80.

Chalupa, L.M., & Rhoades, R.W. Directional selectivity in hamster superior colliculus is modified by strobe-rearing but not by dark-rearing. *Science*, 1978, *199*, 998–1001.

Chance, W.T., White, A.C., Krynock, G.M., & Rosencrans, J.A. Conditioned fear-induced antinociception and decreased binding of [³H] N-Leu-enkephalin to rat brain. *Brain Research*, 1978, *141*, 371–374.

Chapman, W.P. Studies of the periamygdaloid area in relation to human behavior. In H.C. Solomon, S. Cobb, & W. Penfield (Eds.), *The brain and human behavior*. Baltimore: Williams & Wilkins, 1958.

Chappel, S.C., & Barraclough, C.A. Hypothalamic regulation of pituitary FSH secretion. *Endocrinology*, 1976, *98*, 927–935.

Cheng, P., & Casida, L.E. Effects of testosterone propionate upon sexual libido and the production of semen and sperm in the rabbit. *Endocrinology*, 1949, *44*, 38–48.

Christensen, L.W., & Gorski, R.A. Independent masculinization of neuroendocrine systems by intracerebral implants of testosterone or estradiol in the neonatal female rat. *Brain Research*, 1978, *146*, 325–340.

Churchill, J.A., & Schuknecht, H.F. The relationship of acetylcholinesterase in the cochlea to the olivocochlear bundle. *Henry Ford Hospital Medical Bulletin*, 1959, *7*, 202–210.

Clarke, E., & Dewhurst, K. *An illustrated history of brain function*. Berkley: University of California Press, 1972.

Clegg, P.C., & Clegg, A.G. *Hormones, cells and organisms: The role of hormones in mammals*. Stanford, Calif.: Stanford University Press, 1968.

Coburn, P.C., & Stricker, E.M. Osmoregulatory thirst in rats after lateral preoptic lesions. *Journal of Comparative Physiological Psychology*, 1978, *92*, 350–361.

Cohen, M.J., Landgren, S., Strom, L., & Zotterman, Y. Cortical reception of touch and taste in the cat: A study of single cortical cells. *Acta Physiologica Scandinavica*, 1957, *40*, Suppl. 135, 1–50.

Colavita, F.B. Temporal pattern discrimination in the cat. *Physiology and Behavior*, 1977, *18*, 513–521.

Comfort, A. Likelihood of human pheromones. *Nature (London)*, 1971, *230*, 432–433.

Coren, S., Porac, C., & Ward, L.M. *Sensation and perception*. New York: Academic Press, 1979.

Coursin, D.B. Malnutrition, brain development, and behavior: Anatomic biochemical and electrophysiologic constructs. In M.A.B. Brazier (Ed.), *Growth and development of the brain* (Vol. 1). New York: Raven Press, 1975.

Cragg, B.G. The development of cortical synapses during starvation in the rat. *Brain*, 1972, *95*, 143–150.

Crosby, E.C., Humphrey, T., & Lauer, E.W. Blood vessels, meninges, cerebrospinal fluid. *Correlative anatomy of the nervous system*. New York: Macmillan, 1962.

Dacou-Voutetakis, C., Anagnostakis, D., & Matsaniotis, N. Effect of prolonged illumination (phototherapy) on concentrations of luteinizing hormones in human infants. *Science*, 1978, *199*, 1229–1231.

Das, G.D., & Hallas, B.H. Transplantation of brain tissue in the brain of adult rats. *Experientia*, 1978, *34*, 1304–1306.

Dastoli, F.R., & Price, S. Sweet-sensitive protein from bovine taste buds: Isolation and assay. *Science*, 1966, *154*, 905–907.

Davidson, J.M. Activation of male rats' sexual behavior by intracerebral implantation of androgen. *Endocrinology*, 1966, *79*, 783–794.

Davies, V.J., & Bellamy, D. Effects of female urine on social investigation in male mice. *Animal Behaviour*, 1974, *22*, 239–241.

Davis, H. Audiometry. In H. Davis & S.R. Silverman (Eds.), *Hearing and deafness* (Rev. ed.). New York: Holt, 1960.

Davis, H. A model for transducer action in the cochlea. *Cold Spring Harbor Symposia on Quantitative Biology*, 1965, *30*, 181–190.

Davison, A.N., & Dobbing, J. Myelination as a vulnerable period in brain development. *British Med. Bulletin*, 1966, *22*, 40–44.

Daw, N.W., Berman, N.E.J., & Ariel, M. Interaction of critical periods in the visual cortex of kittens. *Science*, 1978, *199*, 565–567.

Delgado, J.M.R. Offensive-defensive behavior in free monkeys and chimpanzees induced by radio stimulation of the brain. In S. Garatlini & E.B. Sigg (Eds.), *Aggressive behavior*. New York: Wiley, 1969.

DeLong, M.R. Motor functions of the basal ganglia: Single-cell activity during movement. In F.O. Schmitt & F.G. Worden (Eds.), *The neurosciences*. London & New York: Cambridge University Press, 1974.

DeLora, J.S., & Warren, C.A.B. (Eds.). *Understanding sexual interaction*. Boston: Houghton Mifflin Co., 1977.

Dement, W.C., Ferguson, F., Cohen, H., & Barchas, J. Nonchemical methods and data using a biochemical model: The REM quanta. In A.J. Mandell & M.P. Mandell (Eds.), *Psychochemical research in man*. New York: Academic Press, 1969.

Dement, W.C., Mitler, M., & Henriksen, S. Sleep changes during chronic administration of parachlorophenylalanine. *Revue Canadienne de Biologie*, 1972, *31*, 239–246.

Dement, W.C., & Wolpert, E.A. The relation of eye movements, body motility and external stimuli to dream content. *Journal of Experimental Psychology*, 1958, *55*, 543.

Dement, W.C., & Zarcone, V. Pharmacological treatment of sleep disorders. In J.D. Barchas *et al.* (Eds.), *Psychopharmacology: From theory to practice*. London & New York: Oxford University Press, 1977.

DeValois, R.L., Abramov, I., & Jacobs, G.H. Analysis of response patterns in LGN cells. *Journal of the Optical Society of America*, 1966, *56*, 966–977.

deWeid, D. Pituitary-adrenal system hormones and behavior. In F.O. Schmitt & F.G. Worden (Eds.), *The neurosciences: Third study program*. Cambridge, Mass.: MIT Press, 1974.

Dicker, S.E., & Nunn, J. The role of anti-diuretic hormone during water deprivation in rats. *Journal of Physiology (London)*, 1957, *136*, 235–248.

Dobbing, J., & Widdowson, E.M. The effect of undernutrition and subsequent rehabilitation on myelination of rat brain as measured by its composition. *Brain*, 1965, *88*, 357.

Doetsch, G.S., & Erickson, R.P. Synaptic processing of taste-quality information in the nucleus tractus of the rat. *Journal of Neurophysiology*, 1970, *33*, 490–507.

Döhler, K.D. Is female sexual differentiation hormone-mediated? *Trends in Neuroscience*, 1978, *1*, 138–140.

Doving, K.B. Studies of the relation between the frog's electro-olfactogram (EOG) and single unit activity in the olfactory bulb. *Acta Physiologica Scandinavica*, 1964, *60*, 150–153.

Dowling, J.E., & Boycott, B.B. Organization of the primate retina: Electron microscopy. *Proceedings of the Royal Society of London, Ser. B*, 1966, *166*, 80–111.

Dröscher, V.B. *The magic of the senses.* New York: Harper, 1969.

Duncan, C.P. The retroactive effect of electroshock on learning. *Journal of Comparative and Physiological Psychology*, 1949, *42*, 32–44.

Dunn, A., & Bondy, S. *Functional chemistry of the brain.* Flushing, N.Y.: SP Books, 1974.

Dunn, A.J. Biochemical correlates of training experiences: A discussion of the evidence. In M.R. Rosenzweig & E.L. Bennett (Eds.), *Neural mechanisms of learning and memory.* Cambridge, Mass.: MIT Press, 1976.

Eaton, G.G., Goy, R.W., & Phoenix, C.H. Effects of testosterone treatment in adulthood on sexual behaviour of female pseudo-hermaphrodite Rhesus monkeys. *Nature (London)*, 1973, *242*, 119–120.

Eayrs, J.T. Functional correlates of modified cortical structure. In D.B. Tower & J.C. Schade (Eds.), *Structure and function of the cerebral cortex.* Amsterdam: Elsevier, 1960.

Eayrs, J.T. Developmental relationships between brain and thyroid. In R.P. Michael (Ed.), *Endocrinology and human behavior.* London & New York: Oxford University Press, 1968.

Eayrs, J.T., & Horn, G. The development of cerebral cortex in hypothyroid and starved rats. *Anatomical Record*, 1955, *121*, 53–61.

Eccles, J.C. The synapse. *Scientific American*, 1965.

Ehrhardt, A.A. Prenatal androgenization and human psychosexual behavior. In J. Money & H. Musaph (Eds.), *Handbook of sexology* (Vol. 1). Amsterdam: Excerpta Med. Found., 1977.

Eichelman, B.S., & Thoa, N.B. The aggressive monoamines. *Biological Psychiatry*, 1973, *6*, 143–164.

Ellison, G.D., & Flynn, J.P. Organized aggressive behavior in cats after surgical isolation of the hypothalamus. *Archives Italiennes de Biologie*, 1968, *106*, 1–20.

Engel, G. Emotional stress and sudden death. *Psychology Today*, 1977, *11*, 114–115.

Epstein, A.N. The lateral hypothalamic syndrome: Its implications for the physiological psychology of hunger and thirst. In E. Stellar & J.M. Sprague (Eds.), *Progress in physiological psychology* (Vol. 4). New York: Academic Press, 1971.

Epstein, A.N. Epilogue: Retrospect and prognosis. In A.N. Epstein, H.R. Kissilett, & E. Stellar (Eds.), *The neuropsychology of thirst.* New York: Wiley, 1973.

Epstein, A.N., Fitzsimons, J.T., & Rolls, B.J. Drinking induced by injection of angiotensin into the brain of the rat. *Journal of Physiology (London)*, 1970, *210*, 457–474.

Epstein, A.N., & Stellar, E. The control of salt preference in the adrenalectomized rat. *Journal of Comparative and Physiological Psychology*, 1955, *48*, 167–172.

Erickson, R.P. Sensory neural patterns and gustation. In Y. Zotterman (Ed.), *Olfaction and taste I.* Oxford: Pergamon, 1963.

Erickson, R.P., & Schiffman, S.S. The chemical senses: A systematic approach. In M.S. Gazzaniga & C. Blakemore (Eds.). *Handbook of psychobiology.* New York: Academic Press, 1975.

Erickson, R.P., Doetsch, G.S., & Marshall, D.A. The gustatory neural response function. *Journal of Comparative Physiology,* 1965, *49,* 247–263.

Erlenmeyer-Kimling, L., & Jarvik, L.F. Genetics and intelligence: A review. *Science,* 1963, *142,* 1477–1479.

Evans, E.F. Cochlear nerve and cochlear nucleus. In W.D. Keidel & W.D. Neff (Eds.), *Handbook of sensory physiology,* (Vol. 2). Berlin & New York: Springer-Verlag, 1975.

Evarts, E.V. Relation of discharge frequency to conduction velocity in pyramidal tract neurons. *Journal of Neurophysiology,* 1965, *28,* 215–228.

Evarts, E.V. Pyramidal tract activity associated with a conditioned hand movement in the monkey. *Journal of Neurophysiology,* 1966, *29,* 1011–1027.

Evarts, E.V. Activity of thalamic and cortical neurons in relation to learned movement in the monkey. *International Journal of Neurology,* 1971, *8,* 321–326.

Evarts, E.V. The Third Stevenson Lecture. Changing concepts of central control of movement. *Canadian Journal of Physiology and Pharmacology,* 1975, *53,* 191–201.

Evarts, E.V., & Tanji, J. Gating of motor cortex reflexes by prior instruction. *Brain Research,* 1974, *71,* 479–494.

Evered, M.D., & Mogenson, G.J. Regulatory and secondary water intake in rats with lesions of the zona incerta. *American Journal of Physiology,* 1976, *230,* 1049–1057.

Everitt, B.J. Cerebral monoamines and sexual behavior. In J. Money & H. Musaph (Eds.), *Handbook of sexology* (Vol. 1). Amsterdam Excerpta Med. Found., 1977.

Everitt, B.J., Fuxe, K., & Hökfelt, T. Inhibitory role of dopamine and 5-hydroxytryptamine in the sexual behavior of female rats. *European Journal of Pharmacology,* 1974, *29,* 187–191.

Everitt, B.J., Fuxe, K., Hökfelt, T. & Jonsson, G. Role of monoamines in the control of hormones and sexual receptivity in the female rat. *Journal of Comparative and Physiological Psychology,* 1975, *89,* 556–572.

Everitt, B.J., Herbert, J., & Hamer, J.D. Sexual receptivity of bilateral adrenalectomized female Rhesus monkeys. *Physiology and Behavior,* 1971, *8,* 409–415.

Famiglietti, E.V., Kaneko, A., & Tachibana, M. Neuronal architecture of on and off pathways to ganglion cells in carp retina. *Science,* 1977, *198,* 1267–1269.

Fann, W.E., Davis, J.M., & Janowsky, D.S. The prevalence of tardive dyskinesias in mental hospital patients. *Diseases of the Nervous System,* 1972, *33,* 182–186.

Fedio, P., & Van Buren, J.M. Memory and perceptual deficits during electrical stimulation in the left and right thalamus and parietal subcortex. *Brain Language,* 1975, *2,* 78–100.

Feinberg, I., Fein, G., Walker, J.M., Price, L.J., Floyd, T.C., & March,

J.D. Flurazepam effects on slow-wave sleep: Stage 4 suppressed but number of delta waves constant. *Science*, 1977, *198*, 847–848.

Fencl, V., Koski, G., & Pappenheimer, J.R. Factors in cerebrospinal fluid from goats that affect sleep and activity in rats. *Journal of Physiology (London)*, 1971, *216*, 565–589.

Fex, J. Neural excitatory processes of the inner ear. In W.D. Keidel & W.D. Neff (Eds.), *Handbook of sensory physiology* (Vol. V, Part 1). Berlin & New York: Springer-Verlag, 1974.

Fibiger, H.C., Zis, A.P., & McGeer, E.G. Feeding and drinking deficits after 6-hydroxydopamine administration in the rat: Similarities to the lateral hypothalamic syndrome. *Brain Research*, 1973, *55*, 135–148.

Fisher, C. Dreaming and sexuality. In L. Lowenstein, M. Newman, M.M. Schur, & A. Solnit (Eds.), *Psychoanalysis: A General Psychology*. New York: International University Press, 1966.

Fisher, G.L., Pfaffman, C., & Brown, E. Dulcin and saccharin taste in squirrel monkeys, rats and men. *Science*, 1965, *150*, 506–507.

Fitzsimons, J.T. The physiology of thirst: A review of the extraneural aspects of the mechanism of drinking. In E. Stellar & J.M. Sprague (Eds.), *Progress in physiological psychology* (Vol. 4). New York: Academic Press, 1971.

Fitzsimons, J.T., & LeMagnen, J. Eating as a regulatory control of drinking in the rat. *Journal of Comparative and Physiological Psychology*. 1969, *67*, 273–283.

Foreman, D., & Ward, J.W. Responses to electrical stimulation of caudate nucleus in cats in chronic experiments. *Journal of Neurophysiology*, 1957, *20*, 230–244.

Fox, C.A., Ismail, A.A., Love, D.N., Kirkham, K.E., & Loraine, J.A. Studies on the relationship between plasma testosterone levels and human sexual activity. *Journal of Endocrinology*, 1972, *52*, 51–58.

Frankova, S. Effect of protein-calorie malnutrition in the development of social behavior in rats. *Developmental Psychobiology*, 1973, *6*, 33–43.

Frederickson, J.M., Schwarz, D.W.F., & Kornhuber, H.H. Convergence and interaction of vestibular and deep somatic afferents upon neurons in the vestibular nuclei of the cat. *Acta Oto-Laryngologica*, 1966, *61*, 168–188.

Frederickson, R.C., Burgis, V., & Edwards, J.D. Hyperalgesia induced by naloxone follows diurnal rhythm in responsivity to painful stimuli. *Science*, 1977, *198*, 756–758.

Freeman, F.R. *Sleep research: A critical review*. Springfield, Ill.: Thomas, 1972.

Freeman, R.D., & Pettigrew, J.D. Alteration of visual cortex from environmental asymmetries. *Nature (London)*, 1973, *246*, 359–360.

Friedman, M.I., & Stricker, E.M. The physiological psychology of hunger: A physiological perspective. *Psychological Review*, 1976, *83*, 409–431.

Fuller, C.A., Sulzman, F.M., & Moore-Ede, M.C. Thermoregulation is impaired in an environment without circadian time cues. *Science*, 1978, *199*.

Fuster, J.M. Effects of stimulation of brain stem on tachistoscopic perception. *Science*, 1958, *127*, 150.

Fuster, J.M., & Alexander, G.E. Firing changes in cells of the nucleus medialis dorsalis associated with delayed response behavior. *Brain Research*, 1973, *61*, 79–91.

Gaito, J. A biochemical approach to learning and memory: Fourteen years later. In G. Newton & A.H. Riesen (Eds.), *Advances in psychobiology* (Vol. 2). New York: Wiley, 1974.

Galaburda, A.M., LeMay, M., Kemper, T.L., & Geschwind, N. Right-left asymmetries in the brain. *Science, 1978, 199,* 852–856.

Ganchrow, J.R., & Erickson, R.P. Neural correlates of gustatory intensity and quality. *Journal of Neurophysiology, 1970, 33,* 768–783.

Gardner, E. *Fundamentals of neurology: A psychophysiological approach.* Philadelphia: Saunders, 1975.

Gardner, B.T., & Gardner, R.A. Two way communication with an infant chimpanzee. In A.M. Schrier & F. Stollnitz (Eds.), *Behavior of non-human primates* (Vol. 4). New York: Academic Press, 1971.

Gardner, R.A., & Gardner, B.T. Teaching sign language to a chimpanzee. *Science, 1969, 165,* 664–672.

Gazzaniga, M.S. The split brain in man. *Scientific American, 1967, 217,* 24–29.

German, D.C., & Bowden, D.M. Catecholamine systems as the neural substrate for intracranial self-stimulation: A hypothesis. *Brain Research, 1974, 73,* 381–419.

Geschwind, N. Disconnexion syndromes in animals and man. *Brain, 1965, 88,* 237–294.

Geschwind, N. The organization of language and the brain. *Science, 1970, 27,* 940–945.

Gesteland, R.C., Lettvin, L.Y., Pitts, W.H., & Rojas, A. Odor specificities of the frog's olfactory receptors. In Y. Zotterman (Ed.), *Olfaction and taste I.* Oxford: Pergamon, 1963.

Gesteland, R.C., & Sigwart, C.D. Olfactory receptor units—a mammalian preparation. *Brain Research, 1977, 133,* 144–149.

Getlein, F. Mind controllers: CIA testing. *Commonwealth, 1977, 104,* 548–549.

Gibson, W.E., Reid, L.D., Sakai, M., & Porter, P.B. Intracranial reinforcement compared with sugar-water reinforcement. *Science, 1965, 148,* 1357–1359.

Glickstein, M., & Gibson, A.R. Visual cells in the pons of the brain. *Scientific American, 1976, 235,* 90–98.

Gold, P.E., Macri, J., & McGaugh, J.L. Retrograde amnesia gradients: Effects of direct cortical stimulation. *Science, 1973, 179,* 1343–1345.

Gold, P.E., & McGaugh, J.L. Neurobiology and memory: Modulators, correlates and assumptions. In T. Teyler (Ed.), *Brain and learning.* Stamford, Conn.: Greylock Publishers, 1978.

Gold, P.E., & Sternberg, D.B. Retrograde amnesia produced by several treatments: Evidence for a common neurobiological mechanism. *Science, 1978, 201,* 367–369.

Gold, P.E., & van Buskirk, R. Enhancement of time-dependent memory processes with post-trial epinephrine injections. *Behavioral Biology, 1975, 13,* 145–153.

Gold, P.E., & van Buskirk, R. Effects of α and β adrenergic receptor antagonists on post-trial epinephrine modulation of memory: Relationship to posttraining brain norepinephrine concentrations. *Behavioral Biology, 1978, 24,* 168–184.

Goldberg, J.M., & Brown, P.B. Response of binaural neurons of dog superior olivary complex to dichotic tonal stimuli: Some physiological mechanisms of sound localization. *Journal of Neurophysiology, 1969, 32,* 613–636.

Goldberg, J.M., & Fernandez, C. Physiology of peripheral neurons innervating semi-circular canals of the squirrel monkey. I. Resting discharge and response to angular acceleration. *Journal of Neurophysiology*, 1971, *34*, 635–660.

Goldfoot, D.A., Essock-Vitale, S.M., Asa, C.S., Thronton, J.E., & Leshner, A.I. Anosmia in male rhesus monkeys does not alter copulatory activity with cycling females. *Science*, 1978, *199*, 1095–1096.

Goldman, P.S. Developmental determinants of cortical plasticity. *Acta Neurobiologiae Experimentalis*, 1972, *32*, 495–511.

Goldman, P.S. Neuronal plasticity in primate telencephalon: Anomalous projections induced by prenatal removal of frontal cortex. *Science*, 1978, *202*, 768–770.

Goldman, P.S., & Rosvold, H.E. Localization of function within the dorsolateral prefrontal cortex of the rhesus monkey. *Experimental Neurology*, 1970, *27*, 291–304.

Goldstein, M. Inhibition of norepinephrine biosynthesis at the dopamine-β-hydroxylase stage. *Pharmacological Review*, 1966, *18*, 177.

Goldstein, M.H., Jr., Hall, J.L., & Butterfield, B.L. Single-unit activity in the primary auditory cortex of unanesthetized cats. *Journal of the Acoustical Society of America*, 1968, *43*, 444–455.

Goodwin, D.W. Alcoholism and heredity. *Archives of General Psychiatry*, 1979, *36*, 57–61.

Goodwin, F.K. Behavioral effects of L-Dopa in man. *Seminars in Psychiatry*, 1971, *3*, 477–492.

Goodwin, F.K., & Murphy, D.L. Biological factors in the affective disorders and schizophrenia. In M. Gordon (Ed.). *Psychopharmacological agents*. New York: Academic Press, 1974.

Gormezano, I. Classical conditioning. In J.B. Sidowski (Ed.), *Experimental methods and instrumentation in psychology*. New York: McGraw-Hill, 1966.

Gorski, R.A. Mechanisms of androgen induced masculine differentiation of the rat brain. In K. Lissak (Ed.), *Hormones and brain function*. New York: Plenum.

Gorski, R.A., Gordon, J.H., Shryne, J.E., & Southam, A.M. Evidence for a morphological sex difference within the medial preoptic area of the rat brain. *Brain Research*, 1978, *148*, 333–346.

Gossop, M.R., Stern, R., & Connell, P.H. Drug dependence and sexual function: A comparison of intravenous users of narcotics and oral users of amphetamines. *British Journal of Psychiatry*, 1974, *124*, 431–434.

Goy, R.W., Phoenix, C.H., & Young, W.C. A critical period for the suppression of behavioral receptivity in adult female rats by early treatment with androgen. *Anatomical Record*, 1962, *142*, 307.

Goy, R.W., Wolf, J.E., & Eisele, S.G. Experimental female hermaphroditism in Rhesus monkeys: Anatomical and psychological characteristics. In J. Money & H. Musaph (Eds.), *Handbook of sexology* (Vol. 1). Amsterdam: Excerpta Med. Found., 1977.

Gradwell, P.B., Everitt, B.J., & Herberg, J. 5-hydroxytryptamine in the central nervous system and sexual receptivity of female Rhesus monkeys. *Brain Research*, 1975, *88*, 281–293.

Graziadei, P.P.C. The olfactory mucosa of vertebrates. In L.M. Beidler (Ed.), *Handbook of sensory physiology* (Vol. IV). Berlin & New York: Springer-Verlag, 1971.

Greenough, W.T. Experiential modification of the developing brain. *American Scientist*, 1975, *63*, 37–46.

Greenough, W.T. Enduring brain effects of differential experience and training. In M.R. Rosenzweig & E.L. Bennett (Eds.), *Neural mechanisms of learning and memory*. Cambridge, Mass.: MIT Press, 1976.

Greenough, W.T. Development and memory: The synaptic connection. In T. Teyler (Ed.), *Brain and learning*. Stamford, Conn.: Greylock Publishers, 1978.

Greenough, W.T., Carter, C.S., Steerman, C., & DeVoogd, T.J. Sex difference in dendritic branching patterns in hamster preoptic area. *Brain Research*, 1977, *126*, 63–72.

Grollman S. *The human body: Its structure and physiology* (2nd ed.). New York: Macmillan, 1969.

Gross, C.G., Cowey, A., & Manning, F.J. Further analysis of visual discrimination deficits following foveal prestriate and inferotemporal lesions in Rhesus monkeys. *Journal of Comparative and Physiological Psychology*, 1971, *76*, 1–7.

Gross, C.G., Rocha-Miranda, C.E., & Bender, D.B. Visual properties of neurons in inferotemporal cortex of the macaque. *Journal of Neurophysiology*, 1972, *35*, 96–111.

Guilleminault, C., Eldreidge, F.L., & Dement, W.C. Insomnia with sleep apnea: A new syndrome. *Science*, 1973, *181*, 856–858.

Gulick, W.L. *Hearing, physiology and psychophysics*. London & New York: Oxford University Press.

Guth, L. Taste buds on the cat's circumvallate papilla after reinnervation by glossopharyngeal, vagus, and hypoflossal nerves. *Anatomical Record*, 1958, *130*, 25–37.

Haberly, L.B. Single-unit responses to odor in the prepyriform cortex of the rat. *Brain Research*, 1969, *12*, 481–484.

Halberg, F. Physiologic considerations underlying rhythmometry with special reference to emotional illness. In J. de Ajuriaguerra (Ed.), *Cycles biologiques et psychiatrie*. Paris: Masson, 1968.

Halberg, F. Chronobiology, in 1975. *Chronobiologia*, 1976, *3*, 1–14.

Hall, C.S. What people dream about. *Scientific American*, 1951, *184*, 60–63.

Halpern, B.P., & Marowitz, L.A. Taste responses to lick-duration stimuli. *Brain Research*, 1973, *57*, 473–478.

Halpern, P.B. & Tapper, D.N. Taste stimuli: Quality coding time. *Science*, 1971, *171*, 1256–1258.

Hamilton, C.L., & Brobeck, J.R. Hypothalamic hyperphagia in the monkey. *Journal of Comparative and Physiological Psychology*, 1964, *57*, 271–278.

Hanby, J.P. Social factors affecting primate reduction. In J. Money & H. Musaph (Eds.), *Handbook of sexology*. Amsterdam: Excerpta Med. Found., 1977.

Harding, J., Graziadei, P.P.C., Monti-Graziadei, G.A., & Margolis, F.L. Denervation in the primary olfactory pathway of mice. IV. Biochemical and morphological evidence for neuronal replacement following nerve section. *Brain Research*, 1977, *132*, 11–24.

Hardy, M. *Anatomical Record*, 1934, *59*, 404.

Harlow, H.F. The heterosexual affectional system in monkeys. *American Psychology*, 1962, *17*, 1–9.

Harris, L.J., Clay, J., Hargreaves, F., & Ward, A. Appetite and choice of diet. The ability of the vitamin B deficient rat to discriminate diets containing and lacking the vitamin. *Proceedings of the Royal Society of London, Ser. B*, 1933, *113*, 161–190.

Hartline, H.K., & Ratliff, F. Inhibitory interaction of receptor units in the eye of *Limulus*. *Journal of General Physiology*, 1957, *40*, 357–376.

Hartline, H.K., & Ratliff, F. Spatial inhibitory influences in the eye of the *Limulus*, and the mutual interaction of receptor units. *Journal of General Physiology*, 1958, *41*, 1049–1066.

Hartline, H.K., Wagner, H., & Ratliff, F. Inhibition in the eye of *Limulus*. *Journal of General Physiology*, 1956, *39*, 651–673.

Hartmann, E. *The biology of dreaming.* Springfield, Ill.: Thomas, 1967.

Hashimoto, T., & Katsuki, Y. Enhancement of the mechano-sensitivity of hair cells of the lateral-line organs by environmental potassium ions. *Journal of the Acoustical Society of America*, 1972, *52*, 553–557.

Hatton, G.I. Nucleus circularis: Is it an osmoreceptor in the brain? *Brain Research Bulletin*, 1976, *1*, 123–131.

Hauri, P. What is good sleep? *International Psychiatry Clinics*, 1970, *7*, 70–77.

Hays, S.E. Stragties for psychoendocrine studies of puberty. *Psychoneuroendocrinology*, 1978, *3*, 1–15.

Hebb, D.O. *The organization of behavior.* New York: Wiley, 1949.

Heck, G.L., & Erickson, R.P. A rate theory of gustatory stimulation. *Behavioral Biology*, 1973, *8*, 687–712.

Heffner, R., & Masterson, B. Variation in form of pyramidal tract and its relationship to digital dexterity. *Brain, Behavior and Evolution*, 1975, *12*, 161–200.

Heimer, L., & Larsson, K. Impairment of mating behavior in male rats following lesions in the preoptic-anterior hypothalamic continuum. *Brain Research*, 1966–1967, *3*, 248–263.

Hensel, H. Cutaneous thermoreceptors. In A. Iggo (Ed.), *Somatosensory system.* Berlin & New York: Springer-Verlag, 1973.

Hensel, H., & Boman, K.K.A. Afferent impulses in cutaneous sensory nerves in human subjects. *Journal of Neurophysiology*, 1960, *23*, 564–578.

Hensel, H., & Kenshalo, D.R. Warm receptors in the nasal region of cats. *Journal of Physiology (London)*, 1969, *204*, 99–112.

Herbert, J. Some functions of hormones and the hypothalamus in the sexual activity of primates. *Progress in Brain Research*, 1974, *41*, 331–348.

Herbert, J. The neuroendocrine basis of sexual behavior in primates. In J. Money & H. Musaph (Eds.), *Handbook of sexology* (Vol. 1). Amsterdam: Excerpta Med. Found., 1977.

Hillyard, S.A., Hink, R.F., Schwent, V.L., & Picton, T.W. Electrical signs of selective attention in the human brain. *Science*, 1973, *182*, 177–179.

Hirsch, H.V.B., & Spinelli, D.N. Modification of the distribution of receptive field orientation in cats by selective visual exposure during development. *Experimental Brain Research*, 1971, *13*, 509–527.

Hite, S. *The Hite report.* New York: Macmillan, 1976.

Hobson, J.A., McCarley, R.W., & Wyzanski, P.W. Sleep cycle oscillation: Reciprocal discharge by two brainstem neuronal groups. *Science*, 1975, *189*, 55–58.

Hoebel, B.G. Satiety: Hypothalamic stimulation, anorectic drugs, and neurochemical substrates. In D. Novin, W. Wyrwicka, & G.A. Bray (Eds.),

Hunger: Basic mechanisms and clinical implications. New York: Raven Press, 1976.

Hohmann, G.W. Some effects of spinal cord lesions on experienced emotional feelings. *Psychophysiology,* 1966, *3,* 143–156.

Holden, C. Pain control with hypnosis. *Science,* 1977, *198,* 808.

Hollister, L.E. Antipsychotic medications and the treatment of schizophrenia. In J.D. Barchas *et al.* (Eds.), *Psychopharmacology: From theory to practice.* London & New York: Oxford University Press, 1977.

Horne, J.A., & Österberg, O. Individual differences in human circadian rhythms. *Biological Psychology,* 1977, *5,* 179–190.

Hornykiewicz, O. Dopamine (3 hydroxytyramine) and brain function. *Pharmacological Review,* 1966, *18,* 925–962.

Houston, J.P., Bee, H., Hatfield, E., & Rimm, D.C. *Invitation to psychology.* New York: Academic Press, 1979.

Howard. E., Olton, D.S., & Johnson, C.T. Active avoidance and brain DNA after postnatal food deprivation in rats. *Developmental Psychobiology,* 1976, *9,* 217–221.

Hubel, D.H., & Wiesel, T.N. Receptive fields of single neurons in the cat's striate cortex. *Journal of Physiology (London),* 1959, *148,* 574–591.

Hubel, D.H., & Wiesel, T.N. Receptive fields, binocular interaction and functional architecture in the cat's visual cortex. *Journal of Physiology (London),* 1962, *160,* 106–154.

Hubel, D.H., & Wiesel, T.N. Shape and arrangement of columns in cat's striatal cortex. *Journal of Physiology (London),* 1963, *165,* 559–568.

Hubel, D.H., & Wiesel, T.N. Receptive fields and functional architecture in two non-striate visual areas (18 and 19) of the cat. *Journal of Neurophysiology,* 1965, *28,* 229–289.

Hubel, D.H., & Wiesel, T.N. The period of susceptability to the physiological effects of unilateral eye closure in kittens. *Journal of Physiology (London),* 1970, *206,* 419–436.

Hughes, J., Smith, T.W., Kosterlitz, H.W., Fothergill, L.A., Morgan, B.A., & Morris, H.R. Identification of two related pentapeptides from the brain with potent opiate agonist activity, *Nature (London),* 1975, *258,* 577–579.

Hutchinson, R.R., & Renfrew, J.W. Stalking attack and eating behavior elicited from the same sites in the hypothalamus. *Journal of Comparative and Physiological Psychology,* 1966, *61,* 300–367.

Hydén, H. Changes in brain protein during learning. In G.B. Ansell & P.B. Bradley (Eds.), *Macromolecules and behaviour.* New York: Macmillan, 1973.

Hydén, H., & Egyházi, E. Nuclear RNA changes in nerve cells during a learning experiment in rats. *Proceedings of the National Academy of Sciences of the United States of America,* 1962, *48,* 1366–1372.

Iggo, A., & Iggo, B.J. Impulse coding in primate cutaneous thermoreceptors in dynamic thermal conditions. *Journal of Physiology (Paris),* 1971, *63,* 287–290.

Iggo, A., & Young, D.W. Cutaneous thermoreceptors and thermal nociceptors. In H.H. Kornhuber (Ed.), *The somatosensory system.* Stuttgart: Thieme, 1975.

Ikeda, H., & Wright, M.J. Receptive field organization of "sustained" and "transient" retinal ganglion cells which subserve different functional roles. *Journal of Physiology (London),* 1972, *227,* 769–800.

Isaacson, R.L. Experimental brain lesions and memory. In M.R. Rosenzweig & E.L. Bennett (Eds.), *Neural mechanisms of learning and memory*. Cambridge, Mass.: MIT Press, 1976.

Ivey, M.E., & Bardwick, J.M. Patterns of affective fluctuation in the menstrual cycle. *Psychosomatic Medicine*, 1968, *30*, 336–345.

Iwai, E., & Mishkin, M. Further evidence on the locus of the visual area in the temporal lobe of the monkey. *Experimental Neurology*, 1969, *25*, 585–594.

Jacob, F., & Monod, J. Genetic regulating mechanisms in the synthesis of protein. *Journal of Molecular Biology*, 1961, *3*, 18.

Jacobson, M. A plenitude of neurons. In G. Gottlieb (Ed.), *Studies on the development of behavior and the nervous system* (Vol. 2). New York: Academic Press, 1973.

Janowitz, H.D., & Grossman, M.I. Some factors affecting the food intake of normal dogs and dogs with esophagostomy and gastric fistula. *American Journal of Physiology*, 1949, *159*, 143–148.

Jarrard, L.E. Selective hippocampal lesions: Differential effects on performance by rats of a spatial task with preoperative vs. post operative training. *Journal of Comparative and Physiological Psychology*, 1978, *92*, 1119–1127.

Jasper, H.H., & Ajmone-Marsan, C. Diencephalon of the cat. In D.E. Sheer (Ed.), *Electrical stimulation of the brain*. Austin: University of Texas Press, 1961.

John, E.R., & Schwartz, E.L. Neurophysiology of information processing and cognition. *Annual Review of Psychology*, 1978, *29*, 1–30.

Jones, B.E., Bobillier, P., & Jouvet, M. Effets de la destruction des neurones contenant des catécholamines du mésencéphale sur le cycle veillesommeils du chat. *Comptes Rendus des Seances de la Société de Biologie et de Ses Filiales*, 1969, *163*, 176–180.

Jouvet, M. The role of monoaminergic neurons in the regulation and function of sleep. In O. Petre-Quadens & J.D. Schlag (Eds.), *Basic sleep mechanisms*. New York: Academic Press, 1974.

Jouvet, M. The function of dreaming: A neurophysiologist's point of view. In M.S. Gazzaniga & C. Blakemore (Eds.), *Handbook of psychobiology*. New York: Academic Press, 1975.

Jouvet, M., & Renault, J. Insomnic persistante après lésions des noyaux du raphé chez le chat. *Comptes Rendus Seances de la Société de Biologie et des Ses Filiales*, 1966, *160*, 1461–1465.

Kaada, B.R. Brain mechanisms related to aggressive behavior. In C.D. Clemente & D.B. Lindsley (Eds.), *Aggression and defense: Neural mechanisms and social patterns*. Los Angeles: University of California Press, 1967.

Kandel, E.R. *The cellular basis of behavior*. San Francisco: Freeman, 1976.

Kare, M.R., & Ficken, M.S. Comparative studies on the sense of taste. In Y. Zotterman (Ed.), *Olfaction and taste I*. Oxford: Pergamon, 1963.

Keesey, R.E., & Powley, R.L. Hypothalamic regulation of body weight. *American Scientist*, 1975, *63* (5), 558–565.

Kenney, F.T., Greenman, D.L., Wicks, W.D., & Albritton, W.L. RNA synthesis and enzyme induction by hydrocortisone. *Advances in Enzyme Regulation*, 1965, *3*, 1–10.

Keverne, E.B. Pheromones and sexual behavior. In J. Money & H. Musaph (Eds.), *Handbook of sexology* (Vol. 1). Amsterdam: Excerpta Med. Found., 1977.

Kiang, N.Y.-S. *Discharge patterns of single fibers in the cat's auditory nerve.* Cambridge, Mass.: MIT Press, 1965.

Kim, Y.K., & Umbach, W. Combined stereotaxic lesions for treatment of behavior disorders and severe pain. In L.V. Laitenen & K.E. Livingston (Eds.), *Surgical approaches to psychiatry.* Baltimore: University Park Press, 1973.

Kimura, K., & Beidler, L.M. Microelectrode study of taste receptors of rat and hamster. *Journal of Cellular and Comparative Physiology,* 1961, *58,* 131–140.

King, M.B., & Hoebel, B.G. Killing elicited by brain stimulation in rat. *Communications in Behavioral Biology,* 1968, *2,* 173–177.

Kinsey, A.C., Pomeroy, W.B., Martin, C.E., & Gebhard, P.H. *Sexual behavior in the human female.* Philadelphia, Pa.: Saunders, 1953.

Klein, K.E., Wegmann, H.M., & Brüner, H. Circadian rhythm in indices of human performance, physical fitness and stress resistance. *Aerospace Medicine,* 1968, *39,* 512–518.

Kleitman, N. *Sleep and wakefulness* (2nd ed.). Chicago: University of Chicago Press, 1963.

Klüver, H., & Bucy, P.C. "Psychic blindness" and other symptoms following bilateral temporal lobectomy in Rhesus monkeys. *American Journal of Physiology,* 1937, *119,* 352–353.

Klüver, H., & Bucy, P.C. An analysis of certain effects of bilateral temporal lobectomy in the Rhesus monkey with special reference of "psychic blindness." *Journal of Psychology,* 1938, *5,* 33–54.

Knibestöl, M., & Vallbo, A.B. Single unit analysis of mechanoreceptor activity from the human glabrous skin. *Acta Physiologica Scandinavica,* 1970, *80,* 178–195.

Knudsen, E.I., & Konishi, M.A. Neural map of auditory space in the owl. *Science,* 1978, *200,,* 795–797.

Köves, K., & Halász, B. Location of the neural structures triggering ovulation in the rat. *Neuroendocrinology,* 1970, *6,* 180–193.

Kramer, M., Hlasny, R., Jacobs, G., & Roth, T. Do dreams have meaning: An empirical inquiry. *American Journal of Psychiatry,* 1976, *133,* 778–781.

Krieger, D.T. Factors influencing the circadian periodicity of plasma corticosteroid levels. *Chronobiologia,* 1974, *1,* 195–216.

Kripke, D.F., Mullaney, D.J., Atkinson, M., & Wolf, S. Circadian rhythm disorders in manic-depressives. *Biological Psychiatry,* 1978, *13,* 335–351.

Kukorelli, T., & Juhász, G. Sleep induced by intestinal stimulation in cats. *Physiology and Behavior,* 1977, *19,* 355–358.

Landgren, S. Convergence of tactile, thermal, and gustatory impulses on single cortical cells. *Acta Physiologica Scandinavica,* 1957, *40,* 210–221.

Larroche, J.-C. Part II. The development of the central nervous system during intrauterine life. In F. Falkner (Ed.), *Human development.* Philadelphia, Pa.: Saunders, 1966.

Larsson, K. Mating behavior in male rats after cerebral cortex ablation. II. Effects of lesions in the frontal lobes compared to lesions in the posterior half of the hemispheres. *Journal of Experimental Zoology,* 1964, *155,* 203–214.

Lashley, K. In search of the engram. *Symposia of the Society of Experimental Biology,* 1950, *4,* 454–482.

Leavitt, F. Drug-induced modifications in sexual behavior and open field locomotion of male rats. *Physiology and Behavior,* 1969, *4,* 677–683.

Lee, S. van der, & Boot, L.M. Spontaneous pseudopregnancy in mice. *Acta Physiologica et Pharmacologica Neerlandica*, 1955, *4*, 442–444.

Legendre, R., & Piéron, H. Recherches sur le besoin de sommeil consécutif a une veille prolongés. *Zeitschrift fuer Allgemeine Physiologie*, 1913, *14*, 235–362.

LeMagnen, J. Les phénomènes des olfacto-sexuels chez le rat blanc. *Archives Sciences des Physiologigues*, 1952, *6*, 295–332.

LeMay, M., & Geschwind, N. Hemispheric differences in the brains of great apes. *Brain, Behavior and Evolution*, 1975, *11*, 48–52.

Lettvin, J.Y., Maturana, H.R., McCulloch, W.S., & Pitts, W.H. What the frog's eye tells the frog's brain. *Proceedings of the IRE*, 1959, *47*, 1940–1951.

Lettvin, J.Y., Maturana, H.R., Pitts, W.H., & McCulloch, W.S. Two remarks on the visual system of the frog. In W.A. Rosenblith (Ed.), *Sensory communication*. New York: Wiley, 1961.

Levine, S. Stimulation in infancy. *Scientific American*, 1960, *202*, 80–86.

Levine, S. *Hormones and behavior*, New York: Academic Press, 1972.

Levitsky, D.A., & Barnes, R.H. Nutritional and environmental interactions in the behavioral development of the rat: Long-term effects. *Science*, 1972, *176*, 68–71.

Levy, J. The origins of lateral asymmetry. In S. Harnad, R.W. Doty, L. Goldstein, J. Jaynes, & G. Krauthamer (Eds.), *Lateralization in the nervous system*. New York: Academic Press, 1977.

Levy, J., & Levy, J.M. Human lateralization from head to foot: Sex related factors. *Science*, 1978, *200*, 1291–1292.

Lewis, S.A., Sloan, J.P., & Jones, S.K. Paradoxical sleep and depth perception. *Biological Psychology*, 1978, *6*, 17–25.

Lewontin, R. Genetic aspects of intelligence. *Annual Review of Genetics*, 1975, *9*, 387–406.

Licklider, J.D.R. Three auditory theories. In S. Koch (Ed.), *Psychology: A study of a science* (Vol. 1). New York: McGraw-Hill, 1959.

Liebelt, R.A., Bordelon, C.B., & Liebelt, A.G. The adipose tissue system and food intake. In E. Stellar & J.M. Sprague (Eds.), *Progress in physiological psychology*, (Vol. 5). New York: Academic Press, 1973.

Liebeskind, J.C., & Paul, L.A. Psychological and physiological mechanisms of pain. *Annual Review of Psychology*, 1977, *28*, 41–60.

Liedgren, S.R.C., Milne, A.C., Rubin, A.M., Schwarz, D.W.F., & Tomlinson, R.D. Representation of vestibular afferents in somatosensory thalamic nuclei of the squirrel monkey *(Saimiri sciureus)*. *Journal of Neurophysiology*, 1976, *39*, 601–612.

Liley, A.W. The quantal components of the mammalian end-plate potential. *Journal of Physiology (London)*, 1956, *133*, 571–587.

Lindsley, D., Bowden, J., & Magoun, H. Effect upon the EEG of acute injury to the brain stem activating system. *Electroencephalography and Clinical Neurophysiology*, 1949, *1*, 475–498.

Lindsley, D., Schreiner, L., Knowles, W., & Magoun, H. Behavioral and EEG changes following chronic brain stem lesions in the cat. *Electroencephalography and Clinical Neurophysiology*, 1950, *2*, 483–498.

Lippa, A.S., Antelman, S.M., Fisher, A.E., & Canfield, D.E. Neurochemical mediation of reward: A significant role for dopamine? *Pharmacology, Biochemistry and Behavior*, 1973, *1*, 23–28.

Lisk, R.D. Diencephalic placement of estradiol and sexual receptivity in the female rat. *American Journal of Physiology,* 1962, *203,* 493–496.

Livett, B.G. Histochemical visualization of adrenergic neurones, peripherally and in the central nervous system. *British Medical Bulletin,* 1973, *29,* 93–99.

Loewenstein, W.R. & Mendelson, M. Components of receptor adaptation in a Pacinian corpuscle. *Journal of Physiology (London),* 1965, *177,* 377–397.

Loewenstein, W.R., & Rathkamp, R. The sites for mechano-electric conversion in a Pacinian corpuscle. *Journal of General Physiology,* 1958, *41,* 1245–1265.

Loewenstein, W.R., & Skalak, R. Mechanical transmission in a Pacinian corpuscle; an analysis and a theory. *Journal of Physiology (London),* 1966, *182,* 346–378.

Lucero, M.A. Lengthening of REM sleep duration consecutive to learning in the rat. *Brain Research,* 1970, *20,* 319–322.

Luine, V.N., Khylchevskeya, R.I., & McEwen, B.S. Effect of gonadal steroids on activities of monoamine oxidase and choline acetylase in rat brain. *Brain Research,* 1975, *86,* 293–306.

Lynch, G. Some difficulties associated with the use of lesion techniques in the study of memory. In M.R. Rosenzweig & E.L. Bennett (Eds.), *Neural mechanisms of learning and memory.* Cambridge, Mass.: MIT Press, 1976.

Lynch, G., & Wells, J. Neuroanatomical plasticity and behavioral adaptability. In T. Tyler (Ed.), *Brain and learning,* pp. 105–124, Stamford, Conn.: Greylock, 1978.

Lynch, G., Deadwyler, S., & Cotman, C.W. Postlesion axonal growth produces permanent functional connections. *Science,* 1973, *180,* 1364–1366.

Lynch, G., Stanfield, B., & Cotman, C.W. Developmental differences in postlesion axonal growth in the hippocampus. *Brain Research,* 1973, *59,* 155–168.

Lynn, P.A., & Sayers, B.McA. Cochlear innervation, signal processing, and their relation to auditory time-intensity effects. *Journal of the Acoustical Society of America,* 1970, *47,* 525–533.

Maas, J.W. Biogenic amines and depression: Biochemical and pharmacological separation of two types of depression. *Archives of General Psychiatry,* 1975, *32,* 1357–1361.

Maccoby, E.E., & Jacklin, C.N. *The psychology of sex differences.* Stanford, Calif.: Stanford University Press, 1974.

Magnes, J., Moruzzi, G., & Pompeiano, O. Synchronization of the EEG produced by low frequency electrical stimulation of the region of the solitary tract. *Archives Italiennes de Biologie,* 1961, *99,* 33–67.

Malamud, N. Psychiatric Disorder with intracranial tumors of limbic system. *Archives of Neurology (Chicago),* 1967, *17,* 113–123.

Manning, A. Animal learning: Ethological approaches. In M.R. Rosenzweig & E.L. Bennett (Eds.), *Neural mechanisms of learning and memory.* Cambridge, Mass.: MIT Press, 1976.

Mark, V.H., & Ervin, F.R. *Violence and the brain.* New York: Harper, 1970.

Marks, W.B., Dobelle, W.H., & MacNichol, E.F. Visual pigments of single primate cones. *Science,* 1964, *143,* 1181–1183.

Marshall, J.F., Turner, B.H., & Teitelbaum, P. Sensory neglect produced by lateral hypothalamic damage. *Science*, 1971, *174*, 523–525.

Mason, W.A. Early social deprivation in the nonhuman primates: Implications for human behavior. In D.C. Glass (Ed.), *Environmental influences*. New York: Rockefeller Press, 1968.

Masters, W.H., & Johnson, V.E. *Human sexual response*. Boston: Little, Brown, 1966.

Masterson, R.B. Adaptation for sound localization in the ear and brainstem of mammals. *Federation Proceedings, Federation of American Societies for Experimental Biology*, 1974, *33*, 1904–1910.

Matthews, P.B.C. Receptors in muscles and joints. In J.I. Hubbard (Ed.), *The peripheral nervous system*. New York: Plenum, 1974.

Mayer, D.J., & Hayes, R.L. Stimulation produced analgesia: Development of tolerance and cross-tolerance to morphine. *Science*, 1975, *188*, 941–943.

Mayer, D.J., & Liebeskind, J.C. Pain reduction by focal electrical stimulation of the brain: An anatomical and behavioral analysis. *Brain Research*, 1974, *68*, 73–93.

Mayer, D.J., Price, D.D., & Becker, D.P. Neurophysiological characterization of the anterolateral spinal cord neurons contributing to pain perception in man. *Pain*, 1975, *1*, 51–58.

Mayer, J. Regulation of energy intake and the body weight: The glucostatic theory and the lipostatic hypothesis. *Annals of the New York Academy of Sciences*, 1955, *63*, 15–43.

McBurney, D.H. Are there primary tastes for man? *Chemical Senses and Flavor*, 1974, *1*, 17–28.

McCarley, R.W., & Hobson, J.A. Single neuron activity in cat gigantocellular tegmental field: Selectivity of discharge in desynchronized sleep. *Science*, 1971, *174*, 1250–1252.

McClearn, G.E. *Introduction to behavioral genetics*. San Francisco: Freeman, 1973.

McEwen, B.S., Plapinger, L., Chaptal, C., Gerlach, J., & Wallach, G. Role of fetoneonatal estrogen binding proteins in the association of estrogen with neonatal brain cell nuclear receptors. *Brain Research*, 1975, *96*, 400–407.

McGaugh, J., & Gold, P.E. Modulation of memory by electrical stimulation of the brain. In M.R. Rosenzweig & E.L. Bennett (Eds.), *Neural mechanisms of learning and memory*. Cambridge, Mass.: MIT Press, 1976.

McGinty, D.J. Effects of prolonged isolation and subsequent enrichment on sleep patterns in kittens. *Electroencephalography and Clinical Neurophysiology*, 1969, *26*, 332–337.

McLennon, H. *Synaptic transmission* (2nd ed.). Philadelphia, Pa.: Saunders, 1970.

Melzack, R. *The puzzle of pain*. New York: Basic Books, 1973.

Melzack, R., & Wall, P.D. Pain mechanisms: A new theory. *Science*, 1965, *150*, 971–979.

Messenger, J. Sex and repression in an Irish folk community. In D.S. Marshall & R.C. Suggs (Eds.), *Human sexual behavior*. Englewood Cliffs, N.J.: Prentice-Hall, 1971.

Meyer, P.M., Horel, J.A., & Meyer, D.R. Effects of dl-amphetamine upon placing responses in neodecorticate cats. *Journal of Comparative and Physiological Psychology*, 1963, *56*, 402–404.

Meyer-Bahlburg, H.F.L., Boon, D.A., Sharma, M., & Edwards, J.A. Aggressiveness and testosterone measures in man. *Psychosomatic Medicine*, 1974, *36*, 269–274.

Michael, R.P., Bonsall, R.W., & Warner, P. Human vaginal secretions: Volatile fatty acid content. *Science*, 1974, *186*, 1217–1219.

Michael, R.P., & Keverne, E.B. Pheromones in the communication of sexual status in primates. *Nature (London)*, 1968, *218*, 746–749.

Michael, R.P., & Keverne, E.B. Primate sex pheromones of vaginal origin. *Nature (London)*, 1970, *225*, 84–85.

Michael, R.P., Keverne, E.B., & Bonsall, R.W. Pheromones: Isolation of male sex attractants from a female primate. *Science*, 1971, *172*, 964–966.

Michael, R.P., & Zumpe, D. Potency in male Rhesus monkeys: Effects of continuously receptive females. *Science*, 1978, *200*, 451–453.

Miczek, K.A., Altman, J.L., Appel, J.B., & Boggan, W.O. Para-chlorophenyl alanine, serotonin and killing behavior. *Pharmacology, Biochemistry and Behavior*, 1975, *3*, 355–361.

Miller, I.J. Peripheral interactions among single papilla inputs to gustatory nerve fibers. *Journal of General Physiology*, 1971, *57*, 1–25.

Miller, N. Learning of visceral and glandular responses. *Science*, 1969, *163*, 434–445.

Milner, B. Intellectual function of the temporal lobes. *Psychological Bulletin*, 1954, *51*, 42–62.

Milner, B. Effects of different brain lesions on card sorting. *Archives of Neurology (Chicago)*, 1963, *9*, 90–100.

Milner, B. Memory and the temporal regions of the brain. In K.H. Pribram & D.E. Broadbent (Eds.), *Biology of memory*. New York: Academic Press, 1970.

Milner, B., Branch, C., & Rasmussen, T. Evidence for bilateral speech representation in some non-right-handers. *Transactions of the American Neurological Association*, 1966, *91*, 306–308.

Mineka, S., & Snowdon, C.T. Inconsistency and possible habituation of CCK-induced satiety. *Physiology and Behavior*, 1978, *21*, 65–72.

Mishkin M. Cortical visual areas and their interactions. In A.G. Karczmar (Ed.), *The brain and human behavior*. Berlin & New York: Springer-Verlag, 1972.

Mishkin, M., Vest, B., Waxler, M., & Rosvold, H.E. A re-examination of the effects of frontal lesions on object alternation. *Proceedings of the International Congress of Psychology*, 1966, *18*, 43.

Mishkin, M., Vest, B., Waxler, M., & Rosvold, H.E. A re-examination of the effects of frontal lesions on object alternation. *Neuro-psychologia*, 1969, *7*, 357–363.

Mitchell, D.E., Freeman, R.D., Millodot, M., & Haegerstrom, G. Meridional amblyopia: Evidence for modification of the human visual system by early visual experience. *Vision Research*, 1973, *13*, 535–558.

Mogenson, G.J. Neural mechanisms of hunger: Current status and future prospects. In D. Novin, W. Wyrwicka, & G. Bray (Eds.), *Hunger: Basic mechanisms and clinical implications*. New York: Raven Press, 1976.

Mogenson, G.J., & Phillips, A.G. Motivation: A psychological construct in search of a physiological substrate. In J.M. Sprague & A.N. Epstein (Eds.), *Progress in psychobiology and physiological psychology* (Vol. 6). New York: Academic Press, 1976.

Mohr, J., Watters, W., & Duncan, G. Thalamic hemorrhage and asphasia. *Brain Language*, 1975, *2*, 3–17.

Møller, A.R., & Boston, P. (Eds.), *Basic mechanisms in hearing*. New York: Academic Press, 1973.

Møllgaard, K., Diamond, M.C., Bennett, E.L., Rosenzweig, M.R., & Lindner, B. Qualitative synaptic changes with differential experience in rat brain. *International Journal of Neuroscience*, 1971, *2*, 113–128.

Monckeberg, F. The effect of malnutrition on physical growth and brain development. In J.W. Prescott, M.S. Read, & D.B. Coursin (Eds.), *Brain function and malnutrition*. New York: Wiley, 1975.

Money, J., Cawte, J.E., Bianchi, G.N., & Nurcombe, B. Sex training and traditions in Arnhem land. *British Journal of Medical Psychology*, 1970, *43*, 383–399.

Money, J., & Ehrhardt, A.A. *Man and woman, boy and girl*. Baltimore: Johns Hopkins Press, 1972.

Montplaisir, J., Billiard, M., Takahashi, S., Bell, I.R., Guilleminault, C., & Dement, W.C. Twenty-four hour recording in REM-narcoleptics with special reference to nocturnal sleep disruption. *Biological Psychiatry*, 1978, *13*, 73–89.

Moore, R.Y., & Eichler, V.B. Loss of a circadian adrenal corticosterone rhythm following suprachiasmatic lesions in the rat. *Brain Research*, 1972, *42*, 201–206.

Morgan, C.T., & Morgan, J.D. Studies in hunger. II. The relation of gastric denervation and dietary sugar to the effect of insulin upon food intake in the rat. *Journal of General Psychology*, 1940, *57*, 153–163.

Moruzzi, G., & Magoun, H. Brain stem reticular formation and activation of the EEG. *Electroencephalography and Clinical Neurophysiology*, 1949, *1*, 455–473.

Motokawa, K., Taira, N., & Okuda, J. Spectral responses of single units in the primate visual cortex. *Tohoku Journal of Experimental Medicine*, 1962, *78*, 302–337.

Mountcastle, V.B., Lynch, J.C., Georgopoulos, A., Sakata, H., & Acuna, C. Posterior parietal association cortex of the monkey: Command functions for operations within extrapersonal space. *Journal of Neurophysiology*, 1975, *38*, 871–908.

Mountcastle, V.B., Talbot, W.H., Sakata, H., & Hyvärinen, J. Cortical neuronal mechanisms in flutter-vibration studied in unanesthetized monkeys. Neuronal periodicity and frequency discrimination. *Journal of Neurophysiology*, 1969, *32*, 452–484.

Mourek, J., Himwich, W.A., Myslivecek, J., & Callison, D.A. The role of nutrition in the development of evoked cortical responses in rat. *Brain Research*, 1967, *6*, 241–251.

Moyer, K.E. Kinds of aggression and their physiological basis. *Communications in Behavioral Biology*, 1968, *2*, 65–87.

Mpitsos, G.J., Collins, S.D., & McClellan, A.D. Learning: A model system for physiological studies. *Science*, 1978, *199*, 497–506.

Myerson, J., Manis, P.B., Miezin, F.M., & Allman, J.M. Magnification in striate cortex and retinal ganglion cell layer of owl monkey: A quantitative comparison. *Science*, 1977, *198*, 855–857.

Nachman, M. Learned aversion to the taste of lithium chloride and generalization to other salts. *Journal of Comparative and Physiological Psychology*, 1963, *56*, 343–349.

Nachman, M., & Pfaffman, C. Gustatory nerve discharge in normal and sodium deficient rats. *Journal of Comparative and Physiological Psychology*, 1963, *56*, 1007–1011.

Nafe, J.P. A quantitative theory of feeling from the psychological laboratories of Clark University. *Journal of General Psychology*, 1929, *2*, 199–210.

Naquet, R., Denavit, M., & Albe-Fessard, D. Comparison entre le rôle du subthalamus et celui des différentes structures bulboméséncéphaliques dans le maintien de la vigilance. *Electroencephalography and Clinical Neurophysiology*, 1966, *20*, 149–164.

Nathan, P.W., & Rudge, P. Testing the gate-control theory of pain in man. *Journal of Neurology, Neurosurgery and Psychiatry*, 1974, *37*, 1366–1372.

Nathan, P.W., & Wall, P.D. Treatment of post-herpetic neuralgia by prolonged electrical stimulation. *British Medical Journal*, 1974, *3*, 645–647.

Nemeroff, C.B., Osbahr, A.J., III, Bissette, G., Jahnke, G., Lipton, M.A., & Prange, A.J., Jr. Cholecystokinin inhibits tail pinch induced eating in rats. *Science*, 1978, *200*, 793–794.

Newman, J.D., & Wolberg, Z. Multiple coding of species-specific vocalizations in the auditory cortex of squirrel monkeys. *Brain Research*, 1973, *54*, 287–304.

Nienhuys, T.G.W., & Clark, G.M. Frequency discrimination following the selective destruction of cochlear inner and outer hair cells. *Science*, 1978, *199*, 1356–1357.

Niijima, A. Afferent impulse discharge from glucoreceptors in the liver of the guinea pig. *Annals of the New York Academy of Sciences*, 1969, *157*, 690–700.

Niki, H. Prefrontal unit activity during delayed alteration in the monkey. I. Relation to direction of response. *Brain Research*, 1974, *68*, 185–196. (a)

Niki, H. Prefrontal unit activity during delayed alteration in the monkey. II. Relation to absolute vs. relative direction of response. *Brain Research*, 1974, *68*, 197–204. (b)

Niki, H. Differential activity of prefrontal units during right and left delayed response trials. *Brain Research*, 1974, *70*, 346–349. (c)

Niki, H., & Watanabe, M. Prefrontal unit activity and delayed reponse: Relation to cue location vs. direction of response. *Brain Research*, 1976, *105*, 79–88.

Norgren, R. Taste pathways to hypothalamus and amygdala. *Journal of Comparative Neurology*, 1976, *166*, 17–30.

Norgren, R., & Leonard, C.M. Ascending central gustatory pathways. *Journal of Comparative Neurology*, 1973, *150*, 217–238.

Novin, D., & Vanderweele, D.A. Visceral involvement in feeding: There is more to regulation than the hypothalamus. *Progress in Psychobiology and Physiological Psychology*, 1977, *7*, 193–241.

Nunez, E., Savu, L., Engelman, F., Benassayay, C., Crepy, O., & Jayle, F. Origine embryonnaire de la protéine serique fixant l'oestrone et l'oestradiol chez le ratte impubere. *Comptes Rendus Hebdomadaires des Seances de l'Academie des Sciences*, 1971, *273*, 242.

Oakley, B. Receptive fields of cat taste fibers. *Chemical Senses and Flavor*, 1975, *1*, 431–442.

Olds, J. Self stimulation of the brain. *Science*, 1958, *127*, 315–323.

Olds, J., & Milner, P. Positive reinforcement produced by electrical stimulation of septal area and other regions of rat brain. *Journal of Comparative and Physiological Psychology,* 1954, *47,* 419–427.

Oleson, T.D., Ashe, J.H., & Weinberger, N.M. Modification of auditory and somatosensory system activity during pupillary conditioning in the paralyzed cat. *Journal of Neurophysiology,* 1975, *38,* 1114–1139.

Oleson, T.D., Westenberg, I.S., & Weinberger, N.M. Characteristics of the pupillary dilation response during Pavlovian conditioning in paralyzed cats. *Behavioral Biology,* 1972, *7,* 829–840.

Oliveras, J.L., Besson, J.M., Guilbaud, G., & Liebeskind, J.C. Behavioral and electrophysiological evidence of pain inhibition from midbrain stimulation in the cat. *Experimental Brain Research,* 1974, *20,* 32–44.

Ottoson, D. Analysis of the electrical activity of the olfactory epithelium. *Acta Physiological Scandinavica,* 1956, *35,* Suppl. 122, 1–83.

Overton, D. State-dependent or "dissociated" learning produced with pentobarbital. *Journal of Comparative and Physiological Psychology,* 1964, *57,* 3–12.

Ozeki, M., & Sato, M. Responses of gustatory cells in the tongue of rat to stimuli representing four taste qualities. *Comparative Biochemistry and Physiology A,* 1972, *41,* 391–407.

Pager, J. Ascending olfactory information and centrifugal influxes contributing to nutritional modulation of the rat mitral cell responses. *Brain Research,* 1978, *140,* 251–269.

Pager, J., & Royet, J.P. Some effects of conditioned aversion on food intake and olfactory bulb electrical responses in the rat. *Journal of Comparative and Physiological Psychology,* 1976, *90,* 67–77.

Parmalee, A.H., Schultz, H.R., & Disbrow, M.A. Sleep patterns in the newborn. *Journal of Pediatrics,* 1961, *58,* 241–250.

Patrick, R.L. Amphetamine and cocaine: Biological mechanisms. In J.D. Barchas *et al.* (Eds.), *Psychopharmacology: From theory to practice.* London & New York: Oxford University Press, 1977.

Pearlman, C. Latent learning impaired by REM sleep deprivation in rats. *Psychonomic Science,* 1971, *25,* 135–136.

Peck, J.W., & Novin, D. Evidence that osmoreceptors mediating drinking in rabbits are in the lateral preoptic area. *Journal of Comparative and Physiological Psychology,* 1971, *74,* 143–147.

Penfield, W. Functional localization in temporal and deep Sylvian area. *Research Publications, Association for Research in Nervous and Mental Disease,* 1958, *36,* 210–226.

Penfield, W. *The mystery of the mind.* Princeton, N.J.: Princeton University Press, 1975.

Penfield, W., & Rasmussen, T. *The cerebral cortex of man.* New York: Macmillan, 1950.

Penfield, W., & Roberts, L. *Speech and brain mechanisms.* Princeton, N.J.: Princeton University Press, 1959.

Perl, E.R. Myelinated afferent fibres innervating the primate skin and their response to noxious stimuli. *Journal of Physiology (London),* 1968, *197,* 593–615.

Perlow, M.J., Freed, W.J., Hoffer, B.J., Seiger, A., Olson, L., & Wyatt, R.J. Brain grafts reduce motor abnormalities produced by destruction of nigrostriatal dopamine system. *Science,* 1979, *204,* 643–647.

Perry, T.L., Hansen, S., & Kloster, M. Huntington's chorea: Deficiency of 8-aminobutyric acid in brain. *New England Journal of Medicine,* 1973, *288,* 337–342.

Persky, H., Smith, K.D., & Basu, G.K. Relation of psychologic measures of aggression and hostility to testosterone production in men. *Psychosomatic Medicine,* 1971, *33,* 265–277.

Petersen, M.R., Beecher, M.D., Zoloth, S.R., Moody, D.B., & Stebbins, W.C. Neural lateralization of species–specific vocalizations by Japanese macaques *(Macaca fuscata). Science,* 1978, *202,* 324–326.

Pfaff, D.W., Uptake of ^{3}H-estradiol by the female rat brain. An autoradiographic study. *Endocrinology,* 1968, *82,* 1149–1155.

Pfaff, D.W., & Gregory, E. Olfactory coding in olfactory bulb and medial forebrain bundle of normal and castrated male rats. *Journal of Neurophysiology,* 1971, *34,* 208–216.

Pfaffman, C. Gustatory nerve impulses in rat, cat, and rabbit. *Journal of Neurophysiology,* 1955, *18,* 429–440.

Pfaffman, C., & Bare, J.K. Gustatory nerve discharges in normal and adrenalectomized rats. *Journal of Comparative and Physiological Psychology,* 1950, *43,* 320–324.

Pfaffman, C., Fisher, G.L., & Frank, M.K. The sensory and behavioral factors in taste preferences. In T. Hayashi (Ed.), *Olfaction and taste II.* Oxford: Pergamon, 1967.

Pfeiffer, C.A. Sexual differences of the hypophyses and their determination by the gonads. *American Journal of Anatomy,* 1936, *58,* 195–226.

Pinget, M., Straus, E., & Yalow, R.S. Localization of cholecystokinin-like immunoreactivity in isolated nerve terminals. *Proceedings of the National Academy of Sciences of the United States of America,* 1978, *75,* 6324–6326.

Pirke, K.M., Kockott, G., & Dittmar, F. Psychosexual stimulation and plasma testosterone in man. *Archives of Sexual Behavior,* 1974, *3,* 577–584.

Pohl, W. Dissociation of spatial discrimination deficits following frontal and parietal lesions in monkeys. *Journal of Comparative and Physiological Psychology,* 1973, *82,* 227–239.

Premack, D. The education of Sarah. *Psychology Today,* 1970, *4,* 54–58.

Preston, F.S., Bateman, S.C., Short, R.V., & Wilkinson, R.T. Effects of flying and of time changes on menstrual cycle length and on performance in airline stewardesses. *Clinical Aviation and Aerospace Medicine,* 1973, *44,* 438–443.

Price, S., "Sweet sensitive protein" from bovine tongues: Stereospecific interactions with amino acids. In D. Schneider (Ed.), *Olfaction and taste IV.* Stuttgart: Wissenschaftliche Verlagsgellschaft, 1972.

Price, S., & Desimone, J.A. Models of receptor cell stimulation. *Chemical Senses and Flavor,* 1977, *2,* 427–456.

Pujol, J.E., Stein, D., Blondaux, C., Petitjean, F., Fromont, J.L. & Jouvet, M. Biochemical evidence for interaction phenomena between noradrenergic and serotonergic systems in the cat brain. In E. Usdin (Ed.), *Frontiers in catecholamine research.* Oxford: Pergamon, 1973.

Quartermain, D. The influence of drugs on learning and memory. In M.R. Rosenzweig & E.L. Bennett (Eds.), *Neural mechanisms of learning and memory.* Cambridge, Mass.: MIT Press, 1976.

Quartermain, D., & Botwinick, C.Y. The role of biogenic amines in the reversal of cycloheximide-induced amnesia. *Journal of Comparative and Physiological Psychology*, 1975, *88*, 386–401.

Rada, R.T., Laws, D.R., & Kellner, R. Plasma testosterone levels in the rapist. *Psychosomatic Medicine*, 1976, *38*, 257–268.

Raisman, G. Neuronal plasticity in the septal nuclei of the adult rat. *Brain Research*, 1969, *14*, 25–48.

Raisman, G. Evidence for a sex difference in the neuropil of the rat preoptic area and its importance for the study of sexually dimorphic functions. *Research Publications, Association for Research in Nervous and Mental Disease*, 1974, *52*, 42–51.

Raisman, G., & Field, P.M. A quantitative investigation of the development of collateral reinnervation after partial deafferentation of the septal nuclei. *Brain Research*, 1973, *50*, 241–264.

Rakic, P. Prenatal genesis of connections subserving ocular dominance in the Rhesus monkey. *Nature, (London)*, 1976, *261*, 467–471.

Ranson, S.W., & Clark, S.L. *The anatomy of the nervous system (10th ed.)*. Philadelphia, Pa.: Saunders, 1959.

Raskin, D.C., Barland, G.H., & Podlesny, J.A. *Validity and reliability of detection of deception*. Washington, D.C.: US Govt. Printing Office, 1978.

Rasmussen, H. Organization and control of endocrine systems. In R.H. Williams (Ed.), *Textbook of endocrinology (5th ed.)*. Philadelphia, Pa.: Saunders, 1974.

Ratliff, F., & Harline, H.K. The responses of *Limulus* optic nerve fibers to patterns of illumination on the receptor mosiac. *Journal of General Physiology*, 1959, *42*, 1241–1255.

Rees, H.D., Brogan, L.L., Entingh, D.J., Dunn, A., Shinkman, P.G., Damstra-Entingh, T., Wilson, J.E., & Glassman, E. Effect of sensory stimulation on the uptake and incorporation of radioactive lysine into protein of mouse brain and liver. *Brain Research*, 1974, *68*, 143–156.

Reeves, A.G., & Plum, F. Hyperphagia, rage and dementia accompanying a ventromedial hypothalamic neoplasm. *Archives of Neurology (Chicago)*, 1969, *20*, 616–624.

Reid, J.E., & Inbau, F.E. *Truth and deception: The polygraph ("lie-detector") technique* (2nd ed.). Baltimore: Williams & Wilkins, 1977.

Reis, D.J., & Fuxe, F. Brain norepinephrine: Evidence that neuronal release is essential for sham rage behavior following brainstem transection in the cat. *Proceedings of the National Academy of Sciences of the United States of America*, 1969, *64*, 108.

Reis, D.J., & Gunne, L.M. Brain catecholamines: Relation to the defense reaction evoked by amygdaloid stimulation in the cat. *Science*, 1965, *149*, 450.

Reivich, M., Isaacs, G., Evarts, E., & Kety, S.S. The effect of slow wave sleep and REM sleep on regional blood flow in cats. *Journal of Neurochemistry*, 1968, *15*, 301–306.

Riege, W.H. Environmental influences on brain and behavior of year old rats. *Developmental Psychobiology*, 1971, *4*, 151–167.

Rigter, H. Attenuation of amnesia in rats by systemically administered enkephalins. *Science*, 1978, *200*, 83–85.

Rimon, R., Roos, B.-E., Rakkolainen, V., & Yrjo, A. The content of 5-hydroxyindoleacetic acid and homovanillic acid in the cerebrospinal fluid of patients with acute schizophrenia. *Journal of Psychomatic Research*, 1971, *15*, 375–378.

Riss, W., Valenstein, E.S., Sinks, J., & Young, W.C. Development of sexual behavior in male guinea pigs from genetically different stocks under controlled conditions of androgen treatment and caging. *Endocrinology*, 1955, *57*, 139–146.

Riss, W., & Young, W.C. Somatic, psychological and androgenic determinants in the development of sexual behavior in the male guinea pig. *American Psychologist*, 1953, *8*, 421.

Roberts, W.W., Steinberg, M.L., & Means, L.W. Hypothalamic mechanisms for sexual, aggressive and other motivational behaviors in the opossum, *Didelphis virginiana*. *Journal of Comparative and Physiological Psychology*, 1967, *64*, 1–15.

Robinson, B.W., Alexander, M., & Bowne, G. Dominance reversal resulting from aggressive responses evoked by brain telestimulation. *Physiology and Behavior*, 1969, *4*, 749–752.

Robinson, B.W., & Mishkin, M. Alimentary responses to forebrain stimulation in monkeys. *Experimental Brain Research*, 1968, *4*, 330–366.

Robinson, D.L., Goldberg, M.E., & Stanton, G.B. Parietal association cortex in the primate: Sensory mechanisms and behavioral modulations. *Journal of Neurophysiology*, 1978, *41*, 910–932.

Rodgers, W., & Rozin, P. Novel food preferences in thiamine deficient rats. *Journal of Comparative and Physiological Psychology*, 1966, *61*, 1–4.

Roffwarg, H.P., Dement, W.C., Muzio, J.N., & Fisher, C. Dream imagery: Relationship to rapid eye movements of sleep. *Archives of General Psychiatry*, 1962, *7*, 235–258.

Roffwarg, H.P., Muzio, J.N., & Dement, W.C. The ontogenetic development of the sleep-dream cycle in the human. *Science*, 1966, *152*, 604–619.

Rose, J.E., Brugge, J.F., Anderson, D.J., & Hind, J.E. Phase-locked response to low-frequency tones in single auditory nerve fibers of the squirrel monkey. *Journal of Neurophysiology*, 1967, *30*, 769–793.

Rose, J.E., Gross, N.B., Geisler, C.D., & Hind, J.E. Some neural mechanisms in the inferior colliculus of the cat which may be relevant to localization of a sound source. *Journal of Neurophysiology*, 1966, *29*, 288–314.

Rose, J.W., Claybough, C., Clemens, L.G., & Gorski, R.A. Short latency induction of oestrous behaviour with intracerebral gonadal hormones in ovariectomized rats. *Endocrinology*, 1971, *89*, 32–38.

Rose, R.M., Bernstein, I.S., & Gordon, T.P. Consequences of social conflict on plasma testosterone levels in Rhesus monkeys. *Psychosomatic Medicine*, 1975, *37*, 50–61.

Rose, S.P.R. *The conscious brain*. New York: Alfred A. Knopf, 1973.

Rose, S.P.R., Hambley, J., & Haywood, J. Neurochemical approaches to developmental plasticity and learning. In M.R. Rosenzweig & E.L. Bennett (Eds.), *Neural mechanisms of learning and memory*. Cambridge, Mass.: MIT Press, 1976.

Rosenzweig, M.R. Evidence for anatomical and chemical changes in the brain during primary learning. In K.H. Pribram & D.E. Broadbent (Eds.), *Biology of memory*. New York: Academic Press, 1970.

Rosenzweig, M.R., & Bennett, E.L. Cerebral changes in rats exposed individually to an enriched environment. *Journal of Comparative and Physiological Psychology*, 1972, *80*, 304–313.

Rosenzweig, M.R., Bennett, E.L., Diamond, M.C., Wu, S.-Y., Slagle, R.W., & Saffran, E. Influences of environmental complexity and visual stimulation on development of occipital cortex in rat. *Brain Research*, 1969, *14*, 427–445.

Rowell, T.E. Female reproductive cycle and social behaviour in primates. In D.S. Lehrman, R.A. Hinde, & E. Shaw (Eds.), *Advances in the study of behaviour* (Vol. 4). New York: Academic Press, 1972.

Rowland, N. Regulatory drinking: Do the physiological structures have an ecological niche? *Biobehavioral Reviews*, 1977, *1*, 261–272.

Rowland, N.E., & Antelman, S.M. Stress-induced hyperphagia and obesity in rats: A possible model for understanding human obesity. *Science*, 1976, *191*, 310–312.

Rozin, P. The psychobiological approach to human memory. In M.R. Rosenzweig & E.L. Bennett (Eds.), *Neural mechanisms of learning and memory*. Cambridge, Mass.: MIT Press, 1976.

Rubinstein, E.H., & Sonnenschein, R.R. Sleep cycles and feeding behavior in the cat: Role of gastrointestinal hormones. *Acta Cientifica Venezolana*, 1971, *22*, 125–128.

Rumbaugh, D.M. (Ed.). *Language learning by a chimpanzee: The Lana project*. New York: Academic Press, 1977.

Russek, M. Hepatic receptors and the neurophysiological mechanisms controlling feeding behavior. In S. Ehrenpreis & O.C. Solnitzky (Eds.), *Neurosciences research* (Vol. 4). New York: Academic Press, 1971.

Russek, M. Current hypotheses in the control of feeding behaviour. In G.J. Morgenson & F.R. Calaresu (Eds.), *Neural integration of physiological mechanisms and behaviour*. Toronto: University of Toronto Press, 1975.

Sachs, C., & Jonsson, G. Mechanisms of action of 6-hydroxydopamine. *Biochemical Pharmacology*, 1975, *24*, 1–8.

Sack, R.L. Side effects of and adverse reactions to psychotropic medications. In J.D. Barchas, P.A. Berger, R.D. Ciaranello, and G.R. Elliott (Eds.), *Psychopharmacology: From theory to practice*. London & New York: Oxford University Press, 1977.

Sackheim, H.A., Gur, R.C., & Saucy, M.C. Emotions are expressed more intensely on the left side of the face. *Sciences*, 1978, *202*, 434–436.

Sagan, C. *The dragons of Eden: Speculations on the evolution of human intelligence*. New York: Ballantine, 1977.

Salama, A., & Goldberg, M.E. Neurochemical effects of imipramine and amphetamine in aggressive mouse-killing (muricidal) rats. *Biochemical Pharmacology*, 1970, *19*, 2023.

Salas, M. Effects of early malnutrition on the development of swimming ability in the rat. *Physiology and Behavior*, 1972, *8*, 119–122.

Salas, M., & Cintra, L. Nutritional influences upon somatosensory evoked responses during development in the rat. *Physiology and Behavior*, 1973, *10*, 1019–1022.

Salas, M., Diaz, D., & Nieto, A. Effects of neonatal food deprivation on cortical spines and dendritic development of the rat. *Brain Research*, 1974, *73*, 139–144.

Salmon, V.J., & Geist, S.H. The effect of androgens upon libido in women. *Journal of Clinical Endocrinology and Metabolism*, 1943, *3*, 275–238.

Saunders, J.C. Cochlear nucleus and auditory cortex correlates of a click stimulus-intensity discrimination in cats. *Journal of Comparative and Physiological Psychology*, 1970, *72*, 8–16.

Savage-Rumbaugh, E.S., Rumbaugh, D.M., & Boysen, S. Symbolic communication between two chimpanzees *(Pan troglodytes)*. *Science*, 1978, *201*, 641–644.

Sawin, C.T. *The hormones.* Boston: Little, Brown, 1969.

Schachter, S. *Emotion, obesity and crime.* New York: Academic Press, 1971.

Schachter, S., Goldman, R., & Gordon, A. The effects of fear, food deprivation, and obesity on eating. *Journal of Personal and Social Psychology*, 1968, *10*, 91–97.

Schachter, S., & Gross, L. Manipulated time and eating behavior. *Journal of Personal and Social Psychology*, 1968, *10*, 98–106.

Schachter, S., & Singer, J.S. Cognitive, social, and physiological determinants of emotional state. *Psychological Review*, 1962, *69*, 379–399.

Scharf, B. Audition. In B. Scharf & G. Reynolds (Eds.), *Experimental sensory psychology.* Glenview, Ill.: Scott, Foresman & Co., 1975.

Schildkraut, J.J. Biogenic amines and affective disorders. *Annual Review of Medicine*, 1974, *25*, 333–348.

Schmidt, E.M., Jost, R.G., & Davis, K.K. Cortical cell discharge patterns in anticipation of a trained movement. *Brain Research*, 1974, *75*, 309–311.

Schmitt, F.O., Dev, P., & Smith, B.H. Electrotonic processing of information by brain cells. *Science*, 1976, *193*, 114–120.

Schneider, R.A. The sense of smell and human sexuality. *Medical Aspects of Human Sexuality*, 1971, *5*, 157–168.

Schuckit, M.A., Goodwin, D.W., & Winokur, G. A half-sibling study of alcoholism. *American Journal of Psychiatry*, 1972, *128*, 1132–1136.

Schwartz, M. *Physiological psychology.* New York: Appleton, 1973.

Schwartz, W.J., & Gainer, H. Suprachiasmatic nucleus: Use of ¹⁴C-labeled deoxyglucose uptake as a functional marker. *Science*, 1977, *197*, 1089–1091.

Sclafani, A. Neural pathways involved in the ventromedial hypothalamic lesion syndrome in the rat. *Journal of Comparative and Physiological Psychology*, 1971, *77*, 70–96.

Scott, J.W., & Pfaff, D.W. Behavioral and electrophysiological responses of female mice to male urine odours. *Physiology and Behavior*, 1970, *5*, 407–411.

Scott, T.R., & Erickson, R.P. Synaptic processing of taste-quality information in thalamus of the rat. *Journal of Neurophysiology*, 1971, *34*, 868–884.

Seligman, M.E.P., & Hager, J.L. *Biological boundaries of learning.* New York: Appleton, 1972.

Selye, H. *The stress of life* (2nd ed.). New York: McGraw-Hill, 1976.

Sfikakis, A., Spyraki, C., Sitaras, N., & Varonos, D. Implication of the estrous cycle on conditioned avoidance behavior in the rat. *Physiology and Behavior*, 1978, *21*, 441–446.

Shepherd, G.M., & Haberly, L.B. Partial activation of olfactory bulb: Analysis of field potentials and topographical relation between bulb and lateral olfactory tract. *Journal of Neurophysiology*, 1970, *33*, 643–653.

Shillito, E. The effect of p-chlorophenylalanine on social interactions of male rats. *British Journal of Pharmacology*, 1969, *36*, 193P–194P.

Siegel, A., & Flynn, J.P. Differential effects of electrical stimulation and lesions of the hippocampus and adjacent regions upon attack behavior in cats. *Brain Research*, 1968, *7*, 252–267.

Singer, J. Hypothalamic control of male and female sexual behavior in female rats. *Journal of Comparative and Physiological Psychology*, 1968, *66*, 738–742.

Sjoerdsma, A., Lovenberg, W., Engelman, K., Carpenter, W.T., Wyatt, R.J., & Gessa, G.L. Serotonin now: Clinical implications of inhibiting its synthesis with p-chlorophenylalanine. *Annals of Internal Medicine*, 1970, *73*, 607–629.

Skoglund, S. Anatomical and physiological studies of knee joint innervation in the cat. *Acta Physiologica Scandinavica*, 1956, *36*, Suppl. 124.

Smith, G.P., & Gibbs, J. Cholecystokinin and satiety: Theoretic and therapeutic implications. In D. Novin, W. Wyrwicka, & G. Bray (Eds.), *Hunger: Basic mechanisms and clinical implications*. New York: Raven Press, 1976.

Snyder, S.H. Opiate receptors and internal opiates. *Scientific American*, 1977, *236*, 44–56.

Sobotta, J., & Figge, F.H.J. Atlas of human anatomy. New York: Hafner, 1974.

Sperry, R.W., Lateral specialization in the surgically separated hemispheres. In F.O. Schmitt & F.G. Worden (Eds.), *The neurosciences: Third study program*. Cambridge, Mass.: MIT Press, 1974.

Spinelli, D.N. Receptive field organization of ganglion cells in the cat's retina. *Experimental Neurology*, 1967, *19*, 291–315.

Spinelli, D.N., & Jensen, F.E. Plasticity: The mirror of experience. *Science*, 1979, *203*, 75–78.

Spoendlin, H. Neuroanatomy of the cochlea. In E. Zwicker & E. Terhardt (Eds.), *Facts and methods in hearing*. Berlin & New York: Springer-Verlag, 1974.

Stein, L., & Wise, C.D. Release of norepinephrine from hypothalamus and amygdala by rewarding medial forebrain bundle stimulation and amphetamine. *Journal of Comparative and Physiological Psychology*, 1969, *67*, 189–198.

Stein, L., & Wise, C.D. Possible etiology of schizophrenia: Progressive damage to the noradrenergic reward system by 6-hydroxydopamine. *Science*, 1971, *171*, 1032–1036.

Stell, W.K., Ishida, A.T., & Lightfoot, D.O. Structural basis for on- and off-center responses in retinal bipolar cells. *Science*, 1977, *198*, 1269–1271.

Stephan, F.K., & Zucker, I. Rat drinking rhythms: Central visual pathways and endocrine factors mediating responsiveness to environmental illumination. *Physiology and Behavior*, 1972, *8*, 315–326. (a)

Stephan, F.K., & Zucker, I. Circadian rhythms in drinking behavior and locomotor activity of rats are eliminated by hypothalamic lesions. *Proceedings of the National Academy of Sciences of the United States of America*, 1972, *69*, 1583–1586. (b)

Sterman, M.B., & Clemente C.D. Forebrain inhibitory mechanisms: Sleep patterns induced by basal forebrain stimulation. *Experimental Neurology*, 1962, *6*, 91–102.

Stetson, M.H., & Watson-Whitmyre, M. Nucleus suprachiasmaticus: The biological clock in the hamster? *Science*, 1976, *191*, 197–199.

Stricker, E.M. Thirst, sodium appetite, and complementary physiological contributions to the regulation of intravascular fluid volume. In A.N. Epstein,

H.R. Kissileff, & E. Stellar (Eds.), *The neuropsychology of thirst: New findings and advances in concepts.* New York: Holt, 1973.

Stricker, E.M. Drinking by rats after lateral hypothalamic lesions: A new look at the lateral hypothalamic syndrome. *Journal of Comparative and Physiological Psychology,* 1976, *90,* 127–143.

Stricker, E.M. The renin-angiotensin system and thirst: Some unanswered questions. *Federation Proceedings, Federation of American Societies for Experimental Biology,* 1978, *37,* 2704–2710.

Stricker, E.M., Rowland, N., Saller, C.F., & Friedman, M.I. Homeostasis during hypoglycemia: Central control of adrenal secretion and peripheral control of feeding. *Science,* 1977, *196,* 79–81.

Stricker, E.M., & Zigmond M.J. Recovery of function after damage to central catecholamine-containing neurons: A neurochemical model for the lateral hypothalamic syndrome. In J.M. Sprague & A.N. Epstein (Eds.), *Progress in psychobiology and physiological psychology* (Vol. 6). New York: Academic Press, 1976.

Stumpf, W.E. Estrogen-neurons and estrogen-neuron systems in the periventricular brain. *American Journal of Anatomy,* 1970, *129,* 207–218.

Suga, N., O'Neill, W.E., & Manabe, T. Cortical neurons sensitive to combinations of information bearing elements of biosonar signals in the mustache bat. *Science,* 1978, *200,* 778–781.

Sutherland, E.W. Studies on the mechanism of hormone action. *Science,* 1972, *177,* 401–408.

Sutherland, S.D., & Gorski, R.A. Intrahypothalamic interaction of steriods and pentobarbital in the neonatal rat. *Anatomical Record,* 1970, *166,* 386.

Swanson, J.M., & Kinsbourne, M. Stimulant-related state-dependent learning in hyperactive children. *Science,* 1976, *192,* 1354–1357.

Sweet, W.H., Ervin, F., & Mark, V.H. The relationship of violent behavior to focal cerebral disease. In S. Garattini & E.B. Sigg (Eds.), *Aggressive behavior.* New York: Wiley, 1969.

Szechtman, H., Caggiula, A.R., & Wulkan, D. Preoptic knife cuts and sexual behavior in male rats. *Brain Research,* 1978, *150,* 569–591.

Talbot, W.H., Darian-Smith, I., Kornhuber, H.H., & Mountcastle, V.B. The sense of flutter-vibration: Comparison of the human capacity with response patterns of mechanoreceptive afferents from the monkey hand. *Journal of Neurophysiology,* 1968, *31,* 301–334.

Tannenbaum, B., & Stillman, M. *Understanding sound.* New York: McGraw-Hill.

Tasaki, I., Davis, H., and Eldredge, D.H. Exploration of cochlear potentials in guinea pig with a microelectrode. *Journal of the Acoustical Society of America,* 1954, *26,* 765–773.

Taub, J.M. Behavioral and psychological correlates of a difference in chronic sleep duration. *Biological Psychology,* 1977, *5,* 29–45.

Teitelbaum, P. Sensory control of hypothalamic hyperphagia. *Journal of Comparative and Physiological Psychology,* 1955, *48,* 156–163.

Teitelbaum, P., & Campbell, B.A. Ingestion patterns in hyperphagic and normal rats. *Journal of Comparative and Physiological Psychology,* 1958, *51,* 135–141.

Teitelbaum, P., & Epstein, A.N. The lateral hypothalamic syndrome: Recovery of feeding and drinking after lateral hypothalamic lesions. *Psychological Review*, 1962, *69*, 74–90.

Teitelbaum, P., & Stellar, E. Recovery from the failure to eat produced by hypothalamic lesions. *Science*, 1954, *120*, 894–895.

Teyler, T.J., & Alger, B.E. Monosynaptic habituation in the vertebrate forebrain: The dentate gyrus examined *in vitro*. *Brain Research*, 1976, *115*, 413–425.

Teyler, T.J., & Alger, B.E. Plasticity in the vertebrate central nervous system. In T.J. Teyler (Ed.), *Brain and learning*. Stamford, Conn.: Greylock Publishers, 1978.

Thach, W.T. Discharge of cerebellar neurons related to two postures and movements. I. Nuclear cell output. *Journal of Neurophysiology*, 1970, *33*, 527–536. (a)

Thach, W.T. Discharge of cerebellar neurons related to two postures and movements. II. Purkinje cell output and input. *Journal of Neurophysiology*, 1970, *33*, 537–547. (b)

Thach, W.T. Correlation of neural discharge pattern and force of muscular activity, joint position, and direction of intended next movement in motor cortex and cerebellum. *Journal of Neurophysiology*, 1978, *41*, 654–676.

Thatcher, R.W. Evoked-potential correlates of hemispheric lateralization during semantic information-processing. In S. Harnad, R.W. Doty, L. Goldstein, J. Jaynes, & G. Krauthamer (Eds.), *Lateralization in the nervous system*. New York: Academic Press, 1977.

Thoa, N.B., Eichelman, B., & Ng, K.Y. Aggression in rats treated with dopa and 6-hydroxydopamine. *Journal of Pharmacy and Pharmacology*, 1972, *24*, 337. (a)

Thoa, N.B., Eichelman, B., & Ng, K.Y. Shock-induced aggression: Effects of 6-hydroxydopamine and other pharmacological agents. *Brain Research*, 1972, *43*, 467–475. (b)

Thompson, R.F. *Foundations of physiological psychology*. New York: Harper, 1967.

Thompson, R.F. The search for the engram. *American Psychologist*, 1976, *00*, 209–225.

Thompson, R.F., Patterson, M.M., & Berger, T.W. Associative learning in the mammalian nervous system. In T.J. Teyler (Ed.), *Brain and learning*. Stamford, Conn.: Greylock Publishers, 1978.

Thompson, R.F., & Spencer, W.A. Habituation: A model phenomenon for the study of neural substrates of behavior. *Psychological Review*, 1966, *73*, 16–43.

Thurlow, W.R. Audition. In J.W. Kling & L.A. Riggs (Eds.), *Experimental psychology* (3rd ed.). New York: Holt, 1971.

Tilley, A.J., & Empson, J.A.C. REM sleep and memory consolidation. *Biological Psychology*, 1978, *6*, 293–300.

Tomita, T., Kaneko, A., Murakami, M., & Pautler, E.L. Spectral response curves of single cones in the carp. *Vision Research*, 1967, *7*, 519–531.

Toran-Allerand, C.D. Sex steroids and the development of the newborn mouse hypothalamus and preoptic area *in vitro*: Implications for sexual differentiation. *Brain Research*, 1976, *106*, 407–412.

Trimble, M.R., & Herbert, J. The effect of testosterone or oestradiol upon the sexual and associated behavior of the adult female Rhesus monkey. *Journal of Endocrinology*, 1968, *42*, 171–185.

Turner, C., Donnell, & Bagnara, J.T. *General endrocrinology* (5th ed.). Philadelphia, Pa.: Saunders, 1971.

Udry, J.R., & Morris, N.M. Distribution of coitus in the menstrual cycle. *Nature (London)*, 1968, *220*, 593–596.

Ungar, G. (Ed.), *Molecular mechanisms in memory and learning*. New York: Plenum, 1970.

Ungerer, A. Nature et ampleur des effets de l'acétoxycycloheximide sur la retention d'un apprentissage instrumental chez la souris *Physiology and Behavior*, 1973, *11*, 323–327.

Ungerstedt, U. On the anatomy, pharmacology and function of the nigrostriatal dopamine system. *Acta Physiologica Scandinavica*, 1971, Suppl. 367.

Ungerstedt, U. Adipsia and aphagia after 6-hydroxydopamine induced degeneration of the nigrostriatal dopamine system. *Acta Physiological Scandinavica*, 1971, *82*, Suppl. 367, 95–122.

Ungerstedt, U. Brain dopamine neurons and behavior. In F.O. Schmitt & W.F. Worden (Eds.), *The neurosciences: Third study program*. Cambridge, Mass.: MIT Press, 1974.

Uttal, W.R. *The psychobiology of sensory coding*. New York: Harper, 1973.

Vahlquist, B. A two-century perspective of some major nutritional deficiency diseases in childhood. *Acta Paediatrica Scandinavica*, 1975, *64*, 161–171.

Valenstein, E.S. Brain stimulation and the origin of violent behavior. In W.L. Smith & A. Kling (Eds.), *Issues in brain/behavior control*. New York: Spectrum, 1976.

Valenstein, E.S., Cox, V.C., & Kakolewski, J.W. Polydipsia elicited by the synergistic action of a saccharin and glucose solution. *Science*, 1967, *157*, 552–554.

Valenstein, E.S., Cox, V.C., & Kakolewski, J.W. Re-examination of the role of the hypothalamus in motivation. *Psychological Review*, 1970, *77*, 16–31.

Valenstein, E.S., Riss, W., & Young, W.C. Experiential and genetic factors in the organization of sexual behavior in male guinea pigs. *Journal of Comparative and Physiological Psychology*, 1955, *48*, 397–403.

Valenstein, E.S., & Young, W.C. Resistance of strain differences in male sex drive and growth to maternal influences prior to weaning in the guinea pig. *Anatomical Record*, 1953, *117*, 604. (Abstract)

van Buskirk, R.L., & Erickson, R.P. Odorant responses in taste neurons of the rat NTS. *Brain Res.*, 1977, *135*, 287–303.

Vance, E.B., & Wagner, N.N. Written descriptions of orgasm: A study of sex differences. *Archives of Sexual Behavior*, 1976, *5*, 87–98.

Vanderweele, D.A., & Sanderson, J.D. Peripheral glucosensitive satiety in the rabbit and the rat. In D. Novin, W. Wyrwicka, & G.A. Bray (Eds.), *Hunger: Basic mechanisms and clinical implications*. New York: Raven Press, 1976.

Van Dis, H., & Larsson, K. Induction of sexual arousal in the castrated male rat by intracranial stimulation. *Physiology and Behavior*, 1971, *6*, 85–86.

Van Harreveld, A., & Fifkova, E. Swelling of dendritic spines in the fascia dentata after stimulation of the perforant fibers as a mechanism of post-tetanic potentiation. *Experimental Neurology*, 1975, *49*, 736–749.

van Wagenen, G., & Hamilton, J.B. The experimental production of pseudohermaphroditism in the monkey. *Essays in biology* (in honor of Herbert M. Evans). Berkeley: University of California Press, 1943.

Vernadakis, A. RNA synthesis in embryonic cerebellar explants cultured with estradiol. In K. Lissak (Ed.), *Hormones and brain function*. New York: Plenum, 1973.

Villescas, R., Bell, R.W., Wright, L., & Kufner, M. Effect of handling on maternal behavior following return of pups to the nest. *Developmental Psychobiology*, 1977, *10*, 323–329.

Volkmar, F.R., & Greenough, W.T. Rearing complexity affects branching of dendrites in the visual cortex. *Science*, 1972, *176*, 1445–1447.

von Békésy, G. *Experiments in hearing*. New York: McGraw-Hill, 1960.

Wada, J. A new method for the determination of the side of cerebral speech dominance: A preliminary report on the intracarotid injection of sodium amytal in man. *Medical Biology*, 1947, *14*, 221–222.

Waddington, C.H. *The strategy of the genes: A discussion of some aspects of theoretical biology*. London: Allen & Unwin, 1957.

Waespe, W., & Henn, V. Neuronal activity in the vestibular nuclei of the alert monkey during vestibular and optokinetic stimulation. *Experimental Brain Research*, 1977, *27*, 523–538.

Wald, G. Molecular basis of visual excitation. *Science*, 1968, *162*, 230–239.

Wall, P.D., & Cronly-Dillon, J.R. Pain, itch, and vibration. *AMA Archives of Neurology*, 1960, *2*, 365–375.

Wall, P.D., & Sweet, W.H. Temporary abolition of pain in man. *Science*, 1967, *155*, 108–109.

Wallace, P. Individual discrimination of humans by odor. *Physiology and Behavior*, 1977, *19*, 577–579.

Walsh, R.J., & Brawer, J.R. Cytology of the arcuate nucleus in newborn male and female rats. *Journal of Anatomy*, 1979, *128*, 121–133.

Walsh, T.E. The surgical treatment of hearing loss. In H. Davis & S.R. Silverman (Eds.), *Hearing and deafness* (Rev. ed.). New York: Holt, 1960.

Wasman, M., & Flynn, J.P. Directed attack elicited from hypothalamus. *Archives of Neurology (Chicago)*, 1962, *6*, 220–227.

Webb, W.B. Sleep as an adaptive response. *Perceptual and Motor Skills*, 1974, *37*, 511–514.

Webb, W.B. *Sleep: The gentle tyrant*. Englewood Cliffs, N.J.: Prentice-Hall, 1975.

Webb, W.B., & Agnew, H.W. Sleep and waking in a time-free environment. *Aerospace Medicine*, 1974, *45*, 617–622. (a)

Webb, W.B., & Agnew, H.W. The effects of a chronic limitation of sleep length. *Psychophysiology*, 1974, *11*, 265–274. (b)

Webb, W.B., & Agnew, H.W. Are we chronically sleep deprived? *Bulletin of the Psychonomic Society*, 1975, *6*, 47–48.

Webb, W.B., & Cartwright, R.D. Sleep and dreams. *Annual Review of Psychology*, 1978, *29*, 223–252.

Wechsler, I.S. *Clinical neurology* (9th ed.). Philadelphia, Pa.: Saunders, 1963.

Weiss, B., & Santelli, S. Dyskinesias evoked in monkeys by weekly administration of haloperidol. *Science*, 1978, *200*, 799–801.

Werblin, F.S., & Dowling, J.E. Organization of the retina of the mudpuppy, *Necturus maculosus*. II. Intracellular recording. *Journal of Neurophysiology*, 1969, *32*, 339–355.

Wever, E.G., & Bray, C.W. Action currents in the auditory nerve in response to acoustical stimulation. *Proceedings of the National Academy of Sciences of the United States of America,* 1930, *16,* 344–350.

Wever, E.G., Rahm, W.E., & Strother, W.F. The lower range of the cochlear potential. *Proceedings of the National Academy of Sciences of the United States of America,* 1959, *45,* 1447–1449.

Whalen, R.E. Gonadal hormones and the developing brain. In A. Vernadakis & N. Weiner (Eds.), *Drugs and the developing brain.* New York: Plenum, 1974.

Whatson, T.S., Smart, J.L., & Dobbing, I. Social interactions among adult male rats after early undernutrition. *British Journal of Nutrition,* 1974, *32,* 413–419.

Wheatley, M.D. The hypothalamus and affective behavior in cats: A study of the effects of experimental lesions with anatomic correlations. *Archives of Neurology and Psychiatry,* 1944, *52,* 296–316.

Whitfield, I.C., & Evans, E.F. Responses of auditory cortical neurons to stimuli of changing frequency. *Journal of Neurophysiology,* 1965, *28,* 655–672.

Whitten, W.K., & Bronson, F.H. The role of pheromones in mammalian reproduction. In J.W. Johnston, D.G. Moulton, & A. Turk (Eds.), *Advances in chemoreception* (Vol. 1). New York: Appleton, 1970.

Whitten, W.K., Bronson, F.H., & Greenstein, J.A. Estrous-inducing pheromone of male mice: Transport by movement of air. *Science,* 1968, *161,* 584–585.

Wiener, S.G., Fitzpatrick, K.M., Levin, W.P., Smotherman, W.P., & Levine, S. Alterations in maternal behavior of rats rearing malnourished offspring. *Developmental Psychobiology,* 1977, *10,* 243–254.

Wiesel, T.N., & Hubel, D.H. Effects of visual deprivation on morphology and physiology of cells in the cat's lateral geniculate body. *Journal of Neurophysiology,* 1963, *26,* 978–993.

Wiesel, T.N., & Hubel D.H. Spatial and chromatic interactions in the lateral geniculate body of the rhesus monkey. *Journal of Neurophysiology,* 1966, *29,* 1115–1156.

Wilson, E.O. *On human nature.* Cambridge, Mass.: Harvard University Press, 1978.

Wilson, R.S. Synchronies in mental development: An epigenetic perspective. *Science,* 1978, *202,* 939–948.

Winick, M., Fish, I., & Rosso, P. Cellular recovery in rat tissue after a brief period of neonatal malnutrition. *Journal of Nutrition,* 1968, *92,* 623.

Winick, M., & Rosso, P. Malnutrition and central nervous system development. In J.W. Prescott, M.S. Read, D.B. Coursin (Eds.), *Brain function and malnutrition.* New York: Wiley, 1975.

Winter, P., & Funkenstein, H.H. The effect of species-specific vocalization on the discharge of auditory cortical cells in the awake squirrel monkey *(Saimiri sciureus). Experimental Brain Research* 1973, *18,* 489–504.

Winter, P., Ploog, D., & Latta, J. Vocal repertoire of the squirrel monkey (Saimiri sciureus): Its analysis and significance. *Experimental Brain Research,* 1966, *1,* 359–384.

Winton, F.P., & Bayliss, L.E. *Human physiology* (6th ed.). London: Churchill, 1968.

Wise, C.D., Baden, M.M., & Stein, L. Post-mortem measurements of enzymes in human brain: Evidence of central noradrenergic deficit in schizophrenia.

In S.W. Matthysse & S.S. Kety (Eds.), *Catecholamines and schizophrenia.* Oxford: Pergamon, 1974.

Wise, C.D., & Stein, L. Facilitation of brain stimulation by central administration of norepinephrine. *Science,* 1969, *163,* 299–301.

Wise, R.A., Spindler, J., DeWit, H., & Gerber, G.J. Neuroleptic-induced "anhedonia" in rats: Pimozide blocks reward quality of food. *Science,* 1978, *201,* 262–264.

Witelson, S.F. Sex and the single hemisphere: Specialization of the right hemisphere for spatial processing. *Science,* 1976, *193,* 425–427.

Woolard, H.H., Weddell, G., & Harpman, J.A. Observations of the neurohistological basis of cutaneous pain. *Journal of Anatomy,* 1940, *74,* 413–440.

Wood, P. *Dreaming and social isolation.* Unpublished doctoral dissertation, University of North Carolina, 1962.

Wyatt, R.J., Schwartz, M.A., Erdelyi, E., & Barchas, J.D. Dopamine-β-hydroxylase activity in brains of chronic schizophrenic patients. *Science,* 1975, *187,* 368–370.

Yamamoto, T., & Ueki, S. Characteristics in aggressive behavior induced by midbrain raphe lesions in rats. *Physiology and Behavior,* 1977, *19,* 105–110.

Yin, T.C.T., & Williams, W.J. Dynamic response and transfer characteristics of joint neurons in somatosensory thalamus of the cat. *Journal of Neurophysiology,* 1976, *39,* 584–600.

Yoss, R.E., & Daly, D.D. Criteria for the diagnosis of the narcoleptic syndrome. *Proceedings of the Mayo Clinic,* 1957, *32,* 320–328.

Zacharias, L., & Wurtman, R.J. Blindness and menarche. *Obstetrics and Gynecology,* 1964, *33,* 603–608.

Zigmond, M.J., & Stricker, E.M. Recovery of feeding and drinking by rats after intraventricular 6-hydroxydopamine or lateral hypothalamic lesions. *Science,* 1973, *182,* 717–720.

Zucker, I., Rusak, B., & King, R.G. Neural bases for circadian rhythms in rodent behavior. In A.H. Riesen & R.F. Thompson (Eds.), *Advances in psychobiology* (Vol. 3). New York: Wiley (Interscience), 1976.

Reference Notes

1. Hornykiewicz, O. *Dopamine and extrapyramidal motor function and dysfunction.* Presented at ARNMD Meeting, New York, 1970.

2. Hohmann, G.W. *The effect of dysfunctions of the autonomic nervous system on experienced feelings and emotions.* Paper presented at the Conference on Emotions and Feelings, New School for Social Research, New York, October 1962.

3. Komisaruk, B.R., Larsson, K., & Cooper, R. *Intense lordosis in the absence of ovarian hormones after septal ablations in rats.* Second Annual Meeting of the Society for Neuroscience, Houston, Texas, 1972.

4. Higgins, E.A., Chiles, W.D., McKenzie, J.M., Iampietro, P.F., Winget, C.M., Funkhouser, G.E., Burr, M.J., Vaughan, J.A., & Jennings, A.E. *The effects of a 12-hour shift in the wake-sleep cycle on physiological and biochemical responses and on multiple task performance.* Document prepared for the U.S. Department of Transportation, Federal Aviation Administration, 1975.

5. Luce, G.G. *Biological rhythms in psychiatry and medicine.* Public Health Service Report, NIH, 1970.

author
index

Analgesia *(cont.)*
    under stress, 201, 203
    rhythmic response to, 370–371, 382
Analog code, 11–12, 30
Anarthria, 531
Anatomical terms, 48–50
Androgens, 327–328, 334, 348, 361, 430
    fetal, 334–341, 343, 431–433
    sexual differentiation of brain
        structures, 341
Anger, 251
Angiotensin, 315–317, 320
Angular gyrus, 533–534
Anhedonia, 298
Animals, language in, 535–538
Anion, 18
Anosmia, 163–165, 168
Anterior cerebral artery, 530
Anterior direction, 48–49
Anterior hypothalamic area, 355, 362
Anterior olfactory nucleus, 162, 168
Anterior pituitary gland, 429, 431
Anterior thalamus, 58–59, 66
Anticipatory neuron, 233–235
Antidepressant drugs, 42, 281–282,
    285–286
    side effects, 283–286
Antidiuretic hormone (ADH),
    313–315, 320
Antidromic invasion, 113
Antipsychotic drugs, 277–280, 285–286
    side effects, 283–286
Aphagia, 291, 294–295, 309
Aphasia, 522, 531–532, 537
Aphrodisiac, 357, 362
Apical dendritic shaft, 445
Aplysia, 461–465, 473
Apomorphine, 262, 274
Aqueous humor, 88
Arcuate fasciculus, 533
Ascending pathway, 49
Association cortex, 56–57, 500–510
Association nuclei, of thalamus, 59
Associative learning, 455–457, 460,
    465
Astigmatism, 443–444, 450
Astrocyte, 51–52
Atlas, human brain, 541–547
Atropa belladonna, 41
Atropine, 41, 44, 264
Attention, 511–515, 519
Audiogram, 121–122
Audiometry, 121
Audition, 117–146
    afferent pathway, 131–132

average evoked potentials, 511–515,
    519
coding of sound, 132–143
ear, structure of, 123–128
efferent effects, 143–145
hearing loss, 122, 124–125
hearing thresholds, 120–122
range of frequencies heard, 134
sound, 118–122
transduction in ear, 128–131
word deafness, 534
Auditory canal, 123, 128
Auditory nerve, 70, 126, 130–133, 137
Autonomic nervous system, 68–70,
    217–218, 249–250, 255; *see also*
    Parasympathetic nervous system;
    Sympathetic nervous system
Autoradiography, 106
Autosomes, 325
Average evoked potential (AEP), 500,
    510–519, 527–529, 537
AXM, *see* Acetoxycycloheximide
Axo-axonic contact, 32, 36–38
Axo-dendritic contact, 32
Axon, 13–16
    sodium–potassium pump, 22
Axonal conduction, 11–13, 16–24
Axon hillock, 12–14, 20–21, 24–26
Axon sprouting, 238–239, 436–437,
    449–450
Axoplasm, 18
Axoplasmic transport, 16
Axo-somatic contact, 32

Barbiturate, 284
Basal cell, of olfactory epithelium,
    160–162
Basal dendrite, 445
Basal ganglia, 57
    extrapyramidal system, 228–229
    voluntary movement, 232–233, 235
Basement membrane, of taste bud, 151
Basilar membrane, 125–126, 128–129,
    131, 134–136, 138, 142
Basis pedunculi, 61–62, 66, 226–227,
    229
Behavior
    and early maternal separation, 435
    and emotions, 242–243
    genetic influences on, 417–424
    and impoverished environment, 448
    instinctive, 457–458
    learned, 457
    localization of function in brain, 4–5

malnutrition's effects on, 426–428
mind-body problem, 2–4
nature versus nurture controversy,
    5–6
and reward, 267–277
Behavioral set, 515–516, 519
Belladonna, 41
Benzodiazepine, 283
Benzotropine, 43–44
Best frequency, 133, 136, 138, 142
Beta brain waves, 384, 398
Binaural hearing, 139, 142
Binocular vision, 106–108, 397, 399, 439
Biofeedback, 250, 255
Biogenic amine theory of depression,
    281–282, 286
Biological clock, 366, 372–373,
    376–377, 383
Biological rhythms, 365–383; *see also*
    Circadian rhythms; Estrus cycle;
    Menstrual cycle
Biological relevance
    chemical senses, 167–175
    sounds, 141–142
Bipolar cell, of retina, 88–91, 93, 98–99
Bipolar depression, 281
Bipolar neuron, 12
Bitter taste, 150, 154–155, 157, 170
Blind spot, 88, 91
Blood–brain barrier, 52–53
Blood groups, genetics of, 415
Blood pressure
    and drinking behavior, 315–317, 320
    polygraph tests, 248–249
Body and mind, *see* Mind–body
    problem
Body fat, regulation of, 301
Body temperature
    circadian rhythm, 367, 369, 380, 382
Bony ossicles, of middle ear, 124–125,
    127–128, 144
Brain, 50–53; *see also* specific parts of
    the brain
    and behavior, 2–4
    blood supply, 529–530
    chemical pathways, 64–65
    development, 411–413
        and malnutrition, 426
    effects of complex environment on,
        445, 450–451
    effects of sensory deprivation on,
        439–444, 450
    electrical stimulation, 198–199, 203,
        256–258, 260, 266, 268–277
    human, and aggression, 264–267

and feeding behavior, 275, 291–295, 298–299, 309
and motivated behavior, 268, 276
and pituitary gland, 330–332
self-stimulation, 268–270, 272
and sexual behavior, 330–332, 334, 337, 353–354, 361–362
and sleep, 403
Hypovolemia, 311, 314–317, 320

Illness, and chronic stress, 246–247
Imipramine, 282
Impotence, 357
Imprinting, 398, 481–482
Incentive motivation, 275–277
Incus, 123–125
Inferior colliculi, of tectum, 61, 63, 132, 134, 137, 139–140
Inferior direction, 49
Inferotemporal cortex, 92, 504–507, 509
Inflammation, inhibition of, 245, 255
Information, 10–11
Information processing, 11–14; see also Coding process
Infrared, 88
Inhibitory postsynaptic potential (IPSP), 33–35, 38
Inner ear, 125–128
vestibular organ, 206–207, 211
Insomnia
central sleep apnea, 391, 399
drug dependent, 389–391, 399
Instinctive behavior, 457–458
Instrumental aggression, 256
Instrumental conditioning, 455–457, 460, 465
Insular-temporal reflex, 144–145
Insulin, 290, 300–301, 304–305, 430
Integration, cellular, 410–411, 413
Integration of information, by neuron, 11–14, 24–26
Intelligence, 418–419, 427
Intensity, of stimulus, 79, 81–82, 86
chemical stimulus, 148
in gustation, 152–153
light, 88, 96–97, 105
olfaction, 166–167
skin senses, 187, 190
sound, 120–122, 132–134, 138–139, 142
Intermale aggression, 256, 262
Intermedius nerve, 61
Internal auditory canal, 123

Internal capsule, of midbrain, 226–227, 229
Internal carotid artery, 529
Internal granular layer, of the cerebral cortex, 55–56
Interneuron
pain transmission, 194–195, 224, 226
Renshaw cell, 225–226
Interposed nucleus, of cerebellum, 232–235
Interstitial fluid, 311
Intestinal stimulation, sleep-inducing, 405–407
Intracellular fluid compartment, 311–312, 319–320
Intrafusal muscle fiber, 220–222
Intromission, 332–334
Iodopsin, 95–96
Ionic movement, during postsynaptic potentials, 34–35, 38
Iproniazid, 281, 286
Ipsilateral pathway, 49
IPSP, see Inhibitory postsynaptic potential
IQ scores
and environment and heredity, 418
and malnutrition, 427
Iris, 88–89, 112
Irritable (shock-induced) aggression, 256, 261–262, 266–267

James–Lange theory of emotion, 251–252, 255
Jet lag, 377–378
Joint receptor, 203–204, 206
Juxtaglomerular cells, 315–316

Kanamycin, 130
Ketone bodies, 304–305
Kidney, and drinking behavior, 315–317, 320
Kinesthetic system, 203–206
Klüver–Bucy syndrome, 58, 504, 509
Knee jerk reflex, 223, 225
Knowing, 500
Krause end-bulb, 180
Kwashiorkor, 425, 428

Labeled line theory of sensory coding in skin senses, 188
Landmark reversal task, 507–508
Language, 57, 525–538

in animals, 535–538
and handedness, 523
split-brain studies, 520–522
Large pyramidal layer, of the cerebral cortex, 55–56
Larynx
taste buds, 152
Lateral direction, 48
Lateral fissure, of the cerebral cortex, 55, 58, 411
Lateral geniculate nucleus (LGN), of thalamus, 59, 62–63, 91–94, 102, 110–111
effect of monocular deprivation, 440, 450
exogenous and endogenous influences, 518
Lateral hypothalamus
and drinking behavior, 319
and food intake, 291, 293–296, 309
Lateral interaction, in sensory pathways, 79, 86
in retina, 101, 103, 105
Lateral leminscus, 132
Lateral olfactory tract, 162–163, 168
Lateral ventricle, of brain, 53, 58
Learned specific hunger, 171–172
Learning, 454–461; see also Memory
and changes in the brain, 479–484, 495–496
and complex environment, 446
in developing organism, 458–459
and drinking behavior, 318
and flavor aversion, 171–172
incentive motivation, 275–277
model systems, 461–473
reward research, 267–277
state-dependent, 493–494, 496
thyroxine's effect on, 432
Left-handedness, 523–527, 537
Left hemisphere, of brain, 520–525
language, 526–531, 537
Lemniscal pathway, 182–185, 197, **202**
Lens, of eye, 88–89
LGN, see Lateral geniculate nucleus
LH, see Luteinizing hormone
LH syndrome, 293–295
Lie detector test, 69
Light, 87–88
and circadian rhythms, 376, 380, 383
Limbic system, of brain, 58–59, 66
brain self-stimulation, 268–269
Lipostatic theory, of food intake regulation, 301
Lithium, 281–282, 284

Myelin sheath, 13–16
Myofibril, 218–219, 222
Myosin myofilament, 218–220, 222
Myotonia, 346, 361
MZ twins, *see* Monozygotic twins

Naloxone, 198–200, 371, 382
Narcolepsy, 391–392, 399
Nature versus nurture controversy, 5–6
NE, *see* Norepinephrine
Neostigmine bromide, 263
Nephrectomy, and drinking behavior, 317
Nervous system, 47–71; *see also* Autonomic nervous system; Central nervous system
   asymmetry, 519–525
   development of, 409–452
      environmental contributions to, 433–451
      genetics, 413–424
      hormonal contributions to, 428–433
      nutritional contributions to, 424–428
   plasticity, 459–461
Neural tube, 412–413
Neurochemistry, and learning, 481–484
Neurogenesis, 412–413
Neuromodulator, 200
Neuromuscular junction, 32, 219
   in myasthenia gravis, 237
Neuron, 9–27, 51, 53
   activity during sleep, 385
   axonal conduction, 16–24
   coding of information, 11
   development of, 412–413
   enkephalins' effect on, 199–200
   information processing, 11–13
   integration of information at axon hillock, 24–26
   receptive fields, 82
   recovery from damage to, 238–239
   structure of, 13–16
   synaptic transmission, 28–45
   topographic organization, 82
Neurotransmitter, 12, 16, 30–44; *see also* specific neurotransmitters
   and aggression, 260–264, 267
   chemical pathways in brain, 64–65
   from hair cells of organ of Corti, 129
   metabolic defects and motor dysfunction, 237–239

photoreceptor cell, 96
   in schizophrenia, 277–280
   and sexual behavior, 355–357, 362
Neurotubule, 16, 30–31
NGC, *see* Nucleus gigantocellularis
Nicotine, 41, 44
Nicotinic receptor, 40–41, 44
Nigrostriatal pathway, 271, 275
   and food intake, 295, 306
Nociceptor, 194–195, 202
Node of Ranvier, 13–14, 16, 182
Nonspecific nuclei, of thalamus, 59–60
Noradrenalin, *see* Norepinephrine
Noradrenergic pathway, 271
   and food intake, 298–299, 306, 309
Noradrenergic synapse, 41
   drugs' effects on, 41–42, 44
   and memory modulation, 490, 496
   and schizophrenia, 279
Norepinephrine (NE), 36, 41–42, 44, 245, 255, 430
   and aggression, 260–261, 267
   in depression, 281–282, 286
   pathways in brain, 64–65
   reward research, 271–276
   in schizophrenia, 279–280
   and sleep, 402, 407
Nose, 161
Nuclei, of thalamus, 59
Nuclei, of pons, 62
Nucleus circularis, 314, 320
Nucleus gigantocellularis, 197, 202–203
Nucleus of the solitary tract, of brainstem, 152, 157–159
   and sleep, 403, 406–407
Nutrition, 449
   and nervous system development, 425–428
   and sense of taste, 170–171, 174

Obesity, 291–292, 298, 307–310
Object alternation test, 502–503
Object reversal task, 507–508
Occipital lobe, of cerebral cortex, 55
Ocular dominance column, 106, 108
Ocular dominance shift, 439, 443, 450
Oculomotor nerve, 61, 70
Off-center ganglion cell, 99, 105
6-OHDA, 261, 273–274, 279
   aphagia and adipsia, 295–296, 298–299
Olfaction, 161–169
   afferent pathway, 162–163

biological relevance, 167–168, 170, 172–175
coding, 166–169
convergence of odor and taste information, 158
olfactory system, anatomy of, 160–161
primary qualities of odor, 149, 163–165
spatial characteristics of odor, 149
stimulus control of sex behavior, 358–359
transduction, 154, 162–165
Olfactory bulb, 160, 162–163, 167–169
Olfactory cilia, 160–161, 168
Olfactory epithelium, 160–161, 168
Olfactory nerve, 70, 162–163, 168
Olfactory rod, 160–161, 168
Olfactory tubercle, 162, 168
Olivary complex, 132
Olivary nucleus, 139, 142
Olivo-cochlear bundle, 143–145
Ommatidia, in horseshoe crab, 101, 103
On-center ganglion cell, 99, 105
Operator gene, 416, 424
Operon model, of gene regulation, 416, 424
Opiate, 198–199, 203
Opponent process theory, of color vision, 109–110, 112
Opsin, 94–96
Optical illusion
   Mach band, 101
Optic chiasm, 61, 91–92, 94
Optic nerve, 62, 70, 88, 90–93
Optic tract, 61–63, 91–92
Organizing effects, of hormones, 336, 343
Organ of Corti, 127–129
Orgasmic phase, of sexual response cycle, 344–348, 361
Orientation, cortex cells sensitive to, 103–104
Orientation, spatial, *see* Spatial orientation
Ornithine decarboxylase, 434
Oscillator (biological clock), 366, 372–373, 376–377, 383
Osmoreceptors, 313–314, 320
Osmosis, 17
Osmotic gradient, 16–17, 23
Osmotic pressure, cellular, 311, 316
Otitis media, 125
Otoconia, of vestibular system, 207–208

Otosclerosis, 124
Outer ear, 123–124, 128
Outer segment, of photoreceptor, 94, 96
Oval window, of ear, 123–128
Ovary, 325–327, 334, 430–431
Oviduct (Fallopian tube), 326–327
Ovulation, 327, 329, 334, 351
Ovum, 410
Oxytocin, 330, 431

Pacemaker, 218
Pacinian corpuscle, 180–182, 185
Pain, 193–203, 224–226
    rhythmic response to, 370–371, 382
Pancreatic islets, 430
Papillae, of tongue, 151, 155–156, 159
Parabrachial nucleus, of pons, 152
Paralysis, 236
Parasympathetic nervous system, 68–70, 243–244, 254
Parathyroid hormone, 430
Paresis, 216, 227–228, 236, 239
Parietal lobe, of cerebral cortex, 55
    association cortex, 507–509
Parieto-occipital sulcus, of cerebral cortex, 55
Parkinson's disease, 43, 62, 65, 229, 237, 239, 284–285, 439
Passive avoidance, 456–457
Pathways, terms for, 49–50
Pattern vision, deprivation of, 440
Pavlovian conditioning, see Classical conditioning
PBZ, see Phenoxybenzamine
PCPA, 198, 262, 299, 355–356, 401–403
Penis, 327
Peptide, 428
Perception, 84–85
Perilymph, 125, 129
Period, of biological rhythm, 366
Period, of sound wave, 119
Peripheralist theory, of hunger, 290, 302, 309
Peripheral nervous system, 50, 67–70
Periventricular area, of hypothalamus, 314, 317, 320
PGO waves, in sleep, 384–385, 396, 398
Pharynx
    taste buds, 152
Phase, of biological rhythm, 366
Phase difference detector, of auditory system, 139–140, 142

Phase-locking
    in auditory system, 136–139, 142
    in kinesthetic system, 205–206
Phase shift, in biological rhythm, 377–380, 383
Phenothiazine, 283–284
Phenotype, 415, 424
Phenoxybenzamine (PBZ), 490–493
Phenylketonuria (PKU), 417, 424
Phenylthicarbamide (PTC), 417
Pheromone, 172–175, 358–359, 362
Phospholipids, of neuron cell membrane, 15
Photopigment, 94–96, 109
Photoreceptor, 94–96, 109–110; see also Cone; Rod
Photosensitivity, and circadian rhythms, 376–377, 380, 383
Phrenology, 5
Physiological signs of emotion, 243–255
Physostigmine, 40, 44
Piloerection, 243
Pimozide, 297–298, 355–356
Pinna, 123, 128
Pitch, of sound, 120, 134
Pituitary gland, 60, 245–246, 255, 328–332, 334, 429, 431–433
PKU, see Phenylketonuria
Placebo treatment, 196
Placenta, 430
Place reversal task, 507–508
Planes of dissection, 49–50
Planum temporale, 522–523, 531
Plasma, blood, 311
Plateau phase, of sexual response cycle, 344–347, 361
Pleasure center, in brain, 276
Polygraph test, 248–249, 255
Polysynaptic reflex pathway, 224–226
Pons, 58, 60–63, 66
    afferent pathway for gustation, 152, 158–159
    efferent input from visual cortex, 113–114
    noradrenergic pathway, 271
    pyramidal system, 226–227, 229
Pontine nuclei, 62
Postabsorptive phase, in metabolism, 299, 301, 309
Posterior cerebral artery, 530
Posterior direction, 48–49
Posterior nuclear group, of thalamus, 187
Posterior pituitary gland, 429, 431

Postsynaptic cell, 30–32
Postsynaptic membrane, 30–33, 38
Postsynaptic potential (PSP), 32–35, 38
Posttetanic facilitation, 462–463, 473
Potassium ions, 18, 23, 34–35, 38
Predatory aggression, 256–267
Premenstrual syndrome, 351–352
Preoptic area, of brain, 313–314, 331–332, 337, 341, 353–354, 361
Prepyriform cortex, 162, 167, 169
Prestriate cortex, 91–92, 103, 504–505, 509
Presynaptic cell, 30–32
Presynaptic facilitation, 37–38
Presynaptic inhibition, 36–38
Presynaptic membrane, 33
Primary drinking, 311–313, 320
Primary qualities, of chemical stimuli, 149–150, 163–165
Principle sulcus, of dorsolateral frontal cortex, 502–503, 509
Progesterone, 327–330, 334, 336, 338, 340, 348–351, 354–355, 362, 430
Progestin, 336, 340–341
Prolactin, 328–329, 431
Proliferation, cellular, 410, 413
Propanolol, 490–492
Proprioceptive information, 203, 210
Prostigmine, 237
Proteins
    of neuron cell membranes, 15
    synthesis, 414–415, 423, 480–481, 486–488, 496
Pseudoconditioning, 456
Pseudohermaphrodite, 335–336, 342
PSP, see Postsynaptic potential
Psychic blindness, 504, 509
Psychosurgery, 266–267
Psychotropic drugs, see Antidepressant drugs; Antipsychotic drugs
PTC, see Phenylthicarbamide
PTZ, 492–493
Pulvinar, of thalamus, 62, 532
Pupil, of eye, 88–89
Pupillary reflex, of cat, 466–467, 473
Push–pull cannula, 272
Putamen, of corpus striatum, 57–58, 66
    dopamine pathway, 271
    self-stimulation, 272
Pyramidal cell, of cerebral cortex, 55, 412
Pyramidal neuron, 12, 14

Pyramidal system, 226–229
Pyramidal tract, 226–229, 236, 239

Quality, of stimulus, 80–82, 86
    chemical stimulus, 149–150
    for color vision, 108–112
    in gustation, 154
    sound frequency, 134–138, 142

Rage, 58
Raphe nucleus, of brainstem, 65, 198,
    203
    and aggression, 262–263
    and sleep, 401–402, 407
Rapid eye movement (REM), 384; see
    also D-sleep
Rapidly adapting mechanoreceptor,
    182, 189–190
Rarefaction, of sound wave, 118–119
Rebound effect, of sedatives, 390
Receptive aphasia, 531, 538
Receptive field, 82, 86
    for auditory space, 140–141
    cortical cells, 103
    ganglion cells, 99–101, 105
    in gustation, 155, 159
    inferotemporal cortex, 505–506
    visual stimuli, in LGN, 102, 110–111
Receptor cell, of sense organ, 76–80
    of ear, 128, 132–133
    in gustation, 151–152, 154–155, 159
    hair cells of vestibular system, 208
    olfactory epithelium, 161–163,
        165–166, 168
    rods and cones of retina, 89, 93
    somatosensory system, 180–181,
        185, 188
Receptor potential, 77–78
    of hair cells of organ of Corti,
        129–130
    photoreceptors, 95–97
    in gustation, 152, 154–155, 159
Receptor site, for neurotransmitter,
    30–34, 38, 40–41
Recessive allele, 415, 424
Recurrent inhibition, 225–226
Red nucleus, of tegmentum, 61–62,
    228–229
Redundancy, in afferent visual
    pathway, 93
Reflex, 78–79, 222–226, 234–235, 455
    pupillary, of cat, 466–467, 473
Refractory period, 21, 23

Regulator gene, 416, 424
Relaxin, 430
Relay nuclei, of thalamus, 59
Releaser, pheromone, 172
REM, see Rapid eye movement
Renin, 315–316, 320
Renshaw cell, 225–226
Reproductive organs, 325–327, 333–334
    sex hormones' effect on
        development of, 431, 433
    sexual differentiation, 335–336, 343
Reserpine, 42, 44, 273, 277, 281, 356
Resistance stage, of general adaptation
    syndrome, 246–247, 255
Resolution phase, of sexual response
    cycle, 344–347, 361
Response to stimulus, 455–457; see
    also Reflex
    delayed, 501–502, 509
Resting potential, 18–19, 23
Reticular activating system, 63
Reticular formation, of brain, 63–64,
    66, 92, 94
    and sleep, 400–401, 406–407
Retina, 88–91, 93
    coding in, 97–101
    color vision, 109–110
    efferent input, 112
    lateral interaction, 101, 103
Retinal, 94–96
Retinal disparity, 106, 108
Retrograde amnesia, 485–488
Re-uptake of neurotransmitter, 35–36,
    38
Reward, 267–277
    and food intake, 297–299
    and mental illness, 277–286
Rhodopsin, 95–96
Rhythms, biological, see Biological
    rhythms
Ribonucleic acid, see RNA
Right-handedness, 523–527, 537
Right hemisphere, of brain, 520–525
    language, 527–529, 537
Ritalin, 493
RNA, 414, 416, 423, 431
    and learning, 480–483, 496
Rod, of retina, 88–91, 93–97
Rostral direction, 48–49
Round window, of ear, 123, 125–127
Ruffini ending, 180

Saccule, of vestibular organ, 206–207,
    211

Sagittal plane, 49–50
Salivation, 248
Saltatory conduction, 22–23
Salty taste, 150, 154–157
Satiety, in eating behavior, 298–299,
    301–304, 309–310
    and sleep, 405
Scala media, 125–126, 129
Scala tympani, 125–127, 129
Scala vestibuli, 125–127, 129
Schizophrenia, 43, 277–280, 285–286
    heredity and, 420–422
Schwann cell, 162
SCN, see Suprachiasmatic nucleus
Scotophobin, 484
Scrotal sac, 326–327
Secondary drinking, 312–313,
    317–318, 320
Secondary sex characteristics, 325–327,
    334
Second messenger hypothesis, of
    hormonal action, 430
Sedatives, 389–391, 399
Selective attention, 511–515
Semicircular canal, 123, 125, 206–207,
    211–212
Semipermeable membrane, 16–19
Sensitization, 455–456, 460, 466
Sensory area, of cerebral cortex, 55,
    57, 507
Sensory deprivation, 439–444, 450
Sensory enrichment, 444–451
Sensory neglect, 296, 507, 509
Sensory nerve fiber, see Afferent nerve
    fiber
Sensory-neural hearing loss, 122
Sensory neuron, 78
Sensory systems, 74–86; see also
    specific systems
Septal area, of telencephalon, 58, 60,
    66
Septal rage, 58
Serotonergic synapse, 43
Serotonin, 43–44, 65, 198
    and aggression, 260, 262–263, 267
    in depression, 281–282, 286
    and food intake, 299
    and sexual behavior, 355–356, 362
    and sleep, 401–403, 407
Sex, of individual
    and hemispheric lateralization of
        function, 524
    and interaction with environment,
        448, 451
Sex chromosomes, 325, 333, 416

A 0
B 1
C 2
D 3
E 4
F 5
G 6
H 7